Bonnie Dahl's
Superior Way
Fifth Edition

The Cruising Guide to Lake Superior

Bonnie Dahl

Kollath+Stensaas
PUBLISHING

Bonnie Dahl's

Superior Way
Fifth Edition
The Cruising Guide to Lake Superior

Kollath+Stensaas Publishing
394 Lake Avenue South, Suite 406
Duluth, MN 55802
(218) 727-1731
kollathstensaas.com

First Edition: 1983
Second Edition: May 1992
Third Edition: June 2001
Fourth Edition: March 2008
Fifth Edition: January 2025

Print management by JS Print Group, Inc. Duluth, MN 55805
Printed in South Korea
5 4 3 2 1 Fifth Edition

Dahl, Bonnie, 1939-
ISBN-13: 978-1-936571-16-1
Design/Graphics: Kollath Graphic Design
5th Edition Editor: Robert Shutes

To our Son Peter
Who continues the dream

Acknowledgments
First Edition

Throughout our years of cruising, there have been a number of people who have contributed information on specific anchorages or particular areas. Others have been instrumental in assisting us in a variety of ways, so that we might pursue our own explorations. Without these people, this book would have never become a reality, and we wish to give the following individuals our sincere thanks:

Hans and Ruth Deller, Minneapolis, Minnesota
Burt and Fran Douglas, Nipigon, Ontario
Sylvia Eby, Rice Lake, Wisconsin
Chuck and Daphne Henderson, Rossport/Lakefield, Ontario
Jim and Shiley Leggit, Thunder Bay, Ontario
Robin Maercklein, National Park Service, Bayfield, Wisconsin
Chuck and Charlene Marcum, Minneapolis, Minnesota
Jim and Phyllis Massey, Thunder Bay, Ontario
Craig and Sue McDonald, Ottawa, Ontario
Jim and Marge Miller, Apostle Islands Marine, Bayfield, Wisconsin
Delores O'Brien, Rice Lake, Wisconsin
Elwyn and Joy Richardson, Otter Head/Wiarton, Ontario
William Ross, Ontario Regional Archaeologist, Thunder Bay, Ontario
Bill (deceased) and Mary Schelling, Rossport, Ontario
Gene and Mary Ann Skadberg, Grand Marais, Minnesota
John W. Smith (deceased), Hancock, Michigan
Colonel Templer (deceased) and Betsy Cawthorne, Detroit, Michigan
Jerry and Susan Ventrudo, Thunder Bay, Ontario
Doug and Edna Vokes, Mamainse Harbour, Ontario

We would like to express our gratitude to Larry and Midge (deceased) Perkins, Evanston, Illinois, for introducing us to the Great Lakes Cruising Club. We are indebted to GLCC because it was the club's Log Book that gave us the confidence to begin exploring the far reaches of Lake Superior's remote areas. We also would like to thank Art Hutchison, Chicago, Illinois, long-time editor of the Log Book, for releasing the material which we have contributed to the club for use in this guide.

Finally, a special thank you to our two children, Peter and Kristin. Many of the points of interest and findings listed in the book are their discoveries, the results of eight summers of exploring Superior's wilderness shores. A distinctive element of our cruising experience has been the ability to participate in it as a family. Through our children's eyes we have come to know the lake in a different light which might have otherwise remained obscured.

Second Edition

In many respects, The Superior Way belongs to us all as there are many, both boaters and non-boaters, who have made valuable contributions to the information contained in these pages. Many of those who gave assistance in the first edition have continued to provide information in the second edition. As the boating community grows, so does the list of those who have provided important leads or taken time out of their cruises to substantiate specific details. I am including a list of those who have freely and unselfishly provided information for the second edition. My sincere apologies to those who may have inadvertently been left out.

Derck and Shirley Amerman, New Brighton, Minnesota
Dennis Bailey, Drummond Island, Michigan
Jonathan and Jerri Boyd, Bayfield, Wisconsin
Chuck Burnside, Fridley, Minnesota
Brad Buck, Wawa, Ontario
Jim Coslett, Thunder Bay, Ontario
Ed and Shirley Erickson, Bayfield, Wisconsin
Barb Foley, Copper Harbor, Michigan
Gerry Gosselin, Thunder Bay, Ontario
Ben and Natalie Heineman, Chicago, Illinois
Emery Jones (deceased) Cornucopia, Wisconsin
Russ and Avis Lindquist, Minnetonka, Minnesota
James R. Marshall, Duluth, Minnesota
Bruce McCuaig, Heron Bay, Ontario
Dave and Bernice Nixon, Bayfield, Wisconsin
Phil Peterson, Bayfield, Wisconsin
Rev. Edward Prinselaar, Nipigon, Ontario
Peter and Rosemary Preuss, Lethbridge, Alberta
Bill and Judy Rhode, New Brighton, Minnesota
Brian Riley, Munising, Michigan
Dan and Marlene Simonson, Duluth, Minnesota
Brach Schnabel, Hancock, Michigan
Gordon Smedley, Sault Ste. Marie, Ontario
Steve Somsen, Superior, Wisconsin
Dick and Marion Sonderegger, Marquette, Michigan
Dave and Sue Steffens, North Oaks, Minnesota
Steve Verbanac, Bayfield, Wisconsin
Peter and Lil Von Straten, Pequaming, Michigan
Gordie Walter, Nipigon, Ontario
Jay Wittak, Black River Ranger, Ironwood, Michigan

There are also a number of staff members in the National Park Service who have given invaluable assistance in providing information and in reading those chapters on the Apostle Islands and Isle Royale for technical error.

Apostle Islands National Lakeshore
Jerry Banta, Park Superintendent
Dick Carrier, Transportation Officer
Kayci Cook, Chief of Interpretation
Jeff Hepner, Acting District Ranger
Neil Howk, Park Ranger
Gary Miller, Foreman: Trails & Docks
Dave Snyder, Park Historian

Isle Royale National Park
Bill Fink, Park Superintendent
Jerry Case, East District Ranger
Larry Kangas, West District Ranger
Elen Mauer, North Shore Sub-District Ranger
Bruce Weber, Park Naturalist/Public Affairs Specialist

Third Edition
The list of people who have contributed information for Superior Way continues to grow. Many are those who also contributed to the first and second editions and continue to have input. I want to thank each person, whether the contribution was large or small, as each is important. I especially enjoy the freshness of others' perspectives as my impressions are often influenced by over familiarity. The following is a list of new contributors for this edition. Once again, I give my sincere apologies for anyone who was inadvertently left out.

Dale Anderson and Rita Cedarhom, Shoreview, Minnesota
Joe Cain, Sault Ste. Marie, Ontario
Rich Clarke, Thunder Bay, Ontario
Jack Culley (Sailboats Inc.), Superior, Wisconsin
Larry and Jan DeMars, Eau Claire, Wisconsin
Mike and Cheri Ditty, Zimmerman, Minnesota
Richard and Donna Fink, La Crosse, Wisconsin
Mark Gainey (pilot & retired Great Lakes captain),
Bayfield, Wisconsin
Bill and Grace Hines, Saxon Harbor, Michigan
Frank and Marilyn Jurgovsky, Brooklyn Center, Minnesota
Neil Kormo (District Ranger), Grand Marais, Michigan
Steve Koski, L'Anse, Michigan
Gary Lange, Nipigon, Ontario

Pete Pierti, Copper Harbor, Michigan
Dan Plescher, Copper Harbor, Michigan
Doug Poulin, Nipigon, Ontario
Bob & Terri Power, Woodville,Wisconsin
Bill Roth, Washburn, Wisconsin
Tom and Regina Shea, East Mariches, New York
Wayne and Edie Spangler, Rice Lake, Wisconsin
Cheryl Sprandel, Princeton, Minnesota
Doug Stuart, Houghton, Michigan
Dave and Mary Beth Tillman, Cornucopia, Wisconsin
Brett Zorza, Marquette, Michigan

Again, there are also a number of staff members in the National Park Service who have given information and read those chapters on the Apostle Islands and Isle Royale for technical error.

Apostle Islands National Lakeshore
Jim Nepstad, Acting Chief of Resources Management
Neil Howk, Assistant Chief of Resources Management
Rusty Rawson, Chief of Maintenance
Mindy Lane, Ranger

Isle Royale National Park
Douglas A. Barnard, Superintendent
Peter D. Armington, Chief Ranger
Stuart Croll, Visitor Services & Resource Protection
Terry Lindsay, Park Naturalist

Fourth Edition
Once again I am indebted to those who provide information from around the lake. As in previous editions, many have contributed to each edition and I give my thanks for their continued efforts. I especially appreciate tips on what is new or if there have been changes from previous editions. The following is a list of new contributors for this edition. Along with my thank you, please accept my sincere apologies to anyone who has been unintentionally left out.

Will and Nancy Borg, Duluth, Minnesota
Doug Caldwell, Terrace Bay, Ontario
Larry Carpenter and Judy Taylor, Minneapolis, Minnesota
Pete Discenza, Eagan, Minnesota
Kevin Duby, Marquette, Michigan
Michael and Patty Facius, Minneapolis, Minnesota
Jim and Cathie Hatch, Bemidji, Minnesota
George Hite, Eagle Harbor, Michigan
Richard D. Kemplin, Mercer, Wisconsin

Niels and Vickie Jensen, Minneapolis, Minnesota
Keith McCuaig, Marathon, Ontario
Tom McMaster and Rose Hansmeyer, Minneapolis, Minnesota
Angie Moen, Superior, Wisconsin
Dave and Brenda Moulson, Thunder Bay, Ontario
Brian and Joanne Novak, Thunder Bay, Ontario
Ron and June Parkila, Baraga, Michigan
Jerry Powlas and Karen Larson, Maple Grove, Minnesota
Joe Radtke, Superior, Wisconsin
Murray and Donna Smeltzer, Red Rock, Ontario
Helge and Judy Swanson, Red Rock, Ontario
Ken Tennant, Hudson, Wisconsin
Dave Tersteeg, Grand Marais, Minnesota
Jack and Wendy Ward, Collingwood, Ontario
John and Carol Zechner, Nipigon, Ontario

Staff members in the National Park Service continue to give information and read the Apostle Islands and Isle Royale chapters for accuracy and technical error.

Apostle Islands National Lakeshore
Bob Krumenaker, Park Superintendant
Neil Howk, Assistant Chief, Interpretation and Education
Steve Kacvinsky, Supervisor Marine and Grounds
Jim Nepstad, Chief of Planning and Resource Development
John Pavkovich, Supervisory Park Ranger

Isle Royale National Park
Phyllis Green, Park Superintendant
Larry Kangas, Chief Ranger
Steve Martin, West District Ranger
Liz Valencia, Chief of Interpretation & Cultural Resource Division

Fifth Edition

Once again, I want to thank those fellow boaters who are still contributing to Superior Way. Throughout the years many of you have freely pointed out updates, changes in home marinas etc. I want to thank those who are *new* contributors. It's amazing how many new contributors, listed below, we get with each edition. Again, a very large thank you goes to the staff members in the National Park Service who continue to give information and read the Apostle Islands and Isle Royale chapters for accuracy and technical error.

Richard Barzyk, Wellington, Ohio
John & Carol Blackburn, Savage, Minnesota
Dave Carr, Port Severn, Michigan
Scott Cheadle, Silver Islet, Ontario

Cathy Collinson, Rossport, Ontario
Liam Giffin, Nipigon, Ontario
Gary & Ann Hay, Coty, Wyoming
Bill & Grace Hines, Saxon Harbor, Wisconsin
Anothy Holland, Black River Harbor, Michigan
Tony Holly, Cornucopia, Wisconsin
Kim Ode, Edina, Minnesota
Devin Olson, Munising, Michigan
Eric Peterson, Saxon Harbor, Wisconsin
Steve Robinson, Thunder Bay, Ontario
Brian & Joanne Norvak, Thunder Bay, Ontario
Nelson Stone, Souix Falls, South Dakota
Dave Tersteed, Grand Marais, Minnesota
Gil Veith & Kay Jacobs, Two Harbors, Minnesota
Frank & Joanne Welsh, Marquette, Michigan
Jim Witz, Skanee, Michigan.
Apostle Islands National Lakeshore

Apostle Islands National Lakeshore
Lynne Dominy , Park Superintendent
Lucas Wescott, Director of Communication & Education
Jennette Gary, Recreation Fee Supervisor & Volunteer Coordinator
Neil Howk, Deputy Program Manager of Interpretation (Retired)
Dave Cooper, Cultural Resource Specialist (Retired)
Isle Royal National Park

Isle Royale National Park
Denice Swanke, Park Superintendent
Jeff Arnst, Lead Park Ranger

Forward 5th Edition

It is hard to believe that once again we are bringing out another edition of *Superior Way*. Who would have thought when we started out with the first edition in 1982 that we would be doing this 5 times. In looking back, it took dozens of log books and hundreds of chartlets written/drawn over almost 50 years that went into the making of Superior Way. We want to thank you, the boating community, for your continued support and acceptance. We could not have done it without you. Because of your support we are able to bring you yet another updated edition, the 5th edition of *Superior Way*.

In looking back over the years since our first year on the Big Lake in 1974, we have seen countless changes in recreational boating. One of the first is that now we know where we are going. In those early years, very little was written up about the wilderness areas. Aside from the odd fisherman, we were the first to visit most anchorages - let alone write up any up for public use. Very little had been written about the North Shore beyond Minnesota and particularly the Canadian waters of the East Shore. GLCC (Great Lakes Cruising Club) had a few Harbor Reports written by paper mill employees, but that was it. Hence our log books, written for our own use so we would have something to go back to. These were soon followed by our own contributions to GLCC Harbor Reports and then soon after — Superior Way.

Another change in those early years was in boat construction where fiberglass was taking its place in the industry, replacing wood. There were also changes occurring in the area of navigation where we went through a number of systems. Loran C (which many of our readers never heard of) was just getting a foothold only to be ousted by Satnav, the first satellite-based navigation system. This was soon replaced by GPS and all the bells and whistles that came with electronic navigation. These years were enhanced by the silicon chip and computers that were simultaneously bringing on an electronics industry never thought of before.

Just since the writing of the last edition, we have seen some of the biggest changes in electronics for the boater, both recreational and commercial. Two of these AIS (Automatic information System) and DSC (Digital Selective Calling) are used with the VHF radio. With AIS, vessels of all sizes are able to exchange identity and position/navigation information with each other and land-based systems. Particularly useful in conditions of reduced visibility, it can also be Interfaced with ship's chart plotters and radar. With DSC, boaters can digitally send pre-determined messages, like a distress call, on channel 70.

One of the biggest and most recent changes to boating is NOAA's announcement that as of January 2025 it would no longer be producing traditional paper copies of its raster nautical charts, that they would be replaced by Electric Navigational Charts (ENC). The ability to get navigational charts on different devices like tablets and laptops will enable flexible use around the boat not to mention all the different attributes that digital brings. The impact on electronic charts and their derivatives such as the chart plotter is going to be phenomenal. The chart plotter differs from ENC by integrating GPS data so that position is determined along with other navigation characteristics on the chart. A lot of combinations are possible such as integrating with other ship's systems like radar. The chart plotter has already seen a lot of use in the two decades since 2000. Now with the elimination of paper charts it is expected to be even larger.

I cannot go into the 5th edition without recognizing Cindy and Paul Hayden, past owners of *Lake Superior Port Cities*: publishers of *Lake Superior Magazine* and *The Lake Superior Travel Guide*. In addition to publishing a number of books, they were also my publishers for *The Superior Way: The Cruising Guide for Lake Superior* 2nd, 3rd, and 4th editions. It was Paul and Cindy's love of Lake Superior, their belief in the book and the need for such a book on this big, beautiful lake that literally put Superior Way on the map. They took Superior Way from a small paperback book and made it into an easy to use spiral bound, double in size cruising manual. Paul has also been the lead editor for 3 editions. Among so many things, I appreciate that he has always been careful in preserving my "writer's voice".

In bringing you this 5th edition there are a number of changes. The first is that we have a new publisher, Kollath+Stensaas Publishing, which includes our new graphic designer, Rick Kollath. Thus, Rick has experience in both publishing and designing numerous books. He also knows Superior well, having boated on the lake for many years, particularly in the wilderness areas. As a graphic designer, Rick conveys a fresh new approach to the book in the layout and presentation of many of the charts and graphics that have been in the book for decades. Within this edition, in opening to almost any page, you will see the addition of full color along with clear representation and easy to understand explanations. It has been a pleasure working with Rick as he brings new ideas from the industry to these pages.

Also new to the team is my editor, Bob Shutes. Bob also knows Lake Superior well, having begun sailing on the lake when he was 16 and owning several different boats on the lake throughout the years. Bob is also a writer who has written both prose and poetry. In particular, I would like to draw your attention to his poem, "A Lady Ice Blue" which I have chosen to introduce the book. Phrases like "Playful in day breeze …", "…memories of glacier days.", "…she will be stalking ships.", portray in succinct description many of the traits Superior has lurking in her waters.

I cannot think of a better way to introduce any book on Lake Superior and his poem is found at the beginning, just prior to Chapter One.

In all 4 editions I dedicated the book to my husband Ron. In each one I wrote a dedication statement. Although they were all beautiful, it's the one in the first edition I like the best:

> "To my husband Ron,
> without whom, the adventure
> would have never begun."

And it is true, in so many different respects. It is especially true in the writing of Superior Way. It was his idea to take all the anchorages I had written up so far in our Log Books along with their charts and put them into a book. He was there at each turn of the way, with each new edition, helping and giving encouragement. But now we are no longer boating, in more than 50 years, we no longer have a boat. And so, it is time to pass on the baton to our son, Peter who spent his summers as a young lad growing up on our boat; who has recently completed his own boat, and launched it just a few months ago (see Appendix V 2024); who has just recently completed his maiden voyage; whose turn is to now - "carry on the dream".

— Bonnie Dahl
August 2024

Table of Contents

Detailed Table of Contents

In the Order of the Book

61 Docking

62 Anchoring

Chapter 3 South Shore
70 Waiska Bay, Michigan, to Washburn, Wisconsin

71 Harbors and Anchorages

Chapter 4 The Apostle Islands
114 A National Lakeshore

Chapter 5 West End
164 Cornucopia, Wisconsin, to Pigeon Point, Minnesota

164 Harbors and Anchorages

Chapter 6 Isle Royale
192 A National Park

199 Harbors and Anchorages

Chapter 7 Gateway to the North
234 Pigeon Point, Minnesota, to Lamb Island, Ontario

236 Harbors and Anchorages

Chapter 8 Across the Top of the Lake
272 Nipigon Strait to Port Coldwell, Ontario

273 Harbors and Anchorages

Chapter 9 East Shore
314 Marathon to Dog Harbour, Ontario

317 Harbors and Anchorages

Chapter 10 East Shore
354 Michipicoten Island, Michipicoten Harbour to Gros Cap

354 Harbors and Anchorages

Chapter 11 Crossroads of the Upper Great Lakes
388 Sault Ste. Marie and St. Marys River

Notice to Mariners

The maps, charts and GPS data contained in this book have been adapted from official NOAA and Canadian charts or from the author's personal experience. However, they are not intended for navigational use beyond as a general background reference for the mariner. We strongly urge acquisition of the proper official U.S. and Canadian charts for any and all navigational needs.

A Lady Ice Blue

Superior is a Lady Ice Blue.
 But she has a glacier heart and her thoughts are glacier thoughts.

Once she made the bedrock groan and crushed the hills without regret.
 Boulders trembled at her approach while the rocks cried out in surrender.
How dreadful this Queen of Snows! Stalking the land with unhurried step.

Look at her now! Her ice feet melted away.
 Hobbled by a shore, her wanderings all ended.
Pebbles and stones gather on her beaches, staring and unafraid.
 Laughing, they skip across her back at the hands of children.

Look at her now! None like Superior! Incomparable, beautiful, cold.
 She has become a lady! Melted to crystal blue.
No more the unbearable crushings of her glacier past.
 She has become beautiful in lakehood, brilliant and shining.

She has been gentle with me at dayspring and twilight.
 Playful in day breeze and splashing sunshine.
I have watched her dancing in moonbeam and starlight.
 When she was contented and her sighs were soft at the shore.

But October winds stir up memories of glacier days.
 Deep in the cold waters where no one sees.
That is when her thoughts return to crushing.

By November she will be stalking ships.
 Men and freighters trembling at her furious step.
No one is safe with her then. The sailors know.

But today she is gracious and lovely.
 So beautiful is this Lady Ice Blue.

Robert S. Shutes c. 2001
rsshutes@aol.com
(612) 845-4520

Chapter One

An Introduction To The Lake

From the beginning of time, Lake Superior has held a certain fascination for all who come to its shores. Early natives painted prehistoric pictographs depicting "sea monsters" on rock-faced cliff walls. Voyageurs chanted of the rigors of living on the water in their boisterous songs as they paddled through pristine wilderness areas. Longfellow wrote of "the shores of Gitche Gumee, by the shining Big-Sea-Water." The Group of Seven (Canadian artists) captured the raw majesty of Lake Superior's Algoma region and north shore in a bold new style on canvas. In the last decades of the 20th century, we listened to Gordon Lightfoot's haunting ballad of the gales of November. And more recently to Ian Tamblyn's "Woodsmoke and Oranges":

"In the land of the silver birch, cry of the loon,
There's something 'bout this country that's a part of me and you."

To those who cruise Lake Superior's waters, the lake evokes a feeling of awe and respect; love and fear. However we try to capture the moods of the lake, whether it is with pictures, words or song, one thing always becomes apparent—the moods of Lake Superior are ever-changing. In fact, they are so different, it is almost as though the lake takes on human qualities and has many different personalities.

For example, there are times when the lake seems quite gentle and almost complacent with an "I don't care" attitude. On days like this you can just about get away with anything, as it is so calm the water becomes almost oily in appearance and a canoe or kayak can take to the lake without fear of turning over. Fishermen especially like the lake when it is like this. During these quiet periods, close to harbor entrances, they can be seen by the dozens in their small open boats—drifting specks on the horizon, like small mosquitoes on a millpond. If the sun is out, sunbathing and

Please Note:
Maps and Charts
in this book are
not necessarily
to scale and are
not intended for
navigation.

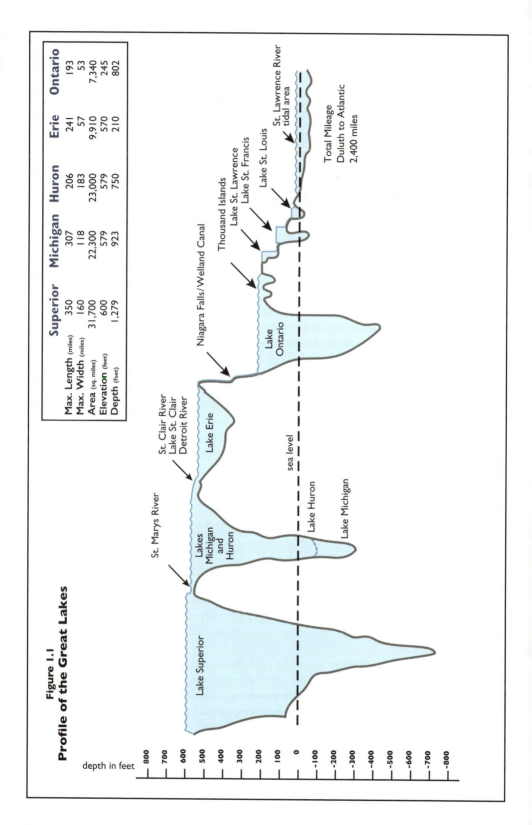

Figure 1.1
Profile of the Great Lakes

	Superior	Michigan	Huron	Erie	Ontario
Max. Length (miles)	350	307	206	241	193
Max. Width (miles)	160	118	183	57	53
Area (sq. miles)	31,700	22,300	23,000	9,910	7,340
Elevation (feet)	600	579	579	570	245
Depth (feet)	1,279	923	750	210	802

St. Marys River

St. Clair River
Lake St. Clair
Detroit River

Niagara Falls/Welland Canal

Thousand Islands
Lake St. Lawrence
Lake St. Francis

Lake St. Louis

St. Lawrence River
tidal area

Total Mileage
Duluth to Atlantic
2,400 miles

Lake Superior

Lakes
Michigan
and
Huron

Lake Erie

Lake
Ontario

Lake Huron

Lake Michigan

sea level

depth in feet

800
700
600
500
400
300
200
100
0
-100
-200
-300
-400
-500
-600
-700
-800

even swimming in the backwaters is possible.

There are also times when the lake is friendly and inviting, such as on a warm fall day in the Apostle Islands when the leaves are beginning to turn or when the fishing is good off the reefs at Isle Royale. Even the rugged north country can be inviting as one protective island chain after another beckons as we skim over the water under an azure sky. Secure in a hidden anchorage by Lake Superior's lush green forest and lichen-painted shoreline, we sit by a shore fire to watch the stars come out. Off in the distance a loon is heard calling hauntingly to its mate.

Would that it were always like this. But just when things are going well and we begin to enjoy the lake too much, Lake Superior pulls the "great deception" — fog.

It may be that Lake Superior likes to keep us on our navigational toes — but does it have to do this so well or so often? Certainly fog adds to the excitement and challenge of a cruise, and it may even make good telling back home, for everyone has a "fog adventure." But to be fogged into an anchorage for days on end can upset the schedule for a whole vacation, if not be just downright boring. Yet wrapped in a cloak of gray mystery, the lake takes on an eerie quality as islands and rocky shorelines become but shadows receding into the distance. Whether we are out on the water or walking on a beach in the mist, fog puts us in a world apart with a silence that is broken only by the lonely cry of a gull or the mournful wail of a distant foghorn.

In addition to being deceptive, the lake is also quite fickle. For just when we've set our light-air sails, the wind pipes up. When we've changed to a working jib, the wind drops back to a whisper. There are times, however, when the lake becomes compassionate as when fog is allowed to lift for just a moment so we can see our way into a tricky anchorage. It can even be forgiving as with a rainbow after a shower or the surprise of sun after a squall.

Sometimes the lake exhibits a temper and shows its anger. Especially in early summer, squalls and thunderstorms become commonplace, and it is not without anxiety that we pilot our small craft between lightning touchdowns. The strong winds in a squall line or the updraft of a thunderstorm make it seem as though the lake is lashing out its anger upon us. Even the water is no longer a friendly deep blue, for without the reflection from a blue sky, it takes on a black, hostile look. Fortunately, as with most tempers, these conditions are usually short-lived — unless they are predecessors to a full-scale storm.

There are times when the lake is downright mean. You only have to look to the carved-out caves in the Apostle Islands or the Pictured Rocks on the south shore to envision the power and treachery of which the lake is capable. For to experience a storm on Lake Superior is to behold the lake with all its latent fury unleashed. Although these storms are not the rule during the summer months, a few may still remember the one that quickly developed during the Trans-Superior

Race in late July 1977. Raging through the Saturday night of that race, seas and winds built to such proportions that at least a quarter of the original boats were forced to retire and turn off into Copper Harbor. And many will not soon forget the wild raging winds that whipped over the western part of the lake the 4th of July, 1999. Now with climate change we are finding that these storms are coming more often and with greater intensity.

Yet on 10 November 1975, such a storm did develop and the *Edmund Fitzgerald* was tragically sunk with her crew of 29 men just a few miles from the relative safety of Whitefish Bay. Before the ship went down, her captain, E.M. McSorley, reported winds of 60 to 70 mph and waves of 30 feet. At one point he must have encountered a rogue wave, for he came over the radio, "...big sea —I've never seen anything like it in my life." On the east shore, which was particularly hard hit, this same storm took out the rock breakwater at Mamainse Harbour and part of the large government dock at Sinclair Cove. Farther up the shore, hurricane-force winds ripped off the siding of buildings at Otter Head Lighthouse, while at Battle Island Light, 500-gallon tanks of diesel were lifted out of their cradles and tossed about like so much driftwood.

As if to show that it has the last word, Lake Superior isn't content with just winter storms. Commercial shipping still continues into December, but the lake knows that in the end it has final control, as all navigation ceases when the ice closes in. Only a couple of times in recent history has the freeze-over been complete —in 1962 and 1979, and almost 100 percent in 1996 and 90 percent 2014. No longer were the rogue waves free to roam; a strange sound of hushed silence settled over the lake as the lonely wind howled across the great expanse of crystalline white.

An Inland Sea

To call Lake Superior a lake is an anomaly, as its size alone dictates that it is an inland sea. Belonging to the largest fresh-water system in the world, Lake Superior has the largest surface area of any fresh-water lake on earth, in excess of 31,000 square miles. It is 383 miles long and 160 miles wide at its greatest breadth. Lake Superior's average depth is 487 feet and in some places exceeds almost 1,300 feet. These dimensions make it the largest volume of fresh water on this hemisphere. Lake Superior is not, however, the largest fresh-water body on the planet. Lake Baykal (Baikal) in Russia, because of its great depths (in some places as much as 5,000 feet) has the greatest fresh-water volume—six quadrillion gallons. Actually when measuring by volume, Lake Superior is only No. 3 with 3 quadrillion gallons and is superceded by Lake Tanganyika in East Africa with almost 5 quadrillion gallons. (See Fig. 1.1.)

Lake Superior's drainage basin is also impressive: 80,900 square miles. More than 200 rivers and streams pour their waters into the lake where the general flow is to the southeast and Sault Ste. Marie.

At 602 feet above sea level, its waters begin the descent to the sea, first via the St. Marys River and the Sault Ste. Marie locks to lakes Huron and Erie, then they plunge over the Niagara Falls into Lake Ontario and finally down the last stretch of the St. Lawrence River into the Atlantic Ocean. Less than 1 percent of Lake Superior's waters leave each year via the Soo. At this rate, it would take almost 200 years to cleanse the lake of any accumulated pollution.

Because of its size, Lake Superior's waters are very cold, usually around 43 degrees Fahrenheit or 8 degrees Celsius. In some of the backwaters and shallow bays, especially on the north and east shores, it is often possible to find much warmer water in midsummer—warm enough for even swimming. This constant water temperature and the fact that it takes enormous amounts of energy to change it even a few degrees has a definite effect on local weather conditions. Summers tend to be cooler than areas inland; winters are generally milder. Spring and fall are often one to two weeks later than in surrounding areas.

An Exceptional Cruising Area

Much of the area surrounding Lake Superior is covered with dense forest, dark with spruce and firs, accented with stands of birch and poplar. Hence it is this vast wilderness of Lake Superior's shoreline—still left largely intact from the impact of man and civilization pursuits—that makes Lake Superior one of the prime cruising areas in the world. Here are the steep cliffs of Old Woman Bay, the raw majesty of Palisade Head and the famed rolling sand dunes of Au Sable. The intricate sandstone caves of the Apostle Islands are only excelled by the grandeur of the south shore's Pictured Rocks.

Waterfalls can be seen falling directly into the lake as at Otter Head. There are high-rising island chains through which one can wander in complete protection from the lake along the northern shore. This is sharply contrasted by the splendor of cruising the open waters of Lake Superior's expansive eastern shore. Against bold headlands such as Cape Gargantua and La Canadienne Pointe, we cruise at land's edge, our small craft insignificant next to these heavily forested bluffs plunging deep into the water.

As rich and diverse as its topography, the wildlife of Lake Superior also greets us with a seemingly endless abundance. Again, it is in the wilderness that we experience Lake Superior at its best. For here moose and deer are common companions. It is not unusual to see beaver and otter scampering on the shoreline as we glide into an anchorage. Chipmunks and red squirrels entertain us with their antics. Occasionally we are able to catch glimpses of wry foxes and shy caribou. Sometimes we may even hear the distant howl of wolves on Isle Royale.

Waterfowl are also present in many varieties and great numbers. Wood ducks and mergansers can be found plying the backwaters.

The stately flight of the great blue heron is often seen overhead. And, of course, there is the ever-present herring gull, always looking for a handout, scolding us when our anchorages invade a rookery. Then, in contrast to the high-pitched screech of the gull, there is that beautiful, haunting call of a distant loon on a still night.

Not only is the Lake Superior wildlife abundant, but the offerings of anchorages to the cruising boater seem endless. Isle Royale alone has more docks and anchorages than one could visit in a single vacation. Likewise, the Apostle Islands and the south shore offer a changing variety to satisfy every sailor's interest. And when you talk about the north and east shores, there are more rivers, bays, inlets, coves and island chains than one could explore in many summers. Each anchorage is a true "hurricane hole" and each seems better than the last.

Setting the Scene: Early Beginnings

Lake Superior is unique among the Great Lakes in that its basin is composed of a bedrock that is far different and older than any of the other lakes. Known as the Canadian Shield, or often called the Laurentian Shield, this very hard rock core extends south from Hudson Bay forming the basin for all but the southeast corner of the lake.

Parts of the shield are rich in metals: iron, copper, silver and nickel. In fact, the word *mesabi* means *great* in Chippewa, referring to those vast areas rich in iron ore to the northwest of the lake. Even today in cruising the lake, we are quickly made aware of the effects that these mineral deposits have had on the history of the lake, past and present. For example, Keweenaw Peninsula is known as "Copper Country," we can explore ancient copper pits of the Native Americans on Isle Royale; Silver Islet entices us with stories of men waging an endless battle against the elements; and we dodge the huge ore carriers as they head out from Silver Bay.

Warm tropical seas and even volcanos all had a part in molding the Lake Superior basin. But it was the glaciers that had the greatest impact in forming the lake as we know it today. These huge ice fields, more than a mile thick, moved out over the region from the northeast several times during the past 2 million years. There were four distinct periods, but it was as the last of the glaciers retreated (approximately 10,000 years ago) that the modern shorelines began to emerge, taking their final shape as recently as 2,500 years ago. Following the paths of major pre-glacial river systems and by glacial excavation of valley floors, the present bodies of water formed as the glacial melt was held between the glacier edge on the north and the high ground on the south. Called Lake Minong, this post-glacial predecessor to Lake Superior was 600 feet higher than the present level. Evidence of these higher lake levels is seen in the old terraced cobbled beaches on the east and north shores. Today, part of the Canadian Shield is once again left exposed. It is interesting to note that as we cruise along the high bluffs of Lake Superior's east shore, or wander through the numerous island chains of the north shore, we are actually seeing the remnants of the oldest highlands of this continent that are formed from its oldest bedrock originating more than a billion years ago.

As the climate continued to warm, it was probably between 9,000 and 9,500 years ago that plants and animals first became permanently established in the area. The vegetation was initially quite sparse, similar to the grasses and dwarf bush of present-day northern tundra. Then came the conifers such as the black spruce, the trademark of the northern boreal forest. Deciduous trees such as white birch and alder invaded from the warmer climates of the south. With the changes in vegetation came the wildlife: caribou, white-tailed deer and later moose. The lakes were first inhabited by cold-water fishes such as whitefish and lake trout followed by northern pike and walleye. The scene was set, and it wasn't too much later that there was another arrival—humans.

Early Inhabitants

Archaeological evidence attributes the arrival of man to the North American continent via the Bering Land Bridge beginning about 11,000 years ago. It wasn't until a couple of thousand years later, however, that these Paleo-Indians (ancient Americans) began to inhabit the Lake Superior area. There are four main periods or cultures of prehistoric occupation (see Fig. 1.2), and artifacts in the Lakehead area indicate occupation of this first group between 9,000 and 8,000 years ago. Although these Paleo-Indians lived along the shoreline, the lake at that time was about 150 feet higher than present-day Lake Superior, so these crude tools are found quite a bit inland. It was a harsh subsistent existence, and stone dart heads tell us that survival was primarily by hunting, since fish populations were still developing.

Sometime in this vague past, the early inhabitants of the region left some puzzling telltale signs of their presence. Known as the Pukaskwa Pits, these curious circular or oblong structures are found on Lake Superior's east and north shores. (See information on Thompson Island in Chapter 7 and Otter Head in Chapter 9.) Often they are merely depressions in the cobble beaches, but on many of the better sites there are actually the remains of rock walls built up from the beach level. They probably date back to

Figure 1.2
Prehistoric Periods and Cultures of Human Occupation

Period	Culture	Approximate Dates
Paleo-Indian	Plano Culture	11,000 - 7,000 years ago
Archaic	Shield Archaic Culture	7,000 - 3,000 years ago
Initial Woodland	Laurel Culture	3,000 - 1,000 years ago
Terminal Woodland	Algonkian Culture	1,000 years ago - early 1600s

somewhere between 5,000 to 2,000 years ago, which would put them in the Archaic period. Lack of artifacts has made it difficult to date them, however, and they are currently under study. For those who venture to Lake Superior's wilderness areas, these curious structures can be found up on the terraced cobble beaches that are also indicative of higher lake levels in millennia past.

The Archaic period roughly spanned a time frame of 7,000 to 3,000 years ago. Dramatic warming changes in climate enabled these people of the Shield Archaic Culture to devote more time to developing tools and living conditions. Birch-bark canoes came into use and weapons for hunting were improved. It was late in this period that the bow and arrow were developed, which greatly enhanced their abilities in obtaining wild game. Fish also became a part of the diet. It is thought that during this time, fishing with fish hooks and nets came into practice.

One of the biggest changes to occur during this period was the mining and use of copper. It is interesting that the first use of any metal in North America took place in the Lake Superior region — the Keweenaw Peninsula. Primitive mining pits left by these Old Copper Indians dating back to 4000 BC have been found here and also on Isle Royale. The copper was heated and hammered into weapons, fish hooks and various tools. Today, those who visit Isle Royale can see many of the primitive pits which are still intact and show extensive engineering techniques such as underground drains and tunnels.

Artifacts found on Isle Royale and Michipicoten Island indicate that these early inhabitants were probably crossing the lake during this period. It is generally believed that there was substantial traffic between the Keweenaw Peninsula and Isle Royale in search of copper. Today, anyone who sails the 50-mile distance over open water can only marvel at these hardy adventurers who made this trip in open bark canoes.

The Woodland period is actually divided into two periods: the Initial Woodland and the Terminal Woodland. One of the main changes in the Initial Woodland period (3,000 to 1,000 years ago) was the introduction of pottery. Another was the widespread expansion of trade. During this time, Lake Superior copper found its way to the Atlantic coast, the Southwest and even as far away as Mexico.

The Terminal Woodland period extended from 1,000 years ago to the coming of the white man in the 1600s. During this time, the tribes in the Great Lakes region had stabilized into a number of territorial units. To the north and far west of Lake Superior were the Cree; to the east and in Georgian Bay the Algonkins (Algonquins); and around Lake Superior's east shore and part of the south shore the Ojibwe (Ojibwa, Ojibway), sometimes known also as the Chippewa. A common language, Algonkian, promoted considerable travel and trade among the three bands. (Note: with a westward expansion closely tied with the coming of the Europeans and the fur trade, the Ojibwe completely dominated all of Lake Superior's shores by the mid-1800s.)

The life of the Ojibwe ("people who have puckered moccasin seams") was a nomadic one existing primarily on hunting and fishing. They were organized into family groups or clans consisting of approximately 30 family groups with around 20 people in each. They usually came together in the summer to traditional campgrounds on major waterways for fishing. But with the approach of the harsh winter, they would disband to spread-out individual camps so that the game could support the smaller units.

Some of the Ojibwe story is told in Indian paintings (pictographs) that are usually found on rock-faced cliff walls. Although there are hundreds of these sites of Shield Art found inland in the Nipigon area and to the northeast of the lake, there are only a few found on Lake Superior's shores. Of these, the best site is found at Sinclair Cove on Lake Superior's east shore (see Chapter 10). The pictures may have been painted at different times, but one is definitely dated, since it shows a man on horseback. It could only have been painted after encounters with Europeans or stories of them. With the coming of the Europeans, the cultures of these first North Americans were to be forever changed.

Early Explorations

The first white man to see Lake Superior is usually considered to be Etienne Brulé, one of Champlain's scouts. Brulé explored the Great Lakes region from 1608 until his death in 1633. Little is known of his adventures, because he spent much of his time living in close contact with the Huron Indians of the Georgian Bay area and kept no written records after 1615. Champlain, however, did record many of Brulé's explorations, and from this we learn that in 1618 he sent Brulé west of Georgian Bay to further explore the area. It is generally assumed that Brulé probably passed along the north shore of Georgian Bay and then entered Lake Superior via the St. Marys River. At this time Brulé and his companion, Grenoble, named this new discovery *la mer douce du nord*—"the Sweet Sea of the North." A beautiful anchorage honoring Brulé's name lies on Lake Superior's eastern shore, just south of Michipicoten Harbour.

There is also some controversy concerning the Vikings, who may have been the first Europeans to see Lake Superior. Recent discoveries have established the existence of small Scandinavian colonies along the Labrador and Nova Scotia coastlines, long before the arrival of Columbus. In addition, early Scandinavian artifacts dating back to 1362, especially the Kensington stone with runic inscriptions, have been found as far inland as northern Minnesota. If authentic (there has been some controversy concerning these findings), these artifacts lead to the assumption that these "Vikings" made their way inland via Hudson Bay and then traveled south

over land. There are two generally accepted routes, one that "could" skirt the northern shore of Lake Superior. However, any evidence confirming the presence of the Vikings on the lake is yet to be found.

After Champlain and Brulé came other explorers, missionaries, fur traders and the voyageurs—all of whom in these early years were French. It was the French who first constructed a map (before 1658) of the area calling the lake *Lac Tracy* in honor of the then Governor General of New France. The name was later changed to *Supérieur,* which meant "upper lake" not "superior" meaning great or grand as the translation eventually became.

It was the French Medard Chouart, Sieur des Groseilliers, and Pierre Ésprit Radisson, who were the first to give any detailed written account of the lake in their epic, but unauthorized, trip along the southern shore to Chequamegon Bay in 1658. When they returned to Montreal expecting a hero's welcome, they were fined for trading without a permit and their furs were seized. In retaliation, they turned to the British and instigated the formation of the Hudson's Bay Company, thus beginning a rivalry that was to last 200 years. Other explorers who opened up vast areas of the lake all bear French names: Sieur du L'hut, Jolliet, Jean Baptiste Péré, Father Allouez and Father Marquette—names which still remain in use around the lake today.

It is interesting that because of easy access to the Great Lakes waterway, this area of the continent was penetrated and explored much earlier than other areas of the New World farther south. Thus, while the British were busily settling the colonies on the eastern seaboard, Jesuit missionaries were establishing missions at Sault Ste. Marie, the Keweenaw Peninsula and the Apostle Islands as early as the 1660s.

With a zeal that was unequalled, these first pioneers, the Jesuits, endured great hardships in the harsh wilderness, often including torture and murder at the hands of the Native Americans. So vigorous were the Jesuits in their pursuits that by 1680 they had the lake completely encircled with their missions. It is because of their detailed narratives in the 73-volume *Jesuit Relations* that we have an articulated documentation of native life and habits, and early French colonial life. There are numerous places around the lake where tribute is paid to these courageous souls, the first true pioneers of the lake.

The Fur Trade

Centuries ago, Lake Superior provided a vital link in the pursuit of one of the New World's most highly sought resources. So important was this precious commodity that it spurred the efforts of three major national powers for more than 200 years and instigated extensive exploration far into the interior while the Colonists were still struggling with survival far to the east. The great treasure? Furs. In particular, the luxurious beaver that was used to make the distinctive tall felt hats of the wealthy and rising bourgeois of the

European countries across the ocean.

So crucial was the fur trade in those early years that it could be compared to the impact of oil and petroleum products in our modern economy. Rivaling an oil cartel, a vast network was developed that linked the merchants or "partners" in Montreal with the traders and trappers in the far reaches of the Northwest Territories, a distance of 3,000 rugged wilderness miles.

Lured by the profits to be made from a lucrative trade in furbearing animals, first the French and then the British and Americans established large fur trading companies that were to become a critical factor in the development of the area. With the arrival of the North West Company, and the subsequent rivalries with the Hudson's Bay and American Fur companies, came the establishment of trade routes and forts that became an integral part in the building of an empire.

At first, in the late 1600s, furs were brought out by *coureurs de bois* (runners of the woods), independent frontiersmen who lived in close harmony with Native American tribes. But as the Montreal partners gained more control, brigades of voyageurs were formed to transport the furs east to Montreal, replacing the frontiersmen.

The voyageurs were boatmen — French canoeists, who with their large Montreal canoes (*canot de maitre* or master canoe) plied the open waters of Lake Superior and portaged the rough terrain of the upper Great Lakes. Leaving in early spring with ice break-up, these Montrealers would be heavily loaded with trade goods for the North American winters.

The life of a voyageur was a rigorous one, often spent paddling or portaging 16 to 17 hours per day to take advantage of the long northern day. The only breaks were "pipes," that were short rest stops to smoke a small clay pipe of tobacco. Portages were especially grueling since 90-pound packs were carried at a running trot, two packs at a time. With routes that were long and dangerous, these hardy men developed a way of life characterized by endless hours of paddling to the chants of their boisterous songs. Living on thin rations and the camaraderie of their peers, the main high point in their lives was the Great Rendezvous which took place in early summer each year.

In the early years, the rendezvous was held at Grand Portage, which is located in the far eastern tip of Minnesota. It was a logical place because it marked the end of open-water canoeing on the lake and the beginning of the inland waterway system to Lake of the Woods and beyond. In the early 1800s, in an effort to avoid American taxation, the rendezvous was moved north into Canadian territory at Fort William (now the large city of Thunder Bay), which was built in the mouth of the Kaministiquia River.

For a few weeks each summer, the harbor would come alive as thousands of Native Americans, trappers and voyageurs would congregate on the banks of "The Kam." At these meetings, the

differences between the lifestyles of the woodsmen and voyageurs often erupted into open conflict. Usually these confrontations were centered around the pride and joy of each — the canoes which had evolved to meet individual requirements of their respective parts in the system.

The voyageur was proud of his large 36-foot Montreal canoe, which had a beam of 6 feet. But because of the intricate waters inland, the smaller 24-foot *canot d'nord* (north canoes) had been developed for the trapper. While the woodsmen argued that their canoes required more skill, the Montrealers argued that theirs required more strength. Thus, the ability to stand up in a good fight became another characteristic of these hardy men.

When the exchange of goods and decisions of business had been completed, each would turnabout, with Native American and trapper heading inland via the boundary waters network and the voyageur east over the open waters of Lake Superior. What a sight it must have been as one brigade after another would leave, dipping their paddles to the chant of their robust songs.

For the modern boater, glimpses into this colorful past are readily visible in the historic displays at Grand Portage National Monument, Minnesota, and Fort William Historical Park in Thunder Bay, Ontario. Today at Fort William Historical Park, both types of canoes can be seen as they are built by skilled craftsmen, using the same materials and methods employed during the fur-trade era.

Opening the Lake: Shipping

As the centuries passed, it became apparent that the population growth on the lake was closely connected to its resources and the various modes of transportation upon its waters. Thus as resources were developed, the need for larger vessels, other than the canoe, grew as well. This part of Lake Superior's history has special interest to the boater who can compare his modern vessel with the early open boats: the bateaux and the mackinaw (late 1770s). Larger than canoes and too heavy to portage, these boats used sails when conditions permitted, otherwise they were propelled with oars.

As cargo needs increased, so did the size of the sailing ships. During the 1800s, several fleets developed, serving the various mining ventures and the fur companies. Square riggers evolved into schooners and then multimasted schooners. The Double Sloop was a rig unique to the Great Lakes. This new rig had no obstructions in the cargo area and was developed to assist loading and unloading of cargo. Steam vessels first appeared on the lake in 1841.

Along with the increased demand in shipping came the need for safe navigation. Lighthouses began emerging around the lake. The first light station was established at Whitefish Point in 1849. Along with the lighthouses came a new breed of pioneer — the light keepers and their families. In many instances the keepers were put

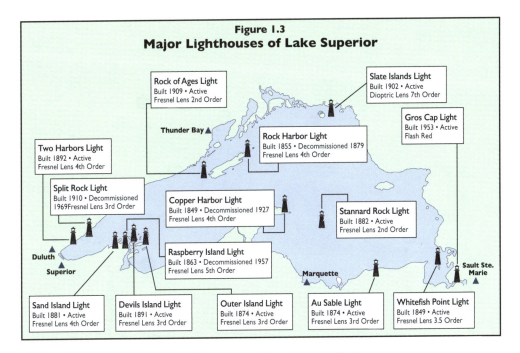

Figure 1.3
Major Lighthouses of Lake Superior

Rock of Ages Light
Built 1909 • Active
Fresnel Lens 2nd Order

Slate Islands Light
Built 1902 • Active
Dioptric Lens 7th Order

Gros Cap Light
Built 1953 • Active
Flash Red

Thunder Bay ▲

Rock Harbor Light
Built 1855 • Decommissioned 1879
Fresnel Lens 4th Order

Two Harbors Light
Built 1892 • Active
Fresnel Lens 4th Order

Split Rock Light
Built 1910 • Decommissioned
1969 Fresnel Lens 3rd Order

Copper Harbor Light
Built 1849 • Decommissioned 1927
Fresnel Lens 4th Order

Stannard Rock Light
Built 1882 • Active
Fresnel Lens 2nd Order

Duluth ▲

Superior ▲

Raspberry Island Light
Built 1863 • Decommissioned 1957
Fresnel Lens 5th Order

Marquette ▲

Sault Ste. Marie ▲

Sand Island Light
Built 1881 • Active
Fresnel Lens 4th Order

Devils Island Light
Built 1891 • Active
Fresnel Lens 3rd Order

Outer Island Light
Built 1874 • Active
Fresnel Lens 3rd Order

Au Sable Light
Built 1874 • Active
Fresnel Lens 3rd Order

Whitefish Point Light
Built 1849 • Active
Fresnel Lens 3.5 Order

on station with ice break-up in the spring only to have to find a way off for themselves in late fall and in a few cases were forced to spend the winter on station. Some stations had additional crew and served also as a lifeboat station such as the one in the Huron Islands. The light keepers became the mainstays of the shoreline and in Ontario waters were even part of the Coast Guard. Many a story has been told about the long and lonely hours in up-keeping the light, rescuing shipwrecked sailors and enduring hardships at these often remote stations.

In the late 1800s, as farmers were turning the prairies into the breadbasket of the world and eastern conglomerates produced an incessant demand for Midwest iron, the demand for increased shipping reached an all-time high. It didn't take steamship owners long to realize that they could greatly increase their profits by towing barges. Just about anything that could float was fair game, and when it became obvious that sail power couldn't effectively compete with steam, many a schooner had its mast cut off and was converted for barge duty. However, skippers soon found that towing an old cumbersome schooner was difficult and time consuming.

About this time one of the most interesting innovations in Great Lakes shipping emerged, the "whaleback" or "pig boat" as it was often called. Designed by Captain Alexander McDougall of Duluth, these cigar-shaped vessels had curved sides with no clear dividing line where the actual deck began. McDougall reasoned that the streamline shape would move through the water easier and provide less resistance in storms by allowing seas to roll over the ship.

The first whaleback was a nonpowered barge, Barge *101*,

An Introduction to the Lake

13

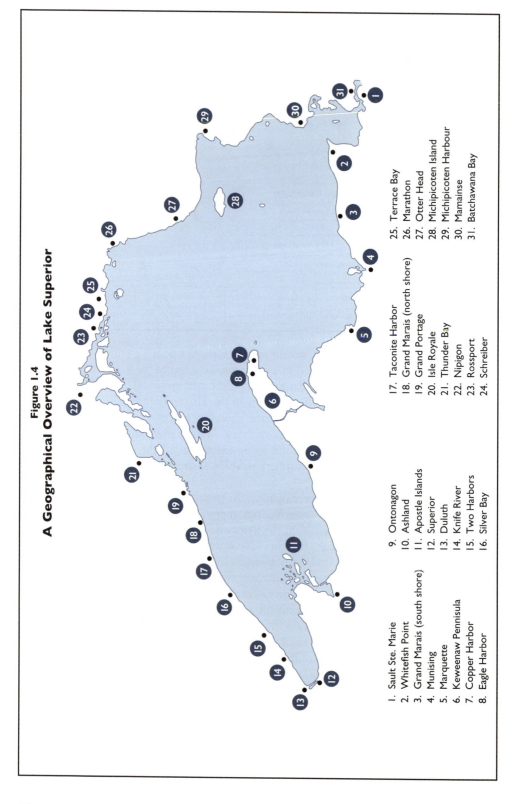

Figure 1.4
A Geographical Overview of Lake Superior

1. Sault Ste. Marie
2. Whitefish Point
3. Grand Marais (south shore)
4. Munising
5. Marquette
6. Keweenaw Pennisula
7. Copper Harbor
8. Eagle Harbor
9. Ontonagon
10. Ashland
11. Apostle Islands
12. Superior
13. Duluth
14. Knife River
15. Two Harbors
16. Silver Bay
17. Taconite Harbor
18. Grand Marais (north shore)
19. Grand Portage
20. Isle Royale
21. Thunder Bay
22. Nipigon
23. Rossport
24. Schreiber
25. Terrace Bay
26. Marathon
27. Otter Head
28. Michipicoten Island
29. Michipicoten Harbour
30. Mamainse
31. Batchawana Bay

which McDougall financed with his own savings. It was launched on 23 June 1888 at Duluth and when heavily laden with iron ore at Two Harbors, McDougall's unconventional ideas about ship construction were quickly proven. John D. Rockefeller was quick to join McDougall in forming the American Steel Barge Company and the whalebacks soon became steam powered with the launching of the *Charles B. Wetmore* on 23 May 1891. The *Wetmore* was the first whaleback to sail on salt water and also the first to go around Cape Horn.

There was a total of 43 whalebacks built, with 40 constructed primarily for Great Lakes shipping. One of the last, the *Frank Rockefeller* (launched in April 1896), had a particularly interesting history. It started out as a bulk carrier for grain and iron ore but was renamed the *South Park* in 1928 when it was refit with sandhoppers for a dredging company. In the mid-1930s it was used to deliver automobiles, and in a November gale in 1942 was stranded near Manistique, Michigan. Purchased by Cleveland Tankers, another refit changed it to an oil tanker with another new name, the *Meteor*. For 25 years, the *Meteor* was the only whaleback roaming the Great Lakes until November 1969 when it went aground near Marquette, Michigan. Unable to pass Coast Guard inspections, Cleveland Tankers presented the *Meteor* as a gift to the city of Superior, Wisconsin. Today, it lies at rest as a fully preserved museum ship at Barker's Island where visitors can get a glimpse into the past and the history of Great Lakes shipping.

The whalebacks were but the predecessors to contemporary Great Lakes ships. Limited by open holds with no interior braces to

Ontario's Old Woman Bay as seen from the Nokomis Hiking Trail in Lake Superior Provincial Park . DAHL

impede cargo handling, the whalebacks couldn't compete with the demands for larger beamed ships. As the size of cargos increased, so did the ships. Today we traverse the shipping lanes with massive 1,000-footers with beams in excess of 100 feet whose size is limited only by the size of the locks at Sault Ste. Marie.

Probably the single greatest change that influenced Lake Superior shipping was the opening of the American Canal in 1855 at Sault Ste. Marie, Michigan. From time beginning, the rapids of the St. Marys River had kept Lake Superior cut off from the rest of the lakes, thus seriously curtailing interlake transportation. Only with great effort and expense could steamships and sailing vessels be hauled on rollers around these treacherous rapids. With the lake open to eastern lakes in the mid-1850s, it only remained for the completion of the St. Lawrence Seaway in 1959 for Lake Superior to take its part in worldwide shipping.

Riding the Rails

Along with shipping another key element in opening up the lake was the building of railroads. Often hand-in-hand with shipping, cargo was transshipped down to the lake only to continue its journey over the open water. The first railways appeared along the south shore in the 1850s to deliver lumber and ore from the Marquette Range to the lake. Within decades, similar rail/ship connections developed along the Wisconsin and Minnesota shorelines. Many towns, such as Ashland and Bayfield, Wisconsin, owe their early development to the arrival of the railroad. But by far the most impressive feat of railroad engineering was the closing of the gap in the transcontinental Canadian Pacific Railroad (CPR) around the north shore of Lake Superior to connect east with west.

It seemed an impossible task. Sheer rock bluffs plunging directly into Lake Superior's waters had to be breached; impenetrable tracks of spongy bog had to be traversed; adverse working conditions in the northern winter had to be endured. The cost in dollars and human life was devastating. It took 12,000 men, 1,500 horses and periodic supply depots, a few of which (Rossport and Peninsula, now Marathon) remain to this day. To blast through the formidable Precambrian Shield required hundreds of tons of dynamite and nitroglycerine. Explosives alone cost more than $7 million requiring three factories built between Jackfish and Coldwell to turn out a ton of dynamite per day. Blasting through just one mile of solid rock near Jackfish cost $700,000. Often whole crews were lost to misjudgment and misplaced explosives. It was not surprising then when the railroad ran out of funds and pressure was exerted to abandon the project. With just four remaining gaps totaling 86 miles, the solution came in an unexpected form in the second Riel Rebellion in the winter of 1885. CPR general manager William Van Horne gambled that if he could demonstrate the use of the railroad with the fast delivery of troops (11 days), funds would be forthcoming. Despite great hardship in crossing those gaps, the troops were delivered, and finally on 16 May 1885, the last spike was driven near the town of Jackfish. Today as we anchor close to shore at Jackfish or at Rossport, we are continually reminded of the CPR presence as trains come roaring through many times a day.

With the establishment of the railroads and the availability of inexpensive water transportation, the scene was once again set. Another key element in the development of the lake and its surrounding areas has been the harvest of its resources. Throughout the centuries, the area's wealth in minerals, forests and fish has significantly contributed to make Lake Superior what it is today.

Mining

With the large mineral deposits surrounding the lake, the Lake Superior area has seen mining of all forms: from the intricate ancient copper mines at Isle Royale to the million-dollar shafts at Silver Islet and the mammoth open pits on the Mesabi Iron Range. All have been instrumental in the development of the lake region. For with the miners came their families and then the towns. Cities and towns such as Marquette, Copper Harbor, Eagle Harbor, Ontonagon, Ashland, Duluth, Silver Bay, Schreiber, Mamainse and Batchawana Bay owe much of their early growth to either mining or the transportation of various ores. Of these, copper and iron lead the list; but silver, lead, zinc, nickel and even gold have also been mined in some quantity.

Copper had been mined early by the Native Americans (Jesuit missionaries reported of spiritual relations between natives and copper) and its various deposits were well-known by early settlers. Yet, it wasn't until the 1840s that serious copper mining began on the Keweenaw Peninsula of Upper Michigan. Substantial amounts of capital were invested by eastern companies, which often yielded returns of 2,000 percent. There were also smaller ventures undertaken on Isle Royale, Michipicoten Island and Mamainse Point in the mid-1800s. However, as competition from mines in the western states grew, production fell off. The peninsula produced only 3.9 percent of the nation's copper in 1970 as compared with 80 percent during 1845-77.

Precious metals have also had their day in Lake Superior's past. As early as 1847, deposits of silver were found in Prince Bay, just south of Thunder Bay. A number of silver mines were quickly established in the area, but none came even close to the miraculous find on a little pile of rock just a mile east of the Sleeping Giant. For 15 years, Silver Islet was the richest producing silver mine in the world, its ore assayed as the richest silver ever found (see Chapter 7).

Lake Superior has even experienced a couple of gold rushes. The first had all the characteristics of a gold stampede, lacking only one thing—gold. It took place on the Vermilion Range in the mid-1800s. A survey had indicated large deposits of iron ore AND gold-

and silver-bearing quartz. The iron ore was ignored and the rush was on. The town of Winston City (no longer exists) was quickly established, along with investment in heavy machinery by at least 15 different companies. By 1866, however, most had abandoned their claims. It wasn't until decades later that miners turned their attentions to the real wealth of the area—iron.

Next to the opening of the Soo locks, the single most important developing factor on the lake was probably the discovery of iron ore. Iron was first mined along the south shore of Michigan's Upper Peninsula and also on the east shore near Wawa (see Chapter 10) in the mid-1800s. But it wasn't until the discovery of the rich deposits in Minnesota's Vermilion and Mesabi ranges in the late 1800s that this natural resource came into its own. In 1884, the first shipment of Minnesota ore left the Vermilion Range.

The first expedition of the Mesabi Range was a clear miss —they missed it by being just to the east of the rich deposits. It wasn't until 25 years later that the full potential of the area became apparent. Then in 1890, after a few initial tests, the results were released—soft ore yielding around 65 percent iron—and the rush was on. In just a few years, more than 100 mining companies were formed, soon to be bought out by eastern investors. In subsequent years, scores of mines were opened and an elaborate rail network was developed to transport the ore to waiting carriers on the lake. The Mesabi Range was an incredibly rich vein, 100 miles long.

With the mines came the railroads—and the people. A true melting pot, thousands of people of all nationalities came to work the mines. Often immigrants or first generation families, these hardworking pioneers became the backbone of the north country. Cities and towns seemed to spring up overnight—a dozen "Range Cities" alone. Along with the more recent discovery of extracting iron from the lower grade taconite rock formations, Lake Superior's iron deposits soon furnished 80 percent of all iron ore produced in the United States.

Although the gold rush on the Vermilion Range was a clear bust, Lake Superior has experienced a full-scale gold rush—and in just the past quarter century. The find is just a few miles inland from Heron Bay in Lake Superior's northeast corner. The presence of gold-bearing veins in the Hemlo-Heron Bay area has been known since the mid-1800s, and at various times attempts were made to extract the precious metal. But it wasn't until 1981 that the extent and location of the deposits were clearly known. With the sophistication of modern-day technology, the rush was on. Gone were the prospector's placer claims and tools of the trade: the pick and shovel. Instead came the metallurgists and engineers of large, well-financed mining conglomerates. Today, there are two mines, the Williams and David Bell that are jointly owned and operated by Teck Cominco and Barrick Gold Corporation. With estimates in excess of $10 billion, it is one of the greatest gold strikes ever—

certainly the largest in Canadian history.

Lumbering

Another major resource, often thought to have contributed as much to the region's growth as mining, is Lake Superior's thick immense forests. It is a region that presents a rich mixture of northern conifers and southern deciduous hardwood trees. As the nation grew, so did the need for building materials. Along with cheap transportation, Lake Superior and its surrounding shores were able to provide both.

Along Lake Superior's southern shores were vast stands of the tall, straight, coveted white pine, the premiere building material. The shoreline north of Duluth produced more white and red pine along with balsam, tamarack, white spruce and cedar, which were used for pulpwood. At Black River Harbor, on the Michigan peninsula, it is possible to see some of this virgin timber still standing straight and tall, to get a small idea of what these massive stands of virgin timber must have been like. The lumbering companies were quick to spot these vast riches as eastern forests became depleted.

Most of the lumbering in the states bordering Lake Superior was done in the 1880s to the 1930s, again beginning in the Upper Peninsula and spreading around the lake. Towns such as Ashland, Superior and Duluth attributed much of their early growth and development to lumbering. Although much of Ontario was devoid of the sought-after white pine, early lumbering here provided timber for railway ties and trestles. But it took a change in the paper industry from using cotton to wood fiber to make lumbering a profitable concern in Ontario. As the pulpwood was harvested, almost overnight towns such as Red Rock, Terrace Bay and Marathon got their start as paper mills. Financed largely by eastern entrepreneurs, again came a corps of skilled and unskilled laborers from many nations. With a new breed of pioneer, the lumberjack, it was a colorful era that rivaled that of the lusty voyageurs.

In many areas, especially along Lake Superior's east shore, the log harvest was brought down to the lake via river drive. Logs were cut during the winter months and skidded to major streams by oxen or horses where they were piled high to await the spring run-off. With the high waters of the snow melt, they were then driven downstream to waiting log booms where they were transported by tugs to sawmills.

At McGreevy Harbour, the large central landlocked basin in the heart of the Slate Islands, logs were brought to be stored and sorted before they made their final journey. Pictures taken as late as the 1940s show the harbor almost completely filled with pulpwood. In giant rafts miles long, the logs were then slowly (one mile per hour) moved to the waiting paper mills. The rafts were susceptible to breaks and often tons of pulpwood would be washed up on the

shore creating income for locals who retrieved them and sold them back to the paper companies. One of these families, the McCuaigs, pursued such an operation out of Heron Bay in Lake Superior's NE corner until the early 1980s.

In some areas, such as the Minnesota shoreline where high elevations resulted in precipitous cascades and waterfalls, river drives were not feasible. One solution was to construct long flumes to bypass the waterfalls, such as those in the lower Pigeon River. It was, however, the railroad industry, developing hand in hand with lumbering, that provided the means via a network of spur lines to transport the logs down to shoreline landings. Later, main lines transported the logs directly to mills in Minnesota and Wisconsin.

The remnants of this era are readily seen in many places around the lake, especially along the Ontario shoreline. For here it is quite common to find pulpwood washed up on the beaches. Sometimes it is possible to see the remains of the large log flumes that were built to transport logs down to the lake, as at Heron Bay. The large chained log booms (bearing individual names for identification), that were used to transport the logs across the lake, are found from time to time at the White River, Pulpwood Harbour, the Pic River and other spots along the eastern shore. There are even the remains of an old Abitibi lumbering village near the Pukaskwa River. All tell the story of when lumber was king and the lake region again gave abundantly of its riches.

Commercial Fishing

When the early Europeans first entered Lake Superior, they found a native population that was heavily dependent on fish for food, primarily whitefish and trout. Early accounts, though often exaggerated, reported of an unusual abundance of this resource. Legendary are the stories of dip netting for whitefish in the St. Marys River rapids. Much of the yearly native life cycle centered around getting food, and each year the Ojibwe would congregate on Lake Superior's shores in summer camps to harvest runs of lake trout that migrated into shallow waters.

Today, Lake Superior and its tributary waters contain a total of 83 different species. Most are native species, but there are also a number that have been introduced either intentionally or accidentally. Two of the native species in particular have been sought over the centuries: the firm white meat of the famed whitefish akin to a chicken's breast and the succulent pink flesh of sweet-tasting trout.

Until the early 1800s, fishing was done largely for local consumption. Then the fur-trading companies established fisheries to supplement their dwindling fur trade. Early stations were at La Pointe on Madeline Island in the Apostles, Isle Royale, Fort William and Michipicoten. As mining and lumbering grew, so did the need for food, and commercial fishing began to thrive. Annual harvests steadily increased, altered only by the ebb and flow of demand, politics and sometimes pollution, due to the various growing industries.

With commercial fishing came another breed of people and boats to pioneer the lake. Using small open boats, powered only by oars and sail, these people developed into a hardy lot. In the early days, there were no diesel-powered tugs equipped with lifters and net pullers, radar, loran and GPS. Everything had to be done by hand in the cold, icy waters—often by husband and wife working side by side in an open boat.

Exploring the sea caves at Woodbine Harbour. DAHL

In the mid- to late 1880s, sailing schooners (followed by the addition of steam power) were adapted to the fishing scene. When the gasoline engine came into use at the turn of the 20th century, followed by the diesel, the greatest improvements for fishing were made. Because of these engines, fishing boats not only had power for locomotion, but also power to run the large drums of the pullers that were used to retrieve the nets. Fishing methods and nets also improved, enabling the anglers to increase their catches. The gill net has been, and still is, the most commonly used. Other types of nets are the pound (sometimes called pond) nets, trap nets and fyke nets. (For diagrams and descriptions of these types of nets, see Chapter 4.)

By the 1880s, as with Lake Superior's other resources, big business began to enter the scene. A large conglomerate, A. Booth and Co. out of Chicago, took over much of the fishing in Lake Superior's waters. On the Canadian shoreline, large stations were established at Gargantua and Quebec Harbour on Michipicoten Island. An independent group, the Nicoll Brothers at Port Coldwell, also established an outlet to market the individual fisherman's catches. In 1934, James and Ivan Purvis bought the Quebec Harbour Station and successfully operated it for the next two decades. Along the south shore, commercial fishing thrived in the Apostle Islands and the villages of Cornucopia and Port Wing became centers for dozens of fish tugs working the surrounding waters. By 1941, commercial fishing reached an all-time high of 25.5 million pounds per year. But this was all to soon change. In a little more than a decade, an invader from the sea all but decimated this, one of Lake Superior's most lucrative industries.

The sea lamprey (*Petromyzon marinus*) is a primitive fish that is now found in both fresh and salt water. It belongs to the family of jawless fishes and has a suckerlike mouth that attaches to its

An Introduction to the Lake

prey much like a suction cup. Inside the mouth are rows of rasping teeth that rasp into the victim's flesh, consequently sucking out blood and bodily fluids. The lamprey attacks are up to 90 percent fatal, and because they seek primarily larger fish that have attained sexual maturity, spawning and continuation of the species is severely affected.

The sea lamprey entered the Great Lakes from the Atlantic Ocean through the St. Lawrence Seaway and were first seen in Lake Ontario in the 1830s. Impeded to further migration by the Niagara Falls, they gained access to the other lakes when the Welland canal, which bypasses the falls, was deepened in 1919. By 1938 the lamprey had invaded all of the Great Lakes with the first Lake Superior sighting at Two Harbors in that year. Within two decades the whitefish and trout stocks were all but depleted. Not only did fishing stations close, but whole towns like the village on Sand Island in the Apostles disappeared.

Initial studies showed that adult sea lampreys migrate up a stream to spawn and then die with the female producing about 65,000 eggs. The nonparasitic larvae burrow into the stream bed where they feed on debris and microorganisms for three to six years before transforming into the parasitic adult and heading back out into the lake where they feed on large fish for 12 to 18 months. Early control attempts in the mid-1950s were to block the lamprey spawning streams with electromechanical weirs, but these proved marginally effective. A breakthrough came in 1958 when the chemical Tri-Fluoro-Methyl-Phenol (TMF) was found that killed the lamprey larvae in the spawning streams without affecting aquatic plants and other wildlife. Another method of control is to collect, sterilize and release males before the spawn. A number of different kinds of barriers are still used and through these combined efforts, there has been a 90 percent reduction of sea lamprey populations.

Today, both commercial and sports fishing are making a comeback. The annual yields, however, are considerably less now (less than 10 million pounds per year for all species) primarily due to conservation control through a quota system, the government buying up commercial licenses on the Canadian shore, and the still present lamprey. Of interest to the fisherman are those species that have been introduced by extensive restocking programs. They include the coho and chinook salmon along with several varieties of trout: lake, rainbow and brown.

Lake Superior Today

Today, Lake Superior is a story of contrasts. Contrasts between the old and the new, contrasts between the wilderness and the urban.

Still-expanding cities such as Marquette, Ashland, Duluth, Superior and Thunder Bay have mushroomed through the decades. Hundreds of thousands of people make their homes here, in these and in smaller towns that dot the shoreline. Industry is booming. Large grain terminals load thousands of bushels per hour. Hundreds of railroad cars, loaded with coal and taconite, can be seen lined up and awaiting unloading. Pulp and paper products are found in the far reaches of two countries. Lake Superior chub makes its way to fine restaurants all along the East Coast. The 1,000-footers, such as the *Mesabi Miner* and the *Columbia Star*, complete the picture as they journey up and down the lake—a vital link in the pursuit of progress. The pulse of the lake is the same as years back, with the lake still giving of its natural resources and providing efficient transportation—only the beat has been stepped up.

However, the story is not complete. Progress and the wilderness are having difficulty existing side by side. Already we have seen hints of a break in the delicate balance between the two. We have only to look to eastern lakes to see that the threats from a growing population, industry itself and poor management have had serious consequences. From time to time, the lake and wilderness have suffered from these effects. But fortunately, our leaders and industry (often at great expense) have seen fit to legislate controls to protect the lake. Large areas have been set aside as parks and national lakeshores to preserve the lake and its wildlife for all to enjoy.

Still, the conflicts persist, and often the solutions are not clear cut as special interest groups meet in open confrontation. It then becomes apparent that the future of the lake rests not only with proper management, but through a combined effort by all to preserve its resources—a legacy for all.

Chapter Two

Cruising Tips for Lake Superior

For novice and experienced sailors alike, there is one characteristic of Lake Superior with which we must all contend:
its size. Lake Superior is big. This single characteristic alone
influences every aspect of our cruising experience. For not only
does this mean the possibility of higher winds and bigger seas,
but also longer distances to travel and fewer supplies. Thus, it
is the prudent skipper who carefully tends to vessel and gear;
who cautiously plans a cruise with an eye to the weather and
navigation; and who wisely provisions the boat with adequate
stores and replacement parts.

Equipping Your Boat for Lake Superior

One of the most frequently asked questions about the type
of boat needed to cruise Lake Superior deals with size. How big
a boat do you really need to cruise the lake? And in truth there
is no hard and fast answer. Today you can see everything from
17-foot canoes and kayaks to powerboats costing six figures in
all parts of the lake. We can recall seeing a 22-foot sailboat, with
but an outboard engine and gerry cans for auxiliary power, that
was well enough equipped to handle most anything that Lake
Superior could toss its way during the summer months. We have
also been on some 35-foot boats on which we wouldn't venture
outside the Apostle Islands, let alone the far reaches of Lake
Superior's wilderness north and east shores.

Safety, of course, is the prime concern. It doesn't take long
for a 6-foot to 8-foot sea to develop on the lake, even during
the summer months. Whether the boat is power or sail, a good
parameter would be that it should be capable of handling the
worst conditions you may encounter for the area in which you
plan to cruise for the time period during which you will be
cruising. For example, a boat that will be staying within the

Please Note:
*Maps and Charts
in this book are
not necessarily
to scale and are
not intended for
navigation.*

protected confines of the Apostle Islands need not have the same considerations as one that will venture across the open water and into the remote areas of Lake Superior's wilderness. Likewise, the time of year in which the boat is used has a profound effect on the type/size of a boat. Even in the Apostles, cruising into the late fall can sufficiently challenge those on power and sailboats alike.

Often what makes a boat adequate to cruise Lake Superior's waters is not the boat itself, but the way in which it is equipped. Certainly, the boats of the 21st century are a far cry from what were being cruised in the 1980s and 1990s. Not only are boats generally larger, but items that used to be thought of as luxuries are now considered necessities and are included as standard equipment. The list may seem endless, but heading the top remains safety gear.

Safety Considerations

It should go without saying that adequate safety equipment should be a part of each cruising boat. This means Coast Guard-approved personal flotation devices (PFDs) for each person on board and appropriate distress signals along with horseshoes/ring buoys or overboard recovery poles. Fire extinguishers for the engine room and galley are also necessities. The Coast Guard has put out two good pamphlets that are helpful in these areas: "Federal Requirements for Recreational Boats" and "Visual Distress Signals for Recreational Boats."

Along with having proper safety gear on board comes the ability to know how to use it. More than anything else, good safety procedures are a state of mind and, thus, the need for safety drills becomes apparent. It doesn't help much if the skipper is the only one who knows how to use the safety gear—if the skipper is the one to go overboard.

A word of caution about going overboard. The water in Lake Superior is very cold. Offshore, rarely does it get much above 40 degrees Fahrenheit. **Hypothermia** takes hold in a matter of minutes, and therefore it is absolutely essential that any overboard person be retrieved as quickly as possible. Here prevention takes on new importance and safety harnesses become just as important as PFDs. The 1990s saw the development of a number of hybrid inflatable vests with safety harnesses such as the Switlik and Sospenders. Generally lightweight and non-cumbersome, we have even seen them used when cruisers are dinghy exploring.

It is also important to note that you don't have to go overboard in order to experience hypothermia. Many a skipper or crew member has suffered its ill effects merely by staying too long on the wheel or exposed to inclement weather. Signs of advancing hypothermia are the inability to shiver, slurred speech, sluggish actions and the inability to think clearly. Note basic treatment for hypothermia: remove wet clothing and cover with dry. DO NOT RUB THE BODY SURFACE; warm the victim gently and slowly, create a vapor barrier (sleeping bag with garbage bags outside) to

Figure 2.1
Different Kinds of Anchors

retain heat. Give only warm milk, water or juice—never alcohol or caffeine. Administer CPR if breathing has stopped. Get medical help quickly.

Finally, it should be mentioned that for those with sailboats, an important safety consideration is to have the ability to reef down for heavy weather conditions and with a variety of sail combinations. Unfortunately, with the advances in roller furler technology and tri-laminate headsails complete with luff-pads, many sailors are putting all their eggs in the reefable genoa basket. What happens when your only headsail is blown out in 30 to 35 knots of wind? Thus, the importance of adding stay sails, storm sails, etc., to one's sails inventory becomes apparent, as a safety consideration.

Danforth

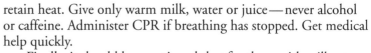

Anchors

An adequate anchoring system is also essential for any boat that cruises the lake. Even if marinas and docks are the main way in which the boat will be used, anchors are needed first for that element of safety. Since there are few docks in many cruising areas, you must be prepared to anchor in a variety of ways. (See the last section of this chapter for possible anchoring techniques.)

Plow
(CQR)

This means not one anchor, but at least two, ready to go with marked rode, not stuck down in the bottom of some locker. (We once saw a boat that had lost its auxiliary power drift up on a sandbar, mainly because the owner couldn't get the anchor out of the sail locker fast enough.)

Bruce

When using traditional anchors, it is important to have more than one type of anchor on board, as there is no traditional type of anchor that works equally well with all types of bottoms. Two types of anchors that work well on the lake are the Danforth and CQR plow. Other anchors that work well are the Bruce or Fortress (a lightweight/very strong Danforth type anchor) and the Delta (a plow type burying anchor that sets quickly). (See Fig. 2.1.) With the turn of the century came two new anchors the Mantus and Rocna and their derivatives. These anchors are characterized by a rollbar/hoop and a three-dimensional scoop design of the fluke which enables them to get a quick bite on most substrates. Although the fluke size is not much different, the longer shank length and larger hoop diameter of the Mantus may account for its slightly easier setting. As these modern anchors and their ability to set well in a variety of conditions catch on, the need for many anchors diminishes. It isn't a bad idea, however, to carry an extra anchor, as many anchorages have deadheads and slash lying on the bottom in which it is easy to lose an anchor.

Fortress

Mantus

Mantus has slightly longer shank & roll bar than rocna

Rocna

Whether you anchor with all chain, or a mix of chain and nylon rode is a matter of personal preference. However, it is important to note that all anchors work better with more chain. For example, with a CQR plow it is necessary to have at least 20

feet of chain to get it to lay right and dig in. Unfortunately, it is in this area of adequate chain that skippers often cut dangerously short corners. There are some distinct advantages to anchoring on all chain (see Figure 2.2). For example, in our earlier years when we were anchoring primarily on nylon, we were picking up a lot of deadheads—at least two or three a season, because nylon seems to float around a lot. Once we changed to all chain, years would go by without our getting caught on deadheads.

Figure 2.3 Illustrates the anchoring system we developed over the years that worked quite well for the Great Lakes. Note that the amount of chain on our primary anchors was increased when we went to the Caribbean. When we came back, even though this amount of chain was unnecessary for most Lake Superior anchoring and meant most of the time we were anchoring on all chain, there was no way we would go back to using less. (See discussion Appendix III.) We particularly liked the flexibility of the system. For example, when we thought we might want more than 12 feet of chain with the Fortress, we simply brought it forward and shackled it onto one of the bow rodes. Although this system seemed a bit of overkill, rare was the season that we didn t use each part in some way. But then we were spending more than 100 nights each season swinging on the hook, and our travels took us to some pretty marginal anchoring situations.

Figure 2.2
Advantages to Anchoring on All Chain
1. Anchoring on reduced scope in tight anchorages.
2. Picking up fewer deadheads.
3. Less drifting around on windless nights.
4. Less skating around in heavier winds.
* Note — you don't have to have 300 feet of chain to be anchoring on all chain. See Appendix III.

Dinghies

Another crucial item that must be added to any boat that explores the outreaches of Lake Superior is an adequate tender. Sooner or later on Lake Superior, you are going to be anchoring and will either wish to simply go ashore or go exploring.

There are basically two kinds of dinghies (tenders): hard and soft (inflatable). Each has advantages and disadvantages, and it is not the purpose of this guide to explain these. There has been a decided increase in the use of inflatable dinghies—especially the sport boat that, with its inflatable keel and floorboards, is able to get up on a plane and cruise at higher speeds than a regular dinghy. There has also been an increase in the use of RIBs (Rigid Inflatable Boat), which are inflatable dinghies with a rigid fiberglass bottom. As with the main vessel, in recent years the trend has been toward larger dinghies with larger motors. It's not uncommon to see a 10-foot dinghy sporting a 15-horsepower motor. Which type of dinghy is chosen depends not only on how it is to be used, but also how it is transported along with the mother ship. The choices here are two: either trail it behind or carry it on the boat.

Figure 2.3
***Dahlfin II's* Anchoring Arsenal**
Bow Anchors – Primary
35 lb Delta – each with 140 ft. chain and 33lb Bruce – 100 ft. 5/8" marked nylon rope
Stern Anchors – Secondary
12 lb hi tensile Danforth – 6 ft. chain, 150 ft. 3/8" nylon line
24 lb Fortress – 12 ft. chain, 150 ft. nylon line
RodeRider with 15 & 25 lb detachable lead weights
Simpson Lawrence electrical (vertical) windlass with rope/chain gypsy stowed off the deck down in divided chain locker
Two floats with trip lines
Detachable electric anchor light (for use in cockpit)
Mast head anchor light run on solar sensors

We have known many who for years have trailed their dinghies, both hard and soft, on long painters (to ride back on the second wave) with no problems. We have also known of others who under adverse conditions have had to cut their dinghies loose for one reason or another and lose them to the lake. Another way of trailing an inflatable dinghy is to snug its bow right up on the transom leaving just the aft end of the dinghy to trail in the water.

There are a number of ways in which a dinghy can be carried on the main vessel. If there is enough space, it can be stored simply on the deck, often in chocks secured with line or bungy cords. Some powerboaters stow it on the cabin top or across the transom on a swim platform. Skippers will often put a dinghy upside down on the foredeck or midship across the cabin top. A main disadvantage with these methods is that the dinghy is then in the way for sail handling. To solve the problem of dinghy storage, many skippers (both power and sail) have taken to transporting their dinghies on davits off the transom.

Another important consideration regarding the dinghy is to have some kind of auxiliary power for the craft. For years, we diligently rowed a mile or more for good fishing or for exploring a particularly interesting area. Often, points of interest were outside our range so we bought a little two-horsepower motor for the dinghy. Then we changed to an eight-horsepower motor and found that those remote places that were formerly outside our reach became everyday experiences. However, with bigger/heavier motors comes the problem of raising them for storage on the main ship. So, another addition on many boats in recent years has been the use of a small crane at the stern rail.

Dinghy on the beach at Cascade Falls across from Old Dave's Harbour in Ontario. DAHL

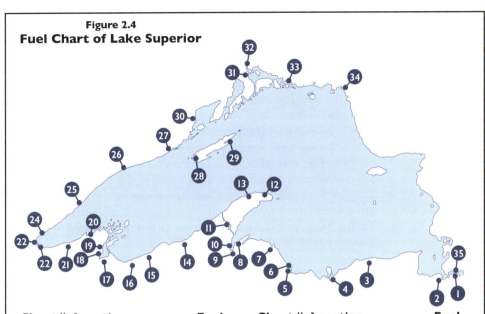

Figure 2.4
Fuel Chart of Lake Superior

Chart #	Location	Fuel
1	Sault Ste. Marie, MI	
	George Kemp Marina	G,D
2	Chippewa Landing	
	Bay Mills, MI	(G)
3	Grand Marais, MI	G, D
4	Munising, MI	G, D*
5	Cinder Pond	
	Marquette, MI	G, D
6	Presque Isle, MI	G, D
7	Big Bay, MI	(G)
8	Pequaming, MI	G
9	L'Anse, MI	G, D*
10	Baraga, MI	G, D*
11	Keweenaw Waterway	
	Lower Entry	G (I)
	H & Y Marina	G (I)
	Houghton Co. Marina	G, D
12	Copper Harbor, MI	G, D
13	Eagle Harbor, MI	G
14	Ontonagon, MI	G, D*
15	Black River, MI	G (I)
16	Saxon Harbor, WI	G, D
17	Ashland, WI	G, D
18	Washburn, WI	G, D
19	Apostle Is. Marina, WI	G, D
	Madeline Is. Yacht Club	G, D
	Port Superior	G, D
	Roy's Pt. Marina	G, D
20	Cornucopia, WI	G, D
21	Port Wing, WI	G
22	Barker's Island, WI	G, D
23	Lakehead Boat Basin, MN	G, D
24	Knife River, MN	G, D
25	Silver Bay, MN	G, D
26	Grand Marais, MN	G, D
27	Grand Portage, MN	G, D
28	Windigo, Isle Royale	G
29	Rock Harbor, Isle Royale	G, D
30	Thunder Bay, ON	G, D
31	Red Rock, ON	G, D
32	Nipigon, ON	G, D
33	Rossport, ON*	G, D
34	Marathon, ON **	G*, D*
	Michipicoten R., ON	(G) (D)
35	Sault Ste. Marie, ON	
	Bondar Marina	G, D
	Bellevue Marina	G, D

G = Gasoline   D = Diesel   (I) = Intermittent   ( ) = Not available to deep draft boats

* = Gerry cans availble. Local transport arranged to Pays Plat (7 miles) for fuel. Fuel at dock possible in a few years.

** = Fuel brought down by taxi, bring own gerry cans.

Note: In Ontario fuel is sold by the liter; 3.78 liters = I US gallon.

Extending Range

Whether the boat is power or sail, inboard or outboard, one of the main criteria seems to be fuel tankage. In other words—range. For anyone who does any extensive cruising on the lake, one thing becomes quickly apparent—there are often few supply depots along the way. For example, between the Sault and Red Rock, there is no place where a large, deep-draft boat can get fuel pumped at a dock. In many areas fuel either must be transported via portable cans or brought in by special order via truck. (See Fig. 2.4.)

We often met boaters each summer who had their cruises severely altered or even curtailed because of this single factor of inability to obtain fuel. Thus, one advantage for the larger boat often means more tankage and subsequently greater range. For smaller boats, it becomes essential to carry extra gasoline or diesel cans on board. We have even seen 50-gallon drums carried in the cockpits of those with power cruisers who plan to be out for extended periods of time. Because of this unavailability of fuel, it became our custom to "top off the tanks" whenever possible, whether we needed it or not.

Adequate tankage for water will also extend one's range. Again, there are few areas—especially in the wilderness—where it is possible to take on water from a dock. However, on fresh-water Lake Superior, this is one problem that is not as important as others. For years we filled our tanks directly from the lake, adding Chlorox and vanilla (1 tsp each per 30 gallons of water), not so much because there is anything wrong with the water, but to keep it fresh while sitting in the tanks. A handy gadget to assist in this is a small submersible pump that will run off the ship's 12-volt system.

Again, because there are large areas of the lake where marinas are simply nonexistent, electrical dependence is a serious detriment to any extensive cruising. Clearly, it is the boat that is closely tied to that long yellow cord that won't venture far into Lake Superior. By paying close attention to our electrical needs, we were able to become electrically independent for the full six-month season, using the power cord only when up on the cradle. This was a fair achievement, because like most boaters we added our fair share of electronic equipment and "gadgets" to the boat inventory over the years. (See Appendix II for some possible solutions on becoming electrically independent.)

Electronics

It is probably in this single area of electronics that we have seen some of the greatest advances in the boating industry. For example, as we entered the 1980s only a handful of boaters had Loran-C on board. Yet, just a little more than a decade later, loran was as common as VHF and many boaters had backup units or additional units in the cockpit. Today, of course, everyone is using the Global

Positioning System (GPS) complete with electronic charts, often with more than one receiver on board.

Basic equipment for any boat on the lake should be a compass and depth sounder. Knot-meters and logs are also high on the list, as dead reckoning is still a good backup for navigation. VHF radio remains essential for weather information and distress assistance even though it continues to gain popular use on the social side of cruising. Many radios now come with an additional remote for use in the cockpit. A handheld VHF is a useful addition as a system backup and in the dinghy. Although not essential, many boat owners (those with both power and sail) are incorporating the use of autopilots.

In the light of advances in radio navigation, use of radio direction finders (RDFs) and Loran-C have become non-existent, replaced by GPS and electronic charts. Without a doubt it was Loran-C that put us in the radio navigation driver's seat in the 1980s, only to be superseded by GPS in the 1990s. Now it is electronic charts that are being added to navigation stations—often with the ability of tying everything (GPS, radar, charts and auto pilot) together.

To pay back the ship's electrical system for the drainage produced by today's electronic gadgetry, there are a number of options. One, of course, is to just add more and larger batteries. In the area of batteries, product technology has given us a number of different kinds. In addition to the traditional flooded batteries, there are the AGM and lithium batteries which have the advantages of no maintenance, faster recharge and longer operation between charges. There are also a number of alternative ways to charge batteries other than with the engine's alternator. Two of these are to use solar cells or wind generators. A very nice backup, especially in the area of safety, is to have a small portable generator on board. However, along with "larger and more," permanent generators are now also becoming a necessity on many larger boats.

Creature Comforts

When all the basic necessities have been added to the boat, one finally comes to the point where any further additions could fall more in the category of luxuries or creature comforts. But again, there is no hard and fast rule. For what may be a luxury on one boat is a basic requirement on another. A case in point: when we bought another boat, we installed a wind-speed indicator just as pure luxury. Now after using it not only to aid in sail-change decisions, but also for getting the most out of the boat under sail, we wouldn't be without one again.

One of these creature-comfort additions for a Lake Superior cruising boat is a dodger and/or weather cloths. For powerboats, this is usually solved in the form of a wheelhouse or a permanent dodger, which is already built into the boat. However, since most

sailboats come without this addition, it takes only one night out on the lake without a dodger, even in midsummer, to realize that some kind of protection is needed against the elements in an open cockpit on these waters. It is also important to have some type of protection against the sun on those hot, sunny midsummer days. Some sort of a boom tent-awning or Bimini top solves the problem nicely. It can also be useful in extending living space in light rain.

Another creature-comfort addition is some kind of cabin heater. Even in midsummer, nights on Lake Superior can become unbearably cold. Especially when fog sets in, a cabin heater comes close to that list of essentials to take the chill off.

We have seen a great variety of heaters in many boats: everything from heating with white gas, kerosene and diesel to wood, charcoal and even coal. To solve our particular requirements, a heater has to be safe enough to use when under way and throughout the night, while the crew is asleep. It also has to be conservative on electrical power and noise and use an easy-to-obtain fuel. This narrowed the offerings down considerably. After trying many different types of heaters, for more than 25 years we have used a forced air system from Sweden (made by Volvo) that runs on either kerosene or diesel fuel.

Finally, it should be mentioned that we are seeing a number of items on today's cruising boats that were almost nonexistent 15 years ago. For example, it is no longer uncommon to see small 12-volt color TVs on both power and sailboats. Many are even adding 12-volt VCR and DVD players along with videotape and disk libraries. In fact, some boaters are now trading tapes like we used to trade paperback books. There are even a number of boats that sport compact microwaves—and not only those that can back them up with big electrical generators. If the item can't be purchased with a 12-volt option, then an inverter can be installed to convert ship's power to 110 volts. And, of course, there are many of us who can't leave the dock without our laptop computer. There are even ways to hook up with the Internet by beaming off a satellite. It would seem that in these days of modern technology there is little that can't be done to make our boats more compatible with the cruising life and our own lifestyle.

Customs

Because Lake Superior's waters are shared by two countries, checking in and out through customs is a common occurrence in the cruising experience. During the covid years this became increasingly complicated for vessels entering or returning to U.S. waters. Now in the aftermath of those years, we welcome new programs to replace those that were discontinued and the stabilization of those programs we had come to rely on.

For U.S. Customs clearance, offices are at Sault Ste. Marie, Michigan; Duluth, Minnesota; Grand Marais, Minnesota; and

Grand Portage, Minnesota. Note that customs clearance can also be obtained at Isle Royale when coming from Ontario to the island. Canadian clearance is available at Thunder Bay, Marathon and Sault Ste. Marie, Ontario.

Americans leaving the United States do not need to declare departure, but customs clearance is necessary to enter Canada. Items that need to be declared are firearms (description and serial number required), tobacco products and alcoholic beverages. Duty free amounts of these last two items are tobacco: 200 cigarettes, 50 cigars, 7 oz manufactured tobacco, 200 tobacco sticks, and alcohol: 50 oz wine, 38 oz alcoholic beverages, 24 cans beer. Pets need to have the required shots (usually distemper and rabies) and a current health certificate. A cruising permit will then be issued for the length of your stay. To leave Canada, no clearance is necessary unless you have brought in articles that were registered with a temporary permit.

During the mid-1990s, through a joint initiative of Canada Immigration and Canada Customs, the **Remote Area Border Crossing** (**RABC**) permit provided an alternative option to onsite clearance for Americans and returning Canadian citizens to clear customs when entering the *remote* areas of the Canadian shore of Lake Superior. With this permit boaters are allowed to enter these areas without reporting to an official port of entry—you don't even have to phone in upon your arrival into the country. To do this, you apply for a permit ahead of time in which you give all the normal information and documentation you would give at any regular port of entry ahead of time. You still have to declare any goods over the personal exemption entitlement by contacting the CBSA (Canada Border Services Agency) prior to leaving the US.

Figure 2.5
Canadian Remote Area Border Crossing (RABC) Permit

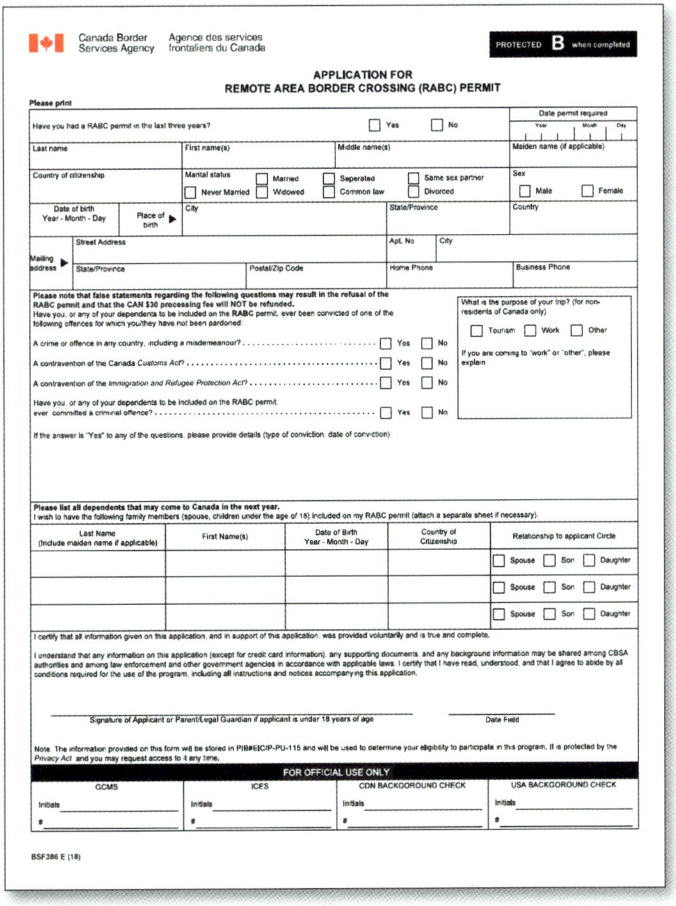
Canada Border Services Agency / Agence des services frontaliers du Canada

PROTECTED B when completed

APPLICATION FOR
REMOTE AREA BORDER CROSSING (RABC) PERMIT

Please print

Have you had a RABC permit in the last three years? ☐ Yes ☐ No

Date permit required: Year Month Day

Last name | First name(s) | Middle name(s) | Maiden name (if applicable)

Country of citizenship | Marital status: ☐ Married ☐ Seperated ☐ Same sex partner ☐ Never Married ☐ Widowed ☐ Common law ☐ Divorced | Sex: ☐ Male ☐ Female

Date of birth Year - Month - Day | Place of birth ▶ City | State/Province | Country

Mailing address ▶ Street Address | Apt. No | City | State/Province | Postal/Zip Code | Home Phone | Business Phone

Please note that false statements regarding the following questions may result in the refusal of the RABC permit and that the CAN $30 processing fee will NOT be refunded.
Have you, or any of your dependents to be included on the **RABC** permit, ever been convicted of one of the following offences for which you/they have not been pardoned:

A crime or offence in any country, including a misdemeanour? ☐ Yes ☐ No

A contravention of the Canada *Customs Act*? ☐ Yes ☐ No

A contravention of the *Immigration and Refugee Protection Act*? ☐ Yes ☐ No

Have you, or any of your dependents to be included on the RABC permit, ever committed a criminal offence? ☐ Yes ☐ No

If the answer is "Yes" to any of the questions, please provide details (type of conviction, date of conviction):

What is the purpose of your trip? (for non-residents of Canada only) ☐ Tourism ☐ Work ☐ Other

If you are coming to "work" or "other", please explain

Please list all dependents that may come to Canada in the next year.
I wish to have the following family members (spouse, children under the age of 18) included on my RABC permit (attach a separate sheet if necessary).

Last Name (Include maiden name if applicable)	First Name(s)	Date of Birth Year - Month - Day	Country of Citizenship	Relationship to applicant Circle
				☐ Spouse ☐ Son ☐ Daughter
				☐ Spouse ☐ Son ☐ Daughter
				☐ Spouse ☐ Son ☐ Daughter

I certify that all information given on this application, and in support of this application, was provided voluntarily and is true and complete.

I understand that any information on this application (except for credit card information), any supporting documents, and any background information may be shared among CBSA authorities and among law enforcement and other government agencies in accordance with applicable laws. I certify that I have read, understood, and that I agree to abide by all conditions required for the use of the program, including all instructions and notices accompanying this application.

Signature of Applicant or Parent/Legal Guardian if applicant is under 18 years of age | Date Field

Note: The information provided on this form will be stored in PIB#EIC/P-PU-115 and will be used to determine your eligibility to participate in this program. It is protected by the *Privacy Act* and you may request access to it any time.

FOR OFFICIAL USE ONLY

GCMS	ICES	CDN BACKGOROUND CHECK	USA BACKGOROUND CHECK
Initials	Initials	Initials	Initials
#	#	#	#

BSF386 E (18)

Note that throughout the years many programs are changed or fine-tuned to meet current needs. For example, the RABC was discontinued during the Covid-19 pandemic only to be resumed in July 2022. As of May 2024 the CANPASS program for private boats no longer exists, yet parts of CANPASS are still found in other programs. This also includes the Small Vessel Reporting System (SVRS). Thus, it is important to check with the Internet for up-to-date Information before any border crossing.

There are a couple of ways to get the RABC application. One is to print it off the Internet. In the Goggle search bar type "remote area border crossing permit application". This will give several choices relating to RABC. The first two that are identified with red maple leaves are RABC web pages that give general Information about the program. The third has the title "Remote Area Border Crossing (RABC) Permit" and a form you can print out. The application is fairly simple to complete. (See Fig. 2.5.) You need to include certain documentation: one primary piece of proof of citizenship (photocopy of birth or citizenship certificate, passport) and one secondary piece of identification (example—photocopy of driver's license) for each person on the application. The permit is valid for one year and there is a processing cost of $30 CAN. Note that credit card authorization is mandatory If applying by mail/email.

There are a couple of ways to submit your application to get the RABC permit. The first way is by email.

Go to: *cbsa.rabcapplications-applicationsprfe.asfc@cbsa-asfc.gc.ca*
Then select:
BSF386: Remote Area Border Crossing Permit - cbsa-asfc.gc.ca

Note that by submitting electronically you consent to having the permit Issued electronically as well.

The second method is to apply by regular mail at least 6 weeks in advance of your trip. The completed application along with photocopies of your supporting documentation should be sent to:

Canada Border Services Agency
RABC Processing Agency
201 North May St, 1st floor
Thunder Bay, ON P7C 3P4

The third way is to present the application in person at one of the following CBSA offices:

Pigeon River Port of Entry:
Monday, Tuesday, Wednesday between 8am - 8pm
Walk-Ins are available, appointments need not be made.

Sault Ste. Marie Point of Entry
Tuesday and Wednesday between 8am - 8pm.
Clients need to call 705-941-3044 to make an appointment.

Within a couple of weeks, the permit will be returned with a cruising permit number. Note: for the permit to be valid, it must then be signed and dated by the applicant. Also, the permit is only valid for a specific geographical location. If you should enter at a designated port of entry, then you have to clear Customs and Immigration as usual.

The NEXUS program is a joint Canada-US program that offers customs clearance for either country for low-risk boaters who preregister into the program. Once you get your NEXUS card it is valid for 5 years and satisfies face-to-face Inspection, but boaters must still phone in. The card costs $50 and is valid for 5 years. There are almost 400 marine telephone reporting centers. To enter Canada, you call 866-99N-EXUS (866-996-3987) at least 30 minutes and up to 4 hours in advance of arrival in Canada. To enter the US, you call the local Customs and Border Protection marine number for the arrival area. Again between 30 minutes and 4 hours of arrival.

For Americans returning to the states by boat there are two ways to receive clearance: by presentation at a port of entry or by telephone. Those who need to clear customs by face-to-face Inspection must report to either an immigration or customs officer at one of the following locations:

Duluth, Minnesota	218-720-5203
Grand Marais, Minnesota	218-387-1148
Grand Portage, Minnesota	218-475-2244
Sault Ste Marie, Michigan	906-632-7221

There continues to be clearance at Isle Royale for boaters returning from Ontario.

Customs & Border Protection (CBP) has developed three different ways/programs to clear back into the US by telephone. They are the NEXUS program which is used for clearing both Canadian and US customs (already discussed), the Canadian Border Boat Landing Permit (I-68) and the CBP Reporting Offsite Arrival - Mobile (ROAM).

To receive clearance by telephone (Ex - call 800-505-8381 when coming into MN) it is necessary to obtain an I-68 form ahead of time. Called the **Canadian Border Boat Landing Program or I-68**, it means that each person (over 14) must apply in person at a Port of Entry sometime before leaving the states to be inspected. Children under 14 can be entered on a parent's form. Unfortunately, Ports of Entry are often in remote locations (ex - the Minnesota/Ontario Border: Warroad, MN; Baudette, MN; International Falls, MN; Roseau, MN and Grand Portage, MN) which for many involves a considerable drive ahead of time. For those going up Superior's East Shore it is a little easier as the inspection can be completed at the Customs Office in Sault Ste. Marie, MI. During this inspection a photo and fingerprint will be

taken. Cost is $16/person or $32/family. The form is only good for one year, but it does enable clearance just by telephone. It is especially useful for those who make many crossings back and forth or who return to the U.S. in remote areas.

Many boaters think the third method for telephonic reporting in offsite areas is the best. Using the CBP Reporting Offsite Arrival4w—Mobile (ROAM), boaters report their U.S. entry to CBP via their personal smart device. To do this a special free app is downloaded from the Apple App Store or the Google Play Store and all relevant information you would normally give at a regular onsite entry is downloaded ahead of time. In addition to boat documentation, you would give photos of passports, birth certificates, driver's license etc. If you didn't get this done ahead of time, there are a few places where this app can also be accessed on tablets at partner locations. For example, in early 2024 a tablet with the app was set up at the Rock Harbor Visitor Center on Isle Royale. When you get back into U.S. remote waters all you have to do is press the "arrival button" and the phone call will automatically be made.

Regardless of which method is used to receive U.S. clearance, most vessels must have a Customs User Fee Decal. All vessels more than 30 feet in length entering the United States (including returning American and foreign vessels) must pay an annual Customs User Fee of a little under $35 (at the time of this writing). It is possible to pay this fee in advance and receive a decal by mail. There are three different methods for obtaining a decal. (See Fig. 2.6). Note that passport requirements for persons entering U.S. waters by boat have been in flux. This includes returning Americans and visiting Canadians. Thus, if you are

---

Figure 2.6
Applying for U.S. Customs Decal

A. Online Method

You must sign up before you can purchase decals online to obtain a 20-digit account number.

1. Go to *cbp.gov/travel/pleasure-boats*
2. Scroll down to *Decal Transponder Online Procurement System DTOPS*
3. Just below that heading click on *Apply On-line for User Fee Decals and Transponders.*
4. Select *Private Vessel* button.
5. Select *Pay Annual User Fee* button.
6. Select either *Returning User- (Log In)* or *New User- (Sign Up)*
7. Complete the registration process.

B. Fax Application

To receive a decal within 5 to 7 days, FAX your application to (317) 290-3219, use a credit card for payment, give a "ship to" address in the U.S. and select the optional overnight courier shipping method for a U.S. address. (Note it will take 3-6 weeks if first class mail is used, payment is by check or the "ship to" address given is out of the U.S.)

C. Mail-in Application

To get the application form go to:
cbp.gov/sites/default/files/2024-05/cbp_form_339v.pdf
Select *Form 339v-U.S. Customs And Border Protection Print-out form*, complete application and mail to:
U.S. Customs and Border Protection
Revenue Division,
Atten: DTOPS Program Administrator
8899 East 56th Street
Indianapolis, IN 46249

getting telephonic clearance, you need: Custom User Fee Decal #, your I-68 #s, and may need passport #s for each person on board. Those reporting for in-person inspection may need passport #s; the Custom User Fee Decal can be purchased at that time if you haven't already done so.

Canadians leaving their country need not declare departure unless they are carrying goods that need to be registered. To enter the United States, the procedures and restrictions are similar to those for Americans entering Canadian waters. A cruising license can be obtained from the first port of entry and usually has a duration of one year. Note: without this license, Canadians must report in each port visited and clear before leaving the States. Restrictions on tobacco and alcoholic products are one carton of cigarettes and one liter of alcoholic beverages per person. On return to Canada, a report must be filed to indicate the vessel's arrival.

When cruising a foreign country, common courtesy requires that you fly the flag of the country that you are visiting. For powerboats, this usually is from the bow staff; for sailboats, the starboard spreader is used. Your own country is identified with a flag flown from the stern.

Communications

The marine VHF radio is a link between you and other ships, and between you and stations on shore. Initial contact is made on Channel 16 and should be kept as brief as possible (less than one minute), because this channel is set aside for safety and calling. Channel 06 is likewise a ship-to-ship channel that is reserved for safety communications. Channel 22 is a Coast Guard working and broadcast frequency. Use by non-government users is restricted to communication with the Coast Guard. Canadian marinas are required by law to monitor and answer only on Channel 68. Common channels used by pleasure craft for ship-to-ship communications are 68, 69, 71 and 72. Note that when sailing in Canadian waters, Channel 68 should be kept clear for marina use. A summary of these and other channels commonly used on the lake is found in Fig. 2.7.

In cases when there is an emergency or matter of safety, it is permissible to use Channel 16 for short transmissions. There are three of these conditions that would apply. The first of these, which is the most serious, involves sending out a Mayday (beginning with the word "Mayday" repeated three times). This type of transmission is used when it is certain that the vessel and/or crew are in grave or imminent danger. To reduce the time taken in relaying pertinent information to the distress, the Coast Guard suggests posting a filled-in Distress Communications Form near your radiotelephone. (See Fig. 2.8.)

The second type of emergency/safety transmission begins with the words Pan! Pan! Pan! and is used when a message that concerns

the safety of a vessel or crew is to be transmitted, usually by Coast Guard station. This includes, but is not limited to, overdue craft, man overboard, vessel fire, grounding or sinking and medical cases. An example of this type of message is when Station Duluth may put out a call for information on an overdue vessel.

The third type of permissible transmission on Channel 16 is the Securité call. The transmission is begun by saying the word "securité" (pronounced "say-cur-i-TAY") three times. This type of message normally consists of a single subject containing important navigational or meteorological warning. These messages are quite often given in restricted waterways and in conditions of reduced visibility. For example, Station Duluth may transmit a securité message as a warning of a storm cell moving out over the lake. Often vessels in commercial shipping can be heard using this type

Figure 2.7
VHF Channel Usage

Channel Numbers	Type of Communication
16	**DISTRESS, SAFETY & CALLING** Intership & ship to coast
6	**INTERSHIP SAFETY** Intership. **Not** to be used for non-safety intership communications.
9	**BOATER CALLING** Commercial and non-commercial
13	**REQUESTING BRIDGE OPENING**
21A, 23A, 81A, 82A, 83A	**U.S. GOV / USCG ONLY**
22A	**COMMUNICATIONS WITH U.S. COAST GUARD** Ship, coast or aircraft.
12, 14, 20, 65A, 66A, 73, 74, 77	**PORT OPERATIONS** Intership & ship to coast
68, 69, 71, 72, 78A, 79A, 80A*	**NON-COMMERCIAL** Intership
7A, 10, 11, 18A, 19A, 79A, 80A	**COMMERCIAL** Intership & ship to coast
8, 67, 88A	**COMMERCIAL** Intership
24, 25, 26, 27, 28, 84, 85, 86, 87, 88	**PUBLIC CORRESPONDENCE** Ship to public coast (marine operator)
70	**DIGITAL SELECTIVE CALLING** Voice communication not allowed
88	**U.S. COAST GUARD ONLY** Coast Guard Liaison & Information
AIS 1, AIS 2	**AUTOMATIC IDENTIFICATION SYSTEM**
WX1 162.550 MHz WX2 162.400 MHz WX3 162.475 MHz WX4 162.425 MHz WX5 162.450 MHz WX6 162.500 MHz WX7 162.525 MHz WX8 161.650 MHz WX9 161.775 MHz WX10 163.275 MHz	**NOAA WEATHER SERVICE** Ship receive only

of transmission as they approach various destinations, especially in congested areas. This type of message is also helpful when crossing the shipping lanes in reduced visibility. After repeating "securité" three times, the boat's estimated position, course and speed is given —all within one minute. Sometimes boaters will ask any vessels in the immediate area to respond and then another channel is used for further communication.

In addition to issuing safety broadcasts (Securité) and urgent broadcasts (Pan), the Coast Guard also transmits scheduled marine information broadcasts. These consist of important notices to mariners, storm warnings, advisories and other important marine information. For information on weather broadcasts refer to the next section on weather.

Another use of VHF radio is to make ship to shore radio telephone calls. However, in recent years with the advance of

Figure 2.8
Distress Communications Form

It is suggested that you fill out this form ahead of time and record it in your DSC so all you have to do is press that button in a distress condition.

DSC DISTRESS COMMUNICATION FORM

Post this form by each permanently installed radio equipped with DSC

Fill in Items 5, 6, 11 and 13 prior to getting underway.

SPEAK SLOWLY – CLEARLY – CALMLY

1. Make certain your radio and GPS are turned on and the radio is on High Power.
2. Send DSC Distress Call – **press Red Distress Button for 5 seconds.** Wait for a DSC Distress Acknowledgement then shift to VHF Ch 16 or SSB 4125 kHz (USB) for voice instructions.
3. If no DSC Acknowledgement is received Select **VHF Ch 16 or SSB 4125 kHz (USB)**
4. Press microphone button and say: **"MAYDAY - MAYDAY - MAYDAY"**
5. Say: **"This is** (Your boat name, MMSI or Call Sign)**"**
6. Repeat once: **"MAYDAY** (Your boat name)**"**
7. **Tell where you are:**
   a. **Latitude and longitude** _____
   b. **Navigation Aids or Landmarks nearby** _____
   c. Direction and distance to a Prominent Landmark _____
8. **State the nature of your distress and the kind of assistance required:**
   _____
9. **Give the number of people aboard and condition of any injured** _____
10. **Estimate present seaworthiness of your boat.** _____
11. **If time allows - Briefly describe your boat:**
    a. **Type –** (Sail or Power) _____
    b. **Length in feet-** _____
    c. **Hull color-** _____
    d. **Trim color-** _____
    e. **Masts-** _____
    f. **Other Identifying Info-** _____
12. Say: **"I will be listening on Channel 16 or 4125 kHz Upper Sideband "**
13. Say: **"This is** (Your Boat Name, MMSI or Call Sign) **OVER"**
14. Release microphone button and **Listen for an Answer.**
15. **Activate 406 MHz EPIRB** by following directions on Beacon Body. Ensure EPIRB remains vertical, antenna pointing upward. Take EPIRB to Survival Craft if abandoning ship.
16. If you do not receive an answer **Repeat Call beginning at Item 3.**
17. If no answer again **Check to see if radio is turned on and VHF is on CH 16, high power** or **shift SSB to higher emergency frequencies for communications with distant shore stations.**

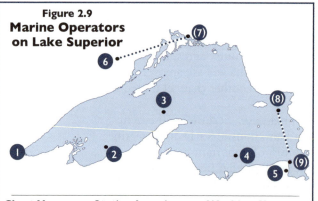

Figure 2.9
Marine Operators on Lake Superior

Chart No.	Station Location	Working Channel
1	Duluth, MN	84
2	Ontonagon, MI	86
3	Copper Harbor, MI	87
4	Grand Marais, MI	84
5	Sault Ste. Marie, MI	26
6	Thunder Bay, ON	16, 85, 83B
(7)	Horn, ON	16, 24, 21B
(8)	Bald Head, ON	16, 27, 83B
(9)	Sault Ste. Marie, ON	16, 24, 21B

( )= Repeater

Figure 2.10
Phonetic Alphabet

A	Alpha
B	Bravo
C	Charlie
D	Delta
E	Echo
F	Foxtrot
G	Golf
H	Hotel
I	India
J	Juliet
K	Kilo
L	Lima
M	Mike
N	November
O	Oscar
P	Papa
Q	Quebec
R	Romeo
S	Sierra
T	Tango
U	Uniform
V	Victor
W	Whiskey
X	X-ray
Y	Yankee
Z	Zulu

cellular technology many boaters have turned to the use of the cell phone which has become an important part of the boater's communication system. Because connections are sometimes sporadic and, in some areas, nonexistent, it is suggested that you contact your provider to get correct information of coverage areas before cruising into a particular area. For those times in which you need to make a VHF phone call, such as cruising in areas with poor cellular coverage or being out of range such as offshore sailing, Figure 2.9 shows a chart of the working channels for Lake Superior marine operators. Note that when making phone calls, because transmissions may be misunderstood, particularly in spelling, it is often preferred to use the phonetic alphabet. See Fig. 2.10.

Two additional uses of the VHF radio which have gained popularity in recent years are AIS (Automatic Identification System) and DSC (Digital Selective Calling). Both systems transmit data over VHF radio and satellite communication. They are both usually tied into the ship's GPS in order to provide position/location and navigation data. Both are identified by a specific MMSI (Marine Mobile Service Identity).

The MMSI is a unique 9 digit number assigned to identify a vessel or coast radio station. To register for an MMSI go to the U.S. Coast Guard webpage *www.navcen.uscg.gov/maritime-mobile-service-identity* and follow the directions. You will need to put in a few details about yourself and your vessel and you will be assigned an MMSI that becomes an integral part of your boat's identification. The same MMSI can be used for multiple devices. If you sell your boat or radio/device or transfer it to another boat, it's important to cancel your MMSI registration or transfer it to the new owner.

AIS is a system that broadcasts continuously routine messages of ship identity and position such as: ship name, call sign, vessel type, MMSI number, position, navigation information (position, speed, course etc.). With AIS vessels of all sizes are able to exchange identity and navigational information with each other and land-based systems. This is especially helpful when navigating in areas of reduced visibility such as storms, fog, or night. There is a whole range of ASI units and depending on the sophistication of your equipment you can get VHF radios that are equipped to just receive-only AIS with units that also are interfaced with ships' radar and chartplotter to an AIS transponder which will also transmit your information/position to other vessels in the area. One decided advantage of using ASI is the general "distress" button which transmits vital information in case of such an emergency.

DSC is a feature built into all fixed mount VHF radios. It is a requirement for all fixed mount VHF's and an optional feature of handheld VHF radios sold in the United States. DSC is another feature of the VHF radio that allows boaters to send and receive digital messages including distress calls. While AIS is continuous, DSC is a system which can use on-demand predetermined messages that can be quickly transmitted over dedicated radio channel 70 to provide a quick and easy method of communication. These messages are usually more distress or emergency related like a grounding, ship fire, taking on water, or man overboard. Again, each DSC unit has a specific MMSI number assigned to allow it to operate. To help in distress each unit has a distress button which immediately broadcasts a generic distress message with basic ship information to all stations in range. Another use of DSC is the "buddy boat" feature which allows those with DSC radios to communicate within a small group (3-10 boats) and periodically and privately exchange AIS type of information to keep track of each other. This is particularly helpful when cruising with a group or on an overnight passage with others.

Weather

It doesn't take long for the cruising skipper to realize that on Lake Superior one is subject to the dictates of weather. There are few of us who blatantly will head out in the lake disregarding the forecasts and weather systems that move across the lake. And wisely so. Because of its large size and long fetch, seas of large proportions can quickly develop, making Lake Superior one of the best proving grounds for blue-water cruising.

Probably the most dramatic example of the effects of weather was the tragic sinking of the Edmund Fitzgerald on 10 November 1975. To envision seas that would make these huge lakers flounder is almost beyond imagination. With this particular winter storm and the full fetch of the lake, the seas built to such tremendous proportions as to give all who were on the eastern end of the lake great cause for concern. It was also during this storm that the gigantic 500-pound diesel storage tanks at Battle Island Light were lifted out of their cradles and tossed about like so much driftwood.

That these winter storms on Lake Superior are treacherous is also readily seen in the numerous cave formations carved out of the northern (lake side) exposures of many of the Apostle Islands.

But it isn't just during the winter storms that the lake can release its latent fury. It is possible for gale conditions to develop in the summer that will keep even hardy skippers in port. Spring and fall have their own special brand of weather systems. Thunderstorms and fog are prevalent in the early boating season as warm, moist air moves out over the cold lake. Small craft advisories and gale warnings become more common the later one cruises into the fall. It is also important to note that weather systems are changing all over the planet. Predictions are for more extremes in temperatures, wind and severe conditions. Already, we are seeing some of this on Lake Superior. In the years following the turn of the century, it became common to see at least one gale or half-gale in August. Fall gales in early to mid-October continued to increase in number and intensity well into the second decade.

Therefore, in addition to relying on the regularly transmitted weather broadcasts, the prudent sailor will always keep an eye open to the weather and quickly develop some self-interpretation techniques. Also, keeping in mind the long distances that may sometimes be involved, a boater will be careful not to get caught out in the middle of the lake where the safety of shelter may be hours away.

Lake Superior is subject to mid-continental weather systems that are not tempered by the moderating effects of the ocean, and it is common to experience abrupt and often severe changes in weather. Because of this, Lake Superior is often labeled as a "fickle lady." It is common to be ghosting along, basking in warm balmy weather one day, only to be thrashing through waves, rail down, the next.

A Few Basics

It isn't within the scope of this guide to provide a complete discussion of all factors that affect Lake Superior weather. But there are a few general principles that may assist a boater in understanding the weather systems and forecasts encountered on the lake.

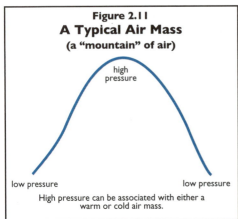

Figure 2.11
A Typical Air Mass
(a "mountain" of air)

high pressure

low pressure   low pressure

High pressure can be associated with either a warm or cold air mass.

The most basic of these principles is that most of our weather systems approach from the west and continue toward the east in the form of air masses controlled by very high winds in the jet stream. The direction can vary from the SW to the NW. Thus, the prevailing winds in the western part of the lake are SW to NW with a little NE thrown in, and NW in the eastern part of the lake. Systems coming in from the SW bring in hot, moist air from the Gulf of Mexico; those from the NW move in cold, dry air from Canada. Air masses coming in from the Pacific usually lose moisture as they pass over the Rockies, so they are usually dry with near normal temperatures for the season.

There are a few basic factors that characterize these air masses: barometric pressure, temperature and moisture. Air masses can be pictured as "mountains of air," with high pressure in the center where the weight of the air is the greatest and low pressure at the periphery where the air mass tapers off. Fair weather is generally associated with the highs and stormy or unsettled conditions in those low-pressure areas between the masses. Whether the air mass is warm or cold, wet or dry, there is an area of contact between it and the next air mass called a frontal zone. If the approaching air mass is warmer, then the zone is a warm front; if it is colder, then it is a cold front. It is where these fronts come together that we have our weather, with each type producing predictable weather patterns. (See Fig. 2.12.)

Since warm air rises and cold air sinks, **an approaching warm front** means that the warm front will climb over the preceding cold front. This usually occurs slowly, so there is less violent weather than what occurs with an approaching cold front. If there is enough moisture in the warm front, a gentle rain will begin that can often last a day or so. Note that often just ahead of a warm front there may be fog and drizzle.

When **advancing cold fronts** come on the scene there is often more violent weather, especially if the front is coming on fast. A cold front will move in under the preceding edge of warm air, pushing it upward and often producing strong winds. One telltale sign of this occurrence is high billowing clouds that build to enormous

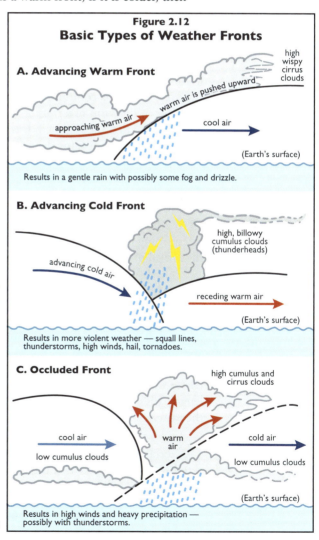

Figure 2.12
Basic Types of Weather Fronts

A. Advancing Warm Front

high wispy cirrus clouds

warm air is pushed upward

approaching warm air

cool air

(Earth's surface)

Results in a gentle rain with possibly some fog and drizzle.

B. Advancing Cold Front

high, billowy cumulus clouds (thunderheads)

advancing cold air

receding warm air

(Earth's surface)

Results in more violent weather — squall lines, thunderstorms, high winds, hail, tornadoes.

C. Occluded Front

high cumulus and cirrus clouds

cool air   warm air   cold air

low cumulus clouds   low cumulus clouds

(Earth's surface)

Results in high winds and heavy precipitation — possibly with thunderstorms.

proportions. It is these conditions that produce potentially dangerous weather systems such as heavy rains, squalls, severe thunderstorms and even tornadoes.

A third type of front occurs when two cool air masses merge and force the warmer air between them to rise. This is called an **occluded front**, and it may also develop thunderstorms with high winds and heavy precipitation. Unfortunately, this type of front may be difficult to spot because the thunderheads that are formed may be hidden by the lower lying clouds of the cold fronts.

Squalls

A squall line will advance ahead of a fast-moving cold front, often by as much as 30 to 80 miles. It also moves very quickly, 35 to 50 miles per hour, so once a squall line is sighted there isn't much time to take in sails, batten down hatches and so forth. However, because of this fast-advancing speed, squalls are short in duration, usually 15 to 20 minutes. Squalls usually contain some type of precipitation, but it is also possible to experience squall lines with just high winds.

Although squalls in themselves are short in length, it is wise to remember that they are often predecessors to larger weather systems. Thus, it is common to have the adverse conditions continue in the form of a thunderstorm or rain. However, it is good to note that the high winds that one usually experiences in a squall are lessened to some degree in the storm that may follow.

If you are out in open water, it is easy to see a squall coming. Usually, it is marked by an abrupt darkening of the sky that is coming on fast. But if you are sailing close to land or among high islands, it is easy to be taken by surprise. Quite often, a noticeable 15 to 20 degree drop in air temperature will be experienced as a forewarning to a squall. This is particularly helpful in anticipating the arrival of a squall that is hidden by land formations.

It is also helpful to remember that most of the weather systems approach the lake from the west and move across in an easterly direction. Thus, a thunderstorm or squall line to the east of your position is *usually* little cause for concern, whereas those to the west of you will usually move across your path. Likewise, thunderstorms and squalls are more readily found on the western end of the lake as the warm weather systems move out from the land over the cooler water. Because of the cooling effect of the lake, and its great length, these storms are usually well spent by the time they reach the eastern shore.

Thunderstorms

Certainly, one of the most awesome experiences for the boater is to be out on the lake in a thunderstorm. To have lightning touching down all around you, while miles away from the nearest harbor of refuge, is not a situation anyone would relish.

In a thunderstorm, not only does one have to contend with lightning, but also the high gusty winds that develop in the updraft of the storm as it feeds upon itself. Therefore, most boaters will try to avoid thunderstorms, preferring to be tucked away into a cozy harbor as opposed to battling the high winds, thrashing through the building seas and hoping to dodge the lightning touchdowns. And as thunderstorms are somewhat easy to predict and spot, this is a viable option.

There are two basic types of thunderstorms. One is the **air mass thunderstorm** in which updrafts of wind are produced by intense heating of air over land. These storms are formed as individual cells that are usually easy to spot by high rising columns of clouds. Thunderstorms that develop over land often lose some of their punch when they move out over water, but not always.

The other type of thunderstorm is the **frontal thunderstorm** that is produced by a cold front wedging in under a warm air mass. These are also easy to spot, since they will form a distinct line of building clouds along the advancing front, as opposed to individual cells of the air mass type. With both types of storms there are three distinct stages that help determine what kind of action to take.

The first stage is when the storm is building. It can be identified by the large, billowy cumulus clouds of thunderheads building with rapid vertical growth. Usually this means that you have at least a couple of hours to reach the safety of an anchorage. However, as the storm matures into its second stage and the bottoms of these clouds blacken with the tops spread out in that characteristic anvil shape, there is little time to seek safety. It is during this second stage that the thunderstorm is at its worst, producing lightning and downward drafts of cold air creating strong surface winds—sometimes with gusts up to 50 or 60 miles per hour. Rain usually occurs and sometimes hail. However, because thunderstorms move very quickly, they are often short in duration, passing through a given area in 20 to 30 minutes. In the third stage, the storm dissipates with most of its energy spent. Although lightning ceases and rain diminishes, there may still be some erratic gusts of wind on the surface of the water as residual downdrafts spread outward.

While most skippers generally prefer to avoid thunderstorms, it should be mentioned that not all low pressure systems are necessarily bad. It doesn't take sailors long to learn that Lake Superior is a fickle lady—not only in her weather systems, but in her wind patterns as well. Rare is the day in which we can make a run without at least one sail change. However, with low pressure, we are often assured of consistent winds, even though they may be strong. Some of our best sailing has been reefed down in low pressure systems, with 20 to 25 knots of wind.

The main problems the skipper has to contend with in these conditions are bigger seas and, if precipitation is present, reduced visibility. Certainly with greater wind strength, the seas are going to build and there comes a point—whether in powerboat or sailboat

—when it is no longer fun and it's time to seek shelter.

Fog

A common occurrence that often comes as the aftermath of rain is the descension of fog. And it is interesting that for many boaters, it is this condition that is disliked most. Even those with extensive radio location systems don't often go out intentionally in fog, for just by accident you get caught out often enough in fog. One thing is for certain: if you cruise Lake Superior, sooner or later you will be traveling in fog.

One reason for this is that not only is Lake Superior the largest of the Great Lakes, it is also the coldest. This contributes to the prevalence of fog as warm, moist air masses move out across the lake and dew point is reached.

Fog is simply a cloud that has touched the earth. There are two conditions that can produce fog:
1. Increasing the water vapor to air mass saturation point (for that temperature).
2. Lowering the air temperature below its saturation point to condense the water vapor.

Thus, fog occurs when the difference between air temperature and dew point decreases. As this difference approaches zero, air saturation occurs, and the result is fog. This can be seen quite readily with a sling psychrometer and by plotting the closing curves.

There are basically three different types of fog that are encountered on Lake Superior. The first of these is **radiation fog**. This is the most common fog encountered during the summer cruising season and occurs when an air mass loses its heat into space as the day cools at sundown. It often forms on clear nights when there are no clouds to retain heat or surface wind. Clear skies, little or no wind and high relative humidity are good signs of fog occurring in the morning. This type of fog is usually a shallow layer over the water ranging from a few feet to 25 or 30 feet above the surface and it rarely spreads far offshore. It usually dissipates early the following morning after the sun has warmed the air mass above its dew point.

Another type of fog is called **frontal or precipitation fog**. It occurs when a warm and cold air mass meets and is found just ahead of an oncoming warm front. As the warm air climbs over the cold, it is cooled below its condensation point and a thin band of fog is formed. It is often accompanied by warm rain. It is not as dense as the other two types of fog, but it often lasts a day or so until the front moves on. If the front contains warm, moist air, the precipitation fog will be replaced by advection fog.

Advection fog is the worst kind of fog, the "pea soup" variety. It is formed whenever warm moist air moves over a cold surface. Thus, cold Lake Superior being in the center of the continent that warms the moving air masses is a prime candidate for this type of fog. It is especially prevalent in the spring and early season when southerly winds bring in the warm moist air from the Gulf, forming very dense fog that covers large sections of the lake. It can also form in midsummer when warm, moist air is condensed below its dew point by cold water that wells up from below. When this happens the fog patches are much smaller, but it may take a while for them to dissipate.

There are a few clues that may be helpful in predicting fog. Quite often if there is rain during the night, due to the increased humidity in the air the possibility of fog the next morning is increased. This type of fog usually dissipates and is burned off by noon as the day warms up. Other signs of the possibility of fog forming are a hazy white sky, a watery sun and a poorly defined horizon. Often, this is accompanied by a feeling of dampness as the relative humidity increases.

Often fog is not consistent in its density. Between particularly heavy patches of fog there may be areas where visibility will be considerably greater. Before we had radio navigation systems on board, we would often sit outside the entrance of an anchorage waiting for the fog to lift, if only momentarily, to give those all-important bearings. Another trick we have used is to turn the gain up on our radar and thus bring in the background noise. Fog will appear on the screen as distinct patches relative to our position and surrounding land masses so that we can determine its extent. We have also used this technique in tracking rain, squalls and thunderstorms.

The basic premise in fog navigation is to know where you are and let others know your position. Thus, it becomes important to know your exact position before the weather closes in and update your position every five to 10 minutes. Radio location systems such as radar and GPS are an unbeatable combination for navigating in reduced visibility.

There are a number of ways in which you can let others know of your position. One is by flying a radar reflector, another is by sounding a foghorn. Regulations state that a boat under engine power must sound one prolonged blast (four to six seconds) at intervals not more than two minutes, while under sail power it must emit one long and two short blasts every two minutes. Although these regulations pertain to vessels more than 39 feet, it isn't a bad idea for those on smaller craft to use them, too. Another way of letting others in the area know of your position is with a "securité call" (see section on communications).

Weather Broadcasts

There are a number of ways to obtain weather information on Lake Superior. Three of the most common ways use the VHF radio: NOAA continuous broadcasts, U.S. Coast Guard scheduled broadcasts and Canadian Coast Guard continuous weather. It is also possible to get valuable weather information on the Internet from a number of different sites. For a listing of these sites, refer to

the Chapter Two section in the Directory of Marine Interests.

The National Weather Service, known as NOAA Weather Radio, transmits a number of continuous weather broadcasts from stations along Lake Superior's south and north shores. They are given in plain language and include both short-range and long-range forecasts. These stations concentrate on a specific area giving the near shore forecast for just that area. For example, WX1 from Duluth gives the nearshore forecast for Two Harbors to Port Wing, while WX7 gives the nearshore forecast for Port Wing to Saxon Harbor. Unfortunately, the offshore/open waters forecast is not given as frequently, and you may have to wait a number of times through the tape to get it. Most stations have a schedule for the offshore/open waters forecast that starts on the top of the hour

Figure 2.13
NOAA Continuous Weather Broadcasts For Lake Superior
I. Stations

Channel	Call sign Freq. (MHz)	Site Name	Area Served	Near Shore Marine Forecast	Open Waters Forecast
WX-1	KIG-64 162.550	Duluth, MN	NE Minn. & NW Wisc.	Two Harbors to Port Wing	Every 20 min.
	KIG-66 162.550	Marquette, MI	North Central Upper Peninsula	*Huron Is. to Marquette *Marquette to Munising	Every 30 min.
	KIG-74 162.550	Sault Ste. Marie, MI	Eastern L. Superior Northern L. Michigan Northern L. Huron	*Whitefish Bay and the Saint Marys River	Every 15 min.
WX-2	WXK-73 162.400	Houghton, MI	Central & NE Wisc. Copper Country & surrounding area	*Ontonagon to UE/ UE to Manitou I. *Manitou I. to LE/LE to Huron I. *Isle Royale Rec. Forecast	Every 20 min.
WX-3	WZ-2514 162.475	Munising, MI	NE Upper Michigan	Marquette to Grand Marais, MI	Every 20 min.
WX-4	WNG-630 162.425	Finland, MN	Minn. Arrowhead Country	Grand Portage to Two Harbors	Every 20 min.
WX-5	KXI-43 162.450	Grand Marais, MN	Minn. Arrowhead Country	Grand Portage to Two Harbors	Every 20 min.
	WNG-576 162.450	Marquette, MI	NE Upper Peninsula	*Grand Marais to Whitefish Point	Every 30 min.
WZ-2513	WXM-91 162.500	Copper Harbor, MI	North/central Wisc. & marine interests in western Lake Superior	Port Wing to Saxon Harbor	Every 20 min.
WX-7	KZZ-78 162.525	Ashland, WI	South shore of western Lake Superior	Port Wing to Saxon Harbor	Every 20 min.

UE = Upper Entry Keweenaw Waterway   LE = Lower Entry Keweenaw Waterway
* Given at same time as Open Waters Forecast

II. Information Given

A. Description of weather patterns affecting the Great Lakes region.

B. Forecasts for the U.S. portion of nearby land area through 5 days.

C. Marine forecasts, advisories and warnings for appropriate lake.

D. Weather observations from selected National Weather Service and Coast Guard stations.

E. Radar reports when pertinent.

F. Local weather observations and forecasts.

G. Special bulletins and summaries concerning severe weather.

and is repeated every 15, 20 or 30 minutes. In addition to the marine forecast, these transmissions also include information on surrounding land formations along with severe weather warnings and watches
(see Fig. 2.13).

Unfortunately, the broadcasts that originate from Sault Ste. Marie, Michigan, also include weather information for the St. Marys River system, Lake Michigan and North Lake Huron. Thus, they become quite lengthy, and it takes some time before information pertinent to your area is given. Likewise, as you travel along the south shore between Marquette and the Soo you will often pick up weather channels that give forecasts just for Lake Michigan.

The weather reports from the U.S. Coast Guard are not continuous but are regularly scheduled broadcasts that are transmitted twice daily. These broadcasts contain the marine forecasts for the American side from Grand Marais, Minnesota, around the west end of the lake to the Soo. They also are quite lengthy giving information on some of the lower Great Lakes and Notices to Mariners for the whole region, so again it may take some listening before getting relevant information for your area. In addition to these regularly scheduled broadcasts, the Coast Guard will relay urgent weather warnings such as a "securité" transmission.

The Canadian Coast Guard provides continuous weather reports from Thunder Bay and with repeaters on the north shore at Horn (near Schreiber) and the east shore at Bald Head and Sault Ste. Marie, Ontario. Thus, it is possible to get coverage for the whole east shore and most of the north. (There are a few spots on the east shore where, tucked in between the bluffs of Otter Cove, Richardson's Harbour and La Canadienne, reception is poor and sporadic.) These tapes, updated every few hours, are also particularly helpful in that they often give actual conditions at various stations around the lake and from ships in transit. Information is given in plain language and the MAFOR code, along with information on aids to navigation. Depending on the area you are in these transmissions are received on WX1, WX8, WX9, 21B (Sault and Bald Head) and 83B (Thunder Bay and Horn). Once again, these broadcasts are lengthy including the St. Mary's River, Lake Huron, North Channel and Georgian Bay.

Fortunately, there are a number of areas along the Canadian shoreline where there are transmitters, owned and operated by Environment Canada, that provide more regional information. These stations broadcast to the city of Thunder

Figure 2.14
Metric Wind Speed Conversions

km/hr	stm/hr	knots
10	6	5.2
15	9	7.8
20	12	10.4
25	15	13.0
30	18	15.6
35	21	18.3
40	24	20.1
45	27	23.5
50	30	26.1
55	33	28.7
60	36	31.3
65	39	33.9

km/hr – kilometers/hour
stm/hr – statute miles/hour
knots – nautical miles/hour

Figure 2.15
Metric Temperature Conversions

°Celsius	°Fahrenheit
0	32.0
3	37.4
6	42.8
9	48.2
12	53.6
15	59.0
18	64.4
21	69.8
24	75.2
27	80.6
30	86.0
33	91.4
36	96.8

$F° = C° \times 9/5 + 32$
$C° = (F° - 32) \times 5/9$

Bay on WX3, to the Nipigon and Red Rock area on WX1, and to Marathon and the Pukaskwa Park area on WX1. Thus, this secondary system provides almost complete coverage from Thunder Bay to Otter Head on the east shore. The broadcasts give local weather conditions and projections in addition to the Marine Forecast for the present 24 hours in both western and eastern Lake Superior and with an outlook for the following 24 hours.

Parts of the Canadian broadcasts are given in metric units, and these may be confusing for most Americans. For example, when they forecast a wind of 34 kilometers per hour that may sound like it's time to get out the storm sails—when in reality it's only 18 knots. Likewise, temperature measurements can be confusing. Although 25° C sounds like it might be kind of cold, it is really a nice day in the upper 70s F. Thus two charts on metric conversions for wind and temperature are included. (See Figures 2.14 and 2.15).

MAFOR Code

The **MA**rine **FOR**ecast is a system that dispenses the marine forecast in coded form, thereby enabling a large amount of information to be transmitted accurately and in short order. The

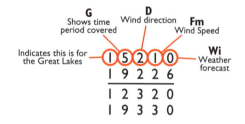

Figure 2.16
The MAFOR Reporting Code

G – Forecast Period	D – Wind Direction	Fm – Wind Force	WI – Forecast Weather
0 – Beginning of period	0 – Calm	0 – 0 to 10 knots	0 – Moderate to good visibility, more than 3 nautical miles
1 – Valid for 3 hours	1 – Northeast	1 – 11 to 16 knots	1 – Risk of accumulation of ice on superstructures (Temp. 23° to 32°F)
2 – Valid for 6 hours	2 – East	2 – 17 to 21 knots	
3 – Valid for 9 hours	3 – Southeast	3 – 22 to 27 knots	2 – Strong risk, accumulation of ice on superstructures (Temp. below 23°F)
4 – Valid for 12 hours	4 – South	4 – 28 to 33 knots	
5 – Valid for 18 hours	5 – Southwest	5 – 34 to 40 knots	3 – Mist (visibility 5/8 to 3 nautical miles)
6 – Valid for 24 hours	6 – West	6 – 41 to 47 knots	
7 – Valid for 48 hours	7 – Northwest	7 – 48 to 55 knots	4 – Fog (visibility less than 5/8 nautical miles)
8 – Valid for 72 hours	8 – North	8 – 56 to 63 knots	
9 – Occasionally	9 – Variable	9 – 64 knots and above	5 – Drizzle
			6 – Rain
			7 – Snow or rain & snow
			8 – Squally weather with or without showers
			9 – Thunderstorms

code consists of groups of five numbers, with each set representing conditions during a specific time period. (See Fig. 2.16.) The code was used a lot in weather broadcasts many, many decades ago. Although its use has declined in recent years, we found after checking it is still given with a number of contemporary broadcasts. Hence, its continued inclusion in this edition.

The first number of the code is always "1," representing the Great Lakes. The second number indicates the period of time covered by the forecast. At the beginning of the forecast, the time for which the code is to be initiated will also be given, because these numbers will have little meaning if you don't know the beginning of the forecast period. In any given forecast, the time periods represented by these numbers should add up to 24 hours. The third number gives wind direction while the fourth number gives the wind speed or force in knots. The last number gives a brief description of what type of weather is forecast for that time period. A typical example of a forecast would be as follows:

For the first 18 hours of the forecast period, the wind will be out of the east at 11 to 16 knots. There will be moderate or good visibility. Occasionally during this first time period, there is a possibility of rain with winds increasing to 17 to 21 knots. During the second time period, which is six hours, the winds will be SE at 17 to 21 knots. Occasionally during this time period, the wind may strengthen to 22 to 27 knots. The visibility will be clear to moderate.

Because the time is often given as Universal Time Coordinated or Greenwich Mean Time (GMT), it is important to be able to convert to your present operating time. In the summer, GMT is four hours ahead of daylight-saving time in the Eastern Time Zone, five hours ahead of daylight-saving time in the Central Time Zone. All of Ontario, Isle Royale and most of the Upper Peninsula of Michigan are in the Eastern Time Zone, Minnesota and Wisconsin are in the Central Time Zone. (In the winter, GMT is five and six hours ahead respectively.) Thus to convert from GMT to your present operating time it is necessary to subtract four or five hours in the summer depending on your time zone. (See Fig. 2.17).

Figure 2.17
Converting From GMT

GMT
10:15
1400 (2:00)

Eastern DST
6:15
1000

Central DST
5:15
0900

Lake Conditions

Next to weather, there are certain lake conditions that also have an effect on the Lake Superior boater. They are seiches, currents and lake levels.

Seiches

Although Lake Superior is not affected by tides, there are often fluctuations of water levels that are not caused by the action of the sun and moon. Called a *seiche* (SAYsh), these normally occur in narrow, constricted anchorages. If you watch the shoreline for 20 minutes or so you can often see water level changes of 6 to 10 inches. In fact, in some anchorages they appear

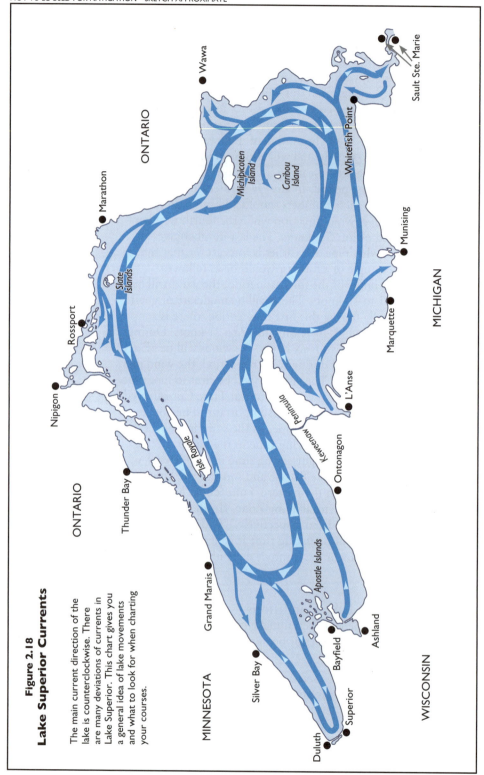

Figure 2.18
Lake Superior Currents

The main current direction of the lake is counterclockwise. There are many deviations of currents in Lake Superior. This chart gives you a general idea of lake movements and what to look for when charting your courses.

almost cyclic, and we have used them to advantage when trying to enter/leave a tight anchorage in low water. We have frequently seen this phenomenon in the long entrance to Brulé Harbour, and in CPR Slip and Ganley Harbour. Historically, much larger seiches of many feet were observed by the voyageurs and recorded at Marquette, Michigan, in 1939 (7 feet), Bayfield and the Apostles in 1968 (4 feet) and more recently in Rossport (3 to 4 feet). When reaching this magnitude, they are thought to be associated with squalls and storm changes caused by a change in wind and an abrupt change in barometric pressure. Fortunately, seiches of these proportions are quite uncommon and not of great concern when out on the open waters of the lake with the most damage occurring near shore, especially when tied up to a dock.

Currents

For years we have known there are currents on Lake Superior and that they are more pronounced in some areas than others. It didn't take us long to find out that when we were going NE up the Keweenaw Peninsula from Upper Entry to Copper Harbor we were literally flying, while coming back the other way it was like a slog to weather, even with the wind off the beam or behind us. We can't count the times that we have crabbed for each mile going around the southern end of Isle Royale from Siskiwit Bay to Windigo. Then a couple of years ago a friend showed us a current chart for the lake (see Fig. 2.18).

Although the initial study was done in the 1890s for all of the Great Lakes, it has been verified in parts by more recent studies: ex—the Keweenaw Current. The general circulation on Lake Superior is cyclonic, or counterclockwise, with variations from less than 1 knot to greater than 3 knots. While currents are more of a concern to slow-moving sailboats where they can affect passage time, even powerboats can be affected by fuel consumption, especially if bucking a 3-knot current. There is also the problem of a wind-against-current situation where an unusually short steep chop may be experienced that could become dangerous depending on the size of the boat.

Lake Levels

Lake Superior is 601.1ft/183m above sea level. This is called Chart Datum and is also known as Low Water Datum. It is the reference point against which lake levels are measured: either above Chart Datum (high water) or below Chart Datum (low water). In normal years the lake can fluctuate by as much as a foot throughout the year with higher levels being in late summer and early fall and lower levels in the winter, with the average over the years fluctuating in this cycle a little above chart datum.

Before the turn of the century boaters hardly gave lake levels a thought. In fact, there are only a few that remember the mid-1980s when lake levels were so high (October 1985 the highest in

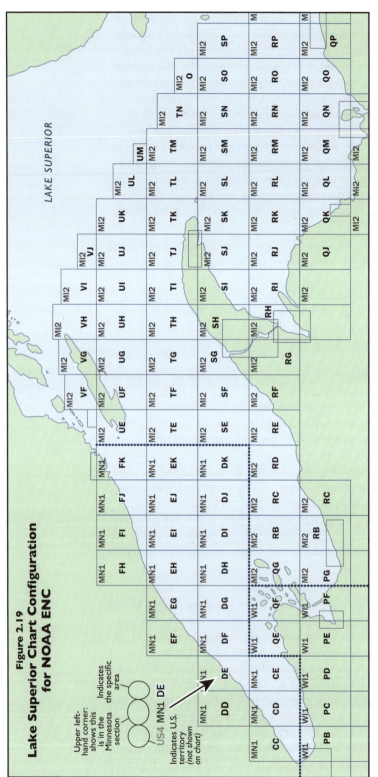

Figure 2.19
Lake Superior Chart Configuration for NOAA ENC

Upper left-hand corner: shows this is in the Minnesota section

Indicates the specific area

US4 MN1 DE

Indicates U.S. territory (not shown on chart)

LAKE SUPERIOR

Lake Superior is divided into 35 sections by state:
- Minnesota: MN1
- Wisconsin: WI1
- Michigan: MI2

Each chart is represented by eight letters and numbers. Example: **US4 MI2 TH** (for simplicity only the two state letters and number are given, along with the last two letters on the above chart).

- The first three spaces "US4" tell that it is a U.S. chart.
- The next three spaces "MI2" tell that it is in the Michigan section.
- The last two spaces identify the specific area.

recorded history at about 2 1/2 feet above Chart Datum) that many marinas raised their docks - only to have to put on bang boards (vertical rub rails) when the lake receded to normal levels.

In 2007 lake levels saw some of the lowest readings in recorded history: in March it was 599.7ft/182.9m above sea level or 17 inches below Chart Datum; in August it was 600.43ft/183.01m above sea level or 8 Inches below Chart Datum, hitting a new low for that month. There is only one other time that lower readings have been recorded and that was in April 1926 with 599.5ft/182.7m above sea level or 19 Inches below Chart Datum.

There are two primary causes contributing to these low lake levels: evaporation and low precipitation. With generally higher temperatures the rate of evaporation increases. In 2006, 2010, and 2024 there were some of the highest water surface temperatures ever recorded. For example, in 2024 as we were working with the present edition, researchers at the University of Minnesota Duluth found summer surface water temperatures have increased by 5 degrees over the past 30 years. When you consider the size and volume of the lake, this is quite a large increase.

Along with increased air temperatures, wind speeds also increase, producing more evaporation. Evaporation even occurs during the winter months and is enhanced by reduced ice cover. The Lake Superior watershed has been running 5 to 12 inches below normal precipitation. In fact, the Midwest has been in a drought and projection models indicate that this drought may be here to stay for at least a few more years.

The impact of these low levels on boaters is seen in many ways. Many are not able to get up to docks that they normally use. If they do, there is the real danger of part of the boat slipping under the dock and being pounded up into the dock with even the smallest wave action. Even in the wilderness, rocks that were normally under water are popping up and there are some anchorages boaters are not able to get into. (Note that most of the soundings in this book were taken in normal water years. In most cases these soundings are clarified by giving the Chart Datum at the time the soundings were taken and it is important to correlate those soundings in light of present Chart Datum water levels.) On an economic level, commercial shipping is forced to take on lighter loads to navigate in harbors and channels.

One of the answers to low water levels for harbors and marinas is dredging. Many marinas are taking on expensive dredging operations to keep their facilities usable for those with moderate to deep draft boats. The Army Corps of Engineers is responsible for dredging commercial and recreational harbors. To find out when the last time a harbor has been dredged or its future dredging schedule, go to *www. lre.usace.army.mil/who/operationsofficehomepage/*, select the state and then the harbor.

In light of these low-water levels it is important that the boater keeps abreast of fluctuating water levels. Fortunately, there are a

number of ways to do this. The Thunder Bay weather station updates the water level in its VHF weather forecast each Tuesday during the boating season. Since this is given in meters, it is important for Americans to be able to convert this to inches. The conversion factor is to take the meter reading times the number of inches in a meter (39.37)—it makes no difference if the reading is a decimal fraction or + or -. For example if the water level is -0.17m (below) Chart Datum: take –0.17 x 39.37 = -6.69 inches or 6.7 inches below Chart Datum. The same information can be obtained by calling this Thunder Bay number: 807-344-3141. On the American side, this information can be obtained at the Army Corps of Engineers Website: *www.lre.usace.army.mil/glhh* then click "water levels," then "current conditions." You can also access historical data and future predictions at this Website.

Navigation
Nautical Charts – U.S.

In November 2019 NOAA announced that all traditional paper nautical raster charts and the associated raster chart products would be cancelled by January 2025. This includes four raster chart formats:

- Paper Nautical Chart
- Full-size Nautical Chart
- Booklet Chart—NOAA paper chart that is divided into a dozen 8.5 x 11 pages
- Raster Navigation Chart (RNC)

The new NOAA Electronic Navigational Chart (NOAA ENC) is NOAA's premier navigation product. You can download an individual ENC and view it for free in a software viewer like the CARIS Easy View or use the online ENC viewer hosted on NOAA's Office of Coast Survey website. You can also access this new tool in custom making your own charts by going to: https://devgis.charttools.noaa.gov/pod. On the map shown use your mouse to select Lake Superior (see Figure 2.19) and zoom in until you get to the area you want. On the left side select either "Quick Start Guide" or "User Guide".

Embracing the functionalities of digital technology, there are many new enhancements implemented in the new NOAA ENC. These include zooming in and out providing larger scale (more detailed) coverage in many areas, resolving discontinuities and properly "edge-matching" data between adjacent

Figure 2.20
CHS Chart Selection for Lake Superior

Minutes	Seconds	Minutes	Seconds
.05	3	.55	33
.10	6	.60	36
.15	9	.65	39
- - - -	- - - -	- - - -	- - - -
.20	12	.70	42
.25	15	.75	45
.30	18	.80	48
- - - -	- - - -	- - - -	- - - -
.35	21	.85	51
.40	24	.90	54
.45	27	.95	57
- - - -	- - - -	- - - -	- - - -
.50	30	1.00	60

CHS Chart Selection for Lake Superior

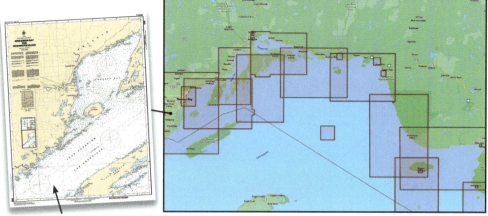

CHS Nautical Chart CHS2314,
Port Of Thunder Bay

**Nautical Charts –
Canadian**

Clicking on a box in the
nauticalchartsonline.com site
will bring you to a page
where you can purchase
that area's CHS chart.

ENC cells by using just 12 standard chart scales. The online
NOAA Custom Chart application enables users to create their own
customized nautical charts directly from the latest official ENC
data. The tool outputs PDF files set to the paper size, scale, and
location selected by the user. Depths can be displayed in meters,
feet, or fathoms. Users may save their charts in a personal chart
catalog as ENC data becomes available. They can even print them
out on home printers or send them out to be printed if larger
charts are needed. Along with these enhancements, ENC can be
downloaded on chart plotters and used with GPS enabled systems.

Nautical Charts – Canadian

The Canadian Hydrographic Service (CHS) produces nautical
charts for the Ontario waters of Lake Superior. These charts can be
bought online by going to: *https://nauticalchartsonline.com/charts/
CHS/Central*. Lake Superior charts can be found either by using the
map and "+" sign and mouse or by using the long list underneath
the map of charts: Lake Superior charts are found on the right side
about 1/4 of the way down. You can select what type of chart and
then "add to cart" and proceed with normal online shopping. See
Figure 2.20.

Aids to Navigation

In addition to charts there are numerous aids to navigation
around the lake, such as buoys, day markers, light beacons and
light stations. It is, however, in electronic navigation that we have
seen the greatest advances in recent years. For in addition to using
our compasses, depth sounders and knot-logs, we are now able to
navigate with a precision that was only dreamed of years ago.

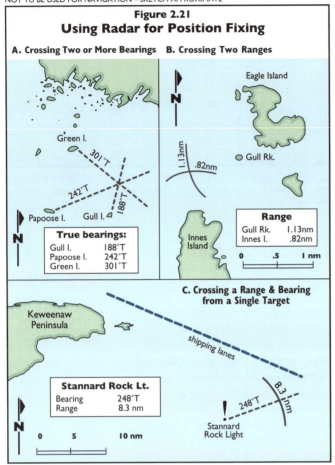

Figure 2.21
Using Radar for Position Fixing

A. Crossing Two or More Bearings   **B. Crossing Two Ranges**

Green I.

301°T

242°T

188°T

Papoose I.   Gull I.

N

True bearings:

Gull I.	188°T
Papoose I.	242°T
Green I.	301°T

Eagle Island

Gull Rk.

1.13nm

.82nm

Innes Island

Range

Gull Rk.	1.13nm
Innes I.	.82nm

0   .5   1 nm

C. Crossing a Range & Bearing from a Single Target

Keweenaw Peninsula

shipping lanes

8.3 nm

248°T

Stannard Rock Light

Stannard Rock Lt.

Bearing	248°T
Range	8.3 nm

N

0   5   10 nm

Radar

The word "radar" is an acronym for RAdio Detecting And Ranging. It basically consists of sending out radio waves that are reflected to the source by distant objects. The amount of time it takes the radio waves to travel to the object and back to the source is a measure of the distance (range) to the object. The principle is the same as that used in depth sounders.

It used to be that radars were seen primarily on powerboats, mainly because of the large size of the radomes. The 1980s, however, saw the development of compact 24-inch and even petite 18-inch radomes. This, combined with smaller display units and drastic price reduction, has made

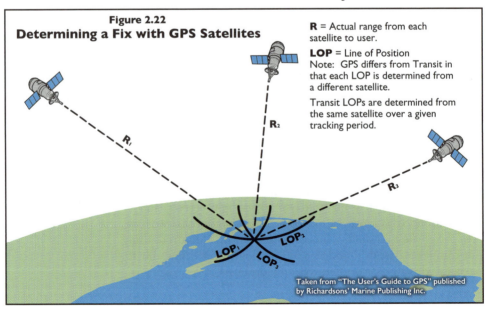

Figure 2.22
Determining a Fix with GPS Satellites

R₁

R₂

R₃

LOP₁

LOP₂

LOP₃

R = Actual range from each satellite to user.

LOP = Line of Position
Note: GPS differs from Transit in that each LOP is determined from a different satellite.

Transit LOPs are determined from the same satellite over a given tracking period.

Taken from "The User's Guide to GPS" published by Richardsons' Marine Publishing Inc.

radar a viable navigational tool for sailboater and powerboater alike.

Radar is used to determine approximate position, your own, other vessels, and range to land masses. It is particularly helpful in situations of reduced visibility like night, fog, and rain. Employing the circular Guard Zone and its alarm is very helpful in these situations as a warning when you are getting too close to land or other vessels. Two other tools that are helpful in determining the position of other vessels and land masses are the Variable Range Marker and the Electronic Bearing Line. It is interesting that in the days before accurate position fixing with satellite navigation these were useful tools in determining more accurate position. This was done by crossing the bearings from two or more different targets, crossing the ranges from two different targets or crossing the range and bearing from a single target. See Figure 2.21.

Satellite Navigation – GPS

To answer the quest for a worldwide navigation system, the Department of Defense turned to satellite-based systems as a means of transmitting radio signals that could be received anywhere, even on the high seas thousands of miles from any land mass. The first system, **SAT NAV**, was an interim system which was in service until 1996.

Where Loran-C (a land based system for signals) was the rage in the 1980s, **GPS** (Global Positioning System) proved to have an even greater impact in the 1990s. It combined the best of both the loran and SAT NAV worlds: continuous navigation, everywhere.

GPS differs from SAT NAV in many respects, one of which is that the satellites are placed in very high (10,800-mile) orbits. Another is that the system consists of a large number of satellites — a "nest" of 24 satellites plus spares. These two differences (high orbits and number of satellites) are what provide continuous navigation. Another basic difference is the way in which position is determined. GPS also uses the concept of satellite ranging, but thanks to some sophisticated technological tricks, this is determined by actual (corrected) transmission time. It also differs from SAT NAV in that more than one satellite (three for a 2-D fix, four for a 3-D fix) is required to determine a fix. (See Fig. 2.22.)

GPS has the inherent potential of providing incredibly accurate fixes (within a few meters) and thus is finding unlimited use in all environments, not just the maritime community. Receiver technology has reached a high degree of sophistication producing numerous "bells and whistles." Where we first started tracking one satellite at a time sequentially, most receivers now come with a 12-channel chip that can track 12 different satellites simultaneously. Initially, accuracy was limited to 100 meters (300 feet) because of an imposed signal degradation, selective availability (SA). Then on 1 May 2000, President Bill Clinton signed a bill to remove SA. Civilian accuracy is now at 10 meters (30 feet).

Chartplotters

Chartplotters are devices used for marine navigation that combine GPS data with electronic navigational charts (ENC). With the cancellation of NOAA paper charts in January 2025, chartplotters have taken on new importance in the navigational arsenal of the Lake Superior boater. The basic chartplotter starts with a simple unit that displays ENC along with GPS data from either an internal or external source so that ship's position, heading and speed can also be displayed. More advanced units accept interfacing with additional components such as radar antennas, sounders, AIS, satellite weather, fishfinder, and sonar with sidescan and downscan to see underwater objects. There are also Network Chartplotters that allow you to have one or more display screens sharing all components that are connected to the "network". This is particularly helpful if you have an upper and lower helm or want screen readouts in the navstation down below and also outside at the helm.

Dead Reckoning

When all is said and done about electronic navigation, it is important to return to the basics of dead reckoning. It shouldn't be surprising that in this age of electronic gadgetry, most skippers don't know how to dead reckon. Yet, it is the rudiment of all navigation. It is also an important technique to master in case you lose your electronics to a major system breakdown or lightning strike. To gain confidence in dead reckoning and to check other systems, a common practice is to periodically keep a separate DR fix from those established with other navigational aids.

Basically dead reckoning involves keeping track of your direction, speed and time under way so that position can be periodically updated. For example, if you are going six knots for a period of two hours, you should have traveled a distance of 12 nautical miles, providing no headwinds or oncoming seas are encountered. A handy device used to determine distance is a pair of dividers, since distance

NOT TO BE USED FOR NAVIGATION – SKETCH APPROXIMATE

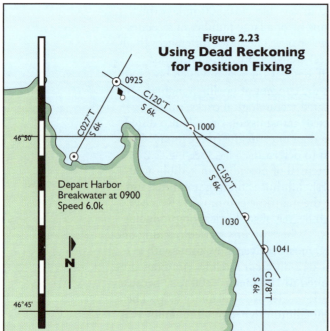

Figure 2.23
Using Dead Reckoning for Position Fixing

can be quickly lifted off from the side/latitude scale of any chart: 1 nautical mile = 1 minute of latitude. Course direction can be determined by using a protractor or a set of parallel rules and a compass rose, which is also printed on the chart.

In plotting position, a track line is drawn which indicates course direction. A direction label is placed on top of the line expressed as a three-digit number in degrees which is preceded by the letter "C" to indicate course. It is also important to mark if the course is true (T) or magnetic (M). The speed (S) is given below the line along with the appropriate unit (knots or mph). A known position is plotted with a dot with a small circle around it; an estimated DR based on running time with a half circle. Either type of position is labeled with the time as a four-digit number in the 24-hour system. Positions are calculated whenever there is a change in course or speed or at desirable intervals. (See Fig. 2.23.)

Once you know your position, you can determine the range and bearing to your destination and even your estimated time of arrival (ETA), just like waypoint navigation in radio-location systems. The only difference is that you do the calculations instead of an onboard computer. A little handheld calculator quickly simplifies the tasks.

Docking

It is assumed in this book that anyone who leaves a marina and heads out into Lake Superior will know how to dock a boat. There are, however a few points that should be briefly mentioned and one technique that bears discussion.

It should go without saying that fenders should be commensurate with the size of the boat. Yet every year we see boats tied up to a dock with incredibly small fenders for their size. Larger fenders may be difficult to store, but they should be able to protect the boat and take considerable pounding in a blow. Extra fenders should also be carried for rafting or in case a fender is lost or collapses from stress. Likewise extra dock lines should be carried for tying off in a variety of situations and conditions. In

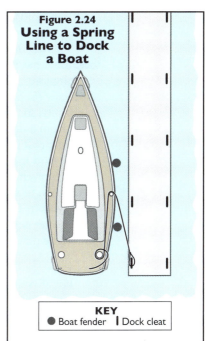

**Figure 2.24
Using a Spring
Line to Dock
a Boat**

KEY
● Boat fender ❙ Dock cleat

1. Before approaching dock run a dock line through a snatch block or ring attached midship. Lead end of line back to a cockpit winch and put on a couple of wraps leaving end free to helmsman.

2. Approach dock and place dock line spliced loop over a cleat with a boat hook. It helps if the loop is quite large.

3. Continue to motor ahead slowly parallel to the dock. When the cleated loop on the dock approaches the winch turn the boat *away* from the dock and start winching the line in while still motoring ahead very slowly. This combined motion will draw the boat onto the dock. (Note that the spring line loop is now well aft of the winch to get the best purchase power on the spring line.)

4. Cleat off the spring line when the boat is next to the dock. Keep the engine in slow forward with the wheel braked hard over away from the dock and the boat will remain in this position.

5. Step off the boat and cleat off bow and stern lines and other spring lines as needed. When the boat is secure, turn off the engine and return the wheel to normal position.

addition, to using bow and stern lines, fore and aft spring lines are equally important in stabilizing a boat on a dock.

There is one docking technique that should be mentioned because it has been gaining popularity in recent years. It is to use a spring line in docking a boat (see Fig. 2.24). This technique is especially useful when trying to dock on a short dock or in adverse conditions such as encountering a beam wind that will blow you away from a dock. It is also useful when docking shorthanded, i.e. with just two people. One crucial part of the technique is to reduce the forward momentum of the boat by approaching the dock very slowly or even going in reverse. The timing used in the technique as to when to start winching in the spring line and turning the boat away from the dock will vary depending on the size and underwater configuration of the boat. So, this technique is one that should be practiced ahead of time in calm, controlled conditions.

Anchoring

For anyone who does any serious cruising on the lake, anchoring will soon become a large part of the cruising experience. Because the anchorages are often constricted and/or so deep that it is difficult to get adequate swinging room, a variety of anchoring techniques will need to be utilized.

Anchoring will usually be done in sand or good holding clay. But sometimes the bottom may be rocky or composed of small gravel. Often, there will be deadheads and slash lying on the bottom, making retrieving anchors difficult. Thus, it may be necessary to use a trip line with a float in some circumstances.

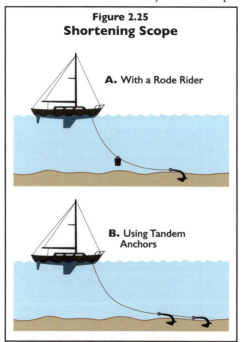

Figure 2.25
Shortening Scope

A. With a Rode Rider

B. Using Tandem Anchors

Older types of anchors that have worked well on the lake are the Danforth, Bruce and CQR plow or Delta. Newer types of anchors that are gaining popularity because they can be used with a variety of substrates and usually set well are the Mantus and Rocna. With the plow, it is necessary to have at least 20 feet of chain to get it to lay right and dig in. The usual 7-to-1 scope is desirable, but with the plow or Bruce and depending on the anchorage and the amount of chain, it may be possible to cheat on this a little. In a heavy blow, it is advisable to let out more scope or put down more ground tackle. As boaters get use to the Mantus and Rocna these parameters may change.

Reducing Scope

Some of the anchorages on Lake Superior are real "hurricane holes." But even though they are snug, there may not be much swinging room. Others might be quite deep, as well as having restricted space, so letting out enough scope may be a problem.

There are a number of ways to safely reduce scope. One is to use a bigger anchor; another is to use more chain. These, however, may not be viable options and there are ways of achieving the same effect with one's present system.

One way is to slide an extra weight down the rode with a rode rider (see Fig. 2.25A). This has the effect of increasing the catenary (sag of the rode) and reducing the angle between it and the bottom which allows the anchor to lie in a more horizontal position, dig in and hold. If a rode rider isn't available, any kind of a weight, such as another small anchor, can be slipped down the rode. One that works very well is the small mushroom anchor which is sometimes used for dinghies.

Another way to reduce scope is to anchor with two anchors set in tandem (see Fig. 2.25B). This method is especially effective in getting the shank of the first anchor to lie parallel to the bottom. Both of these methods have the added feature that the extra weight acts as a shock absorber when the wind pipes up and the boat begins to pull harder on the anchor. A disadvantage with using tandem anchors is that if the wind switches, there is the danger that the two anchors will become fouled on each other and not reset. A disadvantage with both methods is that, should you have to leave an anchorage quickly, there is a lot more ground tackle to bring up, usually when conditions aren't the best.

Figure 2.26
Using an Anchor & Tying On Onshore

A. With a Bow Anchor

Heads the bow into the wind if there is a chance it may funnel in through the entrance.

B. With a Stern Anchor

Provides better protection for the rudder & usually allows one to snug up closer to shore.

Tying Off On Shore

There may be some anchorages that are so restricted that even by reducing scope, there still isn't enough swinging room. Other anchorages may be so deep that the only place where it is shallow enough to get an anchor to set is right up next to shore. A technique that is then very useful is to set out either a bow or stern anchor and tie off on shore.

Which type of anchor is used depends on a couple of factors. If the anchorage is open to the wind, it may be advantageous to set out a bow anchor and tie off on shore so that the bow will ride better to the wind. If the shoreline is led back to the boat, this method has the advantage that, should you have to leave quickly

Dahlfin I ties off on shore in Allouez Bay at the top of Lake Superior. Dahl

(i.e., in the middle of the night), it is a simple matter to release the shore line and bring it back on the boat, motor up to the anchor and retrieve it on the way out. A disadvantage to this method is that often lying close to shore there are underwater rocks and

Figure 2.27
Using a Bridle to Help Position a Boat at Anchor

A. Boat lies to the wind, waves coming around point hit on the beam causing an uncomfortable motion.

B. Boat now lies with bow into the waves with reduced motion.

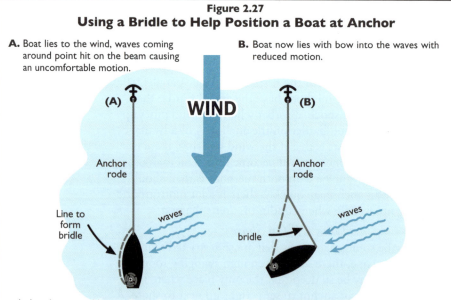

1. Attach a second line to the anchor rode to form a bridle (see text).

2. Run the free end of this line back to a cockpit winch that is on the opposite side as the waves. Put on a couple of wraps and cleat.

3. Let out one or two dozen feet of anchor rode and the bow will swing into the waves.

4. Use the winch to adjust the line until the boat lies into the waves.

* To remove the bridle, simply release the winch end and the boat will swing into the wind. Retrieve the anchor rode back to where the second line is attached and remove the line. CAUTION: it is prudent not to drop this winch end of the line in the water but walk it forward to the bow taking in the excess. Especially if you are motoring forward to take in the anchor rode this second line won't get caught in the prop.

boulders that could do damage to the rudder. In this case using a stern anchor and running a bow line ashore would be a better option. Since the bow usually conforms better to the underwater slope of the shoreline, it is often possible to snug so close to the shore that it is actually possible to step right off the boat. A disadvantage to using either method is that you are in a fixed position and should the wind switch, you may find yourself in a tenuous situation. (See Fig. 2.26).

Anchoring with a Bridle

There are times when it is beneficial to stabilize a boat at anchor without tying off on shore. It may be a tight anchorage where there is little swinging room or it may be desirable to avoid obstacles or merely get a more comfortable position with the boat as in Figure 2.27 A and B. Rigging a bridle may be a viable option in these conditions. It is simple to set up and doesn't have the disadvantages of being in a tightly fixed position or having a lot of gear to retrieve if it is necessary to leave in the middle of the night.

The procedure is really quite simple. Set the main anchor first. To form the second leg of the bridle, attach a line to the rode at the bow and then run it back to a cockpit winch, put on a couple of wraps and cleat it off. If you are anchoring on nylon rode, a rolling hitch works well for securing this second line to the rode. If you are anchoring on all chain, secure the bridle line with a bowline to a shackle that is easily attached to the chain. Before proceeding further it is important that this line is secure on a cockpit cleat.

To form the rest of the bridle, let out on the anchor rode a couple dozen feet. This amount will vary on the length of the boat and conditions so you may need to experiment. This will cause the boat to move more abeam of the wind and become very stable. In fact, one of the advantages of using a bridle is that the boat won't skate around as much at anchor. The beauty of this system is that you are on only one anchor and the boat position can be fine-tuned from the cockpit by taking in or letting out the line on the winch as conditions change. Another advantage is that it is relatively easy to retrieve in case you have to leave in a hurry. (See Figure 2.27).

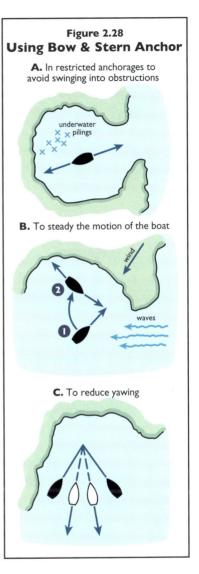

Figure 2.28
Using Bow & Stern Anchor

A. In restricted anchorages to avoid swinging into obstructions

underwater pilings

B. To steady the motion of the boat

wind

waves

C. To reduce yawing

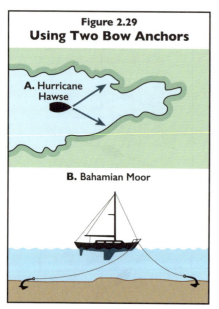

Figure 2.29
Using Two Bow Anchors

A. Hurricane Hawse

B. Bahamian Moor

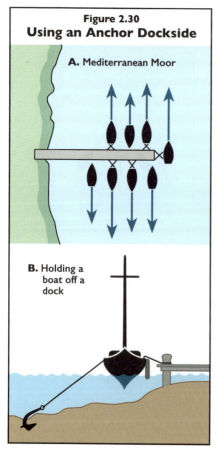

Figure 2.30
Using an Anchor Dockside

A. Mediterranean Moor

B. Holding a boat off a dock

Using More Than One Anchor

Sometimes it may be necessary to use both a bow and stern anchor at the same time. This is another technique that is useful when in restricted anchorages where there is little swinging room. It also comes in handy when you wish to avoid swinging into a particular area of an anchorage where there may be underwater pilings or shoal water. With a bow and stern anchor you can just about position your boat any way you like. (See Fig. 2.28A.)

There are a couple of ways in which using two anchors will help position the boat so it rests easier at anchor. Under normal conditions the boat will lie to the wind. But sometimes eddying effects coming around a point or seas left over from a previous weather system will produce an uncomfortable motion as the waves strike on the beam or quarter. By rowing out a stern anchor, the boat can be made to lie to the waves instead of the wind. The disadvantage with this technique and the previous one is that, again, you are lying in a fixed position and should the wind pipe up or change in the night and you are hit broadside, it can become very uncomfortable. (See Fig. 2.28B.)

Some sailboats, especially those with extreme fin keels, are often quite lively at anchor, literally skating back and forth in a yawing motion. The worst part of this is at the end of the yaw where the boat will snap in a sharp jerking motion as it begins to skate on "the other tack," sending a very uncomfortable motion down below. Sometimes just dropping another anchor over the stern and letting out a little rode can reduce this motion considerably. The anchor doesn't actually set (the scope is much too short), but the added weight dragged along the bottom reduces the yaw considerably. (See Fig. 2.28C.)

There are a couple of ways of setting two anchors off the bow. One is the "hurricane hawse" where two bow anchors are set in a "V." (See Fig. 2.29A.) This anchoring technique is especially useful when a strong blow is expected, since the strain and holding power is now shared by two anchors. Some sailors swear by this technique, others swear at it. For if the two anchors aren't set at least 45 to 50 degrees apart, the "V" is liable to collapse and the boat drags both anchors. Another disadvantage is that you have to be pretty sure on the wind direction. Should it switch, it is highly unlikely that both anchors will reset, and there is the chance that at least one will break out and foul on the other.

Another way of using two bow anchors is to have them set at 180 degrees from each other. This method, called the Bahamian Moor, is particularly useful when there are changes in wind, tide or currents and the swinging room is restricted. Actually, what is done is that bow and stern anchors are set and the stern rode is then led forward and cleated off the bow. The boat is now free to turn on just its own boat length. The trick is to allow enough slack in the unburdened line so the keel and rudder can swing over it freely without getting fouled. One disadvantage to this method is that it takes only a couple of full turns for the two rodes to become twisted enough to complicate retrieval of the anchors. To solve this problem, many skippers who use this anchoring technique frequently will rig some kind of swivel bridle to which each rode can be attached. The Bahamian Moor lends itself nicely to anchoring in restricted anchorages—as long as others are anchored that way so there is no chance of another boat with unrestricted swing moving into your area. (See Fig. 2.29B).

Using Anchors Dockside

Anchors can be used in connection with docks much the same as bow and stern anchors are used along with tying off on shore. This method, called the Mediterranean Moor, is particularly useful in congested areas where there is little dockage, as it allows more boats access to a dock. It is also useful in wilderness areas where there are old docks where there might not be enough depth for your boat. By setting out a stern anchor you may be able to just nudge up enough to the dock and still disembark at the bow.

It makes little difference which is used, a bow or stern anchor. Unless winds dictate otherwise, bow anchors are often preferred, since they are much easier to retrieve should you have to leave in the middle of the night. In this same light, it is prudent to lead the dock lines back onto the boat for cleating off. Not only can they be quickly released without climbing back on the dock, but it's nice to be able to ease off and snug up on the anchor line to move the boat a few feet off the dock before turning in. If the area has heavy boat traffic, this might be a situation in which it is wise to slide that extra weight down the rode to keep it out of the way lying close to the bottom. (See Fig. 2.30A.)

Another way of using an anchor at a dock is to set one out abeam to hold the boat off the dock. This is useful if you are tied up to an old dock that has underwater projections that could

damage the hull. It may be that by being held off, you get a little more depth so the keel won't rub on the underwater slope of the shoreline. Possibly the dock is greasy or soaked in creosote, and you just don't want the fenders to rub up against it, yet you still want to be close enough to step off. In any case, setting out a small anchor via dinghy with a breast line is usually all it takes to keep the boat away from the dock. (See Fig. 2.30B).

Rafting

One of the delights of cruising is doing it with others, and rafting offers the opportunity to socialize within an anchorage. This practice involves two or more boats secured together with fenders in between, on one or more anchors.

There are a number of different ways to construct a raft. Generally the first boat goes into the anchorage and sets an anchor and gets ready to receive (fenders out, etc.) the other boat. The second boat approaches cautiously with docklines in hand which are handed over to the first boat as it comes alongside. Once the bow and stern are secured to the first boat, it is important to add fore and aft spring lines to keep the boats from moving back and forth against each other. Fenders usually have to be adjusted for the amount of freeboard on each boat.

Literally all of the above techniques, such as tying off on shore, setting out a stern anchor and even using a Bahamian Moor, can be used successfully with a raft. Other boats can be added, usually with more anchors—but always with an eye to the weather. It's no fun to be in the middle of a large raft when the wind pipes up from a different quarter at 2 a.m. But when used with caution, rafting can become another enjoyable part of the cruising experience.

The ultimate social gathering is rafting in a remote anchorage. Dahl

Chapter Three

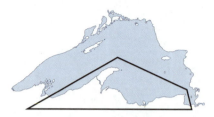

South Shore: Waiska Bay, Michigan, to Washburn, Wisconsin

Please Note:
Maps and Charts
in this book are
not necessarily
to scale and are
not intended for
navigation.

When we leave the Soo and head out into Lake Superior, it is probably a good thing that we meet the lake in stages. For to experience the lake all at once—with its full expanse—would be overwhelming. But as it is, we can get accustomed to the lake gradually. As we leave the broadening upper reaches of the St. Marys River and are guided north by the Gros Cap Light, first the river widens into a bay and this, in turn, widens at Pt. Iroquois into the magnitude of Whitefish Bay.

It is interesting that whenever coming from the Soo, Whitefish Bay always hits one as being enormous. And yet, this is nothing compared to clearing Whitefish Point and taking in the vast immensity of the full lake. To the east are the gargantuan headlands and bays of the Laurentian Plateau. To the north and west are the miles upon miles of open water, revealing Lake Superior as it really is—an inland sea.

The south shore of Lake Superior offers some of the most diverse topography to be found in the lake region. Traveling west from Whitefish Point, you first encounter the lowlands, green with new forests that have recovered from the days of lumbering. In stark contrast, you are next greeted with the dazzling white of the famed rolling Grand Sable Sand Dunes, which, in turn, abruptly change into the magnificent formations of the mineral-hued Pictured Rocks. Cities and towns dot this part of the lake, only to be contrasted with the wild bluffs of the high-rising vistas of the Huron and Porcupine mountains. There is even an inland waterway as we transverse the Keweenaw Peninsula via the Portage River, Portage Lake and the Keweenaw Waterway.

Although this is one of the more populated portions of the lake, it is also one of the most hostile areas to the recreational boater, since there are often long stretches between anchorages. There are no protecting island chains along this part of the shoreline. In contrast with other sections of the lake, there are few inlets or harbors of refuge here where the boater can retreat from foul weather. For example, in the 45-mile stretch from Whitefish Point to Grand Marais there is only one anchorage possibility. This is Little Lake Harbor, which, depending on whether it has recently been dredged or not, may not be open to boats drawing more than 4 feet. Thus, as we head across the southern shore, we follow the same route of Des Groseilliers and Radisson, and with the exception of the towns, we, too, can experience many of the same impressions that must have greeted these first French explorers as they ventured along the remote vast stretches of this sector of the lake.

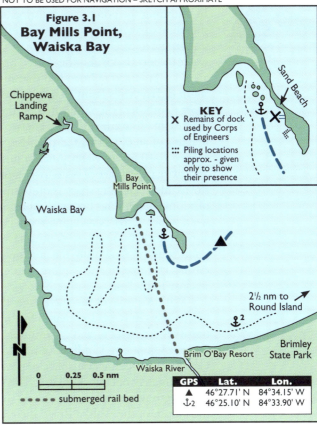

Figure 3.1
**Bay Mills Point,
Waiska Bay**

Chippewa Landing Ramp

KEY
X Remains of dock used by Corps of Engineers
::: Piling locations approx. - given only to show their presence

Bay Mills Point

Waiska Bay

Sand Beach

2½ nm to Round Island

Brimley State Park

Brim O'Bay Resort

Waiska River

N

0   0.25   0.5 nm

• • • • submerged rail bed

GPS	Lat.	Lon.
▲	46°27.71' N	84°34.15' W
⚓2	46°25.10' N	84°33.90' W

Note: a number of harbors along this south shore of the lake are subject to serious silting and require periodic dredging. In particular those harbors subject to silting are Whitefish Bay Harbor, Little Lake Harbor and Big Bay Harbor. Often before dredging they are inaccessible to deep-draft boats. To inquire about a harbor's status, you can access the Website for dredging at: *www.lre.usce. army. mil/who/operationsofficehomepage/*. Select the state and harbor in question. You can also call Operations and Dredging at 313-226-5148. Note that because of funding cuts, dredging is currently concentrated in harbors with commercial shipping.

Harbors and Anchorages

For those who have a late start in leaving the Soo for Lake Superior or want to cut a long day short before entering the Soo from the west, there is an anchorage at the bottom of Whitefish Bay behind **Bay Mills Point** in Waiska Bay. The anchorage is found by heading 212 degrees T from red buoy #32 in the St. Marys River buoyage system. Although the main part of Waiska Bay is very shallow, it is possible to find a narrow slot of adequate depths for anchoring immediately behind and to the west of the point.

In rounding the point, care must be taken to stand off from the shoreline to avoid sunken pilings to starboard. However, it is also important to carefully read the chart (#14884) and avoid the shoal water to port. Note also the dotted line on the chart that represents an old submerged railroad bed that must be avoided, extending south of Bay Mills Point to just west of the Waiska River. There is more depth here than indicated on the charts—10 to 12 feet when coming in. To starboard there are two very large metal pilings, the remains of an old Army Corps of Engineers dock, where a beam there is 8-10 feet of water. Anchor just beyond this structure in approximately 8 feet of water over a sand and mud bottom. Note: the usable anchoring space is quite small, since there are a number of submerged pilings between shore and the shoal water to the west, which restricts swinging room considerably. The bottom is also somewhat uneven, so depths have to be carefully watched. The point/sandspit separating the anchorage from the greater lake is especially interesting to explore, being unbelievably wild for an area so close to the Soo.

Within a mile of the anchorage, there are a couple of places where boats drawing less than 3 feet may access or where it is possible to dinghy in and get minimal supplies. One of these is at the Chippewa Landing Ramp N/NW of the anchorage. Gasoline and ice are available along with a general grocery store approximately one block inland. The small marina provides 10 slips along with water and power. Across the bay to the south, just inside the mouth of the Waiska River, there is the Brim-O-Bay Motel, which also supplies gasoline. Within a short walking distance there are another general store and a couple of good restaurants. With southerly winds, an alternative is to anchor along the southern shore of the bay between Brim-O-Bay Motel and Brimley State Park. There is also good anchoring 2.5 miles to the NE, south of Round Island.

With anchorages few and far between, **Whitefish Point Harbor of Refuge** is an important stopover for those heading to or from the Soo. A day's run from the Soo (33 nautical miles), this harbor is actually located one mile SW of the point and Whitefish Point Light.

One of the problems with many of the smaller harbors along Lake Superior's south shore is periodic silting-in around their breakwaters. The Army Corps of Engineers is responsible for keeping these harbors open and dredges some on a regular schedule and others on a demand basis as the need arises. The entrance to the Whitefish Point Harbor is one of those that often experiences considerable silting-in, and this is important to know should you arrive when it is present. When it occurs, the silting is located around the outer breakwater with the Fl G light, which one keeps to the port when entering. Often the silting is so great extending so far east toward the other breakwater as to almost effectively **close** the entrance. However, by holding **very close** to the starboard breakwater when entering, it is possible to squeeze around the shoal area and maintain 8 feet of depth. See accompanying sketch chart for track to take when this condition is present (Fig. 3.2). It is interesting to note that in the 1970s this harbor was dredged every three years. Then for a number of years it was dredged every 10 years. The last time it was dredged was in 2019.

Although the harbor was constructed in the early 1960s, it wasn't until the mid-1970s that the present slips were added. Three or four of the eight available slips are supposed to be kept open for transients; however, these are often occupied by locals and commercial fishermen, so it may be necessary to tie off on the inside of the uneven iron sheet piling that forms the inner breakwater via large metal rings or cleats. Depths in the slips are approximately 9 feet. Depths throughout the harbor are 12 feet except close into the breakwaters where there are some underwater boulders. There are no supplies here. A sheet piling dock was constructed in the late 1990s between the old fishery dock and small boat ramp to which boats may tie up and have fuel brought in by truck. There are two pit toilets adjacent to the parking lot but no garbage facilities.

An interesting walk can be taken along the sandy beaches or an inland road out to the far end of Whitefish Point. Here it is possible to watch, at close hand, the large lakers as they trek by, converging into the bottleneck toward the Soo. The lighthouse is

**Figure 3.2
Whitefish Point
Harbor of Refuge**

to Whitefish Point

launch ramp

sheet piling dock

fishing station

Fl R

Vis 6 St M

Fl G

Fl R

GPS	Lat.	Lon.
▲	46°45.49' N	84°57.86' W

0   200   400 ft

conditions when silting-in exists

Whitefish Point Harbor.
MICHIGAN WATERWAYS COMMISSION

also of special interest since it is believed to be the oldest lighthouse on the lake, built in 1849. As in the past, the light is a sentinel for passing ships, marking one of the worst areas on the lake for shipping disasters—an area which throughout the decades has become known as the "graveyard of the Great Lakes." For just to the N/NW of Whitefish Point there are more than 500 shipwrecks, including the wreck of the *Edmund Fitzgerald*. To commemorate these and all Great Lakes shipwrecks, the Great Lakes Shipwreck Historical Society has leased the lighthouse grounds and established a very interesting Shipwreck Museum. Key displays are a full scale diorama (three dimensional scene) of two divers realistically suspended over ship wreckage and a central "walk around" display of a 17 Whiteshoal 2nd Order Fresnel Lens that was built in France in 1918. In another building, a small video theater gives short presentations on dramatic aspects of Lake Superior shipwreck history including videotapes made of actual dives on a number of local wrecks. There is also a bird sanctuary here and it is of particular interest as it is one of the nesting areas for the piping plover that is an endangered species. This is an appropriate setting for the complex, out among the sand dunes and sedge grasses, where the whistling wind and gulls circling overhead create a feeling of loneliness and wild mystique.

Along the 45-mile stretch from Whitefish Point to Grand Marais, there is only one anchorage, a harbor of refuge that is marginal because of a shallow entrance and a shifting sandbar. This is **Little Lake Harbor** located approximately 18 nautical miles west of Whitefish Point. The harbor is one that experiences regular silting-in near the entrance and within the entrance channel and thus needs periodic dredging by the Corps of Engineers. However, the last time this harbor was dredged was 2018 making it primarily a harbor for very shoal draft runabouts. Even when dredged, it is not prudent to attempt this shallow entrance if there is any sea running. It is also important to note the approach depths on the inset of Chart #14962. Once inside the harbor, there is 15 to 20 feet of water throughout. Thus, it is possible to anchor or use a small dock that is located in the NE end. If anchoring, be careful of debris and old moorings on the bottom. Depth along the outside of the dock is approximately 7 to 8 feet.

Grand Marais, Michigan, (which should not be confused with Grand Marais, Minnesota, on the north shore) is the next harbor located along this long, lonely stretch of shoreline. The

NOT TO BE USED FOR NAVIGATION – SKETCH APPROXIMATE

Figure 3.3
Little Lake Harbor, Michigan

Fl R

very shallow

Fl G

N

0   400   800 ft

GPS	Lat.	Lon.
▲	46°43.10' N	85°21.80' W

town got its start as a commercial fishing center and later became a lumbering village. In French, the word *marais* means placid—a protected bay or cove.

The entrance is marked by two long breakwaters extending into the lake. The westerly one is equipped with a light (Fl W) and foghorn. Within the harbor, there are ample depths throughout except close-in along the shoreline and in the NE end of the harbor where considerable shoaling is building up. Historically, the Army Corps of Engineers built a breakwater in 1894 to protect this section of the harbor. But with years of maintenance neglect and Lake Superior's harsh storms, the breakwater deteriorated until 1971 when it was completely destroyed. In the early 2000s there were a number of studies done on replacing the breakwater and after the loss of 5 lives and a couple of boats, enough funds were raised for a new breakwater.

Construction began in August 2012 when the remnants of a pile dike breakwater dating back to the 1800s were removed along with part of the southern end of the East entry pier. These were replaced with 370 feet of new stone breakwater which extends from the southern end of the pier in a SE direction towards the southern shore of the harbor. It was constructed with three stone layers, with smaller stones on the bottom Interior and 6-10 ton stones on the exterior sides. After many years of lobbying the new breakwater was dedicated In January 2013.

Within the harbor it is possible to anchor in a number of places. However, there are usually a number of moorings for local boats in the western end that need to be avoided and there is also debris on the bottom in some areas. In the NW end of the harbor

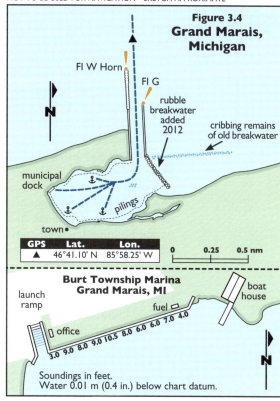

Figure 3.4
Grand Marais, Michigan

Grand Marais Harbor.
MICHIGAN WATERWAYS COMMISSION

there is another Michigan Waterways Commission marina, the Burt Township Marina that provides gasoline, diesel, pump-out, water and electricity (110 V 30 and 50 A). At times there may be no attendant on duty, so it may be necessary to call a posted phone number or inquire at one of the stores uptown. Showers and rest rooms can be obtained in a nearby park. In strong easterly winds being at this dock can become quite uncomfortable. It is possible under these conditions to tie up inside the long eastern entrance breakwater. Note — because of its location between VHF transmitting stations, it is often difficult to get weather information while in the harbor.

Within the town there are groceries, ice and laundry facilities. Out on the peninsula there is an interesting gift shop and excellent restaurant. There no longer is a Coast Guard Station here and the station building has been converted to a Maritime Museum and NPS ranger station. For those who like to hike, the North Country National Scenic Trail passes around the bay heading east or west. If the trail is taken west to the Grand Sable Dunes (one mile), it is important to stay on the trail and not walk under the dunes since they are known to disrupt easily with sand slides.

The stretch of shoreline between Grand Marais and Munising provides some of the most spectacular scenery that Lake Superior has to offer. Beginning one mile west of Grand Marais and extending six miles along the shore toward Au Sable Point are the **Grand Sable Sand Dunes**. A point of interest in connection with these dunes is the Devil's Slide, once used in logging days to transport logs down the dunes to the lake where they were then floated via log booms to the mill at Grand Marais.

Even more spectacular are the **Pictured Rocks** that are made of bold-faced cliffs, caves and arches of soft sandstone carved out by the action of the lake. Many of the caves are large enough that, should conditions permit, they make interesting

NOT TO BE USED FOR NAVIGATION – SKETCH APPROXIMATE

Figure 3.5
The Munising Area

Williams Island

Grand Island

Trout Bay

Fl R 4s Bell

Shipwreck

Murray Bay

"Thumb"

RW Bell

Fl G Bell

Fl 2.5s

Fl R

Fl R

Kimberly-Clark

town with municipal dock

GPS	Lat.	Lon.
▲1	46°27.25' N	86°41.90' W
▲2	46°27.76' N	86°39.40' W
▲3	46°24.86' N	86°39.08' W
▲4	46°27.75' N	86°36.70' W
⚓5	46°29.00' N	86°38.10' W
⚓6	46°29.70' N	86°41.25' W

0   1   2 nm

exploring via dinghy. Varied mineral deposits have also colored large sections of these areas in hues of red, blue, green and white, thus providing the basis for imaginative "pictures" by the viewer. The Pictured Rocks appear approximately four miles NE of Grand Portal Point and are an intricate part of the shoreline for 10 miles toward Munising with special points of interest such as Sail Rock and the Miners Castle, a nine-story rock tower. So beautiful is this section of the shoreline that, in 1966, it was set aside as a protected area, the Pictured Rocks National Lakeshore, the nation's first National Lakeshore.

The natural harbor and bay of **Munising** has long been used by Lake Superior travelers as a resting place. Even before the coming of the white men, this was a favorite camping spot for the Chippewa. Surrounded by high rising hills on three sides, and Grand Island to the north, the area offers protection from most winds.

In approaching Munising from the east, care must be taken to skirt the rather large shoal off Sand Point. This is well marked by a bell buoy. From the buoy you can then line up on a SW range that is on shore. If coming from the west, the channel adjacent to Grand Island should be used—passing between it and Wood and Williams islands. The town is well marked at the end of the bay by a massive structure just to the east of it, a paper mill.

In the past, transient dockage was almost nonexistent at Munising because of the tour boats and local usage. However, in the early 1990s the facilities were improved by dredging and adding a long pier with fingers along its western side. Called the **Bayshore Marina**, it is located to the SE of the range markers between them and the paper mill. The marina monitors channel 16 or can be reached by telephone: 906-387-3445 May-Oct., 906-387-2095 off-season.

In 2017-2918 the marina received quite an uplift with a $3.4 million upgrade. The "L" was extended 110 feet to the East with a new sheet pile wall. This provides better protection for the harbor and room for new docks. A new pier with finger slips as a floating dock system was added which provides 24 new transient only slips. This floating dock has standard utility service with water and 30/50 amp services. The new extension of the L dock Is also for transient use. Tour boats still occupy much of the inside of the original L-shaped breakwater and local boats are on the old finger slips. Water and electricity (110V 30 A; 220 V 50 A) are provided at

NOT TO BE USED FOR NAVIGATION – SKETCH APPROXIMATE

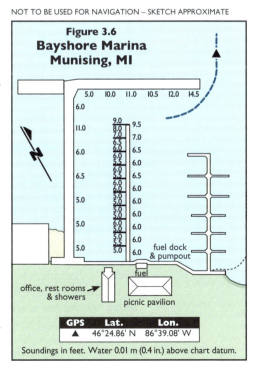

Figure 3.6
Bayshore Marina
Munising, MI

GPS	Lat.	Lon.
▲	46°24.86' N	86°39.08' W

Soundings in feet. Water 0.01 m (0.4 in.) above chart datum.

the slips. Gasoline (no diesel) is onshore at the eastern side of the old pier (see Fig. 3.6). Caution—because of the extreme height of the docks, especially in low water years, it is easy for boats with low decks to slip under the docks. Also note that fluctuations of 1.5 feet may occur in the harbor and it is necessary to take that into consideration and make sure there is ample depth when tying up. Finally, the eastern side of the new pier is wide open to exposure from NE winds and if they are strong it could become quite uncomfortable on this side of the dock.

Within a short walking distance from the marina there are a number of good restaurants, hardware store, grocery store, laundry facilities, Radio Shack and NAPA store. Diesel can be obtained via Gerry cans at nearby gas stations. Ice can also be obtained at the gas stations. Adjacent to the marina is a large open pavilion and picnic area with a playground. The Lakeshore North Country Trail can be followed NE along the shoreline—all the way to Grand Marais. Publications and maps on the area can be obtained at the Pictured Rocks-Hiawatha National Forest Information Center about four blocks SE.

Points of interest are, of course, the Pictured Rocks, to which there are daily tours via the excursion boats. The tours are approximately three hours long and are conducted by experienced captains who describe the different sites and history. The paper mill also conducts daily tours during weekdays in the summer. For history buffs, there are a couple of interesting museums in the town. The waters within the Munising area have been designated as an underwater preserve for scuba diving since there are a number of shipwrecks here, all of which are buoyed with orange markers. Glass Bottom Boat Tours visit some of these wrecks and also explore the Alger Underwater Preserve.

Another alternative to the Munising dock is to anchor across in Murray Bay, which lies under the protection of **Grand Island**. For many years the island served as a resort area and wild game preserve. During the first Bush administration it was purchased by the U.S. Forest Service and a bill was passed making it a National Recreation Area.

Within the bay there are a number of places to anchor depending on wind direction, since it is possible to snug up to most parts of the shore. There are a few docks along the western shore of the bay that in the past were private, belonging to those with summer homes on the island. Many of the docks have been rebuilt, but care should be taken for slash and sunken pilings in some areas. By far the best place to anchor in the bay is behind Muskrat Point on the eastern side of the bay. Because of shoaling, you can't get all the way in. But it is still possible to get good protection behind the sand point and have 10 to 15 feet of depth. It is important to note that there is a shipwreck (a 90-foot schooner, the Bermuda) in the eastern half of the bay that lies in approximately 8 feet to

12 feet of water. It is marked by a buoy and on a calm day can be easily seen from a dinghy. There are a number of old roads and trails on the island that are interesting to hike—or you can even rent bicycles. There is a short walk in the NW corner of the bay to an old cemetery or a little farther east to inland Duck Lake. Another interesting hike is across the land bridge to the beautiful sandstone cliffs in Trout Bay.

There are a few other places in which to anchor around Grand Island, but these are somewhat marginal in that they offer only two- or three-sided protection and are open to the greater lake. One of these is Trout Bay next to a sand beach that is quite unusual for this sector of the lake. Other places to anchor are in the indentation on the western side of the island or in the center of the bay at the north end, adjacent to an old lighthouse that stands high up on the bluffs. These anchorages, however, should be used only with an eye to the weather or possibly as lunch stops.

From Munising to **Marquette**, Michigan, it is another long jump (37 nautical miles) with no harbors or anchorages in between for good protection. Named after the Jesuit missionary, Father Jacques Marquette (who in the 1660s was instrumental in pioneering the south shore), Marquette today reflects its heritage as a mining center and an iron ore shipping port. With the discovery of iron ore on the Marquette Range in 1845, Marquette was first settled in 1849. In 1857, it became the first Lake Superior port to ship iron ore. Today, the town boasts of a population of 22,000 and, with varied industries such as lumbering, machinery and meat processing, retains its position as one of Lake Superior's valued shipping ports.

The harbor is formed by a large breakwater extending southward from its northern end. Key lights on the breakwater are the Outer Light (Fl W) that is also equipped with a red sector to the north. This sector should be avoided because it marks shoal waters that extend east of Marquette Light. On the small peninsula just to the north of the harbor is the Marquette Light, that flashes white. There is no longer a radio beacon for this harbor.

Recent years have seen a number of changes for boaters, and facilities are found in a number of different areas in the harbor. For the transient boater there are two places to obtain overnight accommodations. The main facility in the area is located in the **Cinder Pond** (Tel.: 906-228-0469) in the middle of the north end of the Marquette Harbor complex. The name Cinder Pond comes from the establishment of an iron ore furnace on the site where raw ore was turned into pig iron to be shipped out from the nearby docks. The cinders from the furnace were dumped into the lake at this spot. The marina, which was dedicated in 1995, has a total of 100 slips (wooden floating docks), 10 or more of which are reserved for transient dockage. The entrance is marked with red and green day markers that are lit at night. Entrance depth in normal

water years is 9 feet with 7 to 10 feet within the marina. Note, however, that these depths can change by as much as a foot in storm conditions. The marina provides gasoline, diesel, pump-out, water and electricity (110 V 30 A; 220 V 50 A). Within the office/comfort station there are rest rooms, showers, laundry and small lounge area with cable TV. There is also a double concrete launch ramp within the complex. The marina should be contacted via VHF on channel 71 as opposed to channel 16.

Boats larger than 55 feet can tie up broadside to the old coal

NOT TO BE USED FOR NAVIGATION – SKETCH APPROXIMATE

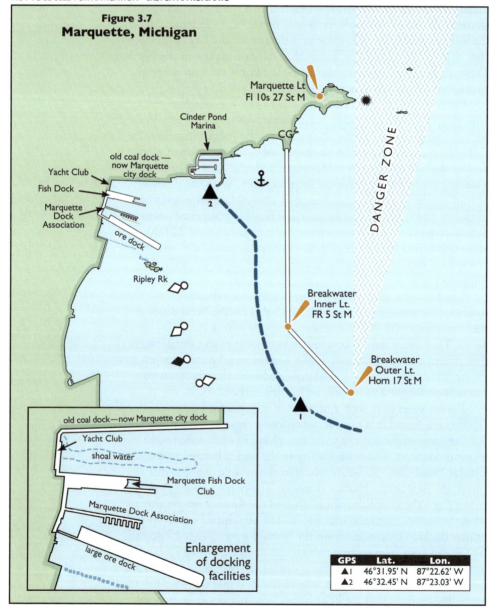

Figure 3.7
Marquette, Michigan

Marquette Lt
Fl 10s 27 St M

Cinder Pond
Marina

CG

old coal dock —
now Marquette
city dock

Yacht Club

Fish Dock

Marquette
Dock
Association

ore dock

▲ 2

⚓

DANGER ZONE

Ripley Rk

Breakwater
Inner Lt.
FR 5 St M

Breakwater
Outer Lt.
Horn 17 St M

▲ 1

old coal dock—now Marquette city dock

Yacht Club

shoal water

Marquette Fish Dock
Club

Marquette Dock Association

large ore dock

Enlargement
of docking
facilities

GPS	Lat.	Lon.
▲1	46°31.95' N	87°22.62' W
▲2	46°32.45' N	87°23.03' W

dock area that is now a beautiful park and City Dock. There are five power pedestals with two 50 A receptacles and water along the City Dock. Note that this section of the dock is exposed to strong S and SE winds. More protection can be achieved by moving farther in along the wall to the west. A reduced cost for dock usage is paid at the Cinder Pond where all facilities are available to

Cinder Pond Marina.
DAHL

those who use the City Dock. The park adjacent to this dock is the Ellwood A. Mattson Lower Harbor Park. There are trees, picnic tables, flower pots and a children's playground.

Along the west side of the harbor there are more marine facilities, but these are used primarily by locals. Just north of the large ore dock is a long dock that has boats on both sides, the Marquette Dock Association, a private organization with no transient dockage. To the north of it is the prominent old Fish Dock. Most of the boats seen at this dock belong to the Marquette Fish Dock Club with the clubhouse about halfway out on the dock. At the base of this dock is the Fish House where fresh and smoked fish can be obtained. Tucked in between the Fish Dock and City Dock there is a small private yacht club. Note the shoal water that exists between the Fish Dock and City Dock, which is primarily silted-in mud.

There is a marine railway on the north side of the harbor about 1,000 feet west of the start of the breakwater. The Marquette Coast Guard Station is located near the inner end of the breakwater. An alternative to docking is to anchor behind the breakwater just south of the Coast Guard station where you can get protection from all winds except those out of the south.

The town provides excellent sources for replenishing supplies with a number of good hardware and grocery stores,

NOT TO BE USED FOR NAVIGATION – SKETCH APPROXIMATE

Comfort Station

Pier 4

Pier 3

fuel
water
pump-out

Pier 2

ramps

Pier 1

green

Figure 3.8
Cinder Pond Marina
Marquette, Michigan

red

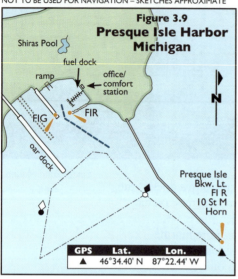

Figure 3.9
Presque Isle Harbor
Michigan

Shiras Pool

fuel dock

ramp

office/
comfort
station

N

FIG   FIR

oar dock

Presque Isle
Bkw. Lt.
Fl R
10 St M
Horn

GPS	Lat.	Lon.
▲	46°34.40' N	87°22.44' W

Figure 3.10
Big Bay Harbor, MI

West Pier Lt. Fl R

G
Bn

N

dock

- - - - - Conditions when silting-in occurs

0   200   400 ft

GPS	Lat.	Lon.
▲	46°49.78' N	87°43.41' W

Dock at Big Bay Harbor

(harbor)

3.0 2.0 4.0 6.0 7.5 8.0 5.5 5.5 6.0 5.0 5.0 5.5 5.5 8.0

launch
ramp   fuel

office/
rest rooms   Seasonal Docking

Soundings in feet.
Water 0.01 m (0.4 in.) below chart datum.

available by using the city transit system. There are also a number of good restaurants, many with varied ethnic cuisines. Points of interest include a statue of Father Marquette at Lakeside Park, the Marquette County History Museum and the John M. Longyear Research Library. These last two provide much information about Father Frederic Baraga, the Snowshoe Priest and the first bishop of the Marquette diocese, whose remains are encrypted at St. Peter's Cathedral. Following the shoreline, there is a bike/hiking trail where it is possible to have a pleasant walk either north toward Presque Isle or south one mile into the Marquette business district and beyond.

Just five miles north of Cinder Pond is **Presque Isle Harbor**, which contains one of the most beautiful marinas on the lake. It is identified by a long breakwater extending to the SE, which is marked by a flashing red light. The marina received a very extensive upgrade in 2019-21. The 3 long piers with finger slips were replaced with a large "T" extending SW from the office/comfort station. On the southern side of the main part of the "T" are the "A" slips, on the northern side of this part of the "T" are "B" slips, with the "C" slips extending out from the top of the "T". Pump-out is on the north end of the top of the "T". The marina monitors VHF channels 9 and 16.

Of special interest is Presque Isle Park, which is just adjacent to the marina. Here there are lovely trails to hike, beautiful picnic areas and a nature reserve. There are also tennis courts and a swimming pool that make the area a very pleasant place to visit.

The next jaunt up the shore is 25 nautical miles to **Big Bay Harbor**, Michigan. Located at the base of the stately Huron Mountains, this harbor provides an excellent all-weather harbor of refuge along this rather wild and forlorn shoreline. It is interesting to note that geologists consider the Huron Mountains to be the oldest mountains east of the

Mississippi River.

Big Bay, which is easy to confuse with the next bay between Salmon Trout Point and Conway Point, is identified by a flashing white light on the end of Big Bay Point. When rounding this point, it is important to give wide berth to the large shoal that extends a good mile out from the point and is marked by a green can. The harbor is in the SW end of the bay with its entrance formed by two long breakwaters, the west or northerly pier being marked by a flashing red light.

Big Bay Harbor.
MICHIGAN WATERWAYS
COMMISSION

Unfortunately, this harbor is one of those that is not dredged on a regularly scheduled basis, so silting-in often occurs and at times, especially with low water, can effectively close the harbor to those with boats drawing more than 5 feet. When the silting occurs, there are basically two "trouble spots," one of which is right at the entrance with the shoal extending west from the eastern breakwater into the channel track. The other again extends west from the small sand point to port farther in the channel (see Fig. 3.10). In both cases, the trick is to hug the starboard breakwater as closely as possible without grounding on those shoals to starboard. Note: the last time the harbor was dredged was in 2000 and considerable silting in has built up in recent years. Depending on funding, the next dredging may occur in 2009.

There is another Michigan Waterways Dock here with gasoline, pump-out, water, electricity, rest rooms and showers. However, because of shallow depths near the gas pump, those with medium-to-deep-draft boats have to obtain their fuel by gerry can. Diesel needs to be brought in by truck from Marquette.

Note that there often is little transient space available at the dock because at least one-half of it is used for local seasonal dockage. (See Fig. 3.10.) The harbor master here is on call at Perkins Park with a phone number posted at the office. If no dock space is available, it is possible to anchor off to the side by using a bow and stern anchor or Bahamian moor, since swinging room is limited.

The town is approximately one mile inland and provides very limited supplies. However, Thunder Bay Inn, which has been recently restored, has an excellent dining room. Its bar has historical interest in that some of the scenes of the motion picture *Anatomy of a Murder* were filmed here. There is also an interesting health club/camp on the road into the town. In the Huron Mountains to the west there are still some of the elite establishments of the once

exclusive Huron Mountain Club.

For those who cruise this section of the lake, it is important to mention the **Stannard Rock Lighthouse**, which marks a particularly dangerous reef in an area of wide open water. Because it stands well offshore (28 nautical miles NE of Big Bay), it isn't often seen by many boaters. However, for those who make the jump from the south shore to the Keweenaw Peninsula, this reef becomes a viable concern.

The reef is named for Captain Charles C. Stannard who discovered it in 1835. Because of its remote location, and difficulties in fighting the elements during construction, the lighthouse was not completed until 1882. This forlorn outpost was staffed until 1961, when the light became automated. (Note: just 25 miles SE of this reef, the water depths plunge to almost 1,300 feet—the deepest in the lake.)

Continuing along this bold expanse of rugged shoreline, we come upon the small group of **Huron Islands**, that are important from a navigational standpoint because of a lighthouse on West Huron Island, which was built in 1868. For years, the light was staffed and its crew of five gave it an additional distinction of being a lifeboat station ready to give assistance to anyone who had the need of it. Today the light is automated.

In the past, these islands were also used as a base for commercial fishing. With the fishermen came the double-crested cormorant, a jet black fish-eating bird and, because of their influx, the islands were set aside in 1938 as a National Wildlife Refuge. Although the cormorants are now all but gone, the islands are still occupied by thousands of herring gulls.

There is a marginal anchorage located at the south end of **West Huron Island**. It is found by coming in from the west or southwest and keeping the smaller island off West Huron's southern tip to starboard. The anchorage area is in a small "harbor" adjacent to a boathouse and cement dock that used to serve the light. For years the dock was unusable because of disrepair. There are reports that it has been completely repaired. However, because of depth and under water boulders it still remains usable for only shallow draft boats. Although there isn't much depth at the dock, not too far out the depths become quite large for the small area making regular anchoring difficult because it's hard to get adequate scope and swinging room. It is still possible to set out an anchor and run a line to the

NOT TO BE USED FOR NAVIGATION – SKETCH APPROXIMATE

Figure 3.11
West Huron Island, South End

West Huron Island
(Lighthouse Island)

trail to lighthouse

boathouse

N

GPS	Lat.	Lon.
▲	46°57.60' N	88°00.10' W

dock. However, this is still a marginal anchorage because of poor holding and it is wide open to the west and SW. Thus, it should be treated only as a lunch stop or when easterly winds are assured. There is an interesting hike on a trail behind the boathouse up to the light.

Southwest of the Huron Islands is **Huron Bay**, a long deep bay that has two possibilities for anchorages. The first of these is located in the sharp indentation just SW of Huron Bay Light at **Skanee**, Michigan. Skanee was Swedish in origin. It is believed that its name is a derivative of Skane, the southernmost province in Sweden. In its early days, the town flourished as a lumber camp. Today there is a small marina, the **Witz Marina** (seasonal Tel: 906-524-7795) in a well-protected basin. The marina has been in the family for 50 years and provides local dockage for approximately 50 boats. There are no entrance markers except for a private white yard light that is on at night on the southern part of the entrance. The marina provides gasoline, electricity, water and a small boat launch ramp with an adjacent campground and picnic tables. Depth in approaching the entrance is 5 feet but there are also some sand bars that have to be negotiated. Within the basin, depths are 4 1/2 to 6 feet, so it is primarily a small boat harbor. Anchoring is possible in the bay, but it should be noted that there is only two-sided protection here.

At the far **SW end of Huron Bay** there is another possibility for anchoring. But, here, care must be taken to avoid the remains of old wharves that extend out from the mouth of the Slate River and the no-longer inhabited village of Huron Bay. Because of the extensive shoaling in the area, and a long open fetch to the NE, this anchorage is marginal at best.

Keweenaw Bay is an even larger and deeper extension of the lake than Huron Bay. Extending 20 nautical miles to the SW, it forms the eastern shore of the Keweenaw Peninsula and offers a couple of interesting harbors and anchorages. To enter the bay from the east, there are no obstructions other than

NOT TO BE USED FOR NAVIGATION – SKETCH APPROXIMATE

Figure 3.12
Huron Bay

Huron Bay Lt.
Skanee

Huron Bay

GPS	Lat.	Lon.
⚓1	46°50.05' N	88°16.30' W
⚓2	46°53.15' N	88°13.00' W

Slate River

0   1   2 nm

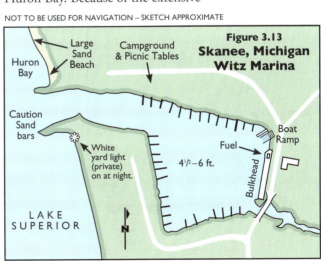

NOT TO BE USED FOR NAVIGATION – SKETCH APPROXIMATE

Figure 3.13
Skanee, Michigan
Witz Marina

Large Sand Beach

Campground & Picnic Tables

Huron Bay

Caution Sand bars

White yard light (private) on at night.

4 1/2 – 6 ft.

Fuel

Boat Ramp

Bulkhead

LAKE SUPERIOR

N

Abbaye Reef, which is buoyed approximately one mile off Point Abbaye. Otherwise, the water is deep and clear throughout the bay.

About 12 nautical miles down the eastern side of Keweenaw Bay from Point Abbaye is an interesting outcropping of land that has an unusually interesting history. Here is the site of the once abandoned village **Pequaming**, which originally began as a saw and shingle mill in 1878. So prosperous was lumbering in those days that at one time there were 500 people working at the site and 400 more out in the woods. In 1923, the mill and associated buildings were bought by Henry Ford to be developed as a model town and to supply lumber for Ford's other enterprises. The village worked under Ford's direction for approximately 26 years until wood was no longer needed for the production of automobiles.

Part of the village still remains intact, even though many of the buildings are in ruin and disrepair. It is possible to see the remains of the large old mill and original water tower. A couple of the buildings have been restored into contemporary dwellings. For example, the old schoolhouse that stands prominently on the south bank is now a spacious permanent residence. The old store has been converted to apartments available for rental to those traveling in the region.

It used to be that the only facilities available to transient boaters were to carefully snug up to one of the old decaying docks or anchor off in the basin between submerged cribs and pilings. However, in the mid-1980s, the area was purchased by Peter Van Straten who through considerable effort not only cleaned up substantial parts of the southern basin, but also put in a number of floating docks for local and transient use. Most of the docks are found along the inner side of the southern arm of the peninsula with well over 10 feet of water leading up to them, providing a mid-channel track is kept. By looking off to each side, pilings and slash on the bottom can be seen, the remains of old docks. Many of those docks were constructed of metal using sections from the mill smokestacks as floaters. In the early 1990s gasoline was added along with water and power at a small gas dock. There is also a 35-ton Travelift available that can haul boats up to 40 feet in length. Today a number of the docks have been removed because of disrepair.

Approximately five miles SW of Pequaming in the far southern end of Keweenaw Bay is **L'Anse**, Michigan. Named by the Jesuit missionary Rene Menard when he wintered here in 1660-

Figure 3.14
Lower End of Keweenaw Bay

Pequaming

Pequaming Bay

N

Sand Pt.
Lt. Fl W
7 St M

Baraga

L'Anse

statue

0   1   2 nm

GPS	Lat.	Lon.
▲1	46°50.80' N	88°24.05' W
▲2	46°45.65' N	88°27.90' W
▲3	46°46.70' N	88°28.60' W

61 (L'Anse means "cove"), the area has had a long and interesting history reflecting, on a small scale, events that were taking place all around the lake. Long before the Europeans arrived, this lower part of the bay was a favorite site among the Native Americans. Here, they established a summer village and cultivated maize. Early missionaries were quick to use this place as a post, only to be followed by the American Fur Company, which established a fishery here for their expanding interests. The settlers (Irish and German immigrants) came with the discovery of copper in the 1840s. They were joined by the loggers when the area became a lumbering center in the late 1800s. But it is probably for the efforts of one man that this area is best known, and that person is Father Frederic Baraga. For just a mile west of the town there is a large 35-foot bronze statue commemorating the work of this famous priest who also became the first bishop in the area. Known as the "Snowshoe Priest," because Baraga often traveled by canoe and snowshoes, this vigorous pioneer worked among the Chippewa, the miners and fishermen from 1830 to 1868, establishing missions at La Pointe in the Apostle Islands, Wisconsin, and Grand Portage, Minnesota, as well as L'Anse.

Figure 3.15
Pequaming, MI

○ old Ford water tower

remains of old Ford Factory

launch well for Travelift

Keweenaw Bay

gas pump

boat house

floating docks

bad water submerged cribs

shrub

old dock

old pilings

shrub

N

GPS	Lat.	Lon.
▲	46°50.80' N	88°24.05' W

• submerged rock buoyed with plastic bottle in 1991

Located at the mouth of the Falls River, the harbor is quite shallow and open to the northwest. However, in the mid-1990s a small all-weather harbor was constructed through the joint efforts of the Downtown Development Authority, Village of L'Anse and the Department of Natural Resources. A large stone rubble breakwater was constructed, the basin was dredged and new slips were installed along with a cement double launch ramp. The entrance to the marina is marked with a red day marker (red light at night) on the end of the stone breakwater that is kept to starboard when entering. Note that in approaching the entrance there are shoal areas to each side and it is important to head on a

L'Anse Village Municipal Marina.
DAHL

narrow course from the outer green buoy, which marks some ruins and submerged cribbing, toward this red marker—but a little to the NE of it. Even within this narrow course there are some shallow areas and it is advised that those with deep draft boats should not attempt this approach or entrance in low water years. Once inside there are 6 feet to 7 feet in most of the basin. Although the docks in the center are used primarily for local seasonal dockage, the periphery of the complex is reserved for transients. The marina provides gasoline, water and electricity. Diesel can be obtained via gerry can from nearby gas stations. There is no dock attendant on duty, but there are provisions for self-registration at the bulletin board by the launch ramp.

Adjacent to the marina there is a lovely park with a picnic/barbecue area and playground. A few blocks into the town is a grocery store, hardware store, pharmacy, bank, laundry and a couple of restaurants. A lovely walk follows the Falls River about one-half mile up to the falls. It is about 1.5 miles west to the Bishop Baraga Shrine and display center. Another point of interest is the lighthouse built into the corner of the closest building to the marina, Indian Country Sports. This lighthouse is an actual working lighthouse with the official Coast Guard designation as "the only new working lighthouse."

Around the bay on the western shore is the small town of **Baraga**, another tribute to Father Baraga. In approaching from the north, it is important to clear the shoal (marked by a red buoy) off Sand Point. There is a natural harbor formed next to the town between two peninsulas that extend into the water. The marina consists of a number of finger docks with slips (26) that are found along the northern shore of the southern peninsula. It is easy to spot by a red, white and blue building (office and rest rooms) and a red gas dock building. In approaching, it is important to avoid a shoal that extends off the smaller northern peninsula the end of which is marked

NOT TO BE USED FOR NAVIGATION – SKETCH APPROXIMATE

Figure 3.16
L'Anse, Michigan

ruins & old cribbing

observation decks

(Caution)

red with light

fuel

7.0 7.0
7.0 5.5 5.5
6.6 6.5 5.5
6.0 6.0 6.0
6.0 6.5 6.0
6.0 6.0 6.0 6.0
6.0 6.0 6.0

6.0 7.0

Double Launch Ramp

shoal—uncovers

Celotex Corp. L'Anse Plant

Falls River

Soundings in feet. Water 0.01 m (0.4 in.) below chart datum

GPS	Lat.	Lon.
▲	46°45.65' N	88°27.90' W

by a "slow wake" buoy. The gas dock is easily recognized, as it is a double "T." The marina provides gasoline, pump-out, water, electricity (110V 30A), ice, launch ramp, rest rooms, showers and security for each slip. Diesel needs to be transported by gerry cans from a gas station right at the marina road entrance. Larger amounts can be brought down from Northern Oil (Tel.: 906-353-6185). Out on the peninsula there is a park with picnic tables, barbecue and playground. The marina is attended from June to October (Tel.: 906-353-8110).

NOT TO BE USED FOR NAVIGATION – SKETCH APPROXIMATE

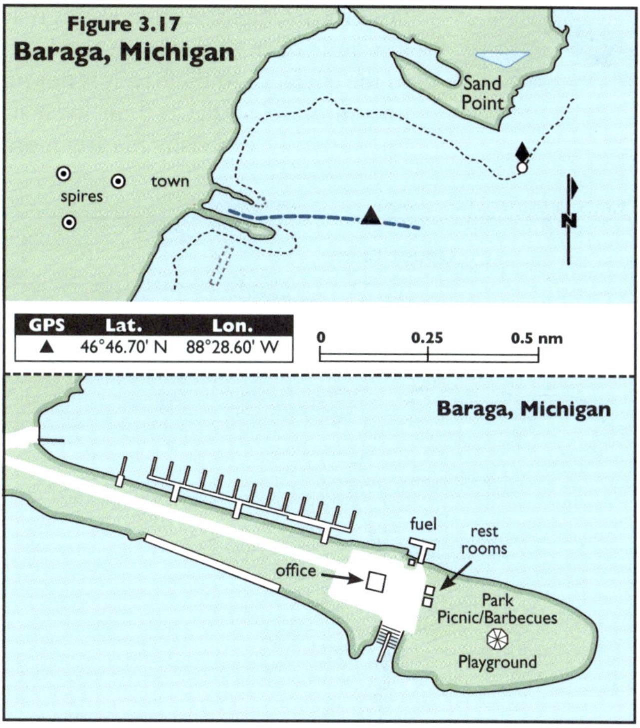
Figure 3.17
Baraga, Michigan
Sand Point
spires
town
N
0
0.25
0.5 nm
Baraga, Michigan
fuel
rest rooms
office
Park
Picnic/Barbecues
Playground

GPS	Lat.	Lon.
▲	46°46.70' N	88°28.60' W

To travel through the **Keweenaw Waterway** is one of the more interesting experiences one finds along the southern shore. The word "Keweenaw" comes from the Ojibwe *Keeywaynan*, which means "the crossing place" or "the way made straight by means of a portage." From the earliest of Lake Superior's history, not only Native Americans, but the voyageurs and other early explorers, too, used the natural basin of Portage Lake and the Portage River. Together they formed a shorter canoe route than the longer way around the peninsula. Dredging and further excavation of the dry areas (completed in 1873) allowed the canal to provide a complete water passage across the peninsula. Today, the controlling depth is well in excess of 20 feet throughout, making the waterway an important refuge in commercial navigation, particularly in the fall months.

The **Lower Entry** is marked by a long breakwater that, at the outer end, has a light on the white octagonal tower (Fl W). The light is also equipped with a foghorn. Pass with the breakwater kept to starboard. Green buoys are kept to port. Note that in accordance with waterway rules of "returning from the sea," all markers to the east of your track are red, and markers to the west of your track are green.

It is possible to tie up on the northern extension of the breakwater just past the green buoys where there is an open grassy area, picnic tables and a sand beach on outer Keweenaw Bay shoreline. There is a nice walk here out on the breakwater to the

Lower Entry light. Although this is a pleasant area to explore, it is quite open to the south and SW. Also, because it is so close to the entrance to the bay, it is not uncommon to experience an uncomfortable wake as those in small powerboats leave and enter the waterway, especially in early morning and evening when the

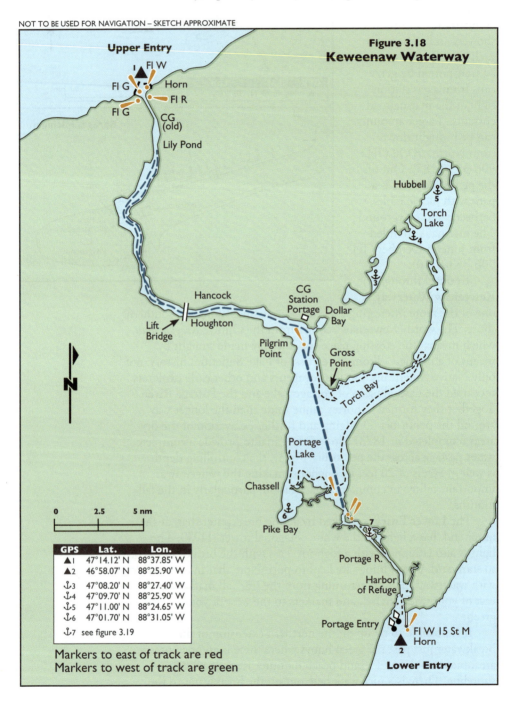

Upper Entry

Fl W

Fl G   Horn

Fl R

Fl G

CG (old)

Lily Pond

Figure 3.18
Keeweenaw Waterway

Hubbell

Torch Lake

Hancock

Lift Bridge   Houghton

CG Station Portage   Dollar Bay

Pilgrim Point

Gross Point

Torch Bay

Portage Lake

Chassell

Pike Bay

Portage R.

Harbor of Refuge

Portage Entry

Fl W I5 St M
Horn

Lower Entry

GPS	Lat.	Lon.
▲1	47°14.12' N	88°37.85' W
▲2	46°58.07' N	88°25.90' W
⚓3	47°08.20' N	88°27.40' W
⚓4	47°09.70' N	88°25.90' W
⚓5	47°11.00' N	88°24.65' W
⚓6	47°01.70' N	88°31.05' W
⚓7	see figure 3.19	

0   2.5   5 nm

N

Markers to east of track are red
Markers to west of track are green

fishing is good. For better protection, both from the weather and passing traffic, it may be prudent to move farther into the waterway.

About a mile into the waterway on the western side, there is the small village of **Portage Entry**, which is made up of a number of homes and summer cottages. In the small basin behind and to the west of the Harbor of Refuge pier there is a small marina and an adjacent gasoline pump. The basin is entered to the south of the pier, which is marked by green day marker #7. (See Fig. 3.19.) When entering and approaching the dock, it is important to skirt the small islands and shoal areas that lie to port by favoring the southern extension of this Harbor of Refuge pier. Although the marina is used primarily for local seasonal dockage, occasionally there may be a transient slip available. The gasoline pump is separate from the marina and the dock, for its use forms the south portion of a hoist well. Note that an attendant may not always be available.

Just north of the village is the **Portage River Harbor of Refuge**. Again found on the western side, here is a long mooring pier complete with a beautiful landscaped area, picnic tables, water and toilets. The water motion against this pier is definitely quieter compared to the mooring pier farther south on the east side. The pier makes a nice stopping off place before venturing to other parts of the lake.

The lower portion of the waterway south of Portage Lake is wild and beautiful. There are few of the cottages and homes that are found farther north and close to Hancock-Houghton. Meandering off from the present-day main channel are swamp-like passages between marshy islands, original tracks of the river. Wildlife abounds. In some of these side channels, shallow depths restrict access to only those with shoal draft boats. There are, however, a number of places where it is possible to pull off from the main channel and anchor. One of these is found on the east side of the main channel between lights marked St M "16" and St M "20" where it is possible to anchor anywhere in the original Portage River, which runs parallel to the dredged channel. (See Fig. 3.20.) In particular, note the small indentation on the east side of the longest island. Depths here are much greater than on the chart (10-12 feet), making this a

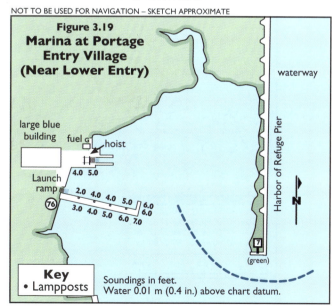

NOT TO BE USED FOR NAVIGATION – SKETCH APPROXIMATE

Figure 3.19
Marina at Portage Entry Village (Near Lower Entry)

waterway

large blue building

fuel G hoist

Launch ramp

4.0 5.0

2.0 4.0 4.0 5.0 6.0 6.0
3.0 4.0 5.0 6.0 7.0

76

Harbor of Refuge Pier

N

7
(green)

Key
• Lampposts

Soundings in feet.
Water 0.01 m (0.4 in.) above chart datum.

very secure anchorage. The other area for anchoring is found behind the island that supports the range lights west of Princess Point, just before the waterway opens up into Portage Lake. With both anchoring areas it is possible to enter from either the north or south. It is an austere area, teeming with wildlife, and very interesting to explore in the backwaters via dinghy.

In Portage Lake, it is possible to anchor in **Pike Bay** at the southern end. To reach Pike Bay it is necessary to cross the southern end of the lake, and here care must be exercised to pass well off the southern shore since the area is swampy and shoaled with numerous deadheads lodged on the bottom. To enter Pike Bay, more depth (9 feet) can be found by favoring the swamp as opposed to mainland. Once inside, stay to the center of the bay anchoring in 15 feet to 20 feet. This anchorage may not be as desirable as it looks on the chart because of the congestion of homes and cabins surrounding the bay (Fig. 3.18). The small picturesque town that lies to the west is Chassell, which was once a great lumbering center, but today is primarily a resort area.

With the exception of a 9-foot shoal extending south of Grosse Point and the shoaling already mentioned at the southern end, **Portage Lake** is free from obstructions. With care, Torch Bay can be navigated, and there are a couple of places in Torch Lake to anchor. Although there is some congestion near the town of Hubbell, it is possible to find some areas where there is more isolation. A point

NOT TO BE USED FOR NAVIGATION – SKETCH APPROXIMATE

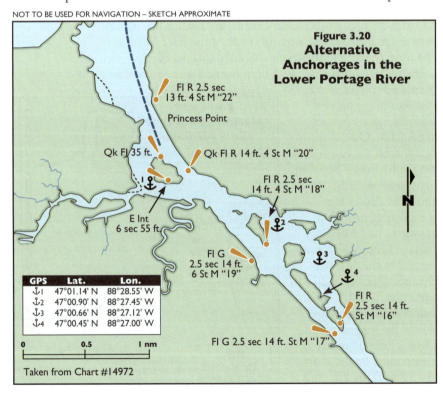

Figure 3.20
Alternative Anchorages in the Lower Portage River

Fl R 2.5 sec
13 ft. 4 St M "22"

Princess Point

Qk Fl 35 ft.

Qk Fl R 14 ft. 4 St M "20"

Fl R 2.5 sec
14 ft. 4 St M "18"

E Int
6 sec 55 ft.

Fl G
2.5 sec 14 ft.
6 St M "19"

Fl R
2.5 sec 14 ft.
St M "16"

GPS	Lat.	Lon.
⚓1	47°01.14' N	88°28.55' W
⚓2	47°00.90' N	88°27.45' W
⚓3	47°00.66' N	88°27.12' W
⚓4	47°00.45' N	88°27.00' W

0   0.5   1 nm

Fl G 2.5 sec 14 ft. St M "17"

Taken from Chart #14972

N

of interest in the long channel on the way to Torch Lake is a good restaurant, the Dreamland. It is found by tying up to a dock that is just past the large point of land on the eastern shore and then hiking a few blocks north on the road that follows the shoreline. To come into the Houghton-Hancock area, keep the Princess Point ranges (SE Portage Lake) on the stern and line up with the Pilgrim Point Light (NW Portage Lake) on the bow.

The twin cities of **Hancock and Houghton** were established in the 1850s largely as supply centers for the growing copper mining industry. For this is the heart of Copper Country. Early reports of missionaries and fur trappers alike record picking up loose nuggets of pure copper by the handfuls. That the Native Americans long knew of and used copper from the peninsula is seen in the numerous copper artifacts that are found around the lake and even far inland. Although the existence of copper was well-known by early explorers and pioneers for 200 years before 1840, it wasn't until reports were initiated by Michigan geologist Douglass Houghton that it became apparent the Keweenaw Peninsula contained a wealth of copper. At first, the copper in the pure metallic veins was mined by hand, literally being chiseled from the rock. Later, as compressed air drills were brought into use, it became obvious that the mining of amygdaloid and conglomerate ores would require large sums of capital. As the mining industry grew, so did the two cities. Today, high on the bluffs on the Hancock side, we can still see some of the remains of a past era in the large silhouette of the Quincy Mine Shaft House, a mine that once was world famous.

On the **Hancock** side just to the east of the Lift Bridge there is a beautiful 54-slip marina, the **Houghton County Marina**. With some transient slips usually available, this all-service marina (Tel: 906-482-6010) provides gasoline, diesel, pump-out, water, electricity (110 V 30 A; 220 V 50 A), showers, rest rooms, laundry facilities and a cement launching ramp. Note that this is the best place in the waterway to obtain fuel and the only place that provides diesel. The people here are most helpful in assisting with transient needs.

It is a short walk up the hill into the town of Hancock, part of which is listed on the National Register of Historic Places. By taking a taxi and continuing on Hwy. 41 out of town you come to the large Quincy Unit of the Keweenaw National Historical Park that was established in 1992. (The second unit includes the historic mining community of Calumet.) The site is of the former Quincy Mining Company and consists of a large steam hoist, an imposing landmark that sits high up on the bluffs. The hoist, which operated from 1921 to the mid-1930s, was the largest steam hoist ever built and was used to transfer the miners to shafts 1.5 miles deep. You can explore the surface area and ride a tram to an underground tour that depicts a first-hand view of the mining operation.

A 30-slip marina, the **H & Y Marina**, is located 2.5 miles east

of the Houghton County Marina in Hancock. It provides primarily local seasonal dockage, but occasionally will take transient boats. They have a pump-out and gas pump, but only have premium gasoline. The marina has built 10 large adjustable trailers that can lift boats up to 40 feet and is one of the few places in the waterway that provides winter storage. It also is one of the few repair facilities in the area providing fiberglass repairs, engine repairs and mechanical repairs—shafts and props.

Between the H & Y Marina and Dollar Bay on the Hancock side is the new site of the U.S. Coast Guard Station. This is the same station that for years was located just one mile inland from the Upper Entry. In summer 1990, it was moved to a temporary location at the old U.S. Naval Reserve just west of the lift bridge and then finally relocated to its new site in the late 1990s just to the west of Dollar Bay. The station monitors Channel 16 and answers to Portage Coast Guard.

On the **Houghton** side just east of the Lift Bridge there is a large **city dock** that is handy for gaining access to the stores and businesses on this side. Note there are no amenities (water or electricity) here. There are a number of interesting shops and good restaurants on this side, many of which specialize in ethnic delicacies. The impressive array of buildings seen on this side belong to the Michigan Technological University. One point of interest is to visit the university's A.E. Seaman Mineral Museum, which is located up the hill between the University football and baseball fields. The museum displays more than 30,000 rocks and gemstones and provides information on the geological forces that produced the largest concentration of pure copper in the world. Also located in the area is the National Park Service Headquarters, which administers the National Park on Isle Royale. A Visitor Center is

NOT TO BE USED FOR NAVIGATION – SKETCH APPROXIMATE

Figure 3.21
Dockage in the Hancock/Houghton Area

Hancock

Houghton Co. Marina

Old Naval Reserve Dock

Lift Bridge

Launch ramp

Houghton City Dock

Houghton

N

City Docks (private)

Broadside Docking

Former Copper Range RR Headquarters/Depot

0   500   1000 ft

located on the premises where there are displays on island flora and fauna and a large collection of related books for sale. The large *Ranger III* disembarks twice weekly from the adjacent docks, taking backpackers and campers across Lake Superior's waters to the island.

Houghton City Dock.
MICHIGAN WATERWAYS
COMMISSION

The large **lift bridge** that spans the waterway and links the two cities has special significance in that it is believed to be the heaviest lift bridge in the world. It is even larger than the lift bridge at Duluth, thus making it the largest lift bridge on the entire lake. Completed in 1959, it has been tagged the "Little Mac" because it is the second largest bridge in the state of Michigan (the largest is the famous Mackinac Bridge that spans the Straits of Mackinac, a distance of five statute miles). Vertical clearance when this bridge is down is 7 feet, with a maximum clearance of 103 feet when fully raised. To get the bridge to rise give a call using a foghorn (one long followed by two short blasts) or call the bridge on VHF marine radio Channel 16. If you call on the radio, your estimated time of arrival and required vertical clearance should be given. Note that initial contact via VHF is preferred when about a half-mile away.

To the west of the bridge on the Houghton side there is a small marina-type complex that is part of a city picnic area and waterfront development. There is no transient dockage here since it is reserved for local use. However, between it and the lift bridge there is a launch ramp and a long dock to which boats can tie broadside. This dock is located in front of what used to be the Copper Range

Houghton County
Marina.
MICHIGAN
WATERWAYS
COMMISSION

RR Headquarters/Depot. A similar dock is across on the Hancock side where the old Naval Reserve and then the temporary Coast Guard Station used to be. One advantage of being at this dock is that just up the hill you'll find a Ramada Inn with an excellent restaurant. Note that there are no services (water or electricity) at either of these docks. Also, it becomes quite

uncomfortable on this side of the bridge if there is a strong west wind blowing, since an uncomfortable chop can quickly develop. There is a little better protection at the Hancock dock in these conditions, but it is much better to be on the east side of the bridge in westerly winds.

North of the lift bridge, the canal and upper entrance are entirely man-made. Here, homes and cottages dot the shoreline. These soon give way to lower land, much of which has been cleared for small farms.

At the northern end of the waterway, approximately 1.5 nautical miles in from the Upper Entry outer breakwater light there is another harbor of refuge, the **Lily Pond**. Located on the east side, this half-mile-long cement mooring pier underwent considerable reconstruction in the late 1980s and early 1990s. Geared for commercial shipping to gain refuge from the greater lake in early and late season storms, there are only large bollards to which you can tie. There are no other facilities here, but it is a welcome respite, especially for those coming into the Upper Entry from the long runs on northern Lake Superior.

Between the Lily Pond and the Upper Entry, also on the east side, are the old buildings of the restationed Coast Guard. At the **Upper Entry** there are four lights, one on each side of the outer breakwater, and one on each side of the inner revetment. Note that the "Red Right Returning" rule does not apply for the outer west breakwater light. This is because Upper entry is part of the Keweenaw Waterway and waterway rules take precedence here, where "returning" takes on different meaning as "returning from the sea." Thus, when approaching Upper Entry from Lake Superior, the light seen on the starboard outer breakwater is **green** not red. The light on the eastern (port) breakwater is flashing white with a foghorn. This can be very confusing when approaching at night. It is important to stay within the center between the two breakwaters when passing through since there is some shallow water to each side close in to the walls. Note also the shoaling approximately one mile NE of the outer breakwater.

Leaving the Lower Entry of the Keweenaw Waterway and heading up the southern shore of the peninsula there are a couple of interesting harbors and anchorages. The first of these is **Little Traverse Bay**, which is 12 nautical miles from the lower entry. This large bay, which opens to the S-SE, has a nice sandy bottom that makes it good for anchoring. However, because it is so open to southerly winds, it should only be used with caution to wind direction. For more complete protection, it is better to use the harbor at Grand Traverse Bay located just a few more miles up the shore.

Grand Traverse Bay Harbor is an interesting, all-weather harbor that has been developed by establishing breakwaters around the long mouth of the Traverse River that flows into Lake Superior.

Established as a small fishing village by Finnish immigrants, the harbor gained importance when a mill was built here in 1880 to process logs that were transported down the river. Today the harbor is mainly used as a base for commercial and sports fishermen who line the shores of the river with their small docks and summer cottages.

Grand Traverse Bay.
MICHIGAN
WATERWAYS
COMMISSION

The harbor is identified by a light (Fl W) on a white skeleton tower, located in the middle of the bay. The light should be kept to starboard when entering. Another light (Fl G) is on the western breakwater and should be kept to port. By staying in the middle of the breakwater channel, in the past it was possible to maintain 9 feet of depth. This is because the harbor had periodic dredging every few years. The last dredging was in 2003 and there is no dredging scheduled for the near future. So with low-water years, this may be a difficult harbor for some boats to enter. Only in the main part of the harbor is it possible to obtain enough water for moderate-keeled boats. The rest of the harbor, particularly going up river, is accessible to only shoal draft boats. There is a cement pier constructed by the Michigan State Waterways Commission that, with care, can be used by boats drawing 5 feet or less depending on water datum. There are no facilities at the pier nor in the harbor. But the people are warm and friendly, making this an interesting place to visit.

From Grand Traverse Bay, it is 20 nautical miles up an inhospitable coast before another suitable anchorage is to be found. This is at **Lac La Belle**, an inland lake that, via a dredged canal into Bete Grise Bay, is accessible to Lake Superior boaters. Originally, this inland lake emptied in Lake Superior only by way of a shallow, winding river. This was replaced by the canal, created in 1866. In subsequent years, the canal fell into disrepair, but since

NOT TO BE USED FOR NAVIGATION – SKETCH APPROXIMATE

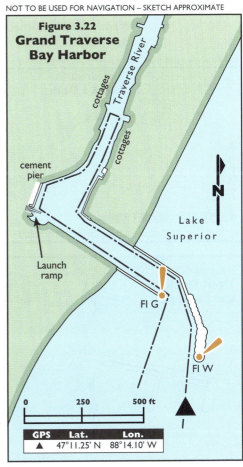

Figure 3.22
Grand Traverse Bay Harbor

cottages
Traverse River
cottages
cement pier
Launch ramp
Fl G
Lake Superior
N
Fl W
0   250   500 ft

GPS	Lat.	Lon.
▲	47°11.25' N	88°14.10' W

1960 it has been restored and maintained by the U.S. government.

The mouth of the canal is marked by two breakwaters extending into Lake Superior. Both piers are marked with lights on 25-foot-high white columns. The southerly light flashes green, the northerly light flashes red. Pass with the red light held to starboard. Passing through the dredged part of the canal is probably the most interesting part of the anchorage. Depths within the canal vary (6 feet to 9 feet) depending on the dredging schedule of the Corps of Engineers. Note that the last time the canal was dredged was in 2006 to 9-10 feet. It is also important to note that in those areas where the original river criss-crosses the dredged canal there is often silting-in, and it is not uncommon for those with deep-draft boats to get hung up on shifting sandbars.

Once inside Lac La Belle, anchoring can be done almost anywhere by watching the shoaling areas that extend out in a few spots along the shore. Because the lake is heavily populated with summer cottages, there are few areas where it is possible to obtain seclusion, should it be desired. There is a Michigan Waterways Commission dock in the NW corner of the lake. In 2005 the outside of the dock was dredged to 9 feet. Note that in recent years this corner of the lake has become quite congested with weeds. There are no facilities at the dock. The nearby resort offers a restaurant, gas and ice (888-294-7634). The wandering river that crisscrosses the entrance canal is interesting to explore with a dinghy. There is an old lighthouse (Mendota Light) half-way through the canal on the southern shore, which has been reactivated as a private aid to navigation (Fl W .4 sec, every 20 sec.).

When you leave Lac La Belle and continue around the Keweenaw Peninsula, there is an abrupt change in shoreline topography. For now we cruise beneath bold and steep-to bluffs. The shoreline becomes more rugged, and only off Keweenaw Point are there any shoals or obstructions and these are well marked by a buoy one-half mile off the point. This buoy bears special interest because on 4 December 1989 it marked the site of the grounding of the 180-foot Coast Guard cutter *Mesquite*.

NOT TO BE USED FOR NAVIGATION – SKETCHES APPROXIMATE

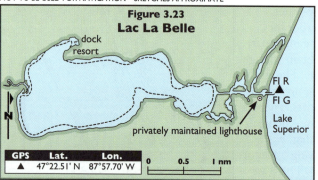

Figure 3.23
Lac La Belle

dock
resort

Fl R
Fl G

Lake
Superior

privately maintained lighthouse

GPS	Lat.	Lon.
▲	47°22.51' N	87°57.70' W

0   0.5   1 nm

Figure 3.24
DNR Dock, Lac La Belle

Small boat launch ramps & dock

125 ft.

N

Ice & gas at Lac La Belle resort ½ mile south.

The *Mesquite* was a
Coast Guard buoy tender
from Charlevoix, Michigan,
that was pulling buoys out
of the lake for protection
from winter ice in place of
the regular Lake Superior
tender *Sundew*, which
was up on dry dock for
repairs. Shortly after the
buoy had been pulled at
2 a.m., due to an error in
navigation, the cutter struck
an underwater rock ledge in
12 feet of water. Immediate

Lac La Belle.
MICHIGAN
WATERWAYS
COMMISSION

damage involved extensive flooding of the engine room and a list
to port. Initially it was hoped that by off-loading some of the deck
load, the cutter could be backed off. However, the hull continued
to disintegrate as the ship pounded on the rocks, and by 6:20 a.m.
the captain gave the order to abandon ship. The 53 crew members
were transferred to the Mangal Desai, a 604-foot grain ship out of
Bombay, India, that had come to their aid a couple of hours earlier,
and then were taken to Duluth. There were only three with injuries
who were medevaced by Coast Guard helicopter to Hancock,
Michigan.

In the days that followed, equipment and diesel fuel were off-
loaded and oil booms were deployed as safety precautions against
a possible oil spill. Attempts to patch the Mesquite's hull and haul
her off were prevented by deteriorating weather conditions, and by
mid-December it was determined that the cutter could not be saved.
Instead of scrapping the vessel, which would have been quite costly,
the decision was made to sink the cutter as a diving attraction in
the proposed Keweenaw Underwater Preserve. On 14 July 1990,
the Mesquite was lifted by a 180-foot crane barge and transferred
approximately one mile to the SW where it now lies in Keystone
Bay in 111 feet of water. For a more thorough and excellent
accounting of the events surrounding the grounding and subsequent
sinking of the Mesquite, refer to the Shipwreck of the Mesquite by
Frederick Stonehouse, published by Lake Superior Port Cities Inc.

Standing off two miles to the east of the Keweenaw Peninsula is
Manitou Island. On the east side of the island there is an anchorage
in the large bay SW of a prominent lighthouse, **Fishermans Bay**.
However, because the anchorage is quite open to easterly winds, it is
marginal. Also, it may be difficult to get a good set with the anchor
because of gravel and some rocks. (See Fig. 3.25.) When entering
this bay, care should be given to take a wide berth around the shoal
extending out from the southern arm of the bay. It is possible to
round the island on either side, but pass well off the shoals on the

west and northwest sides, noting Gull Rock Light and the buoy south of it.

Following around the northern end of the peninsula, the shoreline remains majestic and foreboding with high, towering bluffs that plunge deeply into the water. With no harbors or refuge along this shore, Copper Harbor becomes an important stopover for cruising boaters on the peninsula.

Figure 3.25
Fishermans Bay
Manitou Island

Manitou Island

Fishermans Bay

| 0 | 0.5 | 1 nm |

GPS	Lat.	Lon.
▲	47°24.95' N	87°35.30' W

Copper Harbor lies nestled in the Keweenaw Mountain Range, the oldest exposed volcanic rock on earth. A beautiful natural, all-weather harbor was established early as a fur-trading post by the French hunters and trappers. After Douglass Houghton made his geological survey for copper in 1844, the town literally mushroomed overnight into a boom town. Copper Harbor blossomed as the rush for copper peaked in 1846. It is interesting that the settling of the area is also connected with the completion of the Sault Ste. Marie Canal in 1855. The U.S. government paid the canal company in the form of land grants, many of which were in the Copper Harbor area. Thus, with the mining came the homesteaders; and with men to work the mines, the town rapidly grew. As a result of all the growing pains experienced by this frontier town, troops were brought in to protect the settlers and Fort Wilkins was built on Lake Fanny Hooe. Established in 1844, the fort was maintained until 1870, when it fell into disuse and disrepair. Then, in 1921 it was purchased by the state and finally restored by the Works Progress Administration (WPA) in the 1930s. Today, the fort is part of a state park and is a high point of interest to visitors of the area. Also within the park are abandoned copper

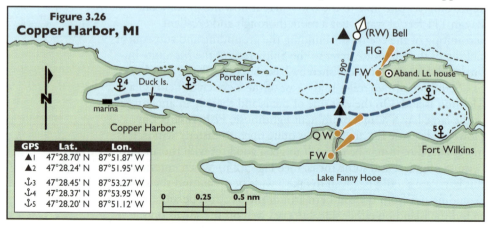

Figure 3.26
Copper Harbor, MI

(RW) Bell
FIG
FW · ⊙ Aband. Lt. house
Duck Is.
Porter Is.
marina
Copper Harbor
Q W
F W
Fort Wilkins
Lake Fanny Hooe

GPS	Lat.	Lon.
▲1	47°28.70' N	87°51.87' W
▲2	47°28.24' N	87°51.95' W
⚓3	47°28.45' N	87°53.27' W
⚓4	47°28.37' N	87°53.95' W
⚓5	47°28.20' N	87°51.12' W

| 0 | 0.25 | 0.5 nm |

mine shafts and the restored Copper Harbor Lighthouse.

To enter Copper Harbor, it is necessary to pass between a wicked outcropping of rock, which lies in the center of the bay, and the extensive shoaling off the eastern arm of the entrance. To do this, it is important to approach the R/W bell buoy that lies outside the harbor, and then follow the range (190 degrees T), which is on the shore past these obstructions. Rounding to starboard will take you to both the marina and the best anchoring, which is in the western end of the harbor. Note: Copper Harbor has its own special brand of welcoming committee. The Harbor Haus, a prominent restaurant on the waterfront, often presents the returning Isle Royale Queen with a whistle salute and a "cancan" dance on the restaurant deck performed by the staff.

At the far west end of the harbor is another Michigan State Waterways Commission marina, the **Copper Harbor State Marina**. Constructed in the early 2000s, it is one of the nicest marinas on the lake. In approaching the marina it is important to note that there is a large rock shoal about 300 feet NE of the marina that in the past has been marked with a danger buoy. The main portion of the marina is a long 160-foot dock extending out into the harbor with four fingers to the west. The fuel dock is on the eastern side along with accommodation for large boats. Most cruising amenities are available: gasoline, diesel, water, pump-out, ice and electricity (30 A and 50A). Within the office building there are rest rooms, showers, telephone and a gift shop. There is a Laundromat about 1/4-mile on the road towards town. Transient dockage is always available except for the 4th of July weekend when reservations are necessary (906-289-4966). The dock master also monitors channel 16. It is about a one-mile walk into town.

There are two other **alternatives for docking in Copper Harbor**, both of which are located closer to town. One of these, the Sixth Street Township Dock, is located behind Duck Island to the west of the Isle Royale Queen dock. The dock is Y-shaped and constructed out of capped

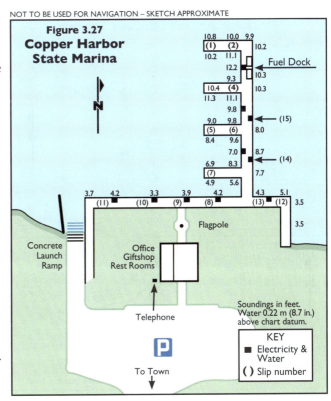

NOT TO BE USED FOR NAVIGATION – SKETCH APPROXIMATE

Figure 3.27
Copper Harbor State Marina

binwalls topped with treated wood. Unfortunately the depths are such that only boats drawing less than 4.5 feet have access to the dock. (See Fig. 3.28.) The second dock is located closer to the marina at 10th Street and in recent years has been taken by local seasonal dockage. This dock, which was completed in October 1996, is 60 feet long with a depth of 5.5 feet to 6 feet at its out end in low water years. Note that Copper Harbor is susceptible to 1-foot seiches and this must be taken into consideration when tying up to any dock. A nominal fee is charged for overnight dockage at both docks. For availability, check with the community center (906-289-4447).

If you prefer to anchor, it is possible to anchor in the western part of the harbor by favoring the NE extension of mainland or Porter Island to stay well out of boat traffic. It is also possible to anchor in the eastern section of the harbor, but care must be taken to stay either north or south of a couple of 4- and 6-foot shoals.

The town of Copper Harbor provides a couple of grocery stores and a number of interesting gift shops, many of which reflect the heritage of when "Copper was King." Ice can be obtained from the fish market down on the waterfront. The harbor is also important as the embarking point for the ferry, the *Isle Royale Queen IV*, which makes the round trip to Isle Royale daily during the peak summer periods, except on Wednesdays or Sundays. There are also several good restaurants, one of which is the previously mentioned Harbor Haus, specializing in excellent German/American cuisine. Another restaurant is found high up in the hills above town, the Keweenaw Mountain Resort. Complete with swimming pool and golf course, this rustic/modern complex was established by the WPA during the Great Depression. The dining room is open to the public, and a phone call for reservations will also bring a car down to the marina dock to take visiting boaters up for dinner.

Fort Wilkins is one of Michigan's most beautiful state parks. To reach the

NOT TO BE USED FOR NAVIGATION – SKETCH APPROXIMATE

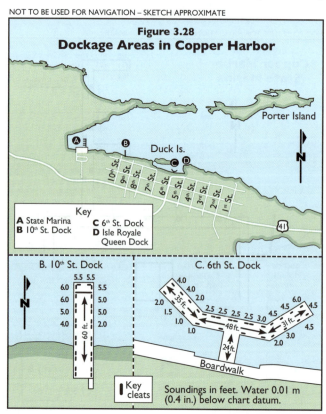

Figure 3.28
Dockage Areas in Copper Harbor

fort from the marina, it is a bit of a walk (two miles). But this can be greatly simplified by taking a motorized dinghy across the harbor and part way up the stream that enters the harbor from Lake Fanny Hooe. There is a convenient landing where the dinghy can be tied off, and then it is but a short walk to the fort.

The fort is bordered on the north and east by a reconstructed palisade, on the west by Fanny Hooe Creek and on the south by Fanny Hooe Lake. Outside of the stockade are two reconstructed quarters for married enlisted men. Also on the outside, about 100 yards east of the fort, are some of the abandoned mine shafts left by the Pittsburgh and Boston Mining Company.

The buildings inside are original structures with varying degrees of restoration. They consist of officers' quarters, company barracks, mess halls, quartermaster's and sutler's stores, a bakehouse and hospital—all finished in stark white clapboard reminiscent of the mid-1800s. Interpretation of what army life was like at a frontier military outpost is vividly portrayed by role-playing docents. Adjacent to the fort on the east is a beautiful Visitor Center with more displays on early frontier life. There are campgrounds to either side of the fort with a number of hiking trails through the woods and along the lake.

Apart from the fort, another structure of historical interest is the old Copper Harbor Lighthouse located on the eastern arm of the harbor entrance. The original light was built in 1849 and then replaced with the present structure that was built in 1866. Today, the lighthouse has been restored as a museum with shipwreck exhibits and is advertised as the oldest working lighthouse on Lake Superior. It can be reached via boat tour in the summer where an interpretative program emphasizes maritime history.

Note that in moving from Copper Harbor there is an east setting current of 1.5-2k. Those in power boats probably won't notice it too much, but those in slow moving sailboats will get a nice boost if traveling from west to east and a noticeable drag when traveling from east to west along the shoreline.

Moving west from Copper Harbor, the shoreline is still bold and inhospitable. Even when one approaches Agate and Little Grand Marais harbors, the area is best avoided by visiting boaters because of shoals and uncharted rocks. Only with local knowledge can these areas be entered safely and then only when there is no sea running.

A few miles farther is **Eagle Harbor** (12 nautical miles west of Copper Harbor), a harbor that is likewise tricky to enter, but because of navigational aids it is possible to get through the closing shoals in clear water. As with Copper Harbor, there are outcroppings of rocks and considerable shoaling in the entrance. Add to this more shoaling outside the entrance and a passage through two partially submerged stone cribs 60 feet apart, and it becomes obvious that this harbor should not be attempted in fog or when there are strong

northerly winds.

The harbor is easily identified by Eagle Harbor Light (Fl W&R), which is on the western side of the entrance. To pass through this hazardous entrance, a range on land as well as an outlying green bell buoy have been provided as in Copper Harbor. Be sure to line up on this buoy before heading in. At times the rear range may be hidden by the trees, so it is important to take a course of 150 degrees T from the buoy to stay on the range. Fortunately the tops of the cribs can be seen if no sea is running. Through the narrow passage, a depth of 12 feet can be maintained. After passing between the stone cribs, there are few places to go in the harbor, since each end is quite shallow and contains many submerged cribs. Turning to port, there is a marina and ramp constructed by the Michigan Waterways Commission on the inside of the eastern arm of the harbor. Note that the western end of the dock is shallow and should be avoided when approaching the fuel pump. There usually is no dock attendant present, but a harbormaster is on call from Copper Harbor via a posted telephone number. Gasoline and pump-out are the only amenities provided and only when an attendant is present. With care, it is possible to anchor in the western end of the bay, but because of shoaling and submerged cribs, it is difficult to get in very far and you are exposed to northerly winds here. For better protection it is better to anchor off just SE of the dock.

NOT TO BE USED FOR NAVIGATION – SKETCH APPROXIMATE

Figure 3.29
Eagle Harbor, Michigan

150 T

Fl W & R

cribs

marina

town

Q G   F G

GPS	Lat.	Lon.
▲	47°27.85' N	88°09.55' W

0   1000   2000 ft

Eagle Harbor Public Dock

P
office/rest rooms

old ramp

fuel G

concrete
launch
ramp

6.0
6.0
5.0
5.5
6.5
5.5
5.0
7.5
5.0
4.0

Soundings in feet.
Water 0.01 m (0.4 in.)
below chart datum.

Eagle Harbor.
MICHIGAN WATER-
WAYS COMMISSION

The stretch from Eagle Harbor to the Upper Entry of the Keweenaw Waterway is 25 nautical miles and again is hostile to small boats, offering no harbors or protecting coves. Because of shoals off the Eagle Harbor and Sand Bay area, it is well to stand off a good mile when traveling along this shoreline. As you pass through this area,

a point of interest is Eagle River, the site of the first mass copper mine on the peninsula. In the mid-1800s, it produced more than 35 million pounds of copper. It used to be a commercial port, but now all that remains are submerged cribs. It is also here that Douglass Houghton, the Michigan geologist who was instrumental in bringing copper mining to the peninsula, was drowned. His canoe swamped in a fall snowstorm (13 October 1845), while he was making further surveys.

If approach to the Upper Entry of the Keweenaw Waterway is made from the east, it is important to give adequate berth to the 8-foot shoal that lies approximately one mile to the NE of the outer breakwater and not close in too fast. For the description of the Upper Entry, see page 101.

From the Upper Entry it is a long 38 nautical miles to Ontonagon, Michigan. With no harbors in between, **Ontonagon**, which is a natural harbor formed by the mouth of the Ontonagon River, is another important port of call along a lonely shoreline.

Ontonagon gained fame early from the first explorations and on through the centuries because of a story that a large "mass of copper ore lying in its bed from which Native Americans would cut chunks of virgin copper when they wanted it" rested here. Even Henry Schoolcraft, later to become the famous Indian agent in the Soo, writes about it in his first exploration on the lake in 1820. This, of course, was the "great Ontonagon boulder," which later gained much publicity when a Detroit businessman tried to move it in the early 1840s to put it on public display in Detroit. (Today, the boulder is preserved at the Smithsonian Institution in Washington, D.C.) Because of all the publicity, along with Houghton's geological reports, miners quickly flocked to the area, and the town was another of those that seemed to "boom overnight." In the second half of the century, lumbering added its part as Ontonagon became one of the early lumber shipping ports.

The entrance of the harbor is marked by two long breakwaters that extend out into the lake, both of which are marked with flashing lights (east breakwater Fl G; west breakwater Fl R). Note that the river is on schedule to be dredged each year because it is a commercial harbor. Controlling depths are 19 feet in the outer section and 15 feet in the inner section. The bridge shown on the charts is no longer there, having been removed in late 2006. It was replaced by a new bridge in October 2006 south of the railroad

NOT TO BE USED FOR NAVIGATION – SKETCH APPROXIMATE

Figure 3.30
Ontonagon Harbor, Michigan

GPS	Lat.	Lon.
▲	46°52.95' N	89°20.00' W

East Pier-
head Light
Fl G 6
St M

West
Pierhead
Light
Fl R 6
St M

town

Abandoned
Light house

marina

ramps

0   500   1000 ft

F – fuel dock

bridge. Thus, there are now no obstructions for boaters to get to the marina. The marina is another quarter mile up the river on the western side. From where the bridge used to be to the marina depths are 8 to 12 feet. Note: due to run-off from the river there is periodic shoaling at the marina entrance, particularly on the north side. The marina puts out red and green entrance buoys, but it is important to favor the green buoy to port when entering.

The marina consists of one long pier with 36 slips and a gas pump at its outer end. Seven slips are reserved at this end along the south side, marked with vertical white signs and black letters on poles. Depths near the outer end are 9 feet, 5 feet next to the office. The marina provides gasoline, pump-out, water, electricity (110 V 30A), rest rooms, showers and a 30-ton Travelift with a large area for winter storage. Diesel fuel can be provided and delivered by the marina with gerry cans that they have on hand. Adjacent to the marina on the south is an elaborate boat launching facility consisting of three sets of two ramps. On the north side of the marina is a large park and picnic area with a playground and public rest rooms. Supplies can be obtained by crossing the new bridge into the town, which is on the other side of the river, and which is now a substantial distance, or you can take a dinghy across where there is a small dinghy dock provided.

Historical note: the old lighthouse that can be seen off the western pier as you enter the river was built in 1866 to replace the original, which had been built in 1852. This second light is three stories high, contains nine rooms and was used out on the west pier until 1964. Now it serves as a station for the Coast Guard Auxiliary.

Continuing west from Ontonagon, there is another barren stretch of shoreline with no harbors, bays or inlets for 35 nautical miles. However, the view is majestic as the rugged Porcupine Mountains, the tallest mountains in the Midwest with some elevations 1,200 feet above the lake, emerge along the shoreline. There are even some stands of virgin timber, left untouched by the big cuts that took place along this sector of the lake in the late 1800s. The area is very wild, and none of the numerous rivers entering the lake along this stretch are navigable.

Black River Harbor has long been a favorite of those who cruise in this part of the lake. Tucked back in the woods among stately tall pines, many of which are virgin timber, this natural harbor is

Ontonagon Harbor.
MICHIGAN
WATERWAYS
COMMISSION

formed where the mouth of the Black River empties into Lake Superior. It is one of the most beautiful harbors in this sector of the lake.

The outer part of the harbor is formed by two breakwaters that extend out into the lake. Both breakwaters have lights on white skeleton towers (Fl G on the east breakwater, Fl R on the west). But despite these markers, the harbor is sometimes difficult to locate

Black River Harbor.
MICHIGAN
WATERWAYS
COMMISSION

since it blends in well with the bold shoreline. There is another marker, a ski jump high in the hills just to the west of the harbor, which is often used as a bearing when closing in. Controlling depths are 10 feet in the entrance channel and 7 feet in the main part of the harbor. (The last time the harbor was dredged was 2001. There is no future dredging scheduled at this time.) Note that deep-draft boats should favor the starboard side after clearing the entrance as there is shoal water to port—even in the channel inside the area marked by a green can. The whole western side of the harbor, from just inside the breakwater to the bridge (clearance 18 feet), is constructed with docks. The first part is a floating wooden dock that has no electricity and will accommodate only boats drawing 5 feet or less.

The main dock up to the launch ramp is concrete, has the best depths and also electricity. Upriver, from the gas pump to the bridge, the depths shoal, making this area usable only by smaller craft. Although the dock space is heavily used by locals, there usually are a number of "slips" open for transients. There is a gas pump and pump-out at the gas dock, but in recent years gas availability has been intermittent. There is also a small concession stand here that, when open, sells sodas and snacks. The harbormaster is part time and when he/she is absent there are envelopes with a fee schedule and container for self-registration on the dock. Note that within this snug harbor there is often poor VHF reception for weather channels.

The U.S. Forest Service has done an especially nice job on developing the

NOT TO BE USED FOR NAVIGATION – SKETCH APPROXIMATE

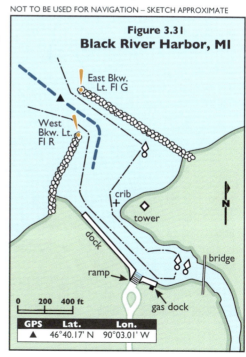

Figure 3.31
Black River Harbor, MI

East Bkw. Lt. Fl G

West Bkw. Lt. Fl R

crib

tower

N

dock

ramp

bridge

gas dock

0   200   400 ft

GPS	Lat.	Lon.
▲	46°40.17' N	90°03.01' W

adjacent recreational area. Along with a campground, there is a lovely picnic area, complete with tables, grills, water and rest rooms. In the surrounding area, there are a number of trails, some of which lead to impressive high overlooks of the lake. Other trails lead inland on both sides of the river to a series of beautiful waterfalls. Many of the large trees seen along these trails are actually virgin timber, the remains of the large stands that once covered the whole southern shore of the lake.

Note: in the early 1990s, two people lost their lives at the waterfalls on the river, one at Rainbow Falls and the other farther upstream at Gorge Falls. The Rainbow Falls accident involved a boater who slipped and fell when trying to cross over to the other side above the falls, plunging to his death in the pool below. The other accident occurred when a young boy was swimming in the pool beneath the falls. It is important to warn crew members not to engage in these dangerous practices.

From Black River, the shoreline takes a dip approximately 17 nautical miles to the southwest until Oronto Bay, at the base of which is another boat harbor, **Saxon Harbor**. The harbor is marked by two breakwaters identified with white day markers (east Fl Gr; west Fl R). in approaching the entrance, it is important to note there is some shoaling around the starboard (red) breakwater and to favor slightly the port (green) breakwater (see Fig. 3.32).

In 2005-06, Saxon Harbor received quite a facelift, doubling its size by dredging and adding a new basin south of the old basin. Then in July 2016, the whole harbor was destroyed by a flash flood. There was considerable boat damage, with boats sunk in the harbor and even swept out into the lake. The whole harbor, marine and campground were rebuilt in 2019-2020. Retaining the original configuration, all docks are now floating with the North Basin taking boats up to 32 feet and the South Basin taking boats up to 45 feet. The harbor has also been completely dredged to a depth of 10 feet throughout. All amenities are provided: gasoline, diesel, pump-out, water, electricity (20, 30 and 50 amps), restrooms,

NOT TO BE USED FOR NAVIGATION – SKETCH APPROXIMATE

Figure 3.32
Saxon Harbor, Wisconsin

LAKE SUPERIOR

Fl G

Fl R

N

Parkers Creek

NOAA weather station

Transient Dockage

launch ramp

North Basin

R/S

PG

R/S

office

South Basin

to harbor lights & campground

Oronto Creek

4.5
5.3
5.1
6.7
Launch Ramp

K

travel lift

F
PO
D, FC

5.3 5.7
4.7
3.9
4.3

D	Dump station	PG	Playground
FC	Fish cleaning	PO	Pump out
F	Fuel dock	R/S	Restroom, shower
K	Kayak launch		

GPS	Lat.	Lon.
▲	46°33.90' N	90°26.30' W

0   200   400 ft

Soundings in feet. Water -0.33 M (13.0 in) below chart datum showers, three boat launch ramps, a Travelift and winter storage. New additions are a kayak launch, playground and WiFi. There is also now an office with an attendant who answers to "Saxon Harbor" on VHF. The Harbor Lights Restaurant and Bar, a short walk up the road, continues to be a pleasant spot to gather with friends and have a good meal. Because Saxon Harbor is less than 25 minutes from Bayfield, it makes a nice getaway weekend from the Apostles, providing a delightful destination and secure harbor for the night.

After leaving Saxon Harbor and rounding Marble Head Point, we come to an especially beautiful area in this part of the lake. The red sandstone cliffs, which took over from the Porcupine Mountains, give way to the low-rolling marshes of **Long Island** that forms the outer extremity of Chequamegon Bay. Up until now, we have traveled along rocky shorelines and majestic forested bluffs. But now the terrain changes abruptly and we get our first glimpse of the beautiful white sand beaches that are one of the enticing characteristics of the Apostle Islands. From time to time, the half-mile gap between Long Island and Chequamegon Point closes, depending on the level of the lake. The name "Chequamegon" is thought to be a distortion of the Chippewa phrases *ha-gua-wan-me-kong*, which, roughly translated, means "a long narrow strip of land running into a body of water," although others translate it to mean "shallow bay."

There are two lights along the northern shore of Long Island, La Pointe Light and Chequamegon Point Light, both of which Fl G. Despite the shoal water around Long Island, it is possible to creep in toward the north side and, while watching the weather, anchor for a lunch stop to do some exploring along the beautiful sandy beaches. However, watch out for poison ivy.

The other (southern) side of Long Island offers more protection for anchoring, but here special care must be taken because of the shoaling waters of Chequamegon Bay. Again, creeping in while closely following the charts, along with using a depth sounder, it is possible to get three-sided protection in 8 to 9 feet of water south of Chequamegon Point.

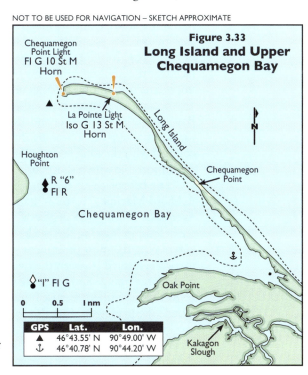

NOT TO BE USED FOR NAVIGATION – SKETCH APPROXIMATE

Figure 3.33
Long Island and Upper Chequamegon Bay

Chequamegon Point Light
Fl G 10 St M
Horn

La Pointe Light
Iso G 13 St M
Horn

Houghton Point

R "6"
Fl R

Chequamegon Bay

Long Island

Chequamegon Point

Oak Point

"I" Fl G

0   0.5   1 nm

Kakagon Slough

GPS	Lat.	Lon.
▲	46°43.55' N	90°49.00' W
⚓	46°40.78' N	90°44.20' W

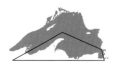

This area is very wild and marshy, the perfect habitat for abundant wildlife, especially in the Kakagon Sloughs south of Oak Point.

This area is a Chippewa Reservation belonging to the Bad River Band of Chippewa, once part of the La Pointe Band. In the late 1800s the La Pointe Band was split up with the residents going to two reservations. The Catholics formed what is now known as the Red Cliff Band; the Protestants, the Bad River Band. Today, this marshy area around Chequamegon Point provides an income source for the tribe in terms of wild rice and guiding for sports fishermen. Although this anchorage is open to the west, it is not too difficult to move to the opposite mainland shore should westerly winds develop.

Chequamegon Bay has long held a place of importance in the history of the lake. For it was here, deep in the interior of the continent that, in the winter of 1659-60, just 50 years after the founding of Jamestown, the first dwelling of white men on the lake was erected by Radisson and Des Groseilliers during their epic exploratory voyage across the southern shore of the lake. Time and again, the name of this bay keeps cropping up, first in the annals of missionaries and then in connection with the fur traders, as posts were established to serve the various disciplines. Although the bay was established early as a key outpost in the development of the western part of the lake, it wasn't until 1854 that the town of **Ashland** was founded. And then the town almost didn't make it, for the financial panic of 1857 and the Civil War left only one family. But when the Wisconsin Central Railroad made the "town" part of its new, expanding line, Ashland was given a fresh start. This was followed by establishing Ashland as the shipping port for the new Gogebic Iron Range along with development of a sawmill to facilitate the lumbering booms. Until the 1960s, Ashland was an important port in ore shipping on the lake.

Because of its large areas of shallow water, Chequamegon Bay is not easy to navigate and attention must be given to the various markers when heading down the bay. These shoal waters, coupled with the long fetch to the NE, make the bay particularly uncomfortable with a short chop when NE winds blow.

The best place for the small boat to berth in Ashland is at the **Ashland Marina** (715-682-7049), which lies at the foot of Prentice Avenue or bearing 158 degrees T from Red Nun #4. Two landmarks are helpful in locating this dock, the coal dock and the ore dock, the latter being the most prominent structure on the waterfront. The marina is located between the two, closer to and just to the west of the large orange and black ore dock. As you near shore, it can be further identified because it lies just in front of the large, white Hotel Chequamegon. It is also marked by a large black stone rubble breakwater that forms the western extremities of the marina. Passage is between this breakwater and a cement breakwater marked with a green day marker, which is passed to port. Note that the rubble breakwater was added in 1999 along with 48 new slips to make a total of 140 slips for the complex. The docks are floating docks with steel frames. They also have a Travelift and provide winter storage. Transient dockage is available along with gasoline, diesel, pump-out, electricity, rest rooms and showers. An attendant is on duty at the office where there is also a ship's store.

The town has excellent shopping with a good grocery store six blocks away and a number of interesting gift shops, many of which display work by local artisans. There are number of marine repair facilities in the area along with stores that provide marine hardware and fishing supplies. By following Hwy. 2 a mile out of town to the east, there are more stores, including a Wal-Mart.

A special point of interest is to visit the Hotel Chequamegon. Designed in the grand tradition of turn-of-the-century hotels with turrets, cupolas and verandas, but built in the late 20th century, the 64-room complex stands out against the shoreline with stark white clapboard siding and bright green roofs. The interior continues the theme with relaxed Victorian elegance reminiscent of the days when the well-to-do from urban centers boarded northbound passenger trains to vacation on Lake Superior's shores. Today, visitors may get a glimpse into the town's opulent past and enjoy an evening out in its formal dining room or relax in the atmosphere of a Victorian pub (Molly Cooper's).

Another point of interest is the Northern Great Lakes Visitor Center, which opened in May 1998 about three miles west of Ashland on Hwy.

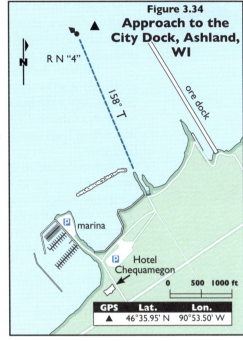

Figure 3.34
Approach to the City Dock, Ashland, WI

GPS	Lat.	Lon.
▲	46°35.95' N	90°53.50' W

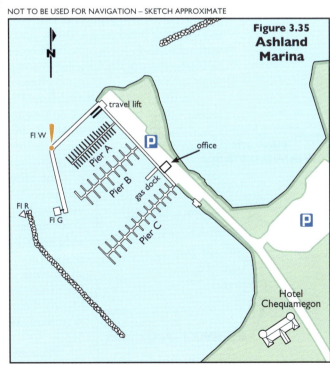

Figure 3.35
Ashland Marina

2. Transient boaters will have to take a taxi, but it is well worth the effort as this is a "must see" attraction. The $8 million complex is designed with regional themes incorporating a brownstone base, dramatic rooflines and a five-story imitation lighthouse tower. With an emphasis on interactive displays, the exhibits are outstanding portrayals of an overview from the Ice Age to the present. Many displays depict the interaction of human cultures with the land and resources of the area. Outside there is a beautiful three-quarter-mile trail, which leads through conifer forest, sedge marsh and grassy field areas.

Across the bay to the north from Ashland, in Vandeventer Bay, lying approximately 10 miles south of the Apostle Islands, is a quaint village reminiscent of the days at the turn of the 20th century when it was a milling center for the area's growing lumber industry. Today, this town of **Washburn**, Wisconsin, is the county seat for Bayfield County. This is personified in one of its attractions, the Bayfield County Courthouse, an imposing domed structure that is made from quarried Lake Superior brownstone.

On the waterfront located just to the west of the C. Reiss Coal dock, there is a large marina that was built in 1982. The entrance to the marina is formed by two long breakwaters, which are marked with red and green day markers with lights. To approach the marina there are no obstructions if a track is made from the east or south. However, because of the ruins of submerged wharves, the western part of Vandeventer Bay should be avoided. The marina has 138 slips, with transient berthing facilities available. Electricity, water, gasoline, diesel and pump-out are available along with showers and rest rooms. It boasts of a 150-ton Travelift, the largest on the lake, with a double-wide concrete launch ramp that can haul boats up to 150 feet in length. Adjacent to and part of the small boat launch ramp are 5 slips for transient dockage.

On the premises there is a large 15,000-square-foot heated indoor storage building and another 15,000-square-foot building added in 2001. The marina is the largest repair facility on the lake, specializing in Awlgrip painting and fiberglass repairs, gel-coat stripping and sandblasting, mechanical and electrical services, woodworking and carpentry, repowering/ repairing gas and diesel motors, and welding and fabrication. A ship's store supplies accessories and yacht gear and has an excellent selection of marine hardware. For further information write: Washburn Marina, One Marina Drive, P.O. Box 482, Washburn, WI 54891. Phone: 715-373-5050.

The town of Washburn, which is

NOT TO BE USED FOR NAVIGATION – SKETCH APPROXIMATE

Figure 3.36
Washburn Marina

N

transient docks

launch ramp

C. Reiss Coal Co.

city dock

hoist well

vessel repair

Fl G

Fl R

0   0.25   0.5 nm

GPS	Lat.	Lon.
▲	46°40.00' N	90°53.25' W

about a two-block walk away, provides a good hardware store, drug store, laundry facilities and an excellent grocery store for replenishing supplies. There are a number of good restaurants here. Other points of interest are the Washburn Historical Museum and Cultural Center located in the old bank building and a hiking trail that follows the shoreline from the West End Park to the marina. This area is particularly reputed for its good sports fishing—and just a few miles to the north lie the red sandstone cliffs and white sandy beaches of the Apostle Islands.

Chapter Four

The Apostle Islands:
A National Lakeshore

There is one area on Lake Superior where there are more pleasure craft per square mile than any other. Not only is the largest charter fleet on the lake located here, but with seven marinas and two yacht clubs, there are more privately-owned boats in this area than anywhere else on Lake Superior. The reason for this high-density boating community — the Apostle Islands.

Located off the Bayfield Peninsula in western Lake Superior, these 22 islands, which cover an area of more than 720 square miles of Lake Superior, offer some of the best cruising on the lake. Sandy beaches and windswept sandspits, red sandstone cliffs and caves, peaceful lagoons teaming with wildlife, deep shoal-free channels — all are a part of the Apostles. Sheltered from the big lake, cruising in the islands not only reduces the chances of encountering big seas, but there is always a shore close by to which one can snug up to get out of the weather. With the close proximity of urban centers, it's not surprising that the Apostles have become a favorite playground for weekend and vacation cruising alike.

Prior to written history, the Apostles were also favored by early Native Americans. Archaeological studies have found artifacts within the islands from these Early Woodland Indians dating as far back as 3,000 years ago. More recently, but still before the coming of early explorers, the islands were inhabited by the Chippewa (Ojibwe) who established a large village on Madeline Island. The village, however, was dispersed shortly before the 1650s due to some grizzly tales of cannibalism accompanied by the hauntings of the spirits of the dead. It was only after a trading post had been established in the late 1600s that the Chippewa felt free to return to the island.

A year after Radisson and Des Groseilliers' trip (1660), the first Jesuit missionary arrived, Father Rene Menard. He was followed by Father Claude Allouez, and shortly thereafter a mission was established at La Pointe on Madeline Island. By the late 1600s, a trading post had been constructed and Madeline Island became an important part of the fur trade. For more than a century, the Apostles were an important outpost serving as a crossroads for further explorations in the western part of the lake and for those on their way to Fond du Lac (Duluth). Both the North West and American Fur companies established posts here.

Following the familiar pattern seen elsewhere in this region, lumbering and the associated arrival of the railroad in 1883 were instrumental in the growth of the area. Commercial fishing and the quarrying of sandstone (brownstone) were also important in bringing in early settlers. An interesting glimpse into the abundance of one of these resources is seen in the late 1700s. At this time, John Johnston, who was later to become an agent in the North West Company, recorded in his journal "seeing a lake trout taken off the NE end of Montreal Island (Madeline Island) which weighed 52 lbs.!"

The town of Bayfield wasn't established until 1856, when Henry Rice, a Minnesota state legislator, began a land company there. The town was named after Admiral Henry Bayfield of the Royal Navy who, in the early 1800s, conducted the first complete survey of Lake Superior, collected geological data for the entire lake shoreline and constructed the first "modern" chart of the lake.

Reflections of the islands' diverse heritage are seen in the variety of names found in the area. The Chippewa, who were closely in tune with their daily experiences, contributed names such as Bear, Otter, Oak, Rocky and Sand. French influence is seen in the names La Pointe and Presque Isle. And it is generally believed that the name "Apostles" came into being in the late 1600s from French missionaries, as a misnomer. Due to the erroneous belief that there were only 12 islands, the missionaries named the islands after the Twelve Apostles. In 1822, Henry Schoolcraft tried to change the name, calling them the Federation Islands, and giving each island the name of a state. The only names that now show this intent are Michigan and York islands — although, oddly enough, these are not the names originally intended by Schoolcraft for those islands.

Today, the visiting boater should note a few general distinguishing characteristics about the area. First, and most important, is that although the cruising is excellent, there are no all-weather anchorages in the islands. Few anchorages have even three-sided protection, and most have only one or two protecting sides. Therefore, it is wise to consider each anchorage with a back-up in mind. In fact, this single characteristic of weather protection is what usually determines which anchorage a cruiser will choose. Note: a common practice when anchoring in the Apostles is to always have alternative anchorages in mind should the wind switch in the night.

Most of the docks within the islands, likewise, offer little protection. Only the dock complex at Presque Isle Bay on Stockton Island, the National Park Service (NPS) Dock at Little Sand Bay on the mainland and the small boat dock at the south end of Devils

Island provide secure protection for all winds. While it is one thing to spend a rough night at anchor should the wind switch it is quite another to be crunched against either a wood or cement dock. It may also be difficult to get off a dock when the wind switches, and each year there are stories of toe rails ripped off, damage to sterns and worse when sailors tried to stick it out at a dock or couldn't get off. Thus, the prudent skipper will also keep a sharp eye to the weather when using docks in the islands.

Another characteristic one should note about the Apostles is that there is precious little dock space within the islands when compared with the high boating density. Therefore, to conserve space and allow others dock usage, it is often customary at some of the docks to use a Mediterranean moor, that is, to set out a bow anchor and tie stern to the dock. This is especially true at some of the more popular spots such as Rocky and South Twin Islands. Because Med-mooring creates navigational hazards at small, shallow docks and harbors, it is not allowed at Little Sand Bay, Stockton Island Presque isle Marina, or areas posted by the Superintendent. Likewise, rafting in tight quarters, which creates congestion and potential hazards is not allowed in these areas or where their non-use is posted.

In some respects, sailing in the islands can be frustrating. For just as you have the spinnaker set and are ready for a nice down-wind run, the wind switches. Or you might be slapping back and forth in an area of calm, only to hear someone remark on the radio that they are having a nice brisk reach in 10 knots just a few miles away. When tacking up channels you may find more wind next to an island, only to have it diminish as you close reach to the other side. The islands do have a decided effect on wind patterns, and experienced sailors learn to use them to their advantage, for unless very strong winds are forecast, rare is the day that you don't have to make some kind of a sail change.

A number of the islands are quite similar in their shoreline topography. With most, the northern shores are rough, rugged sandstone bluffs, many of which are carved into intricate cave formations by the greater lake. In some cases, parts of these caves have broken off to form sea stacks such as those found at the northern ends of Basswood and Stockton. A quick look at the charts shows another distinctive similarity among the islands — many of them have sandspits at their southern extremities. Further examination shows that the spits usually extend quite a way underwater with a fair amount of shoaling. Because of these general island characteristics, it is usually possible to sail quite close to the northern sides of the islands, while off the southern ends near sandspits it's important to stay well offshore.

Another feature important to boaters is the prevalence of fishing buoys and, more important, pond nets (sometimes called pound nets) scattered throughout the islands by the commercial fishing fleet out of Bayfield. The buoys usually mark gill nets which, because of lead weights along their lower side, lie deep in the water and are usually of little concern to the boater (see Fig. 4.1). However, when these buoys are seen close to shore they may lie in relatively shallow waters and could be a problem to boaters.

Although the use of pond nets is now rare, when seen they provide a glimpse into past fishing techniques. The pond net is a formidable structure, only part of which is seen by the passing boater. It consists of a large pen or pot that is marked by extensive poles and nets seen above the water. There is also an even larger portion of the structure lying under the water, the heart and lead (see Fig. 4.2). These can often be distinguished by floats lying just at the top of the water — but they are certainly harder to see than the large stakes above the water. Pond nets are usually placed in relatively shallow water with the underwater parts leading in toward shore — but not always. To get caught in any part of this structure could prove quite hazardous. The pond nets are especially dangerous during night sailing because they are unmarked. The structures, however, involve quite an undertaking to set, so they are usually permanent for the season. Thus, it is often possible to get their locations from marina charts or the Coast Guard.

The Coast Guard in Bayfield is located just southwest of the Apostle Islands Marina. Monitoring Channel 16, they answer to "Coast Guard Station Bayfield." It is also possible to establish contact with the Duluth Coast Guard in this part of the lake. They answer to "Station Duluth." Through the use of repeaters, it is even possible to establish contact

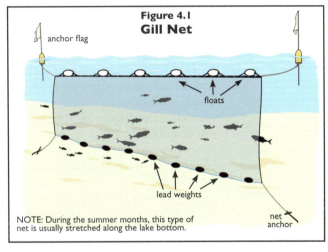

Figure 4.1
Gill Net

anchor flag

floats

lead weights

net anchor

NOTE: During the summer months, this type of net is usually stretched along the lake bottom.

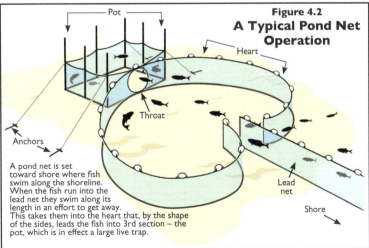

Figure 4.2
A Typical Pond Net Operation

Pot

Heart

Throat

Anchors

A pond net is set toward shore where fish swim along the shoreline. When the fish run into the lead net they swim along its length in an effort to get away. This takes them into the heart that, by the shape of the sides, leads the fish into 3rd section – the pot, which is in effect a large live trap.

Lead net

Shore

with Group Soo, which is located in Sault Ste. Marie, Michigan. Group Soo also initiates a couple of regularly scheduled weather broadcasts each day (see Chapter Two). Once out in the islands, continuous weather can be picked up on numerous weather channels (see Fig. 2.13).

Marine Facilities in the Area

Along with all the boats in use in the area, there are a number of marine facilities that are available for both dockage and repairs. Most offer a wide number of amenities to satisfy transient cruising needs. Some also provide services facilities that can perform repairs on fiberglass, engines, and some electronics. See Figure 4.4 for those facilities in the immediate Bayfield area.

Bayfield City Dock: Right in the heart of the Bayfield waterfront is a major complex consisting of two large breakwaters. These are easily identified from the water by a prominent structure on the shoreline, Bayfield on the Lake, which is a very large three-story gray condominium establishment. The breakwaters are both equipped with lights: the Bayfield Harbor North Breakwater Light flashes red and has a red triangular day marker at its outer end; the Bayfield Harbor South Breakwater Light flashes green, is marked with a black square day marker and is equipped with a foghorn. There is one other light in the immediate vicinity: the Bayfield Municipal Breakwater Light (Iso.G.) located to the north of the two just described. It marks the harbor entrance for the ferry landing which provides ferry service between the mainland and Madeline Island. Note: in approaching or leaving from this area, care must be taken to avoid the ferry traffic which in the height of the season is very heavy with four different ferries making the run to and from Madeline every half-hour. The ferry landing is located just to the north of the north arm of the north breakwater.

Within the Bayfield Harbor there are two places for dockage, the Bayfield City Dock, and the Bayfield City Marina. The City Dock (Tel.: 715-779-5712) offers dockage with electricity and water. There is limited transient dockage on the north side of the pier. There is a container on a post where dockage fees may be deposited in provided envelopes.

Bayfield City Marina: The Apostle Islands Marina, which had been leased from the city and run independently for over 50 years, is now run by the city of Bayfield, and called the Bayfield City Marina. It occupies the whole southern half of the harbor described above. Along

NOT TO BE USED FOR NAVIGATION – SKETCH APPROXIMATE

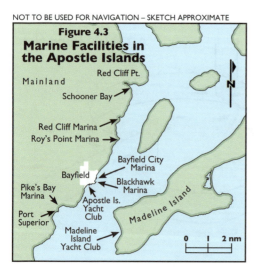

Figure 4.3
Marine Facilities in the Apostle Islands

with the City Dock, it offers the best access to the town of Bayfield and supplies.

With more than 135 slips, the marina (which monitors VHF Channel 16, Tel.: 715-779-5661) usually has transient space available. It is also usually possible to arrange for a long-term transient dockage package. Gasoline, diesel, electricity (30 A & 50 A), pump-out, ice, rest rooms and showers are provided along with a large 30-ton Travelift. It is a full-service facility that provides many maintenance and repair services. Of special note is a complete Rigging Service Center with a swaging machine.

Within the marina area, there is also a launch ramp along with provisions for storing boat trailers, so it is a good departure point for those with trailerable boats. Across the street from the marina is the Sea Store, a marine parts store that has an excellent selection of boat accessories and spare parts. A small city park adjacent to the marina provides picnic tables and playground equipment.

Just two short blocks away is a business district that provides a well-stocked grocery store, hardware store, contemporary bank and even a mini mall. There is a large Community Recreation Center complete with racquetball courts, Olympic-sized swimming pool and whirlpool hot tub. A number of interesting curio and clothing shops along with a half-dozen good restaurants add to the offerings,

NOT TO BE USED FOR NAVIGATION – SKETCH APPROXIMATE

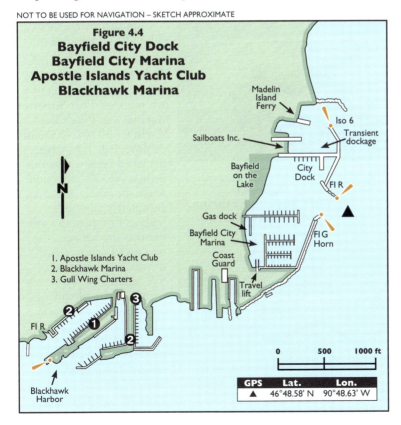

Figure 4.4
Bayfield City Dock
Bayfield City Marina
Apostle Islands Yacht Club
Blackhawk Marina

Madelin Island Ferry

Iso 6

Transient dockage

Sailboats Inc.

Bayfield on the Lake

City Dock

Fl R

Gas dock

Bayfield City Marina

Fl G
Horn

Coast Guard

Travel lift

1. Apostle Islands Yacht Club
2. Blackhawk Marina
3. Gull Wing Charters

Fl R

Blackhawk Harbor

0   500   1000 ft

GPS	Lat.	Lon.
▲	46°48.58' N	90°48.63' W

all within easy walking distance of the marina. Of special interest to the boater is the newly constructed Bayfield Maritime Museum. Located across from the Bayfield City Marina, this museum features marine and historical artifacts from the area.

Apostle Islands Yacht Club: Just a few blocks SW of the Bayfield City Marina there are additional marine facilities in the Blackhawk Harbor: a yacht club, marina, and chartering facility. The Apostle Islands Yacht Club is also within walking distance of the Bayfield business district. It is marked with a flashing red light and a yellow diamond day marker at the end of a long breakwater. Water and electricity (30 A) are provided. Although a private club, slips may be available for transients when vacated by the members. A clubhouse with restrooms, showers and a picnic/barbecue area is also available to those who use the facilities.

To the west and to the east of the Apostle Islands Yacht Club is another marine facility in the area, the **Blackhawk Marina** (717-209-4990). Constructed in 1992, it consists of a 60-slip complex with electricity, water, pump-out, rest rooms and showers. Privately maintained lights mark the entrance on the east side. Transient dockage is sometimes available. Also located In Blackhawk area is the Gull Wing Charters (715-492-7468).

Apostle Islands Marina, Bayfield. DAHL

Approximately three miles SW of the town of Bayfield in Pike's Bay lies the largest marine complex in the area. Consisting of two marinas, **Port Superior Marina,** and **Pike's Bay Marina**, well over 400 slips are provided. Two large, detached breakwaters that lie in a NE-SW direction make the whole area a completely all-weather harbor. Entrance to both marinas lies between the two rock breakwaters, of which the original SW section was built with sunken railroad ore cars filled with rock. The breakwater entrance is marked with day markers with flashing red and flashing green lights. Caution: *be sure to stand off well from each breakwater since what you*

NOT TO BE USED FOR NAVIGATION – SKETCH APPROXIMATE

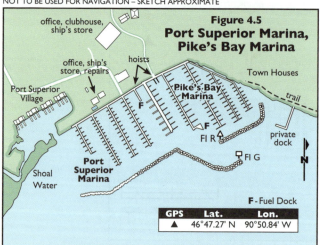

Figure 4.5
Port Superior Marina, Pike's Bay Marina

office, clubhouse, ship's store

office, ship's store, repairs

hoists

Town Houses

Port Superior Village

Pike's Bay Marina

trail

F

F

FI R

private dock

N

FI G

Port Superior Marina

Shoal Water

F - Fuel Dock

GPS	Lat.	Lon.
▲	46°47.27' N	90°50.84' W

see is like the tip of an iceberg and there are more breakwater boulders extending outward slanted underwater from the visual structure. Also, because of shallow depths do not attempt to come in around the far SW end of the breakwater. The controlling depth in both marinas is 8 feet.

Port Superior Marina, Bayfield DAHL

Port Superior Marina: This is the marina seen to the left or port side when entering the harbor. This large 211-slip complex is administered by the Port Superior Marine Association. A little more than half of the slips are owned by members of the association while the rest are rented to non-members on a seasonal basis. Some slips are also usually available for transients (reservations suggested). The marina provides all cruising amenities: gasoline, diesel, pump-out, electricity (30 A and 50 A), rest rooms with showers and Wi-Fi Internet. A large hoist (20-ton) and marine parts store are also available. The ship's store is one of the best-stocked marine parts stores in the area. In 2004, a 30-by- 60-foot building was added to the ship's store. In addition to administrative offices, it includes indoor storage lockers for boaters, segregated workspaces for a mechanics shop, an electronics room and a fiberglass and woodworking shop. With qualified resident technicians that can perform most boat services (electronics; major hull, painting, and fiberglass repairs; rigging maintenance and repair; engine (diesel & gasoline) maintenance, repair and installation) it is one of the best repair facilities in the area. Living up to its motto of Lake Superior's Premier Resort Marina, additional facilities on the premises are a contemporary clubhouse (members only), swimming pool and tennis courts for marina slip owners/renters, their guests, and transients. Within the complex there is an excellent restaurant, Portside (licensed and open to the public), which provides a picturesque view of the marina. The restaurant monitors VHF Channel 9 for dinner reservations — they are not open for lunch. Port Superior is home to Superior Charters (715-779-5124) with both sail and powerboats available for bareboat and captained charter, it's the largest charter operation in the Apostles. Also, within the grounds there is the Brookside Motel with 12 rental units available. The marina office can be contacted by VHF radio (Channel 16) or telephone: 715-779-5360.

Pike's Bay Marina: This is the newest marina in the area. It is the marina that is right in front of you and to starboard when you enter the combined entrance of the two marinas. It is easily recognized by a triangular gas dock on the end of the first dock you encounter. It provides gasoline, diesel and pump-out. The marina

has approximately 200 slips ranging in size from 30 to 60 feet. Transient dockage is usually available. Dockside utilities include water, electricity (30 A & 50 A), telephone and cable TV hookups and Wi-Fi Internet. There is a beautiful clubhouse that has a ship's store, a couple of lounges, a conference room, kitchen, laundry, and rest rooms with separate showers and dressing rooms. Off-season storage is provided with a 35-ton Travelift. A large 120-by-180-foot building provides additional heated indoor storage. As a full-service marina they can provide everything from simple boat maintenance to complete engine (diesel and gasoline) repairs and replacement. Their skilled technicians can perform electrical, plumbing, carpentry, and fiberglass repairs. They can also service air conditioning, electrical power generation, water making, sanitation and other vessel systems. The marina monitors Channel 16 or can be contacted by telephone: 715-779-3900. Adjacent to the marina is Waterford on the Bay, a luxury 49-townhome development built in the New England seaboard style. Of special interest is a lovely walking trail that begins at the eastern end of Waterford on the Bay that follows the lake into town. It runs approximately two miles and parts of it are laid on the old railway bed that used to service the area.

Before leaving the this area it is important to mention that just a few miles inland is the site of the Big Top Chautauqua (715-373-5552) where unique musical productions are produced under an open-air tent during the summer. With a varied schedule featuring local and nationally known artists, performances run Wednesday through Saturday nights with occasional matinees. Some of the programs portray past life in the islands, Bayfield and the surrounding area with song, humor, and visual effects. In particular, the flagship show that started it all, "Riding the Wind," should not be missed. It depicts Bayfield and the Apostle Islands in the early years of lighthouses, sailing ships and logging. It plays about five to 10 times each season. The "Bayfield experience" isn't really complete without a trip to the Chautauqua.

Madeline Island Yacht Club: Across the channel from the mainland on Madeline Island lies one of the most beautiful marine facilities on Lake Superior. This completely landlocked yacht club is located just to the southeast of the small town of La Pointe and is within easy walking distance of the town.

In approaching the yacht club there are three lights. A flashing green light is located at the south end of the city dock approximately one-half mile NW of the

NOT TO BE USED FOR NAVIGATION – SKETCH APPROXIMATE

Figure 4.6
Madeline Island Yacht Club

N

Fl W
*

F

Fl R
*

10

10

10

10

10

8

10

KEY
F Fuel
* Privately maintained

GPS	Lat.	Lon.
▲	46°46.37' N	90°47.03' W

Soundings in feet.

yacht club entrance. An outer detached breakwater is marked with white lights that are privately maintained. The actual yacht club entrance is marked by a flashing white light and a green square day marker on the north breakwater and a flashing red light and red triangle day marker on the south breakwater, all privately maintained. (See Fig. 4.8.)

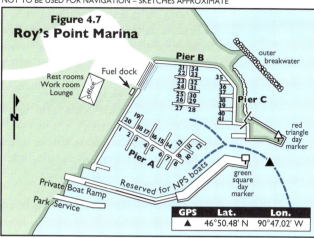

Figure 4.7
Roy's Point Marina

The 150-slip facility is well equipped with diesel, gasoline, electricity, water, pump-out, rest rooms and showers, and often has slips available for transients (contact on VHF channel 16). It also has a very complete marine parts and service department along with a 35-ton Travelift. The service department provides most boat repairs: fiberglass, painting, engine maintenance and welding. Adjacent to the marina is a country club with a beautiful golf course and tennis courts that are open to the public. There are a number of good eating spots within walking distance making the yacht club an attractive place to spend an evening ashore. The marina can be reached by VHF Channel 16 or telephone: 715-747-2655.

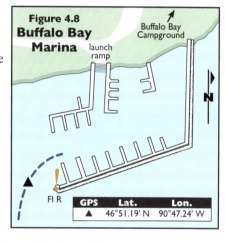

Figure 4.8
Buffalo Bay Marina

Roy's Point Marina: Two-and-one-half miles north of Bayfield there is another marina at Roy's Point (seasonal Tel.: 715-779-5025). Built in the mid-1990s, the marina has 41 slips, a couple of which are rented to the National Park Service. With 8-foot depths throughout, the marina provides diesel, gasoline, pump-out, water, electricity, ice and even cable TV hook-up at each slip. An attractive two-story building houses offices, rest rooms with showers and a pleasant boaters' lounge. In the lower level there is also a workroom where boaters can work on their own projects. There is a small convenience store north of the marina entrance on Highway 13. Note that because of its size, room for maneuvering boats 35 feet or larger may be difficult. This becomes especially apparent if there is any kind of wind blowing.

Buffalo Bay Marina (sometimes called the Red Cliff Marina): This marina (Tel.: 715-779-3712), constructed in the early 1980s, is located on the mainland midway between Bayfield and Schooner Bay approximately one-half mile north of Roy's Point. The marina is formed by a large L-shaped breakwater extending

out from the mainland and is marked with a red flashing light that is kept to starboard when entering. There are approximately 40 slips available with space provided for transients. Electricity and water are provided at some of the slips. Although there are no hauling facilities here, there is a small boat launching ramp and a place to leave boat trailers. (See Fig. 4.8).

Adjacent to the marina is the Red Cliff Campground, which consists of approximately 40 units and provides the use of a beautiful barbecue and picnic area. Within the campground are shower and laundry facilities that are also available to those who use the marina. The area is owned and operated by the Red Cliff Band of Lake Superior Chippewa.

Schooner Bay Marina: This is another small marina located on the Red Cliff or West Channel from Bayfield, just south of Red Cliff Point. The approach and the area rounding the breakwater that forms the harbor was dredged to 7 to 8 feet in 2007. Because of shoaling within the bay just outside the marina, it is important to follow a narrow-buoyed channel going in with the red nun kept to starboard. There is a gate in the middle of the breakwater that is kept in the closed position. For nighttime approaches, there is a reflective chevron on the gate that lines up with a range on shore — course

NOT TO BE USED FOR NAVIGATION – SKETCH APPROXIMATE

270° T. After clearing the buoys, the approach is to hug the breakwater very close around to the north. Even with this track, there will be some 5-foot-plus readings over gravel especially in low water years. (See Fig. 4.9).

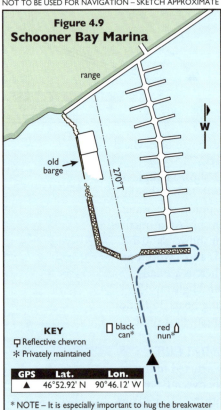

Figure 4.9
Schooner Bay Marina

range

old barge

270° T

KEY
⬜ Reflective chevron
＊ Privately maintained

⬜ black can＊   red 🛆 nun＊

GPS	Lat.	Lon.
▲	46°52.92' N	90°46.12' W

* NOTE – It is especially important to hug the breakwater closely when coming in and rounding up into the harbor.

The marina has approximately 50 slips and provides electricity, water, rest rooms and showers. Launching and haulouts are limited to boats up to 40 feet. The small creek that empties into this bay is very interesting to explore by dinghy and is often abundant with waterfowl and wildlife.

Chartering/Sailing Schools in the Apostles: With more than 100 boats to choose from, numerous fleets and sailing schools, chartering is becoming an increasingly popular way in which to enjoy the islands. The oldest and largest fleet is Superior Charters, (800-772-5124 or 715-779-5124), located at Port Superior. The fleet consists of both power and sail that range from 24 to 44 feet. Boats can be chartered bareboat or with a captain; day or overnight charters including trips. For those who are just beginning sailing or want to brush up on their skills, Superior Charters offers a number of different courses taught by U.S. Coast Guard-licensed captains.

Apostle Islands Charters (612-423-1410) is located next door In the Pike's Bay Marina. It has bareboat and captained charters with boats that are 26 - 41.5 feet, including a catamaran. Lake Superior Tall Ships (262-422-0607) is also out of Pike's Bay Marina providing the large boat experience by sailing one of two 60-foot (60 & 65 ft) boats for captained charters. They have day sails and overnight charters including trips to Isle Royale and Grand Marais.

Other sailing charter fleets in the area are All Hands Sailing (715-861-6699) based at the City Dock in Bayfield. They provide bareboat and captained charters with boats 36-38 feet with day and overnight 3–4-day trips. A couple other charter groups are True North Sailing Charters (715-513-6284) based in the town of Bayfield and Superior Sailing (715-821-1151) in the Schooner Bay Marina. Note that many of the charter fleets also have power boats for charter and then there are also those boats that are offered for fishing charters. In addition to these charter fleets there are a number of independent charter groups and sailing schools within the area. Contact with any of the major marinas can put one in touch with these opportunities to cruise the Apostle Islands.

A National Lakeshore

In 1970, 20 of the 22 Apostle Islands along with a 12-mile sector of mainland were established by Congress as a National Lakeshore to preserve and develop the islands for the enjoyment of all. Madeline and Long islands were the only two that were exempt at that time. Then in early 1986, Congress passed legislation to add Long Island to the National Lakeshore. In 2014 the Ashland Harbor Breakwater Light was also added.

The National Lakeshore is administered by the National Park Service. Park headquarters are in the old Bayfield County Courthouse, located in the heart of Bayfield. Built from brownstone quarried at Basswood Island, the building served as the county courthouse from 1883 until 1893, when the county seat was moved to Washburn. This building now houses park offices and a Visitor Center with an information desk, exhibits, an award-winning introductory film on the islands and sales area. The exhibits are especially well-done depicting

---

Figure 4.10
Apostle Islands Recreational User Fees

Overnight Docking (per night)	**Camping (per party per night)**
$15/boat (less than 40' long)	$10/individual or undesignated site
$30/boat (40' and greater)	$20/group site
Interpretive Fees	**Parking (based on vehicle length)**
Regular guided tours and programs	Meyers Beach
$3/person	$3-5 day use
$8/family	$15-25 annual pass
Longer/more in-depth tours	Park Headquarters
$5/person	$5-8 overnight
$12/family	$10-20 special events

the natural history and flora and fauna of the islands. Permits for camping and scuba diving in the National Lakeshore can be acquired here. There are also offices and a Visitor Center located at Little Sand Bay on the mainland. Before visiting the islands it's not a bad idea to check the NPS website for any changes or updates which may have occurred: *www.nps.gov/apis/planyourvisit.*

Beginning in 2007, a User Fee Schedule was implemented for some of the lakeshore facilities. Boaters are basically affected by overnight docking fees — daytime use of docks remains free. Although the Apostle Islands National Lakeshore has jurisdiction 1/4-mile out from land, there are no fees for boating or anchoring within the lakeshore. Other areas that have user fees are for camping, some interpretative programs and parking on some lakeshore/park property. (See Figure 4.10.) Fees can be paid at Park Headquarters, at Little Sand Bay and possibly some marinas. Boaters also have a couple of additional options since they do not always know ahead of time that they are going to be staying overnight at a dock. Self-payment containers will be established at each dock for cash payment. Again, it's important to periodically check the park website for changes in fee structure/prices and methods of payment.

The fees are used primarily to help defray general maintenance costs of docks, trails, camping/picnic areas and preservation of historic buildings and cultural landscapes. It should be noted that out of response to public input this fee structure is a compromise falling short of needed funds. However, all funds collected in the Apostle Islands will stay in the islands with low overhead to make them go as far as possible. Additional contributions towards these ends can be made to Friends of the Apostle Islands (*www.friendsoftheapostleislands.org*) to become a member and obtain a Voluntary Passport. This group works closely with NPS, and contributions are tax deductible.

It is important to note that although the islands are now part of the National Lakeshore, there are still parts that remain reserved for private use due to the "use and occupancy" provisions provided by the Park Service to those who had holdings before park acquisition. Thus, a few of the small docks and small areas (on Sand, Rocky and Bear Islands) are still private inholdings. These properties will eventually become full parts of the park when the leases expire. There are also certain sections of the islands that are restricted for ecological reasons. Since these are often subject to change, it is wise to confer with park personnel before entering any of these areas.

Figure 4.11
Hiking Trails in the Apostles

Basswood Island – 5.5 mi	Outer Island – 8.7 mi
Devils Island – 5.5 mi	Raspberry Island – 1.75 mi
Madeline Island (*) – @ 1 mi	Rocky Island – 1.4 mi
Manitou Island – 2.75 mi	Sand Island – 2.3 mi
Michigan Island –i @ 1 mi	South Twin Island – 0.25 mi
Oak Island – 11 mi	Stockton Island – 14.5 mi
Otter Island – 1.9 mi	

To assist in preserving the natural beauty of the islands and the safety of those who cruise within them, the National Park Service has established a few guidelines or regulations for those who use the area. Basic to the preservation of the islands is a "pack in & pack out" policy which means that visitors are expected to take all of their garbage and refuse out with them. There are limited garbage facilities at some of the campgrounds, but these are only for campers using the site. Likewise, fires must be contained within established fire rings or grills at most locations. Those who have boat barbecues are asked to use them only at anchor and not at any of the docks. This is not only because most of the docks are constructed of wood, but because they are also areas where there usually is a large congestion of boats within a small, restricted area. Pets are required to be on leashes when on docks and on the islands. Finally, it should be noted that the use of drones, with or without cameras, is catching on throughout the US, both with boaters and campers. However, in keeping with the wildlife emphasis that National Parks support, the use of drones in all National Parks, including the Apostle Islands National Lakeshore, is prohibited.

In the interest of safety, a life jacket must be provided for each person on any boat, including dinghies. Dinghies used after dark must display some type of white light — flashlights are permitted. Anchor lights are required on any anchored boat between sunset and sunrise. This is especially important since more boaters are taking to the islands in the early evening — especially on Friday nights so they can have more time in the islands. And sometimes there is a fair amount of boat movement in the middle of the night when boaters are forced to change anchorages because of changing weather systems. Finally, it should be noted that it is Wisconsin law that any motorized boat, regardless of size (and this includes dinghies with a motor), must have a Wisconsin registration stamp and numbers printed visibly on the hull. The Park Service has been given the authority to see that these regulations are enforced, so boaters should be forewarned that citations may be given when infractions are incurred.

During the cruising season (May to October), naturalists and park rangers may be found throughout the islands to aid the public in their enjoyment of the area. Nature walks, evening campfire programs and natural and cultural history lectures on the islands are all a part of the park's interpretative program. To assist the NPS in this important facet of park management and interpretation is the park's Volunteers In Parks (VIP) program. This program consists of seasonal volunteers who staff various locations in the islands, including several lighthouses. It is important to note that rangers with well-equipped patrol boats roam the islands and often assist visitors during boating and medical emergencies. Rangers monitor marine Channel 16 and work closely with the U.S. Coast Guard in most search and rescue situations that occur in the area.

The NPS has also made a number of improvements throughout the islands that greatly enhance the visitor's enjoyment of the area. Of special interest to the boater are the number of docks that have

been built and renovated on many of the islands. In the mid-1970s there were only a handful of docks that a deep keel boat could be tied to. By the end of the 1980s, depending on boat draft, there were well over a dozen docks that could be used for overnight dockage.

At a number of these spots, the NPS has made special efforts to preserve and restore historical aspects of the islands. Of these, special mention must be made of the restoration of the lighthouse complex on Raspberry Island, the fishing station on Manitou Island and the Hokenson Fishery at the Little Sand Bay docks. With careful attention to authentic detail, these restorations provide a glimpse of what it was like to live and work in the islands in the decades of yesteryear.

Another area in which the National Park Service has done an exceptional job is in the number of campsites and trails it has established throughout the islands. (See Fig. 4.11.) Those without boats can take an excursion boat or a water taxi out to many different islands and experience them through camping in one of the designated sites or backcountry areas. Boaters can dinghy ashore after a brisk sail and hike a trail to an old quarry or through a wild marsh. One of the nicest things about cruising in the Apostles is the variety of experiences that are possible. You can gather at one of the favorite spots in the islands such as the Rocky or Stockton docks and share in the camaraderie of fellow sailors on a Saturday night. Or you can get lost in many of the wilderness areas: walk a lonely beach, hike a trail to a remote lighthouse or watch a great blue heron take flight over a tranquil lagoon.

Islands and Anchorages
(In alphabetical order)

Note: included in this section are sketch charts of public docks with soundings. While every effort has been made toward accuracy, it is important to note that around a number of these docks considerable silting-in has occurred in recent years that affects these soundings. Most noticeable are those docks at Basswood, Michigan, Sand and South Twin. In particular, refer to soundings taken at South Twin (Fig. 4.41) in recent years. The decision was made to include the dock sketch charts and soundings, since they may be beneficial to those with boats of varying drafts, yet boaters should be aware that some of these soundings are subject to change due to silting effects. For a summary of public docks in the Apostle Islands see Figure 4.46. For a full perspective of all the islands, see Figure 4.12.

Basswood Island is the first island one meets when leaving Bayfield and is often passed by boaters seeking spots farther out in the islands. (See Fig. 4.13.) Lying four miles NE of Bayfield, it bisects the two main channels that lead into Bayfield, the North Channel (sometimes called the Main Channel) and the West

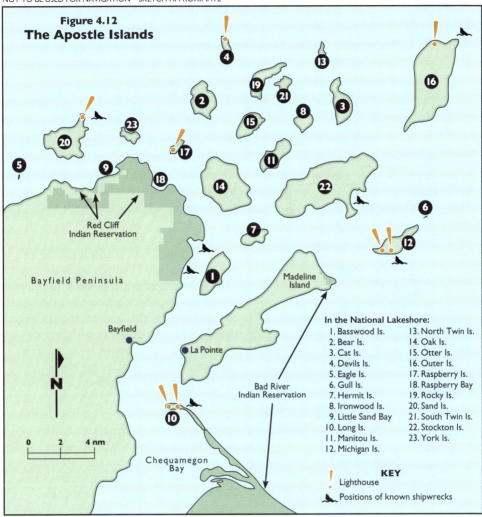

Figure 4.12
The Apostle Islands

Red Cliff
Indian Reservation

Bayfield Peninsula

Bayfield

La Pointe

N

Madeline
Island

Bad River
Indian Reservation

Chequamegon
Bay

0   2   4 nm

In the National Lakeshore:

1. Basswood Is.	13. North Twin Is.
2. Bear Is.	14. Oak Is.
3. Cat Is.	15. Otter Is.
4. Devils Is.	16. Outer Is.
5. Eagle Is.	17. Raspberry Is.
6. Gull Is.	18. Raspberry Bay
7. Hermit Is.	19. Rocky Is.
8. Ironwood Is.	20. Sand Is.
9. Little Sand Bay	21. South Twin Is.
10. Long Is.	22. Stockton Is.
11. Manitou Is.	23. York Is.
12. Michigan Is.	

KEY

Lighthouse

Positions of known shipwrecks

Channel (sometimes called the Red Cliff Channel). At the north end of the island there is a short, picturesque sea stack called Honeymoon Rock. In the past, there were sandstone quarries along the SE end of the island, one of which was the first quarry opened in the islands in the late 1860s. There was also some logging done on the island and even a couple of small farms until the mid-1900s.

Today there are a few trails on the island leading to these areas and a dock. The dock (a 100-foot wooden structure) is found approximately one-third of the way up from the southern tip of the island on its west side. Depending on water depths, boats drawing up to 4 feet can tie up to the outer sides of this dock. (See Fig. 4.14.) Although this dock is often used as a "lunch-stop," it can also be used (with caution to the weather) for those with shoal draft boats who want to get "out into the islands quickly," i.e., first night/late start. It is also not unusual to see boats anchored off to

either side of the dock. A five-and-one-half-mile trail leads north from the dock area to the McCloud-Brigham farmstead then east to the shoreline and south along the east side of the island to the sandstone quarry before turning north to the dock. A short loop off this trail at the south end of the island leads to 4 shoreline campsites, a vault toilet and a natural rock landing the dock area also has 2 campsites, one group campsite, and a vault toilet. Important Note: *the Basswood dock is best used for overnight stays with easterly winds.* The fetch for southerly and northerly winds can make a stay at this dock quite uncomfortable.

NOT TO BE USED FOR NAVIGATION – SKETCHES APPROXIMATE

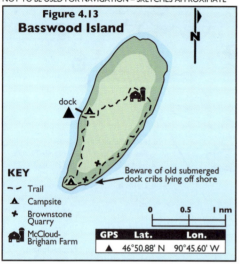

Figure 4.13
Basswood Island

KEY
- ~ ~ Trail
- ▲ Campsite
- ✳ Brownstone Quarry
- 🏠 McCloud-Brigham Farm

Beware of old submerged dock cribs lying off shore

0   0.5   1 nm

GPS	Lat.	Lon.
▲	46°50.88' N	90°45.60' W

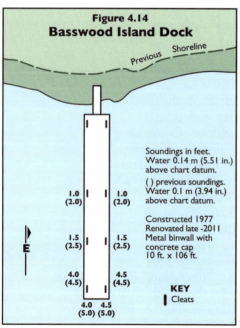

Figure 4.14
Basswood Island Dock

Previous Shoreline

Soundings in feet.
Water 0.14 m (5.51 in.) above chart datum.
( ) previous soundings.
Water 0.1 m (3.94 in.) above chart datum.

Constructed 1977 Renovated late -2011 Metal binwall with concrete cap 10 ft. x 106 ft.

1.0 (2.0)		1.0 (2.0)
1.5 (2.5)		1.5 (2.5)
4.0 (4.5)		4.5 (4.5)
4.0 (5.0)		4.5 (5.0)

E

KEY
❚ Cleats

Another island that isn't often visited by boaters is **Bear Island,** even though there are at least two good spots that provide good anchoring and two-sided protection. (See Fig. 4.15.) The first is to the east of the small sandspit off the SE end of the island. The water shoals rapidly here, but with care it is possible to creep in and get two-sided protection. Best used as a lunch-stop, this is another anchorage that should be used for overnight only with a cautious eye to the weather. The sandspit area is transitioning from "use and occupancy" arrangement and is not open to camping.

The other anchorage on Bear Island is the little "bay" on its NE end that provides protection for SE through westerly winds. There is enough space here for a couple of boats to tuck in with 10 to 12 feet of depth. Note that the bottom here is smooth sandstone covered only by a thin layer of sand, so it should be used cautiously as an anchorage. Eddying currents around the peninsula projecting to the NE, plus the possibility of large rollers off the lake, can make this anchorage uncomfortable (as in Julian Bay off Stockton Island). In the middle of the bay there is a small sand beach and a small stream emptying into the western end. The small peninsula is made of rock ledges that are interesting to walk on. Bear Island is one of the highest in the Apostles, second only to Oak.

Located approximately six miles east of Bear Island is **Cat Island,** which, as far as holding ground is concerned, has a couple of marginal anchorages and a couple of good anchorages. In all of the anchorages but one, the protection is scant two-sided and in the other it is scant three-sided. (See Fig. 4.16.)

The three-sided anchorage lies in the "neck of the cat" in the bight on the island's NE end. This is one anchorage where the protection looks better on the charts than it actually is. Because of the long gradual sweep of the bay to the SE, the protection here isn't as complete as one would expect. The sand bottom near the northern end is also punctuated with small boulders and gravel, so setting an anchor down in the right spot can be a challenge. However, because of the clear Lake Superior waters (if no seas are running), it is usually possible to see and select a patch of sand in which to set an anchor. It is interesting to note that there used to be a fish camp located in this bay with a trail to the other side. It's hard to find much now because of overgrowth. The shoreline here is rugged sand beach with plenty of driftwood. This quickly gives way to a heavily forested area.

The indentation that is located on the other side of the northern end of Cat Island is also sometimes used for anchoring. Again, you have to pick your holding ground, but patches of sand in 15 to 20 feet of water can be found amidst the rocky bottom. There have been reports of a large boulder somewhere near the center, but it's exact location is unknown. With barely two-sided protection, alternative anchorages should be kept in mind.

At the SE end of Cat Island there is a beautiful little sandspit that offers more protection than one would believe by just looking at the charts. On either side, depending on the wind, it is possible to get in close and anchor in 10 feet over a clear, sand-rippled bottom. Although there is little more than one-sided protection in either case, some wind change protection can be regained by simply moving to the other side, thus the spit actually gives protection for all but southerly winds. If this is done, however, care should be taken to give the spit wide berth (at least a quarter mile), since the shoaling does continue out quite a way beyond the point.

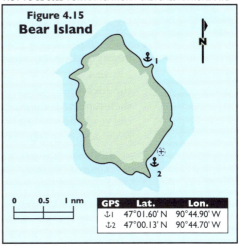

Figure 4.15
Bear Island

GPS	Lat.	Lon.
⚓1	47°01.60' N	90°44.90' W
⚓2	47°00.13' N	90°44.70' W

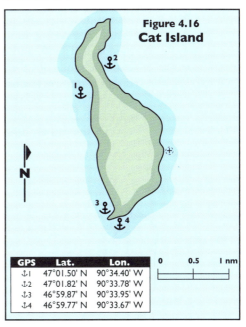

Figure 4.16
Cat Island

GPS	Lat.	Lon.
⚓1	47°01.50' N	90°34.40' W
⚓2	47°01.82' N	90°33.78' W
⚓3	46°59.87' N	90°33.95' W
⚓4	46°59.77' N	90°33.67' W

On shore, there used to be an old fishing shack that showed signs of occasional use by hunters and fishermen. Because of high water in the mid-1980s and subsequent erosion of the shoreline, it began to slide into the lake and was thus condemned and removed. However, in the late 1980s, the NPS built a log cabin structure on the site, fondly called the Cat House by some. It was locked and then removed sometime prior to 2010. There also used to be an old road and a number of trails on this end of the island, remnants from when the island was logged — as recently as the 1950s. These are quite overgrown now and difficult to find.

One of the most distinguishing features of the Apostles is the intricate cave-like formations and arches that are carved in the sandstone by the action of the lake. Many of the islands' northern shores are exposed to the open waters of the greater lake. These areas are the recipients of the lake's unleashed fury in its treacherous winter storms. Although many of the islands exhibit these varied formations, there are none that can exceed the caves at **Devils Island,** the northernmost island of the Apostles. Part of this is that the Devils Island sandstone is more thinly bedded and easily eroded than the sandstone formation of the other islands. Another reason is that it receives the full brunt, force of the high rollers coming off the greater lake before they are broken down by the outer Islands (of which Devils is one) and reach the inner islands. (See Fig. 4.17.)

To the earliest inhabitants, the island seemed to possess supernatural powers. A visit to the caves via a dinghy or small boat quickly reveals why. Large areas open up underneath striated cliffs and awesome overhanging arches, often leading from one "room" to another. Equally dramatic formations can be seen below in Lake Superior's crystal-clear waters reflecting pastel greens, blues and golds. Eerie sounds of water dripping from overhead, combined with the echoes of water surging in and out of the caverns, lend a mystical quality to this whole end of the island. The Ojibwe name for the island is *metchimanitou miniss* meaning Island of Evil Spirit.

Another attraction on the island is the Devils Island Light Station. The light station was established in 1891 and staffed until 1978, when it was automated along with a number of other lighthouses in the U.S. sector of the lake. The light station is also important as the site of a foghorn. The grounds consist of a number of structures that include

NOT TO BE USED FOR NAVIGATION – SKETCH APPROXIMATE

Figure 4.17
Devils Island

RACON
Fl R 10s
100 ft.
23 St M
Horn

caves & arches

Campsite

South Landing

N

GPS	Lat.	Lon.
▲1	47°03.73' N	90°43.70' W
▲2	47°04.83' N	90°43.60' W

0   0.5   1 nm

the fog signal, light tower, tram building, oil houses and two Queen Anne-style brick homes that used to house light-keeping personnel. The NPS has improved a number of the trails that lead to the cliffs and one that goes to a natural landing on the NE end of the island. Note that the rock ledges overhanging the caves are soft sandstone and often under cut, so care should be taken when exploring the cliffs' edges and stay away from those areas marked "hazardous." Sometimes during the summer there has been a resident volunteer on

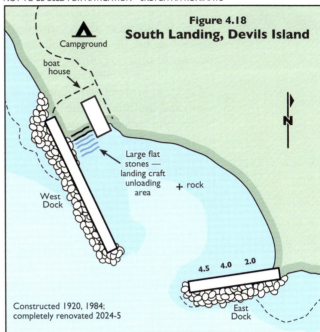

Figure 4.18
South Landing, Devils Island

Campground

boat house

Large flat stones — landing craft unloading area

+ rock

West Dock

N

4.5   4.0   2.0

East Dock

Constructed 1920, 1984; completely renovated 2024-5

station to give guided tours and answer visitors' questions.

To visit the caves and light, there are a couple of options. On a clear day with no sea running, it is possible to anchor off the northern end of Devils Island. It may, however, be difficult to find a patch of sand among the prevalent boulders that are scattered along this section of the shore. It must be emphasized that anchoring here must be done in only calm conditions, since along this northern end of Devils you are also vulnerable to the open lake. Another option lies to the east of the light on the NE end of the island where there are a number of flat rock ledges sometimes called "The Flats." It is possible for boats to edge in closely here for disembarking. Care must be taken if this is done, because a surge can quite easily develop off the lake. It is unwise to leave a boat unattended here. The ledges shift over the winter, so watch the depth very carefully.

At the southern end of Devils there is a small "harbor" that was used by the Coast Guard when it staffed the lighthouse. (See Fig. 4.18.) A road that runs longitudinally through the island connects the harbor with the light on the northern end. Although the harbor is secure for all but strong southerly winds, depending on water depths, its use is limited to boats drawing less than 4 feet. It also must be approached with caution since there are a number of sizable boulders just outside the entrance. The boathouse is of historic interest and has recently been upgraded. There is a small campsite near the dock. Do not attempt to enter or leave this harbor if a strong southerly wind is blowing. Note: this little harbor and docks were completely rebuilt in 2024-25.

The most westerly island of the Apostles is **Eagle Island.** It is also the second smallest, just more than 20 acres. The island is a nesting site for herring gulls and double-crested cormorants. Because of this, no camping is allowed on the island and boaters are restricted from coming closer than 500 feet during nesting periods (May 15 to September 1). Because of shoaling extending to the south and southwest of the island, it is usually given wide berth by boaters and seen only in passing to or from Cornucopia, which lies to the west of the Apostles. Note: on the mainland shoreline south of Eagle Island there is another stretch of beautiful sea caves in the recently renamed *Mawikwe* Bay (which means "weeping woman" in Ojibwe, replacing the former and derogatory term "Squaw"). There is also a trail here following the shoreline. This area (Meyers Beach) can be reached from the highway by car.

Gull Island is the smallest island in the Apostles, a scant 200 yards long. Located off the northern tip of Michigan Island, it often looks like a ship when viewed from the islands looking outward toward the open lake. It is also another nesting site for herring gulls and cormorants, so is restricted to boaters. Therefore, boats are not allowed to approach closer than 500 feet during the nesting season from May 15 to September 1. Nor would you want to. The waters surrounding Gull Island are quite shoaled and to the south fouled with rock. It is not advisable for even very shoal draft boats to try to pass between Gull and Michigan islands. Thus, this is one of the few spots in the islands that is usually given wide berth by passing boaters. It may be of interest to note that this area has also had a history of being troublesome in the past. In 1865, Alexander McDougall (who was then the first mate on the steamer *Iron City*) recorded: "In approaching the Apostle Islands, it was smoky and, my eyes dim, I made a mistake in the island we were to pass and up she slid on the rocky, gravel bottom of Gull Island Shoal among thousands of gulls." Today, the island is marked with a white flashing light.

Hermit Island has some of the most enticing history of all the islands in the Apostles. There are at least two stories of hidden treasure on the island. The first deals with an army payroll, stolen from a French paymaster and supposedly buried on the island in the 1700s.

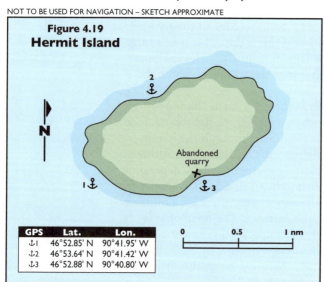

Figure 4.19
Hermit Island

Abandoned quarry

GPS	Lat.	Lon.
⚓1	46°52.85' N	90°41.95' W
⚓2	46°53.64' N	90°41.42' W
⚓3	46°52.88' N	90°40.80' W

0   0.5   1 nm

The second story tells of a hermit (hence the name of the island) named Wilson who moved to the island to live out his days after he had been extradited from the settlement on Madeline Island in the early 1840s. After his death, stories of buried treasure brought many fortune seekers who nearly dug up the entire island. There is little probability that either treasure story was true. Subsequently, nothing was ever found, and today the National Park Service prohibits any further searching. Note: these stories are unsubstantiated. But you have to admit, they do make for a good telling.

The island is also interesting in that along its southern shore, in the middle of the island, a sandstone quarry was established in the late 1800s. At one time there was even a lodge here to house the approximately 100 men who worked at the productive quarry. From time to time, there have been other buildings on the island, the most famous of which was the Cedar Bark Lodge. Built in the 1890s by Frederick Prentice, owner of the quarry, this impressive three-story structure was used until the 1930s. The island was even plotted with streets and names in the early 1900s as part of an enterprise by a land developer.

Today the island has a few overgrown trails on its western side. Remains of the quarry can be seen as huge sandstone blocks when you pass close along the southern shore. The quarry is an interesting place to explore with a dinghy. The huge sandstone blocks are individually numbered and are still piled up, waiting for shipment since the turn of the 20th century. Primitive camping is allowed on certain sections of the island, but not in areas near the quarry.

With stable weather conditions, boats can sometimes snug up to the shores of Hermit for an overnight. Fair holding ground can be found off the SW end and the middle of the island's northern and southern shores. The northeast end of the island displays the usual carved-out formations of sandstone found along the northern sides of many of the Apostles. Care should be taken in approaching these, for there are a number of large underwater boulders. In anchoring off Hermit, it is again important to watch the weather since the protection is one-sided only and weather systems are known to change abruptly in this part of the lake.

Located in the heart of the Apostles there is another island, **Ironwood,** which is often passed by because of the lack of a hospitable shoreline to boaters. There is, however, a small sand point at the southern end, similar to the one on Cat, that does provide good anchoring with a good

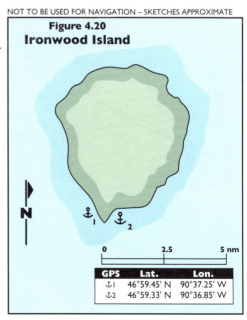

NOT TO BE USED FOR NAVIGATION – SKETCHES APPROXIMATE

Figure 4.20
Ironwood Island

N

0   2.5   5 nm

GPS	Lat.	Lon.
⚓1	46°59.45' N	90°37.25' W
⚓2	46°59.33' N	90°36.85' W

holding sand bottom. (See Fig. 4.20.) Although the protection is only one- or two-sided, it is possible to anchor on either side of the point, getting protection from northerly winds. Because of a sandbar extending quite a ways south of the point, it is important to give this wide berth when changing to the other side in case of a wind switch. There is also a primitive campsite not too far from shore for those who are doing boat camping. All trails on the island have been long overgrown, but the clearing near the sand point is indicative of the days when the island was used for logging enterprises. The name Ironwood comes from an Ojibwe translation that reflects a tree that was once found here with wood as hard as iron.

A manned ranger station and patrol boat are located at **Little Sand Bay** on the mainland at the eastern end of the 12-mile section of shoreline that is also part of the National Lakeshore. (See Fig. 4.21.) Little Sand Bay is of interest to boaters for a couple of reasons. First, there is an all-weather dock complex which is available for overnight transient dockage. (Note: two slips are reserved for NPS boats.) Of the two dock areas one sees in approaching, the Park Service dock is the most easterly one. Although inner harbor depths can accommodate boats drawing up to 5 feet, recent years have seen considerable shoaling at the entrance — less than 4 feet. The National Park Service dredges the harbor every few years to restore the depth to between 4 and 5 feet. In 2024-25 the dock structure in Little Sand Bay was completely renovated. Part of the renovation was the construction of a long breakwater entrance into the lake built perpendicular to oncoming waves to prevent the buildup of silting. For boats drawing more than depths will allow it is possible to anchor off to the side and get protection for south and east winds.

Adjacent to the dock are picnic tables with grills. There is also a Visitor Center, built in 2020, that has a number of outdoor displays illustrating different aspects of the islands' natural and human history. The large anchor seen out in front is from the *Sevona*, an ore carrier wrecked on

NOT TO BE USED FOR NAVIGATION – SKETCH APPROXIMATE

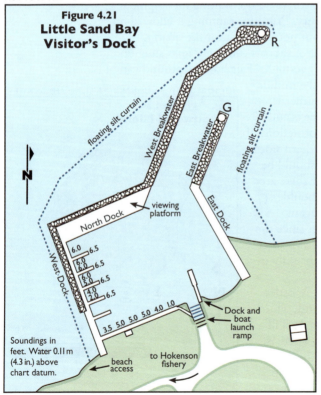

Figure 4.21
Little Sand Bay
Visitor's Dock

the Sand Island Shoals in 1905.

Another attraction to Little Sand Bay is the restored Hokenson Fishery located to the west of the Park Service Dock. This whole complex has been meticulously restored by the Park Service to preserve one of the major fisheries in the area. It is complete with a twine shed, icehouse, dock and herring shed. Of special interest is the *Twilite,* a 38-foot diesel tug that was built in 1937 by the Hokenson brothers and their cousin Halvor Reiten of Bayfield. For more than three decades, the Hokenson brothers successfully fished the surrounding waters, processed fish in the herring shed to prevent spoilage and then marketed them in nearby Cornucopia. Guided tours of the Hokenson Fishery may be available June through September. (Note: the dock that is part of the restoration is not available for transient use.)

Long Island is an interesting place to visit because of its long, low beaches and marshy areas. Although it is just a few miles across the bay from one of the busiest marinas in the area, it remains one of the wilder pristine spots in the Apostles. (See Fig. 4.22.) Depending on lake levels, Long Island is usually an extension of Chequamegon Point on the mainland. However, when the water level rises, it becomes separated from the main point. This low-lying area between the two is an important nesting habitat for a federally protected endangered rare bird species, the piping plover. While dogs must be on leashes everywhere with the National Lakeshore, it is especially important on Long Island to prevent disturbances to the plovers. This is the only place that this bird nests in the state of Wisconsin. Portions of the island are heavily infested with poison ivy, so it's important to be on a careful lookout when going ashore.

In 1986, Congress passed legislation to add Long Island to the National Lakeshore.

The island is marked by two distinctive lights on its northern side. At the far western tip of the island is Chequamegon Point Light, which over the years has withstood considerable damage from high water. In 1987 a new light was established atop a D9 Cylindrical tower at Chequamegon Point. The old iron tower was relocated by helicopter 100 feet inland to protect it from the eroding shoreline.

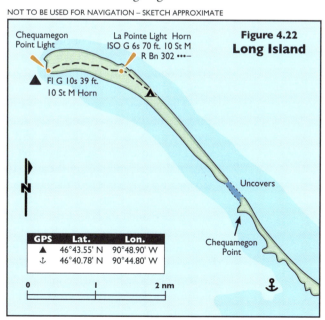

NOT TO BE USED FOR NAVIGATION – SKETCH APPROXIMATE

Chequamegon Point Light

La Pointe Light Horn
ISO G 6s 70 ft. 10 St M
R Bn 302 •••−

Figure 4.22
Long Island

Fl G 10s 39 ft.
10 St M Horn

Uncovers

Chequamegon Point

GPS	Lat.	Lon.
▲	46°43.55' N	90°48.90' W
⚓	46°40.78' N	90°44.80' W

0   1   2 nm

Approximately one mile to the east in the middle of the island's northern side is La Pointe Light. Both lights flash green, and both are equipped with foghorns which by 2024 were no longer working. A boardwalk has been established between the lights.

Because of shoal water around Long Island, it may be difficult to approach and get in very close. An exception is in the area adjacent to the La Pointe Light, where it is possible to anchor somewhat close to shore in 10 to 15 feet of water over a sand bottom. There is a steel dock here that in the past was very high, decayed and a hazard to docking. However, in the winter of 1999/2000 it was renovated by lowering it approximately 4 feet and removing 80 feet of the outer structure. The cut-off steel piles were retained to support a new concrete-and-steel deck. The resulting dock is 60 feet long. However, shore changes in recent years have made the dock unusable and it is recommended using a dinghy to get ashore. This is an interesting place to dinghy in and explore. There is a boardwalk and path over to the other side. There is also a trail from Chequamegon Point Light to slightly past LaPointe Light. This area to the north of Long Island is only considered as an overnight anchorage when southerly winds are assured.

With care, a more secure anchorage can be found on the southern side of Long Island, tucked in behind Chequamegon Point. Although the water is quite shallow, by having someone in the bow, it is possible to creep a good way in and still maintain 8 feet to 10 feet of water for anchoring. For more information on Long Island see Chapter Three.)

Of all the islands, **Madeline Island,** largest of the Apostles, is the most richly steeped in colorful history. In fact, more is probably written about Madeline Island than any other area in western Lake Superior. (See Fig. 4.23.) Long considered the home of the Ojibwe tribe, the southern end of the island was the site of a permanent town for more than three generations (120 years). Only after guilt-ridden dreams from the spirits of the dead were the people dispersed in the early 1600s. (See introduction to this chapter.)

There is some conjecture that Etienne Brulé may have visited this part of the lake around 1620 and was thus the first white man seen by the Native Americans in this area. Following Radisson's and Des Groseilliers' epic trip along the south shore and winter stay in the Ashland area in the mid-1600s, the Jesuits were quick to open up this section of the lake to further exploration. As early as 1663, Father Claude Allouez established a mission on the island which he named La Pointe du Saint Esprits. Following the early explorers and missionaries who had left their mark, a trading post was established in 1693 and then a French fort in the early 1700s. With these crude beginnings, the Chippewa were encouraged to come back, white men continued to arrive, and La Pointe became the key center or crossroads for further exploration and development of the lake.

The fur trading companies, first the North West and then the American Fur Company, headed by John Jacob Astor from 1808 to 1834, chose this port as a central depot for their northern operations. Retired voyageurs and *coureurs des bois* made La Pointe their home, often intermarrying with the Chippewa. Missions were established in the early 1800s, and it was here that Father Frederic Baraga, the "Snowshoe Priest," began his long and selfless work in 1835 as benefactor of the native people. When the fur companies expanded their interests to include commercial fishing in the 1830s, La Pointe was again chosen as a major post in the operations. By that time, a large dock had been built, along with warehouses, cooper shops, stores and even a hotel accompanied by numerous small houses.

As a reflection of its varied history, Madeline Island has had a number of different names in the 300 years since the first explorers arrived on its shores. Before this, the Ojibwe gave the island the special name, *Mon-ing-wun-a-kaun-ing,* which translated means "place of the golden-breasted woodpecker" after the Northern Flicker that is found on the island in large numbers during fall migration. For a long time, Madeline was called the Island of La Pointe because it was located opposite the "long pointe of land which juts out in the lake," Long Island. The name La Pointe also became synonymous with the name Chequamegon, derived from a Ojibwe word meaning "soft beaver dam" in reference to this long spit of land. Eventually, the name La Pointe was used solely for the

NOT TO BE USED FOR NAVIGATION – SKETCH APPROXIMATE

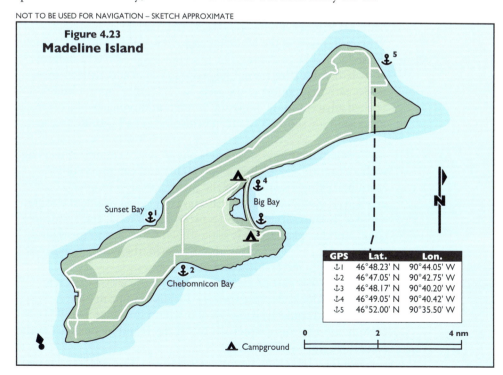

Figure 4.23
Madeline Island

Sunset Bay

Big Bay

Chebomnicon Bay

GPS	Lat.	Lon.
⚓1	46°48.23' N	90°44.05' W
⚓2	46°47.05' N	90°42.75' W
⚓3	46°48.17' N	90°40.20' W
⚓4	46°49.05' N	90°40.42' W
⚓5	46°52.00' N	90°35.50' W

0   2   4 nm

▲ Campground

settlement on the southern end of the island. The name "Madeline" goes back to a man named Michael Cadotte, who, along with John Johnston, was an agent for the North West Company. At the time Johnston visited the island in the late 1700s, it was called Montreal Island. Cadotte married the Native American chief's daughter and changed her native name, *Equaysayway* to the Christian name "Madeline." The chief was so pleased with the marriage that he changed the name of the island to "Madeline."

Today, the island has approximately 300 residents who live on the island year round. Beautiful homes dot the shoreline along the road that circles the island. Big Bay State Park, located on the eastern side of the island, contains a campground, a beautiful sand beach, a lagoon and a shoreline trail and boardwalk. Transportation between the mainland and the island is by ferry and private craft during the summers and as long as Lake Superior's waters remain open. When the lake freezes over, a wind sled and "ice road" marked with Christmas trees are used to cross the channel.

The town of **La Pointe** is a picture of contrasts between the old and the new. Walking down main street, one can easily see how it reflects the characteristics of a rustic New England fishing village. It is not uncommon to see aging, picturesque boats up on the beach in various stages of repair. There is an old log church and a cemetery in which both Native American and white settlers are buried. Michael Cadotte, who died in 1837, and Chief Buffalo, who signed the La Pointe Treaty of 1854, are buried here along with the island's namesake, Madeline. The cemetery has been placed on the National Register of Historic Places. The State Historical Society of Wisconsin operates the Madeline Island Historical Museum, which is also located in La Pointe. The museum has preserved a number of structures (jail, log barn, Old Sailor's Home) and artifacts that reflect early ways of life in the area. In 1991, the Capser Center opened adjacent to the museum. It offers additional exhibits, a lively historical slide show on Madeline's history and a historical research facility.

In sharp contrast, there is the contemporary country club along with a beautiful golf course, tennis courts and condominiums. Within walking distance from the yacht club are a number of excellent restaurants that are well-known for their excellent cuisine and bar. Grampa Tony's provides pizza, Italian food, and a little local color. Another place to eat is at the Beach Club, just to the right of the ferry dock as you land. Within the town, there are a number of interesting gift and craft shops and food stores.

To visit this part of the island by boat, use either the yacht club or city dock. Because the city dock is used primarily by ferries, it is only available for short-term docking. (See introduction to this chapter.) Tours of the island by bus start at the ferry dock during the summer.

Another interesting part of the island to visit is Big Bay, located on the eastern side of Madeline. The bay has three-sided protection with good anchoring throughout over a sand bottom. On shore, spanning the full length of the 1.5-mile bay, there is a beautiful sand beach that provides interesting exploring and walking. Inland from this beach is a large marshy lagoon that is usually abundant with wildlife. Access to this lagoon by

Manitou Island dock and restored fish station. DAHL

dinghy can be found at the northern end of Big Bay where a small stream empties into the lake. A footbridge crosses the stream, but small boats and dinghies are still able to pass under. Note that only electric battery outboards are allowed within the lagoon. Also in this northern section of the bay, there is a long staircase that leads up the cliffs to Big Bay Town Park. Slightly inland from the beach there is a beautiful one-and-one-half-mile boardwalk that meanders among the trees with a couple of loops into the lagoon. There are spurs off the main boardwalk to the beach and these should be used when accessing the boardwalk to avoid damage to fragile vegetation. At the southern end of Big Bay is Big Bay State Park, which also has a picnic area, campground and a number of interesting hiking trails. One goes deep into the interior, another follows the shoreline to the east and south. Although Big Bay does have three-sided protection, it should be remembered that it is wide open to the east, and Madeline Island is a big island to go around, should the winds shift in the middle of the night.

Other areas around Madeline used occasionally for anchoring are found in Chebomnican Bay, which lies SW of Big Bay, Sunset Bay, which lies along the W shore across the island from Chebomnican Bay, and along the NE side of the island. The first two have two-sided protection, the last provides only one. All three have some cottages or homes along the shoreline. The NE anchorage has special importance for those who anchor in Quarry or Presque Isle bays on Stockton. For when a strong SW wind comes raging up the main channel, boaters in these anchorages will often move to this northern end of Madeline Island.

Located in the center of the Apostles, there is another island that reflects an interesting past, **Manitou Island.** (See Fig. 4.24.) This island is of special interest to boaters because of a large dock at its southern end and a restored fishing station. The only hazard found at this end of the island is a formidable shoal extending out from the island's SW point. Fortunately, this shoal is well-marked

by a white flashing, battery-operated light on a pile of rocks, Little Manitou. It is not advisable to pass between Little Manitou and the larger island.

The dock is 165 feet long with approximately 7.5 feet at its outer end, depending on lake levels. (See Fig. 4.25.) The fishing station was in operation at the turn of the 20th century and remained in active use until the 1970s. This station is of particular interest because it was a year-round commercial fishery that endured the hardships of setting nets and lines *under* the ice. Today the buildings and artifacts, including twine sheds, smokehouse, "Governor's" cabin, bunkhouse, windlass, and drying reel, have been restored by the National Park Service and provide a glimpse into the past when commercial fishing was one of the mainstays of the islands. During the summer months, the station may be manned by an volunteer who gives tours of the complex. A couple of trails lead from the station, one, a short way (0.75 miles) along the south shore, leads to a prehistoric fishing camp. The other follows the shoreline for two miles along the island's NW side, to a primitive campsite adjacent to a sand beach. A little farther along the trail, past the campsite, are the remains of an old homestead, including a small cabin and remnants of machinery from an era past.

Alternative anchorages can be found along the western side of Manitou approximately a half-mile NE of the point. Sometimes, boats can be seen anchored farther up this shoreline along the small indentation about midway up the island. Both of these anchorages, however, are marginal being wide open to westerly winds. The name "Manitou" comes from the Ojibwe word that means "spirit."

At the far western end of the Lakeshore is **Mawikwe** (formerly the derogatory "Squaw") **Bay,** which is located on the mainland SW of Eagle Island. It is notable for its caves and rock formations that have been carved out

NOT TO BE USED FOR NAVIGATION – SKETCHES APPROXIMATE

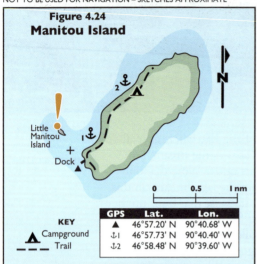

Figure 4.24
Manitou Island

GPS	Lat.	Lon.
▲	46°57.20' N	90°40.68' W
⚓1	46°57.73' N	90°40.40' W
⚓2	46°58.48' N	90°39.60' W

KEY
▲ Campground
- - - Trail

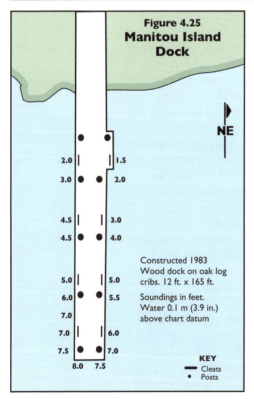

Figure 4.25
Manitou Island Dock

Constructed 1983
Wood dock on oak log cribs. 12 ft. x 165 ft.

Soundings in feet.
Water 0.1 m (3.9 in.)
above chart datum

KEY
— Cleats
• Posts

of the sandstone cliffs by the action of the lake. The area is best enjoyed by passing by, for the rocky bottom is not conducive to anchoring. Often, the caves are visited by boaters traveling to and from Cornucopia. Aside from rock boulders close in toward shore, the only other hazards in the area are the Eagle Island shoals that lie approximately 1.5 miles offshore.

Lying four miles to the NE of Madeline is **Michigan Island**. (See Fig. 4.26.) There is a dock here that is found on the south shore approximately one mile east of the island's SW sand point, beneath the Michigan Island Light. The present dock has seen two recent stages of construction. In 1987, a 202-foot-long structure with steel pilings was constructed. This new dock blocked the along-shore movement of sand from east to west along the south shore of the island. This increased the rate of erosion of the bluffs west of the dock and caused a beach to develop to the east of the dock to the point where the approach to the dock by deep-draft boats was impassable. To alleviate this problem, the dock was reengineered in 1993 and reconstructed in 1995. Seventy-seven feet of the concrete dock were removed and replaced by a 30-foot pier. The pier is less of a barrier to the movement of sediment. To help stabilize the eroding bluffs and resulting silting around the dock, a concrete spur was constructed perpendicular to and extending west from the dock near the

NOT TO BE USED FOR NAVIGATION – SKETCHES APPROXIMATE

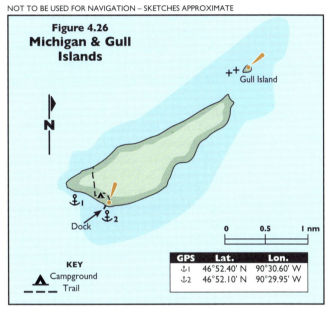

Figure 4.26
Michigan & Gull Islands

Gull Island

N

Dock

KEY	
▲	Campground
---	Trail

GPS	Lat.	Lon.
⚓1	46°52.40' N	90°30.60' W
⚓2	46°52.10' N	90°29.95' W

0   0.5   1 nm

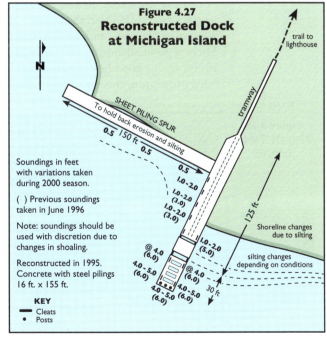

Figure 4.27
Reconstructed Dock at Michigan Island

trail to lighthouse

tramway

N

SHEET PILING SPUR
To hold back erosion and silting
0.5 150 ft 0.5

0.5
1.0 - 2.0
1.0 - 2.0
(3.0)
1.0 - 2.0
(3.0)
1.0 - 2.0
(3.0)

125 ft

Soundings in feet with variations taken during 2000 season.

( ) Previous soundings taken in June 1996

Note: soundings should be used with discretion due to changes in shoaling.

Reconstructed in 1995. Concrete with steel pilings 16 ft. x 155 ft.

KEY	
—	Cleats
•	Posts

@ 4.0 (6.0)
4.0 - 5.0 (6.0)
4.0 - 5.0 (6.0)
@ 4.0 (6.0)
4.0 - 5.0 (6.0)
30 ft
1.0 - 2.0 (5.0)

Shoreline changes due to silting

silting changes depending on conditions

shore. However, despite these efforts, recent years have seen a recurrence of silting and once again, the dock is accessible to only those with shoal draft boats. Refer to Figure 4.27 to see the effects of shoaling in just four years. It is also important to note that these effects change dramatically depending on weather conditions. In particular, strong easterly or westerly winds can change depths by as much as a foot or more. Caution — *the Michigan dock has become especially dangerous because of its height in low-water years.* There have been a number of reports of small boat hulls getting partially trapped under the dock and then pounded in the waves. In 2007, the NPS added "vertical rub rails," which should make the dock safer in low water conditions. A large staircase and tramway lead from the dock up the bluffs to the light station.

There are actually two different lights at the station. The first one, which was built in 1857, consists of a masonry building and tower that have been restored by the Park Service in order to preserve one of the symbols of early Lake Superior navigation. They were replaced in 1929 by a taller steel tower that was automated in 1943. Restored gardens and new exhibits were added in 2016. There are a number of other buildings on the site and an interesting extension of the tramway, a small rail system that circumnavigates the grounds. A trail is found at the western end of the buildings that follows through the forest, past old-growth hemlocks then winds down to the western sand beach and the sand point. It is a pleasant hike that only takes about 20 to 30 minutes. Volunteers may be onsite for lighthouse tours June - September. The sand point at the SW end of Michigan is particularly interesting to explore because it has abundant driftwood washed up on the beach. Inland on the western side of this point, there is an interesting "lagoon" and marshy area, a perfect habitat for wildlife. There is good anchoring off the south side of this point in 10 to 15 feet with a good holding sand bottom. However, with only one-sided protection, this anchorage should only be used when north or NE winds are assured. Protection for east or SE can be obtained by moving to the other side, but this point is wide open to any kind of westerly winds that are quite common in this sector of the lake.

North Twin is a remote island that has received little attention over the years. (See Fig. 4.28.) Because of its distance from the mainland and its relatively small size, this is one of the few islands that didn't experience logging activities and thus remains a prime example of a northern boreal forest. Considerable shoaling at the southern end, and lack of good protection, makes this an island that is best enjoyed just in passing

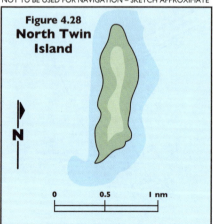

**Figure 4.28
North Twin
Island**

N

0   0.5   1 nm

by. Because of rare vegetation on the island, camping is only permitted in the designated primitive zone.

Standing boldly off the Red Cliff Point shoreline across from Frog Bay on the mainland rises the highest of the Apostles, **Oak Island,** with elevations above 1,000 feet. Oak is unique among the Apostles because it consists of high, steep bluffs and deep cutting ravines and gullies. With few sand beaches, this heavily forested island plunges abruptly into the lake and has a shoreline that can be traversed in only a few areas. Because of its rugged terrain, logging was done in the past only with great difficulty. A fire in the 1940s burned most of the island. Today, Oak has a population of white-tail deer and some bear. Its name comes from a translation of an Ojibway phrase that means "Acorn Island" because of the large number of oak trees present.

The island is of special interest to boaters because of a small wooden dock (see Fig. 4.30.) and trail system that traverses a large part of the island. The dock is located on the western shore, about midpoint on the island, bearing 352°T from the buoy off Red Cliff Point. Approach to the dock should be made with caution since there is sometimes a sandbar found when closing from the west. The dock has approximately 80 feet of usable length with about 6 feet of depth at the outer end depending on present water datum. It is also possible to anchor off to either side of the dock with a good holding bottom. A campground host is stationed near the dock to give information and aid in the enjoyment of the island.

There are two directions one can take from the dock on the trails. One way is to proceed SE along the shoreline to the sandspit at the southern end of the island, which is the site of the first logging camp on the island. This trail then turns deep into the interior of the island where it heads north and rejoins the rest of the trail system in the northern half of the island. Another trail leads north from the dock through a clearing that

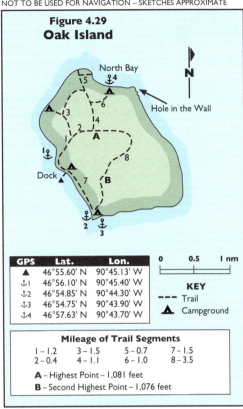

Figure 4.29
Oak Island

GPS	Lat.	Lon.
▲	46°55.60' N	90°45.13' W
⚓1	46°56.10' N	90°45.40' W
⚓2	46°54.85' N	90°44.30' W
⚓3	46°54.75' N	90°43.90' W
⚓4	46°57.63' N	90°43.70' W

KEY
- - - Trail
▲ Campground

Mileage of Trail Segments

| 1 – 1.2 | 3 – 1.5 | 5 – 0.7 | 7 – 1.5 |
| 2 – 0.4 | 4 – 1.1 | 6 – 1.0 | 8 – 3.5 |

A – Highest Point – 1,081 feet
B – Second Highest Point – 1,076 feet

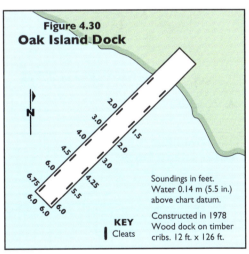

Figure 4.30
Oak Island Dock

Soundings in feet.
Water 0.14 m (5.5 in.) above chart datum.

KEY
❘ Cleats

Constructed in 1978
Wood dock on timber cribs. 12 ft. x 126 ft.

was once part of a logging camp and now serves as a group site for camping. It leads to two magnificent lookouts along the northern shore of the island. This is an especially beautiful island to enjoy inland, as its interior access provides an experience that is in stark contrast to that of walking along the beaches of other islands.

Other places along the Oak Island shoreline that are sometimes used for anchoring are at its southern end to either side of the small sandspit at its SE end, or in the indented "bay" at the northern end of the island. By using sand areas on the shoreline as a guide, adjacent sand bottoms can usually be found. Because of Oak Island's high bluffs, this is an especially good anchorage for strong S and SW winds. A trail can be picked up in this northern anchorage that leads to two of the dramatic overlooks. Because Oak is a large island to go around should winds shift, other anchorages should be kept in mind. For those at the dock, two alternatives for either west or southerly winds are Raspberry or Frog bays on the mainland.

Otter Island's claim to fame is that it was once the site for a National Boy Scouts of America Camporee in 1960. (See Fig. 4.31.) More than 1,000 scouts with their leaders were ferried out to the island by the barge *Outer Island*. The island was divided into sections by an intricate trail system with names and central meeting places. Today, all that remains is another sturdy Park Service dock at the original landing site (which was also used for logging before the Boy Scouts) and the main trail of the system that leads from the dock to the island's northern shore.

The dock is found just to the east of the sandspit on the southern end of the island. It is U-shaped, built around the remains of an old barge that served as a previous dock. (See Fig. 4.32.) Those with deep-draft boats need to confine their use to the outer portion where depths vary from 6 feet to 7 feet depending on lake levels. Those with less draft can use the end sides. A vault

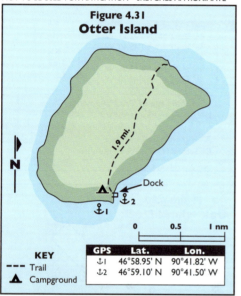

Figure 4.31
Otter Island

1.9 mi.

Dock

0   0.5   1 nm

KEY	GPS	Lat.	Lon.
--- Trail	⚓1	46°58.95' N	90°41.82' W
▲ Campground	⚓2	46°59.10' N	90°41.50' W

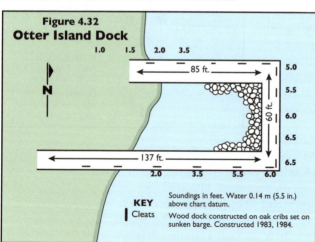

Figure 4.32
Otter Island Dock

1.0   1.5   2.0   3.5

85 ft.

60 ft.

137 ft.

5.0

5.5

6.0

6.5

6.5

2.0   3.5   5.5   6.0

KEY
| Cleats
Soundings in feet. Water 0.14 m (5.5 in.) above chart datum.
Wood dock constructed on oak cribs set on sunken barge. Constructed 1983, 1984.

toilet is available near the dock. The dock has good protection for west and NW winds but is quite open to the east and south. Note of caution: *When clearing the NE end of Otter Island, be sure to stand well off, for there is a rocky shoal area that extends 200 to 300 feet out from this point.*

Because of its distance from the other islands, **Outer Island** is characterized as being one of the most remote and lonely of the islands in the Apostles. (See Fig. 4.33.) Nothing illustrates this better than a visit to that lonely windswept sandspit found at its southern end, a world apart from the congestion often found at the rest of the islands. By watching the weather, good anchoring can be found on either side of this spit in 10 to 12 feet of water over a sand rippled bottom, thus giving protection from all winds except southerly. The anchorage, however, may prove to be uncomfortable because there is often a considerable swell around this point, especially on the eastern side when westerly winds are blowing. On the western side, care must be taken to avoid submerged pilings, a remainder of an old

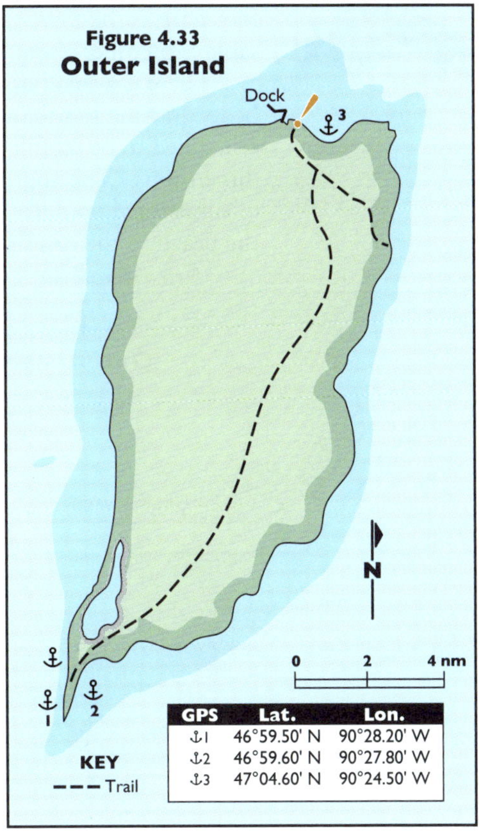

Figure 4.33
Outer Island

GPS	Lat.	Lon.
⚓1	46°59.50' N	90°28.20' W
⚓2	46°59.60' N	90°27.80' W
⚓3	47°04.60' N	90°24.50' W

KEY
– – – Trail

dock from lumbering days, located about three-quarters of a mile north of the point.

The point is particularly interesting to explore, both along the sand beaches and in the interior. There is an old, wrecked boat not too far from where the old dock used to be. Clearings give evidence to the time when the island was used for logging. There is even a "road" through the interior of the island where a small railroad system was built in 1920 to transport logs down to the water. A trail follows this old railroad bed for some way and then continues seven miles to the far north end of the island and the light station. A large inland "lagoon" and cranberry bog (which are now open to the lake) on the western side, north of the sand point, are usually teeming with an abundance of wildlife. With the wind whistling through the sedge grass, the only companions here are sandpipers scurrying in the sand, gulls squawking overhead as their domain on the spit is invaded and possibly a great blue heron spreading its graceful wings as it takes to flight over the bog.

The north end of Outer Island is of interest to the boater because of the lighthouse (built in 1874) that is located there. This is also an area that, because of the shoals lying off the island, has been the site of more than one shipwreck. The wreck indicated on

the charts is the *Pretoria,* a wooden schooner that went down in the same September storm that sank the *Sevona* off Sand Island in 1905.

There is a small dock near the light that can be used by boats drawing less than 5 feet. (See Fig. 4.34.) (Note this dock is scheduled to be rebuilt in 2025-2026 with some change in present dimensions.) The approach to the dock, however, is difficult because of submerged boulders. Marginal anchoring can be found along the beach to the east of the dock. Because this area is exposed to the open lake, it may be uncomfortable when swells develop off the lake, so it is rarely considered for an overnight anchorage. There is a trail (1.7 miles) leading from the lighthouse to the historic Lullaby Lumber Company camp on the east side of the island. The lighthouse is no longer staffed by VIP personnel who used to give tours. For those who ascend the walkway up to the light, the view high up on this end of Outer Island is spectacular. Looking out over the wide expanses of Lake Superior, on a clear day it is possible to see across to the Minnesota shoreline. Closer to the island, huge lakers can be seen as they ply up and down the shipping lanes, only eight miles away.

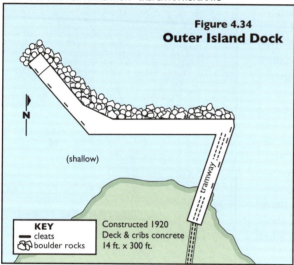

Figure 4.34
Outer Island Dock

(shallow)

N

tramway

KEY
cleats
boulder rocks

Constructed 1920
Deck & cribs concrete
14 ft. x 300 ft.

Raspberry Island has long been a favorite for those who cruise in the Apostles. (See Fig. 4.35.) This is primarily because of the picturesque sand point at its SE corner that provides excellent anchoring on either side. There is unobstructed holding ground here with a good sand bottom and protection for all but south and east winds. This is one of those places where, surprisingly enough, the protection is greater than the chart would indicate. Because the anchorage isn't exposed to the outer lake, the uncomfortable motion often found in many of the outlying anchorages is rarely felt here. Should southerly or easterly winds develop, it is a simple matter to move across to Raspberry Bay on the mainland.

The sand point is one of the more beautiful spots in the islands, but the vegetation here is very fragile, so it is important to stay on the trails and boardwalks provided in the area. One trail leads across the island to the lighthouse on the other side. This light was the third lighthouse built in the Apostles, beginning service in 1863. For almost 100 years, the light was staffed and was a social gathering spot for those who lived and worked in the islands. The station was automated in 1947. Today a ranger is on duty during the boating season to give tours of the complex. For those without boats, Apostle Islands Cruises has 3-4 boat tours to the Raspberry Lighthouse each week during June-August. There is another trail that leads west of the lighthouse up the west side of the island for about a mile.

A special note should be made about the work the NPS has done to restore the light station. Using historic photographs and with meticulous attention to detail, the grounds and the gardens, which were once the showcase of the islands, have been restored to what they were in the 1920s. Inside one of the duplex residences, displays have been constructed that depict various aspects of living on a light station in the early and mid-1900s. Out in the old Fog Signal Building it is particularly interesting to see row upon row of old storage batteries that were used to provide electrical power for the lighthouse.

In recent years, considerable work has been done to stabilize the eroding bank in front of the light station. In 2002-2003 they engaged in a shoreline stabilization project to keep the Fog Signal Building and lighthouse from sliding into the lake. At the base of the light there was a wooden dock complex that in the past was used for unloading supplies for those who were stationed at the light. In the mid-1980s, this dock was repaired and lengthened so, depending on lake levels, it was a viable option for those with boats drawing up to 5.5 feet. In 2016 it was replaced with a metal binwall and concrete dock. (See Fig. 4.36.) In approaching the dock, a lookout should be posted to watch for boulders that lie south of the dock. Note that the west side of the dock is reserved for ferries bringing in lighthouse visitors. It also can become quite "rolly" when tour boats pass by. Thus, it is best used for short stops. The buoy that lies to the west of the dock marks the western end of Marina Shoal that extends out from the island along its southern end.

The bay on the west side of Raspberry Island can also be used for anchoring. However, the shoreline here is steep and quite heavily forested, making going ashore not as attractive as in other areas. The bay gives protection for east and south winds.

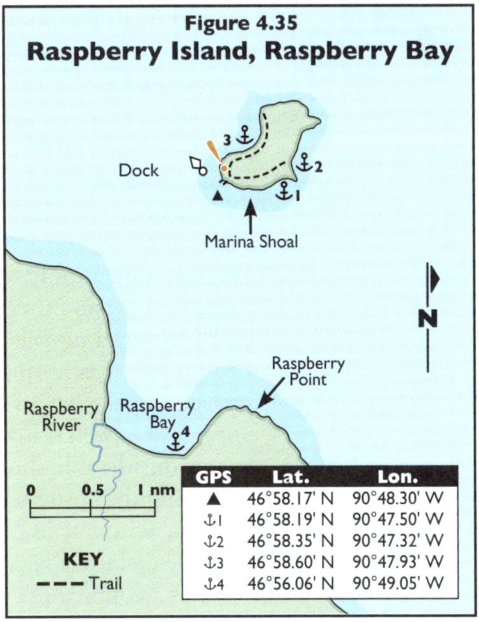

Figure 4.35
Raspberry Island, Raspberry Bay

GPS	Lat.	Lon.
▲	46°58.17' N	90°48.30' W
⚓1	46°58.19' N	90°47.50' W
⚓2	46°58.35' N	90°47.32' W
⚓3	46°58.60' N	90°47.93' W
⚓4	46°56.06' N	90°49.05' W

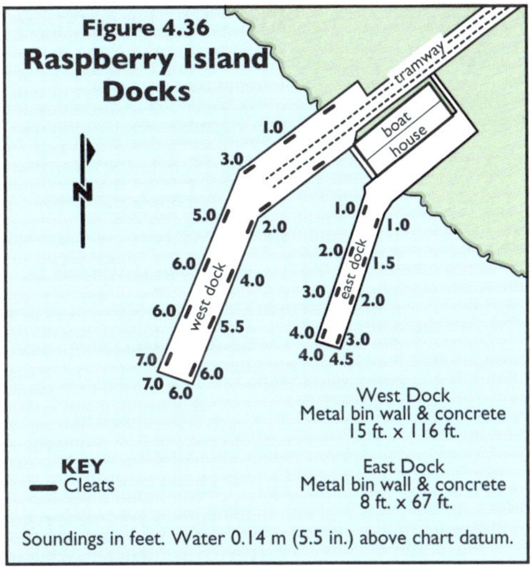

KEY
--- Trail

Figure 4.36
Raspberry Island Docks

KEY
— Cleats

West Dock
Metal bin wall & concrete
15 ft. x 116 ft.

East Dock
Metal bin wall & concrete
8 ft. x 67 ft.

Soundings in feet. Water 0.14 m (5.5 in.) above chart datum.

Although **Raspberry Bay on the mainland** (see Fig. 4.35) is not a part of the Apostle Islands National Lakeshore, it is mentioned here because it is another favorite for boaters who cruise in the area. This segment of the shoreline actually belongs to the Red Cliff Band of Ojibwe and is part of the land that was reserved to them in the La Pointe Treaty of 1854.

This bay is desirable for anchoring because it is one of the few places in the Apostles where there is full three-sided protection. The bay is open only to the north thus, it provides excellent protection for all other winds. The only hazard within the bay is shoaling found off the mouth of the Raspberry River that empties into the bay. Anchoring can be done just about anywhere in the deep end of the bay in 10 to 12 feet of water, the only exception being to stay well off the mouth of the river where silt deposits create considerable shoaling.

Along the entire base of the bay, there is a long sand beach complete with a wild marshy area just inland. Red sandstone cliffs bank the eastern side; a few cottages are along the western side. The river has a couple of channels where, not too far inland, there is a clearing where there used to be a campground that was run by the Red Cliff Band. Going ashore here is not allowed without getting tribal permission.

Passing close along the shoreline of **Rocky Island** it is easy to see how it got its name. (See Fig. 4.37.) This is because along many sections and especially around its long projecting NE tip, there are numerous rocks and boulders lying in the water that were once part of the weather-beaten shore. Therefore, this is an island where it is best to stand well off — especially that NE tip. Although charts show considerable shoaling between Rocky and South Twin, the channel is frequently used by boaters. By staying midway between the two islands, there is clear water with a good 10 feet of depth, which with caution can be successfully navigated. When rounding the NE point of Rocky Island, it is important to note that shoal water does extend out a good half mile.

The southern end of Rocky Island also bears mentioning. Extending south off the sandspit there is again shallow water almost halfway across to Otter Island. The bottom may not be of much concern here because it is clear sand, but many a sailor has met with surprise when sailing well off the point to look down and see sand bottom in what appears to be just a few feet of water.

Rocky Island, along with South Twin, is one of the most popular spots in the islands, competing only with the docks and bays of Stockton Island for overnight boaters. One of the reasons for its heavy use is a large public dock constructed by the Park Service on the eastern side of the island. (See Fig. 4.38.) In the past, on a Saturday night in mid-season, this dock used to resemble a little marina with often as many as 15 boats tied up stern-to. Note however, that Med-mooring is no longer allowed at this dock. So, there are now more boaters who join the group that anchor off to each side with boats standing off as far away as the sandspit to the south.

There are no obstructions in approaching this dock. But because there are other docks along this side of the island, it is helpful to know that the NPS dock is the southernmost one that is seen when approaching. (The rest of the docks seen along this eastern side of Rocky are private.) Depth at the outer end of the dock is approximately 8 feet, with less depths toward shore. It is important to note that this dock becomes most uncomfortable in easterly and NE winds, and a common practice is to move across to South Twin when winds change in this direction.

Adjacent to the dock is an unstaffed ranger station, picnic tables, vault toilets, and fire ring. It's hard to believe that at one time there was even a restaurant here that was quite well known for its specialties of Lake Superior whitefish and lake trout. There are also a number of trails to hike. One of these trails, which at times may be difficult to see, cuts across the island from the ranger station to the other side. Here there is a beautiful overlook high up on cliffs left by the glaciers, which gives a panoramic view of Bear, Devils, and the open lake.

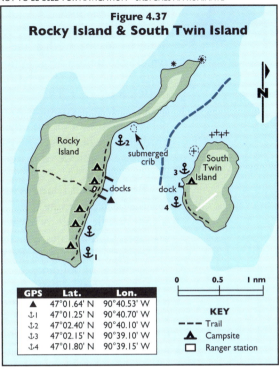

Figure 4.37
Rocky Island & South Twin Island

GPS	Lat.	Lon.
▲	47°01.64' N	90°40.53' W
⚓1	47°01.25' N	90°40.70' W
⚓2	47°02.40' N	90°40.10' W
⚓3	47°02.15' N	90°39.10' W
⚓4	47°01.80' N	90°39.15' W

KEY
- - - Trail
▲ Campsite
☐ Ranger station

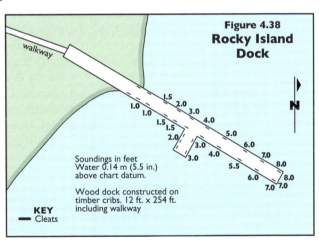

Figure 4.38
Rocky Island Dock

Soundings in feet
Water 0.14 m (5.5 in.)
above chart datum.

Wood dock constructed on timber cribs. 12 ft. x 254 ft. including walkway

KEY
— Cleats

Back at the dock, there are two more trails that follow the shoreline in either direction. Along the northern trail there are a number of cottages and summer homes, most of which are remnants of fishing camps. Some of these continue to have "use and occupancy" rights as determined when the park was established. The trail leading south from the dock is a favorite since it takes hikers out to the beautiful sandspit. Along the way it passes through the former Nies fish camp where there are a number of old decaying boats and artifacts, reminders of an era past. Throughout this area the Park

Service has established a couple of designated campsites.

Another anchorage is found on the eastern side of Rocky Island in the bay to the north at the base of the long "gooseneck." By avoiding some submerged cribs and shoal waters that lie off the northern shore, good anchoring with a sand bottom can be found in 10 feet of water. There is another sand beach along this section of the shore that gives way to rock at the northern end. It is also possible to anchor on the other side of the "gooseneck" along the northern side of Rocky where there is a small sand beach. But this anchorage is considered marginal for anchoring because of exposure to the open lake.

Because **Sand Island** is located so far west, it is often considered "off the beaten cruising track" and sees fewer visitors than those islands that lie closer to Bayfield. Yet Sand Island has much to offer: sea caves, sand beaches, a picturesque lighthouse, less congested anchoring and even remnants of a fishing village. (See Fig. 4.39.)

A cluster of buildings, located along the island's south shore, got started after the Civil War, when a veteran named Shaw was given his veteran's bonus in the form of a land grant on the island. A small village that bore his name developed over the years as fishermen and farmers, predominantly of Norwegian stock, came to the island. At one time there was even a school, cooperative grocery store, post office and an island-to-mainland telephone system. Even as late as the 1930s, when Grace Lee Nute visited the island while doing research for her book, *Lake Superior,* a thriving community could be found. She described in detail the numerous fishing sheds, nets hanging out to dry and the way the whole community came down to the dock to watch the loading of the launch that would transport freshly caught fish to the mainland every other day. However, the Depression, World War II and the presence of the sea lamprey in the 1950s eventually caused the islanders to move elsewhere. Today, all that is left of this once tight-knit community are a few artifacts and some of the original Shaw buildings, many of which have been included on the National Register of Historic Places.

Another point of historical interest is the Sand Island Lighthouse, built in 1881. This lighthouse is unique among those found in the islands since it is constructed of sandstone quarried in the area and was designed in the Norman Gothic style of architecture characteristic of the period. It is identical to several other lighthouses on the Great Lakes,

NOT TO BE USED FOR NAVIGATION – SKETCH APPROXIMATE

Figure 4.39
Sand Island

Sand Island Shoals

Fl 6s 60 ft. 7 St M

Lighthouse Bay

Justice Bay

Swallow Sea Caves

Noring Farm

Docks

East Bay

West Bay

N

GPS	Lat.	Lon.
⚓1	46°58.17' N	90°58.30' W
⚓2	46°59.73' N	90°56.55' W
⚓3	46°59.50' N	90°55.65' W
⚓4	46°58.80' N	90°55.90' W

0   0.5   1 nm

KEY
--- Trail
▲ Campground

including Eagle Harbor Light on Michigan's Keweenaw Peninsula and Passage Island Light at Isle Royale.

Standing off the NE corner of Sand Island is the Sand Island Shoal that is marked with a buoy and has a minimum depth of 15 feet. The shoal is the site of the wreck *Sevona,* which went down in a September storm in 1905. Hatch covers from this old ore carrier were used in building the Sevona Cottage in 1915, which was part of Camp Stella, a summer resort on the island. The cottage is now included on the National Register of Historic Places. The huge anchor from the ship is on display on the grounds of Little Sand Bay on the mainland. Those in pleasure craft can have safe passage between the shoal and Sand Island by favoring the island. However, it is important to not hug the island too closely, especially near the lighthouse point since there are some underwater ledges and boulders just offshore.

The shoal off the SE end of Sand Island also bears mentioning. The fact that the shoal is steadily increasing is borne out by comparing present depths with those in the early 1800s, which were reported as being 40 to 60 feet. Today it is a long narrow sandbar of varying depths that extends from the SE tip of the island to mainland. Those with local knowledge have been known to make passage either to the south of the shoal near the mainland or at its northern end close to the island. In the 1980s, depending on lake levels and weather conditions, boats drawing 5.5 feet were able to successfully navigate right across the middle of the sandbar. Although present-day charts show depths of 6 feet to 7 feet in the middle, these are known to change dramatically in high winds (especially from the NE) since the wave action quickly builds up underwater ridges of sand. Also, recent low water years have compromised these soundings considerably. Thus, passage to the south of Sand Island should be attempted only in calm conditions and when lake levels are up.

There are a number of areas around Sand Island that can be used for anchoring. The first of these is **East Bay** where there is good holding with a sand bottom. Because of shoaling water, it may be difficult to get in close here, especially in the northern end of the bay. There is also a lot of rock close to this northern shore. In the late 1980s, the National Park Service repaired and lengthened two of the main docks in the bay. Unfortunately, shoaling combined with low water subsequently made these docks usable only for shoal draft vessels. Eventually the North Dock was removed, and the South Dock was moved a little further south and enlarged in 2017 to an L-shape with metal bin wall construction and a concrete deck. (See Fig. 4.40). Note that this dock is for NPS use only.

Not far from the dock is a lovely, cleared campground with picnic tables, grills, water pump and vault toilets. A campground host is often on station near the area. There is a trail that leads west from the campground for one-third mile to an old farm site once operated by the Noring family where there are remnants of old buildings and a few artifacts of farm equipment. (Be careful not to stumble into an

old well on the premises.) There is another trail, which once served as a road, that leads north from the campground to Justice Bay and then the lighthouse. On this trail, not too far from the campground, is another clearing, an overgrown field of yesteryear where apples and various crops were grown, the Hansen Farm. This trail from East Bay to Hansen Farm, Justice Bay, and then the lighthouse is being improved with boardwalk. It should be noted that East Bay is quite open to easterly winds and the best alternatives, should these winds arise, are to move around to Lighthouse Bay or over to Little Sand Bay on the mainland.

Figure 4.40
East Bay Dock, Sand Island

Old Shoreline

New Shoreline

Ranger station

N

Dock enlarged 2017.
Metal bin wall consruction with concrete deck.

KEY
— Cleats

Justice Bay, which lies north of East Bay on Sand Island, provides protection for westerly and south winds. There is a small beach here and much of the bay is rock bottom, so it may be difficult to get a good set with an anchor. Often what may feel as a set is merely the anchor hooked on a rock, which could slip off in a wind change. There is also some slash on the bottom that could foul an anchor. Often it is possible to get a better set with the anchor by moving farther out of the anchorage beyond the rocks and slash, where it is still possible to anchor in 15 to 20 feet. Despite this, it is still a lovely little harbor and well worth the effort. Swallow Point has some of the most beautiful and interesting sea caves in the islands. Note that the trail comes very close to Justice Bay and can be picked up just above the beach that leads south to the campground in East Bay or north to the lighthouse. The trail north passes through some magnificent stands of virgin white pines. The trees are about 240 years old and escaped harvest by being under protection of the lighthouse boundaries. Before reaching the lighthouse, the trail comes out to a beautiful overlook of Lighthouse Bay. At the lighthouse, there is often a volunteer on station to give tours and answer questions.

Lighthouse Bay on the northern side of Sand Island can also be used for anchoring if easterly or southerly winds are assured. Because it is exposed to the open lake it is often possible to experience uncomfortable wave action left over from northerly winds. In approaching the bay, it is important to give the lighthouse point adequate berth, since there are a number of submerged boulders. There are also more boulders to the west of this bay, beyond the sand beach. By taking a large wooden staircase found at the eastern end of the sand beach, it is possible to ascend the bluff to a trail that goes to the lookout and the lighthouse. Along the NW end of the island there are more of the carved rock formations and sandstone caves that are characteristic of the exposed shores of the Apostles.

At the SW end of Sand Island is **West Bay,** once the site of a logging camp. Anchoring here is marginal because of underwater rocks and should be done with caution. The bay is open to southerly and westerly winds, and it is a long way in any direction to receive protection, especially from westerly winds. The large log structure seen at the north side of this bay, the West Bay Lodge, is under an exclusive "use and occupancy" agreement with the NPS and is not open to the public.

There are many islands in the Apostles that offer better protection for east winds than **South Twin** (see Fig. 4.37). Yet, when there are forecasts for easterly winds, it is to South Twin that many boaters will flock. Part of the reason is that there is a dock here, along with good holding ground for anchoring. For a long time, this island was privately owned, as were most of the islands. The prominent clearing that one sees was built during that time. Today there are a number of designated campsites and vault toilets.

When cruising around South Twin, it is important to note the shoal waters that extend out from the island along its south and NW shores. The dock, which is "L" shaped, is found in the middle of the western side. This is one dock that has seen considerable shoaling over the years. (See Fig. 4.41.) Anchoring is usually done in the area south of the dock or north of the sand point that is north of the dock. A couple of trails in the area lead to designated campsites. One trail leads south from the dock, past what used to be an overgrown landing strip from a previous owner. It follows the southern part of the island

NOT TO BE USED FOR NAVIGATION – SKETCH APPROXIMATE

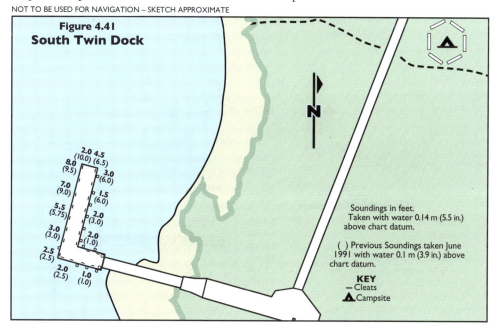

Figure 4.41
South Twin Dock

Soundings in feet.
Taken with water 0.14 m (5.5 in.) above chart datum.

( ) Previous Soundings taken June 1991 with water 0.1 m (3.9 in.) above chart datum.

KEY
— Cleats
▲ Campsite

about 1/4 mile.

If the number of people visiting a particular island is used as the criterion for popularity, then **Stockton Island** by far outweighs all the other islands as being the most popular spot in the Apostles. Part of the reason for its heavy use is that Stockton has two docking areas and three beautiful bays that offer excellent anchoring with three-sided protection. It also has the most campsites, with 17 (campsite #1 accessible by boardwalk with a platform) in Presque Isle Bay, sometimes called Anderson Bay. In Quarry Bay there is one designated and three group sites. Another reason for its popularity is that the island presents a rich diversity in topography, including everything from lagoons and marshy bogs to sandy beaches and heavily forested areas — all accessible because of an extensive trail system put in by the Park Service. (See Fig. 4.42.)

Originally, Stockton was actually two separate islands, with Presque Isle Point being separated from the larger portion of the island. Over many centuries, a tombolo, or sandbar, eventually closed the gap between the two. Today, the delightful Tombolo Trail explores this area. When the French came, they named this outermost portion of the area Presque Isle, which means "almost an island."

NOT TO BE USED FOR NAVIGATION – SKETCH APPROXIMATE

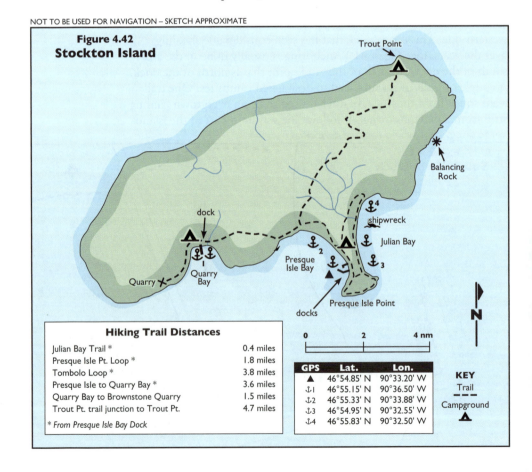

Figure 4.42
Stockton Island

Trout Point

Balancing Rock

dock

shipwreck

Julian Bay

Presque Isle Bay

Quarry

Quarry Bay

Presque Isle Point

docks

N

Hiking Trail Distances	
Julian Bay Trail *	0.4 miles
Presque Isle Pt. Loop *	1.8 miles
Tombolo Loop *	3.8 miles
Presque Isle to Quarry Bay *	3.6 miles
Quarry Bay to Brownstone Quarry	1.5 miles
Trout Pt. trail junction to Trout Pt.	4.7 miles
* From Presque Isle Bay Dock	

0   2   4 nm

GPS	Lat.	Lon.
▲	46°54.85' N	90°33.20' W
⚓1	46°55.15' N	90°36.50' W
⚓2	46°55.33' N	90°33.88' W
⚓3	46°54.95' N	90°32.55' W
⚓4	46°55.83' N	90°32.50' W

KEY
Trail
- - -
Campground
▲

It is **Presque Isle Bay** where the island receives most of its heavy use. This is primarily because of the most complete dock-complex in the islands. It is made up of two docks. The North dock is L shape, and the South Dock is a hybrid between a straight dock and a L shape. The overall effect is a completely weatherproof harbor, which is rivaled only by the harbor at Little Sand Bay. See Figure 4.43. This docking area is not only favored by boaters but is used by excursion boats and water taxis for off-loading backpackers and campers who come to hike the island's many trails and camp in the numerous campsites. Because of this, certain portions of the South Dock are reserved during designated daytime hours. There is also a small portion of this dock reserved for NPS boats near shore. Other than this, the dockage area is available with just a couple of restrictions. To allow free passage between the two docking areas, Med-mooring is not allowed and boaters are asked to tie broadside to both docks. Note again the user fee structure throughout the islands for overnight dockage: boats up to 40 feet, $15; boats 40 feet and larger, $30. Fees can be deposited in self-collecting receptacles. Daytime use of docks remains free.

NOT TO BE USED FOR NAVIGATION – SKETCH APPROXIMATE

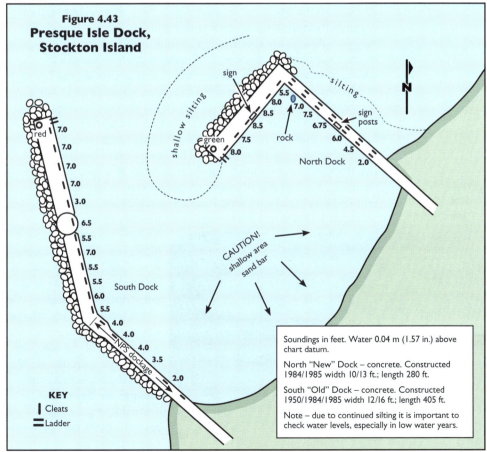

Figure 4.43
Presque Isle Dock, Stockton Island

Soundings in feet. Water 0.04 m (1.57 in.) above chart datum.

North "New" Dock – concrete. Constructed 1984/1985 width 10/13 ft.; length 280 ft.

South "Old" Dock – concrete. Constructed 1950/1984/1985 width 12/16 ft.; length 405 ft.

Note – due to continued silting it is important to check water levels, especially in low water years.

KEY
Cleats
Ladder

There are no hazards in approaching Presque Isle Bay from the SW. When rounding Presque Isle Point, it is prudent to stand off, especially near the SW point, since it gets shallow and there are a number of submerged boulders along the shoreline. The areas just outside of the docks, likewise, have either boulders or are silted in with sand, so it is wise to keep a fair distance off. Note that there has been considerable silting-in around the "L" shaped east dock in recent years. This silting-in not only extends north beyond the dock into the lake, but it also wraps around into the entrance almost closing this harbor off to those with deep draft boats. Those using the east dock with boats drawing 5.5 feet or more need to be careful not to go too far into the harbor because of a sandbar on the side. A good marker to gauge distance is the old signposts on the east dock: don't go inshore of these posts. Depending upon water levels, those with boats drawing 6 feet to 7 feet may be able to use the deeper portion of the west dock. Note that grilling is not allowed when moored to the dock or on the dock itself.

When the Presque Isle dock fills up, as it quickly does, boats will be seen anchoring off in the periphery of the bay. With a good-holding sand bottom, it is quite common to see as many as 20 to 25 boats in the bay on a Saturday night. Note that anchor lights are required from dusk until dawn at this and all other anchorages in the park. Boaters are asked to not anchor in such a way as to impede traffic to or from the dock area. The bay is open to S and SW winds. Should these arise, an alternative is to anchor off the NE end of Madeline or on the other side of Presque Isle Point in Julian Bay.

Stockton Island has been subject to the greatest development by the National Park Service. A Visitor Center and picnic area are located on the bluff between the two Presque Isle docks. Water is available near the North Dock. The campground begins near this dock and extends north for three-quarters of a mile along the shoreline. Each of the 19 campsites has a picnic table, fire ring, tent pad and bear-proof food locker. It is important to note that Stockton Island is home to a significant number of black bears.

Presque Isle Bay dock, Stockton Island. DAHL

Therefore, campers and picnickers should be careful in storing food and cleaning up eating areas, so bears are not attracted to the site.

A number of trails have also been constructed on the island. One of the favorites is the short walk (0.4 mile) across the peninsula from Presque Isle Bay to the other side. At midpoint a dramatic overlook opens on a panoramic vista of a large

marsh bog section of the island. On the other side there are the
long sand beaches and rolling sand dunes of Julian Bay. Particularly
when a northeaster is blowing, it is quite an experience to see and
hear the large rollers as they come in from the open lake and break
upon the beach. This area is very interesting to explore (see write-up
on Julian Bay).

An alternative hike back to the dock is to take the two-mile
loop trail around Presque Isle Point called the Anderson Trail.
Following the shoreline around, there are views of Michigan and
Madeline islands. At one point, the trail goes out on a rock ledge
complete with "tidal pools;" at other points it is possible to hear and
feel the tremendous action of the lake in a number of "blowholes"
that are part of the intricate rock formations.

Another trail leads from the Presque Isle Bay dock northward
through the campground where it splits into three different trails.
The first cutoff is the Tombolo Trail, which heads across to the
north end of Julian Bay through changing inland topography and
includes a boardwalk through an interesting marshy bog area. The
loop is then completed by following the Julian Bay sandy beach
south to the short trail that crosses the peninsula back to the dock.
Just a little farther around the bay from the Tombolo cutoff, the
trail splits again with one branch that leads NE across the deep
interior of the island to Trout Point
where there used to be an old logging
camp. Because of its distance from the
Presque Isle Bay dock (6.5 miles) there
is a designated campsite here. The other
branch continues around Presque Isle
Bay to a clearing where there used to be a
fishing camp. From there it heads inland
for another two miles to Quarry Bay.

Quarry Bay is another favorite for
those who cruise the islands. This is one
of the snuggest harbors in the Apostles,
giving protection for all but southerly
winds. (Note: despite protection from
wind, there is often an uncomfortable swell
in this anchorage.) Deep within the bay
there is good holding with a sand bottom;
along the sides farther out are rocks —
especially on the western side where there
are a number of submerged boulders
beneath the red sandstone cliffs. There
is some deadwood lying on the bottom
that will occasionally foul an anchor. In
the center of the beach shoreline there is
a large dock that the Park Service repaired
and lengthened in two stages. The first was

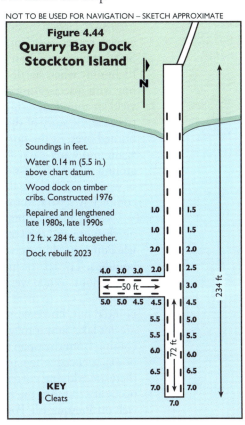

NOT TO BE USED FOR NAVIGATION – SKETCH APPROXIMATE

Figure 4.44
Quarry Bay Dock
Stockton Island

N

Soundings in feet.

Water 0.14 m (5.5 in.)
above chart datum.

Wood dock on timber
cribs. Constructed 1976

Repaired and lengthened
late 1980s, late 1990s

12 ft. x 284 ft. altogether.

Dock rebuilt 2023

KEY
Cleats

in the late 1980s when it was lengthened, and an L was added. The second was in the late 1990s when an additional 72 feet of dock was added. This extension made this dock accessible to those with deep-draft boats. The latest renovation was in 2023. (See Fig. 4.44.)

The area inland from the sand beach is quite picturesque and has been set aside for group camping. Three campsites with picnic tables, grills, bear-proof food lockers and vault toilets can be reserved by groups of eight or more people. Toward the eastern end of the bay there is an interesting beaver pond and a small stream that drains into the bay. Also at this eastern end, the trail can be picked up that leads to Presque Isle Bay. The main attraction of this area, however, is the old sandstone quarry that lies 1.5 miles west of Quarry Bay. A trail leads from the western side of the bay to the quarry, where from a high overlook one can see firsthand the large gorge that was cut into the stone cliffs. This quarry, the largest in the islands, supplied the huge sandstone blocks used throughout the Midwest to construct brownstone buildings that were in vogue at the turn of the 20th century.

Along the eastern side of Stockton Island is one of the most beautiful places in the Apostles, **Julian Bay**. Here is one of the longest sand beaches in the islands, complete with sand dunes and little sandpipers that scurry back and forth, leaving their delicate footprints in the sand. A little farther inland is one of the most extensive "lagoon" systems found among the islands. As one would expect, cranes, mergansers and sometimes geese frequent the area. Stately blue herons can be found walking along the marshes, taking flight only when startled by our intrusion. Farther back, there is a bog with insect-eating pitcher plants and sundew. Low-lying bushes yield an abundant crop of blueberries late each summer. Fire-scarred trees tell the story of the time when this part of the island was burned over. At the northern end of the bay, the shoreline breaks again into water-carved sandstone formations. These continue around the northeast side of the island, the most spectacular of which is Balancing Rock, a sandstone sea-stack that stands completely separated from the rest of the island.

When approaching Julian Bay, both the eastern part of its north shore and the area off the rocky ledges NW of Presque Isle Point should be given adequate berth because of submerged boulders. The rest of Julian Bay is clear with sand bottom throughout. When westerly winds are assured, this is one area of the islands where there will be a congregation of boats. It should be pointed out, however, that this is another anchorage exposed to the greater lake, and it may become uncomfortable because of swells coming from the open water. An uncomfortable motion can also be experienced when anchored near the southern end of the bay if there are eddying currents around Presque Isle Point. Should it be necessary to move the boat in the night, it is important to stand well off Presque Isle Point when rounding to the other side.

It is important to note that there is a shipwreck in Julian Bay that lies in 12 to 15 feet of water and should be given a wide berth when anchoring. It is located a few hundred yards north of the small stream that sometimes opens up through the sand and enters the lake from the lagoon area. In some years the wreck has been buoyed with a white buoy. The shipwreck is the *Noquebay,* a 205-foot wooden lumber schooner that caught on fire while being towed in October 1905. On a good day with no sea running, the ship's donkey boiler, rudder and "steering" wheel are usually visible. It is a great place to snorkel or dive, but a permit is required and that can be obtained at the NPS Headquarters in Bayfield. For more information on this wreck and others within the National Lakeshore, there is a descriptive brochure that includes site coordinates that can be obtained at park visitor's centers or from a ranger.

Another island that is off the beaten track and, thus, doesn't see as many boaters as some of the other islands is **York Island.** (See Fig. 4.45.) This is an island that, like Stockton, was originally two separate islands. It has been only in the last 150 years that they have been joined together by a sandbar or tombolo.

In passing to the south of York Island it is important to favor the mainland, giving the shoal that extends south of the island wide berth since it extends a good way out from the island. The bay on the north side of the island makes a good anchorage for all but NW to NE winds. When approaching this bay, care should be taken to stand off from both ends of the island because of submerged boulders. Along the small sand beach there is sand bottom, however, in a few sections there are some rocks, so it is prudent to be careful where the hook is set. Because of thick vegetation and undergrowth, it isn't as easy to cross the land bridge to the other side as one would think. There are three primitive campsites and a pit toilet here. A rough trail leads across the land bridge to the other side from Campsite #3, the most westward site. This anchorage, like others open to the greater lake, can become uncomfortable from swells.

It is also possible to anchor on the south side of York just to the west of the sand point and get protection from north and NE winds. This anchorage is best approached from the SW, staying well off the western arm of the island where there are a number of submerged boulders.

For a summary of the docks that are available for boater use within the Lakeshore, see Fig. 4.46. Since wind direction is usually the single greatest factor on where one will spend the night in the islands, Figure 4.47 provides a quick reference table for possible docks/

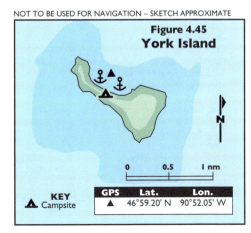

NOT TO BE USED FOR NAVIGATION – SKETCH APPROXIMATE

Figure 4.45
York Island

GPS	Lat.	Lon.
▲	46°59.20' N	90°52.05' W

KEY
▲ Campsite

anchorages that are usable with specific wind directions. For a full perspective of the area, including all the islands and preceding anchorages, see Fig. 4.12.

In closing this section on Lake Superior, no commentary on the Apostles is complete without mention of the annual **Bayfield Apple Festival** that occurs each fall in early October. Originally intended as a grand "farmers' market" for the local apple growers to vend their produce, this event has grown into a weekend of gala festivities complete with queens, parades and that great Lake Superior tradition — the boiled fish supper. Overnight, the town's population of about 600 expands to thousands (as many as 30,000-50,000 over four days) as visitors throng to the streets, delighting in various delicacies and every type of food imaginable that can be made from apples. A carnival atmosphere pervades, and the festive mood continues with the crowds flocking to the banks of the city park on Saturday night to watch a beautiful Venetian Parade put on by boaters from the yacht clubs and marinas. The weekend's celebration is climaxed on Sunday afternoon by a parade that can stand on its own against any other small town parade. Bands, marching groups and various entries come from hundreds of miles around and from three states to participate in this grand event. At the end of the weekend, everyone goes home laden with bags of apples and a feeling that a spark of old mid-American tradition is still alive and well here in the north country.

Figure 4.46
Docks in the Apostle Islands

Name/Location	Length	Description	Depth*
Basswood, West	106 ft..	Wood, Straight	4-4.5 ft.
Devils, South Landing	180 ft.	Wood, Small Harbor	3-4 ft.
Devils, Breakwater	82 ft.	Wood, Small Harbor	2-4 ft.
Little Sand Bay (Visitor)	350 ft.	Wood, Small Harbor	4-6 ft.
Little Sand Bay (Hokenson)	200 ft.	Wood, L-shaped	3-7 ft.
Long Island	60 ft.	Concrete & Steel, Straight	varies
Manitou Fish Camp	165 ft.	Wood, Straight	7 ft.
Michigan, Lighthouse	155 ft.	Concrete, Straight	varies
Oak, West	126 ft.	Wood, Straight	6 ft.
Otter, Southeast	85, 60, 137 ft.	Wood, U-shaped	6-7 ft.
Outer Lighthouse	300 ft.	Concrete, Rocky Bottom	6 ft.
Raspberry Lighthouse, West	116 ft.	Wood, Angled	6-7 ft.
Raspberry Lighthouse, East	67 ft.	Wood, Angled	4-5 ft.
Rocky East	233 ft.	Wood, Straight	7-8 ft.
Sand, East Bay (Campground)	128 ft.	Wood, Straight	4 ft.
Sand, East Bay (Ranger)	70 ft.	Wood, Straight	1.5 ft.
South Twin, North	67 ft.	Wood, Straight	2 ft.
South Twin, South	137 ft.	Wood, L-shaped	2.5-8 ft.
Stockton, Presque Isle West	405 ft.	Concrete, Angled	7-8 ft.
Stockton, Presque Isle East	280 ft.	Concrete, L-shaped	6.5-8 ft.
Stockton, Quarry Bay	296 ft.	Wood, Straight, Side Extension	7 ft.

* Water depths at outer end of docks in normal water years. Depths subject to change due to varying water levels, shifting sediments and sudden storms

Figure 4.47

"When The Wind Blows"

A Quick Reference Guide for Some Areas of Wind Protection in the Apostles

Wind Direction From	Docks	Anchorages
N	Devils (South Landing), Little Sand Bay, Michigan, Oak, Otter, Raspberry, Rocky*, Sand (East Bay), Quarry Bay, Presque Isle Bay	E side of south sandspits on Cat, Ironwood, Oak, Outer; S of Long Is.; Madeline (Big Bay, Chebomnicon Bay); Michigan (S of west sandspit); Raspberry sandspit; Rocky (S of the "neck"); Stockton (Quarry and Presque Isle bays, N end of Julian Bay)
NE	Basswood*, Devils (South Landing), Little Sand Bay, Manitou, Michigan, Oak, Quarry, Raspberry, Presque Isle, South Twin	W side of south sandspits on Cat, Ironwood, Oak, Outer*, Raspberry*; S of Long Island; S of South Twin Dock; Stockton (Quarry and Presque Isle bays)
E	Basswood, Devils (South Landing), Little Sand Bay, Manitou*, Oak, Quarry, Presque Isle, South Twin	W side of south sandspits on Cat, Ironwood*, Oak*, Outer; Cat, W of "neck"; S of Long Island; Oak (N side*); Raspberry Bay (mainland*); Sand Island (Lighthouse Bay); South Twin (S of dock); Stockton (Quarry* and Presque Isle bays)
SE	Basswood, Little Sand Bay, Outer, Presque Isle, South Twin	Bear (hook on NE end); S of Long Island*; Oak (N side); Raspberry Bay (mainland); Rocky (N side of "neck"); Sand (Lighthouse Bay); South Twin (S of dock, N of sandspit N of dock); Stockton (Presque Isle Bay*); York (N side)
S	Little Sand Bay, Outer, Presque Isle	Bear (hook on NE end); Cat (E of the "neck"*); Madeline (Big Bay); Oak (N side); Outer (NE of dock); Raspberry Bay (mainland); Rocky (N side of neck); Sand (Lighthouse and Justice bays); Stockton (S side of Julian Bay), York (N side)
SW	Little Sand Bay, Otter, Outer, Presque Isle, Sand (East Bay)	Bear (hook on NE end); Cat (E of the "neck"); Madeline (Big Bay); Oak (N side); Otter (NE of dock); Outer (E of dock); Raspberry (NE of sandspit); Raspberry Bay (mainland); Rocky (all along east side); Sand (Justice and East bays); Stockton (Julian Bay); York (N side)
W	Devils (South Landing), Little Sand Bay, Otter, Presque Isle, Quarry, Rocky, Sand (East Bay)	Bear (hook on NE end); Cat (E of the "neck," E of south sandspit); Madeline (Big Bay, Chebomnicon Bay); Otter (NE of dock); Outer (E of south sandspit); Raspberry (E side); Raspberry Bay (mainland); Rocky (E side); Sand (Justice and East bays); Stockton (Quarry, Presque Isle and Julian Bay); York (N side)
NW	Devils (South Landing), Little Sand Bay, Otter, Presque Isle, Quarry, Rocky, Sand (East Bay)	E side of south sandspits on Cat, Ironwood*, Raspberry, Oak*, Outer; Cat (E of the "neck"); Madeline (Big Bay, Chebomnicon Bay); Otter (NE of dock); Rocky (E side); Sand (Justice* and East bays); Stockton (Quarry, Presque Isle and Julian Bay)

* Since wind direction is often not exactly N or NE, use of some of these docks and anchorages may become marginal — especially in higher winds.

Chapter Five

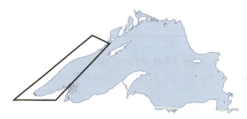

West End: Cornucopia, Wisconsin, to Pigeon Point, Minnesota

When we leave the Apostle Islands and continue heading west, we come to that part of the lake where the north and south shores converge at the twin cities of Duluth/Superior. On a clear day, even well out from this city complex, it is possible to see the bold outlines of both shores as the distance between them decreases. Leading into Superior, Wisconsin, aside from the large headland of Bark Point, the south shore is characterized by relatively low-lying flat land. The north shore, on the other hand, consists of high rolling hills that gradually get steeper as we move NE up the shore. Steep cliffs and jagged rock formations make their appearance as we are greeted by the rough majesty of Castle Danger and Palisade Head.

Once again we reach a section of the lake that is inhospitable to the recreational boater. Here in the western part of Lake Superior are few harbors and anchorages and, often, the distances between them are great. Yet, it is in this section of the lake that we find the largest population and the greatest industrial and shipping activity. Quickly we become aware of the large lakers seen plying the waters to and from the massive grain elevators of Duluth, Minnesota, the loading docks at Two Harbors, and the railroad docks that connect with the interior Mesabi Range. Where copper was king along the southern shore, iron is king on the north. In the days of early exploration and growth, this area of the lake was originally named Fond du Lac (the bottom of the lake). Today, the modern wayfarer quickly becomes aware of the tempo of industrial growth and we can feel the pulse quicken, the closer we come to the west end.

Harbors and Anchorages

Along the south shore, from the Apostle Islands to the city of Superior, there are only two harbors. The first of these is **Cornucopia,** which lies approximately eight miles SW of Sand

Please Note:
Maps and Charts in this book are not necessarily to scale and are not intended for navigation.

Figure 5.1
Siskiwit Bay Marina, Cornucopia, Wisconsin

East Pier Lt.
Fl G 2.5s 20 ft. 8 St M

East Slip

West Slip

South Slip

ramp

Siskiwit River

Key
⭐ Service Dock
▬ Transient Dockage
▬ Dockage

Siskiwit Bay Marina

0   200   400 ft
Soundings in feet.

GPS	Lat.	Lon.
▲	46°51.58' N	91°06.31' W

Island in the Apostles, nestled in the SE end of Siskiwit Bay. This bay is easily confused with Bark Bay, which lies adjacent to the west. The larger headland of Bark Point, which sometimes looks like an island lying next to the shore, can be used to identify this second bay.

Established in 1902, Cornucopia was originally a lumbering center for a number of sawmills and lumbering camps located along this sector of the lake. It also developed as a fishing village and boat-building center, populated largely by Slavic immigrants. Today, the harbor retains much of its early nautical color and natural charm as commercial fishing tugs and small sports fishing boats line its picturesque shores.

The harbor consists of three dredged arms off the mouth of the Siskiwit River that enter Lake Superior via a long dredged channel framed by two breakwaters. The northern breakwater is marked with a Fl G light. The entrance channel and harbor channels are periodically dredged. However, there is often considerable silting due to the Siskiwit River which may impede passage for very deep-draft boats. Thus, boats drawing more than 7 feet should call the marina on VHF before entering. In entering the harbor favor the northern breakwater, then when well into the channel favor the starboard side slightly to the west of the middle.

Of the three harbor extensions, the West Slip has the most depth. The Siskiwit Bay Marina (Tel.: 715-742-3337) is located here and transient dockage is usually available on the service dock. The marina provides gasoline, diesel, pump-out, water and electricity (30 A). See Figure 5.1 Adjacent to the fuel dock there is a small ship's store and gift shop and to the south there is a building that has rest rooms and showers. A 15-ton Mobile Boat Lift and 10-ton hydraulic yard trailer have been added to the premises along with a fair amount of winter storage.

The West Slip at Cornucopia. The Fo'c'sle Inn is housed in the large building. DAH

The marina monitors VHF channel 16 and they appreciate a call ahead from transients coming in. In past years the East Slip has been dredged to depths of 6 feet and greater. A City Dock provides local dockage with a couple of places for transient dockage here. The South Slip, where there is a launching ramp, is only accessible to shoal draft boats. In recent years the addition of a rubble silt-diverter has increased dockage in this section of the harbor.

The most prominent structure in the harbor is a large "barn-like" building that was one of the original buildings built by commercial fishermen who came to this harbor in the early part of the 20th century. A number of boats were built adjacent to it by Tom Jones, a certified Master Shipbuilder. His son, Emory, was the harbor wharfinger who, until the late 1980s, was always on hand to greet visitors – and always with a story to tell about "when the fishing was good." Today the shipwright tradition continues since the lower level of this building has been restored into a boat repair shop where wood, fiberglass and finishing work are available along with engine repairs. The upper level has been converted to a family dwelling for the owner/ dockmaster of the marina and a bed-and-breakfast inn – the Fo'c'sle.

"Corny" is always a fun place to visit. There are a number of interesting gift/curio shops along the NE channel. Just a short walk into town there is a well-stocked general store and bar/restaurant. There is another excellent restaurant, The Village Inn, just a couple of blocks SW on the highway. Today, when we visit this sleepy little harbor, it is hard to believe that at one time there were 22 tugs fishing out of the harbor and that it was also known as an important shipbuilding center on the lake.

The second harbor of refuge along this stretch is **Port Wing,** located at the mouth of the Flag River, approximately 30 nautical miles east of Duluth. Like Cornucopia, Port Wing was established as a logging and fishing village in the early 1900s. It is an important harbor of refuge, because it is the only place to get off the lake between Cornucopia and Duluth, a distance of 43 nautical miles.

The harbor consists of a dredged channel that runs parallel to the lake and is marked by two long piers that extend out into the lake. The eastern pier is marked with a light that flashes green. In approaching the dock area, it is important to turn sharp at the pier to avoid shoal areas to the south.

NOT TO BE USED FOR NAVIGATION – SKETCH APPROXIMATE

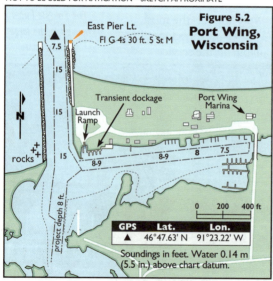

Figure 5.2
Port Wing, Wisconsin

East Pier Lt.
Fl G 4s 30 ft. 5 St M

Transient dockage

Port Wing Marina

Launch Ramp

rocks

15

7.5

15

15

8-9   8-9   8   7.5

project depth 8 ft.

0   200   400 ft

GPS	Lat.	Lon.
▲	46°47.63' N	91°23.22' W

Soundings in feet. Water 0.14 m (5.5 in.) above chart datum.

This is another harbor that needs to be dredged periodically, and depths may vary somewhat from season to season. It used to be primarily a wilderness harbor with no facilities, but then beginning in the early 1980s a number of slips were added each season until there was dockage for more than 40 boats. Although these slips are used primarily by locals with shoal draft boats, there are eight slips adjacent to a launching ramp where medium draft boats can get in. Note that these docks are very short – only about 20 feet – so boats 30 feet or larger don't have much to tie on to and it may be necessary to set out a short-scope stern anchor. Those with deep-draft sailboats often tie off on the inside of the entrance breakwaters. The harbor provides gas, pump-out, water, electricity and rest rooms with showers. Diesel has to be brought in from the town that is approximately one mile inland. The Flag River, which has a number of winding channels, is very interesting to explore by dinghy.

From Port Wing to Duluth/Superior, the shoreline is low and punctuated by a number of rivers that empty into the lake. One of these, the **Brule (Bois Brule) River,** named after the French explorer Etienne Brulé, has historical significance. It is with this river that the early explorers and voyageurs were able to connect Lake Superior with the Mississippi River. They did so by first taking the Brule, and then the St. Croix, inland. Thus the Brule became the most important travel route in the early development of the inland area. Today, it is best known for its excellent trout fishing. It is navigable only by canoe. Note: shallow rocky bars often dot the mouth of the Brule, up to a quarter-mile offshore.

When you approach the twin cities of **Duluth/Superior** by boat, the whole complex at this western end of the lake seems a bit foreboding — especially on the first visit. Large grain elevators shape an industrial skyline, lake shipping is a round-the-clock concern and navigational aids blend into the overwhelming spectacle of the lights and sounds normal to any large urban/industrial center.

One of the largest urban complexes on the lake, the Duluth/Superior area was first visited in the mid-1600s by Father Claude Allouez, who built a mission next to Allouez Bay, and the fur traders Radisson and Des Groseilliers. Sieur du L'hut (for whom Duluth is named) arrived in 1679 on a peace mission to settle a dispute between the Sioux and Chippewa Native Americans. The area was used early as a center for fur trading posts, but it wasn't until the mid-1800s that it gained permanent settlers. Key to the development of the area was the coming of the railroads and the establishment of Duluth as a major grain shipping port. Lumbering and the opening of the Mesabi Iron Range just before the turn of the 20th century quickly assured the establishment of Duluth as the most important shipping port on the lake. Now with the gateway to the oceans through the St. Lawrence Seaway, Duluth takes its place in world-wide shipping, and it is a common occurrence to see foreign ships at the docks taking on grain, coal, iron and even crude

oil from the far fields in Alberta, Canada.

Key to the development of Duluth/Superior as an important shipping port was that it boasts of one of the best landlocked harbors on the Great Lakes. Completely separated from the main lake by two long strips of land, Minnesota and Wisconsin points, Superior Bay has developed into a deep-water harbor that contains 50 docks, some of the largest grain elevators in the United States and the largest iron ore dock in the United States. The Burlington Northern ore docks that are located in Superior are the largest in the world loading taconite ore into the massive 1,000-footers. Within the Duluth area, the Duluth, Missabi and Iron Range Railway Company iron ore docks extend more than 2,000 feet into the harbor. Serviced by six major railroads, the port handles 1,100 rail cars of cargo daily or 40 million tons in a 10-month navigation season. The nine-mile-long sandbar that forms this protected harbor is believed to be the longest fresh-water sandbar in the world.

There are only two entries to the harbor, one at each end. Superior Entry, with controlling depths of 27 to 31 feet, is located

NOT TO BE USED FOR NAVIGATION – SKETCH APPROXIMATE

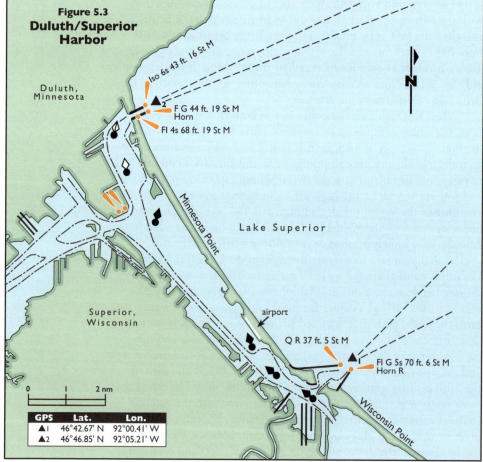

Figure 5.3
Duluth/Superior Harbor

Duluth, Minnesota

Iso 6s 43 ft. 16 St M

F G 44 ft. 19 St M
Horn

Fl 4s 68 ft. 19 St M

Minnesota Point

Lake Superior

Superior, Wisconsin

airport

Q R 37 ft. 5 St M

Fl G 5s 70 ft. 6 St M
Horn R

Wisconsin Point

0   1   2 nm

GPS	Lat.	Lon.
▲1	46°42.67' N	92°00.41' W
▲2	46°46.85' N	92°05.21' W

at the southern end. It is formed by a set of outer and inner breakwaters, both of which are equipped with lights: when entering the harbor, starboard lights flash red, port lights flash green. This entrance is also equipped with a foghorn.

The other entrance to the harbor is the Duluth Ship Canal (controlling depths of 28 to 31 feet) that is located at the northern end of Minnesota Point.

The Dahlfin II *approaches the Aerial Lift Bridge in Duluth.* DAHL

The entrance to the channel is established by two long breakwaters that extend out into the lake. The northern breakwater Fl W, the south breakwater outer light Fl G. It also has an inner light that Fl W. The south breakwater is equipped with a foghorn. The Aerial Lift Bridge that spans this entry needs to be raised for all but small powerboats. To do this, the bridge operator is first called on VHF Channel 16 to provide an approximate ETA. Then when you are at the bridge, signal with a horn – long, short, long (– • –). The bridge can rise to its full height of 138 feet in an impressive 55 seconds. It probably should also be noted that currents as much as six knots are

NOT TO BE USED FOR NAVIGATION – SKETCH APPROXIMATE

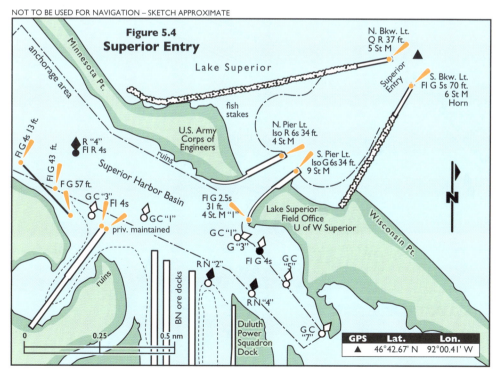

sometimes experienced in the entrance canals, particularly in the Duluth Ship Canal. These are due to changes in the lake's surface as it may temporarily rise or fall.

Within the Duluth/Superior basin there are a number of marine facilities, many of which usually have transient dockage available. Starting at the southern end of the basin near Superior Entry is the largest marina on the lake at **Barker's Island.** The marina, which is operated by Sailboats Inc./SI Marine Management (Tel.: 800-826-7010), has a controlling depth of 8 feet. With accommodations for 420 boats, transient slips are usually available. It is a full-service marina that provides gasoline, diesel, pump-outs (three different stations), water, electricity (30 A & 50 A), rest rooms, showers and even three lighted tennis courts. There is a clubroom where boaters may gather with a kitchen area, TV, WiFi Internet access and a coin-operated laundry. The marina has a 35-ton open-end Travelift and a 35-ton hydraulic boat-moving trailer. They can easily handle

NOT TO BE USED FOR NAVIGATION – SKETCH APPROXIMATE

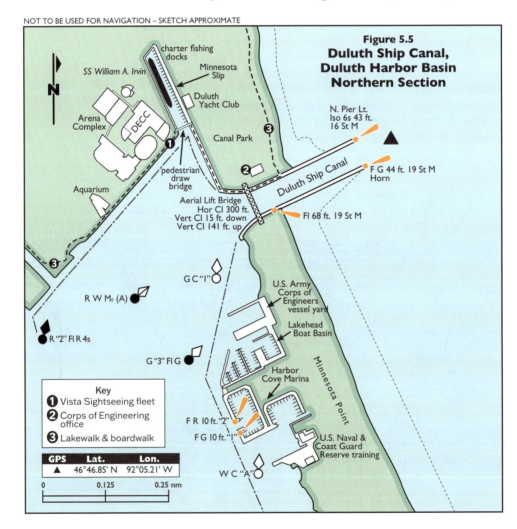

Figure 5.5
Duluth Ship Canal,
Duluth Harbor Basin
Northern Section

powerboats or sailboats for repairs and storage whether on stands or cradles. A 24,000-square-foot heated boat storage building was added in 2005.

Barker's Island Marina is also well known for its 5,000-square-foot repair facility and year-round service and repair capabilities. They have an experienced staff of trained marine repair technicians and are able to handle routine maintenance, major repairs, system upgrades, structural repairs and refinishing or, if necessary, a complete vessel refit. They have a well-stocked parts department open seven days a week during the boating season. Barker's Ship's Store has a large selection of boating equipment, electronic gear, charts and famous name brand clothing and shoes for all seasons. Sailboats Inc., headquartered at Barker's Island Marina, operates the largest sailing school on the lake offering hands-on instruction at both Superior and Bayfield, Wisconsin. To date, more than 10,000 students have graduated from their program, many of whom continue to sail by chartering or owning their own boats.

Adjacent to the marina is a large 115-room hotel, the Barker's

NOT TO BE USED FOR NAVIGATION – SKETCH APPROXIMATE

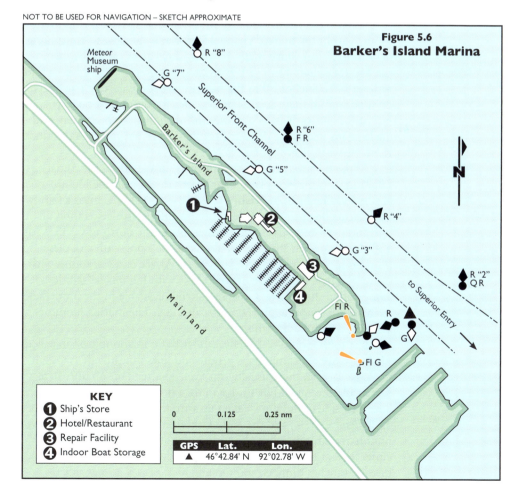

Figure 5.6
Barker's Island Marina

KEY
1 Ship's Store
2 Hotel/Restaurant
3 Repair Facility
4 Indoor Boat Storage

GPS	Lat.	Lon.
▲	46°42.84' N	92°02.78' W

Island Inn, which has an excellent restaurant, lounge and an indoor pool with a whirlpool and sauna. The hotel has bicycles to rent. A number of beautiful townhomes have also been built on the island overlooking the water. Other points of interest in the immediate area are the *SS Meteor* Maritime Museum and the Fairlawn Mansion and Museum. The *Meteor* Museum is comprised of the only surviving whaleback freighter in existence. Built in Superior just before the turn of the 20th century, it was first used as an ore carrier. Then it transported grain and automobiles until it was grounded in 1969.

Across the street from Barker's Island, Fairlawn Mansion and Museum is a restored 42-room mansion of a lumbering magnate built in 1889. The entire house is an exhibit reflecting the days of turn-of-the-century Victorian elegance, maritime commerce and Native American lore. Adjacent to Barker's Island is a beautiful hiking/biking trail that follows the waterfront, the Osaugie Trail. A few blocks NW of Barker's Island the highway splits. By taking Hwy. 2 to the left for four blocks you come to a series of shopping centers, the first of which has a lounge, liquor store and well-stocked 24-hour grocery store.

Traveling north toward Duluth in Superior Bay, it is important to stay within the buoyed channel area that is dredged to controlling depths of 27 feet, since there are many shoal areas off to the side in the bay. (See chart #14975.) With care, however, it is possible to find some areas to anchor off to the side. In fact you will see a few boats on moorings in these areas. The best area for deep-draft boats is NE of R N"4" or R N"8". Those with shallow draft boats may find dockage on a concrete dock at Park Point. The approach to this dock is NE between R N"10" and R N"12".

At the northern end of Superior Bay, just south of the Aerial Lift Bridge, is the best place for transient dockage in the Duluth area at **Lakehead Boat Basin** (Tel.: 218-722-1757). This is a family run marina beginning in 1959 and now into its 4th generation of operation. To enter the marina, enter just to the north of G"3." With 130 slips, transient slips are usually available along with gas, diesel, pump-out, water, electricity (30 A & 50 A), ice and rest rooms with showers. There is a 50-ton Travelift here with full repair facilities along with a ship's store. Groceries are not available in the immediate vicinity. For shopping, it is best to call a taxi. The marina monitors Channel 16 on VHF radio.

Just to the south of Lakehead Boat Basin is a double basin called Harbor Cove. This marina is private and does not provide transient dockage. In fact, there usually isn't even an attendant on duty here. Just inside the Aerial Lift Bridge to the north is the Minnesota Slip. The west side of the slip is taken up with the museum ship, the *SS William A. Irvin*, and the Vista Fleet tour boats. These provide two hour narrated tours of the Duluth/Superior Harbor that include a closer look at the grain elevators and ore docks. Some of the tours provide lunches dinners, and moonlight cruises. The east side is private dockage for the Duluth Yacht Club and some charter boats. There are also a number of fishing and sailing charters at both Lakehead Boat Basin and Harbor Cove Marina.

By staying within the buoyed channel of the St. Louis River it is possible to travel to Spirit Lake, eight miles inland and even a ways beyond. Just before getting to the lake, five miles up river, there is a small marina called Spirit Lake Marina (Tel.: 218-628-3578). Although it is used primarily for small powerboats, there usually is some transient dockage available. Note: there is no fuel here and special arrangements have to be made to have it brought in via truck.

Within the area of the Aerial Lift Bridge there are a number of points of interest for visiting boaters. The Lake Superior Maritime Visitor Center at Canal Park, next to the lift bridge on its northern side, is of particular interest to the boater. For, in addition to presenting the history and growth of Great Lakes shipping, it also displays artifacts and old relics from sunken boats, many of which go back before the turn of the 20th century. Within Canal Park, which used to be a decaying waterfront, old warehouses have been beautifully restored. Here you will find mini-malls with delightful shops and restaurants, business offices and even new hotels. Beginning at Canal Park and following the shoreline approximately one mile to Fitger's Brewery Complex, a renovated 1905 brewery that contains more shops and restaurants, there is a beautiful boardwalk, the Downtown Lakewalk. This total area makes this one of the most beautiful waterfront developments on Lake Superior.

Across the Minnesota Slip on the foot bridge is the *William A. Irvin*, a former flagship of the United States Steel Great Lakes Fleet. Built in 1938, it is one of just two floating museum ships, the other being the *Valley Camp* in the Soo. Complete with rich staterooms that were once used for VIPs, it is one of Duluth's premier attractions. Also located here are the Vista cruise boats that provide two-hour cruises visiting important spots in the harbor and concentrating on the various docks, grain terminals and commercial shipping. If transportation can be provided, it is most interesting to visit one of the observation platforms at the ore docks where you can watch ship-loading operations. The most prominent structure in this area is the Duluth Entertainment Convention Center (DECC) that is built to also look like a ship. To the north of it is an Omnimax Theatre which presents afternoon and nightly programs. This whole area is connected to the downtown Duluth business district via a number of beautiful sky walks.

One of the biggest attractions in Duluth is also the newest, the Great Lakes Aquarium that opened in July 2000. This red, green and blue structure, which was designed to look like an amalgamation of warehouses, steel plants and industrial plants, is easily found on the waterfront just SW of the DECC. Upon entering the complex, the visitor is immediately faced with a uniquely designed waterwall with the word "water" etched into glass in a variety of different languages.

Of special interest are the beautiful displays of different ecosystems around Lake Superior: the falls at Otter Cove; various fish species in the Baptism and St. Louis Rivers; waterfowl in the Kagagon Slough in Chequamegon Bay and at the Pictured Rocks. The aquarium's center piece display is a two-story, three-tank (120,000-gallon) exhibit of Isle Royale that depicts the great sturgeons of the deep and the interaction of wildlife on land and near the water's surface. There are dozens of smaller displays where the emphasis is on "hands-

NOT TO BE USED FOR NAVIGATION – SKETCH APPROXIMATE

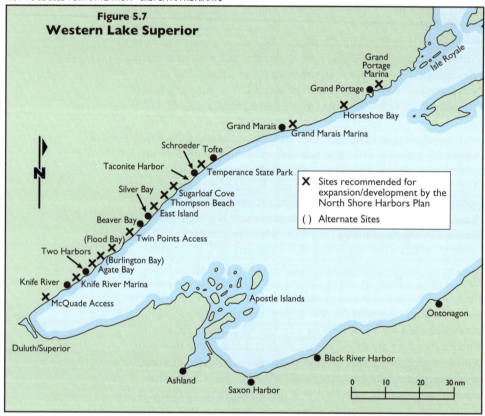

Figure 5.7
Western Lake Superior

X Sites recommended for expansion/development by the North Shore Harbors Plan

( ) Alternate Sites

Figure 5.8
Small Boat Access Sites – Completed or Partially Completed

Name	Location	Lat/Lon	Description
Twin Points Access	Between Two Harbors & Silver Bay	47° 09.81'N 91° 25.52'W	150' crib dock provides protection for 2 launch ramps
Tofte Access	Between Taconite Hbr. and Grand Marais	47° 34.21'N 90° 50.19'W	85' breakwater, new launch ramp, 1 concrete crib dock
Horseshoe Bay Access	Between Grand Marais & Grand Portage	47° 50.90'N 90° 56.04'W	1 ramp, 1 dock, no protection, future plans for a crib dock for protection

on" and interactive learning for both young and old alike. This is a "must see" experience for anyone who visits Duluth whether by land or water.

When we leave Duluth and begin our trek up Lake Superior's northern shore, we are now in that section of the lake which is one of the most inhospitable to the recreational boater. For in the 95-mile stretch from Duluth to Grand Marais there are but two harbors that truly cater to pleasure craft and these are at Knife River and Silver Bay. True, there are a few other harbors, but this is iron country and big shipping takes precedence so, at best, we are talking about harbors of refuge with no cruising amenities. Complete protection may not always be possible, and there is always the probability of an uncomfortable anchorage due to the surge of a passing ore carrier.

In a response to boaters' lobbies for safe harbors of refuge from Lake Superior's unpredictable weather, in the late 1980s the North Shore Management Board directed a study to determine the feasibility of establishing sites for recreational facilities along this inhospitable shoreline. In March 1991, the North Shore Harbors Plan, a 45-page document, was published in which a number of sites were identified for possible development. In some of the sites, the proposal suggested expanding present facilities, in others completely new facilities would need to be constructed. (See Fig. 5.7.)

To date a number of these facilities have been started or completed. The marina at Silver Bay and the safe harbor at Taconite Harbor are direct results of this proposal. However, it is important to note that some of the proposed sites are just points of access with ramps for launching small boats and are not safe harbors. Some do not have protective breakwaters from the lake or the breakwaters are very small. These facilities are very small and confined and thus cater to small trailerable boats and are not feasible for large boat use. (See Fig. 5.8.) Note that further implementation of the plan, particularly for marinas and enclosed harbors for larger boats, remains at the local level as communities, counties and potential owners need to assess individual needs as funding becomes available through the state legislature and other sources.

The newest addition to the program is at **McQuade Access** 10.5 miles NE

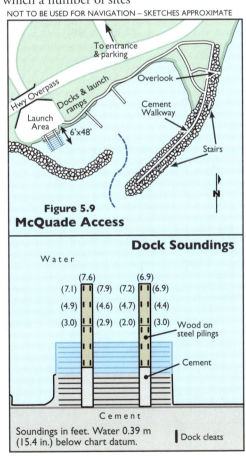

NOT TO BE USED FOR NAVIGATION – SKETCHES APPROXIMATE

Figure 5.9
McQuade Access

Dock Soundings

Water

(7.6)   (6.9)
(7.1) (7.9) (7.2) (6.9)
(4.9) (4.6) (4.7) (4.4)
(3.0) (2.9) (2.0) (3.0)   Wood on steel pilings

Cement

Cement

Soundings in feet. Water 0.39 m (15.4 in.) below chart datum.   ▮ Dock cleats

of Duluth between Duluth and Knife River. Construction of this harbor began in late 2004 and was completed in late 2007. It consists of a three-acre basin protected by two low berm-style breakwaters that have day-markers with flashing lights at the entrance: red triangle to starboard, green rectangle to port. In normal water years the controlling depths are 8 feet. There are two docks with three launch ramps (one double and one single) in the SW corner of the harbor. The docks are constructed in three sections, each 6-by-24 feet. The first section is a cement base and ramp; the other two are wood on steel pilings. Other facilities include rest rooms, public phone, fish cleaning station, a large paved parking area and a cement walkway with an overlook on the eastern breakwater. Two additional 45 foot docks have been added to the middle of the shoreline NE of the launch ramps. A short way down the road is the Lakeview Castle Dining and Lounge. (See Fig 5.9.)

The next harbor we come to after leaving Duluth is the **Knife River Marina,** which was acquired by the DNR in 2001 and is operated by SI Marine Management (Tel.: 218-834-6076). It is located approximately 17 nautical miles NE of Duluth on the north side of Granite Point, a half-mile south of the Knife River. A rock boulder breakwater extending out from Granite Point marks its entrance with a Fl G light at its outer end. Because of the considerable shoaling extending SW from Knife Island, the best approach to the harbor entrance is to keep well to the south of Knife Island. Passage between Knife Island and the mainland is possible, but best done with local knowledge.

Controlling depths in the entrance channel are usually 9 feet, with 8 feet inside the main channel. However, in low-water

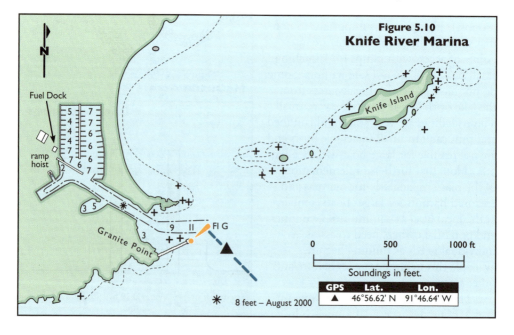

Figure 5.10
Knife River Marina

GPS	Lat.	Lon.
▲	46°56.62' N	91°46.64' W

years these depths are considerably less. When approaching and passing through the entrance channel, it is best to favor the breakwater, since there is shoaling and a sandbar off the other side. There is relatively deep water in the remaining channel except for an 8-foot spot about halfway up the channel. (See Fig. 5.10.) In the docking area, the eastern section has more depth with the western section being used for smaller or shoal draft boats. Of the 100 berths available, some dockage is usually set aside for transients. Electricity (30 A & 50 A), water, gas and diesel fuel, ice, pump-out, rest rooms and showers are provided. There is a small boat launch ramp along with a 20-ton Travelift and full repair facilities available. The marina monitors Channel 16 on VHF radio. There is a terrific smoked fish vendor, Russ Kendall's Smoke House, a few blocks NW on the highway. East down the road there is a small store that makes candy. Note: this is one of the sites along this section of the shoreline where there are plans for future expansion.

McQuade Access just south of Two Harbors, Minnesota.
PAUL L. HAYDEN

A short hop (5.5 nautical miles) up the shore from Knife River lies **Two Harbors,** the first of Minnesota's iron ore ports to open to shipping, receiving shipments from the range as early as 1884. Its name comes from the two bays that are located side-by-side, Agate and Burlington. Only Agate Bay, the western one, was ever fully developed.

Although open to the south, the harbor receives additional protection by a breakwater that extends from the eastern end of the bay and a detached breakwater in the western section. Both are equipped with lights; the eastern breakwater Fl R, the western

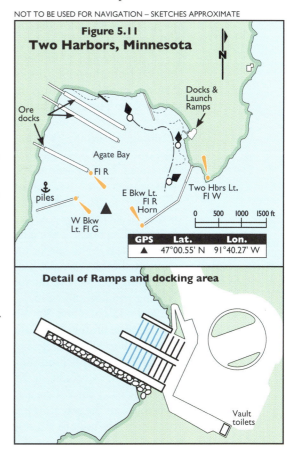

NOT TO BE USED FOR NAVIGATION – SKETCHES APPROXIMATE

Figure 5.11
Two Harbors, Minnesota

Ore docks

Docks & Launch Ramps

Agate Bay

Fl R

piles

E Bkw Lt. Fl R Horn

Two Hbrs Lt. Fl W

W Bkw Lt. Fl G

0 500 1000 1500 ft

GPS	Lat.	Lon.
▲	47°00.55' N	91°40.27' W

Detail of Ramps and docking area

Vault toilets

breakwater Fl G. There is also a light on the mainland at the base of the eastern breakwater that Fl W.

It is important to remember that this harbor was constructed mainly for commercial shipping and remains one of the busiest ore harbors on the lake. Thus, there are no true facilities here for pleasure craft and the harbor should be treated only as a harbor of refuge. It is possible, however, to tie up to the pipe safety rail on the inside of the eastern breakwater for short and even overnight stays. This allows walking access to the town (approximately four blocks) where it is possible to get supplies: groceries, ice, gas in cans. It may be prudent to leave someone on the boat, because an uncomfortable surge can develop from shipping traffic, strong southerly winds or even small boat traffic on weekends. Note that as a part of the North Shore Harbors Plan, a federal grant of $3.5 million has been approved to build a new seven-acre 100-slip marina in the Agate Bayfront area. However, until this happens, provisions for transient boats are marginal at best.

There are three ramps (1 double and 1 single) and two docks for launching small boats in the NE corner of the harbor with a large parking lot for cars and trailers. On the adjacent peninsula, which forms the eastern side of the bay, there is a picnic area with picnic tables and a lovely trail, the Sonju Walking Trail, which follows the shoreline north to a campground.

There are also a number of interesting museums in the area. Not far from the public docks is the Two Harbors Lighthouse Station. Built in 1892, it is the oldest operating lighthouse in Minnesota. Three of its buildings have been converted into a bed-and-breakfast inn and museum that features displays on commercial shipping and fishing. A short walk from this area is the old Duluth and Iron Range Railroad Depot that has also been converted into the Lake County Historical Society depot/museum complete with two steam locomotives that once served the area. One of these is the *3 Spot*, the first steam engine to work in this area. The other is the *Mallet*, the largest of all steam engines. To the north of the huge loading docks is the *Edna G.*, a tugboat museum. Although the emphasis in the harbor today is on shipping and transportation connected to the taconite industry, it is interesting to note that a fledgling company in the manufacture of abrasives, Minnesota Mining and Manufacturing, got its start here. Today 3M operates plants in 32 states and 30 countries.

Because of shipping traffic, anchoring is not allowed in the main harbor. It is possible, however, to tuck down into the SW end of the harbor behind the detached west breakwater to anchor out of the way of traffic. If this is done, be sure to stand well off the breakwater since there are some underwater obstructions about two-thirds of the way in. This breakwater bears special mention because it was built over a shipwreck, the *Samuel P. Ely*, a three-masted schooner converted into a barge. In October 1896, it was being towed to Two Harbors for a load of iron ore only to founder against the original west breakwater in a gale and sink. Years later a new breakwater was built over the site. Plans to rebuild the present breakwater include provisions to preserve the wreck.

From Two Harbors to Silver Bay there are 23 nautical miles of rugged shoreline characterized by steep rocky cliffs and a dozen or more rivers and streams that empty into this portion of the lake. Seven miles NE of Two Harbors, Encampment Island provides limited, but sometimes welcome shelter from rough weather. Though shoaled to the SW, reasonable holding ground can be found. A few miles farther up the shoreline it is important to note that in the area of Castle Danger there is a very shallow and dangerous reef of small boulders that lies fully one-quarter mile offshore. There have been reports in recent years of a number of sailboats that have hit the reef, often with damage.

None of these rivers is navigable except by canoe, but one bears mentioning: the Gooseberry River, named after a crude distortion of the name of an early explorer, Des Groseilliers. Like many of the rivers along this segment of the shoreline, this river was used during the logging operations of the early 1900s. There is a series of beautiful waterfalls located upstream. In 1933, the area was made into a state park and today it is an important stopover for those who circle the lake via land. Despite the scenic attractions here, boaters should not attempt to approach the mouth of this river, for there is an extensive gravel spit that extends out in a southerly direction. Note also the 4-foot shoal approximately one-half mile south of the river mouth.

Perched high on rock cliffs not too far up the shore from the Gooseberry River, there is another point of interest, **Split Rock Lighthouse.** This light was built in 1910 after numerous vessels sank or were stranded near this area. In 1961, it was automated only to be abandoned in 1968. Today it is part of the state park system and is the most widely visited light on the Great Lakes. The *Great Lakes Pilot* reports that, occasionally, the light may be lit for exhibition purposes. The publication also states that it is possible to receive protection from westerly to northerly winds in the indentation where the Split Rock River enters the lake. In calm conditions, it is possible to bring a boat close in to view this picturesque lighthouse.

Immediately SW of the lighthouse, **Little Two Harbors** offers good shelter from W to NE winds, but marginal protection from the SW. Wreckage from an adjacent wreck, the *Madeira*, litters the bottom, so anchors should be buoyed with a trip line.

The story of the *Madeira* is an interesting one as the ship was a 436-foot steel barge that was under tow to Duluth by the *William Edenborn* when they were caught in a blinding snowstorm on 28 November 1905. Note that 29 ships were lost or damaged in this fierce winter storm. The *Madeira* broke loose of the tow around 3

a.m., only to founder a couple of hours later when it was literally battered broadside against a high cliff wall that was as high as its masts. The cliff was heroically scaled by one of the crew members, and all but one of the remaining crew were able to follow suit on a line he tossed back down. The *Madeira* subsequently broke into two parts, and today the debris remains on the bottom, a popular attraction for divers.

Approximately 23 nautical miles up the shore from Two Harbors there are two adjacent bays, the first of which offers only marginal protection as a harbor of refuge. This is **Beaver Bay** which was settled in the 1850s and is one of the oldest settlements on Minnesota's north shore. It was an important center for lumbering because of a sawmill located here.

Although the bay is quite open to the east, there is protection at Beaver Bay for westerly and northerly winds. Anchoring may be difficult because there are a number of large boulders in the bay. There are two docks along the northerly shore, the westerly one having the most depth at its outer end, 9 feet. The bay is marginal at best because of its open exposure to the lake.

When it became apparent that the rich iron deposits of the Mesabi Range were dwindling, the large iron mining concerns began to turn their efforts toward extracting this important metal from a lower grade ore known as taconite. Although taconite was known since the late 1800s, it has only been since the middle of the 1900s that the technology for extracting its iron was developed, thus making its use economically feasible. In this process, the taconite (which is only one-third iron) is crushed and the dust-size particles are extracted with magnets and then compressed into pellets for shipping. To facilitate this dramatic change in the industry, two new plants and harbors were constructed on Minnesota's north shore in the mid-1950s: Silver Bay and Taconite Harbor.

Silver Bay is a privately owned harbor located one mile NE of Beaver Bay. Built by the Reserve Mining Company in 1955, and now operated by Cleveland Cliffs Inc., this harbor's main purpose is to process and ship iron pellets from the low grade taconite transported from 60 miles inland. Adjacent to the harbor is the town of Silver Bay which literally mushroomed into existence overnight to house the company's 3,500 workers.

The commercial harbor consists of a long breakwater that forms its southern end between Pellet Island and the mainland, and, on the north, is Beaver Island with another breakwater to the mainland. There are a number of lights and buoys in the harbor. (See Fig. 5.12.) On Pellet Island the light Fl G; midway on Beaver Island there is a light that Fl R and that is also equipped with a horn. On mainland in the middle of the harbor there is a light that Fl G.

As part of the North Shore Harbors Plan, the newest marina along this shoreline has been built to the SW of the Silver Bay west breakwater. Dedicated in August 1999, the **Silver Bay Marina**

(Tel.: 218-226-3121) has become a welcome safe harbor along this rugged forlorn shoreline. To build the marina was a formidable operation since the huge armor stone for the breakwater was hauled from Babbitt, 52 miles away. It took 25 trucks making two trips a day, seven days a week for three months, with each truck carrying up to four rocks per trip. The entrance of the marina is well-marked with three sets of red and green buoys with red and green lights, a red reflective day marker with a light on the east stone breakwater and green reflective day markers on the port bluff when entering and the smaller inside port breakwater.

Silver Bay Marina is one of the newer safe harbors on Minnesota's shore.
CITY OF SILVER BAY

The marina has 108 slips with 40 slips set aside for transients. This is a full-service marina that provides gasoline, diesel, pump-out, water and electricity – both 30 A and 50 A service. A contemporary Administration Building sits up on the hill. The upper level is open to the public and includes rest rooms and an observation deck with a porch. The lower level provides a laundry, showers and rest rooms for boaters. Adjacent to the marina are a couple of parking lots, a children's playground and lovely picnic areas with tables and grills. A short trail from the western parking lot takes you up to a beautiful overlook of the area. The town of Silver Bay is 2.5 miles NE up the highway. There is a shopping center on Outer Drive near the Mariner Motel with a restaurant, grocery store and hardware store. A little closer (1.5 miles) to the SW is Beaver Bay where there are a couple of excellent restaurants and a liquor store. Located within a wilderness setting, the Northern Lights Roadhouse is especially known for its northern specialties cuisine and they will provide transportation to and from the marina.

Another private harbor, built for the purpose of extracting iron from

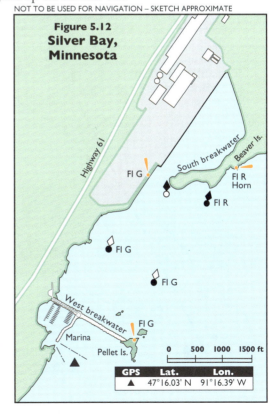

NOT TO BE USED FOR NAVIGATION – SKETCH APPROXIMATE

Figure 5.12
Silver Bay, Minnesota

Highway 61

South breakwater

Beaver Is.

Fl G

Fl R
Horn

Fl R

Fl G

Fl G

West breakwater

Fl G

Marina

Pellet Is.

0   500   1000   1500 ft

GPS	Lat.	Lon.
▲	47°16.03' N	91°16.39' W

taconite ore, is **Taconite Harbor,** 21 nautical miles northeast of Silver Bay. This harbor, which was constructed a few years after Silver Bay, was established by the Erie Mining Company, which was bought out by LTV Steel Mining. After 44 years of ore production, LTV shut down in early 2001. Today, there are still freight vessels going in and out of the harbor, but they are carrying coal for the power plant.

The main portion of the harbor is protected by a breakwater that lies between Gull and Bear islands and then extends NE from Bear Island.

Another breakwater forms the northern section of the bay extending out from the mainland. The harbor is usually entered from the south between Gull Island and mainland, and exited between the two breakwaters on the NE end.

There are a number of lights and lighted buoys in the harbor. (See Fig. 5.14.) The west entrance is marked both with lighted buoys and lights on the mainland and Gull Island. For both sets, keep Fl R to starboard and Fl G to port when entering. There is also a fixed green range on the mainland to line up with when coming in through the entrance. Within the main commercial portion of the harbor, it is

NOT TO BE USED FOR NAVIGATION – SKETCHES APPROXIMATE

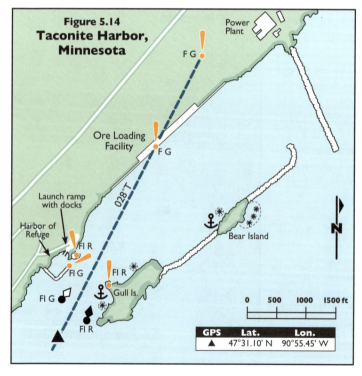

Figure 5.13
Silver Bay Marina

FI G

Pellet Island

lookout

KEY
1 Small boat launch ramp
2 Fuel dock
3 Administration Bldg.
⚓ Red Entrance Marker
⚓ Green Entrance Marker
🔴 Red Buoy with light
🟢 Green Buoy with light

0   250   500 ft

GPS	Lat.	Lon.
▲	47°16.03' N	91°16.39' W

✳ Third Finger with additional slips added in the mid-2000's.

Figure 5.14
Taconite Harbor, Minnesota

Power Plant

F G

Ore Loading Facility

F G

028°T

Launch ramp with docks

Harbor of Refuge

Fl R

Fl G   Fl R

Fl G   Fl R

Bear Island

Gull Is.

Fl R

0   500   1000   1500 ft

GPS	Lat.	Lon.
▲	47°31.10' N	90°55.45' W

possible to anchor just to the west of Bear Island or SW of Gull Island where it gets shallow enough to anchor.

In 2000, a rubble breakwater was constructed to create a Harbor of Refuge adjacent to the southern entrance of the commercial harbor as part of the North Shore Harbors Plan, which was established in 1991. Then in 2001 a large cement double launch ramp with two docks was added. The best entrance into the Harbor of Refuge is to come in from the south in the beginning of the main channel main channel between Gull Island and the mainland between the red and green flashing buoys. The harbor entrance is found NE of the flashing green buoy and is marked by a flashing green marker on the port rubble breakwater and a flashing red marker inside of the starboard rubble entrance.

Within the harbor basin, anchoring is marginal because of a rock bottom. There are, however, three moorings to which you can tie. Note that there is a 24-hour limit on the moorings and this is enforced daily by the DNR. It is possible to tie up to the outside of each of the two docks that are part of the launch complex. Here there is enough room for a 35-foot boat with 7 and 8 feet of water depth depending on lake levels. (See Fig. 5.15.) It is not permitted to tie up on the inside of these docks because of launch traffic. This harbor gets a lot of use by those who launch here with charter fishing boats.

Note that there are no facilities here (electricity or water), only a portable toilet placed on the bank adjacent to the parking lot. Despite this, it is an important Harbor of Refuge in the forlorn 50-mile stretch between Silver Bay and Grand Marais, should it be necessary to get off the lake.

NOT TO BE USED FOR NAVIGATION – SKETCH APPROXIMATE

Although this section of the Lake Superior shore is now primarily characterized by commercial shipping and the iron industry, in earlier years it was commercial fishing and lumbering that brought the immigrant settlers to these shores. A hardy new breed, the Norwegian fisherman, well-adapted to the rigors of open water fishing in small boats, began to dot the shoreline. Names such as Edisen, Tofte, Lutsen and Skadberg became commonplace as these immigrants brought with them their skills from the Old Country. And with

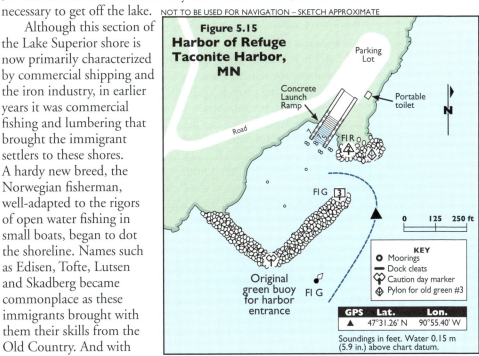

Figure 5.15
Harbor of Refuge
Taconite Harbor,
MN

Parking Lot

Concrete Launch Ramp

Portable toilet

Road

Fl R

Fl G 3

N

0   125   250 ft

KEY
○ Moorings
▬ Dock cleats
✪ Caution day marker
◈ Pylon for old green #3

Original green buoy for harbor entrance
Fl G

GPS	Lat.	Lon.
▲	47°31.26' N	90°55.40' W

Soundings in feet. Water 0.15 m (5.9 in.) above chart datum.

the settlers came a few small towns, some of which never grew large enough to even become incorporated. One, **Grand Marais,** did grow, however, and this was due partly because it is located on a beautiful natural harbor.

Grand Marais was originally named by the French voyageurs who used the bay as a stopover during their travels up and down the shore. With Grand Portage 30 miles to the east quickly becoming a key center in the growing fur trade, less emphasis was placed on developing Grand Marais in these early years (1700s and early 1800s). It wasn't until the mid-1800s that Grand Marais took its place as an important harbor on the shore. This was due to growing activity in commercial fishing and the establishment of large warehouses at Grand Marais for storing fish. At the turn of the 20th century, the town continued to grow as it became an important lumbering center as that industry moved up the shore.

Today, this harbor is formed by two breakwaters that extend the protection achieved by two natural land masses on each side. Both breakwaters have lights, the western one Fl G, the eastern one Fl R. The eastern breakwater is also equipped with a foghorn. There used to be a Coast Guard Station here, adjacent to the east breakwater. After almost 100 years of operation, It closed on Labor Day 2022. For boaters returning from Ontario waters, U.S. customs clearance is available since there is an officer on duty in the Cook County Law Enforcement Center during the summer season: call 218-387-1148 or 218-370-0111 between 9 a.m. and 5 p.m. Depending on how busy they are, the officer will come down to the boat to give clearance, otherwise it is done over the phone. During after hours, call 800-505-8381 for someone who is on border patrol.

There is a marina (Tel.: 218-387-1712) inside the inner breakwater that is often full in the height of the season. When dockage is not available the marina has a number of mooring balls that can be used. The marina provides gasoline, diesel, water, electricity and pump-out. Ice can be obtained at the campground office that is adjacent to the waterfront. The marina has transient moorings: call on Channel 16 and switch to Channel 68 for directions.

To assist in the demand for additional dockage space, the Forestry Department constructed an additional dock in 1989 along the eastern side of the harbor just north of the Coast Guard Station buildings. At the south end of the dock there is a small boat launching ramp. Although the dock can accommodate two or three good-sized boats, depending on water datum, the northern half of the dock can only be used by boats drawing less than 4 feet because of shallow water. Note also the shoal water out from the dock in this area on which boats with greater draft approaching the dock often ground. (See inset, Fig. 5.16.) Note that this dock can become very uncomfortable in strong SW winds. Another alternative to docking is the inside of the eastern breakwater where by climbing up a slanted casement you can reach bollards to tie to. But again, in strong southerly winds, this breakwater can be most uncomfortable as the seas slam against the breakwater sending large amounts of spray up and over onto your boat. The small marina in the SE corner of the harbor is a private establishment constructed in the late 1980s by local boaters and by charter does not provide transient dockage.

The only other alternative is to anchor, and in this harbor anchoring can be tenuous at best. Unfortunately, the eastern half of the harbor which has the best holding ground has become a minefield of local private moorings. Not much space for anchoring is left and since the moorings are positioned on very short scope, it isn't wise to anchor too closely or you may swing into them should the wind shift. It is possible to anchor on the western side, but the holding here is poor due to a gravel bottom and the area is wide open to the SE. The best holding on the west side is just off the little stream that enters the harbor. Still, it is important to keep a watch on your boat while at anchor here.

Grand Marais is always a fun place to visit since the town caters to a thriving tourist trade. There are a number of interesting gift and curio shops, the most prominent of which is the Lake Superior Trading Post, a frontier-style building on the waterfront. For those artistically inclined, there is the Johnson Heritage Post Art Gallery or Sivertson Galleries, which has a very large collection of Lake Superior paintings. There are a number of good eating places: the Donut Shop for early morning coffee; Sven and Ole's Pizza which is done in '50s decor; local cafes such as the Blue Water Cafe or The Angry Trout; The Birch Terrace Supper Club for elegant north woods dining. Within a two- to three-block walk from the harbor there is a variety

NOT TO BE USED FOR NAVIGATION – SKETCH APPROXIMATE

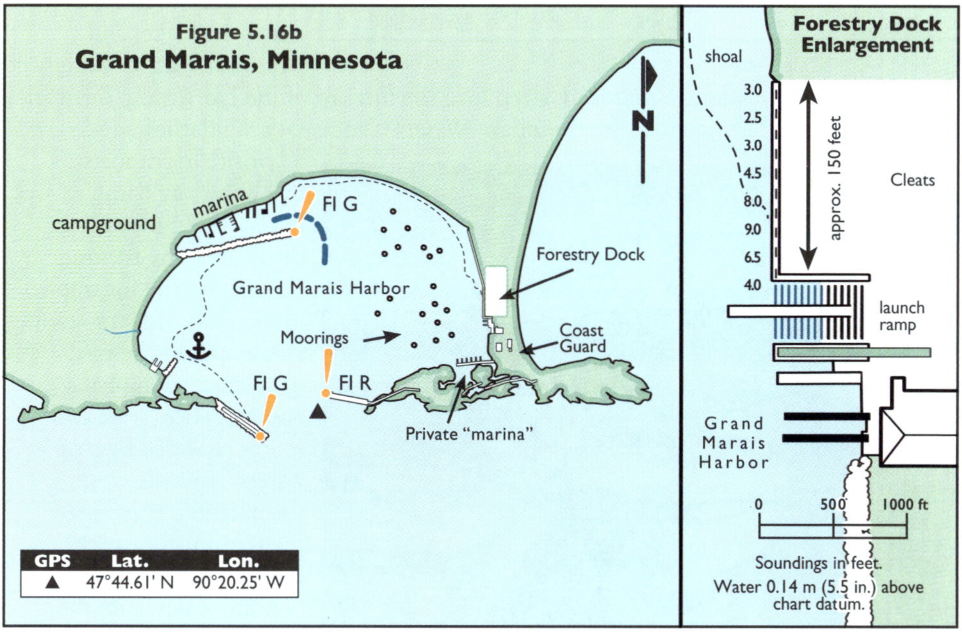

Figure 5.16b
Grand Marais, Minnesota

Forestry Dock Enlargement

store, a hardware store, library, clothing shops and laundry facilities. A little farther up the highway there is an excellent supermarket. A decided attraction is a beautifully designed indoor swimming pool complete with sauna, whirlpool and sunbathing decks, just a short walk from the harbor across from the campground.

Figure 5.16a
Grand Marais Marina & Surrounding docks

North House Folk School

Marina

D C B A

FI G

N

Blowup of Marina docks with Soundings

Marina

Soundings in feet. Water 0.22 m (8.66 in.) above chart datum.

Fuel dock

D C B A

From Grand Marais to Grand Portage, it is approximately 30 nautical miles northeast along a bold rocky shoreline with deep water close in, no protected harbors and few obstructions. Five Mile Rock, which lies approximately five miles NE of Grand Marais, is the only off-shore hazard. However, this segment of the shoreline is well-known for fog conditions (particularly with southerly winds) and because of local magnetic disturbances, it is prudent to stay at least one mile offshore.

The area that forms the border between northern Minnesota and Ontario is interlaced with an intricate network of lakes and streams, a natural waterway passage that leads deep into the interior of the Northwest Territories. Known as the Boundary Waters Canoe Area Wilderness, and now a favorite for canoeists, this waterway complex was once a vital link early in the developing fur trade by connecting the fur trapper in the west with the trading companies in the east.

After leaving Lake Superior there were two routes provided by this waterway to the west: the northern route used the Kaministiquia River inland from Fort William (Thunder Bay) and the

The Forestry Dock in Grand Marais, Minnesota. DAHL

southern route began with the Pigeon River. Although the southern route was shorter and thus was used almost exclusively until the early 1800s, the first 20 miles of the Pigeon River consisted of a series of rapids and waterfalls that were unnavigable and had to be bypassed. Thus, a nine-mile portage trail was established in the early 1700s by the French explorers and fur traders that led from a large bay south of the Pigeon River on Lake Superior's shores and became known as the **Grand Portage** or "great carrying place."

The area grew quickly in importance, and by 1767 it was made a rendezvous point where the trade goods from the east were exchanged for the furs from the west. With elaborate planning each spring, the Northmen (who had wintered inland trading for the precious pelts) would begin their trek down the scores of lakes and streams to meet the voyageurs at lake's edge who likewise had

NOT TO BE USED FOR NAVIGATION – SKETCHES APPROXIMATE

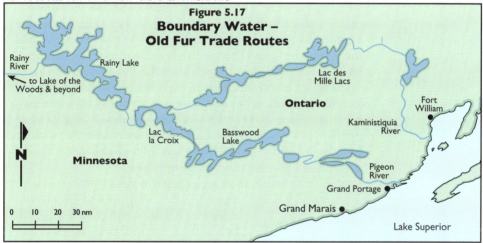

Figure 5.17
Boundary Water –
Old Fur Trade Routes

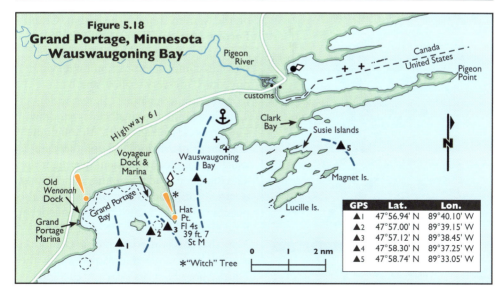

Figure 5.18
Grand Portage, Minnesota
Wauswaugoning Bay

GPS	Lat.	Lon.
▲1	47°56.94' N	89°40.10' W
▲2	47°57.00' N	89°39.15' W
▲3	47°57.12' N	89°38.45' W
▲4	47°58.30' N	89°37.25' W
▲5	47°58.74' N	89°33.05' W

*"Witch" Tree

traveled great distances over land and water to transport agents and trading goods from the east. The rendezvous took place each July and, for two weeks, it was the highpoint for voyageurs and woodsmen alike because it was an occasion of great festivity and merriment. During this time, rivalries between Northmen and voyageurs were paramount, with disputes between their two different lifestyles being settled by boisterous brawls. When the exchange of goods and the decisions of business had been accomplished, each would return along their established routes singing their robust songs and flashing the coveted badges of their office, their feather-plumed hats and long, flowing, brightly colored sashes.

Today, the harbor depicts a much quieter scene with the majority of its activity centered around the Wenonah, an excursion boat which traditionally made the 24-mile trip daily across to Isle Royale, and the Voyageur II, which made the trip to the island three times per week. Those with trailerable boats use the harbor facilities to disembark for their own jump to the island. The harbor is a natural bay, nested between rolling hills on three sides, the land belonging to the Grand Portage Band of Chippewa. The harbor is identified by a flashing white light on the end of Hat Point and Grand Portage Island which lies in the center of the bay. Passage to either side of the island is possible, however, there is a 6-foot shoal between the island and Hat Point which should be skirted. Within the harbor, it is prudent to proceed with caution since the whole area is very shoaled and rocky and has a bottom foul with debris. In only a few areas is it possible to get close into shore.

Within the harbor there are a couple of spots where there is only marginal dockage because of either being open to certain wind directions or lack of sufficient depths. The first of these is a small boat basin with a launch ramp and a gas dock that is located on the western shore of the harbor, **Grand Portage Marina** (Tel.: 218-475-2476). Although this dredged landlocked harbor provides complete protection for all wind directions, it is very shallow and has a narrow entrance channel (12 feet wide). Thus it is limited to small craft that draw 4 feet or less (see Fig. 5.19). Although the slips are primarily for local use, there are usually a couple for transient overnight use. The marina provides gasoline, diesel, water, electricity, rest rooms and showers. It is also possible to get U.S. customs to come down for clearance by calling 218-475-2244. Note that this is another marine facility that has been targeted for expansion by the North Shore Harbors Plan and dredging

NOT TO BE USED FOR NAVIGATION – SKETCH APPROXIMATE

Figure 5.19
Grand Portage Marina

N

Grand Portage Bay

@ 8 ft.

launch ramp   Gas

Customs clearance
218-475-2244

GPS	Lat.	Lon.
▲	47°31.26' N	90°55.40' W

Caution: Bar at entrance approximately 3-4 feet.

and widening the entrance channel would make this marina more accessible to larger boats.

In the NW end of the bay there is a large dock formerly used by the *Wenonah*. It is possible to tie up to the dock (day use only), but because of shoal water boats drawing more than 5 feet will have difficulty getting in. This dock provides the best access to the old fort, museum and heritage center, the Grand Portage National Monument, which is a replica of the first site of the Great Rendezvous. A stockade, the Great Hall and other buildings have been reconstructed to illustrate what life was like in the days of this first white settlement in Minnesota. An interpretative program with tours conducted by the National Park Service, along with displays of local Native American handicraft, provides a brief glimpse into the colorful role that this area portrayed in the past. Within the area, it is also possible to pick up the famous Portage Trail that leads to above the rapids on the Pigeon River.

On the eastern side of the bay is the **Voyageur's Marina** (Tel.: 218-475-2412), which has seen some expansion in recent years. Note that in approaching the dock, about 7 feet from the dock there is a broken spud (a vertical metal beam) stuck in the mud 3 feet under the water surface. It is usually marked with a white plastic bottle and needs to be given wide berth, keeping the obstruction well to starboard. Gasoline, diesel, water, pumpout, electricity (30 A & one 50 A) and limited snack concessions are available. There is a small boat launching ramp here that makes this a common jumping-off place for those making the run over to Isle Royale. Overnight and extended parking for cars and trailers is also provided.

The *Wenonah* and *Voyageur II* both traditionally have reserved dockage here where they load and offload passengers. (See Fig. 5.20.) The *Voyageur II* is another excursion/ ferry boat that makes the run to Isle Royale. Whereas the *Wenonah* makes daily runs to the island, visiting only the southern end at Windigo, the *Voyageur II* makes the run three times each week, completely encircling the island with overnight stays at Rock Harbor on the northern end. The

NOT TO BE USED FOR NAVIGATION – SKETCH APPROXIMATE

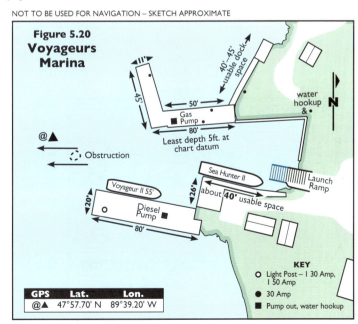

Figure 5.20
Voyageurs Marina

Voyageur II is used primarily to drop off and pick up backpackers and campers at various points around the island.

In leaving Grand Portage and rounding Hat Point to continue up the shoreline, a point of interest is the Spirit Little Cedar Tree (Witch Tree), which is found on the point only a few feet from Lake Superior's waters. Clinging to weather-eroded, lichen-covered rock, this gnarled old white cedar, which has been the guarding sentinel of the harbor entrance for more than 400 years, is still growing. Native Americans both revered and feared it and brought gifts to appease its spirit or gave it wide berth as they passed by in their canoes.

Lying to the east of Hat Point there is a large open bay, **Wauswaugoning Bay,** which provides better anchoring than Grand Portage Bay. By tucking into the NE end of the bay, good anchoring can be found with protection for most winds except SW, where there is a good fetch across the bay. Strong southerly winds can also produce an uncomfortable surge. In entering this area, note the large 5-foot shoal in the western part of the bay and stay clear of the shoal water around Francis Island in the eastern end. The western part of this bay is particularly beautiful with steep, high-rising cliffs that give way to Mt. Josephine, which rises 700 feet above the lake – an indication of the rugged topography that is characteristic as we travel farther up this shore.

Lying to the south of Pigeon Point are the **Susie Islands** that are made up of three main islands and a number of smaller ones. These islands, along with other areas along this shoreline, were once prospected for copper and silver but with minimal rewarding results. Susie Island, which is the largest of the group, has an anchorage in the NE bight of the island that provides protection for all but easterly winds. The approach to the anchorage from the east is clear with no obstructions. From the west it is possible to follow up the western shoreline of Susie Island, between it and the group of smaller islands to the NW, as long as the NW tip of Susie Island isn't hugged too closely since there are some rock shoals there. Note:

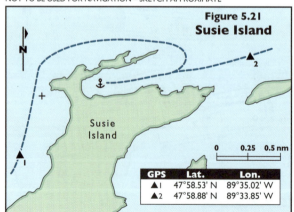

NOT TO BE USED FOR NAVIGATION – SKETCH APPROXIMATE

Figure 5.21
Susie Island

Susie Island

| | 0 | 0.25 | 0.5 nm |

GPS	Lat.	Lon.
▲1	47°58.53' N	89°35.02' W
▲2	47°58.88' N	89°33.85' W

with this approach you will get some 10-foot readings and be able to see the bottom for part of the way. It is possible to go quite a ways into the anchorage and anchor in 8 feet to 9 feet with a bottom of small cobbles and some sand and clay patches. Closer in to the far end there are some large underwater rocks.

The final anchorage in the area before rounding Pigeon Point is **Clark Bay** which is located a little more than a mile N/NE of Susie Island under the high bluffs of Pigeon Point. The anchorage provides good holding ground, but again is open to easterly winds. This is excellent blueberry country on the lower bluffs in early August.

Important Notice: In the area of Pigeon Point, and the islands that lie adjacent, there are strong magnetic anomalies within a mile or so of shore. Therefore, it is wise to stay well offshore when traveling to this area, especially in conditions of reduced visibility and when traveling with compass guidance alone. There have been a number of stories of small craft that have been waylaid in the area and that have even ended up on the rocks.

With eyes turned northward, we now enter one of the best cruising areas of the lake. The bold inhospitable Minnesota shoreline now gives way to a myriad of inlets and bays, quiet coves and protecting island chains. With each wilderness anchorage seeming better than the last, you can get lost here for weeks, if not for a whole summer.

Chapter Six

Isle Royale: A National Park

In the north central part of Lake Superior there is an island that is about 45 miles long and nine miles wide. Surrounding this piece of land, which is often called "The Rock," are approximately 400 smaller islands and islets scattered like pearls off a string, parallel to the deep island ridges. The resulting formations are a series of long narrow channels and deep secure harbors. The wildlife is abundant: waterfowl, beaver, fox and moose. Even the rare haunting call of wolves can be heard on a still night. The fishing on the surrounding reefs and inland lakes is excellent: pike, trout and coho. The land is lush with thick forests, rich with birch and balsam. The island is Isle Royale.

It is believed that the island was first visited by humans as far back as 4,000 years ago when early Native Americans visited it in search of copper. Pieces of Isle Royale copper have been found scattered throughout the United States, and today these prehistoric "mines" can be seen as shallow pits throughout the island. There are at least two writings (Henry Gillman 1873, William P. Ferguson 1923) that tell of finding the remains of a prehistoric townsite on the island's southern shore in the area of Point Houghton. Supposedly these contained a number of "pit dwellings" characteristic of those people known as Mound Builders. To date these findings have not been substantiated and remain an intriguing puzzle of the past. The name these early inhabitants gave to the island was Minong.

In search of furs, the French were the next to have impact on the island. When they claimed it for France, they named the island in honor of King Louis XIV. The fur companies also used the island as a base for commercial fishing to feed their trappers. But it wasn't until the second half of the 19th century that the island became economically important. At that time, several mining concerns were established to extract the native copper

Please Note:
Maps and Charts in this book are not necessarily to scale and are not intended for navigation.

from what were thought to be rich lodes. The most important of these sites was the Minong Mine in McCargoe Cove. Today, by following the trail inland at McCargoe Cove, the pits and excavation along with some of the old machinery can still be seen.

Although the island lies closer to Ontario, it actually is part of the state of Michigan. Since the mid-1800s it has been used as a base for independent commercial fishing, and at one time there were as many as 40 family fisheries. Some of the families wintered on the island, returning to the mainland only when in need of supplies. Today a few of the families remain, coming out to spend summers on the island. But for most of these early homesteads, all that remains are broken artifacts, reminders of an age past.

In the early 1900s the island began to be used for vacation and recreational purposes. A number of steamers made the island a regular port of call bringing tourists and sports fishermen to the lodges that were at Windigo, Rock Harbor and Belle Isle. Through the efforts of Albert Stoll, a Detroit journalist, and other concerned citizens, the island was made a National Park in 1940, set aside for all to enjoy. Now the island is used primarily as a wilderness retreat, as each year thousands of backpackers and boaters alike flock to the island's shores to hike the 165 miles of trails and visit its many protected coves and inlets.

For hundreds of years the island has interested not only those seeking material gains and recreation, but also those interested in studying the intricate ecological relationships of the island. The island is a prime example of a forest in transition, since conifers dot its shoreline and moist lowlands, while pure hardwood stands are found in the interior highland regions. The forest floor abounds with wildflowers of many varieties and in early summer is covered white with Canadian dogwood and the prolific thimbleberry. Insect-eating pitcher plants and sundews are found in the bogs, while there is a large variety of orchids to be found throughout the island. In all, more than 700 different species of plant life have been identified.

The island's fauna is even more interesting, and here there have been many changes in the last century. Separated from the mainland by 15 miles of open water, only those animals that can swim or walk over an ice bridge in cold winters make it to the island. At the turn of the 20th century there were caribou and lynx that have since disappeared. Smaller mammals are still present: fox, beaver, the snowshoe hare, small red squirrel and four varieties of bats. But what interests people most is the fairly recent arrival of moose and wolves, and the intricate relationship that now exists between them.

The moose came to the island in the early part of the last century, probably by swimming, and with no natural predators grew to alarming numbers. By the 1930s, aided by fire destruction of browse, they began to die off in great numbers. One account says that the wolves first crossed over to the island on winter ice in the severe winter of 1948-49 and in approximately 30 years grew

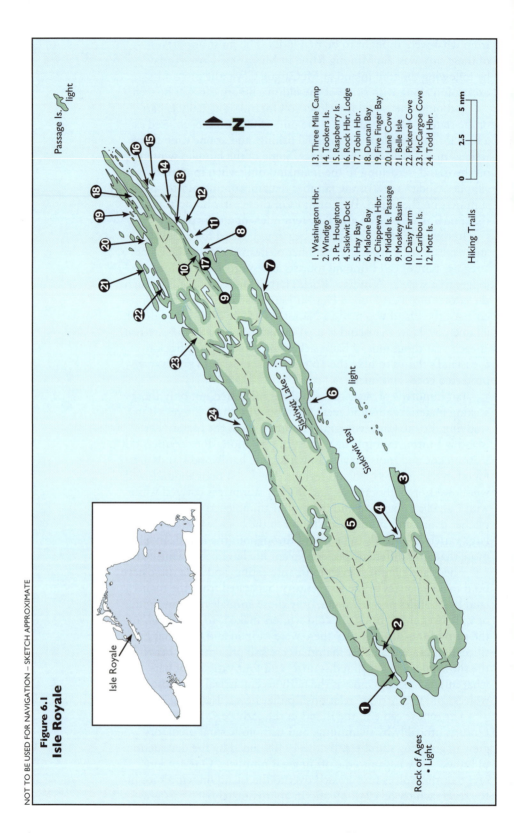

NOT TO BE USED FOR NAVIGATION – SKETCH APPROXIMATE

Figure 6.1
Isle Royale

Isle Royale

Passage Is. light

N

1. Washington Hbr.
2. Windigo
3. Pt. Houghton
4. Siskiwit Dock
5. Hay Bay
6. Malone Bay
7. Chippewa Hbr.
8. Middle Is. Passage
9. Moskey Basin
10. Daisy Farm
11. Caribou Is.
12. Mott Is.
13. Three Mile Camp
14. Tookers Is.
15. Raspberry Is.
16. Rock Hbr. Lodge
17. Tobin Hbr.
18. Duncan Bay
19. Five Finger Bay
20. Lane Cove
21. Belle Isle
22. Pickerel Cove
23. McCargoe Cove
24. Todd Hbr.

Hiking Trails

0   2.5   5 nm

Siskiwit Lake

Siskiwit Bay light

Rock of Ages
• Light

into three packs sometimes numbering in the high-40s. In the late 1980s the wolf population dropped significantly, but in recent years there has been some indication that it might once again increase. The changes in wolf packs and their territories have been under documented study for almost half a century. These studies as well as other interesting aspects of the island's flora and fauna are well presented by the Park Service's evening interpretative programs, daily excursions, and nature walks.

For those people who visit the island without their own boats, there are several different options available to reach the park. These different ferries are also helpful to boaters who wish to use the island as a place to change crews.

The shortest crossing is from Grand Portage on the Minnesota shore, just a 24-mile jump to Windigo on the south end of the island via the *Sea Hunter III*, which traditionally has run daily, or the *Voyageur II*, which makes the trip two to three times a week dependent on the time of year. Although the *Sea Hunter III* only goes to Windigo, the *Voyageur II* circumnavigates the island on each trip, dropping off and picking up backpackers at various predetermined points and spending an overnight stay at Rock Harbor.

For those coming from the south shore, there are several options. From Copper Harbor, Michigan, there is the *Isle Royale Queen IV*, which makes daily round trips to the island. The number of days per week in which the trip is made varies with the season. During peak season from mid-July to mid-August it is made every day, while at the beginning and end of the season it is made only two days per week.

From Houghton, Michigan, the *Ranger III* makes the trip twice a week with overnight stays at Rock Harbor. There is also seaplane service from Houghton, which makes the trip two times per day. Regardless of the method of transportation, reservations are required. For more information, see Figure 6.2.

In coming to the island on your own boat, unless you are making the short jump from Grand Portage, it is important to note that the distances are large and over open water. From Thunder Bay the distance is almost 30 nautical miles, from Copper Harbor and Keweenaw Waterway it is more than 40 nautical miles, from Ontonagon it is 60 nautical miles and from the Apostles it is a good 80 nautical miles. Therefore, only the foolish will make these runs without a cautious eye to the weather. Storms and fog can come up quickly on the lake, and in addition to the lack of protection on open waters, there are shipping lanes to contend with. Often boaters will make these runs at night, with the idea that there is sometimes less occurrence of adverse weather at night. But even in midsummer, it should be remembered that Lake Superior is bitterly cold at night. Sometimes the long distance from the Apostles is cut in half by first crossing to Grand Marais and then heading east to the island making it a two-day trip. However, whatever course is

Figure 6.2
Commercial Transportation to Isle Royale

Name Description	Port Departure Days/Time	Destination	Island Departure Days/Time	Contact Information
Sea Hunter III 63 feet 149 passengers 3 hours one way	Grand Portage, MN Daily-8:30 a.m. CT Mid June–mid July W, F, Sat Mid July-mid Aug. W-Sun Mid Aug.-late Aug. W, F, Sat	Windigo	Windigo to Grand Portage 2 p.m. (3 p.m. EDT) Mid June–mid July W, F, Sat Mid July-mid Aug. W-Sun Mid Aug.-late Aug. W, F, Sat	**Grand Portage/Isle Royale Transportation Line, Inc.** www.isleroyaleboats.com (218)-600-0765 (May-Sept) reservations@isleroyaleboats.com
Voyageur II 55 feet 48 passengers about 8 hours to Rock Harbor	Grand Portage, MN 8 a.m. CT Mid-late May W, Sat Late May-mid Sep M, W, Sat Mid-late Sep. W, Sat	Windigo, around north side of island to Rock Harbor. Overnight in Rock Harbor. Next day: around S. side of island to Windigo, Grand Portage.	Rock Harbor, 9 a.m. ET: Mid-late May Th, Sun Late May-mid Sept. T, Th, Sun Mid-late Sept. Th, Sun	**Grand Portage/Isle Royale Transportation Line, Inc.** www.isleroyaleboats.com (218)-600-0765 (May-Sept) reservations@isleroyaleboats.com
Isle Royale Queen IV 81 feet 90 passengers 3¾ hours one way	Copper Harbor, MI I day round trip, 8 a.m. ET Days/week varies with month in season.	Rock Harbor	Rock Harbor – same day 2 p.m. ET early & late season 3 p.m. ET mid-season	**The Isle Royale Line, Inc.** www.isleroyale.com (906) 289-4437 isleroyalequeen@gmail.com
Ranger III 165 feet 125 passengers 6 hours one way	Houghton, MI 9 a.m. ET June-mid Sept T, Fri Except Widigo trip days on T in mid Jun, Jul, Aug	Rock Harbor or Windego Overnight in Rock Harbor or Windego	Rock Harbor 9 a.m. ET Jun-mid Sept W, Sat Except Widigo trip days on Wed in mid Jun, Jul, Aug.	**National Park Service** www.nps.gov/isro (906) 482-0984 isro).Ranger3Reserve@nps.gov
Seaplane Up to 5 passengers	Houghton, MI On-demand air service daily except Sun.	Rock Harbor and Windigo	Rock Harborand Windigo by reservation	**Royal Air Service, Inc.** P.O. Box 15184, Duluth MN 55815 (218)721-0405 / (877) 359-4754 www.royalairservice.com

taken, weather should be of prime consideration when crossing the open waters of the lake.

When approaching the island from the west, even from far out we are first greeted by that massive structure, **Rock of Ages Light.** On a clear day this light (and foghorn), which stands on a rock reef 117 feet high, can be seen from a distance of 20 miles; at night its light can be seen for 25 miles. The light, which is now automated, is a grim reminder that here as elsewhere around the island there are a great number of rocks, shoals and reefs that are intricately connected with the island. There are a number of shipwrecks in the area (much to the delight of visiting scuba divers) that attest to these hazardous waters. It cannot be emphasized enough to stay clear of Rock of Ages Light, for the shoals here are treacherous.

One does not cruise Isle Royale for long without realizing that it is a national park. The first introduction to this usually comes when you get a Boating Permit and register your boat, the number of people in your party and a float plan of possible destinations and anchorages. Registration can be accomplished ahead of time by calling the Visitors Center at Houghton 906-482-0984 or at the Visitors Centers at Windigo and Rock Harbor. A Daily User Fee per person is required. Depending on your length of stay or for those who plan on more than one trip to the island, you can also obtain an Individual Season Pass for the season. Updated permits (you may encounter changes in your float plan due to weather etc.) should be turned into the Visitor Centers at Rock Harbor, Windigo or Houghton.

For boaters coming from Canadian waters, it is preferred that customs is cleared prior to coming to Isle Royale. This can be done ahead of time in one of three ways: using the CBP Reporting Offsite Arrival—Mobile ROAM App; the NEXUS Program; or the Canadian Border Boat Landing Permit (I-68) Program. As a last resort option customs clearance can be obtained at Rock Harbor. If you do not clear customs prior to your visit you may have to wait for park law enforcement officials to become available.

There are no marina facilities at any of the docks except at Rock Harbor. Rock Harbor provides electricity, water, gasoline, diesel and pump-out. At Windigo, gasoline, diesel and pump-out are provided. Mott Island has a large Travelift and some repair facilities available—but only for emergencies. Except for Rock Harbor all other docks and camping facilities on the island are free. Note that all dock space and individual campsites (including shelters) are available on a first come first serve basis. Boaters who are already set up at a campsite and have a valid boating permit are given priority access to space on the dock. If a boat leaves (to go fishing, on a hike etc.) common practice is to hang out fenders on the dock. There are consecutive night limits (usually three nights) at all docks except those at the Rock Harbor Marina. (See Fig. 6.3.) It is important to note that there is also some dock usage required by

commercial vessels. (See Fig. 6.4.) Those docks that are not adjoined to campgrounds do not allow overnight docking and are open for only daily use. Finally, there are a few docks that are closed to public use. Those docks with limited and restricted usage are found In Figure 6.5.

There are certain sections of the water that are designated as "Quiet/No wake zones" in which boats cannot exceed 5 mph. These areas are conveniently identified for you in those figures where this applies by parallel blue lines in the water. Quiet hours are between10 pm. and 6 am. During this time generator use is prohibited. There are also some areas where generator use is not allowed, see again Figure 6.3. Note that water taken out of Isle Royale's waters should not be consumed without boiling for at least two minutes. This is because of a tapeworm parasite whose life cycle is part of the moose-wolf relationship and is found in wolf feces and thus enters the water. There is a "pack in and pack out" policy since garbage facilities are provided only at Windigo and Rock Harbor. Since fire restrictions change with the site and dryness of the forest, it is a good idea to check if there are any fire restrictions when registering. If allowed, fires must always be at designated sites, contained within a metal fire ring or grill. Pets are not allowed in the park, not even on the boat, for fear of introducing disease and upsetting the delicate balance in the ecosystem. Likewise, motors of any kind are not allowed on any of the park's inland waters such

Figure 6.3
Isle Royale Dockage

Dock Location	Approx. depth in feet	Consecutive Nights Stay	No. of Shelters	Generator Use Permitted
Beaver Island	2-5	3	3	yes
Belle Isle	13	5	6	yes
Birch Island	5	3	1	no
Caribou Island	10	3	2	yes
Chippewa Harbor	7	3	4	no
Daisy Farm	9	3	16	no
Duncan Bay (1)	6	3	2	no
Duncan Narrows	6	3	2	no
Grace Is.	2–4	3	2	yes
Hay Bay	3	3	0	yes
Malone Bay	3–6	3	5	yes
McCargoe Cove (2)	7	3	6	no
Merritt Lane	8	3	1	no
Moskey Basin	8	3	6	no
Rock Harbor	3–12	–	9	yes
Siskiwit Bay (1)	2–6	3	2	no
Three Mile (1)	9	1	8	no
Tobin Harbor	4–11	3	0	yes
Todd Harbor	2	3	1	no
Tookers Is	6	3	2	no
Windigo	4–20	–	10	yes

Figure 6.4
Dock Usage by Commercial Vessels

Voyageur II & other Ferries			M/V Sandy (Tour Boat)		
Dock	Days	Time	Dock	Days	Time
McCargoe Cove	Mon/Wed/Sat	@ 2:30 p.m.	Passage Island	Mon/Fri	2:30-5:30 p.m.
Daisy Farm	Tues/Thurs/Sun	@ 9:30 a.m.		Sat	9:30-12:30 a.m.
Chippewa Hbr.	Tues/Thurs/Sun	@ 10:15 a.m.	Hidden Lake	Tues/Thurs	9:30-11:30 a.m.
Malone Bay	Tues/Thurs/Sun	@ 11 a.m.	Raspberry Island	Tues/Fri	8-9 a.m.
			McCargoe Cove	Wed	11-3 p.m.
			Edisen Fishery	Tues/Thurs/	2:30-5:30 p.m.
(Note: times are given in Eastern Daylight time)				Sat	9:30 a.m.-12:30 p.m.

Figure 6.5
Dock Usage Limits & Restrictions

Limited for Day Use Only		Closed to Public Use
NPS or Concession Fuel Docks		America Dock
Shipwreck Mooring Buoys (for active diving only)		Malone Bay Dock, North Side
Amygdaloid Island	Crystal Cove	Ranger III Dock at Rock Harbor
Edison Fishery	Hidden Lake	Ranger III Dock at Mott Island
Mott Island	Passage Island	Any other dock posted or signed as closed to public entry
Raspberry Island	Wright Island	
Any dock posted or signed as closed for overnight use		

as lakes and streams. Those boaters who carry a drone on board should know that drones are not allowed in Isle Royale like any National Park. All of these issues concerning boaters can be found on the website: *www.nps.gov/isro/planyourvisit/boating.htm.*

Although this book is written primarily for the boating community, it must be noted that there is no other section on the lake where so many different user groups come into such close contact: those who are backpacking/camping; canoeing/kayaking; motor boating/sailing; diving on wrecks. Many come to the island seeking it as a respite from the hectic demands of job-oriented lives. Thus, it becomes each visitor's responsibility to be cognizant of other user group's needs and conduct themselves in a manner to ensure that each can enjoy the island to the fullest. Common courtesy suggests limiting the use of generators, loud music and boisterous gatherings – especially after dusk when the peace and solitude of the island is at its best with the sweet call of bird song and wildlife coming down to water's edge to feed.

Harbors and Anchorages

Washington Harbor is the long deep indentation at the island's southern end, at the base of which is the Windigo Ranger Station. There are three different approaches to entering the harbor. The southernmost approach is to enter through Grace Harbor. This wide deep harbor is easy to enter with no obstructions except for the shoal that extends a good half-mile off Cumberland Point and is marked with a red nun. There is a narrow zig-zag passage between

Washington and Grace islands where, by keeping to the middle of the channel, a minimum of 20 feet of water can be maintained.

The second approach is to enter Washington Harbor directly by passing to the north of Washington Island. This approach is the most difficult because of the shoals around Rock of Ages Light and those extending SW of Washington Island. The light can be passed either to the north or south as long as it is given plenty of berth. However, it is not recommended to use the track indicated by waypoint 2 in poor visibility or if there is a sea running.

North Gap is the approach used most often by those coming from Grand Portage or down along the northern side of the island. This passage is located between Thompson Island and the mainland. The white buoy marks the wreck of the SS America, which is a hazard to navigation since its bow lies a mere 2 feet under the surface of the water. This 183-foot vessel sank in 1928 when it struck a rock reef. Often you will see boats anchored in the vicinity of this wreck, and more often than not this is an indication that there are divers below and common courtesy dictates that you give their operation a wide berth when passing by. Note: Sometimes passage through North Gap can be difficult because of adverse currents that may be running.

It is also possible to enter Washington Harbor from the north between Johns and Thompson islands (see Fig. 6.8). However, because of extensive shoaling out from the eastern end of Johns Island this is not a preferred passage.

Traveling down the long passage of Washington Harbor

NOT TO BE USED FOR NAVIGATION – SKETCH APPROXIMATE

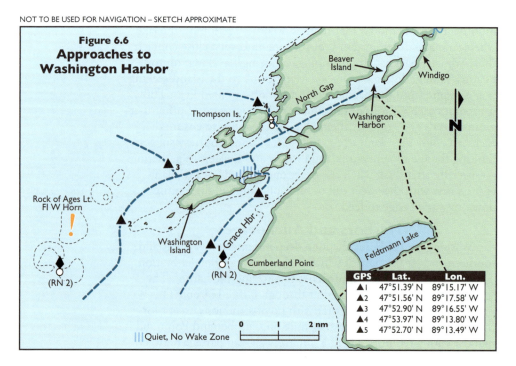

Figure 6.6
Approaches to Washington Harbor

GPS	Lat.	Lon.
▲1	47°51.39' N	89°15.17' W
▲2	47°51.56' N	89°17.58' W
▲3	47°52.90' N	89°16.55' W
▲4	47°53.97' N	89°13.80' W
▲5	47°52.70' N	89°13.49' W

toward Windigo is akin to passing down a fjord – minus the high mountains. There are no hazards except for a rock that is usually awash to the west of the southern tip of Beaver Island. It is possible to pass to either side of Beaver Island.

The name Windigo came from an Ojibwe legend and represented an evil spirit that haunted the natives in the long winters and times of starvation, instilling in them the desire to turn to their brothers for food. When the Windigo was on the prowl, carried by the howling wind on the long, lonely nights, they would retreat into shelter and offer prayers not to be possessed by this awesome evil spirit.

When the American Fur Company expanded its interests to include commercial fishing, a post was established at Windigo. Even after the company no longer supported these interests, the harbor remained important to independent fishermen who established it as their base of operations as early as the mid-1800s. Today the remains of this once important industry can be seen on Washington Island, since the fishery located there is still active in the fall each year.

Before the turn of the 20th century, Windigo was the site of a copper mining concern operated by the Wendigo Copper Company. Resembling a small frontier camp, the "town" in those days even had a different name, Ghyllbank. In the first half of the last century, Windigo was also a tourist spot and boasted of a lodge and dining room. The buildings are no longer present. All that remains today is a small store and gift shop run by Park Concessions.

The main dock at **Windigo** is one of the largest on the island, and you can tie up anywhere as long as the *Sea Hunter II* or *Voyageur II* are not due to arrive. The *Sea Hunter II* has a reserved section along the north side, but only uses it from 1 to 4 p.m. (ET) each day. The *Voyageur II* usually takes the other side, but its stops are only for 15 to 20 minutes to load and unload passengers. Park rangers will be able to tell you if there is a part of the dock that can't be used. There are no facilities at this dock and there is no charge. There are several smaller docks lying to the north of the large main dock. The ones that are closest to the main dock are available for public use. The fuel dock is the one that lies furthest north of all the docks. It provides gasoline (no diesel) and pump-out. The dock just south of the fuel dock is used for park concession. Not too far from the docks is a new store which opened in 2023.

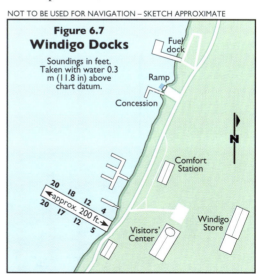

NOT TO BE USED FOR NAVIGATION – SKETCH APPROXIMATE

Figure 6.7
Windigo Docks

Soundings in feet.
Taken with water 0.3
m (11.8 in) above
chart datum.

Fuel dock

Ramp

Concession

Comfort Station

Windigo Store

Visitors' Center

N

20
20
18
17
12
12
4
5
approx. 200 ft.

It is larger than the Rock Harbor store and has some prepared food, pizza, snacks, and some supplies. The area is marked with a light (Fl R) at the outer end of the main dock.

There is a beautiful, contemporary Visitors Center here that displays the history and artifacts of the area including an impressive Fresnel lens from the Rock of Ages Light. Of particular interest are the full-scale displays of wolf, moose, beaver and otter. The center also provides a video viewing area where related videos on the island, national parks and underwater wrecks may be viewed. The Park Service puts on interpretative programs either here or in the outdoor amphitheater, which is on the way up the hill to the store. Minor groceries, mainly canned goods, snacks and a few backpacking supplies, can be bought at the store. It is also possible to arrange for showers at the store.

Windigo is an interesting place to explore, with several good hiking trails in the immediate area. One trail, a mile-long loop, takes you through an interesting change of topography: marshes, woodland and so forth. The trail also goes by a "Moose Enclosure," a small fenced-in area that keeps out the moose. It is interesting to see the impact the moose make on the island's vegetation by comparing the vegetation inside and outside the enclosure. Another trail follows the stream that enters into this bay, passing through a beautiful campground that is used by backpackers who are beginning or ending their trips. For a longer hike of approximately 8.5 miles, there is a loop trail to Huginnin Cove and back. One of the best features of Windigo is abundant raspberries – growing everywhere! In mid-August you can easily get your fill and then some in very short order. Moose can often be seen feeding here, especially in the area where the stream enters the bay.

Besides the main dock at Windigo there are a couple of other docks and anchorages in Washington Harbor where one can stay. A favorite spot is to anchor in the small bay to the NW of Beaver Island. There is good holding ground here with protection for all winds except a very strong SW that gives an uncomfortable surge.

The dock at Windigo, Isle Royale. DAHL

There are docks at the SE end of Beaver Island and the NE end of Grace Island, but these are accessible only to boats drawing less than 5 feet. Note the presence of a Quiet, No Wake Zone in some parts in this area.

Across from Washington Island is Barnum Island, which has historical interest because in the early 1900s there actually was a two-story hotel here, the Johns Hotel named after the Johns family. This area **between Barnum and Washington islands** is sometimes used as another anchorage. It is important, however, not to go too far in because of shoaling. The anchorage must be entered from the east by favoring

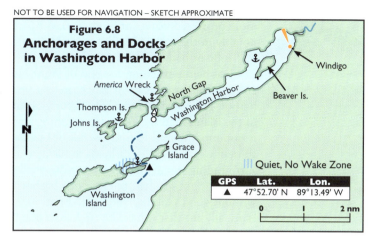

**Figure 6.8
Anchorages and Docks in Washington Harbor**

America Wreck

North Gap

Washington Harbor

Thompson Is.

Johns Is.

Windigo

Beaver Is.

Grace Island

Washington Island

||| Quiet, No Wake Zone

GPS	Lat.	Lon.
▲	47°52.70' N	89°13.49' W

0   1   2 nm

Washington Island since there are shoals extending off the eastern end of Barnum Island. Note: there are several cabins in the basin, and if privacy is desired, this is not a preferred anchorage.

There are also a couple of anchorages near the north exits of Washington Harbor. One of these is the rather long NE indentation on the main island, **NE of North Gap**. By staying in the middle, it is possible to go some way in and get protection from all but W and SW winds. However, since these are prevailing winds in this sector of the lake, a more secure anchorage is to go into the long indentation on the **eastern side of Johns Island**. In entering this anchorage, care must be taken to stand well off from the considerable shoals that extend off the eastern extremities of the opening to the anchorage. Once clear of these shoals it is possible to go quite far in and get protection for all but easterly winds. Even with winds from the east, there is still quite a bit of protection from adjacent Thompson Island. With strong E or NE winds it is possible to get protection on the western side of Thompson Island. The cabins and dock that one sees on the north side of the entrance on Johns Island are private, belonging to those who have special-use permits.

In rounding the southern end of Isle Royale toward Siskiwit Bay there are 20 miles of open water with no possibility of refuge available. Therefore, this is one spot on the island where it is important to pay particular notice to the weather, especially for smaller craft making the run to the

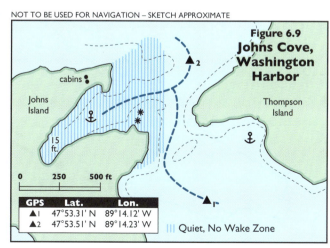

**Figure 6.9
Johns Cove, Washington Harbor**

cabins

Johns Island

Thompson Island

15 ft.

▲2

▲1

0   250   500 ft

GPS	Lat.	Lon.
▲1	47°53.31' N	89°14.12' W
▲2	47°53.51' N	89°14.23' W

||| Quiet, No Wake Zone

more protected waters of Siskiwit Bay. Because of some shoal water, notably in the area of McCormick Rocks, it is best to stand a good half-mile or better offshore.

Just before reaching the end of Point Houghton and the entrance buoys to Siskiwit Bay there is a small, well-protected harbor, **Fisherman's Home**, which for generations has been one of the island's family commercial fishing stations. This harbor is not only difficult to find because it blends in well with the shoreline, but it is also difficult to navigate the entrance because of surrounding shoals and a very narrow, shallow entrance channel. Thus, it is not prudent to enter this harbor with any sea running or without good visibility and sunlight at one's back to see the shoals, especially the first time. The trick is to hug the starboard shoreline *closely* and with that there is but a narrow channel that in low-water years barely has 5 feet of depth. (See Fig. 6.9.) Clearly, this harbor should not be attempted by those with deep-draft boats. There are a couple of docks here, remnants of the fishing station, which are In disrepair and should not be used.

The large expanse of **Siskiwit Bay**, which is located along the middle part of the island's southern shore, offers a number of good anchorages and is

NOT TO BE USED FOR NAVIGATION – SKETCHES APPROXIMATE

Figure 6.10
Fisherman's Home

GPS	Lat.	Lon.
▲	47°53.64' N	88°54.40' W

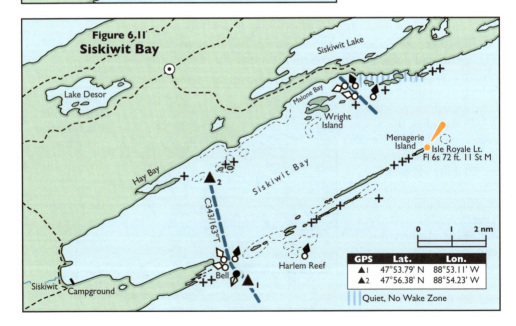

Figure 6.11
Siskiwit Bay

GPS	Lat.	Lon.
▲1	47°53.79' N	88°53.11' W
▲2	47°56.38' N	88°54.23' W

Quiet, No Wake Zone

often a point of entry to the island for those coming from Ontonagon or the Keweenaw Waterway. The bay is well-protected by a long string of islands and reefs that extend NE from Point Houghton. These reefs make this one of the favorite spots on the island for anglers. For here coho and trout abound, making this an area that in the past has been the site of several fishing homesteads. Because of these reefs, this bay should not be approached at night or in conditions of reduced visibility.

To enter the bay on the western end, it is important to line up with the buoys to pass through a break in the reef. The passage is identified by a large outlying red-and-white bell buoy. There are three other buoys, two green cans and one red nun: keep the red nun to starboard when entering the bay. Once clear of the reef, the bay is deep throughout until you approach its northern shore where again there is a string of islands and shoal water.

In entering Siskiwit Bay from the east, there is the Isle Royale Lighthouse on Menagerie Island that marks the northeast extension of the reef. Do not close too tightly to this island since there is a 4-foot shoal, Glenlyon Shoal, which lies approximately one nautical mile NE of the position of the light. Once inside this eastern section of the bay there is deep water until one approaches the shoaling complex around Wright, Malone and Ross islands. Note the individual rocks and shoals extending southward from all these islands. There are four buoys that aid in passing through these foul waters into Malone Bay. Again, the buoys are red and green and are passed by keeping the red to starboard when entering Malone Bay.

Within Siskiwit Bay there are several good anchorages to choose from. Starting at the far western end there is the **Siskiwit dock and campground**. This large cement dock is protected from the eastward fetch of Siskiwit Bay by a rock breakwater that extends out parallel to the east of it. Care should be taken in approaching the dock because of the strong red discoloration of the water from the Big Siskiwit River that makes it impossible to see the bottom.

There is shoaling along the western side of the bay, particularly in the area of the Big Siskiwit River, so approach to the dock should be made straight from the N-NE, taking care not to come in too far to the west. Depths at the outer end of the dock on both sides are 7.5 to 8.0 feet.

The campground here is a favorite for backpackers and anglers alike. There are several trails to hike, one of which leads SW up on the Feldtmann Ridge where there is an old fire tower. Another trail follows around the bay to the north to Carnelian Beach, where beautiful agates can be found, and then heads inland

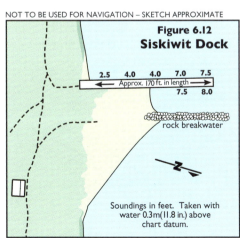

NOT TO BE USED FOR NAVIGATION – SKETCH APPROXIMATE

Figure 6.12
Siskiwit Dock

2.5   4.0   4.0   7.0   7.5
← Approx. 170 ft. in length →
7.5   8.0

rock breakwater

Soundings in feet. Taken with water 0.3m (11.8 in.) above chart datum.

to the Island Mine Campground. (Note: park policy on agates is to leave them on the beach for someone else to discover.) The Big Siskiwit River is interesting to explore by dinghy, with many curves, islands, and abundant wildlife. Separated from the colder Siskiwit Bay by a partial sandspit and just inside the mouth of this river, there is a nice "swimming hole."

This area is also well-known for its large patches of thimbleberries that make up into a delicious jam. Containing its own natural pectin, all that is needed is to boil the berries with equal amounts of sugar for five to seven minutes and then store in clean containers. Straining the pulp will give a delicious syrup to serve over pancakes and French toast.

Nestled in against the north shore of Siskiwit Bay is one of the favorite anchorages of the island. With no trails leading to the dock from the rest of the island, **Hay Bay** is strictly a boaters' anchorage. To enter this long harbor, it is necessary to pass through another set of reefs, those that extend out between Point Hay and Little Siskiwit Island. Actually, quite a wide passage between the two can be found by passing through an area about two-thirds the distance from Hay Point to the island. It may help to run a course of 343 degrees T from the northernmost green spar off Point Houghton. However, since it is a long run across the bay, it is still wise to have someone on the bow as lookout when passing through.

The bay can also be entered by following the north shore of Siskiwit Bay west from Malone Bay and passing through to the north of Wright Island. By staying "midchannel," the shoals off Wright Island and this north shore can be avoided. However, it should be noted that there is quite a "bar" extending from the NW arm of Malone Island west to the main island. In the early 1990s there were reports of at least two boats hitting a 5-foot rock some way out from the island. Once entering the long channel of Hay Bay, it is important to favor Hay Point all the way in, since there is a considerable shoal extending south of Finn Point.

Within Hay Bay, just around the point on the south shore, there is a small wooden dock with room for a couple of boats. There is a pit toilet not too far inland. Because this dock is a favor-

NOT TO BE USED FOR NAVIGATION – SKETCH APPROXIMATE

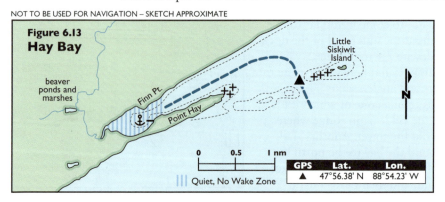

Figure 6.13
Hay Bay

ite for those who fish the exterior reefs of Siskiwit Bay, it often quickly fills up. This dock was rebuilt in 2000.

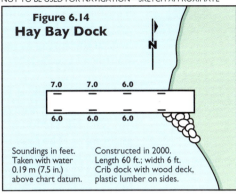

Figure 6.14
Hay Bay Dock

Soundings in feet.
Taken with water
0.19 m (7.5 in.)
above chart datum.

Constructed in 2000.
Length 60 ft.; width 6 ft.
Crib dock with wood deck,
plastic lumber on sides.

It is also possible to anchor here in 9 feet to 10 feet of water, but not too far into the bay since it is quite shallow. However, it should be noted that in unusually warm seasons, the growth of underwater plant life greatly increases and spreads throughout the bay. This may have quite an effect on the difficulty of getting an anchor to dig in and set well in the basin. Where a plow usually is effective, a Danforth, Fortress or Bruce anchor may then be a better choice for this anchorage. The bay is not good for anchoring in strong NE winds because an uncomfortable chop can build quickly with the long fetch here. The best protection for strong NE winds in this area is the bight on the western side of Wright Island.

This area was once the site of a number of fishing homesteads, one of which is located on the Siskiwit Bay side of Hay Point and can be reached by taking a hike across the peninsula from the dock. Another is reached by taking a dinghy toward Hay Point on the Hay Bay side where there is a small clearing and decaying small dock about two-thirds of the way to the point. Within the clearing there are a few remaining artifacts and strawberries growing in the wild. The last site is across the bay just east of Finn Point, and it may be difficult to find any remains here, since in the late '70s the Park Service took down all the buildings. It is of interest that the family who lived here was one of those who wintered on the island for many years, returning to the mainland only when it was necessary to get supplies. Now with the passage of time many of these artifacts, and even parts of the sites are becoming difficult to find.

Hay Bay is well-removed from the hustle and congestion that are often found in other parts of the island. In the quiet backwaters here, waterfowl of many variations can be found. The bay is also a favorite feeding area for moose. Especially at dusk, it is not uncommon to see two or three of these large animals come down to the water's edge, dipping their heads beneath the surface in search of the tender shoots of sedges and elodea. The stream that empties into the bay at the far end is not only sought out by moose, but trout fishermen, too. For by following the stream inland, first with a small boat and then by taking a trail that follows along the right side (when going upstream), a series of beaver ponds and marshes can be found that yield small, speckled trout. Regulations for brook trout on inland lakes and streams are catch-and-release only and the use of barbless hooks. In recent years there have been active eagles' nests high up in the trees approximately midway on Point Hay. As remarkable as it may seem, there have even been times that swans

have been seen elegantly gliding around the bay with their long gracefully arched necks. Apparently, they sometimes come to nest here in the spring as recollected by a past fisherman's son. Recent sightings were in 1999 and the summer of 2000 when there were six swans. For a magnificent view of this peaceful wild area, a hike up to the ridge above Finn Point will display Hay Bay, Siskiwit Bay, Point Houghton and greater Lake Superior beyond.

The NE section of Siskiwit Bay provides several good anchorages. The first of these is at **Wright Island** where it is possible to get good anchoring in either indentation, depending on wind. Hopkins Harbor on the west side is the site of a past commercial fishing station. To approach the harbor, care must be taken to avoid the numerous shoals extending SW of the island and a shoal that blocks the northern half of the entrance. Because of shoaling in the far end of the bay and slash on the bottom, good depth for anchoring and holding is found only halfway into the bay. There is protection here for all but the strongest westerly winds. There is a dock in Hopkins Harbor on the southern shore near the entrance that has approximately six feet on its outer side. The dock is built with wood cribbing and wood decks to keep its historic appearance. It is restricted to daytime use only. In some years this SW end of the island has become a nesting site for eagles. When eagles are nesting, this whole area is off-limits to any kind of boaters from spring until the 3rd week in July.

The eastern indentation of Wright Island also offers good anchoring. To enter this cove, approach should be made from the NE or from the E leaving the track taken through the channel buoys (see Fig. 6.14). Be sure to note the two shoals on the south side of the opening of this cove. There is some shoaling across the entrance width, but by continuing on, 10-foot depths can be found for anchoring. Again, there is some slash on the bottom. This anchorage is more open than the first and is particularly susceptible to easterly winds.

There is a Park Service dock and ranger station on the main island just to the east of the channel buoys. Because of use by park boats on the northern side, there usually is space for only one or two boats along the southern side of the dock. This dock is a little difficult to get into because of a rock shoal spit that extends out from land south of the dock. Thus, approach must be made with wide berth given for the shoal and made pretty much from straight east.

A short half-mile trail leads to Lake Siskiwit, another area known for its untouched wild beauty. Although no motors are allowed on the lake, those who portage over with canoes report excellent fishing, especially in the area of Wood Lake. There is a little "swimming hole" a short way up the Siskiwit River toward Siskiwit Lake. A trail leading to the spot can be found just to the west of a small wooden bridge that crosses the stream on the main trail from the Malone Dock to Lake Siskiwit.

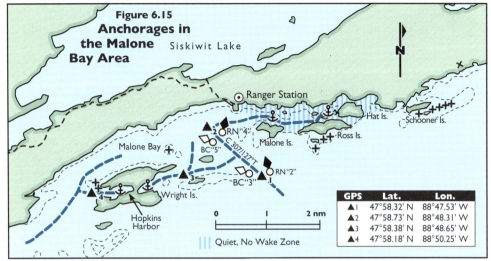

Figure 6.15
Anchorages in the Malone Bay Area
Siskiwit Lake

Ranger Station

Hat Is.

Schooner Is.

RN "4"

Ross Is.

Malone Bay

BC "5"

Malone Is.

C 307/127° T

Malone Bay

RN "2"

BC "3"

Wright Is.

Hopkins Harbor

0   1   2 nm

Quiet, No Wake Zone

GPS	Lat.	Lon.
▲1	47°58.32' N	88°47.53' W
▲2	47°58.73' N	88°48.31' W
▲3	47°58.38' N	88°48.65' W
▲4	47°58.18' N	88°50.25' W

If the small dock at the ranger station is filled, there is an alternative anchorage on the northern side of **Malone Island**. The indentation on this northern side is greater than it appears on the charts, and by hugging up close and anchoring in 10 to 15 feet of water, protection can be achieved for all but very strong winds.

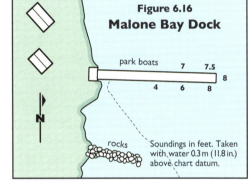

Figure 6.16
Malone Bay Dock

park boats

7   7.5

8

4   6   8

rocks

Soundings in feet. Taken with water 0.3 m (11.8 in.) above chart datum.

There is another anchorage **north of Ross Island to the west of Hat Island**. By passing between the two islands to the north of Ross Island, clear water can be found. However, because of shoaling, you can't go too far beyond these two islands. Good anchoring can be found in 8 feet to 10 feet of water with protection for all but westerly winds.

Important Note: When entering or leaving the Malone Bay area, it is most important to pass through the buoyed channel and not between the islands, since they are fouled with rock and shoal water.

The area behind **Schooner Island** at the far eastern end of Siskiwit Bay looks better on the charts than it actually is. Despite having good protection for all but easterly winds, it is next to impossible to get any holding with an anchor because of a rock bottom.

Heading NE for the next nine nautical miles, the shoreline is bold and deep with no obstructions except close into shore. An abrupt break in this rocky shoreline leads to one of the most beautiful harbors on the island, **Chippewa Harbor**. With its only access through a long narrow channel from the greater lake, it is like an inland lake offering excellent protection in several different anchorages.

The entrance is marked with a white slatted triangular day

marker high up on the eastern side. This is readily seen when approaching from the S or SW but doesn't come into view with easterly approaches until right at the entrance.

Inside the entrance there is a narrows that is tricky to pass through because of blocking islets midchannel and surrounding shoal waters. In order to clear these, an S-shaped track has to be taken, keeping the first all-rock islet to port, the second island, which has trees on it, to starboard. In both cases, it is important to give these islets wide berth since there are rocky projections out from each end underwater. When passing through here it is a good idea to have someone as lookout on the bow.

Chippewa Harbor is divided into two basins, the first of which contains a concrete dock and campground. As the second entrance islet is cleared, the dock that is on the starboard shore will come into view. Do not head directly for this dock since there is a large shoal extending out from the entrance islet that must be given wide berth. The dock is large enough to accommodate two or three boats on the outside. There are several primitive shelters with picnic tables, grills and pit toilets adjacent to the dock.

This area is particularly interesting to explore. A trail from the dock follows the harbor entrance back out to the bigger lake, passing through some clearing and rock bluffs. Another trail, which is picked up on the hill in the campground, leads across a swamp with a boardwalk and then splits, with one trail going to Lake Mason and the other going to Lake Richie. This second trail is of interest because not far from the split there are a series of beaver ponds at varying stages of transition where it is sometimes possible

NOT TO BE USED FOR NAVIGATION – SKETCH APPROXIMATE

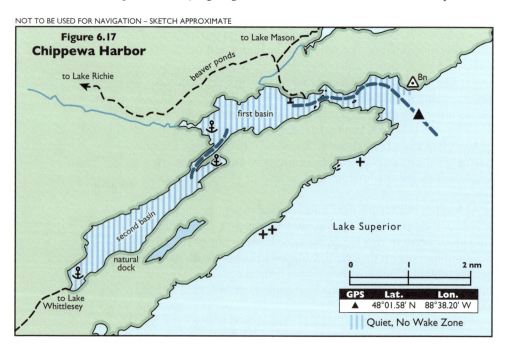

to see beaver at work and possibly even moose.

In the far end of the first basin there is a small stream that can be explored by dinghy. At the mouth of the stream, not too far in because of silting, there is good holding ground for anchoring. Not too far to the east of this stream there is a boat wreck washed up on shore.

To enter the second basin of Chippewa Harbor, it is necessary to go through a second narrows. By staying in the middle, a minimum of 10 to 11 feet of depth can be maintained when passing through the channel. After clearing the narrows there is a secure anchorage in the cove that lies just to the south of the narrows. There is more depth than indicated on the charts and good anchoring can be found in 12 to 15 feet of water. In this snug anchorage there is protection for all but strong westerly winds, and then it is a simple matter to move to the other end of the basin should these arise.

In the far western end of the second basin there is good holding in 20 feet of water with a mud bottom and no obstructions. There is also a natural dock here along the southern shore, a rock-faced wall that falls abruptly into the water enabling a boat to be tied off broadside to the shore. A small clearing here can be used for picnics. In the deepest indentation of this western end of the basin there is a half-mile trail/canoe portage to Lake Whittlesey. The trail also follows around the northern shore of the lake that is one of the more remote spots of the island.

In leaving Chippewa Harbor and continuing NE around the island, the shoreline again is bold, with deep water and no obstructions. Just before coming to Middle Islands Passage there is a deep indentation in the island, **Conglomerate Bay.** Although it looks like it would make a good anchorage, it is rarely used because it is quite open to easterly winds and there are other anchorages in the area that are usually preferred.

Likewise, **Tonkin Bay**, which lies to the north of Conglomerate Bay, is rarely used because it is open to NE winds. If seclusion is desired, anchor in either of these two bays, but only with an eye out for easterly winds.

Rock Harbor is the long 12-mile channel found at the island's northern end that runs parallel to its

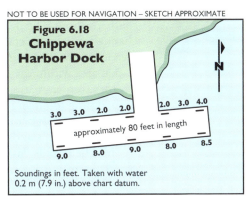

Figure 6.18
Chippewa Harbor Dock

N

3.0 3.0 2.0 2.0   2.0 3.0 4.0

approximately 80 feet in length

9.0   8.0   9.0   8.0   8.5

Soundings in feet. Taken with water 0.2 m (7.9 in.) above chart datum.

The dock at Chippewa Harbor, Isle Royale. DAHL

southern shore. The most populated area of the island, this long channel contains several docks, campgrounds, hiking trails and Park Headquarters at Mott Island. Rock Harbor is also the name given to that area within the channel called Snug Harbor where there is a Visitor's Center, marina, lodge with cabins, campground, store, gift shop, dining room and grill. See further on the section, Port Rock Harbor. The most common used passage to enter the channel is through Middle Islands Passage.

Middle Islands Passage is often a point of entry to the island, especially for those coming across from the Keweenaw Waterway. It is well-marked with a red bell buoy (Fl R) and two green cans. The bell buoy sets just to the west of extensive rock shoals, so if entrance to the passage is from the east, it and the shoal waters should be given wide berth. When going through the passage to enter Rock Harbor channel, keep the bell buoy to starboard and the green cans to port.

By turning SW after entering the channel, one quickly comes to a long dock on the southern shore. Although no overnight dockage is allowed here, it is permissible to tie up here to visit the restored **Edisen Fishery** and the **Rock Harbor Lighthouse** exhibit facility. The Park Service has done an especially nice job of restoring the fishery and thus preserving a part of important island history. It is the best surviving example of a family gill net fishery complete with a dockside "fish house" where the fish were cleaned and stored until being shipped to Duluth. Other structures on the premises include the main residence cabin, a honeymoon cabin, net house, net drying reels and the *Belle*, a gas-powered work boat built around 1900. It is a short walk (one-third mile) to the lighthouse, which likewise as been restored by the Park Service and houses an excellent maritime history exhibit on Isle Royale.

Continuing to the far SW end of the Rock Harbor channel is **Moskey Basin**. Note that about halfway down the channel there is a bar that extends across the width of the channel. However, with a lookout on the bow and by staying in the middle it is possible to maintain a minimum depth of 10 to 11 feet.

Most boaters usually anchor in the far end of the basin where there is a long 144-foot concrete dock and campground. In approaching the dock, have someone on the bow as lookout, since the water does become shallow a good distance out. It is also possible to anchor in most parts at this end of the bay, with the exception of that area between the dock and heading due north toward the northern shore, where there are a number of uncharted rocks. There are also some rocks off to either side of the dock necessitating a straight

NOT TO BE USED FOR NAVIGATION – SKETCH APPROXIMATE

Figure 6.19
Moskey Basin Dock

Length 144 feet, Width 10 feet

Soundings in feet. Taken with water 0.2 m (7.9 in.) above chart datum.

Binwall dock with wood sides and concrete deck.

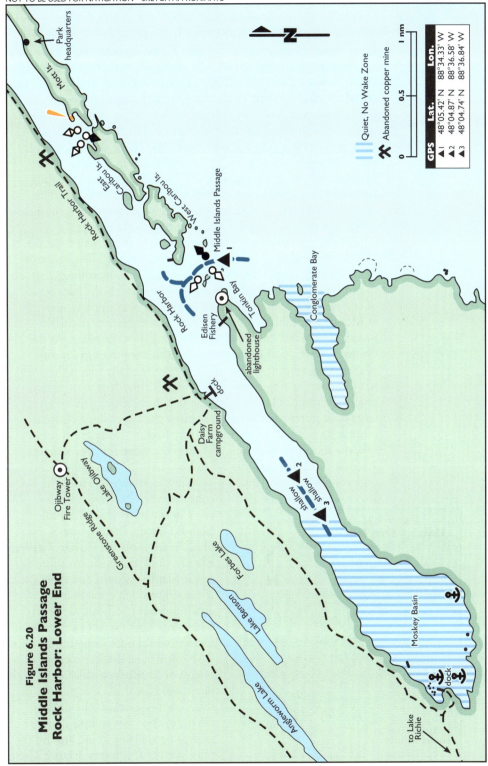

Figure 6.20
Middle Islands Passage
Rock Harbor: Lower End

Park headquarters

Mott Is.

East Carbou Is.

West Carbou Is.

Carbou Is.

Rock Harbor Trail

Middle Islands Passage

Rock Harbor

Tonkin Bay

Edisen Fishery

abandoned lighthouse

Conglomerate Bay

dock

Daisy Farm campground

Greenstone Ridge

Ojibway Fire Tower

Lake Ojibway

Forbes Lake

Lake Benson

Angleworm Lake

shallow

shallow

Moskey Basin

dock

to Lake Richie

GPS	Lat.	Lon.
▲1	48°05.42′ N	88°34.33′ W
▲2	48°04.87′ N	88°36.58′ W
▲3	48°04.74′ N	88°36.84′ W

Quiet, No Wake Zone

⚒ Abandoned copper mine

0   0.5   1 nm

N

in/out approach and departure to the dock. One shoal in particular lies just to the north of the dock with 4-1/2 to 5 feet of water over it, depending on chart datum. The trail here leads NE to Daisy Farm (three miles) and SW to Lake Richie (two miles).

Heading back toward Middle Islands Passage, on the northern shore, NW of the Edisen Fishery, there is another campground and dock, **Daisy Farm**. There is some shoal water just to the east of the dock that is usually marked with a couple of buoys that are privately maintained by the Park Service. The dock is T-shaped with ample water along its outer side. NOTE: It can become very uncomfortable when tied to any of the docks in the long Rock Harbor channel in strong NE or SW winds because of the long fetch and funneling aspects of the wind encountered here. The campground is the largest on the island with 16 shelters and picnic tables and thus is a favorite for backpackers and groups.

There is an interesting trail up to the Ojibway Tower on the Greenstone Ridge, approximately 1.7 miles away. The Greenstone Ridge (which should not be confused with the greenstones that are found on many of the island's exposed beaches) is the backbone of Isle Royale, running its entire length. At many points such as Mount Franklin and Lookout Louise, there are particularly beautiful views of the island and the Canadian shoreline. At the Ojibway Tower, you can usually climb close to the top for one of these magnificent views. Another feature at the top of the island occurs in August when the ridge is abundant with plump blueberries and saskatoons, a colloquial Canadian term for a large dark-purple edible berry. Because the Greenstone Ridge is interesting to hike, an alternative way back to Daisy Farm is to take the loop trail by hiking SW atop the ridge for approximately 1.8 miles and then turning off to head back to the campground on a roughly triangular course totaling around 5-1/2 miles for the complete trip. (See Fig. 6.19.)

On the other side of Middle Islands Passage, there is one of the prettiest spots on Isle Royale, **Caribou Island**. Along the northern shore of the island's western end there is a small wooden dock that can accommodate two boats along its outer side (depth 6 feet to 9 feet) and two shelters. Those using the shelters have priority on dock space, but quite often boat campers with shallow draft boats will take the inside portion of this T-shaped dock. If the dock is filled, It is possible to find a couple of anchoring spots by going around the north end of **Cemetery Island**. These

NOT TO BE USED FOR NAVIGATION – SKETCH APPROXIMATE

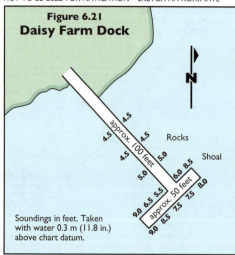

Figure 6.21
Daisy Farm Dock

Rocks

Shoal

Soundings in feet. Taken with water 0.3 m (11.8 in.) above chart datum.

are not to be confused with the basin which lies approximately 500 feet east of the dock which is quite shoaled. The entrance to this area is found by coming in between the NE end of Cemetery Island and Caribou Island where it is important to stay med-channel because there is considerable shoaling to each side. See Figure 6.23. The first anchorage is found by going to port NE towards a small basin on Caribou Island. Because of shoals you may not be able to go too far in. See anchor symbol 1, Figure 23. Two other anchorages can be found by rounding to starboard and snugging up to Cemetery Island. With care, it is possible for shoal draft boats to travel directly to these anchorages from the Caribou Dock.

Caribou Island is actually two islands separated by a small channel of water that is navigable by dinghy and is interesting to explore. The island is also of interest because its outer beaches, along with all the others in this string of islands, yield the famous Isle Royale greenstones. Especially after a storm off the lake, it is possible to find these semiprecious mottled stones at water's edge. Greenstones are made up of a mineral called chlorastrolite that is deposited in the amygdules (holes formed by air bubbles) in lava flows. After being polished by the wave action, the stones display a mosaic-like pattern known as "turtleback." The park policy on greenstone picking is that greenstones, along with other minerals and objects of natural beauty, should be left undisturbed so that others can experience the same sense of discovery.

The next island up the channel from Caribou Island is **Mott Island**, site of the National Park Headquarters. It is from here that the entire island complex is administered. Along with administrative and maintenance buildings there are facilities for park personnel and their families since many of the park officials and maintenance workers live here on the island. There are several docks on Mott Island, one of which is very large to accommodate the Ranger III that stops here twice weekly with supplies from Houghton. The docks are here primarily for park boats and business, but short term visits are permitted. On Mott

NOT TO BE USED FOR NAVIGATION – SKETCHES APPROXIMATE

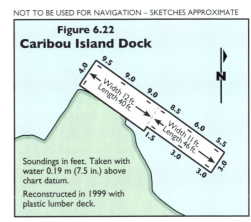

Figure 6.22
Caribou Island Dock

4.0 9.5 9.0 9.0 8.5 6.0 5.5
Width 12 ft.
Length 40 ft.
Width 11 ft.
Length 46 ft.
1.5 3.0 3.0 3.0

Soundings in feet. Taken with water 0.19 m (7.5 in.) above chart datum.

Reconstructed in 1999 with plastic lumber deck.

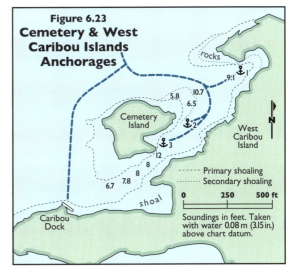

Figure 6.23
Cemetery & West Caribou Islands Anchorages

rocks
9.1 1
5.8 10.7
6.5
Cemetery Island
2
West Caribou Island
3
12
8
8
6.7 7.8
shoal
Caribou Dock

----- Primary shoaling
·········· Secondary shoaling

0   250   500 ft

Soundings in feet. Taken with water 0.08 m (3.15 in.) above chart datum.

Island there is a nice trail that divides the island in half and then circles it. Once again, on the outer beaches, there are areas where greenstones can be found.

Heading up the channel there are a couple of docks that are available for public use. The first of these is at **Three Mile Camp** which is on the northern or main island side of the channel and located about three miles SE of the Rock Harbor Lodge. Actually, there are two docks here: one that runs parallel to the channel; the other is L-shaped and is just a little farther up the channel. The parallel dock is for only shoal-draft boats lying very close to shore. In both cases, care should be taken in approaching these docks because of shoal water. With the L-shaped dock, approach only from the SE not the S or SW. Depending on low-water datum, deep-draft boats may not be able to use these docks, especially the parallel dock. At the campground there are several shelters and picnic tables.

Farther up the channel on the other side there is a dock available for use at **Tookers Island**, which lies in the same string of islands as Caribou and Mott islands. It is another L-shaped dock, that may be difficult to get up to because of shoal water. Depending on chart datum, some years have seen depths of less than 5.5 feet along the outer side of the dock. There are a couple of shelters here along with picnic tables. NOTE: There is little protection at this dock, and it should not be considered for use if strong NE or SW winds are expected.

Although the entire 12-mile channel is called Rock Harbor, what is also meant by the term "Rock Harbor" is the little "metropolis" of the island which is found in the Snug Harbor portion of the channel. Here at **Rock Harbor** is the location of the Rock Harbor Lodge and Dining Room, housekeeping cabins, a gift and coffee shop, small camp store, information center and laundry facilities. Showers are also available and can be arranged for at the camp store. For boaters there is a gas dock that provides gasoline, diesel and pump-out, and a small marina complete with water and electricity. Adjacent to the docking facilities there are picnic tables and grills.

In approaching the Rock Harbor area, enter between the concrete *Ranger III* dock and a small white "no wake" buoy that is kept to starboard. Do not make the mistake of going in behind the large *Ranger III* dock, since there is shoal water here. Note that farther into the harbor, beyond the buoy, there is shoal water to starboard, so it is important to favor the marina side of the harbor when entering and leaving. (See boat track Figure 6.24.)

Because Rock Harbor is such a popular spot, the marina often fills up quickly, particularly in the peak season from mid-July to the end of August. With no reservations taken, the slips are occupied on a first-come basis. When all available dock space is taken, it is possible to go around to the other side and anchor in Tobin Harbor

Ranger III
*at the dock in
Rock Harbor,
Isle Royale. DAHL*

and thus remain in the area and use some of the facilities by taking a dinghy in. There are also a few docks next to the airplane dock In Tobin Harbor that can be used. Then It is about a 1/2 mile walk over to the Rock Harbor side.

Rock Harbor is an interesting place to be because there always seems to be something going on. Mid-June to Labor Day there are

NOT TO BE USED FOR NAVIGATION – SKETCH APPROXIMATE

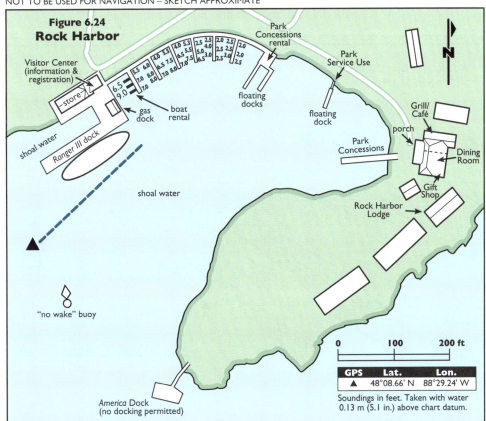

daily nature walks and nightly interpretative programs conducted by the park rangers. Many times a week the lodge runs an excursion boat, the Sandy for tours to the Edisen Fishery, Passage Island or a climb to the top of Lookout Louise from Tobin Harbor. (See Fig. 6.4.) Rock Harbor is also the major center for those coming to or leaving the island. Thus, there is excitement with the arrival of the *Ranger III*, the *Isle Royale Queen IV* or the *Voyageur II* as backpackers, those staying at the lodge, anglers, canoeists and others load and unload their gear. With the many buildings that make up the Rock Harbor Lodge, the housing for staff and park personnel and the large campground, there are more people here than any other area on the island.

Within short distances of Rock Harbor there are many interesting trails to hike. One of the most popular is the Albert Stoll Trail out to the end of Scoville Point. In many places this trail comes out to beautiful overlooks along the Rock Harbor Channel. About halfway to the point there is one of the prehistoric Native American mining pits. The distance out to the day marker at the end of Scoville Point is 2.2 statute miles. On the return trip, an alternative is to take the trail that heads over to Tobin Bay and follow it back to the airplane dock at Rock Harbor. Moose are quite often seen on this trail.

Another trail that can also be taken as a loop is to Suzy's Cave

NOT TO BE USED FOR NAVIGATION – SKETCH APPROXIMATE

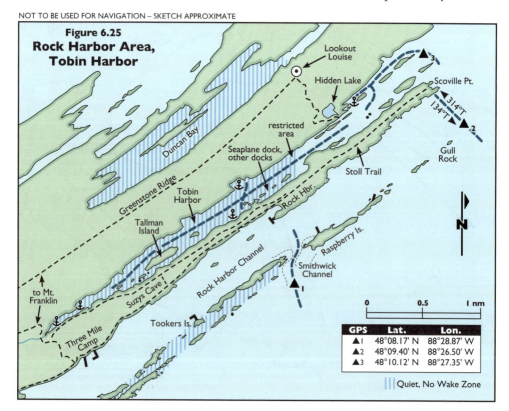

Figure 6.25
Rock Harbor Area, Tobin Harbor

GPS	Lat.	Lon.
▲1	48°08.17' N	88°28.87' W
▲2	48°09.40' N	88°26.50' W
▲3	48°10.12' N	88°27.35' W

||| Quiet, No Wake Zone

and back. This trail follows the shoreline of Rock Harbor Channel SW toward Three Mile Camp and Daisy Farm. There is a turnoff inland about one mile from Rock Harbor to Suzy's Cave. The trail also cuts over to the other side and Tobin Harbor, which can then be followed back to the airplane dock and Rock Harbor.

Just across the channel from Rock Harbor there is another dock on **Raspberry Island**. Although overnight dockage is not permitted, short term visits are allowed. There is a trail here that leads around the island and at one point passes through a bog on a boardwalk where there are a number of different plant species including insectivorous pitcher plants and sundews.

For those wishing to **enter or leave the Rock Harbor Channel**, the **Smithwick Channel** to the SW of Raspberry Island is often used. Because of shoals extending out from both islands in this channel, the "S" track passage needed is difficult and should only be done when there is no sea running and the sun is high at one's back to see the shoals. (See Figure 6.25.) Another way out of this long string of islands is to pass to the **north of Gull Rock** where there is a wide passage with deep water. Taking a bearing off Scoville Point (134 degrees T when leaving the channel, 314 degrees T when entering) is most helpful in establishing this passage. (See again Figure 6.25.) If unsure of the position of Gull Rock, the safest and easiest way to enter and leave the Rock Harbor Channel at this end is between South Government and Edwards/North Government Islands at the NE end of these strings of Islands.

Around the corner from Scoville Point there is a long, beautiful

NOT TO BE USED FOR NAVIGATION – SKETCH APPROXIMATE

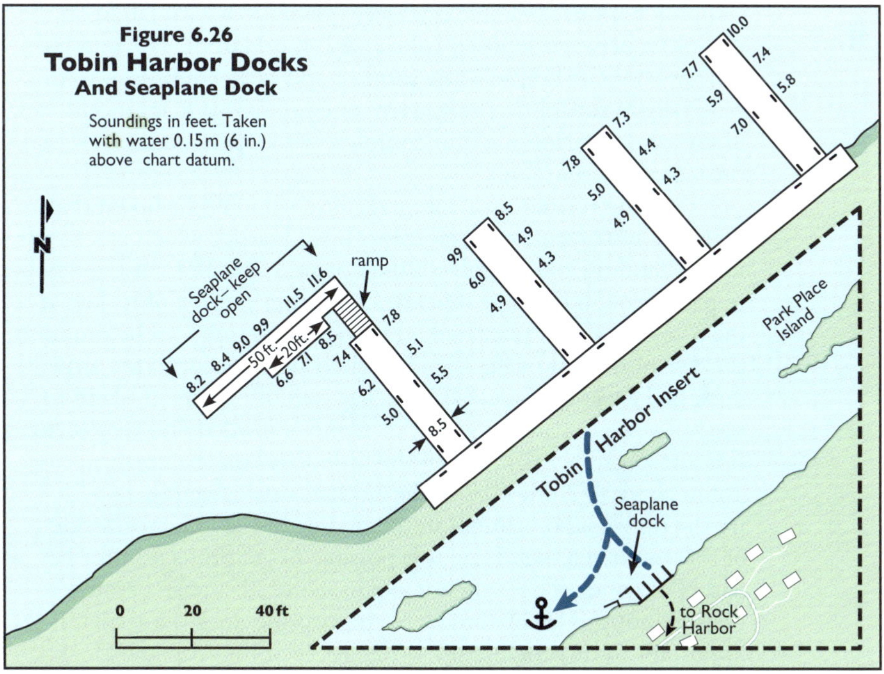

Figure 6.26
Tobin Harbor Docks
And Seaplane Dock

Soundings in feet. Taken with water 0.15m (6 in.) above chart datum.

channel, **Tobin Harbor**, which for years has been a favorite of those who visit the island. As early as the 1900s, this all-weather harbor was the site of many summer homes, with the steamer bringing whole families up from Duluth who would spend their summers living on the island. Today, many of these summer cottages can still be seen, a glimpse into the earlier history of the island, as we pass these picturesque islands. Those who built the cottages were granted a "life lease" on the property until the death of the owner, at which time the property reverts to the Park Service, which is in fact the actual owner. Note that at the time of this writing (5th edition) most of these leases have expired.

The Tobin Harbor area has several good anchorages from which to choose. The first of these is found by bypassing the entrance to Tobin Harbor after rounding Scoville Point and heading in behind the islands that form the northern part of the entrance to Tobin Harbor. (See boat track and waypoint 3 on Fig. 6.25.) The anchorage is behind the last SW island in the chain, and although there is protection here for all but the strongest NE winds, it may take a bit to get the anchor to hold because of some rock on the bottom.

The anchorage is useful because it is a close jaunt by dinghy to the small dock by Hidden Lake and the trail that leads to Lookout Louise. Note that one side of this dock may be used by the Sandy on Tuesdays and Thursdays from 9:30 am to 11:30 am. (See Figure 6.4.) Because of the shoal water surrounding the string of islands adjacent to the dock, this dock is accessible to only very shoal draft boats and then for only short-term stays with no overnight camping permitted. There is a lovely picnic area with tables on the peninsula between Hidden Lake and Tobin Harbor. The one-mile trail to Lookout Louise is the shortest and easiest approach to this especially beautiful overlook. Here one can have a magnificent view of the whole northern island complex, with a panoramic view of the Canadian shoreline.

Heading further into Tobin Harbor, it should be noted that there is a restricted area adjacent to Rock Harbor which is set aside for the landing and takeoffs of float planes. Therefore, it is advisable to pass through this area quickly and anchor outside of it. Just at the SW end of this restricted area, good anchoring can be found to the SW of the last of the islands, which are adjacent to the airplane dock in 15 feet of water. NOTE: stay well off the small island to the NE since the area around this island is shoaled and very rocky. It is also possible to anchor in the little "bay" on the north side of Tobin about 1/2 nm NW of the airplane dock. See Figure 6.25. It's the only anchor symbol in the middle of the long north side of the Tobin channel. Here it is possible to get protection for N and NW winds. These anchorages have the advantage because they are not too far by dinghy to the airplane dock. Note that it is important to tie dinghies up to the inside of the Airplane Dock, leaving the outside open to float planes. The docks adjacent to the Airplane Dock (see Figure 6.26) are available to all boats including boat rentals or those with small boats staying at the Lodge. These docks give access to Rock Harbor by taking the trail (approximately 1/2mile) across the Island.

Deep within the SW end of Tobin Harbor past Tallman Island there are a couple of spots where one can anchor and have good protection for all but the strongest NE winds. One anchorage is in the farthest end just before the water begins to shoal. The other is in the northern "bay" just before entering this far end. In both cases, there is good holding in 10 feet of water.

Besides being more secluded from the rest of the island, these anchorages are of interest because, by taking the dinghy way in on the northern shore, it is possible to hook up with the trail that leads 1.5 miles inland to Mount Franklin. By picking up the trail at this far end of Tobin Harbor, a large part of the distance that is usually covered by backpackers is cut off. Once again, there is a lookout here on top of the Greenstone Ridge that offers a beautiful view of the island and the Canadian shoreline.

Standing off the far NE tip of Isle Royale is the remote island of **Passage Island**, which is off the beaten track for many boaters and thus offers a more secluded anchorage than many of the more commonly used anchorages on the main island. The island gets its name because the commercial shipping lane to Thunder Bay now, as in the past, passes through here, between the island and Isle Royale. At the SW end of the island there is an automated light that is equipped with a foghorn. The only hazards in approaching the island are off the NE end in the area of the Gull Islands where there are a number of rocks and shoal water that should be given wide berth.

In the middle of the island along the SE shore there is a deep bay that offers all-weather protection. Because of a shoal positioned just outside the entrance, this bay is a little tricky to enter. Approach must be from the SW hugging close to the island shoreline in order to pass between the island and the shoal. Once past this outlying shoal, there are two more shoals extending into the entrance off each side of the opening, thus necessitating passing through exactly midchannel. Here a bow lookout is helpful, and with care a minimum depth of 8 feet can be maintained when passing through. Once in the harbor the water becomes very deep, and only at

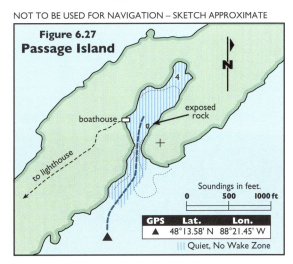

NOT TO BE USED FOR NAVIGATION – SKETCH APPROXIMATE

Figure 6.27
Passage Island

N

boathouse

exposed rock

4

to lighthouse

Soundings in feet.
0   500   1000 ft

GPS	Lat.	Lon.
▲	48°13.58' N	88°21.45' W

Quiet, No Wake Zone

the far end does it become shallow enough to anchor. Note that no overnight docking is allowed here.

On the western shore of the harbor there is a boathouse and a small dock where a trail can be picked up leading 1.5 miles to the lighthouse. At the light, it is possible to sit high up on the rocks with a grand view of the large lakers as they pass between the island and Isle Royale with their diesels throbbing.

In rounding **Blake Point**, there are two reefs, one of which is marked with a buoy: **Five Foot Reef** (buoyed) and an 11-foot reef. Both reefs are noted for good fishing, and only Five Foot Reef is of any real concern to passing boaters and should be avoided. It is possible to pass between Blake Point and the 11-foot shoal with good water, however, note well the rocks that stand off just to the east of Blake Point.

Along the south side of Blake Point is **Merritt Lane** where there is a dock and campground with a shelter. Although it is possible to anchor here, the area is open to the NE. Note that this area, including all sides of Porter Island and adjacent islands, is a Quiet, No Wake Zone.

Following the north side of Blake Point to the SW, there is another of the well-protected bays for which Isle Royale is so well known, **Duncan Bay**. To enter Duncan Bay, there is a very long, narrow entrance that has a long extensive shoal down the middle of its length. Sometimes the top of the shoal can be seen breaking the water, but often the whole shoal is completely submerged. There is another rock shoal predecessor to the larger entrance shoal that is found well before the narrowest constriction of the entrance. To avoid both of these shoals, favor the port shoreline when entering by hugging it *closely* and passing with the shoal water kept well to starboard. However, as you approach the point of land to port there is another shoal extending out into the narrow channel, necessitating a zigzag course between it and yet another shoal to starboard. (See Fig. 6.28.) With a minimum depth of 9 feet, this is one entrance in which it is advisable to enter with no sea running and the sun high at one's back to clearly see the shoal areas. When passing through this entrance the majestic bluffs of Lookout Louise and the Greenstone Ridge welcome one high overhead.

Within Duncan Bay there are two areas to dock and several different anchorages. Because of depths, the two docks are

View of Lake Superior from Mt. Franklin, Isle Royale. DAHL

predominantly for shoal draft boats and are usually used by boat campers who require the use of the shelters on land. The first dock is found just after clearing the long shoal in the entrance and by turning to port. This small wooden L-shaped dock has room for one or two boats. There are two shelters here with picnic tables and grills.

Figure 6.28
Duncan Narrows

GPS	Lat.	Lon.
▲	48°10.43' N	88°28.09' W

||| Quiet, No Wake Zone

The second dock is found at the far end of Duncan Bay on the north side of the northernmost peninsula that extends into the bay. Again, this T-shaped dock is small, only 25 feet along its outer side. With care and depending on low-water datum, boats drawing 5 feet may be able to edge up to this dock. The small campground has two shelters with picnic tables and grills. Those using the shelters have priority on dock usage.

For anchoring, there are even more possibilities in Duncan Bay. One is found in the double anchorage that lies to the north just after passing through the narrows. When entering this double bay, be sure to give wide berth to the 3-foot shoal found south of the eastern arm of this bay. Good anchoring can be found in either end of the bay, with 14 to 15 feet of depth over a mud bottom, the choice dependent only on wind direction. There is some slash lying on the bottom of both bays.

At the far SW end of Duncan Bay there is another excellent spot for anchoring with depths of 8 feet to 12 feet. In passing to the far end of this bay, hold to the middle or slightly favor the southern shore, for there is a large uncharted rock shoal in the middle of the bay off the northern shore that has only 4 feet of water over its rocky bottom. Once the shoal is skirted, there is again deeper water along the northern shore. With excellent holding ground this anchorage is good for all but strong NE winds.

Another anchorage in the SW end of Duncan Bay is to the N-NW of the T-shaped dock. Because of silting from the small stream that enters the bay, it is difficult to go very far in. However, 8 feet to 10 feet of good holding can easily be found here with protection for all but easterly winds.

The stream that empties into the bay is interesting to explore and is navigable for some way by dinghy. The area is very wild, a favorite for moose and beaver.

Following the northern shore of this bay to the NE produces another excellent anchorage behind the long island that bisects much of the length of Duncan Bay. Here 15 to 20 feet of water can be found over a mud bottom. Because of rocks and shoal water, it is impossible to pass around the northern end of this long island to get back into the main part of Duncan Bay. The water often gets

warm enough for swimming here in the back waters of Duncan Bay.

In the Duncan Bay area, there are a couple of canoe portages that make interesting hiking. A short trail of a quarter mile is found where Five Finger Bay comes closest to the northern side of Duncan Bay. Another trail that is considerably more difficult because of height and switchbacks is found in the main part of Duncan Bay along the middle of the southern shore. This trail is marked with a canoe portage sign. It is difficult to imagine how those with canoes and backpacks manage this vigorous ascent to the top of the Greenstone Ridge. Once on the top of the Greenstone, the trail leads 1.5 miles to the NE to Lookout Louise or 3.5 miles to the SW to Mount Franklin.

After rounding Blake Point and continuing on past Locke Point, we come to one of the most beautiful and navigationally challenging sections of the island. For nowhere on the island is the familiar pattern of long island chains, extending rocks and shoals and deep inlets more apparent than along this northern end of the island. Long intricate bays laced with hidden rocks and picturesque islets dominate the scene, again providing some especially beautiful anchorages. Note: there is a particularly wicked extension of the outermost string of islands and shoals here that is known as the **Canoe Rocks**. With very little of the rock shoal breaking surface, this treacherous shoal is difficult to spot since there are no landmarks (islands) close enough from which to get accurate bearings. That the shoal is hazardous is witnessed by the shipwrecks found in the area, one of which is the large steamer *Emperor*, that struck the reef in 1947. It now lies at an angle on the reef with a minimum depth of 35 feet.

NOT TO BE USED FOR NAVIGATION – SKETCH APPROXIMATE

Figure 6.29
Duncan Bay,
Five Finger Bay

Five Finger Bay

Hill Pt.

Stockly Bay

dock

3 ft. shoal

dock

Lookout Louise

Greenstone Ridge

Duncan Bay

canoe
portage

To Mt. Franklin

0   0.5   1 nm

GPS	Lat.	Lon.
▲1	48°10.12' N	88°31.00' W
▲2	48°10.64' N	88°29.73' W
▲3	48°10.43' N	88°28.09' W

||| Quiet, No Wake Zone

The first of the intricate bays to be found in this end of the island is **Five Finger Bay**, which gets its name from the five extensions or bays that are found around its periphery. Most of these can be entered and used as anchorages. However, the center and main part of the bay is made up of a string of small islands and rocky islets that, along with their surrounding shoal waters, create an extensive barrier making it difficult to enter the bay except at the far eastern and western ends. Even then this is an area to stay clear of when there is poor visibility or any sea running.

The longest finger in the complex, **Stockly Bay**, can be navigated successfully by deep-draft boats. Although this is a very snug anchorage, it isn't as pretty as one would expect from the charts, since the area around this end is quite low and, in some places, even swampy. The trail picked up here on the northern side at the far end goes over to the primitive campground on Lane Cove.

The shorter extension to the SE of Stockly Bay can likewise be entered with deep-draft boats, however this bay is more open to NE winds. The small inlet to the north of Stockly Bay is navigable only by dinghy, and the one just north of that can be entered only halfway. The "cove" on the eastern side of the bay is difficult to enter because of rocky shoal water and is quite open to the NW. For those who like seclusion, these extensions of Five Finger Bay are rarely visited and used as anchorages.

The area west of Five Finger Bay is composed of several long channels formed by equally long island chains. The water within each channel when traveling the length of the channel is usually quite deep, however, it should be noted that when cutting across from one channel to the other there are often extensions of shoal water radiating out from each island, sometimes effectively closing the gaps between the islands for clear passage. Here it is important to know your exact position, and thus, counting islands becomes almost a full-time job. With attention paid to the rocky extensions of the chains, each of these channels can be navigated successfully by deep-draft boats.

Lying to the south of the southernmost channel in this area there is a beautiful bay that has two anchorages, **Lane Cove**. Although the eastern end is shallow and foul with debris and deadheads, the western end has two extensions that are good for anchoring.

In the southernmost extension, it is possible to tuck way back in by passing through and beyond the two small entrance islands that lie at the mouth of this inlet. At the

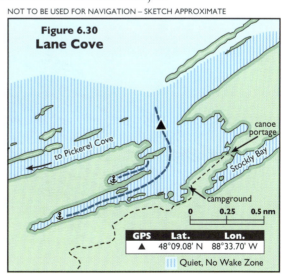

NOT TO BE USED FOR NAVIGATION – SKETCH APPROXIMATE

Figure 6.30
Lane Cove

to Pickerel Cove

canoe portage

Stockly Bay

campground

| 0 | 0.25 | 0.5 nm |

GPS	Lat.	Lon.
▲	48°09.08' N	88°33.70' W

Quiet, No Wake Zone

far end, just before the last constriction, there is a small shoal extending out from the northern shore. Anchor just before this shoal in 15 feet with good protection for all but the strongest NE winds. The shorter extension that lies just to the north of the longer one is more open to NE winds. Good anchoring can be found here with 20 feet of water. There is a primitive campground in the eastern part of the bay. There is a canoe portage here, a short distance over to Stockly Bay, a segment of Five Finger Bay.

By following the long channel that lies immediately north of Lane Cove to the SW, one comes to a narrows that, if navigated carefully, will bring one to another of the more remote spots of the island, **Pickerel Cove**. Because the depths in the narrows may vary from 5 feet to 8 feet, it is important to stay exactly midchannel and have a bow lookout when passing through this very narrow shallow entrance. Once through the narrows there is good water by staying in the middle of the channel until the far end. In fact, in most places the water is so deep that it is difficult to find good anchoring. One spot to anchor is in the indentation on the southern shore just after clearing the shoal water of the narrows. Although this anchorage has good protection for all winds, there may be some difficulty in anchoring because of deadheads. In the far end of Pickerel Cove, the water also gets shallow enough for anchoring. Aside from a short canoe portage to the outer shore of the island, the anchorage has little more to offer than seclusion.

Because **Robinson Bay** is so open to the NE, it is rarely used as an anchorage. It also has a number of rocks and shoal areas that

NOT TO BE USED FOR NAVIGATION – SKETCH APPROXIMATE

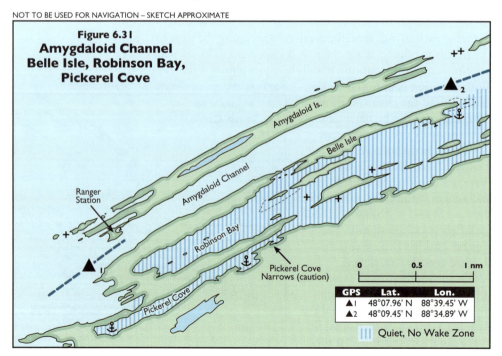

Figure 6.31
**Amygdaloid Channel
Belle Isle, Robinson Bay,
Pickerel Cove**

Ranger Station

Amygdaloid Is.

Belle Isle

Amygdaloid Channel

Robinson Bay

Pickerel Cove Narrows (caution)

Pickerel Cove

GPS	Lat.	Lon.
▲1	48°07.96' N	88°39.45' W
▲2	48°09.45' N	88°34.89' W

||| Quiet, No Wake Zone

0   0.5   1 nm

make navigation difficult. Another reason Robinson Bay is rarely used is that at the NE end of **Belle Isle** there is a dock (see Fig. 6.32), nice picnic area and beautiful campground that make this one of the favorite spots on this end of the island.

It is difficult to believe that where the Belle Isle campground now stands there was at one time a resort—complete with a dance hall and golf course. When Isle Royale was discovered as a recreational paradise in the early 1900s, a new type of visitor – the vacationer—began to flock to its shores, and Belle Isle became *the* night spot on the island. But even before the building of the resort, this little island had gained importance, for in the mid-1800s the American Fur Company established one of its fishing stations here.

Today all that remains of the resort is a large cement shuffleboard court east of the pavilion picnic-grill area. Surrounding this cleared area there is a campsite (1) and a number of shelters (6). Coupled with the fact that this is the only campground that has a 5-night stay limit makes Belle Isle one of the more popular spots for boat camping on the island. Again, It is Important to note that the shelters and campsite are on a first come basis. Boaters do not have priority. Because the small T-shaped dock on the southern shore often quickly fills up, an alternative is to anchor in the small cove that lies just to the east of the campground. Here there is good protection for SW-N winds, but it may be difficult to get a good set with the anchor because of a rocky bottom. There are some rock boulders in the bay off the SW shore that should be avoided when anchoring. This cove is also used by those camping with small boats, who will often run their boats up on shore. Note: both the cove and the dock are especially vulnerable to NE winds.

The **Amygdaloid Channel** is the most often used passage along the northern end of the island. (The name "amygdaloid" comes from the small round cavities that are formed in molten rock by air bubbles, found in much of the rock along this section of Isle Royale.) This channel, which is the outermost in this series of

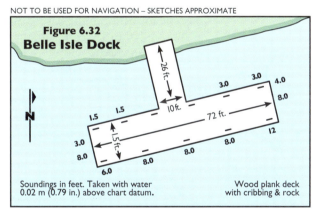

NOT TO BE USED FOR NAVIGATION – SKETCHES APPROXIMATE

Figure 6.32
Belle Isle Dock

Soundings in feet. Taken with water 0.02 m (0.79 in.) above chart datum.

Wood plank deck with cribbing & rock

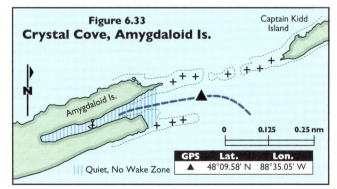

Figure 6.33
Crystal Cove, Amygdaloid Is.

Captain Kidd Island

Amygdaloid Is.

0   0.125   0.25 nm

GPS	Lat.	Lon.
▲	48°09.58' N	88°35.05' W

Quiet, No Wake Zone

parallel running bays and inlets, can be entered from a number of directions. If coming from Blake Point, it is entered by lining up with Steamboat Island. It can also be entered from the channel that forms Robinson Bay if the shoals extending out from both Belle Isle and the small island chain to the NE are given adequate berth. The narrow passage to the west of Belle Isle can even be used by shoal draft boats, but here adverse currents often set up a venturi effect. From the outside, there is a small passage between Amygdaloid and Captain Kidd islands. But this passage should be attempted only when there is no sea running and with the sun high at one's back. From the west, the channel is easily entered by passing to either side of Round Island that lies just off its entrance. Note the shoal water extending to the north of Round Island.

The **Crystal Cove** area on the NE end of **Amygdaloid Island** bears mentioning because originally this harbor was the site of one of the island's family fisheries. This station was run by the same family for decades with family members still visiting the island each summer until the late 1970s. To enter this harbor care must be taken to avoid a number of surrounding shoals, especially those to each side off the eastern end of the entrance. Although it is possible to pass between Amygdaloid and Captain Kidd islands, the best approach into the harbor is from the SE. Because of the extensive shoals, it is important to negotiate this entrance only with no sea running and the sun high at one's back for good visibility. It is possible to anchor in the harbor, since there are good depths for anchoring (10 to 15 feet). Although the wind usually funnels in here (east/west), it probably is best to set out bow and stern anchors or a Bahamian Moor because the area is quite narrow and swinging room is restricted. Many of the original buildings from the fishing station remain along with two docks. In 2005, one of these docks was replaced with a "T" shaped dock constructed of wood cribbing with a wood deck. Note that only daytime use is permitted on this dock. There is little protection for easterly winds. At the south end of Amygdaloid Island there is a ranger station.

McCargoe Cove, which is the very long indentation along the island's northern shore, is probably one of the most historically interesting spots on Isle Royale. For here, not only have the largest

NOT TO BE USED FOR NAVIGATION – SKETCH APPROXIMATE

Figure 6.34
McCargoe Cove
**

G
R
Brady Cove
Birch Island
to Minong Mine
to Chicken Bone Lake

0   0.5   1 nm

||| Quiet, No Wake Zone

copper mining pursuits by both Native American and white men alike taken place, but this deep, long inlet was actually used to hide a British warship in the War of 1812. This ship, which was owned by the North West Fur Company, was the 90-ton *Recovery* and commanded by a Captain McCargoe (hence the name of the cove). It was hidden deep within the cove for the duration of the war and then was used by Admiral Bayfield in the early 1800s in his famous charting expeditions of the lake. The name "McCargoe" shows up every so often in the annals of history written about this era, but little is known about him other than that he went by the singular name of McCargoe, worked for the North West Company – and knew this sector of the lake like no other.

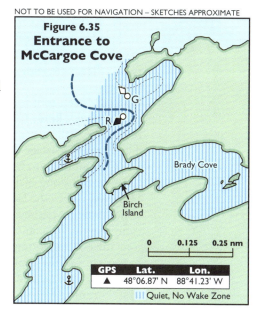

Figure 6.35
Entrance to McCargoe Cove

Brady Cove

Birch Island

0   0.125   0.25 nm

GPS	Lat.	Lon.
▲	48°06.87' N	88°41.23' W

Quiet, No Wake Zone

In coming up to the entrance of the cove for the first time, you can well-see how McCargoe was able to hide such a ship. For this is one of those entrances that "doesn't open up until the last minute" – and then you have to know just where it is. Shoals extending out from each side further make entering the cove difficult, necessitating sharp "S" turns to navigate through these tricky waters.

Fortunately for us, these shoals (and thus the entrance) are now marked with two buoys, a green and a red. To enter, you take a course of 90 degrees T, passing through

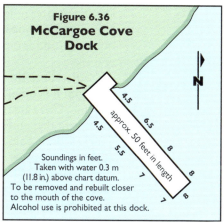

Figure 6.36
McCargoe Cove Dock

N

4.5

approx. 50 feet in length

6.5

4.5

8

5.5

8

7

Soundings in feet.
Taken with water 0.3 m
(11.8 in.) above chart datum.
To be removed and rebuilt closer
to the mouth of the cove.
Alcohol use is prohibited at this dock.

7

8

7

the buoys keeping the outermost green buoy to port. Then, as the red buoy is approached, round it by keeping it to starboard. As you do this and note the shoal water to each side, think of McCargoe bringing in his 90-ton ship—with no engine.

Once the cove is entered, there is deep water to the far end of the inlet. In fact, passing down the length of McCargoe Cove is one of the special treats of visiting Isle Royale, for it is one of the most beautiful spots on the island.

Within this all-weather inlet, there are a number of places in which to anchor or dock. The first of these is found in the small bay that one sees to starboard after clearing the red buoy. Here one can anchor about two-thirds of the way in, in 15 to 20 feet of water over a mud bottom and with protection for all winds.

Just a little farther down the channel on the opposite shore there is a small dock on **Birch Island** that can accommodate two

boats. With care, boats drawing up to 5.5 feet can edge up to the dock and at least tie off the front half of the boat on the dock. In this case it may be desirable to set out a stern anchor. There are two shelters here with picnic tables, and those requiring the use of the shelters have priority on using the dock. At dusk, this is an especially good spot to catch northern pike.

Although **Brady Cove** is very interesting to explore by dinghy, because of shallow depth it is accessible to only shoal draft boats. The southern passage around Birch Island has more depth.

Continuing into McCargoe Cove, there are a number of small indentations along each side that are sometimes used for anchoring. However, it is to the far end that boaters most often tend to go, either to tie up to the large dock that is located next to another campground, or to anchor off in the quiet waters in the base of this long inlet. If anchoring is chosen it should be done off to the side to stay clear of the boat traffic to and from the dock. By not going too close to the far end, it is possible to anchor in 15 feet with a mud bottom.

The small stream at this end can be explored by dinghy for about a quarter mile before it gives way to windfalls. Despite the large amount of boater and backpacker traffic here, the area remains quite wild and is often frequented by moose and beaver, particularly at dusk.

Adjacent to the dock there is a very large, spread-out campground complete with numerous shelters, picnic tables and a firepit. There are many trails to hike in the area. One follows the stream that enters the cove back to its source, beautiful inland Chicken Bone Lake. By following the trail around the western side of the lake, another trail can be picked up along its southern shore that forks at the SE end of the lake heading back to McCargoe on a roughly triangular course that totals approximately seven miles.

Another trail that heads west through the campground leads to the abandoned Minong Copper Mine where there are some of the richest copper deposits on the island. That the prehistoric Native

Americans were well-aware of these is evidenced by a thousand mine pits in this area alone. The pits are from 10 to 30 feet in diameter varying from 10 to 20 feet deep and show the uncanny ability of these early miners to locate the richest veins. The raw copper was "mined" with large stone hammers weighing 10 pounds, fragments of which can still be found. Once free, the copper was hammered into bars and blades for trade.

Like the Native Americans, the early explorers also valued this malleable metal, and with the advent of the copper boom of the mid-1800s, valiant efforts were made to establish and work a mine here in the 1870s. The mine was the largest on the island, and today many artifacts from this venture can still be seen, including remnants of a small railroad.

From McCargoe Cove down the north side of Isle Royale, it is a long 30 nautical miles to Washington Harbor with a bold deep shore and no really good harbors of refuge except one. Therefore a special note to the weather should be given when making this long run, especially to SW winds which here can quickly build into a good sea because of the fetch. With a few outlying shoal areas, it is prudent to stay a good mile offshore, especially on the stretch between McCargoe Cove and Todd Harbor.

Todd Harbor is a large open bay that should be navigated with care, since there are many rocks and shoal areas, especially in the eastern half of the bay. The west end of the bay can be entered to either side of Wilson Island, but again in each case there are shoals that have to be accounted for. If entering to the east of Wilson Island, favor the island in order to avoid the 1-foot shoal located east of the island. If entering between Wilson Point and Wilson Island, favor the point, for there is an unmarked 6-foot shoal between the two. This is another harbor that should not be attempted in rough conditions or without the sun high at one's back.

Within this west end of Todd Harbor there are three anchorages. One is found by following Wilson Point back into **Florence Bay**. Another anchorage is in **Pickett Bay** which is the next inlet to the SE. Although both bays provide good anchoring, both are quite open to NE winds. An alternative is to anchor off or use the small dock that is in the eastern side of this section of Todd Harbor. To reach this dock, be sure to stand well off the southern shore of the harbor because of considerable shoal water along this side. A small island with a tall pine tree is part of this shoal area and should be given wide berth. Deep-draft boats will have difficulty getting up to the dock which lies very low in the water. A trail can be picked up near the shelter that leads to the abandoned Haytown Mine and a small waterfall that are just a little farther west.

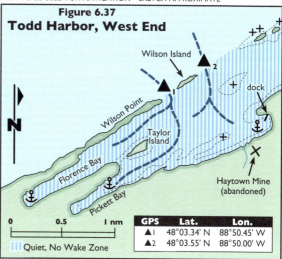

Figure 6.37
Todd Harbor, West End

Wilson Island

dock

Wilson Point

Taylor Island

Florence Bay

Pickett Bay

Haytown Mine (abandoned)

0	0.5	1 nm

Quiet, No Wake Zone

GPS	Lat.	Lon.
▲1	48°03.34' N	88°50.45' W
▲2	48°03.55' N	88°50.00' W

Figure 6.38
Isle Royale Water Mileage Chart

		1	2	3	4	5	6	7	8	9	10	11	12	13	14	15	16	17	18	19	20	21	22	23	24	25	
1	Grace Island	—	3	4	28	26	29	28	36	43	46	43	43	43	46	47	48	49	50	46	49	41	31	33	34	5	**1**
2	Beaver Island	3	—	1	31	29	32	31	39	46	49	46	46	49	49	50	51s	52	52	48	51	43	33	35	26	7	**2**
3	Windigo	4	1	—	32	30	33	32	40	47	50	47	47	48	50	51	52s	53	53	49	52	44	34	36	27	8	**3**
4	Siskiwit Camp	28	31	32	—	6	11	12	20	26	29	26	26	27	29	30	31	32	36	40	43	45	51	53	60	33	**4**
5	Hay Bay	26	29	30	6	—	7	9	16	23	26	23	23	24	26	27	29	29	32	36	39	41	47	49	56	31	**5**
6	Malone Bay	29	32	33	11	7	—	3	10	17	20	17	17	18	20	21	22	23	26	30	33	35	41	43	50	34	**6**
7	Isle Royale Light	28	31	32	12	9	3	—	9	15	18	15	15	16	18	19	20	21	24	28	31	33	39	41	48	53	**7**
8	Chippewa Harbor	36	39	40	20	16	10	9	—	7	10	7	7	8	10	11	12	13	16	20	23	25	31	33	40	41	**8**
9	Middle Passage Light	43	46	47	26	23	17	15	7	—	3	1	1	2	4	5	6	7	9	13	16	18	24	26	33	48	**9**
10	Moskey Basin Camp	46	49	50	29	26	20	18	10	3	—	3	4	5	7	8	9	10	13	17	20	22	28	30	37	51	**10**
11	Daisy Farm	43	46	47	26	23	17	15	7	1	3	—	1	2	4	5	6	7	10	14	17	19	25	27	34	48	**11**
12	Caribou Island	43	46	47	26	23	17	15	7	1	4	1	—	1	3	4	5	6	9	13	16	18	24	26	33	48	**12**
13	Mott Island	43	49	48	27	24	18	16	8	2	5	2	1	—	2	3	4	5	8	12	15	11	23	25	32	47	**13**
14	Three Mile Camp	46	49	50	29	26	20	18	10	4	7	4	3	2	—	1	2	3	6	10	13	15	21	23	30	49	**14**
15	Tookers Island	47	50	51	30	27	21	19	11	5	8	5	4	3	1	—	2	2	5	9	12	14	20	22	29	48	**15**
16	Rock Harbor Lodge	48	51s	52s	31	29	22	20	12	6	9	6	5	4	2	2	—	1	4	8	11	13	19	21	28	47	**16**
17	Raspberry Island	49	52	53	32	29	23	21	13	7	10	7	6	5	3	2	1	—	3	7	10	12	18	20	27	46	**17**
18	Hidden Lake	50	52	53	36	32	26	24	16	9	13	10	9	8	6	5	4	3	—	6	9	12	18	19	28	45	**18**
19	Duncan Narrows Camp	46	48	49	40	36	30	28	20	13	17	14	13	12	10	9	8	7	6	—	3	9	14	16	24	43	**19**
20	Duncan Bay Camp	49	51	52	43	39	33	31	23	16	20	17	16	15	13	12	11	10	9	3	—	12	17	19	27	46	**20**
21	Belle Isle	41	43	44	45	41	35	33	25	18	22	19	18	11	15	14	13	12	12	9	12	—	7	9	15	38	**21**
22	Birch Island	31	33	34	51	47	41	39	31	24	28	25	24	23	21	20	19	18	18	14	17	7	—	2	9	26	**22**
23	McCargoe Cove Camp	33	35	36	53	49	43	41	33	26	30	27	26	25	23	22	21	20	19	16	19	9	2	—	11	28	**23**
24	Todd Harbor	34	26	27	60	56	50	48	40	33	37	34	33	32	30	29	28	27	28	24	27	15	9	11	—	19	**24**
25	Huginnin Cove	5	7	8	33	31	54	53	41	48	51	48	48	47	49	48	47	46	45	43	46	38	26	28	19	—	**25**
		1	**2**	**3**	**4**	**5**	**6**	**7**	**8**	**9**	**10**	**11**	**12**	**13**	**14**	**15**	**16**	**17**	**18**	**19**	**20**	**21**	**22**	**23**	**24**	**25**	

s = via south shore. Add 5 miles more via north shore. NOTE: Mileage is in statute miles.

From Todd Harbor to Washington Harbor the shoreline is even more barren of suitable anchorages. Here there are only two possibilities, and these are so marginal that they hardly bear mentioning. In both cases they should only be treated as harbors of refuge or lunch stops, and then they are accessible to only very small shoal draft boats.

The first of these is **Todd Cove** in Little Todd Harbor which is located approximately 2.5 nautical miles southwest of Wilson Point in Todd Harbor. There are no facilities here, and anchoring is difficult because of a foul bottom, but it is possible to get protection for NE-S winds.

The other marginal anchorage is in Huginnin Cove just around the corner, five miles from Washington Harbor. Although the water is quite shallow, there is protection from southerly winds.

A **water mileage chart** of distances between various points around the island is included in Fig. 6.38. It should be noted that here the distances are given in statute miles and are accurate only to the nearest whole mile. The reason that these distances are not converted to nautical miles is that this would have necessitated using decimals which would imply a greater accuracy than is actually given. To convert to nautical miles divide the statute miles by 1.15.

Chapter Seven

Gateway to the North: Pigeon Point, Minnesota, to Lamb Island, Ontario

When we round Pigeon Point and look up the Canadian shoreline to the north, we catch a first glimpse of the high rolling headlands and dense forests that characterize this wild rugged shoreline of the north. Broken only by the city complex of Thunder Bay with its continuous traffic of commercial shipping, we now come to that section of the lake that is one of the prime areas for wilderness cruising. With much of the shoreline laced with intricate island chains, we can cruise here for days in the protected side channels, a veritable "gateway to the north."

For many, wilderness cruising is cruising at its best. For as we climb this wild shoreline toward the north, the landscape takes on a majestic rugged quality with rocky lichen-painted beaches, high over-towering bluffs and unending forests of spruce and pine. With wildlife and waterfowl abundant, it is not uncommon to be greeted with a slap of a beaver tail or the flight of a great blue heron as we glide into the remote backwaters of a hidden anchorage. Many of these anchorages are secure "hurricane holes" displaying picture postcard scenery, a true photographer's paradise.

Since this section of the lake is a true wilderness area, it is important to note that there are no gas depots or supply stations along the way. In the 90-mile stretch from Thunder Bay to Rossport, there are only two areas to get supplies and these are 30 miles off the beaten track at Red Rock and Nipigon. Therefore when heading up this shoreline, it is important to carry along a full complement of ship's stores, replacement parts and extra fuel. There is little or nothing that can be obtained here.

Another important point to note is that aside from Thunder Bay there are no marinas and few docks in this sector of the lake. Thus you must not only be electrically independent for long periods of time, but you must also be prepared to anchor in a variety of ways. Often it may be necessary to use two anchors or a

Please Note:
Maps and Charts in this book are not necessarily to scale and are not intended for navigation.

trip line to retrieve a fouled anchor. Therefore, it is important to have not only adequate ground tackle, but also to have worked out these systems beforehand.

Many areas in this part of the lake, especially within the island chains, contain hazardous shoals and rock-strewn water. Because there are also many areas of magnetic disturbance, steering a compass course may sometimes be impossible; taking visual bearings may be the only way to navigate. The prevalence of fog, especially along Lake Superior's northern shore, will often compound these problems of navigation. Even with radar and GPS, there are some areas that should not be navigated without good visibility, and the prudent course may be to just snug up to an island and wait for better conditions. In the long run, it is important to be prepared for fog, which can descend in minutes, and cautious boaters should cruise this area with alternative anchorages always kept well in mind.

To address the concerns of wilderness cruising in this area, the mid-1990s saw the establishment of the North of Superior Marina Marketing Association. By pooling resources of communities from Thunder Bay to the Sault, a key mandate of this group is the development and promotion of marinas along the north and east shores of Lake Superior. They put out a helpful booklet that describes Ontario marine facilities from Thunder Bay to Sault Ste. Marie (*www.tbaytel.net/marinas*).

Another development in this section of the lake that will affect the recreational boater is the establishment of a National Marine Conservation Area (NMCA). It is not within the scope of this book to present the total NMCA with all its ramifications. The following is but a summary of the possible impacts it may have on the boating community. Basically, the goal of the plan is to "optimize use while protecting natural and cultural heritage values." Core areas, generally small in size, will protect critical habitats, endangered species and outstanding natural or cultural features. Other elements involve environmental education and interpretative programs. The Lake Superior National Marine Conservation Area extends from Thunder Cape on the Sibley Peninsula to Bottle Point past Terrace Bay, including both Nipigon

---

Figure 7.1
NMCA Zones

Zone I (Preservation) – a highly protected core which would make up approximately 1% of the total area. Example: this might include nesting locations of peregrine falcons and extremely sensitive archaeological sites. Renewable resource harvesting (hunting & fishing) would not be permitted, nor would visitor access be allowed.

Zone II (Natural Environment) – moderately protected areas comprising 2-5% of the total area. These would be buffer zones used to enhance protection of special habitats or features while encouraging recreational use and public education. Example: might be the nesting habitats for great blue herons which are sensitive during egg incubation and the rearing of young and would be restricted during these times, i.e. seasonal zoning. Renewable resource harvesting would not be permitted, but low-intensity outdoor recreation would be allowed.

Zone III (Conservation) – multiple-use areas which are managed for conservation and make up the rest of the NMCA. Would allow shipping, commercial and sport fishing, hunting and outdoor recreational activities.

and Black bays. A key element of the NMCA is the division of the area into zones for protection purposes. (See Fig. 7.1.) Within the NMCA there are 70 different fish species and 50 shipwrecks. There are two Visitor Centers, one at Terrace Bay (seasonal, June – mid-October) and one at Nipigon Administrative Office (open all year).

The NMCA is under the administration of Parks Canada, but in cooperation with other governmental agencies. At present there is no plan for a user fee structure in the proposal. It is expected that the restrictive zone impact to the recreational boater will be small in comparison with the total area. Yet, it is an area on the lake that is bound to have some changes and bears watching in the coming years.

A final comment. One thing we have noticed about our Canadian Brethren over the years is their incredible ingenuity in using floating docks. You have to admit, it's reasonably easy to bring them into remote areas over the water. Attaching them to shore can vary from trying off on a few trees to the elaborate structures in Thunder Bay. And they certainly are adaptable to use in the North Country. When winter comes, all you have to do is unhook them and drag them up on shore. We are making every effort in this guide to be as accurate as possible, both with texts and charts. However, this versatility in dock usage means that you may use a dock in a nice cozy anchorage one season only to find it gone when you come back the next.

Harbors and Anchorages

The area around **Pigeon Point** is one of those which often exhibits magnetic anomalies, especially in those waters SW of the peninsula. This disturbance increases the closer one gets to shore. Therefore, in conditions of reduced visibility, it is wise to stand off

NOT TO BE USED FOR NAVIGATION – SKETCH APPROXIMATE

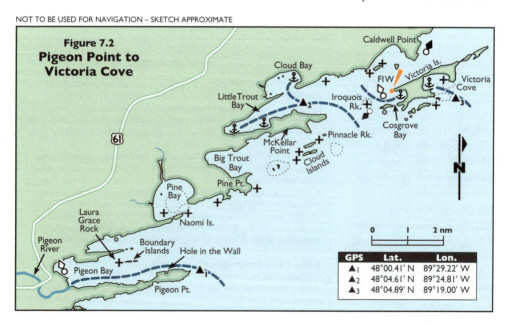

Figure 7.2
Pigeon Point to Victoria Cove

GPS	Lat.	Lon.
▲₁	48°00.41' N	89°29.22' W
▲₂	48°04.61' N	89°24.81' W
▲₃	48°04.89' N	89°19.00' W

from shore at least a couple of miles.

On the north shore of Pigeon Point, approximately a half mile west of the point, there is a small indentation in the sheer rock-faced wall. Aptly named **Hole in the Wall,** this small constricted area can be used as an anchorage. However, the area is quite small and, because of deep water, adequate swinging room is a definite problem. Thus it is almost essential to use two anchors or one anchor and tie off on shore to restrict swinging.

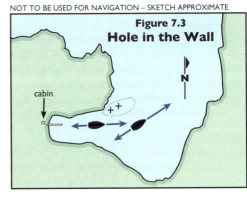

Figure 7.3
Hole in the Wall

cabin

A large rock boulder and shoal just inside the entrance on the west side further restricts swinging. Shoal draft boats can skirt around this shoal and anchor in the "thumb" by using a bow and stern anchor. There is a small cottage here, and reports in recent years indicate that the owners prefer not to have lines tied across this small section of the harbor so they can have free access to the outer lake. Because the rest of the anchorage is deep, it may be necessary to tie off on shore. This anchorage is quite snug, giving excellent protection for all but north winds, which can cause an uncomfortable surge.

At the far western end of Pigeon Bay it is also possible to anchor near the mouth of the **Pigeon River.** To reach this end of Pigeon Bay, it is important to favor the Pigeon Point shoreline to avoid the very large shoal surrounding Boundary island and the smaller shoals, Acadia and Laura Grace rocks. With care, the mouth of Pigeon River can be entered and navigated a short distance, depending on boat draft.

Following the shoreline NE from Pigeon Point, there are a number of small bays that are sometimes used as anchorages, particularly by those who sail out of Thunder Bay. Although most of these are open to at least one side, by watching the weather they can be used successfully as overnight anchorages.

Almost a perfect circle, **Pine Bay** looks on the charts as though it would be a good anchorage. However, because of very shoaled water and a rock-strewn entrance, it is rarely used and then only with shoal draft boats. The bay is also quite open to SE winds.

Farther up the shore there is a similar bay, **Cloud Bay,** which is used more often because greater depths allow boats to get farther in for protection. The bay is still shallow, especially in the western end. Thus it is in the eastern end where boats most often anchor.

In approaching this area from the south it is important to strike a course midway between McKeller Point and Victoria Island, in order to avoid the shoal water surrounding and adjacent to the Cloud Islands and Iroquois Rock, which is buoyed. This west end of Victoria Island is marked with a light (Fl W). The channel north of Victoria Island can be successfully navigated as long as the shoal

south of Caldwell Point, which is marked by a red buoy, is avoided by hugging close to Victoria Island.

The entrance to Cloud Bay is wide and free of obstructions. There is more depth in the eastern side, and thus it is easier to get close into shore at this end. With care, the western side can also be used for anchoring, but here the water shoals rapidly because of silt deposits from the Cloud River which empties into the bay at its NW corner. There is a small public wharf in the mouth of the river, but it is accessible to only very shoal draft boats. Parts of this bay are dotted with cottages and summer homes.

Adjacent to Cloud Bay to the SW is **Little Trout Bay,** which in the far end gets shallow enough to anchor in. The bay has protection for all but NE winds, but even other winds can sometimes cause problems. Because of the very high, steep surrounding hills, winds often build to significant proportions as they sweep down over the bluffs into this long valley. Because of these high surrounding bluffs, this is a particularly beautiful anchorage. This is a Conservation Area which provides concrete launch ramps and docks for small boats behind a large breakwall. Although overnight mooring is not allowed at the docks, it is possible to anchor at the far end. It is also possible to anchor snugged up midway on the south shore behind the rounded point

NOT TO BE USED FOR NAVIGATION – SKETCH APPROXIMATE

Pie Island

Campbell Island

Steamboat Island

Flatland Island

Sturgeon Bay

Wyllie Point

Dog Is.

Alexander Reef

Deadman Island

Figure 7.4
Spar & Thompson Islands, Jarvis, Prince & Sturgeon Bays

Sturgeon Point

▲3

Thompson Island

▲4

Mink Island

Fl W

Mink Point

Jarvis River

N

Prince Bay

▲1

Jarvis Bay

▲2

Spar Island

GPS	Lat.	Lon.
▲1	48°06.95' N	89°19.40' W
▲2	48°07.30' N	89°15.80' W
▲3	48°10.72' N	89°17.33' W
▲4	48°10.35' N	89°08.70' W

Fl W

Jarvis Is.

Spar Channel

0   1   2 nm

that extends into the bay to get protection from easterly winds.

In the string of islands that extends NE from McKeller Point, there are a couple of bays that can be used for anchoring. The first of these is the large bay on the southeast side of Victoria Island, **Victoria Cove.** Although it looks like it would be a good harbor on the charts, it is best used only as a lunch stop. This is because it is quite deep and has a rock bottom, so it is difficult to get a good set with an anchor. In fact, the bay is so deep that there are some places where it is possible to tie right up to shore. To enter the cove, it is important to note the rock shoals that extend out from each side of the entrance and head into the bay in a roughly NW course. This bay is quite open to S and SE winds, which also limits its use.

Thompson Island is a popular destination for Thunder Bay boaters. DAHL

Another anchorage that is best used as a lunch stop is the bay found at the west end of Victoria Island, **Cosgrave Bay.** It is identified by a light tower off the NW point of Victoria and two buoys: a green off this point and a red marking Iroquois Rock. Passage into the bay is between these two buoys favoring the green to avoid the shoal area around Iroquois Rock. Do not pass between the green buoy and the light tower point as it is shoal water. Anchoring depths and holding ground are better here than at Victoria Cove, but the anchorage is quite open to west and SW winds.

A more secure anchorage is the small bay on the **north side of Spar Island.** There are two small islands in the entrance, one larger than the other. Enter with both islands kept to port since the water on the other side of the islands is quite shoal. Deep draft boats will not be able to go much farther in than the middle of the bay. There is good protection here for all but N and NW winds. There used to be a dock, sauna, and shelter built by local boaters in the SE end of the bay which has been removed. There are still a couple of trails here extending from where the dock used to be. One goes across to the other side of the island and one goes to the "Top of a World" lookout for a beautiful view of the city of Thunder Bay to the north. Local sailors take their boat camps and saunas very seriously and you will see them cozied Into anchorages up and down the shoreline. However, few can match the extensive building that is found on Thompson Island.

Thompson Island is the next island in the chain and along its

southern shore approximately two-thirds of a mile from its NE tip there is a long narrow bay that is used as an overnight anchorage and gathering spot for boaters. This is another area that has seen significant development by those who cruise out of Thunder Bay. There is an extensive dock structure and boardwalk that has evolved over the years and now is in excess of 240 feet. (See Fig. 7.6.) The complex also contains a barbecue area with a fire pit, benches, shelter, and sauna. Since the supply of surrounding deadwood has been depleted over the years, it is greatly appreciated that you bring your own firewood to the island if you plan on using the sauna or having a fire. If seclusion is desired, this is not the place to come, especially on weekends, since it is a favorite gathering place for those who cruise the area. Note: if all the docks are filled, rafting is expected.

Again, the Thunder Bay folk must take their hiking very seriously, for they have put in a rather vigorous trail system that provides some beautiful overlooks. One of these looks down into the anchorage and docking area, another looks off the north side of the island toward mainland and Thunder Bay. In the past, these trails have been complete with knotted "rope-downs," tree ladders and even a rope bridge.

This end of Thompson Island is also of interest in light of recent archaeological discoveries. In 1980, a number of man-made pit-like structures were discovered on a series of terraces in a tiny clearing in the middle of the island. Resembling those formations that are known elsewhere on the lake as the Pukaskwa Pits, this site has archaeological significance because it is the first find of this type of activity this far west on the lake. Until now, these pit-like structures have been found confined to Lake Superior's NE shore where there are as many as 50 different locations, some of which have as many as 70 separate structures.

The Thompson Island site consists of 14 structures, 12 of which are circular pits, with the largest measuring 3 meters

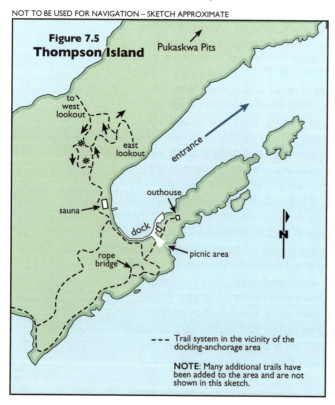

NOT TO BE USED FOR NAVIGATION – SKETCH APPROXIMATE

Figure 7.5
Thompson Island

Pukaskwa Pits

to west lookout

east lookout

entrance

sauna

outhouse

dock

rope bridge

picnic area

N

- - - Trail system in the vicinity of the docking-anchorage area

NOTE: Many additional trails have been added to the area and are not shown in this sketch.

in diameter and almost 1 meter in depth. This largest pit also has a low wall around it and a "doorway" toward the NE. The other two structures are a small rock cairn and a rectangular shape of coarse sand.

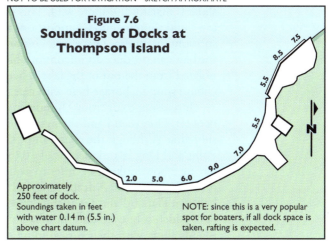

Figure 7.6
Soundings of Docks at Thompson Island

Approximately 250 feet of dock.
Soundings taken in feet with water 0.14 m (5.5 in.) above chart datum.

NOTE: since this is a very popular spot for boaters, if all dock space is taken, rafting is expected.

To date, archaeologists have been unable to date the Pukaskwa Pits or determine their function, particularly because of the scarcity of artifacts at the sites. Thus, they could have been constructed by prehistoric natives or even the historic voyageurs. The function of these pits likewise remains an enigma, and debate persists on whether they were used as bases for shelters, caches for food, hunting blinds, ceremonial lodges or even voyageur rifle pits.

In continuing up the mainland shoreline toward Thunder Bay there are a couple of more harbors that can be used as overnight anchorages. One of these is **Jarvis Bay,** which is located north of Victoria Island. The southern part of this bay is formed by a long extension of land, Jarvis Point. By going way in, adequate depths for anchoring can be found. However, do not go too close to the mouth of the Jarvis River where there is shoaling. This anchorage has protection for all but north to east winds, to which it is quite open.

A more secure harbor lies in the same Jarvis Bay complex, but in the NE corner. This snug little bay is **Prince Bay** and is one of the nicest harbors in the area. There is a small dock here that is in some disrepair but still can be used by boats drawing up to 5 feet. Five-foot draft boats may be able to edge up by setting out a stern anchor and tying off just the bow. It is also possible to anchor here since there is a good-holding blue clay bottom. A trail can be picked up behind the cabin that leads to a lookout behind the Old Jarvis Mine. This was the first silver mine to be constructed on the north shore. There are several mines in this area between Prince Bay and Mink Point.

Another harbor in this area is **Sturgeon Bay** which is a completely landlocked bay surrounded by majestic high cliffs and bluffs. To enter this bay, it is necessary to pass through a constricted channel, but by staying in the middle there are no hazards. However, in years of low water, boats drawing more than 5 feet will have difficulty getting in through the channel. Within Sturgeon Bay it is possible to anchor in most areas depending on wind direction. The west and northern shores are ringed with cottages; the eastern shore is marshy and more wild. This is another spot where winds can build to tremendous proportions as they sweep down over the surrounding bluffs. This effect, combined with the large size of the bay, can produce an uncomfortable chop despite the bay being isolated from the rest of the lake. Therefore, it is important to choose your anchorage here with care.

In passing to or from Thunder Bay, it is possible to pass between Dog Island and the mainland and follow the mainland shoreline. Although the charts show shoal water between Wyllie Point and Dog Island, depths of 10 to 12 feet can be maintained by having a bow lookout in order to avoid the shoal water that extends out from each side. A deeper channel to Thunder Bay is found between Flatland and Pie islands. Here, be sure to note Alexander Reef which is buoyed and the very small Steamboat and Deadman islands along with their surrounding shoal waters.

Although much of the water surrounding **Pie Island** is quite deep right up to shore, there are a couple of spots where it is possible to obtain sufficient depths for anchoring. But since these areas are quite open to certain wind directions, the anchorages are marginal and should only be considered as lunch stops or if wind direction is assured. A couple of these are located in Dawson Bay where it is possible to snug up to shore and get protection for all but southerly winds. Another anchorage is just to the north of Turtle Head which provides protection for south and westerly winds. The best approach is to come In from the east south of the small exposed rock off shore to avoid shoal water.

When you approach **Thunder Bay** from the open water of the south, the total effect can be somewhat overwhelming. This is another section of the lake where everything strikes one as being enormous—and it is. Not only is the bay large, 15 by 30 miles, but its entrance is guarded by those two towering massive sentinels, Pie Island and Cape Thunder. It doesn't take long cruising these waters to know where the name "thunder" comes from, since strong winds are a common occurrence roaring down these gargantuan bluffs onto the lake. It seems that here, there is either lots of wind or none at all, and these conditions are known to vacillate with a most frustrating consistency. We have made more sail changes in this single area than any other on the lake and have quickly come to

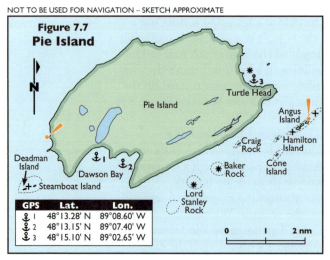

NOT TO BE USED FOR NAVIGATION – SKETCH APPROXIMATE

Figure 7.7
Pie Island

N

Pie Island

Turtle Head

Angus Island

Craig Rock

Hamilton Island

Deadman Island

Dawson Bay

Baker Rock

Cone Island

Steamboat Island

Lord Stanley Rock

GPS	Lat.	Lon.
1	48°13.28' N	89°08.60' W
2	48°13.15' N	89°07.40' W
3	48°15.10' N	89°02.65' W

0   1   2 nm

admire and respect those hardy sailors who sail out of Thunder Bay and call this "home cruising ground."

The awesome **Thunder Cape** is not only one of the most spectacular headlands on the lake, but it also has a rich history steeped in local color and legend. Originally called Cap de Tonnerre by the French voyageurs, today this 25-mile-long peninsula is called the Sibley Peninsula after the one-time president of the Silver Islet Mining Company which was based at its southern end. The peninsula has been made into a provincial park that boasts of numerous hiking trails, campsites and inland lakes.

But what the peninsula is most known for is the distinguishing southern five miles at its tip which are known as "The Sleeping Giant." According to Chippewa legend, the giant is the famed Naniboujou who once lived on the peninsula. There are at least two different legends. One relates that Naniboujou, who was supposed to be protector of the Chippewa, was turned to stone by the Great Spirit when the presence of silver on this shoreline was revealed to the early explorers. Another story tells how Naniboujou killed his wife in a fit of temper when she was nagging him in a time of hunger and starvation. Horror stricken, he ran out into the night, but could not escape the haunting visions of his murdered wife and, in terror, staggered and fell backward into the lake. The Great Spirit took pity on him and turned him into everlasting stone. Today the Giant still rests, a distinguishing landmark guarding the entrance to this awesome bay.

The entrance to Thunder Bay between Pie Island and Thunder Cape is wide and clear except for Hare Island Reef and the shoal water around Hare Island itself. There are lights at the tip on the cape, Trowbridge Island and Angus Island to the SE of Pie Island, all of which flash white.

In crossing Thunder Bay toward the city complex, the water is deep and free from obstructions with the exception of Schwitzer Shoal and the waters surrounding the **Welcome Islands.** Aptly named, this small group of islands stands out five miles from the city greeting those who make their approach from the water.

The islands consist of two larger islands and two small islets. They are marked with a white flashing light on the north side of the largest eastern island and a red flashing buoy which marks the southern end of shoal water that extends south from the group about one-third mile south of the large western island. There is a small harbor on the SE end of the eastern island that gets considerable

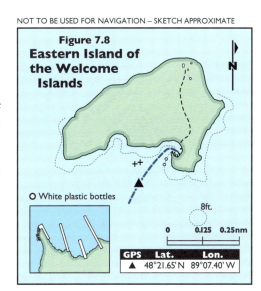

NOT TO BE USED FOR NAVIGATION – SKETCH APPROXIMATE

Figure 7.8
Eastern Island of the Welcome Islands

N

O White plastic bottles

++

8ft.

0   0.125   0.25nm

GPS	Lat.	Lon.
▲	48°21.65' N	89°07.40' W

use, especially by locals. There are a number of docks here, but only the southernmost one which is actually part of a rubble breakwater has enough depth for a 5.5-foot draft boat, the other docks being accessible to boats drawing less than 5 feet.

In approaching the bay there is considerable shoal water off the eastern arm of the bay, which is often marked with white plastic bottles that are privately maintained. Without going too far in, it is possible to anchor in 9 feet of water. But because of the small area, anchoring may block the passage area to and from the docks and should be done when there are few boats present. Transients may use the two most southern docks. The others are reserved for private use. There is protection here for NW to SE winds, but the bay becomes quite uncomfortable with S and especially SW winds. There are a few cottages and summer homes on the island along with a number of trails, one of which leads over to the light.

When you clear the Welcome Islands and the extended skyline of the city of **Thunder Bay** unfolds, it is difficult to believe that just 150 years ago this massive complex, the largest city on Lake Superior, was getting its start. Although there were beginnings of a white settlement at the mouth of the Kaministiquia River in the late 1600s when Sieur du L'hut built Fort Camanistigoyan in 1679, it wasn't until the early 1800s that the area really began to grow. At this time, in an effort to escape American taxation at Grand Portage, the North West Company moved its post inland

NOT TO BE USED FOR NAVIGATION – SKETCH APPROXIMATE

Figure 7.9
Thunder Bay,
Middle Entrance &
Prince Arthur
Landing Marina

Perry's Marine Centre

booming ground

seaplane base

G

R "6"

CPR station

CNR station

R "8"

R "4"

R "2"

Fl R

Fl R
fog sig.

floating breakwater

Prince Arthur
Landing Marina

Qk Fl G

G "3"   G "1"

Fl G

R "10"

G "5"

G "7"

0	0.25	0.5 nm

GPS	Lat.	Lon.
▲	48°25.86' N	89°11.74' W

to a location on the north bank of the Kaministiquia River near its mouth. But the voyageurs and fur traders never did like this longer northern route (see Fig. 5.17) and this, coupled with the merger with the Hudson's Bay Company in 1821, proceeded to de-emphasize the Lake Superior outlet and brought decline to the importance and use of the fort.

Thunder Bay's Fort William Historical Park celebrates the fur-trading days of yesteryear. DAHL

Hopes of renewal for the area came with the discovery of mining prospects in the mid-1800s. However, it took two major events to assure Thunder Bay of its position on the map. These were the opening of the Sault Locks in 1855 and the completion of the Canadian Pacific Railway to the prairies in the West. With the railroad, the town of Prince Arthur Landing came into existence as a key terminal. The name was soon changed to Port Arthur and, along with Fort William, these two towns stood side-by-side for more than 100 years, growing into prosperous cities as the area became the main transshipment harbor for the golden wealth of the West—grain. In 1970, the two cities merged and, by popular vote, became known as Thunder Bay.

Today, this important port boasts the largest grain elevator and grain shipping complex in the world. It has also been a center for the production of Canadian paper, especially newsprint. Along with other pulp products, it supports a large industry consisting of a number of paper, pulp and sawmills. Both the paper mills and some of the grain elevators offer daily tours for visitors.

The harbor itself is formed by a long 4.5-mile breakwater that extends from the north, south to the mouth of the Kaministiquia River. This whole harbor complex is known as the **Lakehead Harbour** and is administered by the Lakehead Harbour Commission, which monitors a VHF radio station and answers to "Lakehead Harbour Control" or "VDX 30." All commercial shipping entering or leaving the harbor must report to this station.

Another marine radio station, "Thunder Bay Coast Guard Radio," is also important in handling ship communication, especially ship-to-shore phone calls, and it is this station you call when you wish to place a phone call. With repeaters at Horn (located on the north shore near Schreiber, Ontario) and Bald Head (on the east shore north of the Sault), this station gives good coverage all the way from Thunder Bay to the Sault. It also provides continuous weather coverage on weather channels WX1, WX8, WX9 and channels 21B and 83B depending on your location.

Unfortunately, this weather coverage extends all the way into lakes Michigan and Huron, and North Channel and Georgian Bay. So, it may take a while for the recording to come around to your area. There are, however, more localized forecasts given by Environment Canada, which are also broadcast on the weather channels WX1 and WX3. For example, WX3 broadcasts specifically to the city of Thunder Bay and WX1 to the Nipigon and Red Rock area.

To enter the harbor, there are three entrances in the breakwater, with the middle entrance being most often used by recreational

NOT TO BE USED FOR NAVIGATION – SKETCH APPROXIMATE

Figure 7.10
Prince Arthur Landing Marina

Children's Pond

Splash Pond/ Ice rink

Waterfront Plaza

Transient Dockage

Pier 3

Breakwater

Floating

Old Marina

Pier 2

Park

Comfort Station

Pier 1

Thunder Bay Yacht Club

2 launch ramps

Fuel Dock

Wilson Street Headland

N

Tugboat Basin

Daymarkers
When entering between
Piers 1 & 2 and Piers 2 & 3

▲ to starboard: red triangle

◉ to port: black bull's-eye

Park

0   500   1000 ft.

Cruise Ship Dock

boaters and the other two by commercial shipping. All three entrances are marked with red and green flashing lights and foghorns. In all three cases the red lights are kept to starboard when entering. In the middle entrance the fog signal is connected with the red light, in the other two entrances the fog signals are connected with the green lights.

Within the harbor there is sufficient depth in most areas, but without local knowledge it is best to stay within the buoyed channels. For example, there is considerable shoaling where McVicar Creek enters the harbor and in other areas that are unmarked on the charts.

With the advent of the Jeux Canadian Games in the summer of 1981, Thunder Bay constructed one of the most beautiful and well-facilitated marinas on the lake. This complex, which is called the **Prince Arthur Landing Marina,** is found by heading due west after passing through the middle entrance in the breakwater. The marina monitors Channel 68 (Tel: 807-345-2741). In addition to the forest of masts, the marina is easy to spot as it lies just in front of two prominent buildings on the waterfront. One of these is the old Canadian National Railway station which is made of red brick. Behind it is a large white and glass Ontario Government Building, which was constructed in the early 1990s.

In 2007, Thunder Bay began a project to expand the marina and provide extensive development to more of the waterfront. A 10-year project, the plan provided for additional docks and another basin between Pier 1 and the Wilson St Headland. New dock additions began in 2008. To date much of the marina has been restructured with new docks using existing parts of the marina. At the time of this writing, plans were to look at the options of expanding into Pool 6, also known as the Tugboat Basin. (See Figure 7.10.)

The total marina complex consists of three main piers with a number of finger piers extending out from the sides and the Wilson Street Headland. In addition to a forest of masts, the marina is easy to spot as it lies just in front of two prominent buildings on the waterfront. One of these is the old Canadian National Railway station which is made of red brick. Behind it is a large white and glass Ontario Government Building, which was constructed in the early 1990s. The entrances between the headland and piers are marked with black (to port) and red (to starboard) day beacons which are positioned on rubble breakwaters. The small building at the end of Pier 1 is private, a clubhouse for the Thunder Bay Yacht Club.

A service dock is located SW of Pier 1 and provides gasoline, diesel and pump-out. Adjacent to the dock there is a beautiful comfort station which provides rest rooms, showers, laundry facilities and a place for sailors to gather. It is from this comfort station that you call to clear customs. Water and electricity (30 A &

50 A) are provided at the slips. With more than 200 slips, there is always room for transient dockage, which is usually along the SW side of Pier 3. The marina also provides a 24-hour security guard. This whole area is tastefully landscaped with boardwalks and an adjacent park, making Thunder Bay's waterfront one of the most enjoyable on the lake.

Another facility for boaters is at the **Thunder Bay Yacht Club** which is located on the southern shore of Mission Island in the mouth of the Mission River, which is the southernmost arm of the Kaministiquia River. To get to this marina it is necessary to enter the Mission River via a buoyed dredged channel. This channel is marked with two flashing buoys, red and green; enter with the red kept to starboard. The power line reached just before the marina has a clearance of 140 feet. The club has a visitors dock, and transient slips are usually available. One of the docks is equipped with water and pump-out. Electricity is also available, 110-volt plug-in. Diesel and gasoline have to be delivered via truck. One advantage of staying at the Yacht Club is that they honor reciprocity with other yacht club memberships. A disadvantage of staying here is that the location is somewhat removed from shopping areas.

For those who should require **marine repairs** while in Thunder Bay, there are two excellent facilities. McKellar Marine (Tel.: 807-622-3864) in the McKellar River is equipped with a hydraulic lift and crane. They can provide full repair services and specialize in engine repairs. The other facility is Morton's Boat Yard at Current River which specializes in fiberglass repairs.

Thunder Bay is an exciting place to visit with good shopping adjacent to the waterfront (use pedestrian overpass), ethnic restaurants and beautiful parks, most of which are within walking distance of the Prince Arthur Landing Marina. In August 2000, a new casino opened just a few blocks from the waterfront. By following the road along the waterfront about a mile SW, there

Prince Arthur Landing Marina in Thunder Bay. DAHL

is a shopping center and Wal-Mart. There is a well-stocked Safeway about six blocks from the marina. For those activities outside of walking distance there is an efficient city transit system.

Of all the points of interest that Thunder Bay has to offer, probably the one that attracts most attention is the restored Old Fort William. Located on the Kaministiquia River a few miles from the original

site, the fort can be reached by using the city transit system. For information on the city transit system, check with the Visitors Information Center, a small spotted domed building that is also in the waterfront area.

The restored fort is a meticulous reconstruction of the old, with attention paid to such details as the original plans and even the 19th century methods of construction. The site is made up of a stockade, wharf and some 40 structures that are staffed by "coopers, bakers, blacksmiths, gunsmiths, company partners," all depicting the lifestyles of another century. Of special interest to the boater is the canoe shed where it is possible to see, at various stages of construction, the 24-foot North canoes that were used inland and the large 36-foot Montreal canoes that plied the waters of the Great Lakes. At the Naval Shed, ship's carpenters can be seen actually building a large schooner and bateau using only the methods of yesteryear.

Within the remaining complex of the north and eastern sections of Thunder Bay, there are just a few anchorages, some of these being marginal because of exposure to certain wind directions. Two of these bays are located side-by-side in the middle of the northern shoreline. Because of close proximity to the railroad and housing, they are not all that desirable. However, they do make a nice day-sail destination for those wishing to stay in the Thunder Bay area.

One of these anchorages is **MacKenzie Bay** which, although shallow, has adequate depths for anchoring behind Bacon Island. The best approach is to the west of Bacon Island since there is shoal water between the island and Conmee Point. The western end of the bay is foul with rock. The harbor is marginal because it is quite vulnerable to southerly winds.

Amethyst Harbour, which lies adjacent to the east, offers more protection but is difficult to enter because of rocks and shoal water. The easiest approach is to enter with Buck and Kent islands kept to port. Once north of Lambert Island, it is important to take a zigzag course to weave in between the rock shoals that lie to the north of the island. This area is not conducive to seclusion for it is ringed with cottages, and the railroad runs close to the shoreline. It also gets a lot of use as a swimming area at the sand beach in the far eastern end. There is a wooden dock with metal rings to tie to in the center of this beach that is approximately 300 feet long with a short "T" on the end. Although boats can tie up to it, there is no docking on the north side

NOT TO BE USED FOR NAVIGATION – SKETCH APPROXIMATE

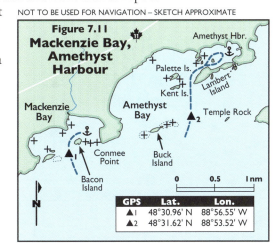

Figure 7.11
Mackenzie Bay, Amethyst Harbour

Amethyst Hbr.
Palette Is.
Kent Is.
Lambert Island
Mackenzie Bay
Amethyst Bay
Temple Rock
Conmee Point
Buck Island
Bacon Island

0   0.5   1 nm

GPS	Lat.	Lon.
▲1	48°30.96' N	88°56.55' W
▲2	48°31.62' N	88°53.52' W

during the summer swimming season, since this area is reserved for swimming.

Along Thunder Bay's eastern shore at the head of The Giant, there is a deep bay, **Sawyer Bay,** that can be used for anchoring if close attention is paid to the weather. This harbor also has a number of moorings for use that are privately maintained. The harbor is marked by two day beacons along the northern shore of its wide mouth. By going way in, good anchoring can be found in 10 to 15 feet with a mud bottom. The anchorage has good protection for all but N-NW winds. With northerly winds, it is possible to get protection by tucking in close to the small bay with the fishing dock and cottage. However, you are at the mercy of NW winds here, and it is a long way in any direction to find protection from the NW.

The bay is of special interest because of the number of good hiking trails in the vicinity, all part of the Sleeping Giant Provincial Park system. One trail that follows the shoreline around the foot of The Giant is a loop trail of approximately nine miles. A shorter trail, two miles round-trip, takes you to the top of the chest of The Giant for a spectacular "helicopter-like" view of Sawyer Bay and the whole Thunder Bay area — 1,200 feet up. To reach the top it is necessary to take a spinoff trail to the right in a fork from the main trail. This trail acquires quick elevations in a number of fairly aggressive switchbacks. Note: in order to get to the panoramic view of the Thunder Bay area it is necessary to continue on from the "high point," which is a clearing back in the woods, and descend slightly to an abrupt drop-off at the bluff's edge.

When you clear the foot of the Sleeping Giant and begin the NE trek up the shore, you can't help but feel that at last you are entering the wild north country. To port are the rugged towering bluffs of the Sibley Peninsula, to starboard are the wide open waters of Lake Superior, interrupted only by the distant blue of the northern end of Isle Royale, and ahead lie the protected waters of sheltering island chains. Although the expanses here are

NOT TO BE USED FOR NAVIGATION – SKETCHES APPROXIMATE

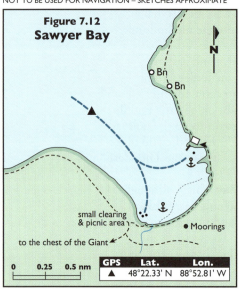

Figure 7.12
Sawyer Bay

o Bn
o Bn

small clearing & picnic area
to the chest of the Giant
• Moorings

0	0.25	0.5 nm

GPS	Lat.	Lon.
▲	48°22.33' N	88°52.81' W

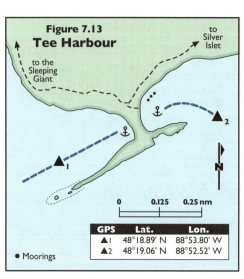

Figure 7.13
Tee Harbour

to Silver Islet
to the Sleeping Giant

▲2
▲1

0	0.125	0.25 nm

GPS	Lat.	Lon.
▲1	48°18.89' N	88°53.80' W
▲2	48°19.06' N	88°52.52' W

• Moorings

immense, the distances between anchorages are small. For unlike other sections of the lake where the shoreline is barren and hostile to the recreational boater, the shoreline here is broken up into bays and inlets providing numerous natural harbors and picturesque anchorages.

It is hard to believe that just a short day's sail out of the city (17 nautical miles) takes one to the first of these beautiful wilderness anchorages, **Tee Harbour.** Basking in the shadow of The Giant, the "T" actually forms two harbors, one on each side. The west harbor has good protection for all but westerly winds, the east harbor has good protection for all but easterly winds. Should these winds arise, it is quite easy to move to the other side.

To enter either harbor, stay clear of the points since there are some rocks and shoal water off each. The western arm of the "T" especially has to be given wide berth since there is a 6-foot-high rock with shoal water extending approximately 600 feet out from the point. In both anchorages there is good holding ground where you can anchor in 15 to 20 feet. The eastern anchorage has a little more depth enabling one to get closer into shore. In this eastern anchorage, there are a number of moorings for use that are privately maintained. On both sides there are beautiful beaches to explore and trails that are part of the Sibley Peninsula Trail System. A four-mile trail follows the shore NE to Silver Islet, a two-mile trail west takes one to the foot of The Giant. For the hardy, this trail continues up for a majestic view of the bay and this area of the shoreline.

Up the shore 2.5 miles NE from Tee Harbour there is a public wharf and government dock. Known as **Silver Islet,** this area has a history that is one of the most exciting on the lake. For in 1869, an unbelievably rich vein of silver was found on a small island lying approximately two-thirds mile offshore. At that time the island was owned by the Montreal Mining Company, but it was soon bought out by an American syndicate, whose president was Alexander Hamilton Sibley, brother of the first governor of Minnesota. The chief mining engineer was a Captain William Frue who built the extensive cribwork that was needed to support the shaft house and various buildings required in the venture. The whole structure was so large that it loomed well over the actual periphery of the island, much like a mushroom with its base anchored in the small island. A constant battle was fought against the

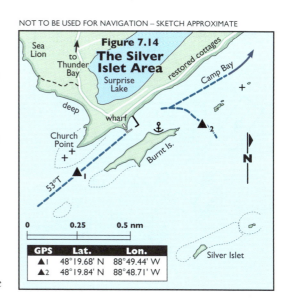

NOT TO BE USED FOR NAVIGATION – SKETCH APPROXIMATE

Figure 7.14
The Silver Islet Area

GPS	Lat.	Lon.
▲1	48°19.68' N	88°49.44' W
▲2	48°19.84' N	88°48.71' W

The government dock at Silver Islet.
DAHL

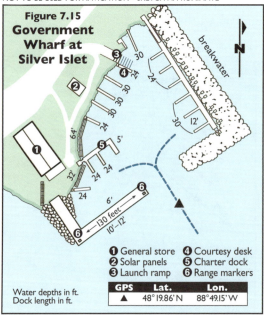

Figure 7.15
Government Wharf at Silver Islet

N
breakwater

30
24
30
30
24
64'
5'
32'
24 24
24
6'
10'-12'
130 feet
12'
30
5'

❶ General store ❹ Courtesy desk
❷ Solar panels   ❺ Charter dock
❸ Launch ramp   ❻ Range markers

Water depths in ft.
Dock length in ft.

GPS	Lat.	Lon.
▲	48°19.86' N	88°49.15' W

lake that repeatedly would undermine this extensive structure. But these valiant efforts paid off, for in 14 years, the mine yielded $3.25 million of silver and was the richest silver mine in the world. On the mainland, the area quickly grew into a little village to house the miners' families and provide supplies for the mine. The area became well-known for its high lifestyle, and many fortunes were made in but a short time. But these years of glory were short-lived, for the mine was soon depleted of its precious ore and the lake quickly reclaimed the island. Although it was the island that was originally called Silver Islet, today this area on the mainland is also called Silver Islet.

The wharf is located on the mainland behind **Burnt Island.** It can be approached from either east or west—with care, as in both cases there are rocks and shoal water that need to be avoided. When coming from the SW there is a set of range markers on the main outside dock that line up on with a course of 53 degrees T. However, it has been discovered that if this track and range are used it will take one dangerously near an underwater rock shoal. Therefore, it is important to steer somewhat to starboard of this range when approaching the dock and yet keep in mind the shoals that extend SW of Burnt Island.

In 2021 and 2022 the Silver Islet dock received quite an upgrade by putting in a new marina. The project was initiated with a generous donation ($26,500) to the Silver Islet Harbour Association from the Great Lakes Cruising Club Foundation (Port Huron, MI). This Initial donation generated others along with teams of volunteers to help in the installing of docks for both seasonal and transient boaters. The first stage of the project was to rebuild the rock breakwater and attach a header-dock along the inside. The header forms the basic dock to attach 6 finger docks. The three fingers closest to the entrance are 30' (water depths > 12') for larger boats and the remaining three are 24'.

The second stage of building the marina was to add a number of docks attached to the shore NE of the large building which is a Country Store. To gain access to this area and inside the main dock a large section of the original dock, which was 'U' shaped, was removed making it 'L' shaped. When all the docks are in there are a total of 7 shore docks including a courtesy dock next to the launch ramp. An 'L' shape Charter Operators' Dock with 2 finger docks was also added yielding moorings for more than 36 craft. Those with very large, deep draft boats can find good mooring on the outside of the main dock which is 130'. However, it may become uncomfortable in strong easterly or SW winds Note they are also certified to handle cruise ship visits, so occasionally one of these larger boats may be on the outside of the main dock. Finally as if all this is not enough, plans are underway to bring Starlink Internet into the harbor to enable Wi-Fi cell phones calls and e-transfers.

A new fee structure has been developed to help pay for additional docks that were purchased. For launching boats, the fee is $5 for a paddle boat and $10 for a powerboat. For transient boats it costs $1.20/foot and for a seasonal mooring it is $20/ft/. Drop boxes with pay envelopes are found at the top of the Launch Ramp and the outer end near the mouth of the Main Dock.

If the marina is full there is a marginal alternative to the marina by anchoring off the northern end of Burnt Island where some protection can be obtained for SW winds. However, it may take a bit of effort to get the anchor to set here since there is some rock mixed with the sand. An alternative for easterly winds may be to anchor off the fishing docks in Camp Bay, one mile NE of the Silver Islet wharf. This bay should be entered with caution because of shoal water. Note also, the shoals NE of Burnt Island. The bay NW of Church Point also looks like it could be used as an alternative since it is marked with 2 fathoms on the charts. However, it is much deeper (10 fathoms) right up to shore and has

a cobble bottom making it unusable for anchoring. Actually, when you can't get into Silver Islet for whatever reason and you want a secure anchorage regardless of wind, you can't beat Tee Harbour 2.5 miles to the SW. By switching sides you can get protection for all winds. You might even be able to pick up a mooring.

Silver Islet is interesting to visit because it has become a picturesque summer colony with residents occupying the restored original old cottages. Adjacent to the dock there is a restored building, the Old General Store. In addition to the new marina, the General Store was purchased and received new owners. It too received a new facelift and will continue to be open in the summer providing limited groceries as well as ice, ice cream and rest rooms. The much-loved tearoom that overlooks the docks and provides a place for locals and visitors to gather will also be back.

A short walk from the dock there is an inland lake where local residents have set up a swimming beach. The lake can be reached by taking a road that also leads up the length of the Sibley Peninsula and then into Thunder Bay, a distance of approximately 50 statute miles. Another point of interest is the Sea Lion, a beautiful sea-stack/rock formation found at water's edge northwest of the wharf. It can be found by taking a fork in the road approximately a quarter mile past the lake to the left and then after a "block" or so, a path that leads off to the right. The path continues about one-quarter mile and then comes out on a scenic overlook of Lake Superior, the Sea Lion and the Sleeping Giant in the background.

A trip out to Silver Islet itself is a most interesting experience and, by staying clear of the shoal water along its NE and western sides, it is possible to get up quite close. When you look at this small island, which measures approximately 90 feet in diameter, it is difficult to imagine that there was at one time a platform of cribwork here that was much larger than the island and that supported not only the shaft house, but four large boarding houses, a lighthouse, storehouses, machine shops, carpenter shops, offices and club rooms, a blacksmith and large docks for shipping the ore.

Bordering the eastern side of the Sibley Peninsula there is a large extension of water, **Black Bay,** which gets little use from those who visit the area. If seclusion is desired, Black Bay is the area to cruise, for it is off the beaten track for most of those who head up and down this segment of the lake. However, because Black Bay is so long and fairly shallow, it doesn't take long for it to build into an uncomfortable chop, especially with northerly and southerly winds. Because the anchorages here are quite open to at least one wind direction, this area should be cruised with a cautious eye to the weather.

The first of these somewhat marginal anchorages is **Squaw Bay,** which lies on the eastern side of the Sibley Peninsula approximately nine miles up the shoreline. This large bay, which is

1.5 miles in length, is also quite shallow (9 feet to 12 feet) and is wide open to E and SE winds. There is a rock shoal in the middle of the northern half of the bay that needs to be skirted. There are a couple of streams that enter the bay at its SW end. This bay may be of importance because the only road in the area, the one which travels the length of the peninsula, comes quite close to its SW end.

Along the peninsula that forms the eastern side of Black Bay, there are a number of bays that, if the wind directions are right, can be used as anchorages. Starting with the northernmost bay that lies approximately halfway up the peninsula, there is good anchoring for all but northerly winds. Secure behind Copper Point, **Louise Bay** lies at the base of high steep bluffs. With good holding clay, there are 9 feet to 12 feet of water for anchoring. Here it is important not to go all the way in, for there are remains of sunken cribs close to shore, especially in the SE corner.

Lying three miles south of Louise Bay there is another small bay that is also surrounded by particularly high hills, **Miles Bay.** Tucked in behind George Point, this bay has protection for all but S and SW winds. By staying in the center of the bay it is possible to maintain depths of 12 to 15 feet.

Two miles farther south from Miles Bay, there is another bay that is open to S and SW winds, **Cowie Bay.** In approaching this small bay, it is important to note the detached rock shoals that lie approximately one-half mile S-SW of Cowie Point. By staying in the center of this bay, 9 feet to 12 feet of water can be maintained.

When southerly winds blow, there are two alternative anchorages on the **north end of Edward Island.** One of these is found between Edward and Ariel islands where there is good holding clay. Because of shallow depths, it is not possible to go into the far end of the bay; however, by

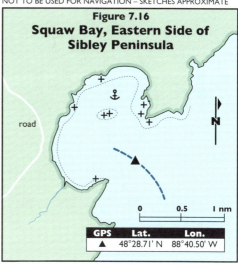

Figure 7.16
Squaw Bay, Eastern Side of Sibley Peninsula

GPS	Lat.	Lon.
▲	48°28.71' N	88°40.50' W

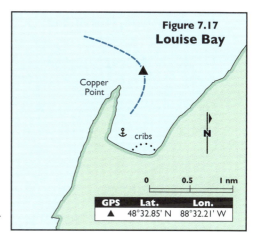

Figure 7.17
Louise Bay

GPS	Lat.	Lon.
▲	48°32.85' N	88°32.21' W

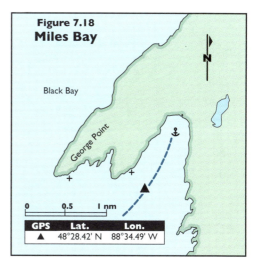

Figure 7.18
Miles Bay

GPS	Lat.	Lon.
▲	48°28.42' N	88°34.49' W

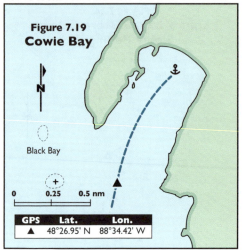

Figure 7.19
Cowie Bay

Black Bay

| 0 | 0.25 | 0.5 nm |

GPS	Lat.	Lon.
▲	48°26.95' N	88°34.42' W

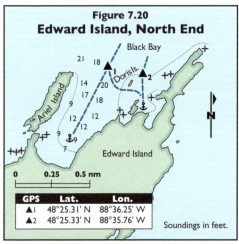

Figure 7.20
Edward Island, North End

Black Bay

Doris Is.

Ariel Island

Edward Island

| 0 | 0.25 | 0.5 nm |

GPS	Lat.	Lon.
▲1	48°25.31' N	88°36.25' W
▲2	48°25.33' N	88°35.76' W

Soundings in feet.

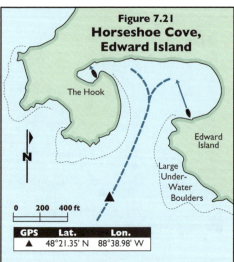

Figure 7.21
**Horseshoe Cove,
Edward Island**

The Hook

Edward
Island

Large
Under-
Water
Boulders

| 0 | 200 | 400 ft |

GPS	Lat.	Lon.
▲	48°21.35' N	88°38.98' W

keeping to the Edward Island side of the bay, it is possible to get quite a ways in. Note also the rock shoals in the western side of the bay south of Ariel Island.

The other anchorage is to the SE of Doris Island behind a small island that is detached from the main island. It is possible to pass to either side of Doris Island but note that this anchorage is much shallower so it is prudent to proceed with caution. The southerly indentation seen a little farther to the east cannot be entered because of shallow depths. With either anchorage, should the wind start to blow from the north, it is easy to move up to Cowie Bay which is just three miles to the NE.

Probably the main reason that these Black Bay anchorages are not used more often is that one of the favorite anchorages of cruising skippers is in the area, lying at the southern end of Edward Island approximately one mile north of the Porphyry Light. This is **Horseshoe Cove,** a snug little harbor that, if "The Hook" is used, gives protection for all winds. (See Fig. 7.21.)

Approach can be made to either side of Hardscrabble Island as long as the island is not hugged too closely. This is one of those anchorages where the entrance is very difficult to spot since it blends in with the shoreline and does not open up until the last minute. Taking a 15 degree T bearing off the eastern end of Hardscrabble Island is a big help in identifying this difficult entrance. Because there is considerable shoaling here on each side of the entrance, it is very important to enter exactly mid-channel.

Once inside the cove, because of deep water and exposure to southerly winds, there really are only two options for anchoring. One is to round up to starboard favoring the eastern section of the bay, setting out a stern anchor and tying the bow off on shore. This will give good protection for all but very strong SW winds.

The other option is to maneuver into the hook, set out a stern anchor and edge the bow up to the southern shore. Although the quarters are close and there are some deadheads on the bottom, we can attest that 35-foot boats drawing 5.5 feet can use this hook nicely. In fact, this is such a favorite spot that at times with good weather forecasts, as many as three boats have been known to stack up in here. Over the years, attempts have been made to assemble a small dock out of pieces of driftwood, but it usually is in disrepair. There is a small campsite here that is a nice spot for picnics.

North of Horseshoe Cove there is a large harbor, **Edward Harbour,** which although quite open to the SW will often get used, especially if Horseshoe Cove is filled up. By tucking down into the far SE corner, it is possible to get protection for even SW winds. For protection from west through easterly winds, the northern part of the harbor is used. It is, however, important to note the rocks and shoal water that lie off the northern shore in the harbor. There is also some shoaling to the S and W of the small island that lies in the southern half of the harbor.

On the western side of **Porphyry Island** there is a deep bay that in the past served as an off-loading site for the lighthouse station at the southern end of the island. The entrance of the harbor is marked by a white diamond day marker on the port side when entering. Because there are a number of shoals on each side, it is important to come in dead center. There is a range hidden in the trees ahead on shore that helps, but the rear range comes into view only when you are right on. If it disappears, you are off course. Because of these shoals, this is another harbor where it is important to enter with clear visibility and no sea running

In the late 1980s, the personnel of the Porphyry Light Station were removed, and the docks fell into disrepair. However,

Figure 7.22
Edward Harbour, Edward Island

Edward Harbour

Horseshoe Cove

0   0.25   0.5 nm

GPS	Lat.	Lon.
▲	48°21.93' N	88°39.21' W

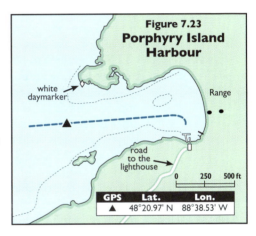

Figure 7.23
Porphyry Island Harbour

white daymarker

Range

road to the lighthouse

0   250   500 ft

GPS	Lat.	Lon.
▲	48°20.97' N	88°38.53' W

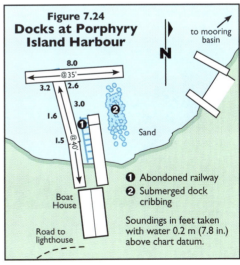

Figure 7.24
Docks at Porphyry Island Harbour

to mooring basin

8.0
@35'
3.2   2.6
3.0
1.6
1.5
Sand

Boat House

Road to lighthouse

❶ Abondoned railway
❷ Submerged dock cribbing

Soundings in feet taken with water 0.2 m (7.8 in.) above chart datum.

like other harbors in the area, beginning around 2018 the docks and whole harbor received a lot of repairs. Some of the old dock structures were removed and new ones were put in their place. The main dock, a structure of about 40', had a 35 ft "T" placed across its' outer end providing dockage for larger/deep draft boats. Quite close to this main dock is a smaller one of about 20 ft. There are two additional docks further away from this Initial complex on the east side of the bay, but further Into the bay. A couple of mooring balls have also been put in to supplement the limited dockage in this popular harbor. On the premises there is a new sauna, a boathouse maintained by CLLS (Canadian Lighthouses of Lake Superior) and a fire pit and picnic tables.

There are a couple of interesting hiking trails in the area. One leads across the island to the eastern side where there is an unusual black sand beach. The other is a mile-long road that runs from the docks to the light station at the southern tip of the island. In the early 1990s, the buildings were still in good condition (complete with gardens and rose bushes) and it was possible to stroll the grounds and get a glimpse of yesteryear to see what it was like to live in a Lake Superior light station. More recently part of the CLLS program is to have Host Lightkeepers who give very nice tours and help with building maintenance.

Heading NE up the shoreline from Porphyry there are two options. One is to go on the outside around Porphyry Point, the other is to pass through the long channel between Edward and Porphyry islands, **Walker's Channel.** Walker's Channel is used extensively by those who cruise out of Thunder Bay, and it is possible for those without local knowledge to also use it if caution is taken for one troublesome area. This area is near a small low dock that is located on the west shore in the northern quarter of Porphyry Island. As you enter the area from the south, there will be a long island to port. Just to the NE of this island there is a shoal that, when abeam, you will be in the least depth encountered, 10 feet in low-water years. At this point it is important to take a bearing on a rock seen ahead to get around a grassy shoal area to starboard. Once abeam of the dock it is necessary to aim for the dock in a zigzag fashion to avoid the shoal water around the rock. Before reaching the dock, resume a NE course to pass between the rock and the dock on a small point of land. It helps to have a

A bow lookout is recommended in Walker's Channel.
DAHL

sharp lookout on the bow with good sunlight and no seas running, especially the first time through. Note that the dock and adjacent buildings are private and not available for transient use. However, the little "bay" south of the dock can be used for anchoring. (See Fig. 7.26.)

Within the Walker's Channel area there is a beautiful anchorage that gets little use, probably because of its proximity to Horseshoe

NOT TO BE USED FOR NAVIGATION – SKETCH APPROXIMATE

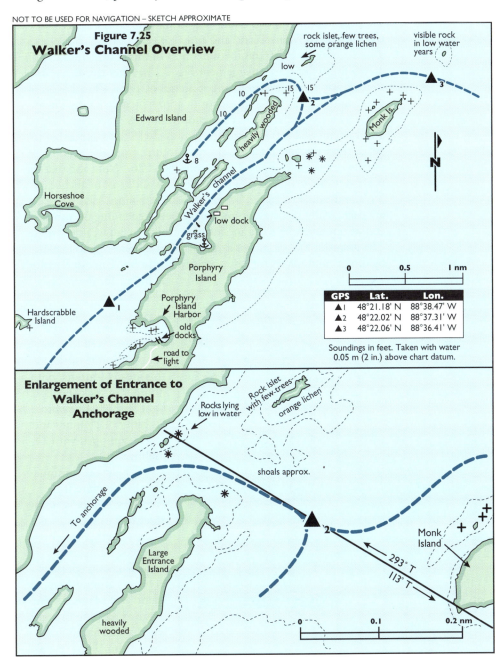

Figure 7.25
Walker's Channel Overview

rock islet, few trees, some orange lichen

visible rock in low water years

Edward Island

heavily wooded

Monk Is.

N

Horseshoe Cove

Walker's channel

low dock

grass

Porphyry Island

GPS	Lat.	Lon.
▲1	48°21.18' N	88°38.47' W
▲2	48°22.02' N	88°37.31' W
▲3	48°22.06' N	88°36.41' W

Soundings in feet. Taken with water 0.05 m (2 in.) above chart datum.

Hardscrabble Island

Porphyry Island Harbor

old docks

road to light

Enlargement of Entrance to Walker's Channel Anchorage

Rock islet with few trees, orange lichen

Rocks lying low in water

shoals approx.

To anchorage

Large Entrance Island

Monk Island

293° T
113° T

heavily wooded

Cove and other anchorages in the area. It is found behind the string of islands that form the main part of Walker's Channel. Since there is usually quite a bit of shoaling between these islands, the entrance is found at the north end of the channel lying W of Monk Island. It is easy to spot, since it passes between a large heavily wooded island to port and a small, low rock islet with few trees and some orange lichen to starboard. Note that there is a lot of shoal water extending S and SW of the orange lichen islet. This can be avoided by favoring the large heavily wooded island to port: line up with the stern on the SW end of Monk Island and run a tangent bearing course of 293°T going in/113°T on the way out. On this course, least depths are 19 to 20 feet. (See enlargement Fig. 7.25.) After this it is possible to tuck way in behind the chain of islands carrying 10 to 12 feet of water until the far end and anchor in approximately 8 feet. There are at least two other places to anchor in the area. (See Fig. 7.26: anchor symbol **2** -10 feet; anchor symbol **3** -15 feet.) Note that to get to these anchorages it is important to turn from the main track in between the two islands. (See again Fig. 7.26.) Note also that the passage to the main channel between the islands east of anchorage 3 is significantly restricted by considerable shoaling. All of these are particularly picturesque anchorages and depending on wind conditions and where the anchor is set, this is an all weather area. The long slot SW of anchor symbol 1 is very interesting to explore by dinghy and makes for easy access to Horseshoe Cove or Porphyry Harbour for the walk to the light station.

In rounding the southern end of Porphyry Island it is well to stand a good half-mile offshore, for this area is scattered with a number of rock shoals. The light flashes white with a visibility of 15 miles and is also equipped with a foghorn.

When you continue NE up the shore from Porphyry Island, you now enter one of those areas of the lake that is known for excessive magnetic disturbances. Especially in waters around Magnet Island and Magnet Point, it doesn't take long to realize where these names have come from. Thus "eyeball"

NOT TO BE USED FOR NAVIGATION – SKETCH APPROXIMATE

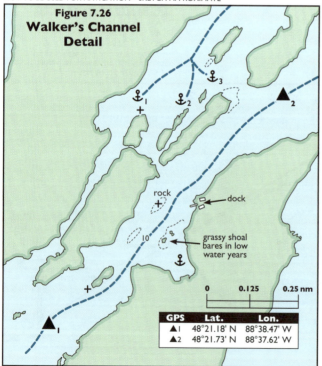

Figure 7.26
Walker's Channel Detail

rock

dock

grassy shoal bares in low water years

| 0 | 0.125 | 0.25 nm |

GPS	Lat.	Lon.
▲1	48°21.18' N	88°38.47' W
▲2	48°21.73' N	88°37.62' W

Soundings in feet. Water 0.22 m (8 in.) above chart datum.   *Bonnie Dahl's Superior Way / Chapter 7*

navigation becomes essential here, and a quick glance at the charts shows that this isn't an area that one would want to navigate in the fog. For although you enter one of Lake Superior's most beautiful cruising areas, when you tuck in behind Shaganash and take the inside channel up through the maze of island chains, you also encounter one of the most rock-strewn and shoal-punctuated sections in the lake.

Before reaching this inside channel there is another anchorage on the eastern side of Edward Island, **Pringle Bay.** Although this anchorage looks quite open to easterly winds on the charts, a large rock shoal that blocks a good half of the entrance of the bay is quite effective in breaking up seas from the east. This anchorage is particularly hard to find since its entrance blends in well with the shoreline and requires close attention to one's navigation. In approaching this harbor, we have also had our autopilot swing off by as much 10-15 degrees because of magnetic anomalies around Magnet Island.

To enter the bay, it is most important to favor the southern shore (but not too close - see mention of shipwreck below) to avoid the very large rock shoal that extends south into the entrance from the northern shore. The anchorage is found by rounding to port where there is 10 to 12 feet of water with good holding ground. The small cove in the NE section of the bay is shallow and accessible to only dinghies or shoal draft boats. Within the harbor about two-thirds in along the south shore of the bay and 50 feet out from shore there is a shipwreck. It lies in about 5 feet of water and you can see tin plating on the remaining hull and lots of debris: pipe, tanks and a motor off to the north. You can even see where the bedding bolts were bent when the motor was torn off. Ashore there is an interesting area of reduced vegetation to explore resulting from a fire that was about 30 years ago. Adjacent to this area there is a moose trail where the moose occasionally come down to drink.

Shaganash Island, which forms the beginning of the inside channel, has an

NOT TO BE USED FOR NAVIGATION – SKETCHES APPROXIMATE

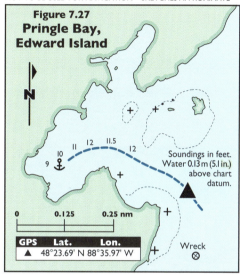

Figure 7.27
Pringle Bay, Edward Island

Soundings in feet.
Water 0.13 m (5.1 in.) above chart datum.

Wreck

GPS	Lat.	Lon.
▲	48°23.69' N	88°35.97' W

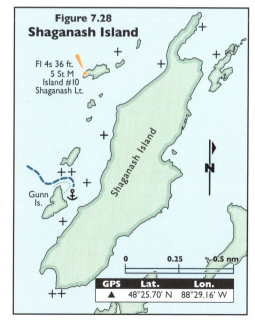

Figure 7.28
Shaganash Island

Fl 4s 36 ft.
5 St M
Island #10
Shaganash Lt.

Shaganash Island

Gunn Is.

GPS	Lat.	Lon.
▲	48°25.70' N	88°29.16' W

anchorage along its western side that gives protection for all but NE winds. The anchorage lies approximately a half mile south of Shaganash Light on Island #10 and is entered by passing to the north of Gunn Island. Because of extensive shoaling around the NE point of Gunn Island, it is important to give this point a very wide berth when entering. The bottom is rock and sand, so it might take a bit to get an anchor to set. Gunn Island provides excellent protection for even very strong SW winds. The island to the north gives more protection for N winds than one would expect, but with NE winds this anchorage becomes very uncomfortable. The interesting hook at the north end of Shaganash, that looks like it would be a good anchorage for south and westerly winds, is not. This is because the bottom is foul with rock, and it is just about impossible to get an anchor to set.

NOT TO BE USED FOR NAVIGATION – SKETCH APPROXIMATE

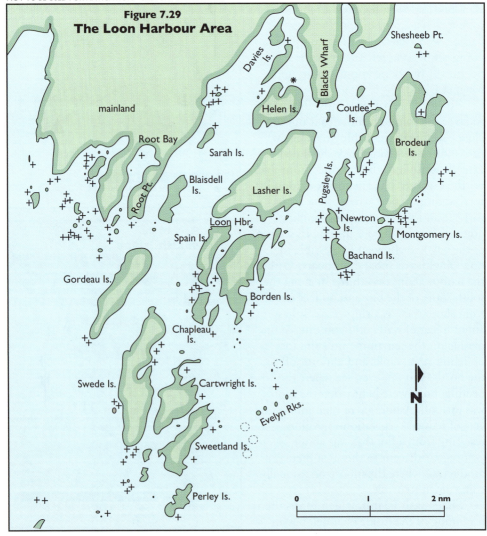

Figure 7.29
The Loon Harbour Area

Continuing up the inside channel, we now come to one of the most beautiful areas on the lake, one that has long been a favorite of those who cruise this shoreline. Known as the **Loon Harbour Area,** the channel now narrows as it becomes banked by heavily forested, high rising islands. This is another of those areas where the deep winding channels and the towering bluffs give one the awesome feeling of wandering down a fjord. Between the islands are intricate bays and coves that, dotted with smaller islets, make up some of the most picturesque anchorages on the lake. The numerous side channels and backwaters teem with wildlife, providing some of the most interesting areas to explore on the lake.

The first of the anchorages in this area is located on the eastern side of **Swede Island** where a deep bay forms a perfect all-weather anchorage. However, because of shoal water across its entrance, this land-locked bay is accessible only to boats drawing 4 feet to 4.5 feet or less. And even then the entrance is so tight that boats may ground. To enter, it is necessary to pass between two small islands. The island to port is right next to the main island point and may be difficult to identify. The starboard island has shoal water extending south, thus further restricting the entrance passage way. Thus this harbor should not be attempted when there is any sea running or without the sun high at one's back. Inside, the water gets deeper and it is possible to anchor anywhere. Northwest of the entrance there is a small dock and nice sauna.

Behind **Chapleau Island** 1.5 miles NE of the Swede Island anchorage there is another secure spot in which to anchor. This is an especially nice alternative to Loon Harbour, which often becomes quite congested in the height of the cruising season. The area is best approached from the west by passing to either side of Rex Island. With surrounding shoal water, this island should not

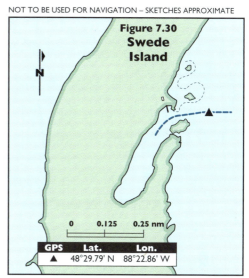

Figure 7.30
Swede Island

| 0 | 0.125 | 0.25 nm |

GPS	Lat.	Lon.
▲	48°29.79' N	88°22.86' W

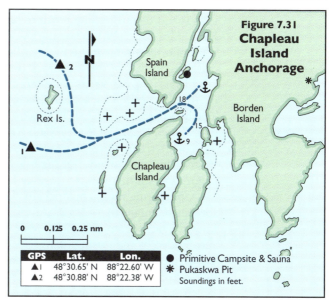

Figure 7.31
Chapleau Island Anchorage

Spain Island

Rex Is.

Borden Island

Chapleau Island

0   0.125   0.25 nm

GPS	Lat.	Lon.
▲1	48°30.65' N	88°22.60' W
▲2	48°30.88' N	88°22.38' W

● Primitive Campsite & Sauna
✳ Pukaskwa Pit
Soundings in feet.

be passed too closely. The SW end of Spain Island has even more extensive shoaling that needs to be given wide berth by favoring the Chapleau side of the entrance. With a bow lookout, it is possible to follow the Chapleau shoreline in and still avoid the shoal water that lies to the west of Chapleau Island. The small islet north of Chapleau Island likewise has shoal water that needs to be skirted.

Figure 7.32
Root Bay

10-20 ft.

⚓ 10

N

Root
Point

Shoal

0   0.25   0.5 nm

GPS	Lat.	Lon.
▲	48°31.41' N	88°23.52' W

The best area for anchoring is found by rounding to starboard and heading south to snug up to Chapleau Island where there are 8 feet to 9 feet of water. There is another anchorage in the area about .25 nm north, between the southern ends of Spain and Borden Islands. By favoring the Borden Island side, there are a number of rock shoals that can be avoided. There is a primitive campsite and sauna on one of the small islands near this anchorage. The sauna is difficult to spot since it is well hidden in the trees and it is painted in camouflaged colors. There is a plank over the sauna that reads *Bahia Espanona* or Bay of Spain. This area is very interesting to explore by dinghy, especially the narrow slot that passes between Spain and Borden islands into Loon Harbour.

Across the main channel from Chapleau Island toward the NW, there is another bay that provides good anchoring but receives little use, probably because of its closeness to Loon Harbour. This is **Root Bay**, which is found by passing between Gourdeau and Blaisdell islands and then rounding north to pass on the west side of Root Point. (See Fig. 7.29.) In passing through the entrance of this bay it is important to favor the starboard shore to avoid a shoal area extending N/NE of the small rock islet to port. (See Fig. 7.32.) The rest of this long bay varies with depths of 10 to 20 feet and has no obstructions except for a small islet and a rock in its northern end. The best place to anchor is in the eastern extension of this north end where there is 10 feet of water with a mud bottom.

An alternative anchorage in the area is to tuck in behind the western entrance island. But because of shallow water as you first begin to go in, this area is accessible to only very shoal draft boats.

Continuing up the main channel, we now come to that very special anchorage that is so beautiful it almost defies description. How do you portray this picturesque lake-like harbor that is surrounded by high rising islands? Where are the words to describe the smaller islands scattered like green jewels in the sparkling blue crystalline water? Now add to this the final touches of rocky, lichen-painted shores, forests heavy with spruce and balsam, the haunting loon's song, and it is no wonder that **Loon Harbour** stands high on the list of those who cruise Lake Superior's waters.

This secure harbor that is formed by Spain, Borden and Lasher islands can be entered from either the east or west. The west entrance that leads off the main island channel is the easiest, for here the water is deep and clear with the entrance banked by steep bluffs.

The eastern entrance is used by those who make the approach off the greater lake or the channel between Brodeur and Lasher islands. There is some shoal water here, particularly off to starboard when entering, just after clearing the small island that one passes to starboard. There are also some islets standing off the long inlet that is found east of Borden Island, but by staying midchannel these should present no problem.

The most popular anchorage in the harbor is to anchor in the area between Spain and Borden islands, just north of the long slot that passes down between the two. Here there is good holding clay with depths that vary from 10 to 20 feet, shoaling toward the inlet. There is a small section of the shore just south of the clearing on Spain Island where it is possible to set out a stern anchor and tie off on the trees on shore. The clearing is a favorite spot for boaters to gather for shore fires. There are some remnants of the lumbering era on shore from a portable sawmill, parts of a pulpwood loader and a rusted boiler. The long channel that leads south toward Chapleau Island is interesting to explore by dinghy.

An alternative anchorage in the area is to find one's way down to the slot between **Borden Island** and the long island that borders it on the east. At the entrance, the port shoreline should be slightly favored since there are some rock shoals off Borden Island's NE tip. Then by staying midchannel, there are no further hazards until the southern part of the channel at the constriction, where the water becomes so shoaled it is navigable only by dinghy. The anchorage is in the widest part of the channel where there is good holding ground with 20 feet of depth. Just to the north of a sheer cliff wall on the long island bordering on the east, there is a path that comes down to the water.

NOT TO BE USED FOR NAVIGATION – SKETCH APPROXIMATE

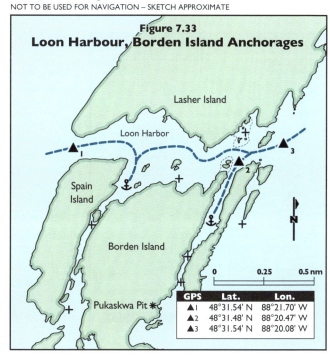

Figure 7.33
Loon Harbour, Borden Island Anchorages

Lasher Island

Loon Harbor

Spain Island

Borden Island

Pukaskwa Pit

0   0.25   0.5 nm

GPS	Lat.	Lon.
▲1	48°31.54' N	88°21.70' W
▲2	48°31.48' N	88°20.47' W
▲3	48°31.54' N	88°20.08' W

This is another area where water depths allow setting an anchor and tying off on the trees on shore. The path leads to the other side of the island where there is interesting walking among rock pools and varied rock formations. There is also a short path leading south to a primitive fire pit on top of the cliffs. Taking a dinghy S/SW through this slot there is a Pukaskwa Pit on the SE side of Borden Island. It is found up on the first terraced beach seen after transiting the slot (see Fig. 7.31). In fact, it can actually be seen from the water. The pit is so well defined that it almost suggests contemporary construction. Unfortunately, the pit has been recently tampered with as non-lichen stones have been removed and put up on the sides. We strongly suggest that, whether old or new, these pits be left untouched by those who are fortunate to find them in the wilderness.

North of Loon Harbour, the channels to either side of Lasher Island can be easily navigated; both are very beautiful. The inlet on the north end of Helen Island, that looks as though it would make a good anchorage on the charts, is quite shallow and has a rock-strewn entrance. The area behind Davie's Island is reputed to have good fishing. At the end of the long mainland peninsula that lies east of Helen Island there is a dock, **Black's Wharf.** This is a remnant of a fishing station that for years was occupied by a husband-and-wife team, Norwegian immigrants. At one time there was an old ice shed and even in midsummer you could still find blocks of Lake Superior ice packed in sawdust. The old dock is now in complete disrepair and the camp has been considerably improved with a new dock added. The new dock is approximately 16 x 100 feet with approximately 6 feet of depth at its outer end. The name posted on the camp is "Nuttaus Fishery."

Just around the corner from Black's Wharf there is a long northerly indentation in **Shesheeb Point** that gets little use on the well-traveled track from Loon Harbour to Otter Cove. To enter, it is important to stay midchannel to avoid shoal water that is to each side — especially that off the extreme SW end of Shesheeb Point. By staying midchannel, it is possible to carry 10 feet of water until about two-thirds of the way in, where the water then shoals to 8 feet and less. There are remnants of a fishing/moose camp on the west shore. Although the bay is open to the south, it really doesn't get uncomfortable unless there are very strong southerly winds.

The last anchorage found in the Loon Harbour area is the deep indentation on

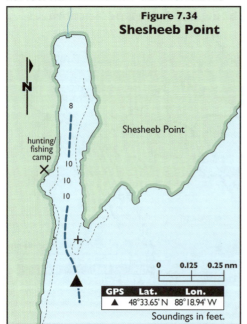

NOT TO BE USED FOR NAVIGATION – SKETCH APPROXIMATE

Figure 7.34
Shesheeb Point

N

8

hunting/
fishing
camp

Shesheeb Point

10

10

10

0   0.125   0.25 nm

GPS	Lat.	Lon.
▲	48°33.65' N	88°18.94' W

Soundings in feet.

the north end of **Brodeur Island.** Secure beneath the high bluffs of the island, the anchorage provides protection for all but N and NE winds. There are no hazards here except for a large rock at the far SW end. However, because of poor holding ground and slash lying on the bottom, it may be difficult to get a good set with an anchor. Because of the close proximity of Loon Harbour and Otter Cove, this anchorage gets little use and is another of those areas where it is possible to obtain seclusion.

Heading north from Brodeur Island there is another large bay, **Shesheeb Bay.** There is a nice sand beach at the far end, and the water here is considerably warmer than that of the larger lake. Although there are no all-weather anchorages here, this can be solved by anchoring in the far north end where there is protection for all but southerly winds and switching to the large bay on the western side near the opening to Shesheeb Bay for southerly winds.

Lying to the east of Shesheeb Bay, between it and the entrance to Otter Cove, are a couple of anchorages that provide nice alternatives to Otter Cove, which can become quite congested in the height of the season. The only hazard in approaching either of these is Manuel Rock which lies approximately one-half mile west of Otter Island.

One of these anchorages is in **Marcil Bay,** a deep indentation on the mainland opposite Shesheeb Point. Although it is quite open to the south, it is a particularly beautiful anchorage with high surrounding bluffs. There are no problems in entering the bay and adequate depths can be found for anchoring.

The other anchorage is found just to the **east of Marcil Bay.** It is found on a bearing of 316 degrees T from the northernmost tip of Otter Island. There are 12 to 15 feet of water throughout the

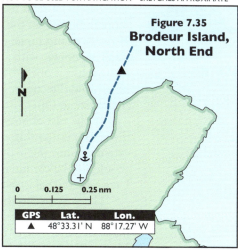

Figure 7.35
Brodeur Island, North End

| 0 | 0.125 | 0.25 nm |

GPS	Lat.	Lon.
▲	48°33.31′ N	88°17.27′ W

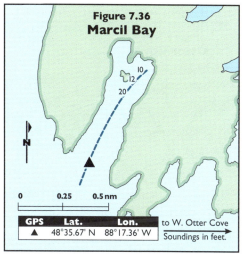

Figure 7.36
Marcil Bay

| 0 | 0.25 | 0.5 nm |

GPS	Lat.	Lon.	
▲	48°35.67′ N	88°17.36′ W	to W. Otter Cove Soundings in feet.

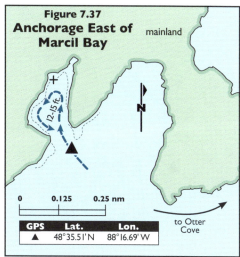

Figure 7.37
Anchorage East of Marcil Bay mainland

| 0 | 0.125 | 0.25 nm |

GPS	Lat.	Lon.	
▲	48°35.51′ N	88°16.69′ W	to Otter Cove

cove except close in to shore. The rock shoal against the northwest shore indicated on the charts is actually farther into the NE part of the cove and presents no problem in the main area. This is a small anchorage with adequate swinging room for only one boat. Although it is open to S and SE winds, it provides protection for all other wind directions. If seclusion is desired, this anchorage is a nice alternative to Otter Cove.

To the east of Shesheeb Bay there is another favorite of those who cruise this northern shoreline, **Otter Cove.** This deep extension into the mainland that forms a perfect natural harbor should not be confused with the other Otter Cove that is found on Lake Superior's East Shore at Otter Head.

The entrance to this long bay is identified by a high dome-rounded island that lies in its center, Otter Island. Passage can be made to either side of this island, however, it is important to note Manuel Rock and shoal that lie approximately 0.4 nautical miles west of the island. Within the outer section of the cove the water is deep and clear, except close into shore. At the narrows, shoals extend from both sides, but with a bow lookout it is possible to maintain depths of 9 feet to 10 feet when passing through. The water gets deeper in the main part of the inner section. The favorite place for anchoring is in the northern arm of this section, where there is a good mud/clay bottom with 12 feet to 15 feet of water throughout until the last one-third of the anchorage where it begins to shoal. It is in the marshy waters of this far northern end that moose often come down to feed.

An alternative anchorage is in the far SE end of this inner section where there is good holding ground. This anchorage would be more secure than the first

NOT TO BE USED FOR NAVIGATION – SKETCHES APPROXIMATE

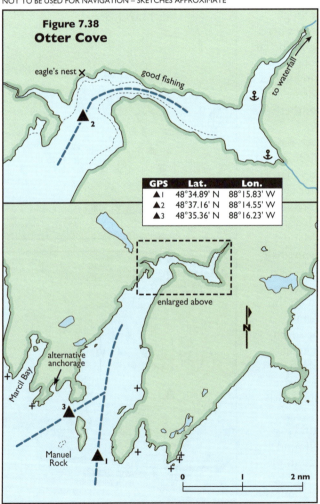

Figure 7.38
Otter Cove

eagle's nest

good fishing

to waterfall

GPS	Lat.	Lon.
▲1	48°34.89' N	88°15.83' W
▲2	48°37.16' N	88°14.55' W
▲3	48°35.36' N	88°16.23' W

enlarged above

N

alternative anchorage

Marcil Bay

Manuel Rock

0   1   2 nm

in a strong southerly blow, however, there is quite an open fetch to the west with this second anchorage.

In addition to being a secure anchorage, Otter Cove is well-known for good fishing. Especially in early summer, lake trout of good size are found to congregate in these waters, particularly in those areas adjacent to the narrows. Another point of interest is a pair of nesting bald

The Lamb Island light station is a popular stopping place. DAHL

eagles seen for many years on the west bank of the narrows. (See Fig. 7.38 for location of nest.) But what Otter Cove is mainly known for is its beautiful waterfall, which is found by taking the stream that empties into the anchorage approximately one-half mile north. Because of shallow water, it is necessary to beach the dinghy and then walk up to the falls for a better view. Depending on the amount of runoff and the water level of the stream, it may even be necessary to get out of your dinghy and walk it in to shore. There are trails that lead to the top on both sides, however, the trail on the right has become quite overgrown. In the summer of 2004, the approach and trail on the left side of the falls was considerably brushed out. This trail can be reached via dinghy in two spots on the western shore of the stream. The first is just inside the mouth, another is just before you reach the falls. Both are marked with orange flagging tape. The trail continues up the left side of the falls

to about 50 feet beyond the second smaller falls where it crosses over to the other side via a couple of large cedar windfalls across the stream. From here, the trail follows the stream for about a mile to a lovely inland lake. Where this trail used to be difficult because of the number of windfalls, it also has been brushed out by some of the boaters who have done so much work on CPR Slip.

Heading up the shoreline around the corner from Otter Cove there are a couple of marginal anchorages that bear mentioning. The first of these is in **Agate Cove,** which is best used as a lunch stop because it is wide open to westerly winds. The beach, however, is interesting to explore and often will

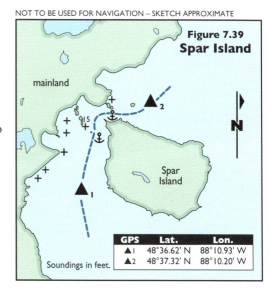

NOT TO BE USED FOR NAVIGATION – SKETCH APPROXIMATE

Figure 7.39
Spar Island

N

mainland

Spar Island

Soundings in feet.

GPS	Lat.	Lon.
▲1	48°36.62' N	88°10.93' W
▲2	48°37.32' N	88°10.20' W

yield beautiful agates.

The channel between the mainland and the north end of **Spar Island** is navigable and is actually easier than it looks on the charts. By staying midchannel, 40 to 45 feet of water can be maintained when passing from east to west. Just to the SW of the sand/rock spit there is a section with 15 feet of water. It is possible to anchor on either side of the spit with the northern side providing more protection than the southern side, which is quite open to westerly and southerly wind. However, this is another spot in which it is difficult to get a good set with the anchor because of a rock bottom. The northern side also drops off quickly making it difficult to obtain adequate scope.

Lying at the base of the Nipigon Strait is a light station at **Lamb Island.** Many years ago it used to be a popular place for boaters to stop off and visit with the light keeper and his wife. This station, however, was unstaffed in the late 1980s along with most of the other Ontario light stations. It does still have some interest to boaters, since there is a small dock at its SW end where those with boats drawing less than 5 feet may tie up. Although the dock provides protection for most wind directions, it is best used as a lunch stop because it is wide open to westerly winds.

The waters around Lamb Island need to be navigated with care, since there are some large shoals both to the north and SW of the island. To the north of Lamb Island is a breathtaking view of the Nipigon Strait, banked by the majestically high-rising bluffs of the mainland and Fluor Island. It is but a brief glimpse of the continuing wilderness waters that extend across the top of the lake.

Chapter Eight

Across the Top of the Lake:
Nipigon Strait to Port Coldwell, Ontario

Please Note:
Maps and Charts in this book are not necessarily to scale and are not intended for navigation.

It is hard to tell which sector of Lake Superior provides the best cruising. A lot depends on individual interests. Yet, if exploring Lake Superior's wilderness backwaters or getting lost in the far reaches of remote areas is your forté, then that section that stretches across the top of the lake from the Nipigon Strait to the east shore presents some of the best cruising the lake has to offer. For here we can cruise for days between protective island chains or head out across the open waters to the remote high-rising vistas of the Slates and Pic Island. Here our constant companions are moose and deer, beaver and otter, herons, and gulls. Here we can get lost in the "outback," fishing and beach combing, hiking an old moose trail back to an inland lake, rediscovering a past rich in logging and commercial fishing or just taking in the quiet serenity of a secluded anchorage.

Fog is prevalent in these parts of the lake, with mid-July to the end of August having the most fog-free days. Yet, within any two-week vacation, it is common to experience at least a couple of days of fog. The area also has some large iron deposits that result in magnetic anomalies, so the need for constant and precise navigation becomes apparent. There are also few areas where it is possible to obtain fuel and supplies. Yet these are small deterrents to those who cruise the north shore. For there is a well-beaten track from Thunder Bay to Rossport, with the "cruising crowd" only thinning out the farther east one goes beyond Rossport.

A large part of this section of the lake is also a continuation of the National Marine Conservation Area (NMCA) — through to Bottle Point, east of Terrace Bay. The impact on the boating community continues to remain uncertain before the full management plan is in place. (See Introduction to Chapter Seven.)

Harbors and Anchorages

Nipigon Strait is the large passage that extends northward between mainland and the western end of St. Ignace Island. Banked by high-rising bluffs to each side, this wide, deep "river to the north" makes an interesting cruise for those who wish to make the side trip into the towns of Red Rock or Nipigon. The base of the strait is marked by two distinguishing landmarks: the high-domed bluffs of Fluor Island and Lamb Island Light.

Located at the bottom of Nipigon Strait is **Moss Island**, which is approximately two miles north of Lamb Island. There are three excellent anchorages to choose from behind the island, one at each end and one in the middle. Because there are few adequate anchorages in Nipigon Strait or in Nipigon Bay, Moss Island becomes one of the important last stops for those who are making the 25-mile run up to Red Rock or the 30-mile run to the town of Nipigon.

Either the north or south anchorage is excellent, with choice dependent only on wind direction. In both cases it is wise to give Moss Island adequate berth when entering due to a few underwater rocks. Also note the small islet and rock shoal that must be avoided when entering the southern anchorage. There is an inland lake that lies quite close to the mainland shoreline of the southern anchorage. It is but a short walk over a narrow land bridge (just north of a

NOT TO BE USED FOR NAVIGATION – SKETCH APPROXIMATE

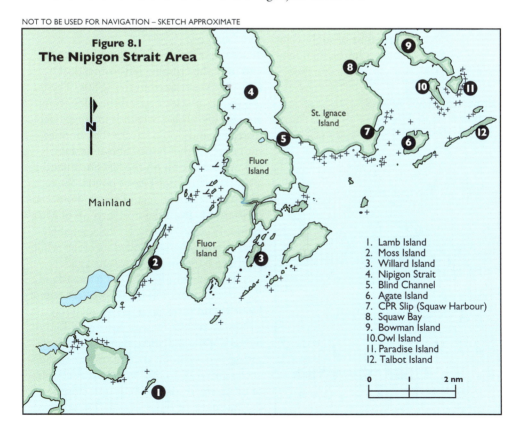

Figure 8.1
The Nipigon Strait Area

N

St. Ignace Island

Fluor Island

Mainland

Fluor Island

1. Lamb Island
2. Moss Island
3. Willard Island
4. Nipigon Strait
5. Blind Channel
6. Agate Island
7. CPR Slip (Squaw Harbour)
8. Squaw Bay
9. Bowman Island
10. Owl Island
11. Paradise Island
12. Talbot Island

0   1   2 nm

small hook of land) that isn't too difficult to bring a dinghy across. We can attest that it has good fishing for pike. The passage between the north and south anchorages should be attempted only with a shallow draft boat and local knowledge since there are a number of rocks and boulders strewn throughout.

Coast Guard cutter Samuel Risley serves Canadian light stations. DAHL

To reach the inner middle anchorage, there is a shoal that is not marked on the charts, which needs to be skirted in the approach. It lies just before a constricted passage, next to a sand beach and private fishing camp on the west side of Moss. Passing to the west of the shoal there is more open surface water with minimum depths of 7 feet to 8 feet (water 0.57 m above chart datum). Locals appear to favor passing to the east of the shoal, between it and Moss Island, where the passage is more constricted but appears somewhat deeper. (See Fig. 8.3.) The fishing camp was established on Moss Island in the 1990s for patrons brought down from Nipigon.

On the mainland side are the remains of a much older camp and only the cribbing left from a dock that was constructed in the 1980s. There is a trail that leads beyond this older camp across a log bridge, which is in considerable disrepair, and over a stream that empties into the lake mentioned above. It then follows the stream on the left side inland to a swamp with some beaver ponds. There is a shipwreck in 108 feet of water about one-quarter mile from the northern tip of Moss Island. It is the *Neebing,* a 193' Canadian steel steamer then exploded its boiler while pulling a barge in heavy seas in 1937.

A couple of miles NE of Moss Island, the large indentation on the **western end of Fluor Island** provides a secure anchorage for all but W to NW winds. It is easily found by noting the red and green spars that are just to the west of a small group of islands at the entrance to this large bay. A couple of other small islands are found close to the shoreline of Fluor Island. The track

NOT TO BE USED FOR NAVIGATION – SKETCH APPROXIMATE

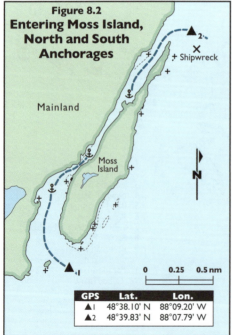

Figure 8.2
Entering Moss Island, North and South Anchorages

Mainland

× Shipwreck

Moss Island

N

0   0.25   0.5 nm

GPS	Lat.	Lon.
▲1	48°38.10' N	88°09.20' W
▲2	48°39.83' N	88°07.79' W

to take into the anchorage is to pass midway between these two sets of islands and then favor the southern shore of the large bay. Once in the bay, there are depths of 10 to 12 feet along the southern shore until way back in, where one can anchor in 8 feet to 9 feet of water over a mud bottom. The stream that bisects Fluor Island at this end is quite clogged with debris and impossible to navigate via dinghy. Because this anchorage is so open to the NW, it is good to have an alternative in mind, in which case the anchorage at the north end of Moss Island would offer the closest choice.

Figure 8.3
Moss Island, Middle Anchorage

Mainland

old cribbing

Moss Island

N

8
8
shoal 8
7   9
8   10
       11

fishing camp

Soundings in feet. Taken with water 0.16 m (6.3 in.) above chart datum.

KEY
Flag
Buoys

North of Fluor Island there is a side channel in the Nipigon Strait that extends SE between Fluor and St. Ignace islands, **Blind Channel**. Although it is very shallow and rock-strewn in some spots, it is used frequently by those who cruise out of Nipigon. By holding close to the Fluor Island side of the channel it is possible to maintain 7 feet of water in normal water years. However, this is one passage that is best used only with local knowledge and when no sea is running.

Nipigon Bay is that large expanse of water (20 miles in length) that lies to the north of St. Ignace and Simpson islands. Nipigon Bay is relatively shallow and because of this it has a reputation for treachery, since it can be whipped into a short, steep chop that can make cruising uncomfortable for any boat in short order.

The bay provides a few anchorages that are marginal because they are open to certain wind directions and thus best used as lunch stops. One of these is **Caribou Cove**, which is found on the NW end of St. Ignace Island just after clearing the strait and

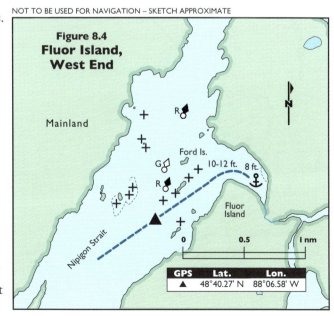

Figure 8.4
Fluor Island, West End

Mainland

N

R
Ford Is.
G
R
10-12 ft. 8 ft.
Fluor Island

Nipigon Strait

0   0.5   1 nm

GPS	Lat.	Lon.
▲	48°40.27' N	88°06.58' W

entering Nipigon Bay. It's important to stay away from the small island on the eastern side, especially south of the Island because there is a sand bar extending south between the island and St. Ignace. Adequate depths for anchoring can be found in the middle of the bay, but it is quite open to northerly winds. Caribou Cove was once a base camp for commercial fishing. Now all that remains are the remnants of a small cabin and a steam bath. Another marginal anchorage is found on the southern side of the west end of **Vert Island**, where it is possible to obtain wind protection from all but southerly winds in approximately 8 feet of water. Probably the best area for anchoring is in **Kama Bay** (also known as Mazokamah Bay) along the mainland north shore of the bay. Although the bay is quite large, it is possible to achieve protection from all but strong SW winds simply by moving around the bay. Note that a road comes down the eastern side of the bay and there are a number of cottages and family camps here.

On the western side of Nipigon Bay, south of the mouth of the Nipigon River, is the small town of **Red Rock** with the newest marina in this segment of the lake. The town is easily identified by a huge mill set on its eastern side in front of a gargantuan rock-faced bluff. The mill, which was initially constructed in the mid-1930s, has had an interesting history. In 1939, after going into receivership, the property was purchased by the government for a prisoner of war camp — Camp R. It was short-lived, however, due to tensions within the camp from diverse inmates: merchant seamen, German Jews, Nazis, and anti-Nazis. In 1941, these factions were separated and sent to other camps and the camp was closed. In the following decades, the mill was purchased by a succession of owners and closed in November 2006.

The marina (monitors VHF 68/Tel.: 807-886-2126) is found toward the western end of the town in front of two rather prominent structures: the Red Rock Inn (red and white with white verandas) and, to the west of it, a large white church. The entrance to the marina breakwater is marked with a red triangle/red fixed light (held to starboard when entering) and a black

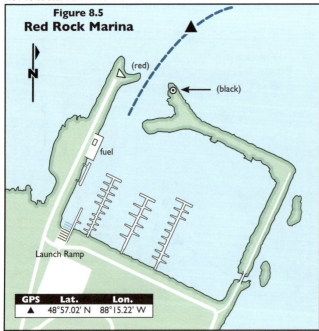

Figure 8.5
Red Rock Marina

GPS	Lat.	Lon.
▲	48°57.02' N	88°15.22' W

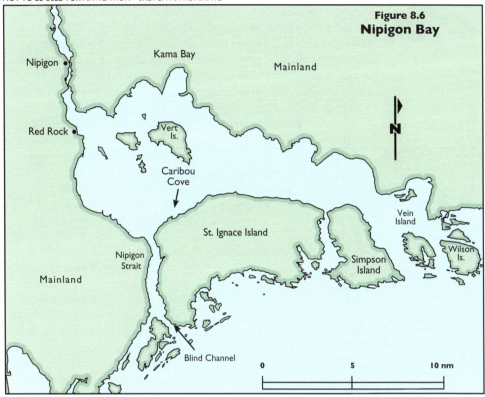

Figure 8.6
Nipigon Bay

bull's-eye/two white fixed lights (held to port). Although there is only 7 feet of water at the entrance, there are 8-9 feet in the outer docking area. Because there are other areas in the marina with less depth, it is a good idea to head straight for the gas dock to get instructions and check in. The marina (82 slips) provides gasoline, diesel, water, pump-out and electricity (30 A).

Adjacent to the marina is a campground, restaurant, gift shop, and Interpretive Center with interactive displays about Lake Superior including a virtual underwater tour. Within the complex are restrooms, showers, laundry, pavilion, picnic tables, all connected with a beautiful boardwalk.

It is but a short walk into town where there is a supermarket, beer and liquor store, bank, convenience store and hardware store. A point of interest is the Red Rock Inn, which has also had an interesting history. In the early years it served as a mess hall for mill employees, and during the prisoner of war camp period it served as a mess hall and officers' quarters. It has also housed a school, drugstore, laundry facilities, credit union and dentist office. The inn was purchased in 1995 and underwent extensive restoration and then was sold in 2004 to its present owners. The dining room is one of the most elegant on the north shore, with diverse entrees to satisfy any palate, large or small.

Before leaving the town of Red Rock, it is important to

mention the Red Rock Folk Festival that has been gathering here the second weekend of August each year since 2003. It attracts new and top-name folk singers from all over Canada. For three days, a festive atmosphere pervades in the park adjacent to the marina. In addition to those who come by land, boaters from up and down the shore attend, so marina reservations are required for this weekend.

Another point of interest is the Nipigon-Red Rock Hiking Trail that connects the two towns along the western side of the Nipigon River over Paju Mountain. This well-maintained trail, which is 8 km (4 miles) long, is particularly beautiful at the Red Rock end, where it passes high up on the bluff for magnificent overlooks of Nipigon Bay and the town of Red Rock. The middle section is vigorously challenging as it passes up and down through deep ravines, while the Nipigon end winds through scenic forest and wild marshlands.

The town of **Nipigon**, which is located on the Nipigon River between Nipigon Bay and Lake Nipigon, is the farthest point north that can be reached from Lake Superior's waters without portaging. This area was first visited by the French in the mid-1600s. Early explorers were Father Claude Allouez who, in 1667, made his epic trip up the river to Lake Nipigon, and Sieur du L'hut, who made the trip in 1678. With an expanding fur trade, the area gained importance as forts and trading posts

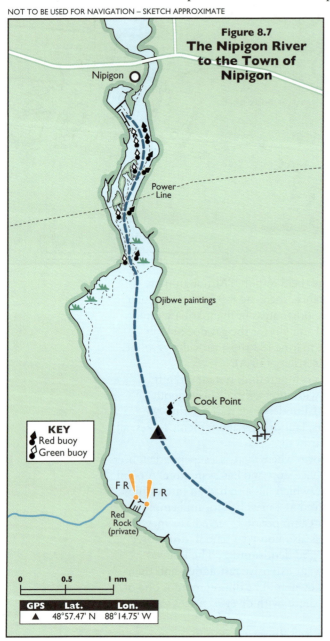

Figure 8.7
The Nipigon River to the Town of Nipigon

were established by the Hudson's Bay Company and the North West Company. One such post was the Red Rock Trading Post of the Hudson's Bay Company that was established in the mid-1800s where the present-day Nipigon town dock is located. The original purpose of the post was to serve as a lookout to prevent outsiders from heading up the river and cutting into the fur trade farther north.

The town itself got its start when the Canadian Pacific Railway completed the north shore section of its line in 1883-1885. During the construction, the town and river became important links for bringing in supplies to the railroads. By the turn of the 20th century, Nipigon had become a significant center for logging and pulpwood activity. Although the use of log booms is now prohibited by the Canadian government, pulpwood and its products still remain one of the largest industries on the north shore.

Located in the farthest northern reaches of Nipigon Bay off Lake Superior, the town is reached from the south via the Nipigon Strait or from the east by traveling through the length of Nipigon Bay. If coming up the strait, it is important to line up with the buoys and range, which are NE of Moss Island. (See Canadian charts #2302, #2312.) The rest of the strait is deep and offers no obstructions if a midchannel course is kept. If coming from the east through Nipigon Bay, it is best to pass to the north of Vert and Ile La Grange islands since the southern part of the bay is more shoaled.

The Nipigon River is buoyed with six sets of red and green spars. When heading upstream, pass in between, keeping the red buoys to starboard. Just before reaching the second set of buoys there is a power line that spans the river at a height of 79 feet. It is important to stay well within the channel since there have been a few reports of some shifting bars in recent years. The water depth in the river varies with minimum depths of 7 feet. After clearing the last set of buoys, the minimum depth is 6 feet.

A special point of interest in the Nipigon River is a spot midway between Red Rock and the town of Nipigon on the eastern shore of the river. Here is one of the few known sites of First Nation (the Canadian term for Native People) pictographs to be found on Lake Superior shores. Although the vast area north of Lake Superior abounds with more than 250 sites, only three or four are actually found on Lake Superior's shores. The paintings are usually found on rock wall faces or steep cliffs at water's edge. The site at Nipigon is typical in that it consists of a half dozen or so paintings on a sheer

SKETCH APPROXIMATE

Figure 8.8
Ojibwe Pictograph, Nipigon River

rock wall that rises some 400 to 500 feet above the water. The cliff is located a little more than a mile from the Cook Point buoy and is recognized as a rock-faced jagged cliff with pine trees growing on the top and also about halfway down. The paintings are found at the northern end of the cliff below this second line of trees about 6 feet above the water. They can readily be seen by boat since the depths are quite deep right up to the cliff, which drops off abruptly in the water. However, because of other red streaks and markings in the rock, the paintings may be difficult to spot.

Many of the paintings are abstract art forms, looking much like hieroglyphics, and defy interpretation. Some look like canoe forms with upright strokes that could represent men. But the most predominant painting of the group is a squatting human-like figure that is generally thought to be one of the mythical *Maymaygwayshi* or Rock Medicine Men who lived in the rock cliffs and were thought to steal fish from nets and bother natives canoeing by. The reverse position of the heart is believed by some to be an indication that

NOT TO BE USED FOR NAVIGATION – SKETCH APPROXIMATE

Figure 8.9
Nipigon, Ontario

The Lagoon

Nipigon River

floating docks

main dock gas & pump-out

shoal water (varies)

to business district

Launch ramp

red

picnic area

marina office showers & rest rooms

Nipigon River Recreational Trail

N

Launch ramp

Picnic Shelter

green   red

the pictographs were meant to be viewed as reflections in the water. The paintings are made from a bright red pigment (now weathered) made from red ochre (the mineral hematite), which was possibly mixed with a grease or glue from sturgeon fish. There has been no effective way of dating these paintings. Although this area is believed to have had inhabitants as early as 7000 BC, it is doubtful that the paintings could survive the rigors of weathering in the harsh northern climate for much more than 1,000 years. Thus, they were probably constructed no earlier than AD 1000 by Algonkian speaking ancestors of the modern Cree or Ojibwe.

In approaching Nipigon's dock, it is wise to proceed with caution since depths vary between 6 feet and 7 feet. Note: after clearing the last set of buoys, it is important to favor the dock side of the channel since there is a large sandbar that extends out from the natural breakwater.

Nipigon is another town that has seen tremendous expansion of its marine facilities (monitors VHF 68/Tel.: 807-887-3040) in recent years. In addition to the old dock (180 feet), which can accommodate up to 10 boats, a finger of floating docks has been added to provide an additional 16 slips. There are 20-foot depths at the gas dock. Gasoline, pump-out, water and electricity (30 A) are provided along with restrooms and showers. Diesel fuel has to be brought down via taxi and gerry cans from nearby gas stations. Within the town there are a couple of excellent supermarkets, restaurants, two hardware stores, laundry facilities, liquor store and bakery.

The Nipigon folk take their history very seriously and a number of years ago established an excellent museum that displayed past and modern history with collections reflecting prehistory archaeology, historic artifacts, local railway history, logging and geology. Of special mention is a collection of Paleo-Indian artifacts of large copper tools that includes axes, knives, needles, and spear points from the Archaic Period. The original museum was located in a turn-of-the-century building that was an engineering office for the CN railroad. Although a fire destroyed the building in February 1990, 75 percent of the collection was saved, and plans are under way to establish another museum on one of the other historic sites near the waterfront.

Back at the lower end of Nipigon Strait there begins an inside passage between Fluor Island and the outlying chain of islands along St. Ignace's southern shore that is one of the more interesting stretches in this part of the lake. The channel is deep and, with the exception of Dacres Rock (which extends south from the southern tip of Fluor Island) and Shank Rock (SW of Willard Island), is free from obstructions if one stays midchannel. Banked by the high rising vistas of Fluor Island to the north and Puff Island to the south, it is one of the more beautiful channels on the lake.

To the west of Puff Island is **Willard Island**, which isn't as heavily forested as the surrounding islands. This is because of a fire in late-June 1988 that burned nearly three-fourths of the island.

The fire apparently was started by lightning and smoldered for many weeks before it crested and burned most of the island. Even though the forest has come back, years later you can still see that it isn't as thick as on other islands.

Behind the northern end of Willard Island there is a nearly all-weather anchorage that can be approached from either side. The easiest approach is to come up the eastern side of Willard Island hugging close to the island in order to avoid the shoaling that extends southward from the small islands to the north. Twenty feet can be carried as one rounds to the west into the anchorage.

If coming up the western end of Willard Island, care must be taken to avoid Shank Rock, which lies SW of Willard. This shoal is usually just awash, spotted only by breaking water, and it is best to pass between the shoal and Willard — again favoring the island. To round up to the NE into the anchorage, it is necessary to pass through a small opening between Willard and the island to the north. There is a considerable shoal off the little island one passes to port that can be avoided by favoring the Willard Island side of the channel. (See insert on Fig. 8.10.) With care, 8 feet of water can be carried through. Anchor in 12 to 15 feet in the indented bay on the north side of Willard.

Although the anchorage is good for most winds, a strong NE wind could prove uncomfortable. Alternative anchoring can then be found snugged up to the smallest section of Fluor Island in 20 feet. Do not attempt to pass through the small islands north of Willard since the water is shoaled and fouled with rock.

The streams bisecting Fluor Island make for interesting exploration. The western arm quickly becomes closed with swamp; the eastern arm is navigable with a small boat. There are the remains of a fishing station along the eastern shore of this smallest section of Fluor Island.

Heading northeast a little farther up the

NOT TO BE USED FOR NAVIGATION – SKETCH APPROXIMATE

Figure 8.10
Willard Island

Fluor Island

fishing camp

Blow-up of Willard Island Anchorage Entrance

fishing station

Fluor Island

Willard Is.

Fluor Island

N

Fluor Island

Puff Island

Willard Island

Shank Rock

GPS	Lat.	Lon.
▲1	48°39.24' N	88°04.45' W
▲2	48°38.79' N	88°05.15' W

0   0.25   0.5 nm

channel is **Agate Island**. The anchorage on its northern end is marginal because it is quite open to northerly winds, and it is difficult to get a good set with the anchor because of deadheads and slash. In approaching this anchorage, it is best to come up the eastern side of Agate Island, because between the western end of Agate and St. Ignace there are numerous shoals, some of which this writer and others have felt over the years are unmarked on the charts. In fact, those waters close to the St. Ignace side are fondly called "the minefield" by locals. Those waters just to the west of Agate should be navigated only when there is little sea running and the sun is high behind one's back.

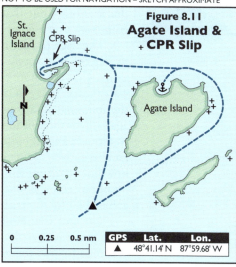

Figure 8.11
Agate Island &
CPR Slip

St. Ignace Island

CPR Slip

Agate Island

	GPS	Lat.	Lon.
▲		48°41.14' N	87°59.68' W

0   0.25   0.5 nm

CPR Slip, which is also called **Squaw Harbour**, has become one of the more popular spots on the North Shore. This is because a particularly energetic group of boaters out of Nipigon and Red Rock have spent a lot of time cleaning up the area, putting in a number of trails and docks, and more importantly, building one of the nicest steambath/saunas on the shoreline.

The name CPR comes from the Canadian Pacific Railway and goes back to the early 1900s when the railroad operated a lodge (now the Nipigon Hotel) for wealthy sportsmen in the town of Nipigon. Around 1927-28, the company built a couple of overnight cabins in this secluded little harbor and took their guests out there for three-to-four-day fishing parties. Thus, it became a wilderness hideaway for the rich. When the fishing died off and people stopped going to the lodge, the cabins deteriorated and eventually burned down. Today there is a newly constructed cabin and a number of docks along with a steambath/sauna.

This little all-weather harbor is located on St. Ignace Island one mile W-NW of Agate Island. It should not be confused with Squaw Bay two miles farther north on the same St. Ignace shoreline, which has a similar shape on the charts. In approaching the harbor, great care must be taken to avoid the surrounding shoals that are in the area — especially those west and north of Agate. Some of the shoals have markers similar to fishing buoys placed on their north side by locals. Because of these shoals and a narrow shallow entrance, this is a tricky anchorage to enter. Therefore,

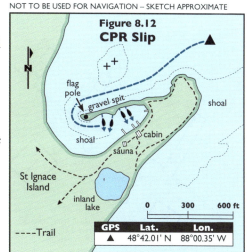

Figure 8.12
CPR Slip

flag pole

gravel spit

shoal

shoal

cabin

sauna

St Ignace Island

inland lake

----Trail

0   300   600 ft

	GPS	Lat.	Lon.
▲		48°42.01' N	88°00.35' W

this is another one that should not be attempted without the sun at your back or if a good sea is running.

The trick to rounding the gravel spit that forms the harbor is to hug the spit closely by holding off a scant 9 feet to 10 feet from shore. Close to shore there is an abrupt 8-foot drop-off (in normal water years) that can be followed around the spit. Farther out from the spit, boats drawing more than 5 feet will ground. Once inside, again favor the spit to the middle of the anchorage for 8 feet of water over a mud bottom. Because the docks often quickly fill up, an alternative is to set out a short scope stern anchor and run a bow line to one of the trees on shore. (See Fig. 8.12.) Note — this harbor often experiences seiches — as much as 6 to 8 inches that can be helpful in getting in/out of the harbor.

The area is interesting to explore, particularly on a number of trails that have been put in. One trail leads across to the "outside" and then follows the beach around the peninsula. Another trail leads across the north end of the "inland lake" and splits into two trails. One leads through the forest across to Blind Channel, the other up to a series of dramatic overlooks providing helicopter views down into the harbor and a breathtaking panorama of the islands and surrounding area. In the cabin there is a table, some bunk beds, and kitchen-like cabinets. In good Canadian fashion, there is a logbook for visitors to sign, and it's interesting to read and find out who has been up the shoreline during the season. The steambath is open to the public. All that is asked is that you cut firewood to replace that which you used and that you leave the area cleaner than you found it. The front halves of the cabin/bunkhouse and steambath are nicely enclosed with screened-in porches, favorite places to congregate for those who use the harbor. If seclusion is desired, this is not the place to come, especially on weekends, since it's not unusual to pack in half a dozen boats or more into this secure little harbor.

A little more than a mile north of CPR slip there is the **Squaw Bay**

NOT TO BE USED FOR NAVIGATION – SKETCH APPROXIMATE

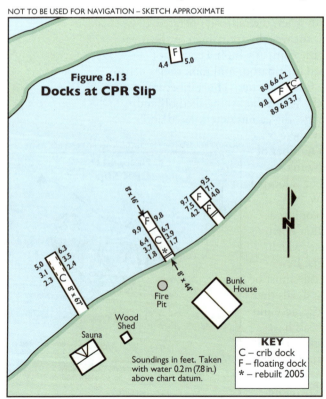

Figure 8.13
Docks at CPR Slip

KEY
C – crib dock
F – floating dock
* – rebuilt 2005

Soundings in feet. Taken with water 0.2 m (7.8 in.) above chart datum.

(mentioned above with CPR Slip/Squaw Harbour) that for years we didn't go into because of reported shallow water and it being so open to the east. Then a local fisherman told us that it wasn't all that shallow if you stayed in the middle and that it was a very nice anchorage. Sure enough, we found a beautiful anchorage heading north between CPR and Owl and Bowman Islands.

Dahlfin II tied off on gravel spit at CPR. DAHL

There are many ways to approach the anchorage. The trick of course is avoiding the shoal spots in the area. The one we used is to come up the east side of Agate Island — not too close, you don't want to come close to land here until you are coming into an anchorage. Once you have passed Agate hold a course of 350 degrees true until you are well past Owl Island. Then you can head directly to the anchorage. With this course you should be able to avoid the shoals, especially the one out in the middle about 1/2 mile off. The sand spit is much small than the one in CPR and unless you have a small shoal draft boat you can't get in behind to tie off. This anchorage is good for all but easterly winds in which case it wouldn't be too difficult to go across to Bowman Island and anchor off the northern half, Just don't get close to land in this area — especially the point extending south from St. Ignace that you will pass on your port side. There is an extensive shoal passing south from it into the bay and you want to be sure and clear it before heading NE to Bowman.

Bowman Island has long been a favorite stopover for boaters coming up the shoreline. As early as prehistoric times, the island received visitors as evidenced by some of the best-defined Pukaskwa Pits on raised cobbled beaches in this sector of the lake.

It is possible to pass

NOT TO BE USED FOR NAVIGATION – SKETCH APPROXIMATE

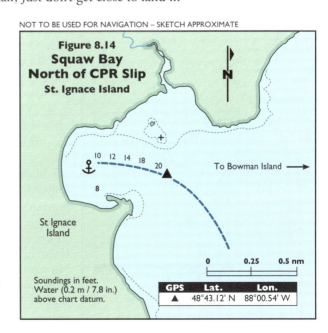

Figure 8.14
**Squaw Bay
North of CPR Slip**
St. Ignace Island

N

10 12 14 18

20

To Bowman Island ⟶

8

St Ignace
Island

0   0.25   0.5 nm

Soundings in feet.
Water (0.2 m / 7.8 in.)
above chart datum.

GPS	Lat.	Lon.
▲	48°43.12' N	88°00.54' W

between the northern end of Bowman Island and St. Ignace Island where there are two camps. The one on St. Ignace is private. The one on the NW end of Bowman Island is a fishing camp, Bowman Island Charters. The fishing camp operates for only a few weeks In the spring and is private for the rest of the year.

The southern end of the island is the site of a past commercial fishing station that goes back to the late 1800s. It is here at these docks, remnants of an era past, that boaters would often congregate. The docks and buildings used to belong to Bill Schelling (deceased 1990) of Rossport, who for years fascinated boaters with tales of an age when people made their living in small engineless open boats — rowing on the stormy waters of Lake Superior.

In approaching the docks, the western approach is the easiest with no obstructions. It is possible to pass to either side of Owl Island, however it is important to note the rocks and large shoals that extend southward from both Owl Island and Paradise Island. In using the eastern approach, care must be taken to give the shoal and rocks off the northeastern end of Paradise Island a *wide* berth.

Where there used to be two docks, there is now only one that over the years has fallen into great disrepair and is no longer usable. It is possible to anchor off and run a bow line ashore and tie off on part of the dock remains. Even the cabin where Bill Schelling used to stay has fallen into great disrepair. About the only thing that remains is an interesting gravesite on the island, on a path just NW of the remains of a couple of buildings. The grave belongs to Thomas Lampshire (French: Lamphier) who died in 1869. He was the light keeper at Talbot Island. Stories tell us that in those days the light keepers were put on the islands largely to fend for themselves. With no way off

NOT TO BE USED FOR NAVIGATION – SKETCHES APPROXIMATE

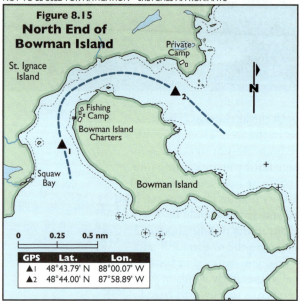

Figure 8.15
North End of Bowman Island

GPS	Lat.	Lon.
▲1	48°43.79' N	88°00.07' W
▲2	48°44.00' N	87°58.89' W

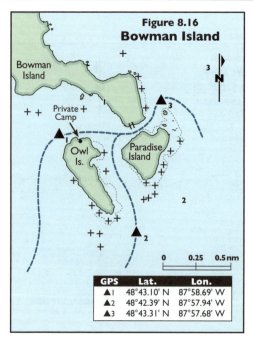

Figure 8.16
Bowman Island

GPS	Lat.	Lon.
▲1	48°43.10' N	87°58.69' W
▲2	48°42.39' N	87°57.94' W
▲3	48°43.31' N	87°57.68' W

the island, Lampshire and his wife were forced to stay on the island through the winter of '69. When he died sometime during this winter, his wife was unable to bury him because Talbot Island is solid rock. She kept the body until spring, when it was moved to Bowman Island where there was enough soil to dig a sufficient grave. Three light keepers lost their lives on what came to be called the "Island of Doom" and the lighthouse was abandoned after only six years of operation. When we read between the lines of this story and others, it takes little imagination to envision some of the struggles our Lake Superior forefathers must have endured. Note: the white marker and bronze plaque marking the gravesite were added in the late 1970s by Bill Schelling and the priest from Rossport.

Across the channel from Bowman Island, **Paradise Island** has quite different terrain from the surrounding islands and thus makes for interesting exploring and walking. The eastern end is especially open with an austere windswept quality. There is a shale-rock beach

NOT TO BE USED FOR NAVIGATION – SKETCH APPROXIMATE

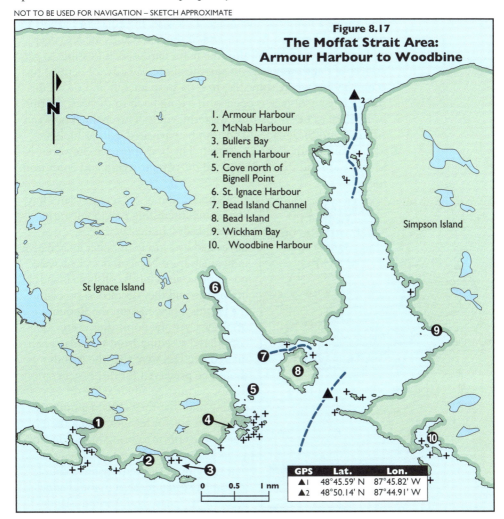

Figure 8.17
The Moffat Strait Area:
Armour Harbour to Woodbine

N

1. Armour Harbour
2. McNab Harbour
3. Bullers Bay
4. French Harbour
5. Cove north of Bignell Point
6. St. Ignace Harbour
7. Bead Island Channel
8. Bead Island
9. Wickham Bay
10. Woodbine Harbour

Simpson Island

St Ignace Island

GPS	Lat.	Lon.
▲1	48°45.59' N	87°45.82' W
▲2	48°50.14' N	87°44.91' W

0   0.5   1 nm

across the channel from the Bowman dock where you can beach a dinghy. A trail leads through the middle of the island to the SE side. Paradise Island is known for its raspberries and especially abundant blueberries in the open areas.

There is marginal anchoring in the small "bay" on the northern end of the east side of **Owl Island** where it is possible for a shoal draft boat to sneak in among the shoals. The anchorage, however, is open to the east and doesn't get much use because of its close proximity to CPR Slip. The dock and camp seen on the north end of Owl are private.

Nearing the eastern end of St. Ignace Island is the **Moffat Strait Area**, where there are a number of interesting little anchorages, many of which receive little use by transient boaters. (See Fig. 8.17.)

Tucked in behind Armour Island is the first of these anchorages, **Armour Harbour**. Surrounded by very high bluffs, this is a particularly beautiful harbor. Because it is considerably open to the west and the bottom is quite deep and laden with deadheads, this can be a marginal anchorage. Likewise, the adjacent harbors in the channel between Armour and St. Ignace islands are also deep and open to the west. Within the main harbor, it is possible to get 20 feet of depth way back in close to shore. Because of depths, this is one harbor where some like to set a stern anchor and tie off on shore. The anchorage is open with a long fetch to the west, so this is no place to be with strong westerly winds. The channel between Armour and St. Ignace islands can be navigated using a lookout with a minimum depth of 20 feet. The best approach, however, is to come around the northern end of Armour Island and enter from the west.

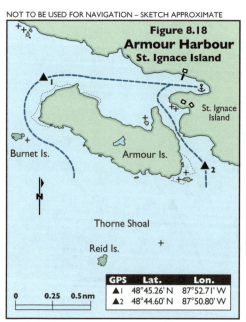

Figure 8.18
Armour Harbour
St. Ignace Island

GPS	Lat.	Lon.
▲1	48°45.26'N	87°52.71'W
▲2	48°44.60'N	87°50.80'W

This section of St. Ignace Island has seen some interesting developments in recent decades. In the late 1970s, it was discovered by a group of rather imaginative individuals from Nipigon that there were no written claims for the offshore islands in this area and they decided to proclaim the islands a new nation, the Republic of Nirivia. At one point they even considered seceding from Canada. Their main objectives were that the islands should be preserved for future generations by not permitting any logging or mining and that they remain a multiuse recreation area. A few years back there were some efforts to bring in patrons for a "back to earth experience." Today, all that remains of the venture are a couple of domed structures seen in the channel between St. Ignace and Armour islands.

) Cabins

Note: when cruising in this area, Thorne Shoal, lying approximately one mile south of Armour Island, needs to be skirted. By taking bearings off Reid Island, just to the west of the shoal, it can easily be avoided.

A mile east of Armour Harbour lies a more secure anchorage, **McNab Harbour**. It is one of the more beautiful harbors in the area, banked by high-rising wooded bluffs. It is, however, very difficult to spot, since the entrance doesn't open up until you are almost in it and you feel that you are heading right into shore. The harbor is secure for all winds, but it is one where depth versus scope is a problem, since in the main harbor there are 25 feet to 30 feet close into the eastern shore. Along the northern shore there is a small "bay" where it is possible to get 15 feet, but with no swinging room. The harbor has a number of deadheads lying on the bottom, and we can attest that this is a place where it may be helpful to use a trip line. Because McNab lies so close to Woodbine, it doesn't get much use, and it's one of those harbors that you can usually have to yourself.

The small lake to the north can be reached via a small land bridge. It's an easy matter to carry over a dinghy, and on a hot sunny afternoon, in a short time it isn't difficult to pick up more northern pike than you can eat. On the southern shore of the anchorage near the entrance is an old aluminum "wreck" washed up on the beach.

Around McNab Peninsula and Bullers Island there is a deep cove, **Bullers Bay**, in which one can also anchor. However, because it is wide open to the SE and very deep, this bay is best used only as a lunch stop. Because of some rocks and shoaling along the shorelines, anchoring is further made difficult with only the far western indentation giving 20 feet of depth for anchoring. Do not attempt to pass between Bullers Island and McNab Peninsula, since it is shoaled and rock-strewn. It is also possible to access the lake,

NOT TO BE USED FOR NAVIGATION – SKETCH APPROXIMATE

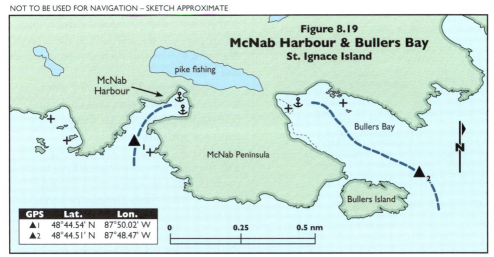

Figure 8.19
McNab Harbour & Bullers Bay
St. Ignace Island

pike fishing

McNab Harbour

Bullers Bay

McNab Peninsula

Bullers Island

GPS	Lat.	Lon.
▲1	48°44.54' N	87°50.02' W
▲2	48°44.51' N	87°48.47' W

0   0.25   0.5 nm

which has pike, from this anchorage.

Between Bullers Bay and French Harbour there is another anchorage in the **Cove NE Bullers Bay** where it is possible to get protection for all but S and SE winds. It is easy to recognize by a large free-standing rock on the starboard point when entering. By staying in the middle of the bay to avoid the shoreline shoals to each side, it is possible to go all the way in and anchor in 15 feet. However, like Buller's Bay this anchorage is also open to SE winds, and even southerly winds.

The next harbor, **French Harbour,** which lies approximately one-half mile farther up the shoreline just south of Bignell Point, offers good protection and holding ground. By going way in behind the "entrance island," that lies to the south of Bignell Point, almost all-weather protection can be achieved. Only a strong southerly wind might produce an uncomfortable surge. The anchorage is entered from the south by keeping the "entrance island" close to starboard. There is a small rock shoal, that is usually awash, which must be kept to port — thus passing between this shoal and the "entrance island." There are also some more rocky shoals close along the St. Ignace shoreline, but these give little interference with anchoring that can be found in 15 to 30 feet of water. Note that at "A" it may be difficult to get the anchor to set because of rock bottom. It is also quite deep here – 39 feet. At "B" there is less depth, approximately 13 to 15 feet and there still is some rock. This area is particularly interesting to explore by dinghy. On the SW side of the largest of the St. Joe Islands there is a picnic table and outhouse.

The **cove north of Bignell Point** is another that offers marginal anchoring, being open to the NE. (It should not be confused with the smaller cove that lies immediately to the south, between itself and Bignell Point.) If approaching from the NE, there are no hazards. However, in an approach from the east between the outlying small islands, care must be taken for a shoal extending south from the northernmost island. Once inside the

NOT TO BE USED FOR NAVIGATION – SKETCHES APPROXIMATE

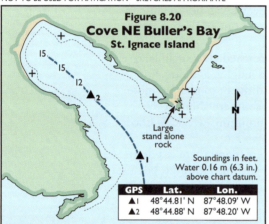

Figure 8.20
Cove NE Buller's Bay
St. Ignace Island

Large stand alone rock

Soundings in feet. Water 0.16 m (6.3 in.) above chart datum.

GPS	Lat.	Lon.
▲1	48°44.81' N	87°48.09' W
▲2	48°44.88' N	87°48.20' W

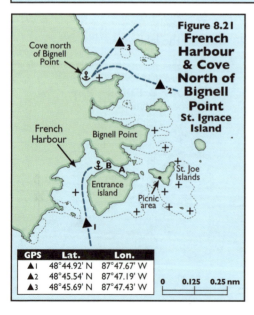

Figure 8.21
French Harbour & Cove North of Bignell Point
St. Ignace Island

Cove north of Bignell Point

French Harbour

Bignell Point

St. Joe Islands

Entrance island

Picnic area

GPS	Lat.	Lon.
▲1	48°44.92' N	87°47.67' W
▲2	48°45.54' N	87°47.19' W
▲3	48°45.69' N	87°47.43' W

0   0.125   0.25 nm

cove, 10 to 11 feet of water is available throughout for anchoring with some rocky shoals close in by the shoreline. Note: the water in and around the St. Joe Islands is particularly foul with rocks and shoals and should be given a wide berth.

St. Ignace Harbour is the very large indentation extending up into the SE end of St. Ignace Island. It is quite large and open to the SE, so special attention needs to be paid to the weather when anchoring here. Sky Lake, inland to the west of the anchorage, is reputed to have good fishing.

In **Bead Island Channel** between the island and St. Ignace, it is possible to find protection from southerly winds. However, because of the great depths in this channel, anchoring is marginal. The wharf indicated on the chart (Canadian chart #2312) is no longer existent — just pilings and the debris left from a few tumbled down buildings, remnants of a past fishing station.

The little cove on the NE end of **Bead Island** doesn't offer anchoring as good as it would appear on the charts, and it is quite shoaled and rock-strewn. It is also open to the NE.

With CAUTION and strict adherence to the navigational chart, especially at the northern end, **Moffat Strait** is navigable through to Nipigon Bay. By taking bearings off the small islands in the northern part of the channel, a minimum of 15 feet can be maintained through the strait. There are, however, shoals to each side in this tight part of the channel and this is not an area to navigate in rough conditions or reduced visibility.

Wickham Bay, one-third of the way up the strait on Simpson Island, is another marginal anchorage primarily because of its wide exposure to the west. Also because of silting from Wickham Creek, it is difficult to tuck way back in.

Woodbine Harbour has long been known as one of the most beautiful

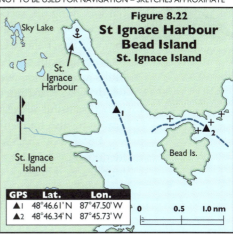

Figure 8.22
**St Ignace Harbour
Bead Island**
St. Ignace Island

GPS	Lat.	Lon.
▲1	48°46.61'N	87°47.50'W
▲2	48°46.34'N	87°45.73'W

0   0.5   1.0 nm

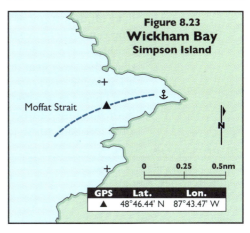

Figure 8.23
Wickham Bay
Simpson Island

Moffat Strait

0   0.25   0.5nm

GPS	Lat.	Lon.
▲	48°46.44'N	87°43.47'W

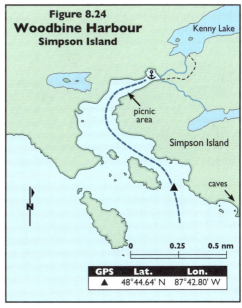

Figure 8.24
Woodbine Harbour
Simpson Island

Kenny Lake

picnic area

Simpson Island

caves

0   0.25   0.5 nm

GPS	Lat.	Lon.
▲	48°44.64'N	87°42.80'W

harbors along this section of the lake and has been a great favorite of those who cruise this area. It is probably because of Woodbine that many of the anchorages in the immediate area are often bypassed by cruising skippers. For Woodbine is surrounded by high towering bluffs heavily laden with a forest of hardwoods and conifers. It winds its way past interesting islands and rock formations way back into a beautiful all-weather harbor. Along with boaters, moose and beaver are also frequent visitors to the area.

Located on the SW end of Simpson Island, Woodbine is identified by the large domed bluff that is a characteristic landmark for the area. However, spotting the actual entrance may be a little more difficult since the opening that lies between the outlying islands and the main part of Simpson Island doesn't open up until the last minute. Here entry is made by keeping these outlying islands to port and Simpson Island to starboard. The only hazard is a rock shoal lying off the SE end of the island that is closest to Simpson Island. This can easily be avoided by favoring the Simpson Island shoreline. Because of great water depths, the best anchorage is found deep into the harbor, way in at the far end. There are several places here where it is possible to set out a stern anchor and tie off on shore.

There are two good places for shore fires in the anchorage, both along the southern shore. One is on a little clearing, up on a hill just adjacent to the anchoring area. The other is on the

NOT TO BE USED FOR NAVIGATION – SKETCH APPROXIMATE

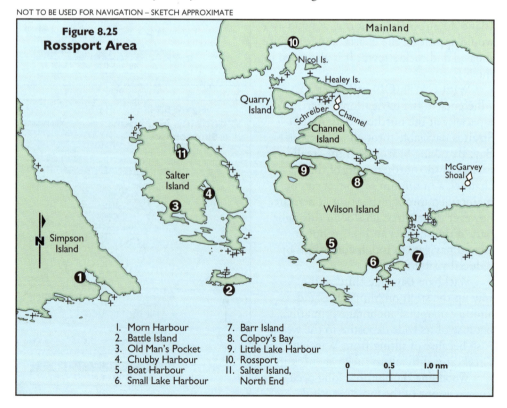

Figure 8.25
Rossport Area

1. Morn Harbour
2. Battle Island
3. Old Man's Pocket
4. Chubby Harbour
5. Boat Harbour
6. Small Lake Harbour
7. Barr Island
8. Colpoy's Bay
9. Little Lake Harbour
10. Rossport
11. Salter Island, North End

last rocky point one leaves to starboard just before reaching the anchoring area. Another interesting feature of the anchorage is that the trail at the far end leads inland approximately one-half mile to Kenny Lake that years ago was stocked with trout. There are some interesting caves along the Simpson Island shoreline that are passed just before coming into the outer entrance making for interesting exploring via dinghy.

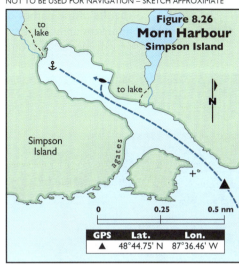

Figure 8.26
Morn Harbour
Simpson Island

GPS	Lat.	Lon.
▲	48°44.75' N	87°36.46' W

The Rossport Area: Within a short distance of the town of Rossport, many excellent anchorages can be found. In fact, one could cruise within 10 miles of Rossport for a week and be in a different anchorage every night.

Starting from the west, the first of these anchorages is **Morn Harbour**. Located on the SE end of Simpson Island, this deep natural harbor has good protection, with good anchoring at the far end (15 feet) for all but strong SE winds. By setting a stern anchor and running a bow line ashore just around the inside end of the long entrance, protection can be obtained from even SE winds. (See Fig. 8.26.)

It is possible to hike back to a couple of lakes in the area, the trails being used by moose and moose hunters in the fall. There are a number of boats up at the lake NW of the anchorage.

The stone beaches here, along the Lake Superior shoreline, are well-known for their agates. If you come prepared with a hammer and chisel, try splitting the rocks for "thunder eggs" (stones that have agates in the center).

Battle Island gets its name from an apparent skirmish in 1885 between troops who were marching across ice to suppress an uprising against the Ojibwe during the Riel Rebellion. The "battle" probably didn't take place this far offshore from the mainland — yet the name stuck on the island. Perched high on a bluff (118 feet), the first lighthouse was built in 1877. It was then replaced with the present reinforced structure in 1911. The light flashes every 24 seconds with a visibility of approximately 18 miles and is equipped with a foghorn. The station was one of the last in the Ontario sector to have personnel removed. Beginning with the 1992 season there were no light keepers officially stationed at the light. However, one of the last light keepers resided here for a number of years in an unofficial position during the summer months and was helpful In answering questions and showing visitors around.

On the north side of the island there is a nice anchorage for those who wish to anchor for the night or merely stop off for a visit to the light. It is found by passing between two small islands

that lie in the harbor on the north side of the island. Depths of approximately 15 feet are found between the islands, but then it gets deeper as you round into the anchorage. There are a couple of moorings that may be used by visiting boats (limit 24 hours), or you can anchor in 15 feet over a mud bottom. Note that there is a submerged electric cable in the harbor that should be avoided when setting an anchor. This harbor gives a lot more protection than indicated on the charts and is good for all but the hardest northeasterly blow.

A trip to the lighthouse is a "must-see" experience.

The view from the top of Battle Island Lighthouse. DAHL

There is a road that can be taken for approximately one-half mile up to the light and adjacent buildings. The view from the light is breathtaking — a picturesque panorama looking out on all sides of the island and beyond.

Old Man's Pocket is the local name given to the long narrow harbor on the SW end of Salter Island. It is a harbor that is easy to find and enter with no obstructions. Approach is made from either west or east along the southern end of Salter Island; under no conditions should passage be attempted between Harry and Minnie islands. If the eastern approach is used, care must be taken to avoid the rock outcroppings that lie along both the shorelines of Salter and Minnie islands.

Because the anchorage is very deep, anchoring is found in only two places: the far end, where it may be necessary to tie off on shore, and in the "thumb," where there are 10 feet to 15 feet of water over a mud bottom. This is another all-weather anchorage, and there is little that can reach you in here.

Chubby Harbour is the very deep indentation along the southern shore of Salter Island that lies just east of Old Man's Pocket.

NOT TO BE USED FOR NAVIGATION – SKETCH APPROXIMATE

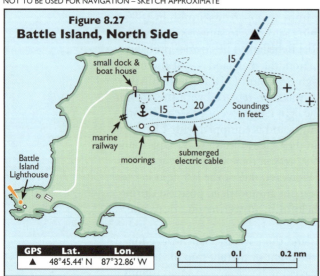

Figure 8.27
Battle Island, North Side

small dock & boat house

15

20

Soundings in feet.

marine railway

moorings

submerged electric cable

Battle Island Lighthouse

GPS	Lat.	Lon.
▲	48°45.44' N	87°32.86' W

0   0.1   0.2 nm

Although a fine harbor, because of excessive depths and being open to southerly winds, it is not used as often as Old Man's Pocket, which offers better protection. There is, however, an anchorage in the small bay at the far NW end where it is possible to anchor in 18 to 20 feet of water. This anchorage provides protection for all but strong SE winds. It is not uncommon to see deer feeding in the marshy area at this end.

Wilson Island has a number of anchorages that are all within an easy day's sail from Rossport. The first of these is **Boat Harbour**, an all-weather harbor that is located at the SW end of Wilson Island. In entering this harbor, it is most important to favor the large headland of Wilson Island that lies to starboard to avoid the rock shoals that are off the entrance island and extend NE into the entrance channel. Keeping this entrance island well to port should avoid this rather extensive shoal. The anchorage is found by rounding to starboard into the second bay, anchoring in 15 feet of water over a mud bottom. Note: it is not uncommon to see deer come down to feed in the SE marshy corner.

Moving east along the southern shore of Wilson Island, there is another of the Wilson Island anchorages, **Small Lake Harbour**. In entering this harbor, there is quite a bit of shoaling along the shore to starboard, thus a midchannel to port track should be favored. Because this anchorage is wide open to the SW, it is best used as a lunch stop. Just to the west of the anchorage there are a number of agate beaches that locals indicate yield greenstones. However, it should be noted that these greenstones are not the true mottled variety that one finds on Isle Royale. The water between Cobinosh and Wilson islands is clear with no obstructions.

Another anchorage along this southern shore of Wilson Island is found at the SE corner, behind **Barr Island**. The approach to the anchorage is made by giving wide berth to the small islets and surrounding shoal area that extend to the east of Barr Island, thus heading in behind Barr Island from a northeasterly direction. There is a small dock on the Wilson side of the channel along with a couple of cabins. To get beyond the dock into the anchoring area it is necessary to snake around a couple of shoals, first by heading

NOT TO BE USED FOR NAVIGATION – SKETCHES APPROXIMATE

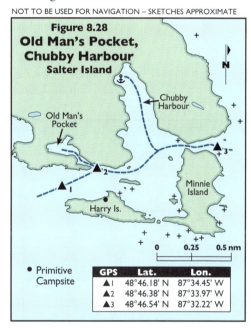

Figure 8.28
**Old Man's Pocket,
Chubby Harbour**
Salter Island

Chubby Harbour

Old Man's Pocket

Minnie Island

Harry Is.

▲3

▲2

▲1

0   0.25   0.5 nm

• Primitive Campsite

GPS	Lat.	Lon.
▲1	48°46.18' N	87°34.45' W
▲2	48°46.38' N	87°33.97' W
▲3	48°46.54' N	87°32.22' W

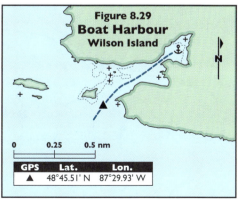

Figure 8.29
Boat Harbour
Wilson Island

0   0.25   0.5 nm

GPS	Lat.	Lon.
▲	48°45.51' N	87°29.93' W

directly toward the dock to avoid shoal water to port and then heading toward the Barr Island shoreline to avoid shoal water just SW of the dock on the Wilson Island side of the channel (see Fig. 8.30). By taking this track it is possible to maintain a minimum depth of 9 feet and anchor in approximately 13 feet to 14 feet. The southern entrance to the anchorage is foul with rock and shoals and should not be attempted with a deep-draft boat.

The area around Barr Island is especially interesting to explore by dinghy. There are several beaches along its southern and eastern shores. Some of these are very old as indicated by the terraces of lichen-covered beach material that extend deep into the island. On the easternmost beach there is the rare site of a Pukaskwa Pit. Note: the passage between Wilson and Copper islands is navigable only by extremely shallow draft boats and dinghies since it is littered with rocks and numerous shoals.

On the north end of Wilson Island, there are two more anchorages, both of which give all-weather protection. **Colpoy's Bay** at Wilson's NE end has good holding over 17 feet of water. However, to get to 17 feet, you have to go over a shoaling (9 feet), which is closer to the opening into the channel. Also, there is quite a bit of slash and what looks like old pilings way deep in, particularly along the SE shoreline. Deeper water can be found along the western shore.

NOT TO BE USED FOR NAVIGATION – SKETCHES APPROXIMATE

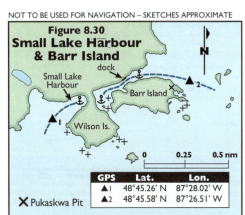

Figure 8.30
Small Lake Harbour & Barr Island

GPS	Lat.	Lon.
▲1	48°45.26' N	87°28.02' W
▲2	48°45.58' N	87°26.51' W

✗ Pukaskwa Pit

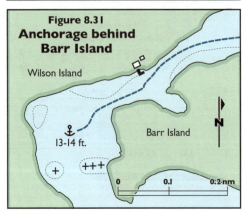

Figure 8.31
Anchorage behind Barr Island

The last of the Wilson Island anchorages, **Little Lake Harbour**, is located in the NW corner of Wilson Island. Although the entrance looks a bit tight, passage can be obtained for boats drawing up to 6 feet or so since water varies from 8 feet to 10 feet depending on low water datum. There is a rock shoal in the center just before entering the harbor with 5 to 5.5 feet of water in low-water years. It can be cleared by keeping the shoal to port and hugging the starboard shore very close when entering. Although the harbor gives perfect all-weather protection, anchoring is made difficult by great depths throughout. Only in the far SE end of the harbor is it possible to get 30 feet, and then this is so close to shore that it may be necessary to set out two anchors or tie off on shore.

The last harbor found in the Rossport vicinity lies in the deep indentation on the **north side of Salter Island**. Although quite open to N and NW winds, the

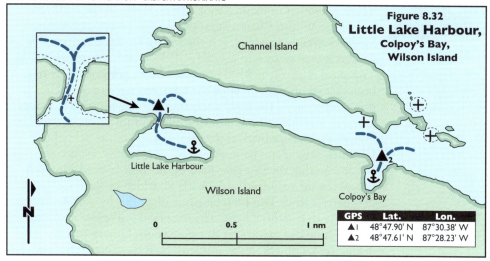

Figure 8.32
Little Lake Harbour,
Colpoy's Bay,
Wilson Island

Channel Island

Little Lake Harbour

Wilson Island

Colpoy's Bay

N

| | 0 | 0.5 | 1 nm |

GPS	Lat.	Lon.
▲1	48°47.90' N	87°30.38' W
▲2	48°47.61' N	87°28.23' W

harbor is secure for all other wind directions. By going way in, it is possible to get adequate depths (20 feet) for anchoring. This harbor isn't used very often because of its close proximity to Rossport.

A visit to the town of **Rossport** is a highlight of any cruise on Lake Superior's north shore. Rossport got its start when the railroad came through (you will be reminded of this daily) and the town was named "Ross Port" after Walter Ross, the contractor responsible for this sector of the line. The Rossport Inn (originally named Oriental Hotel) was built in 1884 to serve as a pay station and hotel. The town soon became one of the largest commercial fishing centers on the lake when the CPR station master, J.A. Nicol, founded the Nipigon Bay Fish Company in 1903. At one time the town boasted of 20 fishing tugs that worked out of the harbor and shipped 375 tons of fish annually by rail.

Today Rossport is a delightful little village that in many ways is reminiscent of a quaint New England fishing village. For many it is the final destination or turning point of a cruise. The townsfolk are most congenial, and a couple of excellent restaurants provide the opportunity for a "night out" right in the heart of the wilderness. Because of the adjacent highway and bus route, Rossport is an excellent place to change crew or leave a boat if a cruise needs to be split up into segments. There is also a small boat launching ramp here. So those with short time blocks and trailerable boats can gain access to a section of the lake that otherwise would be out of reach for them.

In coming to Rossport there are many approaches. If Nipigon Bay is used, Barwis Rock, which is marked with a red buoy (Fl R), should be noted. If coming up the Simpson Channel, there are no hazards within the channel, however Rolette Shoal, which is unmarked off the NW corner of Salter Island should be given a wide berth when rounding to the NE toward Rossport.

There is another unmarked shoal, Tracy Shoal, in the northern end of the Wilson Channel that should also be avoided. Coming up the Schreiber Channel, it is the McGarvey Shoal, responsible for sinking the steamship *Gunilda* in 1911, that is the main obstacle. This shoal is usually marked by a green buoy, however, there has been at least one season when the buoy was not in place. Therefore, it is good to avoid the shoal altogether by hugging close to Copper Island or staying well off, into the middle of the channel. Another buoyed shoal, Breadrock at the southern end of the Schreiber Channel, should also be noted.

In entering the Rossport harbor, the most favored approach is between the mainland and the island, which lies just north of Quarry Island. This island is easily identified by a white day marker with a flashing light. The mainland is likewise identified by a flashing day marker on Rossport Point. Quarry Island is a distinctive landmark in the area with high towering cliffs. It is also possible to enter between Nicol Island and the entrance island with the flashing marker. The passage between Quarry and Healy islands is clear, and there is no rock shoal in the middle as indicated on Chart #2303. The usual track taken is midchannel, slightly favoring Healy Island. There is much deeper water around the north of Boone Island than the south where there is a pretty good shoal extending north of Healy Island. Within the Rossport harbor there is ample depth throughout, except the NE corner adjacent to and north of Nicol Island, where it is so shoaled that even dinghies have difficulty getting to the causeway that connects the island to the mainland.

Most of the docks in Rossport are private. There is, however, a large dock that is run by the town, the Rossport Harbour Non-Profit Marina incorporated in 1995. Since then, Rossport has had

NOT TO BE USED FOR NAVIGATION – SKETCH APPROXIMATE

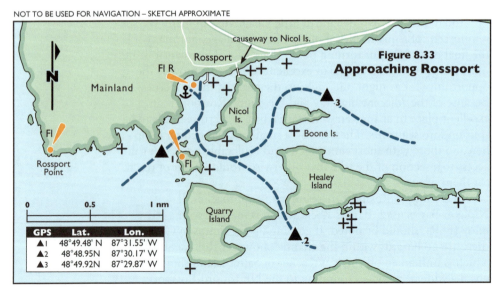

Figure 8.33
Approaching Rossport

GPS	Lat.	Lon.
▲1	48°49.48' N	87°31.55' W
▲2	48°48.95N	87°30.17' W
▲3	48°49.92N	87°29.87' W

some ups and downs in providing fuel from a pump to boaters. They were able to provide gasoline beginning in 1996 and diesel in 1998. Then in 2013, as a non-profit operation, they were unable to afford the government standards to repair the fuel pumps so they could no longer provide fuel. In 2021 the Marina Board started the marina revitalization process due to the deterioration of the dock which was more than 40 years old. A two stage capital plan was developed with Stage 1 beginning fall 2024 and completing by June 2025. This involved removing the east-west dock section, stabilizing the north-south dock section, underpin the dock building, repair boat launch area, and remove outdated gas/diesel tanks. In 2025 there would be less docking space but the docks would be safer with pumpout, water, ice and Internet provided. Stage 2 involves the construction of a new dock with fuel, showers, and laundry facilities. This is a longer term goal requiring capital funding applications beginning in 2026-27. The marina can be contacted by phone in season: 807-824-1143, out of season: 807-823-0883. It is also useful to get marina updates before coming by going to their website: *www.rossportmarina.ca*.

Within the village there are a couple of interesting gift shops: The Raven's Nest and Island Pottery. Island Pottery is located on Nicole Island which is connected to mainland by a short road. Another attraction for boaters is the Serendipity Gardens, located a short walk up the hill from the dock. This delightful restaurant specializes in different Mediterranean-type dishes and also prime-rib on the weekends. Reservations are suggested on the weekends. You can eat inside or out-of-doors on the patio overlooking the harbor amidst a most beautiful array of flowers and shrubbery. Serendipity has become a great spot to get off the boat for a relaxing lunch or dinner.

Leaving Rossport and heading down the Schreiber Channel you come close to the site of an interesting underwater shipwreck, the *Gunilda*. The *Gunilda* was a custom-built Scottish luxury yacht, owned by an executive of the Standard Oil Company, having just completed a circumnavigation a few years prior. In 1911, after the owner refused the aid of a local pilot (cost $15), the steel-hulled vessel hit McGarvey Shoal, which at that time was uncharted on U.S. charts. After the passengers and crew of 21 were safely taken ashore, the tug *James Whalen* out of Port Arthur attempted to salvage the 195-foot vessel. Unfortunately, it slipped off the reef and plunged to a depth of 280 feet where it lies today. In the past it was a favorite dive for deep divers, but to date at least two lives have been lost on the wreck. There are some interesting photographs and artifacts from the wreck at the Rossport Inn. Today, the wreck is privately owned and unauthorized diving is prohibited. The *James Whalen* has been resurrected as a museum ship and can be visited in Thunder Bay.

The mainland shoreline from the Schreiber Channel to

Marathon has a number of anchorages, many of which are often passed by in favor of visiting the Slate Islands and Allouez. However, the first of these, **Les Petits Ecrits**, makes a nice stopover en route from Rossport to the Slates.

This small group of islands is easy to spot lying off the rather bold mainland shoreline just east of the Schreiber Channel. However, when coming from the west the entrance doesn't open up until you are almost directly south of It. Although the chart (Canadian #2303) shows a number of rocks and shoals in the immediate area, the islands are quite easy to navigate within. By holding to the center of the two entrance islands there is no difficulty in carrying deep water through. In fact, the deep water makes finding a suitable anchorage within the islands difficult. The best spot is a small bay against the mainland following a course NW of the entrance, where it is possible to get 20 feet over a sand bottom. The anchorage is good for all but hard easterly winds. The narrow channel between the westernmost island and mainland is too deep (40 to 60 feet) for anchoring. Do not attempt to enter or leave by this entrance since the western end is shoaled and rock-strewn.

From the anchorage it is possible to gain access to a trail that follows along the shoreline here. It was developed by local residents as part of the Voyageur Trail Association. It extends to the west around Schreiber Point and east to Schreiber and Terrace Bay. By taking a 30-minute hike toward the east you come to a lookout with a beautiful view of the anchorage and surrounding islands.

Although the name "Les Petits Ecrits," which translated means "the little writings," might suggest that the area may be a place where Ojibwe rock paintings could be found, to date there have been none reported within this small island group. This is because it is now believed that they were not the usual paintings of red ochre, but rather lichenographs, which were dramatic figures carved into the orange and black lichen and subject to diffusion by creeping overgrowth with the passing of time. There is, however, a small site of the red ochre paintings in the adjacent Worthington Bay, but because they are a little inland, they cannot be viewed from the water as at Agawa and Nipigon. Due to the bold shoreline and wave action of the water, this area is difficult to approach by boat.

Terrace Bay is located approximately two miles to the east of Les Petits Ecrits. Marginal anchoring can be achieved behind and to the north of the small islets that are midway along the eastern shore. This area is open to the west and

NOT TO BE USED FOR NAVIGATION – SKETCH APPROXIMATE

Figure 8.34
Les Petits Ecrits

⊗ lookout

Mainland

| 0 | 0.25 | 0.5 nm |

GPS	Lat.	Lon.
▲	48°45.04'N	87°12.66'W

somewhat to the north, but should these winds develop, it isn't too hard to move to another part of the bay.

The anchorage shouldn't be confused with the town of Terrace Bay that lies inland and approximately two more miles to the east. Because Highway 17 comes down fairly close to the water here (approximately one-quarter mile), it would be possible to hike inland to the highway and take it into town to get supplies. The town is considerably larger than Rossport and well-stocked with a number of different stores.

There is a beautiful anchorage that provides protection for most winds in the **cove SE of Terrace Bay.** It is found by passing through a small group of islands that lie just offshore. The easiest approach is from the south, which, by staying in the middle, is deep and clear of obstructions. It is possible to go way in and anchor next to a small sand beach over a sand-rippled bottom. This anchorage is open to the S and SW winds. By not going so far in and anchoring behind the islands, you can also get protection from the SW. It is possible to exit and enter in the western channel as long as a zigzag course is taken to avoid a shoal that lies off the mainland. This is a little-known anchorage that receives little use so seclusion is usually assured.

About two miles east of Terrace Bay inside the mouth of the **Aguasabon River** there is a small boat landing and a number of floating docks. This is a favorite jumping off spot for those with small powerboats who make the run out to the Slate Islands — only seven miles. The mouth of the river is formed by a long sand spit that is marked by a red triangle day marker and a white flashing light that are held to starboard when entering. Caution: it is important to note that conditions at the mouth of the river change each year. Especially with recent low-water conditions it is important to navigate the mouth only with local knowledge and only very shallow draft boats. Once inside the river, depths vary from 4 to 10 feet. Small boats can usually find space at one of the floating docks or anchor off in sand. There is a road (about one mile) that goes into the town of Terrace Bay where there are grocery stores, hospital, post office and more.

Jackfish Bay is another deep indentation into the mainland shoreline much like Terrace Bay. It is marked by Victoria Cape, a rather bold headland on the west, and a day marker (Fl W) on St. Patrick Island that lies in the middle of the entrance of the bay. The best approach into the bay is to pass with St. Patrick Island to starboard, giving good

NOT TO BE USED FOR NAVIGATION – SKETCHES APPROXIMATE

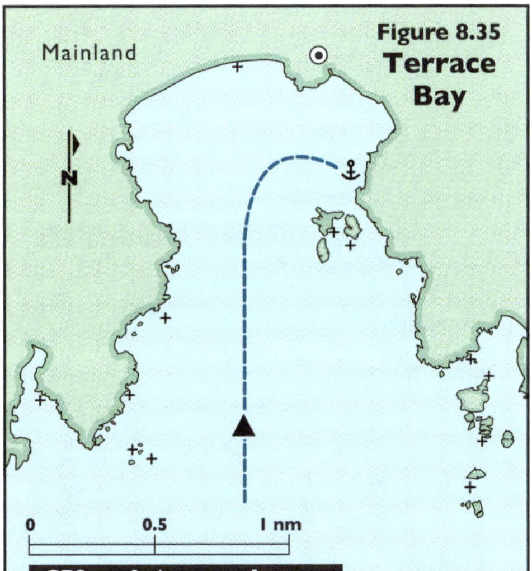

Figure 8.35
Terrace Bay

Mainland

0   0.5   1 nm

GPS	Lat.	Lon.
▲	48°45.95' N	87°10.05' W

water tower – conspicuous

berth to the shoals that extend SW from St. Patrick. Once past St. Patrick, be sure to avoid Little Nick Rock that lies in the middle of the bay. The best anchoring is in the northeast arm, but even this is marginal because it is quite deep and open to the southwest. The western arm of the bay (Moberly Bay) can also be used for anchoring. It can be entered either to the north of Bennett Island or in the middle, south of Bare Rock. The bay is very deep, except at the far northern end. The Canadian Pacific Railway follows the shoreline quite closely around the bay. It is still heavily used, with trains passing many times a day, and for some this may be a negative aspect of the anchorage. The town of Jackfish no longer exists: the wharves have also been destroyed (1967) with only dangerous pilings remaining. It is best to stay clear of this area.

When you look at the circular shape of the **Slate Islands** on a chart, it is easy to see how they could have resulted from the impact of a huge (19-mile-wide) asteroid. Today this group of eight islands lying approximately five miles south of the northern mainland are all that remain of the crater cone from the impact. In the 1930s these islands were the site of an extensive logging operation conducted by the Pigeon River Paper Company. In the late 1980s, the Slate Islands were made into a Provincial Park. Today the islands serve primarily the recreational interests of boaters and fishermen. Particularly in the interior of the Slates, there are a number of cottages set up by mainlanders that are used as hunting and fishing camps. The islands have also become ecologically important, since the largest herd of caribou remaining on the lake is located here.

The approaches to the interior of the islands are basically from the east and west since this is the way in which the islands are divided. If the approach is from the west there are no obstructions, however it is good to note the rocks and shoal that stand off from the northern side of the islands. (No — Dahl Shoal was not named after this writer, and you can be sure that

NOT TO BE USED FOR NAVIGATION – SKETCHES APPROXIMATE

Figure 8.36
Cove SE of Terrace Bay

sand
Mainland
Terrace Bay
12
20
2
shoal
0   0.125   0.25 nm

Soundings in feet. Taken with water 0.14 m (5.5 in.) above chart datum.	GPS	Lat.	Lon.
	▲1	48°45.70' N	87°08.44' W
	▲2	48°46.01' N	87°08.94' W

Figure 8.37
Aguasabon River

Mainland
Docks
N
0   0.125   0.25 nm

GPS	Lat.	Lon.
▲	48°46.05' N	87°06.95' N

Floating Docks with Launch Ramp

@ 6'
@ 5'
Cement launch ramp
@ 5'

any shoal with one's name on it is given wide berth.) Once in the main channel, Kate Rock, which is well into the interior of the Slates, must be given adequate berth. There is a day mark high on the bluff on Mortimer Island, which is helpful to line up on, since there is a large shoal extending off the NW end of McColl Island. It is possible to pass between Bowes and the long extension of Patterson Island. But again, care must be exercised to wind one's way around the shoals. Aside from these few areas, the water is very deep throughout the Slates.

The approach from the east requires even more caution, particularly if one passes through the rocky shoal area south of Dupuis Island. This shoal is actually marked, because the northern end of the southern half is marked by a large rock that extends approximately 8 feet above the water. By aiming for and holding close to this rock when passing through, it is possible to maintain deep water. Pass with the rock kept to

Figure 8.38
Jackfish Bay

Moberly Bay

mainland

Bennett Is.

Little Nick Rock

St. Patrick Island

Cape Victoria

| | 0 | 0.5 | 1 nm |

GPS	Lat.	Lon.
▲	48°46.89' N	86°59.40' W

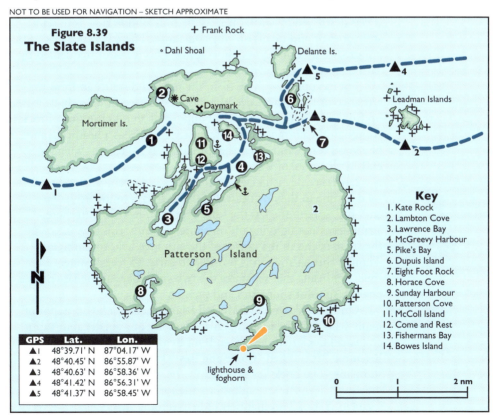

Figure 8.39
The Slate Islands

Frank Rock

Dahl Shoal

Delante Is.

Leadman Islands

Cave

Daymark

Mortimer Is.

Patterson Island

lighthouse & foghorn

Key
1. Kate Rock
2. Lambton Cove
3. Lawrence Bay
4. McGreevy Harbour
5. Pike's Bay
6. Dupuis Island
7. Eight Foot Rock
8. Horace Cove
9. Sunday Harbour
10. Patterson Cove
11. McColl Island
12. Come and Rest
13. Fishermans Bay
14. Bowes Island

GPS	Lat.	Lon.
▲1	48°39.71' N	87°04.17' W
▲2	48°40.45' N	86°55.87' W
▲3	48°40.63' N	86°58.36' W
▲4	48°41.42' N	86°56.31' W
▲5	48°41.37' N	86°58.45' W

| | 0 | 1 | 2 nm |

port when entering the Slates from the east. This passage should not be attempted when there is a sea running or without the sun at one's back. In foul weather, it is safer to enter around the north end of Dupuis Island, between Dupuis and Francois islands.

Entering the Slates is always dramatic, since the steep high-rising bluffs plunge abruptly into winding fjord-like channels. The interior of the Slates offers some interesting exploring, so here it is convenient to have a dinghy that is powered by a small motor. The reputation of fishing in the islands and out by the surrounding reefs is well-known. It is not uncommon to see caribou running along the beaches here. In fact, in recent years there have been a number of research teams here studying the habits and behavior of these shy animals. Because of the great depths throughout the islands, anchoring in many of the bays is often marginal.

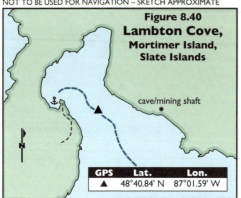

NOT TO BE USED FOR NAVIGATION – SKETCH APPROXIMATE

Figure 8.40
Lambton Cove,
Mortimer Island,
Slate Islands

cave/mining shaft

GPS	Lat.	Lon.
▲	48°40.84' N	87°01.59' W

Lambton Cove, which almost bisects Mortimer Island, has marginal anchorages for anchoring because of its great depths, as well as being quite open to the S/SE. There used to be a small dock around the corner on the west side. But it was destroyed by winter ice, so the only option now is to set a stern anchor and tie off on rings on shore. There is a nice place for a shore fire here and a few short trails. This is a spot frequented by caribou, especially at dusk.

On the opposite shore from the dock, a distance in from the entrance of Lambton Cove, there is an old cave/mining shaft. It is up from the shore about 15 feet and SE of an outcropping of rock. Although the entrance is short, the cave itself has a head clearance of a good 6 feet and extends approximately 50 feet in, where it ends with a pool of water.

Lawrence Bay is likewise quite deep and open to a long fetch — this time to the northeast. Of the two bays found at the far end, the eastern one has the least depth, 30 feet close to shore, again necessitating tying off on shore. To enter this bay, pass with the small island in the center of the entrance held to starboard. Though this narrows, it is possible to carry 35 feet of water. The small peninsula that separates the two small bays at the far end is a favorite spot for shore fires and picnics.

On the SW corner of **McColl Island** there is a favorite spot of many who visit the islands. This is because of a small cabin/camp and small dock that have been built by the Ministry of Natural Resources. It is called "**Come and Rest**" by many who cruise this shoreline. The dock lies very low to the water, but with care boats drawing 5 feet can set out a stern anchor and snug up to the dock. (See Fig. 8.41.) The channels in between the islands here are very interesting to explore by dinghy. In years past, along the northern shore of Burke Island, it has been possible to see one of the caribou live-traps that are constructed on the island for the purpose of caribou study.

McGreevy Harbour, which in the past was the site of lumbering activity, has now become the center of a number of hunting and fishing camps. Until the early 1980s, there was an old derelict barge tied to shore that was a favorite tying off spot for boaters. However, a very large fire in the spring of 1981 all but leveled the barge to the water, making it now unfit for tie-offs. There is, however, good anchoring in 17 to 20 feet of water behind the small island that lies just SW of the barge. The large clearing adjacent to the barge is often a good place to see caribou, especially at dusk. The small bays in the eastern end offer water that is shallow enough for anchoring, but the solitude here is restricted because of the cottages and fishing camps. The northernmost cove, **Fishermans Bay**, is sometimes used for anchoring. Another place in McGreevy Harbour where it is possible to anchor is in the bight on the east side of McColl Island next to a small island.

Pike's Bay is by far the best anchorage within the interior of the Slates. Located in the southwest extension from McGreevy Harbour, this all-weather anchorage provides depths of 10 feet to 15 feet, which are more suitable for anchoring. Because of a number of deadheads and slash on the bottom, it is wise to use a trip line for your anchor here.

The entrance is quite narrow, marked by a small island dead center. It is possible to go around either side of the island, however the passage most often used is the southern one, keeping the island to starboard as you enter. It is prudent to have someone in the bow here, since there is some shoaling extending out from the island. By favoring Patterson Island, it is possible to carry 9 to 10 feet of water in normal water years through this narrow entrance. Unfortunately, the large schools of fish that one sees in these narrows are suckers, not trout. However, it is not uncommon to see caribou on these beaches, right in the heart of the Slates.

Along the southern shore of the Slates there are a few additional anchorages, two of which are marginal

NOT TO BE USED FOR NAVIGATION – SKETCHES APPROXIMATE

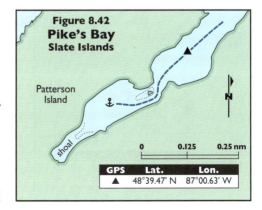

Figure 8.41
"**Come and Rest**" **Dock**
Slate Islands

Mortimer island

N

Single floating wood dock with wood ramp. 10ft.

1.5   1.5
4.5   4.5
6.0

Soundings in feet. water 0.18 m (7 in.) above chart datum.

Figure 8.42
Pike's Bay
Slate Islands

Patterson Island

N

shoal

0   0.125   0.25 nm

GPS	Lat.	Lon.
▲	48°39.47' N	87°00.63' W

because of being open to southerly winds, the other of which provides more protection and anchoring off the beaten track.

Starting from the west, the first anchorage is **Horace Cove**. This large indentation into the SW end of Patterson Island actually has two bays. The first bay that extends quite a way in toward the north is deep and open to southerly winds. In the far end it is possible to get 12 feet for anchoring, but you are still wide open to southerly winds. There is complete protection around the hook. But unfortunately, the water quickly shoals to 3 feet or less.

Within the eastern arm of Horace Cove it is possible to snug up to shore between the shoals to get adequate depths for anchoring. But it is marginal as an anchorage since it is wide open to the SW, and it is difficult to get a good set with the anchor.

Sunday Harbour is likewise open to the SW, and because of great depths and poor holding ground, it is even more marginal as an anchorage. There is a light station here with a foghorn. The first light keeper and his family came on station in 1902, but since the early 1990s it has no longer been staffed. Behind the peninsula on which the light is located there is a small beach and dock for shoal draft boats adjacent to one of the houses that used to be for the light keepers.

On the SE end of Patterson Island there is a delightful little cove that provides more protection than is indicated on the charts. For lack of a name, we have called this **Patterson Cove** (aka "South Bay" by locals), and it is easily identified by the small group of islands that are just south of its entrance. By staying midchannel between these islands and Patterson Island to the north, it is possible to enter with no hazards. Note a number of rather sizable rocks and surrounding shoal water lying just offshore of Patterson Island. It is possible to go quite far in and get protection from all but the strongest S/SE winds. The area is very interesting to explore, and if seclusion is desired, this anchorage is well off the beaten track for those who cruise this northern shoreline.

NOT TO BE USED FOR NAVIGATION – SKETCHES APPROXIMATE

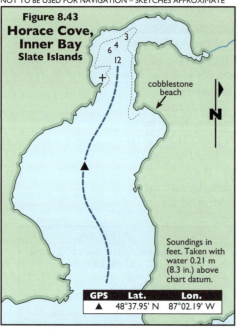

Figure 8.43
Horace Cove, Inner Bay
Slate Islands

cobblestone beach

Soundings in feet. Taken with water 0.21 m (8.3 in.) above chart datum.

GPS	Lat.	Lon.
▲	48°37.95' N	87°02.19' W

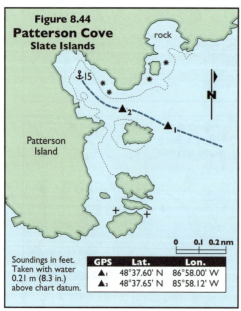

Figure 8.44
Patterson Cove
Slate Islands

rock

Patterson Island

0   0.1   0.2 nm

Soundings in feet. Taken with water 0.21 m (8.3 in.) above chart datum.

GPS	Lat.	Lon.
▲₁	48°37.60' N	86°58.00' W
▲₂	48°37.65' N	85°58.12' W

It is also a nice jumping off point for anchorages on the East Shore.

Northeast of the Slates on the mainland shoreline there are a number of anchorages, many of which are off the beaten track for those who cruise this section of the lake. One of these is **Bottle Cove** which lies just 5 nm NE of the Slates. The approach is free and clear of any obstructions with Entrance Island identified by many trees on the top half and adjacent low-lying rocks with no trees. The "Thumb "is not as prominent as it shows on the charts, blending in with the mainland shoreline. This is a beautiful harbor with rugged high surrounding bluffs and good protection for any kind of northerly or easterly winds. It is however quite open to SW winds. While there is moderate protection for south winds, waves from strong south winds may wrap around the Entrance Island, and because of shoaling you can't snug up to the SE shore as much as you would like to get protection from that shore. The large cove (Cork Cove on some charts) which lies 1/2 nm to the east is not suitable for anchoring being quite deep and open to the greater lake.

Continuing along the mainland shoreline approximately 15 miles NE of the Slates in Ashburton Bay there are a couple of interesting anchorages. The area is well-marked by Barclay Island which stands well out from the mainland.

The first of these harbors is a beautiful, little used harbor that lies approximately 1.5 miles SW of McKellar Harbour, **Claw Harbour.** It is difficult to spot because the small islands that form the harbor blend well up against the shoreline. Taking a bearing of 296 degrees T off the south end of Barclay Island takes you to the Entrance Island of the anchorage. Because there are so many small islands in the vicinity, it is easy

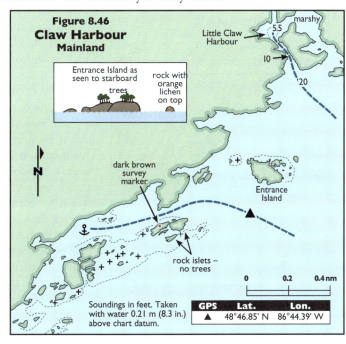

to get confused. The Entrance Island, which is held to starboard, has a decided elongated shape with two split-tree sections on it (see sketch diagram, Fig. 8.44). Another helpful marker is found on the two rock islets (no trees) that are kept to port where there is a brown survey marker on the second islet. Anchor a little farther in, with 15 feet of water over a good holding clay bottom.

This area is most interesting to explore by dinghy. The harbor that lies to the NE and looks like it would be a good harbor on the charts (which for lack of a better name we call Little Claw Harbour) is marshy and quite shallow with mud and silt from the small stream that enters the bay. It is possible to spend hours exploring the dozen or so small islands and rock islets lying to the SW, which are also reputed to have good fishing in the myriad of channels in between.

The **Prairie River**, which enters the lake approximately one mile west of Claw Harbour is also interesting to explore. It is marked by a white sandbar in the front which often changes position with the seasons (see Fig. 8.47). With care it is possible to navigate the entrance of the river with a dinghy and then follow the river approximately three miles upstream through some very wild country teeming with lots of waterfowl. At that point, the river widens to a small pool beneath some small rapids that come out of a rock tunnel underneath the tracks of the Canadian Pacific Railway.

Another anchorage along this northern shoreline is **McKellar Harbour**. The best approach is through the western channel, since in the eastern channel there are a number of rocks and shoals. Note that the shoal in mid-channel towards the northern end of the eastern entrance is quite wicked, lying just below the surface. This shoal can be avoided by favoring the eastern side of this eastern entrance. Likewise, there is an extensive shoal lying off the NE corner of the central islands complex that needs to be given a wide berth when using the eastern entrance.

The anchorage is made up of a number of small bays that can be used depending on the wind. There is a sand beach in the easternmost bay, but this area is quite open to the S and SW. The main part of this bay is quite deep, but

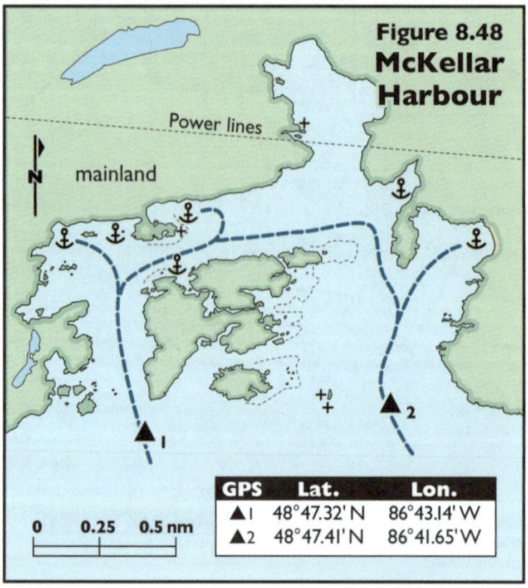

NOT TO BE USED FOR NAVIGATION – SKETCHES APPROXIMATE

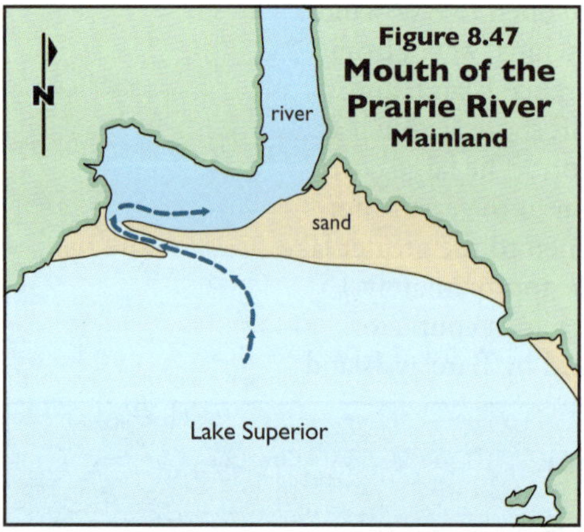

Figure 8.47
Mouth of the Prairie River
Mainland

river
sand
Lake Superior
N

Figure 8.48
McKellar Harbour

Power lines
mainland
N

GPS	Lat.	Lon.
▲1	48°47.32' N	86°43.14' W
▲2	48°47.41' N	86°41.65' W

0   0.25   0.5 nm

close to the sand beach it is possible to get 10 to 15 feet of water. Large power lines span across the large bay to the north. According to the navigation chart, vertical clearance is 110 feet. Although much of this northern bay is too deep for anchoring, it is possible to get suitable depths in the small "bays" on the east and west sides. There are also a couple of anchorages in the NW corner of McKellar where it is possible to work your way in between rock islets and shoals. The most western anchorage lies adjacent to a small sand beach where there is good holding with a clay bottom. To reach the second anchorage to the east you have to tuck in behind a rock shoal. Both of these anchorages are good for northerly winds. The third anchorage to the east along this shoreline doesn't offer as much protection because you can't get very far in due to shoaling water depth. In the bight on the northern end of the main island in the center it is possible to gain protection from southerly winds. However, it does shoal up rather quickly with only 8 feet of water not too far in.

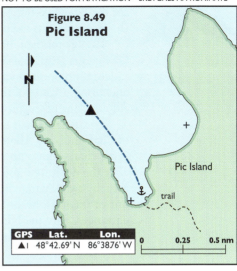

Figure 8.49
Pic Island

Pic Island

trail

GPS	Lat.	Lon.
▲ I	48°42.69' N	86°38.76' W

0   0.25   0.5 nm

In the far northeastern end of Lake Superior lies **Pic Island**, a massive silhouette on the horizon. Its high peaks make it a characteristic landmark for miles around.

It is important to note that there are very strong magnetic variations in the area, with the strongest lying east of Pic. We have seen variations here of as much as 20 degrees. (Also note that to the east of Pic Island there are a number of rocks and small islets.) On the western side of Pic, we have noted variations of as much as 7 degrees. Add to this the fact that this sector of the lake is notorious for fog — especially with southerly winds — and it becomes obvious that this area should be navigated with extreme caution. Here "eyeball" navigation becomes paramount, taking constant bearings off the headlands. One such bearing that is very helpful is Craigs Pit, located on the eastern mainland shore just a few miles south of Marathon. It is quite a conspicuous landmark.

Because the water around Pic Island is quite deep and rocky, anchoring next to this large island is impossible with the exception of the large bay that opens on its northwest side. Within the southern part of this bay it is possible to get 12 feet of water over a sand bottom, next to a lovely sand beach. Anchor just west of the point that bisects the bay. The anchorage is only marginal since it is quite open to the northwest.

Recent years have seen quite a lot of research activity in tagging caribou on the island. There is a trail that leads from the beach up into the high ridges on the island, and on the way it is possible to

see the large live-traps and pens that have been constructed to aid the researchers in the tagging process.

Passage on the north side of Pic through the Thompson Channel is possible if Nicoll Shoal is noted. The large deep indentation on the southern side of Pic Island is inadequate for anchoring because of the extreme depths. Here it is best to tuck into Allouez, one of the most secure all-weather harbors on the lake.

Located one-half mile south, under the large protecting bluffs of Pic Island, lies **Allouez Island** (pronounced "Al-o-WAY"), that on some charts shows up as a mere speck of dust. This island, named after the dedicated Jesuit missionary Father Claude Allouez, is actually two separate half-moon islands forming a natural "lagoon," one of the most beautiful anchorages on the lake. Of the two entrances, only the NE can be navigated successfully by a cruising boat — and then care must be taken to avoid the rather extensive shoal that one sees to starboard when entering. This can easily be avoided by hugging the port shoreline when one enters. The entrance will be tight and because there are some large boulders to port farther in, it is wise to have someone on lookout on the bow. A slight zigzag course will have to be taken, but with care it is possible to carry 10 to 12 feet through the long entrance. The harbor itself is small, and it may be difficult to get adequate scope for the depth, thus necessitating tying off on shore or using a Bahamian moor. It may also be difficult to get a good set with an anchor because of a rock bottom.

Due to its picturesque high surrounding bluffs, Allouez is the spot to take that beautiful photo of your boat at anchor. Allouez is also a herring gull rookery, and by walking out on the outlying rocks, especially in early summer, it is possible to observe the newly hatched gulls. There is a small pulpwood beach here reminiscent of logging days. The rocky point just inside the entrance gets frequent use for shore fires.

Lying a couple of miles NE of Pic Island are a couple of nice anchorages found snugged up to the mainland. The first of these lies in a well-protected **cove just NE of Foster Island**. It is possible to approach the entrance coming from the east or by going to either side of Sullivan Island. However, if the western approach (designated "1" in Fig. 8.51) is used, be sure to favor Foster Island to avoid shoal water off Sullivan Island. The best anchoring area is found by rounding to starboard between a small island and the mainland. There is an exposed rock (1 foot above the surface/water;

NOT TO BE USED FOR NAVIGATION – SKETCH APPROXIMATE

**Figure 8.50
Allouez
Island**

N

| 0 | 400 | 800 ft |

GPS	Lat.	Lon.
▲	48°41.25' N	86°36.73' W

0.34 meters (13.4 inches) above chart datum) and surrounding shoal water off the NW end of this island that need to be skirted before rounding into the anchorage. The area north of Foster Island is very shallow and foul with rock and can be navigated only by dinghy. It is, however, interesting to explore by dinghy and there is good hiking on the rocks on the W and SW shores of Foster Island and on the smaller island that lies off the S/SW end of Foster Island.

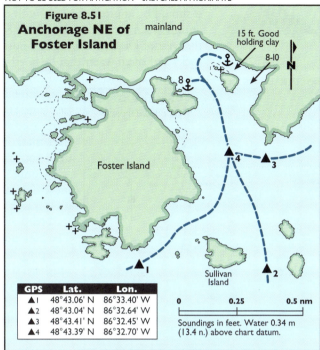

Figure 8.51
Anchorage NE of
Foster Island

GPS	Lat.	Lon.
▲1	48°43.06' N	86°33.40' W
▲2	48°43.04' N	86°32.64' W
▲3	48°43.41' N	86°32.45' W
▲4	48°43.39' N	86°32.70' W

Soundings in feet. Water 0.34 m (13.4 n.) above chart datum.

Heading around the peninsula from Foster Island toward Port Coldwell there is another small anchorage just to the **west of Detention Island**. To enter, there is a small island in the center that can be passed to either side with more water in the southern entrance. In the middle of this small bay it is possible to anchor with 15 to 18 feet of water. Although the anchorage is open to the east, there is some protection for easterly winds from Detention Island that lies a little less than one mile away. However, the anchorage is quite open to the NE.

A more secure anchorage is found 1.5 miles to the north at **Port Coldwell**. Port Coldwell got its start in the early 1880s as a supply depot for the construction of the railroad. Its history mirrors that of so many other villages along this shoreline. After the construction workers left, subsequent growth evolved as a commercial fishing depot that resulted in a general store, chapel, school, boarding house, and summer camp for First Nation people. The closing of the fishery and resulting decline of the village came with the destruction caused by the lamprey in the late 1950s and early 1960s.

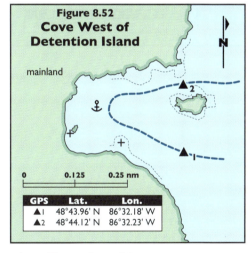

Figure 8.52
Cove West of
Detention Island

GPS	Lat.	Lon.
▲1	48°43.96' N	86°32.18' W
▲2	48°44.12' N	86°32.23' W

In approaching this part of the mainland from offshore, be sure to note the number of rocks and shoal areas that lie in the area. This is also an area of considerable magnetic disturbance, so

it should be approached only with clear visibility. The harbor entrance can be reached by taking either the channel that lies to the west of Detention Island or north of Detention by giving the rocks and shoal water that lie north of the island a wide berth.

Figure 8.53
Port Coldwell

N

high
cliffs

beacon

| 0 | 0.25 | 0.5 nm |

GPS	Lat.	Lon.
▲	48°44.85' N	86°31.94' W

The entrance to Port Coldwell is marked by a white diamond day beacon on the east side. However, it is only readily seen if the approach is from the south since the trees mask it with an easterly approach until you are almost abeam of the marker.

Coming into Port Coldwell is much more dramatic than the actual harbor itself, since there are high bluffs to starboard and steep rock cliffs to port. The best anchoring area is found by rounding to port and snugging up to the southern shore where there are 15 feet to 20 feet of water. These last two anchorages provide nice alternatives to Marathon, that lies just six miles to the east.

Chapter Nine

East Shore: Marathon to Dog Harbour, Ontario

For years, the northern half of Lake Superior's Ontario east shore has been one of the most remote and challenging areas of the lake to cruise. It is remote because its distance from urban and boating centers permits only those with somewhat long time blocks the possibility of reaching its wild shores. It is also remote, because there are few roads here that come down to the lake or even close to it. In the 90-mile stretch from Marathon to Michipicoten Harbour, there is only the road extension that touches in at Heron Bay, the Pic River and at Hattie Cove, a mere 15 miles south of Marathon. The rest of the shoreline is accessible only by boat or, in a few places, by seaplane.

This section of the lake is challenging because it is another area where there are no fuel stops and no amenities attainable. Even at Marathon and Michipicoten Harbour, often little is available, with fuel having to be carried in gas cans or trucked in, and with special parts difficult to obtain. It is also challenging because here there are no protecting island chains, and to get from one anchorage to another, the only course is to travel on the open lake. With this side of the lake receiving much of the weather that moves across from the west, seas of good proportions often develop because of the long westerly fetch. This end of the lake is not without fog either, especially when southerly winds bring in the warm moist air from the Gulf and it flows over Lake Superior's cold waters.

Please Note:
Maps and Charts in this book are not necessarily to scale and are not intended for navigation.

Because the area is so remote, communications become of vital importance. With the repeater from Thunder Bay Coast Guard at Horn near Schreiber, this shoreline is well-covered down to Otter Head. After rounding the bend in the area of Pointe La Canadienne and the Pukaskwa River, better coverage is usually obtained by picking up the Bald Head repeater, which is also controlled by Thunder Bay Coast Guard. However, sometimes in this area from Otter Head to the Pukaskwa, reception is poor because it lies approximately halfway between the two repeaters. Both repeaters dispense continuous weather via international Channel 21 and weather Channel 8. In the northern part of this section of the lake there is a nice alternative for picking up weather information. Weather Radio Canada broadcasts weather information to Pukaskwa Park on weather Channel 1 from a tower located in Marathon. This information is an important addition to this remote area of the lake, covering the area from Terrace Bay to Wawa.

At first glance at the charts, this segment of Lake Superior's shoreline looks rather bold and foreboding. But a closer look, especially at the large scale charts, reveals that rarely does one have to travel a long distance between anchorages, and the anchorages are as plentiful here as on the north shore. There are rivers to enter, coves extending back in off the lake and sometimes even small islands behind which one can tuck to find protection from the greater lake.

The theme is still wilderness cruising with anchorages shared with moose, great blue herons and even an occasional caribou. Sometimes old trappers' cabins can be found, but more often, all that is left of people's intrusions are pulp logs washed up on the beach or remnants of log booms chained to the shores in the backwaters. The area is still as wild as in the early 1800s when Major Delafield and Louis Agassiz led their famous canoe explorations up this side of the lake, enthralled with the grandeur of mountainous terrain and awed by the majestic capes and headlands that form this rugged shoreline.

Historically, this area of the lake has seen little development. Again, this is probably due to its remote location and formidable topography. We do know, however, that this section of the lake was important to prehistoric natives, for it is along these shores that we find the greatest concentration of those curious structures known as the Pukaskwa Pits.

An even more intriguing mystery concerning the early inhabitants in this area are a number of reports in the early 1800s of a major site of old paintings on these shores somewhere between Otter Head and the Pic River. These "paintings," which were reported by Dr. Bigsby in 1823, Major Delafield as "the picture gallery of Lake Superior" in 1823 and the famous naturalist Agassiz in 1849, to date have yet to be found. The paintings are known as lichenoglyphs and differ from the red ochre paintings found at Nipigon and Agawa in that they are made by scraping off the coarse dark leafy lichen known as rock tripe from the rocks. The paintings are now long gone, but it is believed that the site was located in the Picture Island/Pitch Rock Harbour area.

In addition to the early natives, this shoreline was also well used by the voyageurs, since it was an integral part of the 3,000-mile-long fur trade route used in the 18th and 19th

centuries. It is interesting to note that many of the anchorages that we use today—the University River, the White River—were also favorite stopovers for these hardy men as they traveled up the shore. In fact, in the early 1800s the Pic River was the site of a large fur trading fort built by the North West Company that consisted of eight different buildings, some of which were divided into as many as five rooms.

At the turn of the 20th century there was some interest in lumbering, with the Pigeon Timber Company operating in the area of Pulpwood Harbour and the Abitibi Lumbering Company working the areas around the White and Pukaskwa rivers. Like lumbering, commercial fishing also had its day on these shores. It was not uncommon to see fishing tugs working out of Marathon, Michipicoten Harbour and the remote station at Otter Head in the 1970s and 1980s. In recent years, however, they have become a rare breed seen only occasionally on the open waters setting/retrieving nets, traveling from one spot to another.

Today, much of the area is a Canadian National Park, for in 1971 the creation of Pukaskwa National Park was agreed upon

NOT TO BE USED FOR NAVIGATION – SKETCH APPROXIMATE

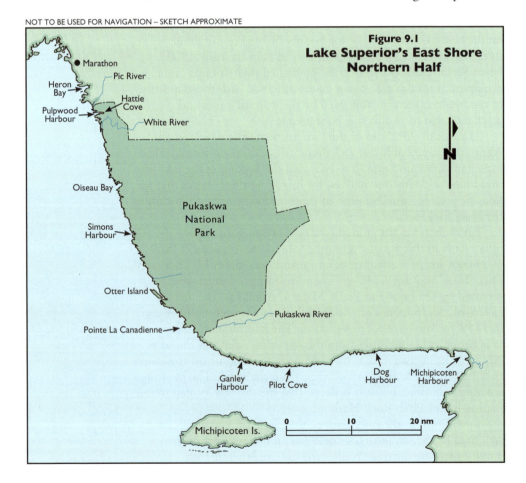

Figure 9.1
Lake Superior's East Shore Northern Half

through a "Memorandum of Intent." The area of the park covers some 725 square miles and extends south from the Pic River to the Pukaskwa River. Although this step is bringing more people to this remote area of Lake Superior, the theme still remains a wilderness refuge accessible only by boaters, canoeists and backpackers. Plans are to keep the area strictly a wilderness park with most of the development restricted to the Hattie Cove area where the road south of Marathon has been extended across the Pic River. Within the cove, a Visitor Information Centre and campground have been established, along with the beginning of a Coastal Hiking Trail that follows the shoreline approximately 47 miles to the North Swallow River. At the Pic River, near the park entrance, there is a launch ramp, which is of interest to those with short time blocks and trailerable boats, since it opens up a whole new section of the lake that is otherwise inaccessible. For further information write: Superintendent, Pukaskwa National Park, P.O. Box 550, Marathon, Ontario P0T 2E0; 807-229-0801.

Harbors and Anchorages

In the NE corner of Lake Superior lies the town of **Marathon** nestled between the surrounding hills and two outreaching peninsulas that form this natural harbor. Originally known as Peninsula Harbour, the town first got its start in the mid-1880s when it served as a supply depot for the construction of the Canadian Pacific Railway. Growth, however, was sparse and Marathon has the unique distinction of being an "overnight boom-town" — twice over.

The first growth spurt came in the mid-1940s when the town was selected as the site for a mill, which was to utilize sawmill residues that were originally classed as waste and burned. These chips, which make up about half of the mill requirement along with pulpwood, are converted into high-grade pulp used in the manufacture of packaging materials, tissue products and fine papers. The mill was originally operated by the Marathon Paper Mill of Rothschild, Wisconsin. In 1967, ownership was changed to American Can of Canada Limited and then in 1983 was bought by the James River Corporation along with a multimillion dollar commitment toward expansion and modernization. It then operated as the Fort James Marathon pulp mill until It closed In 2009.

The second growth spurt occurred in the mid-1980s, with all the trappings of a "California-style" gold rush. Although there had always been rumors of gold

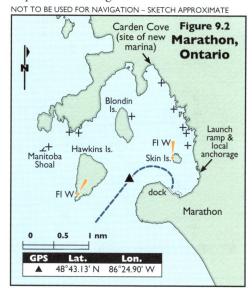

NOT TO BE USED FOR NAVIGATION – SKETCH APPROXIMATE

Carden Cove **Figure 9.2**
(site of new **Marathon,**
marina) **Ontario**

N

Blondin Is.

Launch ramp & local anchorage

Manitoba Shoal

Hawkins Is.

Fl W

Skin Is.

Fl W

dock

Marathon

0   0.5   1 nm

GPS	Lat.	Lon.
▲	48°43.13' N	86°24.90' W

in the area, it wasn't until the last quarter of the 20th century that serious exploration began. An unbelievably rich deposit (the largest in North America) was discovered at Hemlo, approximately 25 miles east of Marathon. Once again, the town mushroomed overnight as surveyors, construction workers and engineers descended on the area. There were two mines extracting the gold: the Williams Mine and the David Bell Mine, both of which were jointly owned and operated by Teck Cominco and Barrick Gold Corporation. The David Bell was scheduled to close in 2009 and the Williams Mine in 2011.

Today Marathon boasts of a population of approximately 4,000, complete with several motels, restaurants, grocery stores, department stores and two shopping malls. In the 1990's a Recreational Complex boasting an arena for roller and ice skating, a theater and a large swimming pool with a sauna and whirlpool was built. At the time of this writing (5th edition), there are plans for building a new Family Living Center on the waterfront.

Because of the distinctive landmarks in the area, Marathon is quite easy to locate. In particular, there is Craigs Pit, a large white cliff area on the shoreline that lies approximately 2.5 miles SE of the large domed peninsula, Peninsula Hill, that forms the southern side of the harbor. Hawkins Island is another identifying landmark. Approach to Marathon is usually between this island and the peninsula.

Add launch ramp text

Because the harbor was primarily committed to the industry of the mill, there are few facilities available to recreational boaters. Since the closing of the mill, the long commercial dock (old coal dock) found in the SW part of the harbor is no longer available to tie up to. There are, however. a number of docks and two launch ramps (see Figure 9.3) on the mainland a little less than 1/2 nm SE of Skin Island. Built in 2023, the design and wood of these docks and connecting boardwalk are quite beautiful. However, they are open to strong westerly winds and there are plans for putting in a breakwater to secure this area from these winds.

Although it is a bit of a walk (one mile) into town: groceries, ice, laundry, hardware store, post office, a mall, Canadian Tire (propane and some boat parts), library (internet access) and a number of restaurants are all available. Gas and diesel can be obtained from gas stations and then brought to the boat via taxi (807-229-1009). If you come without gerry cans, they can be purchased at Canadian Tire. it is also

NOT TO BE USED FOR NAVIGATION – SKETCH APPROXIMATE

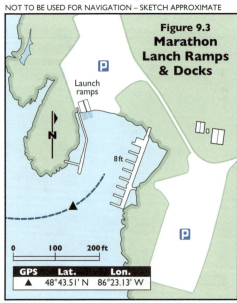

Figure 9.3
Marathon Lanch Ramps & Docks

GPS	Lat.	Lon.
▲	48°43.51' N	86°23.13' W

important to note that it is possible to get customs clearance here. Usually this is accomplished by contacting the local law enforcement officials.

There are a couple of alternatives to tying up at the Marathon docks. Another alternative would be to anchor two miles to the north in **Carden Cove.** It is, however, quite open to southerly winds and even a longer trek around the harbor into town. It is of special interest to boaters that in the late 1990s plans were under way to construct a breakwater across the southern end of this cove with a marina inside, complete with fueling facilities, *pending funding*. We continue to hear plans for some kind of marine facilities along with the pursuance of funding.

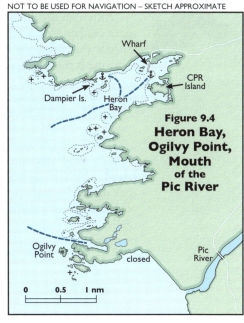

Figure 9.4
Heron Bay,
Ogilvy Point,
Mouth
of the
Pic River

Other alternative anchorages would be Port Coldwell, six miles to the NW, and Allouez Island, nine miles to the SW (see end of Chapter 8). Note that when navigating in this area between Marathon and Pic Island, there are not only a number of shoals and rocks, but the area is also known for considerable magnetic disturbance.

Lying six miles SW of Marathon there is another alternative at **Heron Bay**, which is easily identified by large gray silos of a cement plant at the far end. The anchorage is somewhat marginal because the mouth of the bay is very large and is quite open to westerly winds. The bay also has a number of rocks and shoal areas along its northern half and adjacent to the southern side of the mouth, which must be given wide berth. These can be avoided by entering the bay roughly in the middle until Keating Rock is approached, which is marked with a green buoy. Northeast of Keating Rock there is a large wharf located on the northern side of the bay. To approach the dock there are two more green buoys marking shoal areas. Pass with all buoys kept to port when approaching the dock.

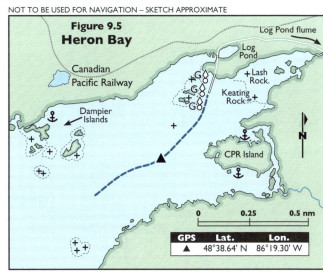

Figure 9.5
Heron Bay

GPS	Lat.	Lon.
▲	48°38.64' N	86°19.30' W

Although the dock is still used commercially, there usually is space available for transient boats. However, there is a large gated fence at the end of the dock that prevents shore access unless someone is there to open the gate. There is an alternative around the corner to the west of the Log Pond where there are a couple of old docks put in by locals. The depth at the docks is approximately 5 feet and they are open to westerly winds. The road to Marathon, approximately 10 miles, comes close to the lake at this point.

There are a couple of alternative anchorages in Heron Bay. If westerly winds develop, it is possible to tuck in behind **Dampier Island**. The holding here, however, is marginal because of a lot of rock on the bottom. Across the bay to the east, **CPR Island** offers a couple of better anchorages. It is possible to tuck in to the south of the island for protection from northerly winds. However, because of shoaling you can't go very far in and this anchorage is really open to the west. A better anchorage is on the north side of CPR Island where you can go much farther in to anchor in 15 feet and get protection for all but NW winds. Those with shallow draft boats can continue around the peninsula on the NE end of the island for complete protection. (See Fig. 9.6.)

Another anchorage lies two miles south of Heron Bay at **Ogilvy Point**. Here there is a long indentation behind the point that gives protection for all but the strongest NW winds. See Fig. 9.7, GPS #1, #2. Ogilvy Point is easily identified because it consists of a number of low rounded domes, with the farthest one out being longer than the others, extending into the lake with a long slope toward the point. By staying midchannel when entering, there are no obstructions, and it is possible to go about three-quarters of the way in before reaching shoal water. There are good depths for anchoring (10 feet) over a mud bottom, but it is wise to use a trip line on your anchor here, for the bottom is also foul with deadheads and debris from logging. The far SE end is not open as it shows on the charts, and the interesting little pond to the NE is clogged with pulpwood.

NOT TO BE USED FOR NAVIGATION – SKETCH APPROXIMATE

Figure 9.6
**CPR Island,
Heron Bay**

N

CPR Island

⚓ 15

⚓ 18

▲ 2

▲ 1

0   0.125   0.25 nm

Soundings in feet. Water 0.19 m
(7.5 in.) above chart datum.

GPS	Lat.	Lon.
▲1	48°38.10' N	86°18.95' W
▲2	48°38.79' N	86°18.77' W

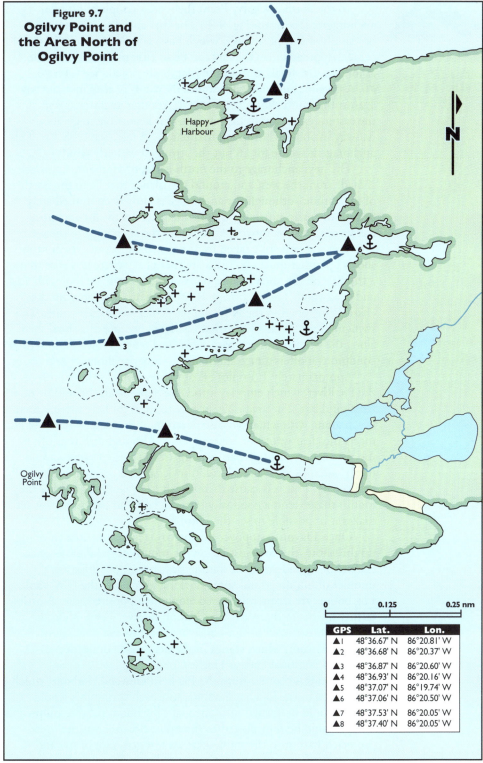

Figure 9.7
Ogilvy Point and the Area North of Ogilvy Point

Happy Harbour

Ogilvy Point

| 0 | 0.125 | 0.25 nm |

GPS	Lat.	Lon.
▲1	48°36.67' N	86°20.81' W
▲2	48°36.68' N	86°20.37' W
▲3	48°36.87' N	86°20.60' W
▲4	48°36.93' N	86°20.16' W
▲5	48°37.07' N	86°19.74' W
▲6	48°37.06' N	86°20.50' W
▲7	48°37.53' N	86°20.05' W
▲8	48°37.40' N	86°20.05' W

To the **north of Ogilvy Point** there are a couple additional anchorages. (See again Fig. 9.7.) The first anchorage is in a large bay south of Prospect Cove, which has a couple of islands in the center. Approach into the bay can be to either side of these islands as long as the shoals around the islands are noted. See GPS #3 #6. A possible anchorage for southerly winds is deep into the bay against the south shore. See GPS #4. Another anchorage is in the eastern extension of the bay where it is possible to go about halfway in and anchor in approximately 15 feet. See GPS # 5. This anchorage is secure for all but the strongest westerly winds.

The next anchorage to the north is **Happy Harbour.** Approach is made from the west and around the islands that lie to the north of the harbor. Although the anchorage is fairly deep immediately behind the main northerly island, adequate depths for anchoring can be obtained by moving farther into the anchorage to the west. However, care must be taken to not go too far in since the bottom shoals up rather quickly. This is another place where it is wise to use a trip line on the anchor since parts of the bottom are foul with slash and deadwood. The anchorage is not as secure as it looks on the chart, being open to the NW and particularly to NE/E winds. The swinging room is also somewhat restricted because of a shoal shelf along the whole southern part of the anchorage. However, in settled conditions it offers a nice alternative to other anchorages in the area.

Approximately 1.5 miles SE of Ogilvy Point is the mouth of the **Pic River**, which empties into Lake Superior in the middle of a large sand bay. The area is again easy to spot, for here there is a sand beach along with a marked discoloration of the water where the Pic meets the clear waters of Lake Superior. Although fish tugs often use the entrance and go part way upstream, this entrance should not be attempted without local knowledge and reasonably shoal draft boats. This is because there are shifting sandbars outside the mouth that extend a good way into the lake and the muddy water makes it impossible to see the bottom.

Once a favorite stopover for the voyageurs and those traveling up this shore, this area just inside the mouth of the Pic was once the site of a good-sized fur trading post/fort. Now there are a number of buildings and some docking area along the NW bank. Log booms are frequently stored along the opposite shore. A little farther upstream there is a First Nation reserve. There is also a recently constructed bridge constructed across the river about a mile upstream, which brings in the only road connection to Pukaskwa National Park at Hattie Cove.

Around the corner from the Pic lies **Pulpwood Harbour**, which was named in the logging days, because each spring this whole harbor would be turned into one giant log boom to store pulpwood until it could be transported to the mills. Because it is the most protected harbor in the immediate area, it gets a lot of use and is a favorite for those who cruise these shores. It is also the first anchorage you come to within the jurisdiction of Pukaskwa National Park.

In approaching the harbor from the north or west, it is important to note the "entrance island" that stands farthest out from shore and the rock islets and shoal water that lie to the S and SE of it. Passage can be to either side of the island as long as this shoal water is skirted. The opening to Pulpwood Harbour is on a bearing of approximately 100 degrees from the entrance island. In approaching from the south, the water is deep and clear, and the entrance is found by passing the large peninsula that forms the northern side of Playter Harbour and then rounding to the north of the islands that lie north

NOT TO BE USED FOR NAVIGATION – SKETCH APPROXIMATE

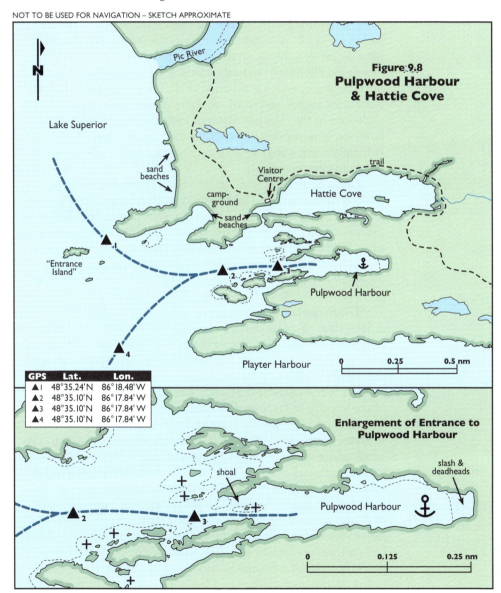

Figure 9.8
Pulpwood Harbour & Hattie Cove

Pic River

Lake Superior

sand beaches

camp-ground

Visitor Centre

trail

Hattie Cove

sand beaches

"Entrance Island"

Pulpwood Harbour

Playter Harbour

GPS	Lat.	Lon.
▲1	48°35.24'N	86°18.48'W
▲2	48°35.10'N	86°17.84'W
▲3	48°35.10'N	86°17.84'W
▲4	48°35.10'N	86°17.84'W

0   0.25   0.5 nm

Enlargement of Entrance to Pulpwood Harbour

shoal

slash & deadheads

Pulpwood Harbour

0   0.125   0.25 nm

of this peninsula. Note: do not hug these islands too closely since there are some rocks and shoal water adjacent to them.

The first time through the narrow entrance to Pulpwood may appear impossible, but by taking a midchannel course between the large island to starboard and the long shoal and rock islet to port, it is possible to carry 30 feet of water through this constricted passage. Here it is wise to have a bow lookout and note that there is shoal water extending out from each end of the rocky shoal and the starboard island. (See enlargement for Fig. 9.8.)

Once inside the harbor, there is good anchorage throughout, with better depths in the eastern end. There is some slash lying on the bottom, especially at the far end, so this is another anchorage where a trip line on the anchor may be desirable. Although the harbor looks like it is open to the west, the outlying rocks and islets do much to break up any seas coming in off the lake. For more protection from westerly winds, it is possible to tuck behind the long island, which was passed in the narrow entrance and set out a stern anchor and tie off on shore. There is also an alternative anchorage in the inlet just south of Hattie Cove. This anchorage, however, is more open to westerly winds and, because of constricted swinging room, it may be necessary to use a bow and stern anchor or a Bahamian moor.

Points of interest: from time-to-time log-booms are seen chained to this harbor. These remind us of the days when logging was at its peak, and the small pulp logs were hauled corralled inside the booms from one part of the lake to another. Often the booms were identified with names carved into their sides such as Max or Frank. Many of these booms were large enough to support the weight of two or three men, measuring 30 inches in diameter or greater.

The Pulpwood Harbour area is interesting to explore by dinghy since there are many little hidden coves here and sometimes even sand beaches. On some of the small ridges, especially on the northern side of Pulpwood Harbour, there are blueberries growing in the wild.

It is hard to believe that just a short dinghy ride to the north of the serenity of Pulpwood Harbour lies a 67-site semiserviced campground (29 electrical sites) and contemporary Visitor Centre in **Hattie Cove**. Note: motorized vessels are allowed only up to the beach adjacent to the Visitor Centre and not in the rest of the cove.

Since Pukaskwa National Park had its official opening in July 1983, it has been the Hattie Cove area that has seen most of the park development. The campground is especially beautiful, with each unit tastefully separated from the others by trees and shrubs, along with centrally located showers and rest rooms. At the Visitor Centre there are attractive and informative displays depicting the area's historical and natural history. Evening programs on pertinent topics relating to park flora and fauna are also given in the center.

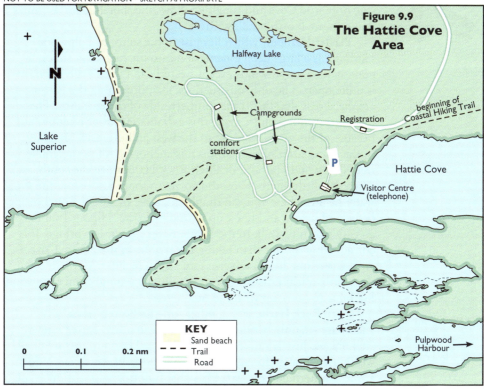

Figure 9.9
The Hattie Cove Area

Halfway Lake

Lake Superior

Campgrounds

Registration

beginning of Coastal Hiking Trail

comfort stations

P

Hattie Cove

Visitor Centre (telephone)

KEY
Sand beach
Trail
Road

0   0.1   0.2 nm

Pulpwood Harbour

Another interest for boaters is that there is a public telephone located on the water side of the center.

One of the best features of park development in the area is the number of self-guiding nature trails that Parks Canada has put in the area. Some of these involve bridges and intricate boardwalks that take you out on rock ledges or through areas of fragile vegetation. Others go down to the three beaches in the area. An especially interesting trail circumnavigates Halfway Lake with a number of spectacular overlooks of the lake and beyond to greater Lake Superior. The Coastal Hiking Trail also begins on the north

Figure 9.10
Playter Harbour

high bluffs

dinghy harbor

Coastal Hiking Trail

10 ft.

0   0.25   0.5 nm

GPS	Lat.	Lon.
▲	48°34.63' N	86°17.60' W

N

side of Hattie Cove and roughly follows the shoreline for 47 miles down to the North Swallow River.

Playter Harbour, which lies just to the south of Pulpwood Harbour, is a large deep indentation into the mainland that is a good harbor for all winds except westerly and in this direction, it is quite open. The only obstructions in approaching the harbor are the shoals that lie off the southern side of the entrance. The high surrounding bluffs make this a dramatic harbor to enter, but because of the open exposure to the west and extensive shoaling in the last quarter of the harbor, this anchorage is less preferable than Pulpwood Harbour or Pitch Rock Harbour to the south. There is a little "harbor" on the northern shore just before the shoal water begins where you can dinghy in, leave the dinghy on a nice little sand beach, and hook up with the Coastal Hiking Trail for an easy two-mile walk to the White River suspension bridge. It is considerably shorter than taking the trail from the Hattie Cove area, where one has to traverse some steep inclines. With an eye to the weather, it is possible to run the dinghy around from Pulpwood Harbour to hook up with the trail here.

Pitch Rock Harbour is another "off-the-beaten-track" anchorage, mainly because it lies so close to other, better-known anchorages. Just 1.5 miles south of Playter Harbour, this small all-weather anchorage for all but the strongest NW winds lies hidden at the southern end of a large bay that is dotted with a number of islands and smaller islets. This is another anchorage that remains hidden until you are almost upon it. The best approach is made from straight west, and here it is important to take bearings off the islands to make sure of one's position. In particular, note the shoal water surrounding the "entrance rock", which one leaves to port when coming through the entrance. By staying midchannel, between this rock shoal and the island to starboard, there is no difficulty in entering this secluded harbor. Rounding up to starboard brings one into one of the prettiest, little-known harbors on the east shore. There is good anchoring over a clear sand bottom in 10 feet to 15 feet of water. There is a lovely sand beach to explore along with the remnants of an old cabin from the days of beachcombing for stray pulpwood. The rest of the large bay to the north is also very interesting to explore by dinghy.

A high point for anyone who cruises Lake Superior's east shore has to be a trip into the **White River** and subsequently to the rapids and waterfalls 2.5 miles upstream. The entrance is tricky to find

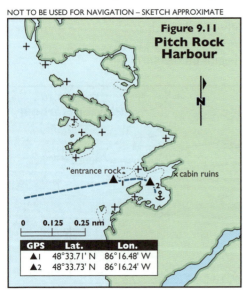

NOT TO BE USED FOR NAVIGATION – SKETCH APPROXIMATE

Figure 9.11
Pitch Rock Harbour

N

"entrance rock"

✕ cabin ruins

0   0.125   0.25 nm

GPS	Lat.	Lon.
▲1	48°33.71' N	86°16.48' W
▲2	48°33.73' N	86°16.24' W

and a challenge to navigate at the river's mouth with the venturi effect of fast moving currents in narrow spots and underwater rock shoals lurking in the murky waters near the entrance. Yet, with care, the entrance can be safely negotiated by deep-draft boats.

The first challenge is to just find the river entrance since it blends in well with the bold landscape of the rocky shoreline. Even

The view just before making the turn to port into the White River. DAHL

when standing on top of GPS numbers it's hard to believe you are there and you feel like you are heading right into shore. It helps in identifying the opening to this river to note that the west bank has a decidedly red color, whereas the east side of the entrance is in sharp contrast, being gray, due to a stone-cobbled beach.

The entrance is approximately 100 feet wide at its narrowest width and should not be attempted if there is any sea running as the waves will stack up against the outgoing current. A rather sizable rock shoal was discovered in the middle of the entrance in the late 1980s, so the preferred approach is to favor the reddish (port) side of the entrance. This is done by coming in well to the west of the river entrance until you are about 75 feet from the reddish shoreline and following it around, keeping 50 feet to 75 feet off the shoreline with depths of 15 feet to 20 feet. As soon as you round the point, it is important to head straight toward the gray cobbled beach to avoid more rocks to port. Continue to hug the starboard shoreline just after the entrance, since there is another rock to port. The least depth in the narrowest width is approximately 9 feet.

NOT TO BE USED FOR NAVIGATION – SKETCH APPROXIMATE

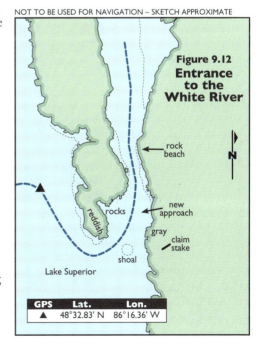

Figure 9.12
Entrance to the White River

Once inside the White, the river widens and there is a half mile or so of water where it is possible to anchor. The water is usually warm, and you can dive Bahamas-style right off your boat, something that is rarely done in the cold frigid waters of Lake Superior. The fishing is also excellent — pickerel (walleye pike to Americans) is abundant. You can take the dinghy a couple of miles up to The

Pool that lies at the base of the Chigamiwinigum Rapids/Falls and then take a mile hike up to a unique suspension bridge (part of the Coastal Hiking Trail), which spans a dramatic 200-foot gorge of the rapids.

Caution

It is important to take discretionary caution in taking any boat up the White River. Because of tight turns and a number of underwater rock shoals, we do not advise taking deep-draft boats (greater than 5-foot draft) or boats longer than 30 feet up the river. Nor is it prudent to take a large boat upstream when there is a strong current running, for it becomes difficult to steer and it is easy to be taken broadside downstream. A better choice would be to anchor in the large open area before "The Narrows" and take a dinghy up. The following directions are given for those with shoal draft boats that are less than 30 feet.

In heading upstream there are three known trouble spots that are encountered soon after leaving the initial anchoring area. Trouble spot No. 1 is found just after The Narrows and is easily identified by a sheer rock cliff to starboard and a small rock islet to port when heading upstream. The starboard shoal, which extends out from the rock cliff, comes almost out to the middle of the river. Thus, it would seem prudent to favor the small rock islet to port. However, there is also a shoal around the rock islet that extends toward the middle of the channel, especially after passing the rock islet. It is possible to avoid both shoals and maintain 9 feet to 10 feet of water by first favoring the small islet until abeam of it and then slowly edge back into midstream.

Trouble Spot No. 2 is a little farther upstream and well in sight of the first. It is identified by another small rock islet to port when heading upstream. The shoal extends from the rock islet well into the middle of the river, so you have to really hug the starboard shore (going upstream) to get around it — approximately 12 feet from the starboard

NOT TO BE USED FOR NAVIGATION – SKETCH APPROXIMATE

Figure 9.13
White River

9 feet

In 1988 red plastic marker in overhanging tree at 50 ft. before shoal but absent in subsequent years.

❸

10 feet

underwater ledge

❷

Hold 10-12 ft. from rock wall. Can carry 9 ft. in low water year.

rock cliff

The Narrows

NOTE: Soundings were taken in 1988 when water was 2 feet below normal.

❶

to river entrance

❹ numbers denote "trouble spots" described in text.

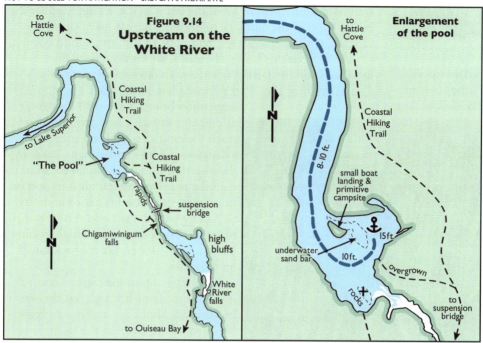

Figure 9.14
Upstream on the White River

Enlargement of the pool

side. Unfortunately, there is another smaller shoal coming out from the starboard side just as you clear the first shoal, so the trick is to kind of snake around them.

Trouble Spot No. 3 is really wicked because it is quite large and lies well enough below the water to be difficult to be seen, yet it is shallow enough to give boats drawing more than 5 feet problems. (On some charts the river is called the White Mud River, and the coffee color water is so bad that there is a saying of those who traverse the White: "When you see it, you're on it.") This shoal is also bad because there are no distinguishing landmarks in this section of the river to identify it as with the other two spots. The shoal is located approximately one-third of a mile upstream from No. 2 and is long and narrow, lying in most of the port half of the river when heading upstream. By keeping to the starboard half of the river it is possible to maintain 9 feet of water. As far as we know the rest of the river is deep and clear with 15 feet to 30 feet of water by maintaining a midchannel course until just before reaching The Pool, where there are a couple of 8-foot readings that appear to be over sand. Note: these Trouble Spots were discovered in low-water years. In average to high runoff from rain, the river water level changes dramatically and these areas are of less concern.

Rounding the bend and coming up on that last stretch approaching The Pool can be a little unnerving. For straight ahead is the rushing torrent of the lower rapids of the White. The current really isn't as bad as one would expect. In fact, you have to head straight for the rapids, turning just at the last minute to hug the

The suspension bridge over the Willow River. DAHL

starboard shore *closely* to avoid the last obstacle, a large sandbar that blocks most of the entrance to the anchorage. Once behind the sandbar, you can anchor in tranquility 15 feet over a mud bottom.

Aside from this being a beautiful anchorage, the main attraction still lies farther upstream. In developing part of the Coastal Hiking Trail, Parks Canada has constructed a unique suspension bridge over a 200-foot gorge of dramatic rapids. There are two ways to reach the rapids via trails on either side, a distance of a little more than a mile. If the eastern trail is used, which connects with the main hiking trail, it is important to mark it, since it is little used and easy to pass by on the way back. A nice way to make the trip is to use two dinghies and go up on one side and come back down on the other.

Walking out on the suspension bridge is not for the faint-hearted. But the view is breathtaking, both up- and downstream. When you look down at this deep gorge, it is exciting to imagine the river swollen with spring runoff carrying thousands of logs downstream, pitching and being thrown about like so many match sticks. Until 1960, this river was used by the Abitibi Lumbering Company to move logs from its inland cut near White Lake to Lake Superior. Once the logs reached the mouth of the White, a waiting raft crew would assemble them within the large booms and then tow them all the way down the shore to Sault Ste. Marie.

By following the trail farther upstream, one comes upon even larger falls at the base of a massive, towering cliff wall. Pieces of pulpwood jammed in between the rocks remind us of the powers of this wild river, and again we can imagine the logs literally flying over these magnificent falls. It is here, beneath the spray of the falls with torrents of water rushing to the side and the gargantuan cliffs overhead, that we experience this northern wilderness at its best.

Approximately three miles south of the White River, there is another river that empties into Lake Superior's waters,

NOT TO BE USED FOR NAVIGATION – SKETCH APPROXIMATE

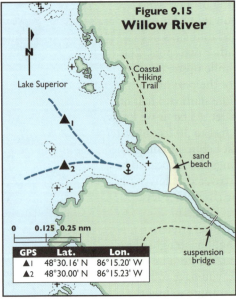

Figure 9.15
Willow River

GPS	Lat.	Lon.
▲1	48°30.16' N	86°15.20' W
▲2	48°30.00' N	86°15.23' W

the **Willow River**. Although this river is not navigable by deep-draft boats, it is possible to anchor in the large bay that forms at its mouth. To pass into this bay, a large rock shoal that guards its entrance needs to be skirted. Because of shoaling off the river, it is possible to go only about halfway into the bay. Here you can anchor in 8 feet to 10 feet of water over a sand bottom with protection for all but W to NW winds to which the harbor is very open. The large sand beach, which is helpful in identifying the harbor from offshore, is interesting to explore along with the river. This beach area is a favorite camping spot for backpackers and those who travel these shores by canoe.

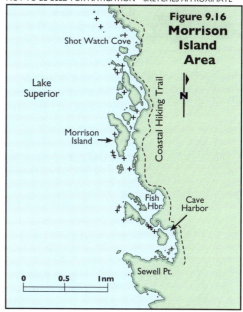

Figure 9.16
Morrison Island Area

A few miles south of the Willow River there is a small stretch of the shore where there are a number of islands lying just offshore, a rare occurrence in this section of the lake. Identified by the largest island, Morrison Island, which lies approximately in the center of the group, it is possible to tuck in behind some of these islands and find anchorages with some protection from the greater lake.

The first of these anchorages is a little-used harbor that is found about one mile north of Morrison Island in **Shot Watch Cove**. A trapper used to have a line shack here, and stories tell of an old pocket watch that was found with a bullet hole in it, hence the name. The anchorage is marginal because it is quite open to NW winds, however by passing between the two small islands that stand offshore

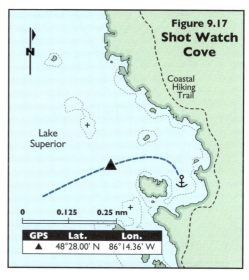

Figure 9.17
Shot Watch Cove

GPS	Lat.	Lon.
▲	48°28.00' N	86°14.36' W

and then rounding to starboard, it is possible to anchor in 8 feet to 10 feet of water and receive protection for all other winds. This is one of the areas where the Coastal Hiking Trail closely follows the beach.

Continuing south, the long channel behind the next long island is navigable only by shoal draft boats. Each end of this passage is quite rock-strewn, which also makes navigation difficult. This long island should not be confused with the next larger island, Morrison, behind which there are two good anchorages, one at each end.

Of the two anchorages behind **Morrison Island**, the northern one offers more protection. The north end of Morrison may be

difficult to spot since it blends in well with adjacent islands, some of which are similar in appearance. To help identify Morrison there is a bare rock island lying to the north of it that looks something like a whale heading south, complete with a darkened spot for an "eye." (See Fig. 9.19.)

This anchorage is found by coming down the NE side of Morrison well into midchannel to avoid some rocky water close into shore. Another island will be passed to port, and just south of this island is a smaller island. To enter the anchorage, round up to port (NE) midchannel between the smaller island and the rock/shoal water to starboard, favoring the rock shoal. Through this narrow passage the least depths will be approximately 9 feet and you will be able to see the bottom. This whole area is quite shallow with anchoring in 8 feet to 15 feet over a sand bottom. Most people seem to anchor tucked way in at anchor symbol #1. However, with W or NW winds, this anchorage can become rolly with waves marching in between the slot. A more protected anchorage for NW winds is at anchor symbol #2. (See Fig. 9.18.)

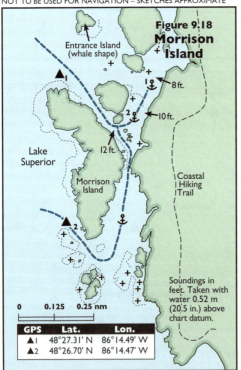

Figure 9.18
Morrison Island

Entrance Island (whale shape)

8 ft.

10 ft.

Lake Superior

12 ft.

Morrison Island

Coastal Hiking Trail

Soundings in feet. Taken with water 0.52 m (20.5 in.) above chart datum.

| 0 | 0.125 | 0.25 nm |

GPS	Lat.	Lon.
▲1	48°27.31' N	86°14.49' W
▲2	48°26.70' N	86°14.47' W

This area is interesting to explore, with the high bluffs on the long island to the north offering a dramatic view of the anchorage. The Coastal Hiking Trail comes down to the mainland beach across from this island, and by following the trail south for a quarter mile you will come upon clearings that display hundreds of orchids growing beautifully in the wild.

With care, boats can pass behind Morrison to the anchorage at the southern end. But the water here is rock-strewn, and passage should only be attempted with a bow lookout and the sun high at one's back. Another approach is to come into this anchorage from the south between the southern end of Morrison and the rock islets that lie south of it. Because of this extensive shoal area, this entrance should not be attempted when there is any sea running or without good visibility. Rounding to the north, there are good depths for anchoring (20 feet) just before the narrows between Morrison and the mainland. There is protection here for all but

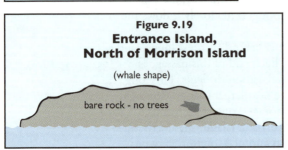

Figure 9.19
Entrance Island, North of Morrison Island

(whale shape)

bare rock - no trees

southerly winds, to which the anchorage is quite open.

For more protection from southerly winds, there is a beautiful all-weather harbor that lies approximately three-quarters of a mile SE of Morrison Island, **Fish Harbour**. The harbor is easily found by using Morrison Island as a reference point, and just as easily entered, as long as the shoal water south of Morrison is given wide berth. The preferred entrance is to come in from the north with a number of islands passed to starboard and then the harbor will open up to the south. The anchorage is found by rounding to the SW and tucking in behind these islands, anchoring in 15 to 20 feet over a sand bottom. It is also possible to enter the anchorage from the SW/W by passing between the large island to port and the all-rock islet to starboard. As tight as it may seem, it is possible to carry at least 15 feet through this entrance (see Fig. 9.20). However, this entrance should only be used with no seas running and when the sun is high at your back so you can see the adjacent shoal water.

This is another area that is interesting to explore. On the mainland there is a nice sand beach that hooks up with the Coastal Hiking Trail. You can hike north toward Playter Harbour or south to Oiseau Bay. There is an old cave, which can only be reached from the water, SE of the anchorage. The area SE of this cave is aptly called **Cave Harbour**. Because this area is rock-strewn and gets shallow behind the island in the bay, at best this is an anchorage for only shoal draft boats.

A scant mile SE of Sewell Point there is a deep indentation into the mainland that offers protection for all but the strongest NW winds, **Gids Harbour**. This secure anchorage is rarely used by visiting boaters, probably because it is so close to the better-known Oiseau Bay. The anchorage is easily entered by passing to the north of the two small islands that stand offshore. It is possible to tuck way back in, anchoring in approximately 10 feet to 20 feet of water.

Located two miles south of Sewell Point is the largest bay in this area, **Oiseau Bay**. "Oiseau" in French means "bird," and the

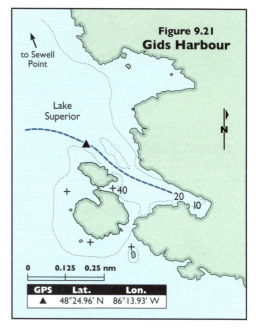

Figure 9.20
Fish Harbour,
Cave Harbour

GPS	Lat.	Lon.
▲₁	48°26.40' N	86°14.12' W
▲₂	48°25.95' N	86°13.87' W

Figure 9.21
Gids Harbour

GPS	Lat.	Lon.
▲	48°24.96' N	86°13.93' W

area is aptly named, for many of the islets here are well-known as rookeries for different species. The bay is another of those areas on this shoreline that saw extensive logging activity, and it is difficult to imagine, when we explore its wild shores, that there once was a logging camp here complete with a sawmill.

Figure 9.22
Oiseau Bay Area

new shoreline
old course
stream diverted to new course
Oiseau Bay
Coastal Hiking Trail
Lake Superior
Dampier Cove
Nichol's Cove

0   0.25   0.5 nm

GPS	Lat.	Lon.
▲	48°23.69' N	86°12.61' W

▲ Campsites

Although the bay is moderately studded with rocks and shoals, it and the immediate area offer a number of interesting anchorages. The first of these is found in the northern end of the bay. To enter the bay, it is necessary to pass between the mainland (to port) and several small islands (to starboard), some of which are heron rookeries. Note the shoal water that lies off the mainland point and some more shoal water off the islands, necessitating a midchannel course. Due to flash flooding and a tremendous spring runoff in 1986 from the little stream that used to enter the bay, this segment of the shoreline was changed considerably resulting in the sand beach that was literally moved quite a way out into the bay. (The destruction was so complete that the mouth of the small stream that was responsible for the torrents of water and debris is completely closed, and the stream now enters the main part of Oiseau Bay.) For years after, it was impossible to anchor very close to the beach because the bay had become quite shallow and strewn with huge trees and debris. Then in the years following, the lake cleaned out the area and it is once again possible to go in close to the "new" beach and anchor in 10 feet to12 feet of water over a sand-rippled bottom. Note that this anchorage is somewhat open to the west and in strong westerly blows, and even with southerly winds, a most uncomfortable swell occurs. If this happens, it may be best to move to a more secure anchorage.

The beach is still an interesting place to explore and a nice place to have a shore fire. It is important to note, however, that up from the beach among the sedge grasses there is a rare form of beach thistle that is under study by Parks Canada. It is requested that people stay away from this area and do not disturb or tramp on these rare plants. Along the main sand beach of Oiseau Bay, there are a couple of nice campsites for canoeists and backpackers using the Coastal Hiking Trail.

Soundings in feet.

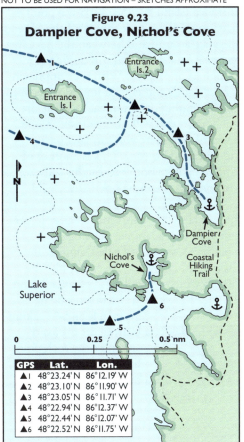

Figure 9.23
Dampier Cove, Nichol's Cove

GPS	Lat.	Lon.
▲1	48°23.24'N	86°12.19'W
▲2	48°23.10'N	86°11.90'W
▲3	48°23.05'N	86°11.71'W
▲4	48°22.94'N	86°12.37'W
▲5	48°22.44'N	86°12.07'W
▲6	48°22.52'N	86°11.75'W

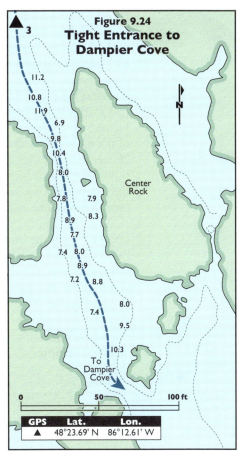

Figure 9.24
Tight Entrance to Dampier Cove

GPS	Lat.	Lon.
▲	48°23.69'N	86°12.61'W

Dampier Cove, which is located on the southern side of Oiseau Bay, has to be the most secure anchorage in the area, if not this whole section of the lake. However, to reach this "hurricane hole" there are a number of outlying rocks and shoal areas that need to be "danced" around. Thus, this is another anchorage that should not be attempted with running seas or without the sun high. Note: Polaroid glasses are a big help on this one, since it is difficult to line up islets and rock shoals here.

There are two different ways to approach Dampier Cove. The first, which comes in from the north and passes on the north side of Entrance Island #1, is probably the most straightforward. Here the shoal areas are well-marked by exposed rock islets and, by following a rough SE course (see Fig. 9.23, GPS waypoints 1, 2 & 3), you can enter the area with a minimum of 20 feet to 25 feet of water. Then steer S-SE down the slot through a narrow channel between two islands. Midway, there is again a rock shoal and, as impossible as it may seem, pass with it to port and you should be able to clear through with 8 feet of water. See Figure 9.24. Continue on the same track, keeping the next two islets to port, to enter the anchorage. The second approach is from the south and

enters the area south of Entrance Island #1. (See GPS waypoint 4.) With this approach you need to skirt the rock shoals off the SE end of the Entrance Island and snake around and between the next two rock islets. (See GPS waypoint 2.) Clearly, with this approach it is important to have the sun high at one's back. With each approach just after waypoint 3, you head south and enter a long slot between two islands with shoal water extending out from each. See again Figure 9.24. Within the anchorage, you will find yourself in one of the most secure anchorages of all, where you can anchor in 20 feet of water over a sand and mud bottom. This is another of those areas that is interesting to explore both via dinghy and on the Coastal Hiking Trail. In some of the more open areas, wild blueberries can be found.

There is another anchorage close by that is much easier to get into but is not the hurricane hole that Dampier is being open to the NW. It doesn't have a name, so we call it **Little Dampier**. It is found to the N/NE of its parent, Dampier Cove, and like the parent it has an entrance island which we will call Entrance Island #2, see Figure 9.23 & 9.25. Head E/SE over the north side of

NOT TO BE USED FOR NAVIGATION – SKETCH APPROXIMATE

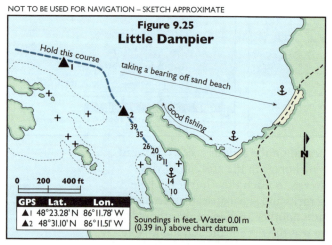

Entrance Island #2 taking a bearing off the sand beach past the rock point which is easy to spot and a distinctive landmark in the area. The trick is to not turn until you are close to the rock point because there is a shoal extending east of Entrance Island #2. When Little Dampier has opened up, you can turn SE and head down into the anchorage. You can anchor along the sand beach, but it has much less protection than Little Dampier being wide open to northerly winds.

A short distance to the SW of Dampier Cove lies another anchorage, **Nichol's Cove**. To reach this anchorage from Dampier, it is necessary to go out and around the mainland point giving wide berth to the large shoal area that lies north of the point. If coming from the west or south, there are no obstructions as long as one stays a half mile offshore.

The anchorage is in the northern extension of the three arms that form this

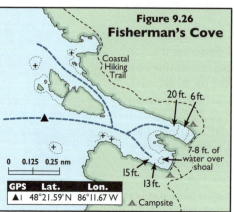

bay. To enter the cove, passage is again through a narrow entrance with a rocky bottom. Because of the clear water, it will appear that you are going to ground, but by staying midchannel, 10 feet of water can be carried through. The area here is small, and it may be necessary to set out more than one anchor to reduce swinging room. This anchorage is secure for all but the strongest southerly winds. With southerly winds an alternative anchorage is in the middle arm next to a small sand beach.

Two miles south of Oiseau Bay, tucked in behind a large island there is another indentation into the mainland that offers anchoring possibilities— **Fisherman's Cove** (called Split Cove in the 2nd edition of this book). There are actually two anchorages here split by a small peninsula of land.

The cove is identified by the high rounded island that stands in its entrance. Passage can be to either side of this island as long as the shoal areas are skirted. Anchoring can be done in either of the two coves with the northern cove being longer and more constricted, thus possibly requiring the use of two anchors. The southern cove is less desirable because there is a rock shoal right in the center

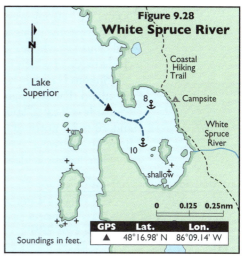

Figure 9.27
One Lake Island

shoal water

One Lake Island

| 0 | 0.25 | 0.5 nm |

GPS	Lat.	Lon.
▲1	48°19.82' N	86°10.94' W
▲1	48°19.23' N	86°11.81' W

Figure 9.28
White Spruce River

N

Lake Superior

Coastal Hiking Trail

8 ⚓ ▲ Campsite

White Spruce River

10 ⚓

shallow

| 0 | 0.125 | 0.25nm |

Soundings in feet.

GPS	Lat.	Lon.
▲	48°16.98' N	86°09.14' W

that has 7 feet to 8 feet of water over it. Both coves are open to westerly winds.

At **One Lake Island**, approximately three miles south of Oiseau Bay, there is another bay that is formed between the mainland and three islands, One Lake Island and two smaller islands. The water here is either very deep or very shoaled, so this harbor is not suitable to be used as an anchorage. However, it is possible to make the narrow passage behind One Lake Island, which is very beautiful because of the high surrounding bluffs. Even at the most narrow constriction, the water is very deep. At the southern end of the passage there is a spot where it is possible to set out a stern anchor and tie off on shore. As an anchorage, it is quite open to southerly winds and should be treated only as a lunch stop.

The area offshore from the White Gravel River to the White Spruce River is studded with small islets and rocky reefs. When no seas are running it is possible to travel through this "inside

passage." However, in rough weather, it is best to stand a good mile offshore in this area. In particular, note Stench Rock, which is located near the southerly end of a long row of rock islets a good half mile off shore near the White Spruce River.

The small harbor that is formed at the mouth of the **White Spruce River** is a beautiful, little-known anchorage. Lying about one mile north of Simons Harbour, it can be approached from the north by taking the mentioned inside passage or from the south by skirting Stench Rock. To avoid the rock islets and shoal water that lie just outside the southern part of the entrance, approach into the harbor should be made from the NW.

Within the bay there are 8 feet to 10 feet of water in the center and the northern half over a sand bottom. Although the bay is open to westerly winds, more protection can be achieved by anchoring in the northern end. However, even here an uncomfortable surge occurs with strong westerly winds. Although this bay is not well-known by most boaters, it is frequently used by sports fishermen and canoeists who are boat camping and require a sand beach or cleared area in which to set up their camps.

Simons Harbour is a deep "two-fingered" indentation into the mainland that offers good protection for all but the strongest NW winds. It is located approximately eight miles south of Oiseau Bay and 10 miles north of Otter Head, so it is a nice stopping-off place between the two.

The harbor is identified by a number of outlying islands and a white triangular day beacon on one of its more prominent points. However, if approach is made from the S or SW, because of the approach angle and some of these islands, this day beacon usually doesn't come into view until you are well-committed into the harbor. If coming from the NW, the beacon is more readily apparent, but even in this direction it can be masked by some of the islands. This entrance can also be confusing since it often is difficult to identify the entrance islands just to the north of waypoint 1. They appear as one when coming from the south and don't separate until you are abeam of them. To help with identification, the first island is a bare salmon-colored rock, and the second island has many trees on the top half.

Of the two anchorages, the easterly one is more secure, and here you can anchor in 15 to 20 feet of water depending on how far you go in. The

NOT TO BE USED FOR NAVIGATION – SKETCH APPROXIMATE

Figure 9.29
Simons Harbour

N

Is. 1

Is. 2

Bn

Lake Superior

Coastal Hiking Trail

0   0.25   0.5 nm

GPS	Lat.	Lon.
▲1	48°15.44' N	86°08.81' W
▲2	48°15.77' N	86°08.56' W
▲3	48°15.87' N	86°08.30' W
▲4	48°16.11' N	86°08.87' W

KEY
Is. 1 Many trees top half
Is. 2 No trees, bare rock–salmon color near water
● Sunken boat

western harbor is quite a bit deeper, except at the far end, and this anchorage is more susceptible to an uncomfortable surge from strong NW winds. There is a sunken 12-foot boat at the right fluke of the anchor symbol. Although it is too deep to cause any worry, an anchor line could get caught if a boat drifted over it. Climbing to the top of the high western bluff provides a spectacular view of the anchorage and the shoreline to the north.

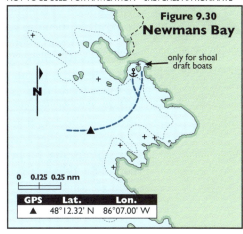

The Coastal Hiking Trail comes down right along the eastern shore of the east anchorage and it is easy to dinghy over and access it near the small stream that enters the harbor. Taking the trail north leads to a lovely little inland lake and then back out to a bluff overlooking the Simons Harbour complex. Continuing north, the trail becomes more difficult, traversing a number of ridges and ravines. Heading south on the trail from Simons for about two miles toward English Fishery brings one up on a high ridge that gives a helicopter view of a chain of three beautiful inland lakes, the grandeur of the Lake Superior shoreline and down into English Harbour. It is some of the most spectacular scenery we have seen on all of our travels on Lake Superior.

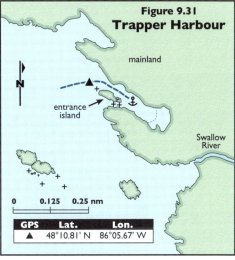

English Fishery, which lies two miles south of Simons Harbour, is at best a marginal anchorage that should be used primarily as a lunch stop. This is because it is quite open to westerly winds and most of the harbor is very deep. By going way in, particularly in the SE corner, it is possible to find less depth, however it is quite rocky and really unsuitable for anchoring. There are a number of campsites here, part of the Coastal Hiking Trail.

Another two miles down the shore, there is another anchorage, **Newmans Bay**, that offers protection for shoal draft boats, but is marginal for deep-draft boats. The harbor is easily recognized by its triangular shape consisting of three smaller "bays," of which the northern one gives the most protection. In this northern bay there is a small rock island behind which very shoal draft boats can tuck for complete protection. Other boats will have to anchor to the west of the rock island in 15 feet of water. The area is marginal because it is quite open to southerly winds and even NW winds

will cause an uncomfortable surge as waves eddy around the point. It may be difficult to get a good set with the anchor here because of a rock bottom. Note: the Coastal Hiking Trail ends just north of Newmans Bay at the North Swallow River.

One-and-one-half miles down the shore and four miles north to Otter Island there is a more secure anchorage, **Trapper Harbour**. All-weather protection is possible here because of an island and extensive shoaling that all but block the mouth of the harbor. Thus, Trapper is another anchorage that should not be attempted with any sea running, for here this already narrow entrance is further complicated by a large rock shoal that blocks a good half of this tight channel.

The harbor is difficult to spot because its narrow entrance and the island blend in well with the bold landscape. A good reference point is the conspicuous white day marker on the south side of Triangle Harbour that is a little more than a mile SE of Trapper Harbour. Other reference points are the small rock islands that lie outside the entrance to the Swallow River. Trapper is just N-NE of these. To enter the harbor, the shoal that lies NW of the entrance island should be kept to starboard, with passage between it and the mainland. This is another entrance where you will be able to see rocks to each side, but by staying in the middle of them depths of 14 to 17 feet can be carried through. There is another shoal off the inner end of the island that also has to be skirted. Because of shallow depths in the second half of the harbor, anchoring is usually done just behind the island with the shoals effectively breaking up anything that comes off the lake.

Around the corner to the south of Trapper Harbour lies the **Swallow River** that, because of a very shallow rock bottom and a spit that almost cuts off the mouth, can only be entered with a dinghy or a flat-bottomed boat. However, the river is interesting to explore and in calm conditions it is worth the trip around. There is an old cabin inside the mouth on the northern shore and farther upstream there are a number of waterfalls. The river is reputed to have good fishing—pickerel and northern pike. As you face the falls, there is a trail up on the left bluff that can be taken, following the river farther upstream.

There is one more harbor on this stretch of the shore before reaching Otter Island, but it is rarely used because much of it is very shallow, and it is so close to Otter Head. This is **Triangle Harbour**, which is identified by a slatted white triangular day beacon that sits on the long extension forming its southern shore.

NOT TO BE USED FOR NAVIGATION – SKETCH APPROXIMATE

Figure 9.32
Triangle Harbour

N

Beacon

22
12
10

sand beach

shallow

0   0.125   0.5 nm

Soundings in feet.
Water 0.14m (5.5 in.)
above chart datum.

GPS	Lat.	Lon.
▲	48°09.85'N	86°05.12'W

error

Note: this day beacon is readily seen when approaching from the north but doesn't come into view until you are almost abeam of it when coming from the south. Entrance should be made in midchannel because of rocks and shoaling to either side, especially along the south shore. It is possible to round up and tuck behind the land projection on this shore and anchor over a sand bottom. This will give protection against moderate west winds, but this anchorage would become very uncomfortable in strong W-NW winds.

Otter Head has long been one of the favorites for those who cruise this shore. This is because there are two snug harbors amidst some of the most beautiful scenery in this sector of the lake. There also used to be a commercial fishing station and manned light station located at the northern end of Otter Island. The light station used to be a favorite gathering spot for those who traveled up and down the east shore. That is, until the personnel were removed beginning with the 1988 season. Now the light has reverted to an isolated solitude, a lonely sentinel standing out high on the bluffs of Otter Island. Even the docks and buildings of the fishing station have fallen into disrepair from disuse.

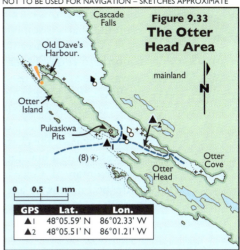

Figure 9.33
The Otter Head Area

Figure 9.34
Old Dave's Harbour, Otter Head

The area consists of the large Otter Island that lies offshore, a natural extension of the mainland, and a deep inlet, Otter Cove, which tucks in behind the protecting hills of Otter Head. At the north end of Otter Island, there is another, smaller island that, along with Otter Island, forms one of the most secure harbors on the shore, Old Dave's Harbour. By locals and those who cruise this shore, this whole complex is called Otter Head.

In approaching the area from north or south, the light, which stands out on the NE end of Otter Island, is readily visible. The light flashes white and is also equipped with an automatic foghorn. Another landmark for those coming from the north are the beautiful Cascade Falls on the mainland that plunge directly into the lake. The main channel behind Otter Island can be entered from either end of the island. If coming from the north, note that the area to the NW of the light is quite rock-strewn and should be given a wide berth. At the south end of Otter Island it is important to favor the island to avoid the rocks and shoal water off the

mainland in this entrance. Note that the rock that is marked 8 feet on the charts is sometimes awash and difficult to spot.

Within the area there are a couple of good anchorages. At the northern end of Otter Island there is **Old Dave's Harbour**, which was named after a fisherman who fished out of here in the early 1900s: "Big Dave." Although there are two entrances, the eastern one is preferred since the western one contains a number of large boulders that make passage difficult. Even then, when coming in from the east, the channel is tight with shoal water to each side necessitating a bow lookout. With care, 8 feet to 9 feet of water can be maintained. Once in the harbor, there is very deep water with the best depths for anchoring at the SW end. The deteriorating dock at the northern end is part of a once-active fishing station that is located on the small island. The small cement dock at the southern end is used primarily for dinghies and flat-bottomed boats. The house at this end used to be for the assistant light keeper. Often in the harbor it is possible to see caribou grazing on the bluffs since each season there are a number of caribou that inhabit Otter Island.

The trail, picked up at the assistant light keeper's house, leads across the island to the Otter Head light and a magnificent view of the shoreline. (Note that off this trail a distance in from the assistant lightkeeper's house there is a site of Pukaskwa Pits located in old, cobbled beach material.) Due to the efforts of the Canadian Coast Guard, the light station has remained in remarkably good condition, despite its abandoned status. Even the small gardens that were planted within the rock ravines in soil carried in from the surrounding woods are still present. When you roam the grounds, it is possible to catch another glimpse into the lives of the former light keepers, the mainstays of Lake Superior's wilderness shorelines. In stark contrast are the solar panels brought in to run the light, a product of modern technology.

Across from Old Dave's on the mainland is **Cascade Falls**. Although boats will occasionally be seen anchored off just to the west of the falls, it should be noted that the bottom here is very rocky, and it is sometimes very difficult to get an anchor to set. By watching the weather, the falls can also be visited by taking a motorized dinghy across from Old Dave's Harbour. It is possible to land on either side and climb up along the falls for many different views. In doing this, you will discover more falls, and by continuing upstream on the right side, you can follow the river quite a ways back into even more falls. Going up on the left side of the first falls, there is a picturesque "swimming hole" between the upper and lower falls that

NOT TO BE USED FOR NAVIGATION – SKETCH APPROXIMATE

Figure 9.35
Otter Island, South End

N

valley

terraced cobblestone beach

high cliffs

high rock cliff

0   0.25   0.5 nm

X Site of "The Fort"

provides a unique experience when swimming, with water coming down from overhead combined with the roar of the falls below. By staying to this western side of the pool, there is little danger of being taken down over the first falls.

Otter Island is also of special interest, because toward its southern end there is one of the largest known sites of the Pukaskwa Pits. The area is accessible only by dinghy since there really isn't good anchoring due to submerged rock boulders. The pits can be found by hiking in either from the north or south shores, but they are much closer to and easier to find from the southern shore. The area is easily marked by a terraced cobblestone beach lying next to some high rock cliffs. Toward the western end of the beach there are a number of smaller pit structures. The major site lies inland to the NW and is found backed up against a high cliff wall. If you reach the small inland lake, you know you have to go farther to the west and also to a higher elevation. (See Fig. 9.35.)

The site consists of a number of structures with a large ring of piled rocks more than 100 feet long and a good 50 feet wide that contains several internal rings. When you look at it, it looks ever so much like a fort, with the smaller internal structures resembling foundations for what could be taken as lodges. There is even an obvious entryway in the outer ring. It puzzled us for years that such a major site should be so far inland when all other pit sites were found on old, terraced beaches not too far in from the shore. Then one season we were privileged to be working with a team studying the site. When hiking up on the ridges with a geologist, he pointed out that the area was what is called a "saddle" with a valley in the center. When the waters of Lake Superior were higher, this lower end of Otter Island was actually two islands and "The Fort" would have been near the water's edge in the passage between the two.

Although this site and others along this shoreline have been studied in recent years, their usage and even their dating remains an enigma. One of the problems is the absence of historic artifacts, which leads many to believe that these structures belong in a prehistoric period. Although the structures are formed primarily by the moving and piling up of rocks on cobbled beaches, they take many different forms varying from depression pits and built-up walled structures to simple cairns.

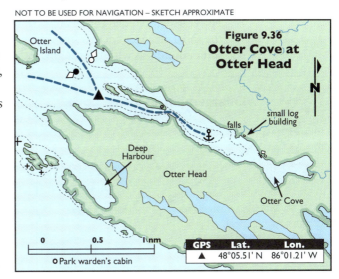

NOT TO BE USED FOR NAVIGATION – SKETCH APPROXIMATE

Otter Island

Figure 9.36
Otter Cove at Otter Head

N

small log building

falls

Deep Harbour

Otter Head

Otter Cove

0   0.5   1 nm

o Park warden's cabin

GPS	Lat.	Lon.
▲	48°05.51' N	86°01.21' W

The shapes and sizes likewise vary, from rectangular to conical to elongated ovals. Current theories on their usage differ from foundations for lodges and fire pits to religious uses for invocation and dedication. On the mainland shore across from Otter Island there are a few more of these pits, but they are much smaller in size. It is probably because this area was the last on the lake to be opened up to development through the logging operations in the 1940s that accounts for these pits still being intact. Thus, it is important that they be left undisturbed, for they are still under study and remain one of the few keys to the past of those who were the first inhabitants of this rugged shoreline. In light of this concern for preservation, Park Service has limited access to Otter Island only to the Assistant Lightkeeper's House in Old Dave's Harbour, and the path to the Otterhead Light itself.

That this area has been so remote until recent years is also illustrated by the fact that a distance in on this part of the mainland across from Otter Island there are the remains of a German prisoner-of-war camp. With no roads in the area, and hundreds of miles of austere forest, this forlorn area was the perfect location to keep prisoners of war in the 1940s. Today all that remains of the camp are some old pieces of lumber, a stove and other small artifacts.

One of the most beautiful spots at Otter Head is **Otter Cove**, which is found at the far SE end of the area. This completely land-locked harbor, which lies at the base of majestic towering bluffs, is well-sheltered from all winds. (Note that because of these bluffs, often reception of VHF weather channels is very poor and sporadic.) To enter, passage is to the south of the long island (Weidman's) that bisects the channel leading into the cove. By staying midchannel there are no obstructions even at the narrows just before reaching the wider cove. Anchoring is possible anywhere in the NW 2/3, although because of great depths it may be desirable to favor one of the shorelines, preferably the south shore. For years we avoided the shallow SE third of the Cove thinking the shoal area went across from shore to shore. Then we made some soundings with the dinghy and found we could get much better depths for anchoring and adequate swinging room by entering the middle of the shoal area, but not going too far in before it starts to get too shallow. See Figure 9.37. It continues to get quite shallow, especially in the area adjacent to the dock and buildings on the north shore. However, if you can get by these, there is good anchoring in both SE basins with 10 to 17 feet

NOT TO BE USED FOR NAVIGATION – SKETCH APPROXIMATE

Figure 9.37
Enlargement of Otter Cove Anchorage

Weidman's Island

Small dock warden's cabin helicopter pad

Old log cabin

Large dock & Park Buildings

N

0   0.25   0.5 nm

GPS	Lat.	Lon.
⚓	48°02.19'N	85°59.74'W

of water. There is a small waterfall a little way inland a little more than halfway down the north shore. The stream can be entered by dinghy right next to the small deteriorating log cabin. The buildings here were once private family camps but are now owned by Parks Canada. There is also a small cabin on the SE end of Weidman's Island that is frequently occupied by park wardens.

A Classic Pukaskwa pit on the mainland near Richardson Island. DAHL

There is even a small helicopter pad that has been built out on the point. The cove is another area that is reputed to have good fishing. It is not uncommon to see moose feeding along the shoreline in the cove, especially in the small bays at the far end.

Deep Harbour, which is the long indentation into the end of Otter Head, is another well-named harbor. For it is so deep that it is next to impossible to set an anchor here. However, the harbor is interesting to explore and can be entered by a large boat as long as the shoal water off the harbor's mouth is given adequate berth.

Five miles down the shoreline from Otter Head, there is another prominent landmark, **Pointe La Canadienne**. Just to the north of this headland there are two anchorages, one behind Richardson Island and Richardson Harbour.

Richardson Island used to be called Cairn Island because there are at least two rock cairns piled high on top of its bluffs. That the island was used in the past for fishing operations is witnessed by a few sunken cribs and remaining artifacts.

The island is difficult to spot since it blends in well with the bold landscape on the mainland. Thus, the easiest approach is to follow along the western side of La Canadienne toward the mainland until the entrance behind Richardson Island opens up. If this approach is used, note the rock shoal and small rock islets that lie off the west point of La Canadienne. By noting the rock islets that lie NW off

NOT TO BE USED FOR NAVIGATION – SKETCHES APPROXIMATE

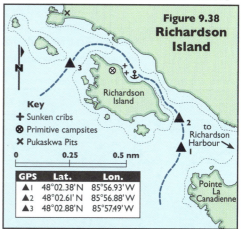

Figure 9.38 Richardson Island

Key
+ Sunken cribs
⊗ Primitive campsites
✕ Pukaskwa Pits

0   0.25   0.5 nm

GPS	Lat.	Lon.
▲1	48°02.38'N	85°56.93'W
▲2	48°02.61'N	85°56.88'W
▲3	48°02.88'N	85°57.49'W

to Richardson Harbour

Pointe La Canadienne

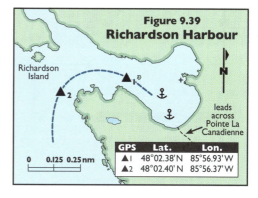

Figure 9.39 Richardson Harbour

Richardson Island

leads across Pointe La Canadienne

0   0.125   0.25nm

GPS	Lat.	Lon.
▲1	48°02.38'N	85°56.93'W
▲2	48°02.40'N	85°56.37'W

Richardson Island, it is also possible to tuck in from this direction.

The anchorage is found by anchoring close in to the island, but not so close as to swing into the sunken cribbing. Because of a gravel bottom it may be difficult to get a good set. Modern anchors like the Rocna will do better with this type of bottom.

The anchorage has good protection for all but exceptionally strong NW and SE winds, and even with these the island gives more protection than one would expect. There is a small beach across the channel on the mainland where there are a couple of trails leading a short way inland to a couple of lakes. On the mainland shoreline to the NW and to the other side of the point there are a couple of Pukaskwa Pits. One of the structures has "walls" that are so high that it is almost impossible to believe it is of prehistoric vintage.

Richardson Harbour, which on some charts is also called Bonamie Cove, has also seen some fishing activity in the past. It is another harbor that can be used for anchoring, but because of shoal water it is difficult to go very far in, thus it is necessary to anchor close to the harbor entrance just behind the small rock island, which leaves one vulnerable to westerly winds. Shallow draft boats may be able to go farther in toward the SW end of the harbor and thus get more protection.

There is a sand beach here that makes the harbor a nice place for boat camping. Toward the SW end of the beach, a trail can be picked up that leads across Pointe La Canadienne to another sand beach. Note: be sure to wear waterproof boots on this trail, since it follows a small stream and much of it leads through swampy areas. On the other side, by following the sand beach farther SE, one comes to a small river that is not too difficult to cross because of sandbars. Following the trail upstream along the southern side brings one quickly to **Puckasaw**, an old, abandoned Abitibi lumbering village. The foundations of many of the buildings along with rusted tools and other artifacts are readily found. There is even one building still left intact, complete with mud plaster between its log walls. When you look at these remnants of this once village, it is difficult to believe that at one time it housed as many as 1,500 men.

South of Pointe La Canadienne there are a number of very beautiful, but little used anchorages. One of these is to anchor in the bay on the

NOT TO BE USED FOR NAVIGATION – SKETCH APPROXIMATE

Figure 9.40 Puckasaw, Pukaskwa River

Pointe La Canadienne

sand beach

Imogene River

Puckasaw

Davis Island

Imogene Cove

sand beach

Pukaskwa River

N

| | 0 | 0.5 | 1 nm |

GPS	Lat.	Lon.
▲1	48°00.97' N	85°55.07' W
▲2	48°01.38' N	85°55.43' W
▲3	48°00.87' N	85°54.57' W
▲4	48°00.25' N	85°53.92' W

south shore of Pointe La Canadienne. To enter the bay, it is necessary to give good berth to a rather sizable shoal off the SE extension of the point since it is foul with rock. To do this, approach from the south and head directly for the western end of Davis Island (within 200 feet) before rounding to port and heading into the anchoring area. (Note: if the approach is from the W or SW, heading for the western end of the island will take one dangerously close to the shoal water off La Canadienne.) It is possible to go quite a ways in and anchor over a sand-rippled bottom beneath the majestic cliffs of La Canadienne.

NOT TO BE USED FOR NAVIGATION – SKETCH APPROXIMATE

Figure 9.41
South of Pointe La Canadienne

Puckasaw (old Abitibi lumbering village)

sand beach

high bluffs

La Pointe Canadienne

Davis Island

Imogene River

GPS	Lat.	Lon.
▲1	48°00.97' N	85°55.07' W
▲2	48°01.38' N	85°55.43' W

0   0.25   0.5 nm

It is also possible to find good protection by rounding to starboard and anchoring **behind Davis Island** or off the sand beach. The dock indicated on some of the older Canadian charts is no longer present, now just ruins and submerged cribs. Both anchorages are open somewhat to SE winds. Should these occur, it is possible to get better protection in **Imogene Cove** that lies to the SE.

From either anchorage, it is possible to dinghy ashore and explore the beach and old Abitibi lumbering village. Parks Canada has set up an especially nice display on an old log boom just up from the beach and east of the small stream, the Imogene River that enters the lake.

The **Pukaskwa River**, which is the southern boundary of Pukaskwa National Park, lies 1.5 miles SE of the old village of Pukasaw emptying into the lake between two large headlands. It is marked by a large sandbar that extends almost across the mouth of the river from the south. Extending out from the sandbar toward the lake is a large cobblestone shoal that makes entrance into the river difficult for deep and shoal draft boats alike. In low-water years the entrance is navigable by only those with boats that

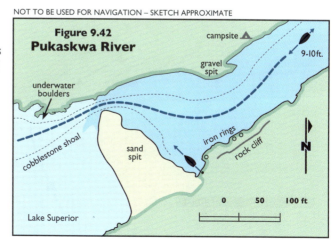

NOT TO BE USED FOR NAVIGATION – SKETCH APPROXIMATE

Figure 9.42
Pukaskwa River

campsite ▲

9-10 ft.

gravel spit

underwater boulders

iron rings

rock cliff

cobblestone shoal

sand spit

N

Lake Superior

0   50   100 ft

draw less than 5 feet. In high-water years it is possible to squeak in with 7- to 8-foot depths. Therefore, it is most important that the entrance to this river is not attempted with any sea running and only in calm conditions with a bow lookout. The cobblestone shoal is kept to starboard (when entering) and large underwater boulders will be seen to port off the north shore, leaving a narrow navigable track. A midchannel course is carried right into the entrance and then an abrupt turn to starboard is made to avoid another shoal off the gravel spit ahead.

Within the river it is possible to head a short way upstream and anchor beyond the gravel spit in approximately 9 feet to 10 feet of water. Both bow and stern anchors are recommended so the boat doesn't swing around in the currents. It is also possible to set out a bow anchor and tie off on some iron rings that have been driven into a rock wall along the south shore. The problem with this is that you have to be careful not to block the area near the mouth for the passage of other boats.

Near the gravel spit there is a primitive campsite that is sometimes used by those traveling via canoe or kayak. On occasion there have been reports of black bears that come down to the river. This river is interesting to explore by dinghy, and just a short way upstream you come to a waterfall. The falls are particularly beautiful, rushing between high jagged cliffs. By beaching the dinghy on the right side (as you face the falls), a trail can be picked up that follows the river a mile or so upstream to another set of waterfalls and a primitive campsite.

For those who want to visit the Pukaskwa River but can't

NOT TO BE USED FOR NAVIGATION – SKETCH APPROXIMATE

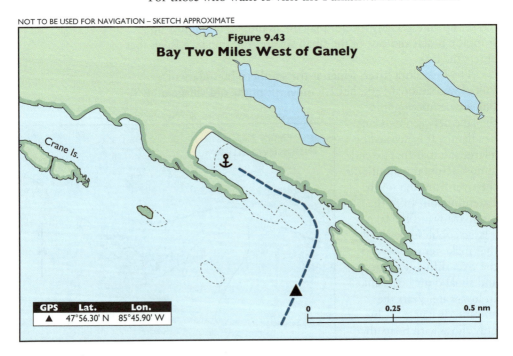

Figure 9.43
Bay Two Miles West of Ganely

Crane Is.

GPS	Lat.	Lon.
▲	47°56.30' N	85°45.90' W

0   0.25   0.5 nm

enter because of boat draft, there is an alternative marginal anchorage one-half mile north of the river's mouth behind a few small islands, see Figure 9.40. Here it is possible to tuck in next to the islands adjacent to a small sand beach. Note the rock shoals that lie NE of the small island that will be abeam. There is good holding here with protection for all but southerly winds. If no sea is running, it is then easy to dinghy into the Pukaskwa River for exploring. Because the anchorage is so open to southerly winds, it is best used as a lunch stop.

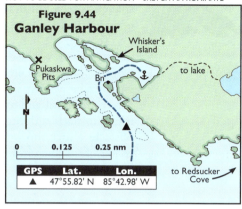

Figure 9.44
Ganley Harbour

From the Pukaskwa River to Michipicoten Harbour, the shoreline once again becomes rugged with few all-weather harbors and a couple of marginal ones. To the west of Ganley Harbour there are three look-alike NW/SE harbors on the shoreline that on the charts look like they may be possible anchorages. However, only the most westerly one, the **Bay Two Miles West of Ganley**, is a viable anchorage and this is somewhat open to the E/SE. On the charts it is the first anchorage to the east of Crane Island and shouldn't be mistaken for False Ganley Harbour or the one in between. In approaching the anchorage, note the offshore shoals to the SW and SE of the entrance. There is also extensive shoaling off the peninsula that forms the southern part of the anchorage, so the approach is to favor the island that is seen to starboard since this shoal extends more than halfway between the peninsula and the island (see Fig. 9.39). Once inside the shoal it is possible to go about halfway in beyond the point to anchor in 10 feet over a sand-rippled bottom. There is a lovely little sand beach at the far end of this bay.

Ganley Harbour, which lies 11 nautical miles from Pointe La Canadienne and 35 nautical miles from Michipicoten Harbour, is one of the few anchorages along this lonely section of the lake. Long recognized as an all-weather harbor, it has been a favorite refuge for commercial fishermen and from time to time is still used by fishing tugs in the area.

This snug harbor is formed by a few small islands that lie close into shore and blend in so well with the shoreline that the harbor is very difficult to spot. Because of this, there is a day beacon on one of the entrance islands that can be seen a good mile offshore. However, because there are no other obvious landmarks on this stretch of the shore, this is another area where it pays to know your exact position and accurate navigation becomes important. The day beacon is a white triangle with a red border. Because the triangle faces to the SE, it can't be seen from off shore when approaching from the west. The beacon is placed in this position so when the

triangle is seen full straight on, it marks the entrance slot right between the islands to port and the mainland shoreline.

To enter the harbor, head for the section of mainland that lies just to the east of the day marker. When coming from the west, it won't be until you come right up to the mainland shore that the entrance between it and the islands will open up to the NW. Follow this course until you reach the island with the day marker and then round to starboard into the anchorage. There is one remaining obstacle, a rock shoal that will be seen to starboard close to the center of the anchoring area. Rounding this, it is possible to anchor in behind the shoal in 10 to 12 feet of water.

At the far SE end of the harbor there is a rudimentary dock that is sometimes used by fishing tugs. A fire pit and other debris indicate occasional use. A little to the NE of this area there is a trail that leads approximately one-quarter mile to the inland lake that opens up from Redsucker Cove. On the small western peninsula that forms Ganley Harbour, there are more of those curious prehistoric structures known as the Pukaskwa Pits. There are approximately seven pits, which are found inland past the tree line on a terraced cobble beach that was once a water's edge in an era when the lake was much higher. Whisker's Island is a nice place for a shore fire.

An interesting area to explore is **Redsucker Cove**, which is the long indentation that lies halfway between Ganley and the Pipe River. In calm weather a dinghy can be taken around into this inlet. It is also possible to anchor in the mouth of Redsucker Cove, but only about one-third of the way in since it begins to shoal up quickly farther in. Although the anchorage is open to the south and SE, it provides protection for all other winds including SW. It is also possible to anchor in the cove just to the east of Redsucker Cove where there is a nice sand beach in the far end. However, you can only go about halfway in, again because of shoaling, and this anchorage is really open to southerly winds. For more complete protection, Ganley Harbour remains the preferred anchorage in the area.

The six-mile stretch of shoreline from Ganley to Pilot Harbour is studded with numerous small islets and rock shoals. Therefore, it is important to stand a good half mile out when traveling this section of the lake. There are, however, a couple of marginal spots where it is possible to

NOT TO BE USED FOR NAVIGATION – SKETCH APPROXIMATE

Figure 9.45
Halfway between Gangley Harbor & Pilot Cove

N

30 ft.

only for shoal draft boats

85°38.90' W

85°37.30' W

| 0 | 0.25 | 0.5 nm |

GPS	Lat.	Lon.
▲	47°55.30' N	85°38.61' W

sneak in when there is no sea running and with the sun high at one's back to spot the shoal areas.

Two of these marginal anchorages are found **Halfway between Ganley and Pilot Harbour** between longitudes 85°38.90' W and 85°37.30' W. The approach to the first anchorage is free of obstructions if coming from the S or SE. It is found behind two adjacent islands where it is possible to go way back in. In fact, because of depth, you have to get in right next to shore before you can get adequate depths for anchoring. The anchorage is marginal because it is quite open to E and SE winds. It does, however, provide good protection for a westerly or northerly blow.

The second anchorage lies a little less than a mile to the east and has to be approached with caution since there are a number of surrounding shoals. It has considerably less depth and should only be used by those with shoal draft boats. With care, it is possible to sneak in behind two small islands. Protection here is marginal for all but northerly winds and should thus be used primarily as a lunch stop.

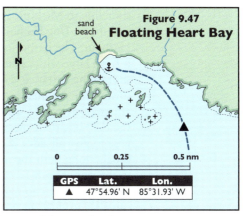

Figure 9.46
Pilot Harbour

GPS	Lat.	Lon.
▲	47°55.06' N	85°34.64' W

Figure 9.47
Floating Heart Bay

GPS	Lat.	Lon.
▲	47°54.96' N	85°31.93' W

Pilot Harbour is the last all-weather harbor on this stretch of the shore to Michipicoten Harbour, a distance of 28 nautical miles. Although there are a couple of more areas in which to anchor along this shoreline, these are open to at least one wind direction.

The harbor is marked with a white rock cairn and a white slatted day beacon built on the western side of its entrance. Depending on the angle of approach, these white markers may not come into view until you are close to the entrance. For example, when approaching from the west, the rock cairn is hidden and only the white slatted day beacon is visible. In approaching the entrance, it is important to note the extensive shoal water that extends out into the lake SW from the islands that lie east of the harbor opening. Giving this shoal wide berth, the islands are passed to starboard. A midchannel course between these islands and the mainland, which is to port, will give a clear track free from the smaller shoal areas that extend out from each side. Although it is possible to anchor anywhere in the harbor, the best protection is found by rounding into the extension to port, where there is good holding in 10 to 15 feet of water. In this far end there once were

remnants of a small cabin and fishing camp.

One and one-half miles east of Pilot Harbour there is a little-known harbor that offers good anchoring, but is open to southerly winds, **Floating Heart Bay**. Although much of this bay contains little islets and rock shoals, by favoring the starboard shoreline when coming in it is possible to sneak in around these and anchor behind the shoals in 15 feet of water with a good holding sand bottom. Although the anchorage is open to the south, the outlying rocks and shoal water are fairly effective in breaking up small seas from the S and SW. There is no protection, however, for wave action from the SE. Although this anchorage has seen little use by those who cruise with deep-draft boats, it is a favorite for canoeists and those who are boat camping because of its beautiful sand beach and small clearing. There is also a small stream that enters this bay that is interesting to explore.

There is only one other harbor along this long stretch of shoreline to Michipicoten Harbour that offers suitable anchoring and that is **Dog Harbour,** 14 nautical miles west of Michipicoten Harbour. The harbor is quite easy to spot from all directions since it has a large white slatted triangular day beacon marking its outer shore. The entrance is found by heading a little east of the beacon toward the mainland shore and then rounding up to port. There are no obstructions except around this point on which the beacon stands. Here there are rock shoals on all sides of the point, and it is wise to give all sides wide berth. Within the harbor, there are some shoals along both the north and south shores, so it is best to anchor in the center with 10 to 12 feet of water and a good holding sand bottom. The anchorage is secure for all but east winds. A SW wind can also produce an uncomfortable surge as waves eddy around the point, and it may be necessary to use two anchors to position the boat for better motion. There is a nice sand beach here and the shoreline is interesting to explore, especially out on the point. In some years this harbor has seen extensive use by those who are boat-camping with small runabouts out of the Michipicoten River. Often the camping facilities are extensive with many tents and eating areas, some of which are erected on semi-permanent platforms. If seclusion is desired, this may not be the harbor to visit.

An alternative to Dog Harbour is **Little Dog Harbour**, which lies just adjacent to the east. The channel is quite narrow, but it can be entered by boats drawing 5 feet. However, once inside there is little space to anchor or maneuver. Shallow draft boats can continue into the

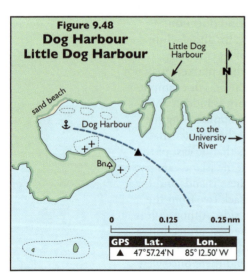

Figure 9.48
Dog Harbour
Little Dog Harbour

Little Dog Harbour

N

sand beach

⚓ Dog Harbour

to the University River

Bn

0   0.125   0.25 nm

GPS	Lat.	Lon.
▲	47°57.24'N	85°12.50'W

small bay at the far end. The only option for deep-draft boats is to set out a stern anchor and nose up into the long arm that extends to the west and tie off on shore using the iron rings that are in the rock to port. This is a very constricted anchorage, and it is best used by those with small boats.

The **University River,** which lies two-thirds of a mile east of Dog Harbour, is a favorite for fishermen and those who are boat camping, often making the run out from Michipicoten Harbour. In the past, it was also a favorite stopping-over place for the voyageurs.

Because of a large sandspit that all but blocks the mouth of the river and very shoal rock-strewn water in the remaining small entrance, this river is accessible only to dinghies and flat-bottomed boats. Passing through this narrow entrance, there are often adverse currents set up where the river current meets the wave action of the lake. The river is very interesting to explore and, depending on the water level, it is possible to take a dinghy a good distance in.

From Dog Harbour to Michipicoten Harbour, a distance of 14 nautical miles, the shoreline is bold and offers no suitable anchorages or harbors of refuge.

Chapter Ten

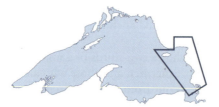

East Shore: Michipicoten Island, Michipicoten Harbour to Gros Cap, Ontario

Please Note:
Maps and Charts
in this book are
not necessarily
to scale and are
not intended for
navigation.

From Michipicoten Harbour to Sault Ste. Marie, Lake Superior's east shore remains wild and exhibits a bold topography. The Laurentian Plateau, which before was indented with predominantly small bays and dotted with equally small islands, is now broken into large capes, towering headlands and deep bays. Once again we come to a section of the lake where everything strikes one as being on a grand scale. Here are the towering cliffs of Old Woman Bay, the massive headland of Cape Chaillon, the intricate rock formations of Cape Gargantua and the large bays such as Batchawana and Goulais. Even the islands are enormous, for it takes hours to skirt Montreal Island, and for days we cruise in the shadow of the mysterious Michipicoten.

There are only a few places here where roads come down to the lake and with few supplies available between Michipicoten Harbour and Sault Ste. Marie, this is another section of the lake where it pays to be well-provisioned and to be prepared for long intervals between fuel stops. With the establishment of three provincial parks — Lake Superior Provincial Park, Pancake Bay Provincial Park and Batchawana Provincial Park — the wilderness theme continues. There are inland lakes to fish, sand beaches to walk and interesting channels and inlets to explore. The shoreline here also boasts the most spectacular site of First Nation paintings on the lake, at Sinclair Cove. With anchorages still plentiful and the scenery spectacular, this is another area on the lake that provides beautiful wilderness cruising.

Harbors and Anchorages

Michipicoten Island has long fascinated those who have traveled up and down Lake Superior's eastern shore. Standing off in the distance, this second largest island on the lake takes on a blue-grey hue and will sometimes seem to rise out of the water and at other times seem to recede into the mist. It was this mysterious quality of undulating appearance that made the early natives awe-struck and superstitious of this island that they called *Michipicotou*.

Despite their fear of the island, early inhabitants often braved Lake Superior's open waters in search of Michipicoten's precious copper. The copper was important to them because they used the nuggets, which heated faster than their usual stones, to cook their food and boil water in birch-bark containers that would otherwise burn if placed directly over a fire. But because of superstition, they were reluctant to remove copper from the island, since some legends told of warriors who did and then died (probably of copper poisoning) before they reached the mainland.

The island also found importance to the early explorers, for as

NOT TO BE USED FOR NAVIGATION – SKETCH APPROXIMATE

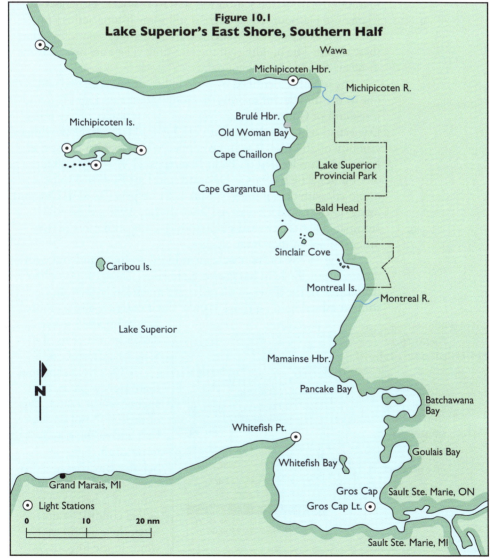

Figure 10.1
Lake Superior's East Shore, Southern Half

Wawa

Michipicoten Hbr.

Michipicoten R.

Michipicoten Is.

Brulé Hbr.

Old Woman Bay

Cape Chaillon

Lake Superior
Provincial Park

Cape Gargantua

Bald Head

Sinclair Cove

Caribou Is.

Montreal Is.

Montreal R.

Lake Superior

Mamainse Hbr.

Pancake Bay

Batchawana
Bay

Whitefish Pt.

Goulais Bay

Whitefish Bay

N

Grand Marais, MI

Gros Cap   Sault Ste. Marie, ON

⊙ Light Stations

Gros Cap Lt. ⊙

0   10   20 nm

Sault Ste. Marie, MI

East Shore: Michipicoten Island, Michipicoten Harbour to Gros Cap, Ontario

early as 1647 Michipicoten found its place on French maps. Like the natives, these explorers and the Jesuit missionaries were quick to acknowledge the importance of copper deposits on the island. It wasn't until the mid-1800s (1853, 1863 and 1881) though, that any serious mining was done on the island. Although millions of dollars were spent in the ventures, the mines were never very productive and, combined with some disasters, the mines seemed to substantiate the legend that the island was guarded by evil spirits.

After copper, it was commercial fishing that beckoned many to the island's shores. With a succession of owners—the Dominion Fish Company, Booth and then Purvis—Michipicoten grew to become one of the largest and better-known stations on the lake. For many decades there was even a small fishing village in Quebec Harbour. In 1959, the station was sold to Ferroclad Fisheries of Mamainse Harbour. Today there is still some fishing activity on the island, as tugs out of Mamainse are sometimes seen to frequent these shores. The buildings of the one-time village are now in some disrepair and are no longer used.

The island is identified by three lights, one at each end and one in the middle, off its southern shore. West End Light is found just south of Cotton Cove (Fl W) and has a visibility of five miles. Davieaux Light, which lies south of Quebec Harbour, Fl W with a visibility of 20 miles. It is also equipped with a foghorn. East End Light, which is located on Point Maurepas, Fl W with a visibility of 14 miles. The stations at Davieaux and East End used to be occupied, with one of the Davieaux light keepers (Gordon Dawson) being on the island 22 seasons. Since the late 1980s, these fully automated lights have had no personnel along with most of the other stations in the Ontario sector.

In the 1970s, caribou were introduced on the island and with no predators, the herd has grown quite large. These caribou differ from those in the Slates in that they are much larger than the stunted inbred herd on those islands. Their coats are also a mottled grey as opposed to the darker brown coats of the Slate Islands caribou.

With a bold shoreline, there are few places to anchor on the island. One of these is found on the west end of the island, north of the light, in **Schafer Bay**. Because this bay is open to westerly winds, it is best used in settled conditions and when there are no west winds in the forecast. It

NOT TO BE USED FOR NAVIGATION – SKETCH APPROXIMATE

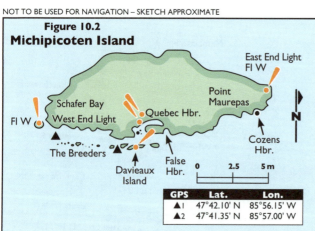

Figure 10.2
Michipicoten Island

East End Light
Fl W

Point
Maurepas

Schafer Bay

West End Light

Fl W

Quebec Hbr.

Cozens
Hbr.

N

The Breeders

Davieaux
Island

False
Hbr.

0   2.5   5 m

GPS	Lat.	Lon.
▲1	47°42.10' N	85°56.15' W
▲2	47°41.35' N	85°57.00' W

does, however, provide good protection for all other winds and the outlying rocks and islets even provide some protection for NW and SW winds. In approaching the bay from the south, it is important to stand off a good half mile from the island to avoid outlying rocks and shoals. When coming from the north, there a number of rocks and in particular, a rock shoal that is normally just awash and that must be

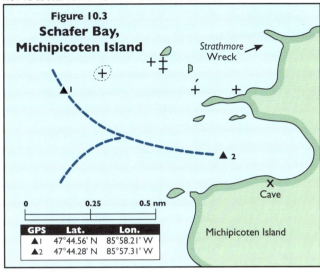

Figure 10.3
Schafer Bay, Michipicoten Island

GPS	Lat.	Lon.
▲1	47°44.56' N	85°58.21' W
▲2	47°44.28' N	85°57.31' W

kept well to port. (See Fig. 10.3, GPS waypoint #1.) A reminder that these rocks to the north are a hazard is the wreck of the Strathmore, a 205-foot wooden steamer that sank in November 1906. Remains of the wreck can still be seen lying 6 feet below the water's surface, where you can see the boiler that is fairly close to the surface and the keel and parts of the ribs that lie a little deeper in the water.

There is good deep water way into the anchorage and you can anchor quite close to shore in 10 feet to 12 feet of water where there is excellent holding over a sand-rippled bottom. This is a very dramatic wilderness anchorage snugged beneath the rugged bluffs of the island and surrounded by interesting rock formations. Because of its remote location, it is often possible to see caribou coming down here to the beach. Despite its remoteness, it is interesting to note that Schafer Bay was once the site of a farm and portable lumber mill that supplied milk, meat, grain and wood to the nearby mine. This is an interesting place to explore by dinghy.

The best place to anchor on the island is in **Quebec Harbour**, the large bay that lies close to the center of the island's southern shore. This harbor should not be confused with False Harbour that lies approximately 1.5 miles to the east but because of shoal water is accessible to only dinghies and flat bottom boats. If approaching Quebec Harbour from the SE there are no obstructions. However, if a SW approach is used, The Breeders, a particularly foul extension of islets, rocks and shoal water lying to the west of Davieaux Island, must be noted and given wide berth. Note: the foghorn on Davieaux Island is self-activated by rapidly keying the mike six times on VHF channel 19.

The passage into Quebec Harbour lies toward the eastern side of the opening, east of the small islets that one sees in the center. Because of shoal water to each side and considerable magnetic

disturbance in the area, the entrance to this harbor should not be attempted in fog or foul weather. A small channel through this shoal water has been dredged and marked with buoys along with a range that has been established on the far side of the bay. The easiest course is to line up on the range (00°45' T/Track A) and enter with the first buoy (GRG) kept to port and then head north with the red buoys kept to starboard. An alternative approach is to line up on a secondary range approximately 50°T at the first green buoy (GPS/Track B) and pass with the GRG buoy to starboard until the north range lines up. Then continue north on the main range with red buoys to starboard, green buoys to port.

Depending on wind direction, either end of this large harbor can be used as an anchorage. Be sure to note the shoaling water along the northern shore and at each end. The docks at the old fishing wharf are now in such disrepair that they are a hazard to tie up to. The small dock directly north of the entrance channel and adjacent to the range is accessible only to boats drawing less than 5 feet. The few buildings seen dotting the periphery of the harbor are private summer fishing camps, some of which go back more than 50 years.

The buildings at the old Purvis fishing station are quite interesting to explore. One of the older buildings has special interest since it once was the old jailhouse that stood at Quebec Mines on the NW end of the island. This log structure was disassembled, hauled to Quebec Harbour by barge and then reconstructed at the station. The east end of Quebec Harbour is also interesting to explore by dinghy since there are a number of small streams that enter the harbor at this end, a favorite feeding area for caribou. Along the south shore of this end of the harbor there are three shipwrecks: the *Big Jim*, *Billy Blake* and *Dixon*. The *Hiram R. Dixon* is of special interest because it is very old, being constructed in the 1870s. It was a 149-foot, 329-ton wooden steamer formerly

NOT TO BE USED FOR NAVIGATION – SKETCH APPROXIMATE

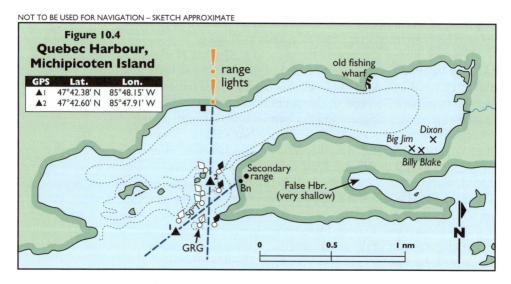

Figure 10.4
Quebec Harbour, Michipicoten Island

GPS	Lat.	Lon.
▲1	47°42.38' N	85°48.15' W
▲2	47°42.60' N	85°47.91' W

range lights

old fishing wharf

Dixon
Big Jim ×
××
Billy Blake

Secondary range
Bn
False Hbr. (very shallow)

50°T

GRG

0   0.5   1 nm

N

of the Booth Packing Company Fleet. On 18 August 1903, it caught on fire in Quebec Harbour and was subsequently moved off to the side where it now lies just under water. Today it is possible to look down into this massive structure and to see the large wooden ribs reminiscent of the construction methods of yesteryear, complete with the large rocks that were used for ballast in those days.

Outside Quebec Harbour, a trip to Davieaux Island is also interesting. The name "Davieaux" comes from one of the first light keepers to operate the station. There is a small dock that used to serve the light on the north end of the island just east of the light. Boats drawing less than 5 feet can approach and tie up to the outer end of this dock. Note: there is foul water off the NE end of the dock. Because it is quite open here, the dock should be treated primarily as a lunch stop and used only for a visit to the light. The light station grounds are still intact with an excellent view of the surrounding area from the light. The beaches on Michipicoten, the chain of islands along its southern shore and Agate Island in Quebec Harbour entrance yield beautiful agates. The fishing is also good among the outlying reefs, as well as within Quebec Harbour itself. In fact, during the last week of July and the first week in August, the island comes alive with fishermen who come up from Sault Ste. Marie, with the hub of activity centering around the dock of the old fishing station.

Another anchorage on Michipicoten Island is **Cozens Harbour**, which is located at the SE corner of the island. Because of its strategic location in this corner of the lake, Cozens is often used by those who want to make fast passage up/down the lake. This secure little harbor is good for all but strong southerly winds. With care, it is possible to pass to either side of the small island that lies in the center of the entrance. Note: shoal water extends south of this island. The best place to anchor

Figure 10.5
Entrance to Quebec Harbour, Michipicoten Island

range lights

Secondary range

Bn

GRG

| 0 | 0.25 | 0.5 nm |

GPS	Lat.	Lon.
▲1	47°42.38' N	85°48.15' W
▲2	47°42.60' N	85°47.91' W

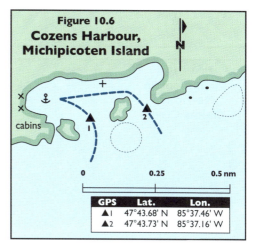

Figure 10.6
Cozens Harbour, Michipicoten Island

N

cabins

| 0 | 0.25 | 0.5 nm |

GPS	Lat.	Lon.
▲1	47°43.68' N	85°37.46' W
▲2	47°43.73' N	85°37.16' W

is snugged up to the western end, since the eastern end is quite deep and foul with rock. The high bluffs provide blueberries and a spectacular vantage point from which to take panoramic pictures of the area. A family camp with a number of buildings was established in the 1990s in the west end of the harbor.

Beginning as a fur trading post for the French in 1725, **Michipicoten Harbour** was one of the first areas to be settled on this end of the lake. In 1763 the post came under British jurisdiction and was established as a key outpost for the North West Company in the 1780s. Then, in a merger with the Hudson's Bay Company in 1821, it again changed hands and remained an active post until 1863.

With a dwindling fur trade, it took the discovery of iron ore in 1897 to rekindle growth in the area. Twelve miles inland, a body of hard hematite was found under Lake Boyer, and this quickly became the well-known Helen Mine. Later, a second mine was found another 10 miles inland. Under the direction of Francis H. Clerque, an efficient way of transporting the ore to Sault Ste. Marie was developed, and by 1900 the first ore made its way to Michipicoten Harbour via rail and then was loaded to waiting ships to be further transported down the shore. In building his industrial conglomerate, Clerque also constructed a large blast furnace and the famous Algoma Steel Company that today is still an imposing structure on the Canadian Sault shoreline. The town of Wawa (population 5,000), which lies approximately 10 miles inland from Michipicoten Harbour, owes much of its growth to the development of this important industry. Today all that remains in the Michipicoten Bay area is a commercial fishing station, a First Nation mission, and a marina and a few homes a short way up the Michipicoten River.

Lying in the NE corner of this section of the lake, Michipicoten Bay is easy to spot, for it is marked with a lighthouse perched out on the end of Perkwakwia Point. With a visibility of 15 miles, the light is also equipped with a foghorn, which is activated by rapidly keying VHF Channel 19 six times.

Because the ore docks are quite high

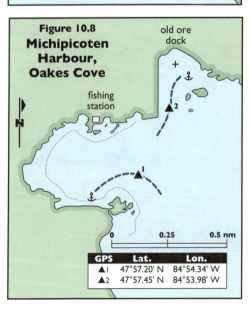

Figure 10.7
The Michipicoten Bay Area

Oakes Cove

Michipicoten Hbr.

Fl 30s 88 ft

Perkwakwia Pt.

Michipicoten Bay

Michipicoten R.

0   0.5   1 nm

Figure 10.8
Michipicoten Harbour, Oakes Cove

old ore dock

fishing station

0   0.25   0.5 nm

GPS	Lat.	Lon.
▲1	47°57.20' N	84°54.34' W
▲2	47°57.45' N	84°53.98' W

and still used commercially, the best spot for visiting boaters to anchor is in **Oakes Cove**. Although this part of the bay is quite open to easterly winds, it is possible to receive some protection from even these winds by tucking in close to the southern shore of the cove. Note that there is substantial shoaling in the western end of Oakes Cove. For protection from N/NE winds, it is possible to come in alongside the ore dock and anchor in the area east of the dock next to a small sand beach. This second anchorage has protection for all but southerly winds.

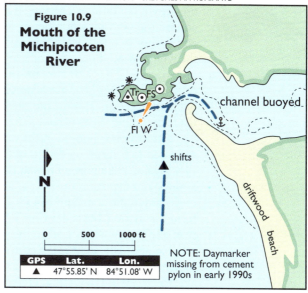

Figure 10.9
Mouth of the Michipicoten River

channel buoyed

Fl W

shifts

driftwood beach

GPS	Lat.	Lon.
▲	47°55.85' N	84°51.08' W

NOTE: Daymarker missing from cement pylon in early 1990s

Within Oakes Cove there are no facilities except to buy fresh or frozen fish from the fishing station on the northern shore. There is, however, an excellent marine facility across the harbor, one mile up the Michipicoten River at **Buck's Marina**. Unfortunately, because of water depths both in the mouth of the river and the river itself these facilities are often available to only those with boats drawing less than 5 feet. In some years, boats drawing more than 4.5 feet could not make it through the

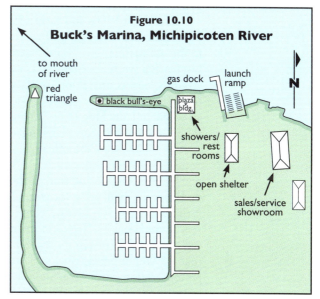

Figure 10.10
Buck's Marina, Michipicoten River

to mouth of river

red triangle

black bull's-eye

gas dock

launch ramp

plaza bldg.

showers/rest rooms

open shelter

sales/service showroom

entrance, in other years boats drawing 5.5 feet have made it all the way up to the marina fuel dock.

The first obstacle is at the entrance to the river, since shifting sandbars can alter the depths considerably. In some years the best course is to go north of the cement base that supports a light (Fl W); in other years it is best to go south of the base. If the southern track is used, it helps to come in on a closing angle toward the sandspit, roughly on a course of 45° true. But even this varies, and the best course is to call Brad Buck at the marina (they monitor Channel 68 or call 705-856-4488 or 705-256-9021) for directions

on current conditions. Drawing 6 feet, we have been able to squeak around the sandspit a number of times with a minimum of 7 feet and anchor in 8 feet behind the spit. (Note: if you can't make it into the river and need fuel, the folks at Buck's will bring it out to you in gerry cans! They also have on-the-water pump-outs and will even come over to your boat in Oakes Cove.) Large amounts of fuel can be brought by truck to the old ore dock. Again, arrangements are made by calling the marina.

The river was buoyed in the mid-1980s, and although there are supposed to be limiting depths of 6 feet to 7 feet, the river levels do vary. Again, it's important to call Buck's for help getting up the river as the water depths in the river are independent of the lake, due to the amount of rain and runoff. In recent years, with assistance from the marina, boats drawing 5 plus feet have made it up the river and then anchored off to the side adjacent to the marina. A sandbar approximately 100 feet from the marina has been dredged, so depending on water levels, boats drawing 5 to 5.5 feet have been able to get up to the marina. Note that is important to call ahead If you need fuel.

In the late 1980s and early 1990s the marina saw considerable expansion and remodeling of facilities. A basin was dredged adjacent to the old marina, breakwaters were constructed and a new 100-slip marina (with electricity) was added to the facility. On the grounds, new construction involved the addition of an open air picnic pavilion, a new gas dock (gasoline, diesel and pump-out), an excellent launching ramp, a new building with showers and rest rooms and an impressive large repair facility that also contains an open-air showroom and offices. Ice and snacks including sandwiches and ice cream are also available. Buck's specializes in all types of boat repairs, both engine and hull. If they don't have a replacement part on hand, they will get it for you. Of special interest to fishermen is the Wawa Salmon Derby, which is sponsored by Buck's each year in mid-August. Begun in the mid-1980s, this event has grown each year with teams in more than 150 boats competing for more than $5,000 in prizes. Buck's Marina is a long-awaited facility in a remote section of the lake, and the people here are congenial and accommodating to boaters.

Ten miles south of Michipicoten Harbour there lies one of the most beautiful harbors in this section of the lake, **Brulé Harbour.** Surrounded by high towering bluffs, heavily laden with dense forest, the awe and majesty of entering Brulé Harbour is hard to beat.

Although the harbor is named after Etienne Brulé, the first explorer usually credited with seeing Lake Superior, it is not certain that Brulé ever got this far north on Lake Superior's eastern shore or actually saw the harbor that was eventually to become his namesake. Because Brulé reported back to Champlain that he had reached an area where natives were mining copper, it is often assumed that his travels took him along Lake Superior's south shore to the Keweenaw

Peninsula or possibly even to Isle Royale. He did, however, explore this region for 20 years, and in that length of time it certainly is probable that he saw many other areas of the lake. Because he left no written records, we have only a few sketches on Champlain's maps upon which to rely.

Today the anchorage is as wild and untouched as it was in the days of these first explorers. An all-weather natural harbor, it blends in well, tucked into the high surrounding hills that sometimes make it difficult to spot. The best identifying landmark in the area is the deep indentation and high cliffs of Old Woman Bay that lies two miles to the SE. Within the entrance of the harbor there is a large island that also blends in well with the shoreline. On the headland, which one passes to port when entering, there is an anchor symbol and arrow painted on the rock. This has a tendency to fade if it hasn't been repainted, so the approach to the harbor is largely by land recognition and strict adherence to navigation. The harbor is entered by passing between the island and the mainland, keeping the island to starboard.

After clearing the island, there are actually two harbors in which to anchor. The western harbor is more open and is quite deep, so it is the eastern harbor that is usually used by those who cruise this shore. In passing through the long channel into this eastern harbor, it is important to stay in the middle, for there is some shoal water off to each side — especially to starboard, just after you clear the long entrance and get into the harbor itself.

Although this beautiful harbor is completely landlocked, there are some restrictions in anchoring. This is because along the southern shore there are numerous submerged pilings, and in the center of the eastern end there is a deadhead of considerable size. (It is possible to anchor to either side of this deadhead by making provisions for reducing swinging room.) The rest of the harbor is quite deep, which leaves the small bay to the NW for the best anchoring. Because of water depth and restricted swinging room, this is one of

Figure 10.11
Brulé Harbour

best anchorage
Deadhead
submerged pilings

white mark
beach

2nd terrace: 3 pits, I very large

1st terrace: 7 pits

driftwood then tree line

| 0 | 0.25 | 0.5 nm |

GPS	Lat.	Lon.
▲1	47°48.43' N	84°56.42' W
▲2	47°48.55' N	84°55.87' W

N

Dahlfin II in Brulé Harbour. DAHL

those anchorages where it may be advisable to set out a bow and stern anchor or a Bahamian moor.

Points of interest: the marsh at the eastern end of this smaller harbor is a favorite feeding area for moose. The southern end of the large island in the entrance is a herring gull rookery and, if visited in early summer, allows a chance to see the nests, eggs and newly hatched young.

Another point of interest is just across the channel from the entrance island where there is an old cobblestone beach on the mainland in which there is a large collection of Pukaskwa Pits. The site is unusual in that it is much farther south than other sites that are found farther up the east shore and on the north shore. That these pits have been under study is also evident by a flat rock painted yellow on one side in the center bottom of each, apparently to give depth perception in photographs. The pits are found above the most southern beach of the two lying in this segment of shoreline. This beach is easily identified by a number of large rock boulders in the water that you have to go around to reach shore. To reach the pits you have to climb over a sizable layer of driftwood and then go a number of feet through a treeline. The terraces here are some of the best examples of old beach material on the lake. There are seven pits found in the first terrace and three in the second, one of which is very large. When you view the pits, keep in mind that they are thousands of years old and probably in no way resemble the original structures.

On your way south of Brulé, you get a spectacular view of the rugged towering cliffs on the eastern shore of **Old Woman Bay**. The water here is quite deep, almost up to the base of the cliffs. By watching for a few large boulders, you can bring your boat quite close in. With an eye out for the weather, it is possible to anchor in Old Woman Bay close to a sand beach for a lunch stop. There is an interesting stream to explore that enters the bay. There are also a number of trails connected with the Lake Superior Provincial Park, one of which, the Nokomis Hiking Trail, is a self-guiding nature trail up to an inland lake. Note that if you go ashore here, there is an hourly/daily fee that is enforced. There is a self-registering box next to the toilets that are near the highway that comes down close to the water here.

Cape Chaillon is another distinctive landmark in the area. Because of deep water and no obstructions, it is possible to cruise quite close to this massive headland.

Six miles south of Cape Chaillon there is another large cape that offers some of the best anchorages and most interesting exploring in the area, **Cape Gargantua**. Pronounced "Gar-gun-TWA," this area of intricate rock formations and deep bays has long been of interest to First Nation people and those who have explored the shoreline in centuries past. Names such as the Devil's Chair and the Devil's Warehouse reflect a First Nation heritage. The Devil's Chair was said to be the spot where Naniboujou, the giant who protected the Ojibwe, rested after jumping over the lake. The Devil's Warehouse is thought to have had mythical significance, and some even think it may have been a mine for the red ochre that was used in the Ojibwe rock paintings farther down the shore.

The area's protected harbors have long been used as a refuge from the lake. There was once a small fishing "village" tucked way back in at Gargantua Harbour. A resident light keeper also used to have his home in this harbor. In the first half of the 20th century, the wharf in Gargantua Harbour was also a favorite stopping-off place for the wealthy who ventured up this shore in their large yachts. Today all that remains of the fishing station is a single deteriorating building and a couple of decaying docks. At the southeast end of the harbor, there is a dirt road that connects to Hwy. 17 (8 to 9 miles), which in recent years has seen a lot of use by backpackers and those with canoes and kayaks to gain access to the area.

On the north end of Cape Gargantua there are a number of anchorages, some of which are marginal depending on wind direction. This end of the

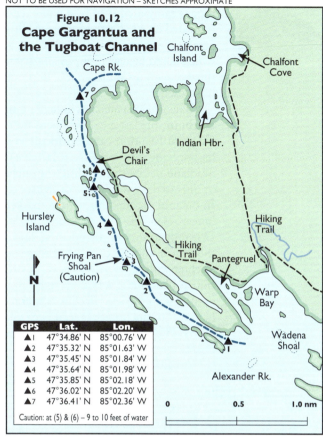

Figure 10.12
Cape Gargantua and the Tugboat Channel

GPS	Lat.	Lon.
▲1	47°34.86' N	85°00.76' W
▲2	47°35.32' N	85°01.63' W
▲3	47°35.45' N	85°01.84' W
▲4	47°35.64' N	85°01.98' W
▲5	47°35.85' N	85°02.18' W
▲6	47°36.02' N	85°02.20' W
▲7	47°36.41' N	85°02.36' W

Caution: at (5) & (6) – 9 to 10 feet of water

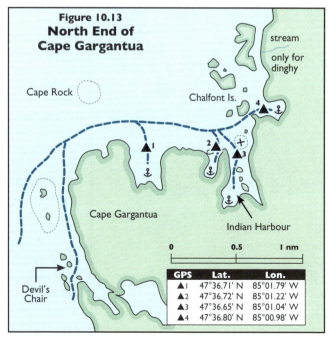

Figure 10.13
North End of Cape Gargantua

GPS	Lat.	Lon.
▲1	47°36.71' N	85°01.79' W
▲2	47°36.72' N	85°01.22' W
▲3	47°36.65' N	85°01.04' W
▲4	47°36.80' N	85°00.98' W

cape is easily identified by a white day marker, which also Fl W, that is located on the northern side of Hursley Island. Note that off this northern end of the cape there is a 1.5-fathom shoal, Cape Rock, which could be hazardous in a heavy sea. There are also some rock shoals close into shore, so it is important to not hug the shoreline too closely.

The most favored anchorage on this end of the cape is **Indian Harbour**, the last area that opens up to starboard directly south of Chalfont Island. It can be difficult to spot since there is a similar harbor lying just to the west. It helps to note that on the last headland before turning into the anchorage there is a "thunderbird" or distorted cross in white or lighter color up on the rock bluff. In the mid-decade, this natural marker was painted white so it no longer resembles a thunderbird, but looks more like a white cross. Down the center of the opening, leading south into the harbor, there are a number of shoals, rocks and little islets. It is important to enter with these held to port, favoring the starboard shoreline. Indian Harbour is very deep right up to shore, and the best holding ground with the least decline is found in the far SW dip of the harbor. The anchorage is secure for all but the strongest northerly blows. The long inlet to the east is accessible to only very shoal draft boats.

An alternative anchorage is found in the bay to the **east of Chalfont Island**. To enter, pass just to the south of Chalfont Island. Although it is open to the west, Chalfont is quite effective in breaking up most seas from the west. It is also possible to snug down into the SE corner of the bay to get more protection. The area north of Chalfont Island is very interesting to explore by dinghy. The island NW of Chalfont is often used for camping by those in canoes and kayaks. There are a couple of more islands to the north of Chalfont that form a perfect all-weather harbor. Unfortunately, the entrance between them and the mainland is foul with rock and suitable for only dinghy passage. It is possible to climb up on the rock bluffs of these islands for a dramatic view of the shoreline and down into Indian Harbour.

Another alternative anchorage is in the smaller southerly indentation in the cape, which lies just **west of Indian Harbour**. Unfortunately, there is a small island at its southern end right where you would want to anchor. It is possible

NOT TO BE USED FOR NAVIGATION – SKETCH APPROXIMATE

Figure 10.14
Indian Harbour, Cape Gargantua

Chalfont Is.

only for very shoal draft boats

N

0   0.125   0.25 nm

GPS	Lat.	Lon.
▲1	47°36.72' N	85°01.22' W
▲2	47°36.65' N	85°01.04' W
▲3	47°36.80' N	85°00.98' W

● "Thunderbird"

to squeeze into the NW of the island by reducing scope, but SE of the island is again foul with rock. It is also possible to anchor in the next harbor to the west, the largest one on this end of the cape. But anchor only with an eye to the weather, as it is quite open and exposed to the north.

If weather permits (no strong winds or fog), a trip through the **Tugboat Channel** is an interesting experience. (See Fig. 10.11.) Here one gets the best views of the spectacular rock formations that make Gargantua famous, particularly the Devil's Chair, which is located close to the northern entrance of the channel. The indentation directly SE of the Devil's Chair gives close access to an inland lake where a dinghy can be easily carried across (a short half block). In this lake and the one directly to the south, there is good fishing for northern pike. Continuing through the channel, it is possible to safely carry approximately 40 feet of water in most parts. Two exceptions are at the Devil's Chair and the narrow passage south of the Devil's Chair where there is 8 to 9 feet of water (see GPS waypoints #5 and #6), and particular care must be exercised when winding through this constricted part of the channel. Note that waypoint #5 is just on the edge of a shoal extending SE from a small rock islet seen to port when heading north through the channel (see Fig. 10.14). It is possible to get more water depth by heading just to the east of the waypoint and hugging the cape to starboard by holding approximately 30 feet off this starboard shore when heading up the channel. Going down the channel, hug the port shoreline in this area. Because there are a number of rock islets that form the outer (western) side of the Tugboat Channel, it is best to make the passage with a bow lookout and with the sun high at one's back.

Lying along the south side of Cape Gargantua there are two good anchorages, Pantegruel Harbour and Warp Bay. In approaching these, it is important to note that the area to the north of Dixon Island and the Devil's Warehouse toward the cape contains many rocks and shoals (Alexander Rock, Wadena Shoal), some of

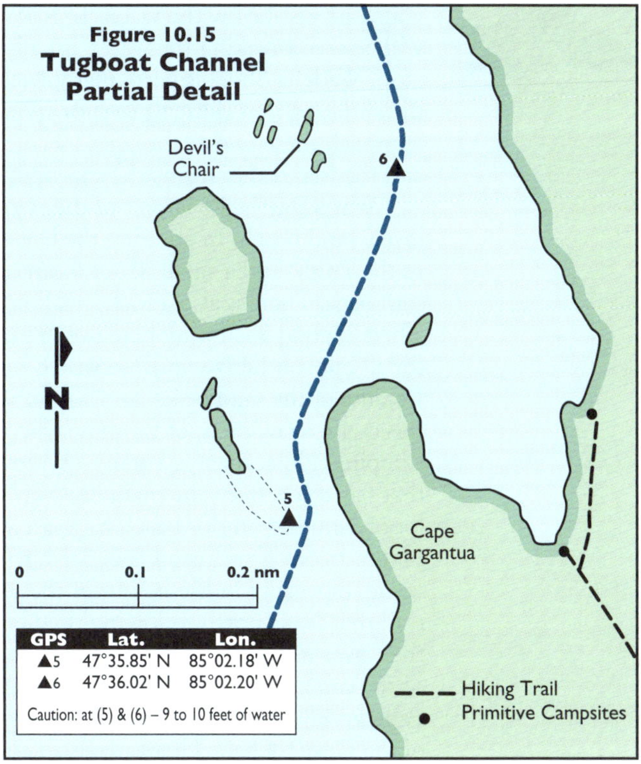

Figure 10.15
Tugboat Channel
Partial Detail

Devil's Chair

N

Cape Gargantua

0   0.1   0.2 nm

GPS	Lat.	Lon.
▲5	47°35.85' N	85°02.18' W
▲6	47°36.02' N	85°02.20' W

Caution: at (5) & (6) – 9 to 10 feet of water

– – – Hiking Trail
• Primitive Campsites

which lie just below the water. In low water years, Alexander Rock will be seen breaking the water, usually with dozens of sea gulls atop. Wadena Shoal is particularly wicked since it lies well below the surface and is difficult to spot. Therefore, it is important to approach these two anchorages by coming in close to the mainland and the island that forms the southern end of the Tugboat Channel.

Warp Bay is the largest of the two bays, and it lies next to a lovely sand beach. In entering the bay, note Wadena Shoal, that lies to the south, and a small island, both of which should be left to starboard. There is also a rock shoal on the eastern side of the bay. There is good anchoring here over a sand bottom with protection for all but southerly winds, to which the anchorage is quite open. Because of the sand beach and a number of primitive campsites, this is also a favorite spot for those who are back packing and boat-camping. Note: there is a trail to Warp Bay from Gargantua Harbour that has access from the main highway. Thus, recent years have seen a lot of camping on this beach by those who hike over from Gargantua Harbour. So, if seclusion is desired, this may not be the place to come, especially in the height of the season. There is also another trail that leads north following the Gargantua River for a ways and then over to Indian Harbour and Chalfont Cove on the other side of the cape. The newest trail in the area begins in the shallow cut to Pantegruel and crosses the cape between two lakes for a nice lookout of the Devil's Chair. There are also a couple of designated campsites in this area. (See Fig. 10.14.) Gargantua River is very interesting to explore by dinghy, and it is possible to take it a good distance upstream. There is a "swimming hole" just inside the mouth where the water gets fairly warm. Unfortunately, the large numbers of fish seen here are suckers, not trout.

A more secure anchorage, **Pantegruel Bay**, lies to the west of Warp Bay, tucked in behind the islands that are found along Warp Bay's western side. (The name Pantegruel comes from the 16th century writings of François Rabelais who wrote a satirical fantasy in which the main characters were the giants, Gargantua and his son, Pantegruel.) To get into Pantegruel it is a little tricky because there are two rather extensive shoals that lie in the middle of this long channel. These usually lie just underwater and can best be seen with Polaroid glasses. To get by these shoals it is important to hold close to the port shoreline (30 feet) so the

NOT TO BE USED FOR NAVIGATION – SKETCH APPROXIMATE

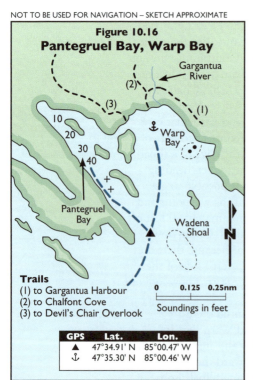

Figure 10.16
Pantegruel Bay, Warp Bay

Gargantua River

(2)

(3)

(1)

10
20
30
40

Warp Bay

Pantegruel Bay

Wadena Shoal

N

Trails
(1) to Gargantua Harbour
(2) to Chalfont Cove
(3) to Devil's Chair Overlook

0   0.125   0.25nm

Soundings in feet

GPS	Lat.	Lon.
▲	47°34.91' N	85°00.47' W
⚓	47°35.30' N	85°00.46' W

shoals are passed to starboard. With this track, 20 feet of water can be maintained.

Despite its beauty, this anchorage is frustrating because of depth versus lack of swinging room. Add to this a tendency to drag anchor through a gravel bottom, and it is not surprising that many decide for the more open Warp Bay. However, with care in anchoring (a Bahamian moor works well here), this anchorage is well worth the effort.

Within this area there is much to explore by dinghy. An interesting short trip follows through the island passage to Warp Bay. Note: at one place this passage is known to partially open and close as the water fluctuates by rising and falling—often within the hour. There is a longer trip across the bay to the **Devil's Warehouse** where it is believed the Ojibwe kept sacred birch-bark scrolls of pictographs depicting religious and historical events. There is a large cave on the northern side of the island. The cave is about 200 feet inland, slightly to the east of the middle of the island's northern shore. The area along the SW shore of the Devil's Warehouse is interesting to explore by dinghy and hike along the rocky shoreline. Adjacent to the Devil's Warehouse, on the eastern side of **Dixon Island** there is a private fishing camp. Shoal water in the area and in approaching the dock limits its use to shoal draft boats.

Gargantua Harbour, the last anchorage in the area, is the large harbor located approximately two miles south of the cape. Established in 1871, it became the site of a sizable fishing station with extensive docks and a small village by the early 1900s. Now, there is little left of the buildings, since most have been cleared and the lumber carried off. In the early part of the 20th century, when the harbor was a favorite rendezvous for cruising skippers, these docks were used as a dance pavilion when couples would gather and socialize under a canopy of twinkling stars. An integral part of the community were also the light keepers and their families who served a lighthouse on Gargantua Island from 1889 to 1948.

To enter the harbor, you can pass to either side of Gargantua Island that is marked with a white day beacon (Fl W) on a skeleton tower. If the passage between the island and the long mainland peninsula is chosen, care should be taken to remain in the center, since there is some shoaling SW of the peninsula and just west of the island.

Once in the harbor, hold close to the peninsula, which will be off to port, since there is some shoaling on the eastern side

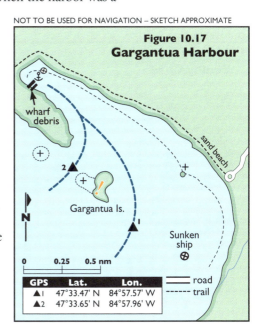

NOT TO BE USED FOR NAVIGATION – SKETCH APPROXIMATE

Figure 10.17
Gargantua Harbour

wharf debris

Gargantua Is.

Sunken ship

0   0.25   0.5 nm

GPS	Lat.	Lon.
▲1	47°33.47' N	84°57.57' W
▲2	47°33.65' N	84°57.96' W

road
trail

of the bay, along with a wreck that lies in the NE part of the far end. Anchor in 10 to 20 feet of water over a good holding sand bottom. There are remains of two docks from the old wharf to which shoal draft boats may tie. It should be noted that this harbor is also open to a hard southerly blow.

There is a nice sand beach in the far end where the water often gets warm enough for swimming. The large sand beach along the eastern side of the harbor, which one sees when coming in, is a favorite spot for canoeists and those who are boat-camping. There are a number of campsites and pit toilets that have been constructed in cleared areas, a couple hundred yards inland. Note that this is one of the few places along this segment of the shore where there is access to the lake via a side road that comes to the harbor at the SE end off the main highway. Because of this, this harbor has become an off-loading point for those with canoes and small boats and has seen increased use in recent years. The wreck that lies off the NE shore in the far end of the harbor is interesting to explore via dinghy. It is the *Columbus*, a 139-foot wooden tug that caught fire while tied to the dock in 1910. In Lake Superior's clear waters, much of the wreck, including the propeller and boiler, can readily be seen as it lies on its side in 10 feet to 30 feet of water.

Six miles down the shoreline from Gargantua Harbour, there is a little-known and used harbor, **Beatty Cove**. Although open to S and SE winds, this snug little bay offers good anchoring with a sand bottom and protection for all other winds.

The cove is easy to locate, since it lies to the NE of Leach Island, which is quite a large landmark in the area. In approaching this area, there are no hazards except for the shoal water surrounding Ella Islet that lies to the north of Leach Island. Note also that there is a small shoal extending out from the SW end of the peninsula that forms the west side of Beatty Cove.

To enter the cove, take a midchannel course. Because there are some rocks and shoaling in the middle of the cove, swinging room in the middle is cut down considerably. However, it is possible to anchor to either side of the shoal, with more protection to the SW of the shoal. Here, there is protection for all but SE winds, but even S and SW winds can give an uncomfortable surge.

Because of the small sand beach, the cove will sometimes be used by canoeists and those who are boat-camping, especially those who make the 10-mile run out of Sinclair Cove. On the northern shore there is an old trapping cabin that

NOT TO BE USED FOR NAVIGATION – SKETCH APPROXIMATE

Figure 10.18
Beatty Cove

N

15
10
15
20
20

0   0.25   0.5 nm

Soundings in feet.

GPS	Lat.	Lon.
▲	47°29.88' N	84°52.65' W

shows signs of occasional use.

Continuing down the shoreline toward Sinclair Cove there is an area of bad water surrounding the **Lizard Islands**. Because of this, the Lizards are usually given wide berth by those with deep-draft boats. The islands are, however, used by those with flat-bottomed boats making the five-mile run out from Sinclair Cove. In recent years the old fishing station on the north side of South Lizard Island has been occupied with a fairly permanent summer family camp.

Snugly tucked in between large rugged bluffs, **Sinclair Cove** has long been a favorite for those who cruise Lake Superior's eastern shore, since it is one of the most beautiful harbors in this section of the lake. It is also one of the few places where a road comes down to the lake, and there is a small boat launching ramp here that makes it a popular jumping off spot for those who wish to gain access to the water. There used to be a substantial Government Dock here that was partially destroyed in the storm that sank the *Edmund Fitzgerald* in November 1975. The initial breach was never repaired and each subsequent season saw further deterioration until the dock was finally removed in late fall 1991. Despite this, Sinclair Cove has much to offer the transient boater since there are trails to hike, rocky bluffs to climb and even a small sand beach for a shore fire. But the main highlight of this lovely anchorage is the most spectacular site of Ojibwe rock paintings to be found on the lake.

The cove is identified by a white day marker that also flashes white on the SW end of Sinclair Island. If coming from the north, there are no hazards except for those areas adjacent to the Lizard Islands. Also note the shoal areas near Ganley Rock. With southerly approaches, it is important to give the Agawa Islands, where there are some rock shoals, and Griffon Reef, that lies north of Montreal Island, adequate berth.

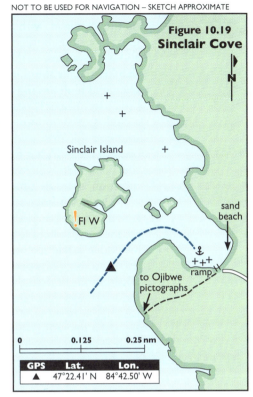

NOT TO BE USED FOR NAVIGATION – SKETCH APPROXIMATE

Figure 10.19
Sinclair Cove

N

Sinclair Island

Fl W

sand beach

to Ojibwe pictographs

ramp

0   0.125   0.25 nm

GPS	Lat.	Lon.
▲	47°22.41' N	84°42.50' W

View from the bluff above Sinclair Cove.
DAHL

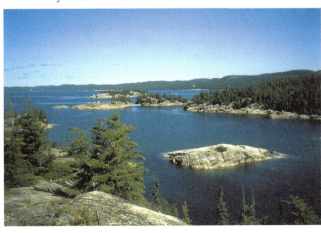

To enter the cove, pass between the island and the large bluffs on the mainland, with Sinclair Island kept to port. The anchorage doesn't open up until after you are well-committed into the entrance and it may appear as though you are going to end up on the rocks that lie straight ahead in the center of the bay. But by following the mainland bluff around to starboard, you will come into a quaint little bay where it is possible to anchor in 10 to 20 feet of water over a sand-rippled bottom. Note that there are a few rocks along the southern side that need to be avoided. The anchorage is partially open to the NW, but for most summertime weather, the outlying rocks and islets will give sufficient protection. Depending on wind direction, there are times when an uncomfortable swell develops.

The area is interesting to explore by dinghy, especially Sinclair Island and the beaches to the north of the cove. In one spot there are the shreds of old fish nets that have been left out on racks to dry — all that is left of a once active fishing station. On a calm day with no sea running it is possible to pull a dinghy up on the rocks on the outside and climb to the top of the southern bluff that overlooks the anchorage for a bird's-eye view down into the anchorage and a panoramic view of the shoreline to the north. It is also possible to reach the top of this bluff by taking a spinoff trail from the trail that leads from the launch ramp parking lot to the pictographs.

The Ojibwe pictographs are found at the water's edge beneath high overhanging cliffs, just around the corner toward the Agawa Islands. There are a number of ways in which to see the paintings. If conditions are calm, it is possible to take a dinghy around and see the paintings from the water. Two other alternatives are to take the trail from the launch ramp parking lot or follow the road to another parking area where there is another trail that leads over to the rock ledges. The trail begins at the parking lot near some display cases. Be sure to wear shoes with a good grip, for the only way to see the paintings is to walk out on a rock ledge that slants into the water. Note that there is a daily fee that is collected by a dropbox near the bulletin board next to the main parking lot.

The red ochre (red pigment made from the mineral hematite mixed with grease) paintings tell a story of a canoe trip "four days over the water" from the Carp River (Porcupine Mountains on Lake Superior's southern shore) to the Agawa Rock — a distance of 215 nautical miles. The expedition/war party was led by the great chief Myeegun who, with the help of the great panther water-lynx Misshepezhieu, was able to lead his five canoes safely to the east shore. One of the pictures, a horse and rider, clearly dates at least some of the pictographs, indicating that they were painted after the coming of the white explorers in the 1600s. Other pictographs, with variations in style and levels over the water, indicate that the paintings were not all done at once, but probably appeared over a great expanse of time.

Although the site was long acknowledged by locals, its modern-day discovery is usually attributed to Selwyn Dewdney (1901-1979), a leading authority on Shield Rock Art in Canada, who came across a reference to the site in the 1950s when he was reading material written by Henry Schoolcraft, the well-known Indian agent in Sault Ste. Marie in the early 1800s. Schoolcraft had been given sketches of the paintings on a birch-bark scroll by a Native American named Shingwauk. Along with the sketches, there were two descriptions of sites, the one at Agawa and one on the south shore. More than 100 years later in 1958, Dewdney finally found the Agawa site after 14 months of searching. The south shore site has never been found. Note that in just the 40-plus years that we have been viewing the pictographs, they have faded considerably. It is important not to touch them since body oils break down the pigment.

Behind **Ganley Island**, which lies approximately two-thirds of a mile SE of Sinclair Cove, there is an area where it is possible to anchor and get good protection for all but the strongest NW winds. Although this area behind the islands is open at both ends, the best approach is to come in from the NW, since the SE entrance contains a number of rocks and shoal water that need to be skirted. Because the islands blend in well with the bold mainland shoreline, they are difficult to spot, and coming in along the mainland from the NW is quite helpful in finding the anchorage. Recent years have seen a lot of activity on Ganley Island since the extended family of a past commercial fisherman now uses the fishing station as a summer camp.

From Sinclair Cove to Mamainse Harbour, a distance of 21 nautical miles, there are no all-weather facilities for keel boats. The **Agawa River**, which is located three miles SE of Sinclair Cove, is only navigable by dinghy; just outside of the mouth it is quite shallow and clogged with deadheads and debris. It is possible to take a dinghy about one-half mile upstream where it again gets very shallow just before coming to a bridge that is used by highway traffic. Beaching a dinghy about one-half mile NW of the river and cutting through the woods to the highway gains access to the Awausee Hiking Trail. This is a very vigorous trail (4 to 5 hours) that follows an old logging road and then climbs high in the hills to offer spectacular helicopter views of the Agawa Valley and Lake Superior.

Another three miles down the shoreline there is a place where deep-draft boats can get marginal protection for

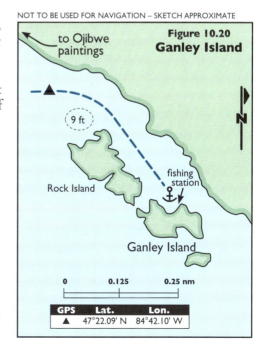

NOT TO BE USED FOR NAVIGATION – SKETCH APPROXIMATE

Figure 10.20
Ganley Island

to Ojibwe paintings

9 ft

N

fishing station

Rock Island

Ganley Island

| 0 | 0.125 | 0.25 nm |

GPS	Lat.	Lon.
▲	47°22.09' N	84°42.10' W

anchoring in **MacGregor Cove** or on the other side of the peninsula headland. In either case these anchorages should be used primarily as lunch stops because they are open to at least one direction.

A very limited possibility along this stretch of shoreline is at the **Montreal River**. In extremely good conditions with no sea running, very shoal draft boats or small powerboats drawing less than two feet can negotiate the mouth of the Montreal River where there are limited supplies. In low water years, the mouth of the river is not navigable by any boat. It is possible for deep-draft boats to anchor south of the southern arm of the river and then dinghy around, but only with an eye to the weather, since one is very exposed to most wind directions here.

In traveling this segment of the shoreline it is important to note Montreal Shoal, a sizable formation of underwater rock that is split into two main shoals. The shoal is difficult to spot because it lies in a section of wide-open water with no nearby distinguishing landmarks. Although its minimum depths are 7 feet, it could cause problems to deep-draft boats with even a small running sea. Thus this is one area where it pays to be diligent with navigation and it helps to establish a waypoint with a safety line of position to track in order to avoid the shoal.

In **Mica Bay**, the first bay north of Mamainse Harbour, there is a small site of rock paintings. Once again, these are on a rock face wall about 20 feet above the water. These differ from known Ojibwe paintings in that they show thick brush marks and use different pigments, namely yellow ochre along with some white and black. Thus aboriginal origin seems suspect and it is now believed that they were painted by a passing artist in the late 1950s.

The area between Mamainse Harbour and the Montreal River first gained importance in the late 1700s when two miners (Alexander Baxter and Alexander Henry) who, having met with bad luck on Lake Superior's south shore, turned their efforts to this area. Looking for copper and silver, they did a lot of searching and dug many tunnels, but never realized any great profits. These pursuits were revived by the Montreal Mining Company in the 1850s, but again with little luck. The Mamainse Mine operated for about five years in the early 1880s a couple of miles north of Mamainse, but the copper soon ran out. However, had these early miners known about, or had they been looking for uranium, their hard efforts would not have been wasted. For in 1948, Robert Campbell used a Geiger counter to discover pitchblende in the area of Theano Point. When we look at this rugged shoreline, it is hard to believe that at one time hundreds of prospectors' tents lined Alona Bay and in just three short years there were about 5,000 claims filed. Today, there is an abandoned mine located here on Highway 17, the Ranwick Uranium Mine.

This section of the lake has also had its share of logging activity mixed with commercial fishing. With the large fishery located at

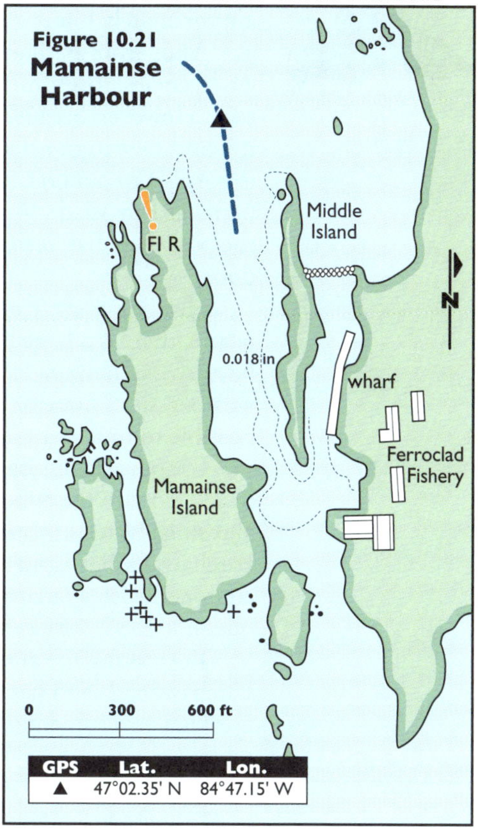

Mamainse Harbour, commercial fishing has become one of the most important industries on this eastern shore. The hub of the industry for this whole section of the lake, from Sault Ste. Marie to Thunder Bay is here. Individual fishing tugs bring in their catches to be packed and shipped to numerous markets throughout Canada and the United States. Trucks are also sent along the shoreline as far away as Thunder Bay, 12 months of the year, making Ferroclad's, the fishery located here, one of the largest on Lake Superior.

Mamainse Harbour is also an important harbor of refuge in the 60-mile stretch from Sinclair Cove to Sault Ste. Marie where there are few well-protected anchorages and the distances between them are often great. An all-weather harbor with a well-built government dock, Mamainse gets heavy use by local tugs that fish the area. There usually is some transient space left on the dock. However, the tugs do have priority on dock usage and when all are in, it can become quite congested and tight to maneuver.

Figure 10.21
Mamainse Harbour

Middle Island

Fl R

0.018 in

wharf

Ferroclad Fishery

Mamainse Island

GPS	Lat.	Lon.
▲	47°02.35' N	84°47.15' W

0   300   600 ft

In approaching Mamainse Harbour from the north, the only obstruction is Mica Shoal, which lies four miles NW of the harbor. From the south it is important to note Hibbard Rock that stands one mile offshore. The entrance to the harbor is well-marked with a large red and white diamond day marker, which flashes red and is equipped with RACON (– –). The marker and the entrance to the harbor are at the north end of Mamainse Island.

When coming in for the first time, it should be noted that this is one of those harbors where the harbor does not "open up" until the last minute. Although in moderate water years a depth of 7 feet may be found in the entrance channel toward the south end of the "middle island," it should be remembered that the *Last Time*, an 80-foot tug that draws close to 6 feet, used this harbor regularly in the past. In order to maintain clear water when passing through this narrow channel, it is important to stay well in midchannel, for there is considerable shoaling to each side and at the southern end of the "middle island." The wharf is found by rounding to port and heading back to the north between the "middle island" and the mainland. Just as you are making this turn there is a shallow spot that may give those with deep-draft boats problems in low water years. Because of constricted space and tug traffic, there really is no place to anchor within the harbor. Depth at the dock is

approximately 6 feet.

Aside from fresh and smoked fish, there are no supplies here. In emergencies, it is sometimes possible to obtain diesel from the fish tugs. However, because of high-pressure hoses and tug dock usage, it works best to transfer the diesel via portable gas cans. At times it is possible to obtain small amounts of gasoline from a hand-cranked barrel at Ferroclad's — again transfer has to be made via cans. In the past there has been a nominal charge for use of the government dock.

Heading down from Coppermine Point south toward Sault Ste. Marie, there is a large bay that is actually made up of many smaller bays by Batchawana Island that lies in the center. By watching the weather, since none of the anchorages have complete protection, it is possible to find a number of places to anchor in the area.

In approaching **Batchawana Bay**, it is important to not come in too close to the Sandy Islands since there are a number of rocks and shoal water surrounding them. The western extremity of Batchawana Bay is marked with a bell buoy that flashes red and is equipped with a radar reflector. The buoy is located approximately one mile S-SW of Corbeil Point.

In entering the area, the first bay that lies to the NW of Batchawana Island has a couple of anchoring possibilities. There is even a government dock here, not too far from the First Nation

NOT TO BE USED FOR NAVIGATION – SKETCH APPROXIMATE

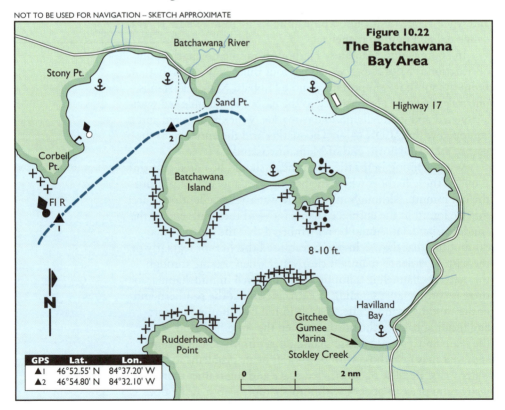

Figure 10.22
The Batchawana Bay Area

Batchawana River

Stony Pt.

Sand Pt.

Highway 17

Corbeil Pt.

Fl R

Batchawana Island

8-10 ft.

N

Havilland Bay

Gitchee Gumee Marina

Rudderhead Point

Stokley Creek

GPS	Lat.	Lon.
▲1	46°52.55' N	84°37.20' W
▲2	46°54.80' N	84°32.10' W

0   1   2 nm

village that lies on the western shore of the bay. The dock is just inside the point that lies 1.5 miles NE of Corbeil Point. It's best to approach the dock "straight on" as there are some underwater obstructions between it and the old dock seen to the south. In the shape of an "L," the dock, which is in some disrepair, has good depths on both sides along its outer end. If seclusion is desired, this is not the place to be, since the local residents are often very curious about visiting boats.

Within this first bay it is also possible to anchor off Stoney Point and to the NW of the Batchawana River. This second anchorage is of interest, for here it is possible to take a dinghy approximately one block upstream to where Highway 17 crosses the river. (Note: the mouth of the Batchawana River is quite shoaled with silting and fouled with deadheads. Locals will often buoy an entrance through this shoal area, but it still should be entered only with dinghies and flat-bottomed boats.) Just before the highway bridge there is the Sunset Motel, which has a number of docks for small boats. Gasoline can be obtained here. One block east on the highway there is a small general store where ice, gasoline and diesel can be obtained — an important supply depot on a shoreline where little else is available. (When leaving your boat in this area, it is advisable to have it locked up.)

In the next bay to the east, there are a couple of more possibilities for anchoring. To enter this bay it is necessary to pass through a constricted area between Sand Point on the mainland and Batchawana Island. Note in particular the extensive shoaling that lies to the west of Sand Point. This can be avoided by favoring the Batchawana Island side of the passage. Within this second bay there is exceptionally good anchoring along the north side of Batchawana Island. Here it is wild and marshy with more seclusion than other spots in the area, since there are many cottages on the mainland.

Another good place to anchor is to the NW of the mouth of the river (incorrectly named "Harmony River" on the charts) that empties into the NE section of this second bay. Be aware, however, that there is shoal water to the south of the river mouth. Note: when anchoring in the Batchawana Bay area, protection is usually one or two sides. Therefore, these anchorages must be used with a cautious eye to the weather and with alternatives kept well in mind, should the winds change.

Another anchorage is found by following around Batchawana Island to Havilland Bay that lies in the southern extremity of the area. A short way up Stokely Creek there is the only marine facility in the area, the **Gitchee Gumee Marina** (Tel.: 705-649-2101). Although depths are 7 feet in this long narrow marina, there is a bar that often forms at the entrance. In the winter of 2006/07, the entrance was dredged to a depth of 6 to 7 feet. There used to be a popular restaurant here, but it is now closed. Likewise, there are no longer any cruising amenities (fuel, pump-out), except electricity.

In entering or leaving Havilland Bay it is possible to pass south of Batchawana Island as long as a midchannel course is taken to avoid the rocks and shoal water south of the island and those offshore of the mainland. However, there is an 8-foot bar that needs to be crossed that could give deep draft problems in low water years.

Twelve miles to the south of Batchawana Bay there is another large bay, one of the largest on Lake Superior, **Goulais Bay**. Banked by massive headlands, this bay is easy to spot since it extends deep into the mainland. The bay is also marked by a light (Fl W) that is located 1.5 miles NE of Goulais Point.

Although this bay is quite open to the SW, it is possible to get protection from all other winds by anchoring in various parts of the bay. However, if the wind should switch, especially from the SW, there is no alternative protection in the immediate area. There is another government wharf here, on the west shore just north of the light adjacent to a First Nation mission. The dock is unusable by those with deep draft boats, since there are large rocks on the outside and less than 3 feet on the inside. It is possible to anchor just to the north of the dock where there is some protection from SW winds but not S.

In a westerly blow, the eastern side of **Ile Parisienne** provides good protection. It is also the only place on this side of Whitefish Bay where there is protection from SW winds. If approach to the island is made from the north, note Parisienne Shoal that lies approximately two miles north of the island. It is possible to anchor anywhere in the indentation along the eastern side of the island. The southernmost part is an especially nice anchorage where it is possible to get in quite close to shore and anchor over a sand bottom. An interesting trip is to take a dinghy around the southern end of the island to visit the light that has one of the most beautiful tower structures on the lake. This lighthouse, which was built in 1911, is of special interest because the tower lantern room was built of reinforced concrete, a new approach in building material for that time. Note: the Isle Parisienne anchorages

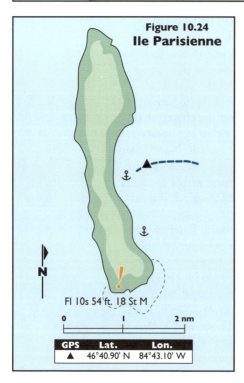

Figure 10.23
Goulais Bay

Goulais Point

Fl W

GPS	Lat.	Lon.
▲	46°41.50' N	84°30.80' W

Figure 10.24
Ile Parisienne

Fl 10s 54 ft. 18 St M

GPS	Lat.	Lon.
▲	46°40.90' N	84°43.10' W

Gros Cap Light in Whitefish Bay. DAHL

should only be used in settled conditions or when westerly winds are assured, since it is a long way to go to get protection from other wind directions.

Whether entering or leaving Whitefish Bay, there is one "landmark" that stands out abruptly on the horizon and that is the distinctive structure that houses the **light at Gros Cap Reefs**. This large sentinel, which marks the reef and stands watch over the beginning of the constricted shipping lanes, flashes red and is readily seen for miles around. Equipped with RACON (– • –), it makes a good target for homing.

There is one last anchorage/dock on the east shore before reaching Sault Ste. Marie. It is located at **Gros Cap on the mainland** approximately 1.5 miles NE of Gros Cap Light. In the early 1980s new docks were added along with an additional rubble breakwater making this an all-weather harbor. The only problem is that it is very shallow both at the entrance and within the harbor itself. In high water years those with deep-draft boats (5.5 feet) can safely get in and tie off on one of the outer docks — as long as no sea is running.

To reach the harbor a course of 65

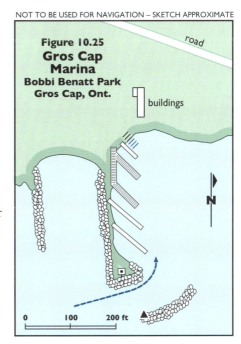

NOT TO BE USED FOR NAVIGATION – SKETCH APPROXIMATE

Figure 10.25
Gros Cap Marina
Bobbi Benatt Park
Gros Cap, Ont.

road

buildings

N

0   100   200 ft

degrees T is taken from Gros Cap Light, keeping the light squarely on the stern. The harbor is marked by two rubble breakwaters with day beacons on each, a red triangle on the south (starboard) breakwater and a black bull's-eye on the north (port) breakwater. It is important to favor the port breakwater, being careful of a 7-foot spot (rock) just before the entrance. It is also important to turn quickly to port once the entrance is cleared since there is shoal water along the southern portion. The harbor is very small, and there is little room for large boats to maneuver. Although a number of locals keep their boats here, there is often room for transients. The harbor provides a welcome stopover on what is often a long day coming into or leaving Sault Ste. Marie. Because of limited space, however, alternatives should be kept in mind in case there is no room. Also, do not attempt this harbor if there is any sea running.

When you come down into Whitefish Bay from the north and join the merging traffic in the shipping lanes, the pulse of the lake is once again deeply felt. With the wilderness left behind, we return to enter the fast stepping pace of the world of industry and progress. Within the buoyed channels, we edge over to the side to allow the huge lakers and ships from all over the world to pass us. The resonating throb of their diesel engines again reminds us of Lake Superior's legacy to us all: an inland sea that gives abundantly of its resources — a vital link in the greatest fresh-water system in the world.

Chapter Eleven

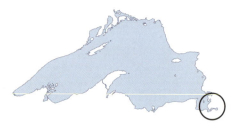

Crossroads of the Upper Great Lakes:
Sault Ste. Marie and St. Marys River

From the time of discovery, the rapids of the St. Marys River have served as a crossroads for all who traverse the Upper Great Lakes. For more than 2,000 years, *Bawating* (water pitching over rock) was a great meeting place for thousands of Native Americans who gathered each spring and fall for prodigious whitefish runs in the river's rapids. Legendary are the early French accounts of these *saulteurs* (people of the rapids) who ran the rapids in birch canoes scooping up great numbers of whitefish with their long-handled dip nets.

The French, arriving on the scene in the early 1600s, were quick to realize the value of this strategic location between lakes Superior and Huron. Fathers Isaac Jogues and Charles Tambault are credited for giving the rapids and river the name of their patron, Sainte Marie, in 1641. In 1668, the Jesuit Pere Jacques Marquette was sent to establish a mission at the base of the rapids, and in the historic Pageant of the Sault (1671) the entire northern Great Lakes were declared as part of the realm of the king of France. Lured by a lucrative trade in furs, the French established a trading post in the next century and Sault Ste. Marie became the gateway for exploration between east and west.

Three different rival powers, the North West Fur Company (French), Hudson's Bay Company (English) and the American Fur Company, had at one time or another posts at this strategic crossroads. One notable fur trader bears special mention. John Johnston first established a trading post on Madeline Island in the Apostles in 1791. After marrying Chief Wauk-O-Jeeg's daughter, he returned to Sault Ste. Marie with his young wife to build a home and trading post. One of his daughters, Jane, married Henry Rowe Schoolcraft, the famed Indian agent, interpreter, explorer, and author who established the first Indian agency in Sault Ste. Marie. Both the Johnston and Schoolcraft dwellings remain standing

Please Note:
Maps and Charts in this book are not necessarily to scale and are not intended for navigation.

today, restored for all to enjoy, a brief glimpse back into the rich history of the area.

To ensure the peace after the War of 1812, Colonel Hugh Brady was sent from New York with a contingent of infantry men to build a fort on the American side. Interestingly, Fort Brady, as it came to be known, was constructed on the same site as the original Marquette mission built in 1669. Despite a dwindling fur trade, the American Fur Company established a post in 1836 just below today's MacArthur Lock where the U.S. Army Corps of Engineers Warehouse now stands.

Throughout the centuries, the nearly mile-long rapids with their 21-foot drop remained a formidable obstacle to all who traveled to and from Lake Superior's waters. In 1789, the North West Fur Company built a 2,500-foot canal and a single 8-foot-by-38-foot wooden lock bypass around the rapids on the Ontario side. This structure, however, was burned by the Americans in the War of 1812 and never rebuilt. In 1839, on the American side, a brief attempt to build a canal by a private firm authorized by the state of Michigan was brought to a quick halt by Fort Brady soldiers in an effort to protect their millrace that provided power for a sawmill. The next solution was the "strap railroad" built in 1845 on the American side by newspaperman Sheldon McKnight (founder of present-day Detroit Free Press). Consisting of a wooden railway covered with metal to reduce wear by horse-drawn carts, it extended from the American Fur Company headquarters to the head of the rapids. By 1850, 6,000 tons of cargo were hauled over this inland bypass per season.

The discovery of copper and iron on Lake Superior's shores,

NOT TO BE USED FOR NAVIGATION – SKETCH APPROXIMATE

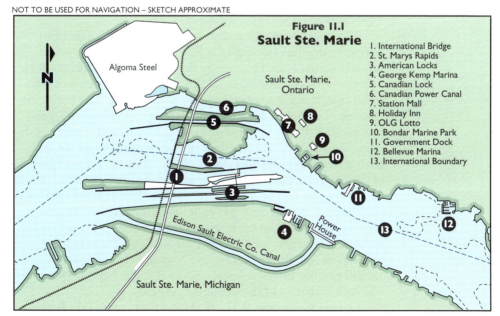

Figure 11.1
Sault Ste. Marie

1. International Bridge
2. St. Marys Rapids
3. American Locks
4. George Kemp Marina
5. Canadian Lock
6. Canadian Power Canal
7. Station Mall
8. Holiday Inn
9. OLG Lotto
10. Bondar Marine Park
11. Government Dock
12. Bellevue Marina
13. International Boundary

Algoma Steel

Sault Ste. Marie, Ontario

Edison Sault Electric Co. Canal

Power House

Sault Ste. Marie, Michigan

needed to feed the metal-hungry industrial conglomerates of the East, provided the incentive for a more efficient means of circumventing the rapids. The first lock on the Michigan side was constructed by Charles T. Harvey of the Fairbanks Scale Company, which had extensive mining interests in the Keweenaw Peninsula. Consisting of two 350-foot locks in tandem, it took two years (1853 to 1855), 1,000 men and approximately $1 million to at last open Lake Superior to the other Great Lakes.

At first the State Lock, as it was called, was administered by the state of Michigan, and boats were required to pay a toll of 4 cents per ton. The importance of this strategic canal to the national economy quickly became apparent, along with the need for additional locks, which exceeded the state's funding capabilities. Thus in 1881, the building, operation and maintenance of the locks were turned over to the U.S. government under the jurisdiction of the U.S. Army Corps of Engineers.

In the decades that followed, additional locks were added and upgraded to meet the demands of Great Lakes shipping. By 1881 a second lock, the Weitzel, was constructed parallel to the original State Lock. The original Poe Lock was completed in 1896, and in 1908 the construction of a third lock, the Davis, was begun and completed in 1914. A fourth lock, the Sabin, was started in 1913 and completed in 1919. In 1943, the MacArthur Lock was constructed to replace the aging Weitzel Lock, and in 1961 a new Poe Lock was ordered, the largest on the Great Lakes, and completed in 1968. (See Fig 11.2.) By 2000 the Sabin was unused, and the Davis was seldom used leaving the MacArthur and Poe locks heavily used carrying the brunt of commercial traffic. There were plans to combine the Sabin and Davis locks to make a duplicate Poe Lock.

The impetus for a Canadian lock occurred when Canadian troops, in an effort to curtail the Riel Rebellion of 1870, were denied westward canal passage by the Americans. Construction on a single Canadian lock began in 1887 and was completed in 1895. In its time, it was the largest lock in the world and represented the epitome of advanced waterway engineering technology, being the first canal in the world to utilize electrically operated machinery. In recent decades this lock was the main facility used by recreational boaters, reserving the larger American locks for the congested traffic of Great Lakes commercial shipping. In the summer of 1987, it was discovered that part of the inner wall was giving way and the lock was closed. A smaller lock was built inside the first in 1996 and 1997 to accommodate recreational vessels. The repair cost $10.3 million and the new lock reopened in July 1998. Although the upper gates run off the new system, interestingly, the lower gates are still running on the original gearing that was built in 1890. The new lock is about half the size of the original lock.

During World War II, the St. Marys River carried the heaviest ship canal traffic in the world, with iron ore transported from Lake Superior's north shore to build a nation's navy. Today, the Sault Locks are one of the largest and busiest locking systems in the world and are a part of the St. Lawrence Seaway. Gargantuan

"thousand-footers" squeeze tightly into the largest Poe Lock and old "salties" are seen flying flags from ports of distant countries. Spanning the locks and linking two countries is an impressive landmark, the two-mile International Bridge. Traversing the bridge, a helicopter-like view of locking operations can be seen along with both sides of the river: the Canadian Sault to the north and the American Soo to the south.

Artistic rendering of the new lock at the Soo Locks in Saulte Ste. Marie, Michigan. U.S. Army Corps of Engineers photo by Ricardo Garcia-Diaz.

Long before the close of the 20th century it became apparent that with the increased number of thousand footers and larger vessels in general something had to be done to take the pressure off the Poe Lock, the only lock large enough to accommodate these larger modern cargo vessels. Often called the "linchpin" of Great Lakes navigation, by 1986 plans were already in progress to merge the Davis and Sabin Locks, now both over 100 years old, into a Super-lock. The plan calls for a lock that is 1,200 ft long, 110 ft wide and 32 ft deep. (See a photo rendition of the New Lock.) It consists of 3 phases.

Phase 1: Includes deepening the upstream approach to the northern channel from 24 to 30 ft deep so modern vessels could approach the New Lock. This phase was completed in August 2022.

Phase 2: Includes rehabilitating the upstream approach walls. In addition to guiding vessels into the New Lock they will also allow vessels to tie up on the wall while waiting their turn to lock through. This phase is expected to be completed in the summer of 2024.

Phase 3: Includes demolishing the Sabin Lock, excavation of bedrock, constructing the New Lock at the Soo chamber walls and floor, fabrication and installation of miter gates, installation of mechanical and electrical systems, constructing a new pump well, and rehabilitating downstream approach walls. This phase is expected to be completed by summer 2030.

Locking Through

The American Locks

Although the American Locks are used primarily for commercial vessels, recreational vessels may also use the MacArthur locks. Note, however, that it may take longer to transit the American Locks than the Canadian locks. The locks are easily identified by the two adjacent arched spans of the International Bridge. The southernmost arch spans the MacArthur and Poe locks, the northern arch of the two spans the Davis and Sabin locks, now under construction for the New Lock. (Note: the single bridge arch that lies close to the Canadian side spans the Canadian Lock.) To "lock through" there are a couple of basic steps to simplify the procedure.

The first step is to contact the Control Tower when you are within a quarter mile of the locks. This is done by calling American Locks or their callsign WUD31 on VHF Channel 16 or preferably 14. Next identify your vessel (example — 35-foot power cruiser) and tell whether you wish to lock up to Lake Superior or lock down. You should also be prepared to give your boat registration number: either documentation number or boat license. At this point the lockmaster will then direct you to the MacArthur Lock since the Poe Lock is used primarily for large ships and thousand-footers.

Sometimes you can motor right into a waiting lock, but often there is a short wait as another vessel is locking through to your side. Red and green traffic lights will tell you whether to wait or go ahead. An amber light means the lock is being prepared (either filling or flushing) for an incoming vessel. Fenders should

NOT TO BE USED FOR NAVIGATION – SKETCH APPROXIMATE

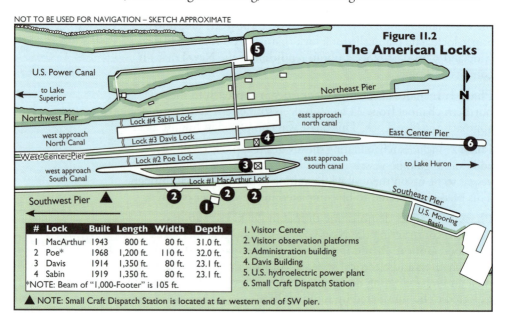

Figure 11.2
The American Locks

#	Lock	Built	Length	Width	Depth
1	MacArthur	1943	800 ft.	80 ft.	31.0 ft.
2	Poe*	1968	1,200 ft.	110 ft.	32.0 ft.
3	Davis	1914	1,350 ft.	80 ft.	23.1 ft.
4	Sabin	1919	1,350 ft.	80 ft.	23.1 ft.

*NOTE: Beam of "1,000-Footer" is 105 ft.

1. Visitor Center
2. Visitor observation platforms
3. Administration building
4. Davis Building
5. U.S. hydroelectric power plant
6. Small Craft Dispatch Station

▲ NOTE: Small Craft Dispatch Station is located at far western end of SW pier.

be placed on the south side (starboard when locking down, port when locking up). You may use your own dock lines (80 feet are recommended) or those provided by the lock attendants. If you should choose the latter, be sure to request two lines, one each for bow and stern, otherwise you may be provided with only one. Whether you are going up or down, it is important to have crew members stationed on deck to fend off (a boat hook is very helpful), since the motion from the water flow can be fairly active).

Once the gates are closed and all the boats are positioned and secured, it takes approximately 20 minutes for the actual locking up or down. When the gates are opened and the green light is on, the dock lines can be released, and you can proceed out of the lock.

The Canadian Locks

It is by far preferred that recreational vessels use the Canadian Locks since they are much easier and quicker to use than the American Locks, which are busy with large commercial traffic. Initially there was a fee for locking through, but this was relinquished after the first year of reopening. Procedure is to approach a red triangular sign with L/A (Limit of Approach) in white letters. Contact the lock by calling "VDX 23 Canadian Canal" on VHF Channel 14 and inform the lockmaster whether you wish to lock up or down. The lockmaster will then inform you on the condition of the lock and the time to wait. Note: the traffic light interpretation on Figure 11.3. Proceed into the lock when the signal changes to green.

Recreational vessels are requested to use the north side where there is a series of plastic-coated vertical steel cables along the wall. Have the fenders on the starboard side locking up, on the port side locking down. Position the boat between two cables and LOOP (don't tie) lines around the cable fore and aft so they can easily slip up or down. Again, a boat hook is most helpful in keeping a boat off the wall since there is some motion as the water flows in or out. The south wall is used primarily for larger tour boats. If you should have to use this wall, there are no cables, and bow and stern lines (75 feet each) must be run to bollards on shore. Do not release lines until the gates are opened and the green light flashes on. Then exit the lock slowly.

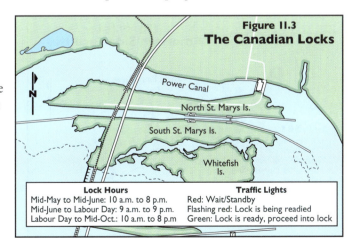

Figure 11.3
The Canadian Locks

Power Canal
North St. Marys Is.
South St. Marys Is.
Whitefish Is.

Lock Hours	Traffic Lights
Mid-May to Mid-June: 10 a.m. to 8 p.m.	Red: Wait/Standby
Mid-June to Labour Day: 9 a.m. to 9 p.m.	Flashing red: Lock is being readied
Labour Day to Mid-Oct.: 10 a.m. to 8 p.m	Green: Lock is ready, proceed into lock

The American Soo

When the transient boater approaches the Soo for the first time, the effect can be somewhat overwhelming. Large lakers of commercial shipping ply their ways to and from the locks, tour boats with waving passengers pass to either side, buoys must be accounted for, tugs and work boats line commercial slips. Until the mid-1980s , transient dockage was almost unavailable—especially on the American side.

Dockage

Note: to obtain U.S. Customs clearance, call 906-632-7221.

From the water, the most outstanding landmark and structure on the American side is the Edison Sault Hydroelectric Plant. Its Romanesque masonry spans 1,500 feet over a millrace that feeds dozens of turbines. Just to the west of it is the Valley Camp Museum Ship. Adjacent to the ship is the newest marina in the area, the **George Kemp Downtown Marina** (VHF channels 9 & 16/Tel.: 906-635-7670). Named after the owner of the property and the Kemp Coal Dock, the 62-slip marina was constructed in the late 1990s. This beautiful marina provides all cruising amenities: gasoline, diesel, pump-out, electricity, water, showers, and laundry facilities. Dockside telephone connections and cable TV are also in the plans. The marina even provides free bicycles, a nice alternative for getting around town and seeing the sites. Note: because of the strong river current, it is helpful to approach the marina entrance from downstream parallel to the outer bulkhead before swinging into the entrance. This gives a more controlled entry presenting the boat broadside to the current for as little time as possible.

Another marina that is used primarily by locals is four miles southeast of the city at a **Michigan Waterways Commission Marina** named after **Charles T. Harvey** who built the first American lock. It is found by leaving the main shipping channel of the St. Marys River at Frechette Point south of Buoy #93 and passing through a small buoyed secondary channel leading NW behind three islands (Unnamed Island, Island #2 and Island #3). (Note: be sure to heed the shallow water indicated on the chart south of Buoy #93 and give it good clearance.) The marina is found well into this secondary channel behind Island #2. The

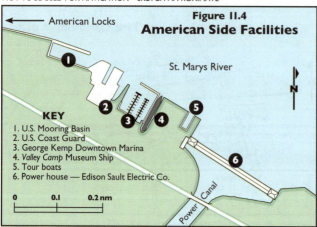

NOT TO BE USED FOR NAVIGATION – SKETCH APPROXIMATE

← American Locks

Figure 11.4
American Side Facilities

St. Marys River

N

KEY
1. U.S. Mooring Basin
2. U.S. Coast Guard
3. George Kemp Downtown Marina
4. *Valley Camp* Museum Ship
5. Tour boats
6. Power house — Edison Sault Electric Co.

0   0.1   0.2 nm

Power Canal

marina provides pump-out, water, electricity, rest rooms and showers. The main disadvantages to this marina are its distance from town facilities and its shallowness, being open to boats drawing less than 5 feet to 5.5 feet.

Points of Interest

The main attraction on the American side is the locks. With the Sabin and Davis Locks being made into the New Lock, only the MacArthur and Poe Locks are operating. The U.S. Army Corps of Engineers has done an especially nice job of making the grounds attractive and providing an excellent Visitors Center and viewing stations. The stations are adjacent to the MacArthur Lock and are constructed on two different levels making it possible to look down into the lock as a ship moves up or down. Within the Center there is a working model of the lock operation as well as numerous displays depicting the history of the locks. An excellent 25-minute film, "The Great Lakes Connection," further illustrates the operation and importance of the locks as an integral part of the waterway system.

Adjacent to the lock complex there are a number of interesting curio/gift shops and restaurants. There is also a well-stocked grocery store in this area for replenishing ships' stores. A few blocks farther from the river is the business district complete with the usual array of clothing, variety, hardware, and auto parts stores. By following the main street, a couple of miles out of town, you come to a group of shopping centers, including Kmart and Wal-Mart stores — another nice use of the bicycles.

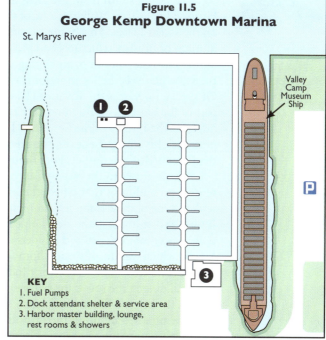

Figure 11.5
George Kemp Downtown Marina

St. Marys River

Valley Camp Museum Ship

KEY
1. Fuel Pumps
2. Dock attendant shelter & service area
3. Harbor master building, lounge, rest rooms & showers

George Kemp Marina is nestled next to the Valley Camp in Sault Ste. Marie, in Michigan. DAHL

Extending south from the locks along the waterfront is the Historic Locks Park Walkway, one of the most beautiful waterfronts on the Great Lakes. This ongoing community effort features a number of historic structures and reconstructions that depict parts of the 350-year story of Sault heritage. A prominent site is old Fort Brady, which was the location for both American and French forts. Of special interest is the River of History Museum, which occupies part of the old Federal Building on East Portage Avenue. The exhibits interpret the history of the St. Mary's River from the glacial era to the presence of Native Americans, the French traders and missionaries, the French/British conflict, Fort Brady, and early settlers.

A little closer to the Valley Camp Museum Ship there is a series of historic buildings that reflect the lives of some of the earliest settlers. One of these is the Johnston House that was built in 1795-96. It was the first house in the area, home for the Johnston family and a trading post for explorers and trappers to meet. Next to it is the Agency House, which was the office and home of Johnston's son-in-law, Henry Rowe Schoolcraft, who was the first Indian agent for the area. The third building in the row is the Baraga House, home of Father Frederic Baraga, the beloved Snowshoe Priest.

The final attraction in the Historic Walkway is the Valley Camp Museum Ship, a historic Great Lakes freighter that was built in 1917 and decommissioned in 1968. Points of interest aboard the vessel are a Marine Hall of Fame, six large aquariums, boardwalk exhibits, and a special exhibit of artifacts recovered from the Edmund Fitzgerald — the crumbled remains of two of its lifeboats. The Ship's Store gift shop is adjacent to the museum ship.

Within sight of the Valley Camp is the contemporary Tower of History that was originally constructed in 1967-68 as a bell tower for a proposed reconstruction of the adjacent St. Mary's Pro Cathedral. The cathedral bears special mention in that it is the third oldest Catholic parish in the United States, with the first mass given in 1641 by Saint Isaac Jogues, and the first church structure built in 1668 by Father Jacques Marquette. When plans for the contemporary complex fell through, the bell tower was converted to a museum to celebrate the city's 1969 Tricentennial and to commemorate the first Jesuit missionaries who founded the settlement. Within the tower a number of displays, including a 12-minute multimedia program, recreate the captivating story of the early history of the region. From the top of this 21-story structure a panoramic view looks across to the Canadian Sault and beyond.

The Canadian Side

Originally, Sault settlements were primarily on what is now the American side since the northern shore of the river was considered undesirable due to swamps. The Ontario Sault got its beginnings after the decision in 1783 to establish the U.S./Canadian boundary

through the middle of lakes Superior and Huron. At this time
the North West Company, which was originally located on the
American side, moved over to the Canadian side. In the next
decade, the company built the first canal and small lock for canoes
and *bateaux* to go around the rapids.

After the dwindling fur trade of the 1800s, it was the vast
mineral and lumbering resources that contributed to the city's
growth. One man in particular stands out—Francis Hector
Clergue. He was an eastern entrepreneur who established a
hydroelectric power generating canal along with a large pulp mill
in the late 1890s. Clergue was also interested in the vast mineral
wealth of Ontario and established iron mines located near Sudbury
and Wawa. He connected his famous Helen Mine by railroad to
Michipicoten Harbour in Lake Superior where freighters then
transported the raw material to his steel mill in the Sault. In 1912,
this large syndicate was reorganized into Algoma Steel Corporation
Ltd., which is now the third largest steel plant in Canada.

Today the Canadian Sault is a bustling, thriving city that
reflects the melding of many cultures. West of the International
Bridge, the massive conglomerate of Algoma Steel dominates the
skyline. East of the bridge, contemporary buildings of concrete
and glass rise along the shoreline. In the early 1990s, the skyline
changed dramatically with the addition of the new Canada
Lotto complex, an impressive modern red-brown structure.
The 1990s have also seen the continuation of a new Waterfront
Redevelopment Project that established a boardwalk and park-like
grounds along much of the waterfront.

Dockage
Note: to obtain Canadian Customs clearance call
888-CAN-PASS (888-226-7277).

The best place for transient dockage is at the **Bondar Marina**
(Tel.: 705-779-5430/800-361-1522), which was renamed in
1992 after Roberta Bondar, Canada's first female astronaut, who
participated in the Discovery space shuttle mission in February

*Bondar Marina, Sault
Ste. Marie, Ontario.
DAHL*

1992. The facility is
found just east of a
large white tent-like
structure and is the
result of extensive city
planning and part
of the Waterfront
Redevelopment Project.
Development of the
area has been in stages
beginning with the 1989
season when the basin was
enlarged by a third with

a completely new configuration of docks and slips. (See Fig. 11.6.) Subsequent seasons saw the addition of a fuel dock (both gasoline and diesel), pump-out, electricity, laundry, and rest rooms/showers. Adjacent to the marina is a delightful park-like area with the tent-like structure (previously mentioned) that is used as a theater and Farmer's Market.

The marina is easily identified from the water by a white building with a bright "lighthouse red" roof that houses the marina office, rest rooms, showers, and laundry. Note: when approaching the marina, the river current, which is very strong from the Canadian power canal in this section of the river, must be taken into consideration. The current travels from west to east and is in excess of 1 knot. If taken on the beam, it is difficult to enter the marina straight-on. Likewise, if the approach is from the west heading downstream, the acceleration of boat speed from the current makes for a very fast entry. A more controlled approach is to approach the marina from the east by heading upstream and then turning in when adjacent to the entrance. Once well into the marina there are few effects of river current.

Approximately one mile farther east is the **Bellevue Marina**, see Figure 11.7 (Tel.: 705-759-2838). Although it is used primarily for local dockage, transient dockage is often available. It is located to the north of red buoys #104 and #106 and is identified by two large, white high-rise buildings that are located behind and slightly to the west. Although the chart shows shoal water in the area, there is a buoyed channel (red and green) with a minimum depth of 8 feet to 9 feet into the marina. (Note: to reach the first of these entrance buoys, head on course NE of red Buoy #104 toward a white pyramid beacon on the peninsula out from the Algoma

NOT TO BE USED FOR NAVIGATION – SKETCH APPROXIMATE

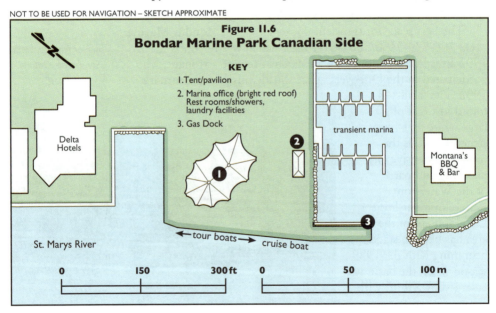

Figure 11.6
Bondar Marine Park Canadian Side

KEY
1. Tent/pavilion
2. Marina office (bright red roof) Rest rooms/showers, laundry facilities
3. Gas Dock

Delta Hotels

transient marina

Montana's BBQ & Bar

St. Marys River

← tour boats → cruise boat

0   150   300 ft   0   50   100 m

Sailing Club.) A complete service dock provides diesel, gasoline, pump-out, electricity (30 A) and water. There is also a substantial launch ramp here. The main disadvantage of this marina is its distance from shopping, however, adjacent to the marina is a beautiful park.

Figure 11.7
Bellevue Marina
Canadian Side

GPS	Lat.	Lon.
▲	46°30.03' N	84°15.35' W

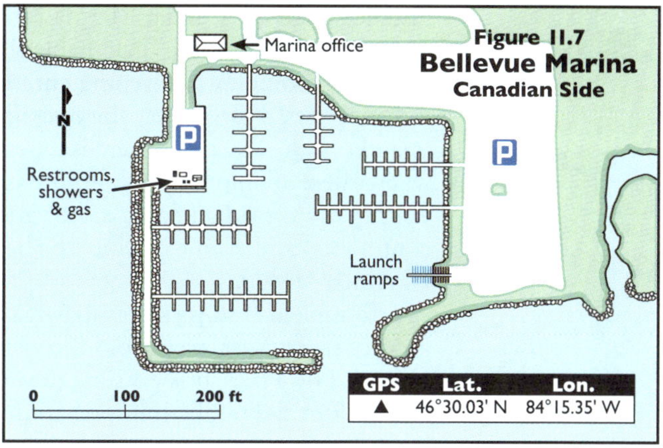

Approximately one-half mile to the east of the Bellevue Marina is a private operation, the **Algoma Sailing Club**. It is found just behind a prominent point, Topsail Island, that extends out into the river from the north shore. There are two basins here: inner and outer. Because of mooring balls for members, anchoring is not allowed in the inner basin. It is possible, however, to anchor in the outer basin. Because of shoal water in this area, it is best used by those with boats drawing less than 5 feet and preferably with local knowledge. There is a dock for loading and off-loading boats along with a very nice clubhouse. As with the Bellevue Marina, its main disadvantage is that it is a long way to shopping and the commercial areas of the city.

Points Of Interest

A visit to the Canadian Lock has special interest, where there is an excellent museum at the site and a trail system that leads across to Whitefish Island and a good view of the turbulent waters of the St. Marys Rapids. Not too far from the Canadian lock at the Abitibi Paper Company is a reconstruction of the first lock that was built in the late 1700s. Slightly more than 8 feet wide, this lock was used to transport sailing *bateaux* and the large 36-foot *canot de maître* (Montreal canoe) of the voyageurs. Another historical interest spot Is the Sault Ste. Marie Museum. The museum displays prehistoric artifacts, fur trade goods and pioneer implements. About one-half mile east of the Bondar Marina on the waterfront is the very interesting Canadian Bushplane Heritage Centre.

A unique experience is to take the Algoma Central Agawa Canyon train trip 114 miles north into the rolling hills and canyons of Canadian wilderness. Dramatic views of Lake Superior and inland lakes and traversing a mile-long trestle over a canyon gorge highlight the trip. There is a midtrip stopover in the Agawa Canyon where there are a couple of waterfalls and an observation tower.

Some of the biggest attractions for the transient boater in the Canadian Sault are the stores and excellent shopping. Just a short

distance from the Bondar Marina is the Station Mall, complete with every kind of shop imaginable. It also has a food court and an 11-theater complex for evening entertainment. Common practice is to trek over shortly after the dock lines are tied. A few blocks inland on Queen Street, there is a beautiful urban renewal project where there are more shops and restaurants. One of the pleasures of visiting the Canadian Sault is the variety of restaurants that provide continental and ethnic cuisine, the best of Italian, Chinese and Ukrainian dishes.

To replenish ship's stores may take a little bit of doing as the grocery stores are a ways from the waterfront at Cambrian Mall or Church Hill Plaza. It is possible to walk one way and then take a taxi back or use public transportation. The store in Cambrian Mall, Rome's, is especially nice with an excellent deli and outstanding produce. You can even have lunch in the store, up on the mezzanine. There is also a Canadian Tire store here where you can get propane tanks filled.

Sault Ste. Marie is an exciting place to visit whether you are on the Canadian or American side. The pulse of commercial shipping is always present and the sights and bright lights of two cities provide numerous activities and points of interest. For the transient boater, as with wayfarers from ages past, it is an important stop to replenish supplies and take a respite from the days of traveling on the water.

The St. Marys River

A key element in contributing to Sault Ste. Marie becoming the crossroads of the Upper Great Lakes has been the navigable waters of the St. Marys River. Throughout the ages this natural waterway has become a literal two-way highway for those traveling up and down the Great Lakes.

It is difficult to tell exactly where the St. Marys River begins as it collects the waters leaving the lower SE end of Lake Superior. But if we assume it starts at Gros Cap Light where the buoyage system begins, it runs a distance of 60 miles to DeTour Passage where it empties into Lake Huron.

The river consists of a number of natural channels and one man-made channel separated by three large islands: Sugar, Neebish and St. Joseph islands. The islands are connected to the mainland via a ferry at the NW end of Sugar, a ferry at the west end of Neebish and a bridge on the north side of St. Joseph. At certain points the river branches out into large and sometimes very shallow lakes: George, Nicolet and Munuscong. The river system embraces the International Boundary with the Ontario mainland and St. Joseph Island on the Canadian side and Michigan mainland, Sugar Island and Neebish Island on the U.S. side. (See Fig. 11.8.)

Commercial shipping is divided into a downbound channel and upbound channel separated by Neebish Island, with the

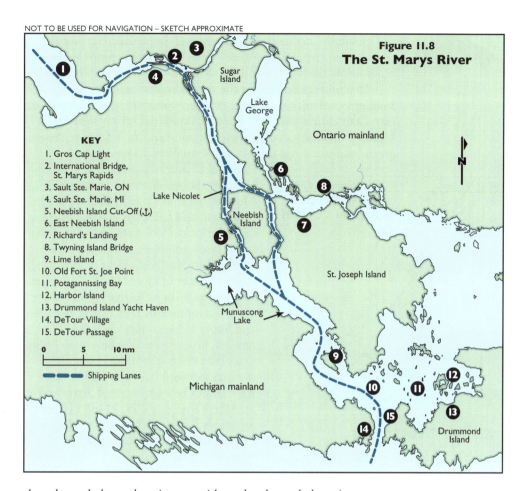

Figure 11.8
The St. Marys River

KEY

1. Gros Cap Light
2. International Bridge, St. Marys Rapids
3. Sault Ste. Marie, ON
4. Sault Ste. Marie, MI
5. Neebish Island Cut-Off (⚓)
6. East Neebish Island
7. Richard's Landing
8. Twyning Island Bridge
9. Lime Island
10. Old Fort St. Joe Point
11. Potagannissing Bay
12. Harbor Island
13. Drummond Island Yacht Haven
14. DeTour Village
15. DeTour Passage

0   5   10 nm

━ ━ ━ Shipping Lanes

Sugar Island

Lake George

Ontario mainland

Lake Nicolet

Neebish Island

St. Joseph Island

Munuscong Lake

Michigan mainland

Drummond Island

N

downbound channel on its west side and upbound along its east side. In lakes Nicolet and Munuscong, commercial shipping shares the same widened channels. Note: it is not necessary for recreational boats to abide by upbound and downbound channels, and they may travel in either direction. However, the current in the man-made cut to the west of Neebish Island is strong (up to 3 knots) and it may be best to take this one when headed downstream. The channel that passes through Lake George is used exclusively by recreational boats. Because the lower end of Lake George is extremely shallow (1 to 2 feet), it is absolutely necessary to adhere to the buoyed channel when traversing. There is another channel that passes between the northern end of St. Joseph and the mainland, but it is limited to only those with powerboats and sailboats with mast heights of less than 38 feet because of the Twyning Island Bridge that connects the island to the mainland.

Although some areas of the river system are extremely shallow (2 to 4 feet), it is the responsibility of the Corps of Engineers to keep the shipping channels open to a minimum of 27 feet deep. Historically, this has involved some interesting dredging and blasting operations. In the early 1930s the Middle Neebish,

or Upbound Channel, was widened and deepened. To create a downbound channel, the West Neebish Channel, approximately 15 miles below the locks, had to be dynamited and opened in 1931.

The buoyage system for the river complex begins at its southern extremity at DeTour Passage, where the river empties into Lake Huron with Red Buoy #2 opposite DeTour Reef Light. Heading upstream, red buoys (even numbers) are kept to starboard, green (odd numbers) to port. Buoy numbers increase until the shipping channel separates into upbound and downbound channels in Lake Munuscong where the numbering begins over again and converges in Lake Nicolet until the locks. At the western side of the locks, buoy numbering begins over and continues to the "top" of the St. Marys River adjacent to Point Iroquois near Gros Cap Light. Within the river system there are also a number of midchannel markers and buoys along with range lights. The range lights are especially helpful in lining up correct channel position when the distance between buoys is so great that they cannot be readily seen. Charts for the St. Marys River are U.S. #14884 (Upper St. Marys River); U.S. #14883 (Middle St. Marys River); and U.S. #14882 (Lower St. Marys River).

NOT TO BE USED FOR NAVIGATION – SKETCH APPROXIMATE

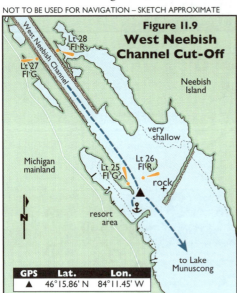

Figure 11.9
West Neebish Channel Cut-Off

GPS	Lat.	Lon.
▲	46°15.86' N	84°11.45' W

In some respects, navigating the river at night is almost easier than in the bright of day, since the lit buoys and ranges stand out nicely against the dark of night. However, to navigate the river in the blind of fog is not only foolhardy but extremely dangerous. In fact, when visibility is so reduced, Soo Control closes all navigation on the river system, and everyone sits and waits for the fog to lift: huge lakers and recreational vessels alike.

Anchorages/Points of Interest

The run from the Soo to the south end of the St. Marys River in Potagannissing Bay or DeTour can make for a long day (40 to 45 miles), especially if you have a late start. Going downstream you can usually count on an additional boost of current (0.5 to 1.5 knots in narrow spots or even more due to a venturi effect) but coming upstream makes the going a little slower. While it's absolutely necessary to stay within the buoyed channels (it isn't hard to be going along in 30 feet of water and then hit 5 feet just a few feet outside of the buoys), there are a few places where it is possible to leave the main channel for overnight dockage or anchoring.

One of these is on the downbound channel just south of the **West Neebish Channel Cut**. Coming down this channel is one of the more interesting parts of the St. Marys River since to each side you can see massive piles of the huge stone blocks that were removed to construct this man-made part of the channel. The anchorage is found on the Michigan mainland side just inside the breakwaters of a small resort area (markers #25 and #26). By anchoring close to the southern breakwater, you can stay off the harbor entrance out of the way of incoming/outgoing traffic and still anchor in 9 feet over a mud bottom. Since the harbor is a point of departure for recreational fishing traffic in the early morning and evening to Lake Munuscong, common courtesy and safety would suggest use of an anchor light. (See Fig. 11.9.)

Convenient for those using the upbound channel are a couple of anchoring alternatives found in the area of **East Neebish Island**, not to be confused with the larger Neebish Island that separates downbound and upbound traffic.

The main track is left, just to the east of the Middle Neebish

NOT TO BE USED FOR NAVIGATION – SKETCH APPROXIMATE

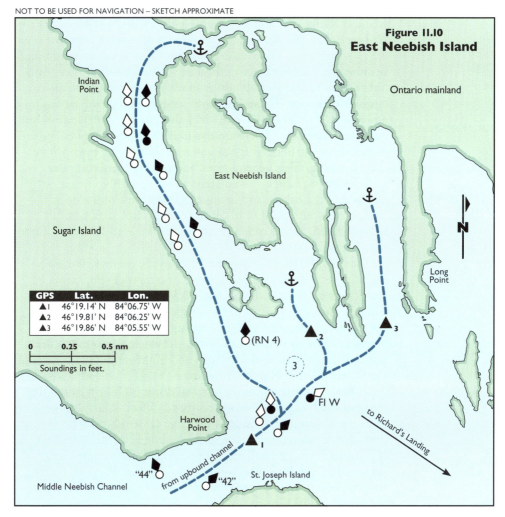

Figure 11.10
East Neebish Island

GPS	Lat.	Lon.
▲1	46°19.14' N	84°06.75' W
▲2	46°19.81' N	84°06.25' W
▲3	46°19.86' N	84°05.55' W

0   0.25   0.5 nm
Soundings in feet.

Channel, which lies to the south of Sugar Island between red buoys #42 and #44. The anchorage is quite easy to find by following the buoys off Harwood Point on the SE end of Sugar Island. The only hazard is a 3-foot shoal to the SE of RN Buoy #4 and this can be avoided by giving wide berth and heading north toward the two long points of land before rounding to the NW into the anchorage. Depending on how far you go in, you can anchor in 9 feet to 15 feet of water.

Another alternative is to anchor between the long points of East Neebish Island and Long Point, that extends south from the mainland in approximately 12 feet of water. Finally, it is possible to find suitable anchoring to the north of East Neebish Island by following the buoyed track toward Lake George and then rounding to the NE when adjacent to Indian Point on Sugar Island. This latter anchorage is especially attractive when winds are blowing hard from the south. (See Fig. 11.10.)

Three-and-a-half miles SE of East Neebish Island on St. Joseph Island is **Richard's Landing Municipal Marina** (Lat 46°17.70' N; Lon 84°02.28' W). Although off the beaten track for those who are traveling up and down the St. Marys River, it bears mentioning because it is the only place in the area where deep-draft boats can obtain fuel from a dock. It also is another point for Canadian customs clearance. The marina consists of the original East Basin and a new West Basin. Facilities include gasoline, diesel, pump-out, water and electricity. There are also limited marine supplies and a restaurant at the dock. It is but a short walk into the town where there is a post office, general store, and grocery store. Laundry facilities are available in an adjacent trailer park. If you can't get into one of the basins, and because the outer side of the dock is exposed to northerly winds, it may be advisable to anchor in behind the SE corner of Hattie Island in 10 feet to 12 feet of water over a mud bottom.

Toward the lower end of the St. Marys River there is a spot that is of interest particularly because of certain developments in recent years. This is at the old fuel dock on the western end of **Lime Island**, that used to be one of the primary sources of fuel for the large lakers that traversed up and down this waterway. No longer used by commercial shipping, the whole complex has been purchased by the state of Michigan and is now under the control of the Department of Natural Resources.

There have been a couple of small docks built or repaired that are available for boats drawing less than 5.5 feet. Boats drawing more can tie up to the inside of the large cement breakwater/ dock that forms the outer side of the harbor. Overnight dockage is permitted, with a small fee charged. The basin is completely protected except for strong southerly winds. (See Fig. 11.11.) A resident host is often present who can provide information about the island and its history.

Flint knappings, found up on an old beach near the present-day cottages from when the lakes were much higher, indicate human presence on the island as early as 4,000 to 6,000 years ago. The early French were quick to realize the island's value when they found that it was composed almost entirely of lime (they called it Island of Plaster) and set up quarries and kilns on the north side of the island. It is believed that some of the cement for the early Soo locks came from these sites. A short 10-minute trail takes one to the kilns that are accessed by a boardwalk constructed by the DNR. Another longer trail on an old roadbed leads approximately two miles to the other side of the island, where it is possible to look across to St. Joseph Island. There is a wooden observation deck on one of the beaches here for observing wildlife.

In the late 1800s there was a large hotel on the island, the St. Marys Club, visited by the wealthy from Detroit and Chicago. But it was the island's strategic location right on the shipping lanes that provided its prime function in the 1900s as a fuel depot. Owned first by Consolidated Coal and then Northwestern Hanna, first coal and then bunker fuel were dispensed to the passing lakers. To run the operation there was a small village, complete with a schoolhouse that at one time served 28 children. A number of the houses, including the Big House, which was brought over the ice with horses and block and tackle from Point aux Frenes at the turn of the 20th century, are under restoration, some of which are available for rent. The large million-gallon storage tanks that stored the bunker fuel are still standing, indicative of an age past in Great Lakes shipping.

Just a few miles to the east of Lime Island at the southernmost extremity of St. Joseph Island there is another point of interest that reflects the area's rich historic heritage, **Old Fort St. Joe Point**. For boaters passing by in the St. Marys River, the fort can be accessed by anchoring off to either side of the point, depending on wind direction. However, because it shoals up quite quickly you really can't get very close in. Because of this and the fact that you are really exposed in most directions, this should only be considered as a lunch stop and then under stable weather conditions. (See Fig.

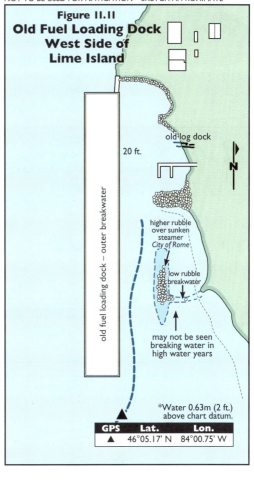

Figure 11.11
Old Fuel Loading Dock
West Side of
Lime Island

old log dock

20 ft.

old fuel loading dock – outer breakwater

higher rubble over sunken steamer *City of Rome*

low rubble breakwater

may not be seen breaking water in high water years

*Water 0.63m (2 ft.) above chart datum.

GPS	Lat.	Lon.
▲	46°05.17' N	84°00.75' W

11.12.) Note: there is a dock on the eastern side of the point that visitors with boats drawing less than 5 feet can tie up to. The dock is adjacent to a small picnic area.

Located at the crossroads of important canoe and fur trade routes from Montreal, the fort was under British command in the late 1700s and early 1800s until 1814, when it was burned by the Americans and never rebuilt. Today the main grounds of the fort are found in a large clearing on the hill. Many of the original foundations and structures have been preserved during excavations in the 1960s and '70s. Some of these are the remains of a large blockhouse, old bakery, a lime kiln, guardhouse, and powder magazine.

A trail leading from the picnic area follows close to the eastern shoreline to an especially beautiful Visitor Reception Centre. The displays inside are extremely well-done and depict life on these shores in the early days —both garrison life and local native culture. There is also a small theater that shows a number of different slide programs on request.

At the bottom of the St. Marys River there are two good marinas and at least a couple of anchorages for the transient boater. To the east in Potagannissing Bay there is an excellent full-service marina, **Drummond Island Yacht Haven** (Channel 16/Tel.: 906-493-5232). This family-owned marina since 1945 is found on Drummond

NOT TO BE USED FOR NAVIGATION – SKETCHES APPROXIMATE

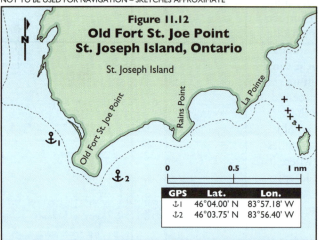

Figure 11.12
Old Fort St. Joe Point
St. Joseph Island, Ontario

St. Joseph Island

Rains Point

La Pointe

Old Fort St. Joe Point

GPS	Lat.	Lon.
⚓1	46°04.00' N	83°57.18' W
⚓2	46°03.75' N	83°56.40' W

Figure 11.13
Drummond Island Yacht Haven

8.0
8.0 8.0 7.5 8.0
6.0
6.5
6.0
6.5 6.5
6.2 6.2
6.2

KEY
1. Office, Marine Store
2. Fuel Pumps
3. Boat storage
4. Rest rooms, showers, boat storage
5. Concrete boat launch
6. Travelift well
7. Water covered boat storage
8. Large heated winter storage facility inland

Soundings in feet. Water 0.24 m (9.4 in.) above chart datum.

Island eight miles east of the DeTour Channel and 1.5 miles SE of Harbor Island. The marina provides transient slips (depths 6 to 10 feet), both covered and uncovered seasonal slips and all cruising amenities: gasoline, diesel, pump-out, water, electricity (30 A & 50 A), crushed and block ice, scuba tank refills, rest rooms, showers, Laundromat, bicycle rental and WiFi Internet. A well-equipped dock store provides a full range of yachting and fishing equipment along with an excellent selection of navigational charts and books. Customs officers are on station noon to 8 p.m. seven days a week for those who need to clear U.S. Customs. Shuttles are available to the airport and nearby restaurant.

At the turn into the 21st century, the Yacht Haven underwent considerable expansion resulting in 50 percent increased dockage, multiple fueling areas, a 75-ton Travelift, a 40-ton hydraulic trailer and a 20,000-square-foot heated winter storage facility. With certified marine technicians on staff, it is one of the best repair facilities in the area, if not all of North Channel, providing electrical, mechanical, fiberglass, sail/canvas and gas/diesel engine repairs. It also provides towing, salvage, and diving service for damage assessment.

Drummond Island Yacht Haven is an excellent place to change crew. It is also a secure marina in which to leave a boat for a period of time. This is especially important since a practice that is gaining popularity for those with restricted time blocks is to have their boat delivered to the Yacht Haven and then picked up by an owner for a cruise in North Channel and Georgian Bay. For those with trailerable boats this is a good place to leave a car and trailer and thus gain access to the North Channel area. Note: to reach Drummond Island by car it is necessary to take a ferry from DeTour on the Michigan mainland.

There are at least a couple of good anchorages in Potagannissing Bay. Favorites are the two natural harbors at **Harbor Island**, 2.5 miles NW of the Yacht Haven. The inner harbor is good for all but the strongest SW winds. Most of it is quite shallow, however, and those with deep-draft boats have to anchor fairly close

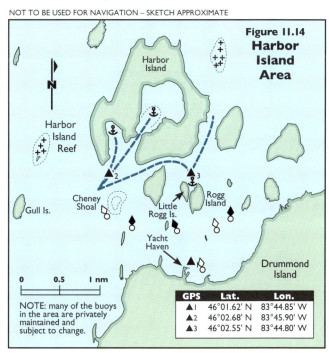

NOT TO BE USED FOR NAVIGATION – SKETCH APPROXIMATE

Figure 11.14
Harbor Island Area

Harbor Island

Harbor Island Reef

Gull Is.

Cheney Shoal

Little Rogg Is.

Rogg Island

Yacht Haven

Drummond Island

0   0.5   1 nm

NOTE: many of the buoys in the area are privately maintained and subject to change.

GPS	Lat.	Lon.
▲1	46°01.62' N	83°44.85' W
▲2	46°02.68' N	83°45.90' W
▲3	46°02.55' N	83°44.80' W

to the entrance. Tucking way into the outer anchorage provides more protection from the SW, but is open to the S and SE. A nice alternative for protection from southerly winds is to anchor between the northern ends of the two Rogg Islands. (See Fig. 11.14.)

Figure 11.15
DeTour Harbor

Rest rooms, showers

Office

to DeTour Village

Fuel Dock & Dock House

DeTour Passage

FIR

N

0   500   1000 ft

The second marina in the area is **DeTour Harbor,** which is adjacent to DeTour Village on the Michigan mainland on the west side of DeTour Passage. The marina has 78 slips and provides gasoline, diesel, water, electricity, pump-out and rest rooms with excellent showers. It monitors VHF Channel 16. The early 1990s saw considerable expansion of available docking facilities. Within a short walking distance into the village there are a couple of good restaurants, a bakery, and a general store for stocking up on ship's supplies. One-half mile away is a full-service boat yard, Passage Boat Works. This yard has a 25-ton Travelift and provides repairs to boats of all sizes. They also have indoor and outdoor storage.

As in ages past, the bottom of the St. Marys River is a turning point for those who traverse the Great Lakes. To the east is another boaters' paradise, the playgrounds of the North Channel and Georgian Bay. To the west is Mackinac Island and then, passing through the Straits of Mackinac under the great expanse of the Mackinac Bridge, the waters of Lake Michigan. To the south lie the open waters of Lake Huron, the lower Great Lakes —and the waters beyond.

Appendix I (1982)

In this appendix, I would like to share some information about some of our sailing background, and more importantly, some of the decisions we made to outfit a stock boat for extended cruising on the Great Lakes.

The adventure began in 1971, when on a lark we bought a 12-foot sailboat at the Minneapolis boat show. Our proving ground became the Wisconsin inland lakes, and with a sailing manual in hand, we quickly learned the joy of slipping through the water under sail power alone. Dinghy sailing is still the best teacher. Mistakes are easy to identify (forgiveness is an unknown word on a dinghy), and when you make a mistake, you pick yourself out of the water and start again. We loved it.

Within months we wanted more. More sailing, more boat, more time on the water. In October 1973, we purchased a Coronado 30. This boat, built by the Columbia Yacht Corporation in Costa Mesa, California, was well suited for our needs. It was big enough for two adults and two children, sailed reasonably well and gave us the confidence to begin exploring Lake Superior. It was a big step for us. Going from a 12-foot dinghy made of foam to a 30-foot fixed keel fiberglass sailboat requires experience and luck. We had little experience, so with the help of good and dear friends, we went heavily on luck. We sailed the Coronado for four seasons, all over Lake Superior, and even the distant waters of North Channel and Georgian Bay.

As the length of our trips increased and our children, Peter and Kristin, grew, it became apparent that a little more room would be nice. We used to joke about it and say that for every two-week period that we sailed, the boat shrunk in size by two feet. At the end of a 12-week cruise, that leaves you with a mythical boat six feet long.

We began to search in earnest for a new boat. Some things had become clear to us over the years. We wanted a boat less than 40 feet overall that could be easily managed by two adults. It had to be able to sail well — and carry weight — which is like putting two antagonistic forces into the same entity. And we were finding that it was in the area of sail performance that we were becoming the most critical. With abrupt weather changes, Lake Superior can be both light and heavy on wind. Thus we found ourselves looking intently at efficient hull construction. What we wanted was a boat that could carry sufficient stores for cruising and still sail well in both light airs and heavy weather. We also wanted good tracking capabilities and the ability to maneuver in tight quarters.

Many would say that these opposing qualities are not available in the same boat. Possibly so — but we think we have come close to finding them in our present boat. In January 1978 we bought Dahlfin II, another Columbia, which is 10.7 meters or 35 feet long. The designer is Alan Payne who also designed Gretel, an Australian contender for the America's Cup. This boat has satisfied all of our requirements and more.

First, the boat can carry weight. It came equipped with a 22-horsepower diesel engine and tankage for 30 gallons of fuel. We added another 30-gallon tank for diesel. To the original 60-gallon capacity for water we added an additional 30-gallon tank. Even when all tanks were filled, the boat wouldn't float on its waterline. However, after adding ships' stores for three months, including 60 quarts of canned meat, along with all our ground tackle, we were finally able to make the boat rest on its waterline. We quickly found that the boat actually sailed better when heavily loaded, and I discovered the advantage of adding moveable ballast for our lighter weight, fall sailing months—a trick learned from reading Eric Hiscock's books.

Sailing performance with the new boat left nothing to be desired. With the modified long keel we could turn in tight quarters and still have good tracking capabilities, as we witnessed with the small electrical expense from our autopilot. By adding a cruising spinnaker, we were able to increase our boat's speed in light airs. In heavy weather, 30 to 35 knots, we learned to appreciate the reefed-down capabilities of our new boat.

Then we began in earnest to change this stock boat to meet our individual cruising needs. To our mind's eye, a cruising boat is a little different than a racer. Things that we would normally put up with on a weekend or two-week cruise became intolerable month after month. So in addition to extra tankage, we added a dodger, cockpit cushions, cockpit grate, cockpit table—and propane. For years Bonnie had cooked with

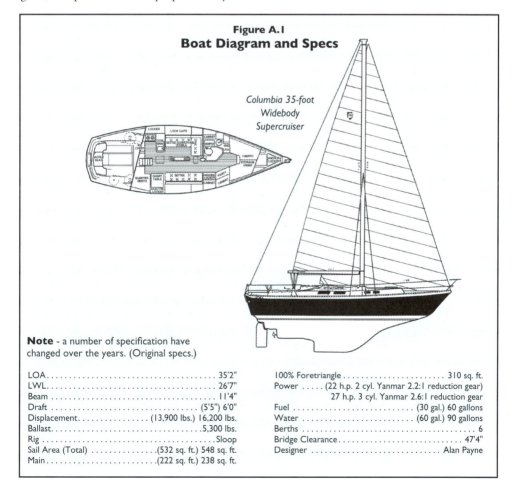

Figure A.1
Boat Diagram and Specs

Columbia 35-foot
Widebody
Supercruiser

Note - a number of specification have changed over the years. (Original specs.)

LOA	35'2"	100% Foretriangle	310 sq. ft.
LWL	26'7"	Power	(22 h.p. 2 cyl. Yanmar 2.2:1 reduction gear)
Beam	11'4"		27 h.p. 3 cyl. Yanmar 2.6:1 reduction gear
Draft	(5'5") 6'0"	Fuel	(30 gal.) 60 gallons
Displacement	(13,900 lbs.) 16,200 lbs.	Water	(60 gal.) 90 gallons
Ballast	5,300 lbs.	Berths	6
Rig	Sloop	Bridge Clearance	47'4"
Sail Area (Total)	(532 sq. ft.) 548 sq. ft.	Designer	Alan Payne
Main	(222 sq. ft.) 238 sq. ft.		

an alcohol stove and oven. Although she never complained and provided us with good meals complete with fresh bread baked, it took only one fire and the beautiful convenience of propane to realize what we had been missing. Fortunately, the Payne boat came equipped with two self-venting lockers in the stern for two 20-pound propane bottles. We are finding in a summer's cruise we take a little less than three tanks. Of course we are also heating water for dishes, as we have no hot water pressure system aboard.

I think one of the areas where we have made the biggest change is in sail stowage. A good friend once pointed out to us that even though you go to a bigger boat with larger sails, the width of the openings of the sail lockers remains the same. Thus we turned to roller furling for the huge genny — simply as a means of stowing the large sail. We do not use it in a reefed down situation for fear of stretching out the sail. We were quick to realize this on/off proposition of using the genny, and thus had a second forestay designed at the same time we put on the furler. This second forestay takes the 115 lapper (which also has reef points) or any other sail that we wish to hank on. This double forestay system has another advantage in that, should you lose one of the stays as we had the unfortunate experience to do, the whole rig is not lost. By positioning the two stays side by side, approximately six inches from each other, we have seen minimal chafe on sails, even when tacking. The lapper is left hanked on the second forestay, ready to go, and is stored in a sausage deck-bag. We liked this method of sail stowage so much that we had another deck-bag made for the spinnaker. This put all our sails on the deck and freed up the "sail" locker for all the other gear we needed for cruising.

It is difficult to know which change was the most important addition to our cruising. The children say the sport boat dinghy and a faster motor. Bonnie says the Loran-C. But I think they are forgetting those long hours on watch day after day, before we had the autopilot. The autopilot did more than anything else to free us up so we could enjoy cruising. We still have watches, but now we don't get so tired because we can read and move around — and this relaxed atmosphere spreads to the others who are not on watch. With the autopilot we began to live on our boat while under way.

When we changed to a sport boat for our dinghy, we could no longer tie it across the cabin top as we had done with the Avon. From past experiences, we were reluctant to be committed to towing the boat. We also like the convenience of having the sport boat pumped up, ready to go. So we made another addition, davits for transporting the dinghy. Once again we were thankful to Alan Payne. For along with the wide body design concept came a wide stern. That beautiful wineglass transom, which was so sea kindly, especially with following seas, now gave us the width we needed for davits. This system: sport boat, fast motor and davits, has greatly increased our enjoyment of each area we visit.

One of the most important systems to be worked out on a boat is choosing what you will be using for anchoring. We have three anchors on board, two 35-pound CQR plows on the bow and a 24-pound Danforth type on the stern. The plows each have 50 feet of 5/16-inch chain and 200 feet of 5/8-inch nylon line. The stern anchor, which is used more as a lunch hook and in well protected anchorages, has six feet of chain and

200 feet of half-inch nylon line. All rodes are marked, ready to go. We also have capabilities of rigging a trip line with a float. Two extra lead weights of 15 and 25 pounds along with a rode rider complete our anchoring system. Although we rarely use all this gear, it is nice to have when we need it and to have the capabilities to anchor in different ways. (For update on our present anchoring system, see Chapter 2.)

Last but not least is the cabin heater. This single subject has probably been the most challenging and frustrating problem for us to solve. And it is one we found that is shared by sailors everywhere. When Bonnie wrote an article on fall weather sailing and mentioned our small kerosene heater, we were besieged with letters and phone calls from all over the country asking what make of heater we used. Over the years we have used a variety of different heaters and fuels — Bonnie is fond of reminding me that we have "gone through" nine different heaters.

So the work on the boat continues. Along with maintenance, I doubt if this work will ever end. Nor would I want it to. Keeping the boat in good working condition and performing at its best is one of the areas of the cruising venture that I enjoy.

Ron Dahl
January 1982

Appendix II (1992)

It seems incredible that 10 years have gone by since The Superior Way was first published, and in that time work to improve and maintain our boat Dahlfin II has not stopped. In this appendix to the second edition, we would like to share some of the upgrades we have found helpful as well as some of the frustrations we have encountered.

General Maintenance:

As our boat became older and technology advanced, it became clear to us that an epoxy barrier job was an inevitable project in our pursuit of preventive maintenance. The task seemed straightforward enough, but proved to be lots of work as the bottom was ground down well into the gel coat and then layer upon layer of epoxy was applied.

We then turned our attention to painting the rest of the boat, hull and deck with Awlgrip. By doing all of the initial prep and prep in between primers for each coat ourselves, we learned first hand how large a job this is. True to the domino effect seen so often in boating, taking off all the deck gear opened up a new can of worms, since we now had the opportunity to evaluate and change existing systems. One of these was to change the existing non-skid to a glued-on product called TBS. It not only proved to give the finishing touch in making the boat look like new, but after a number of seasons of hard use continued to make the deck a much safer place to be. The paint-job project also provided the opportunity to add some new systems such as a four-man off-shore life raft. Since our goal in the whole project was to decrease maintenance, we eliminated much of the exterior teak that came with the original boat in favor of a life rail safety system. With stainless steel cars riding on a stainless hand rail, it is now possible to snap on our lifelines and go anywhere forward to do deck work.

Sail Management

While we have always had roller furling on our boat, we have used it primarily as an "in or out" system. Again the advances in modern technology have improved fullers and sail construction so that reefed genoas are now a viable option. Recently we upgraded to a Profurl system. With the use of a luff pad in our genoa we are able to reef the sail up to 30 percent. This innovation has been used in the charter business for years, and we feel it is effective to about 20 knots. In conditions of sustained winds of 15 to 20 knots, we still use a hanked-on lapper (115 percent) on a second forestay, which is adjacent to the furler.

We also added an inner forestay system for heavy weather sailing with a stay that is stored along the mast and brought forward when needed. A removable inner forestay on a sloop is dynamite in winds 20 to 35 knots. The hank-on sail we use is nearly bullet-proof and stands up well in storms on Lake Superior. On a sloop, the center of effort is brought closer to the mast in this kind of arrangement, motion is eased and there is usually enough power to punch into waves.

Engine

Our boat is powered by a small 22-horsepower engine. This little powerhouse drives the boat, runs the freezer, heats water for dishes and showers, provides electricity and does it all on less than two quarts of fuel per hour. At one point we took a serious look at getting a larger engine, particularly after a couple of experiences in combating adverse strong currents such as in the White River. However, we were reluctant to give up our little workhorse, which is so miserly on fuel — 700-mile range with our present tankage. So after a lot of talking and much research, we changed to a Max Prop. This three blade feathering wonder gives us a full three-quarters of a knot increased speed with the engine and also has improved our performance under sail. Another advantage is that the propeller gives the same power and control in reverse as it does in forward. We quickly learned what those in racing circuits have known for years — any sailboat can benefit greatly from a feathering propeller.

Keeping the main engine working also has become a high priority, since most of our cruising is spent in wilderness areas away from docks and replacement parts. We found that Murphy has a special set of rules for boaters, one of which is: "If you have a replacement on board, it won't break down." So our list of replacement parts continues to grow. Finding parts and making repairs in remote places is difficult and costly. An example comes to mind when we experienced one of our most serious repairs where our engine broke off from all four of its mounts. Fortunately we were able to sail to a small town 50 miles away. After three days we were able to obtain and install new mounts and continue with our cruise. To ensure that this wouldn't happen again, we have now installed soft engine mounts, which allow the diesel more vibrating freedom and a constant velocity joint, which connects it with the shaft.

Cabin Heaters

We have had nine heaters on our boat. Many of these devices were dangerous on a boat and many have been withdrawn from the market. This is an area of marine engineering that still needs some work. Our present heater is a forced air system that runs off kerosene or diesel fuel. It is designed by the people at Volvo and has worked reasonably well. If you plan to be on Lake Superior at night or if you would like to extend your season by three to four weeks in the fall, a cabin heater is high on the list of essentials.

Refrigeration

Aboard Dahlfin II we have compressor driven refrigeration. The main reason we have refrigeration is for long-term food storage and the fact that ice is often not available in the wilderness areas where much of our cruising is done. After years of carrying melting ice around the lakes, we found that our independence was often severely curtailed by "the ice connection."

Again after considerable research, we opted for mechanical refrigeration as opposed to electrical because we valued our independence from the electrical cord and engine running time to keep the batteries up. When we decided to pursue refrigeration, we found that the few mechanical systems that we thought might meet our needs were well out of our price range, so we made our own. This entailed first rebuilding the box with a minimum of four inches of foam insulation. Since we really wanted a freezer, we divided the box into 70 percent freezer with a cold spill-over into a 30 percent refrigerator box. (It's amazing how little refrigeration space you actually need when you aren't carting around ice.) Holding plates were made out of stainless steel and filled with coiled copper tubing surrounded by a eutectic solution. After some experimentation, we found that three small plates in the freezer work nicely to keep approximately 80 pounds of food frozen. Even in the warmer waters of North Channel, the water cools the Freon nicely with 20 to 30 minutes engine running time each day.

Electrical

By far some of our greatest efforts have been made in achieving electrical independence. Since the first edition we have added another loran, SAT NAV, radar and GPS. We also do more than 80 percent of our sailing with an autopilot. Add to that Bonnie's computer, printer, a small TV and VCR and it is clear we needed to have additional power to run things.

Our first approach was to install two small solar panels as kind of an experiment. The results were incredible and we quickly added another set. We were fortunate in that the four panels mount nicely off the dinghy davits well out of the way of deck work and sail handling. We then installed a System 7 built by the Ample Power Company. This system allows complete monitoring of even the smallest electrical drain in the boat along with a very efficient charging system when motoring. Our total battery bank consists of four lead-acid deep cycle batteries: three to run ship's systems and one dedicated for engine starts. Now on a moderately sunny day the solar runs the autopilot, sailing instruments, radio and all navigational instruments except the radar. At anchor the solar charges the batteries or runs the computer and printer—in fact the only time we use the electrical cord is when up on the cradle doing winter work. One side benefit of the solar panels is that they keep the batteries perfectly charged through the winter, and it is one of those systems you can install and forget. You can probably tell that we are very enthusiastic about solar power.

We have a very dear sailing friend who has a much larger boat than ours who once said, "You know, we all have the same problems, the same challenges on our boats—regardless of their size." Yet there is an endless variety in the solutions—as varied as individual sailors themselves. We would never say that ours are the only solutions, but only a few of the many options that are available to boaters everywhere. One of the delights of boating is in this variety and individualism that we meet in fellow boaters. There is not yet a boat we have been on or a skipper we have met from whom we haven't learned something new, a different way of doing things.

Ron Dahl
June 1992

Appendix III (2000)

Much of what we have done to our boat since the second edition of The Superior Way has been to prepare for extended cruising in salt water. While many of these changes are not necessary for cruising Lake Superior, it has become apparent that a large number of Lake Superior sailors have intentions of doing some salt-water cruising at some point. Therefore, we decided to pass along some of the things that worked for us—many of which we are retaining on fresh water simply because they make our cruising easier and more enjoyable.

Engine

Because our boat was almost 20 years when we left, we upgraded our 22-horsepower Yanmar to a Yanmar 3GM30F with 27-hsp. In hindsight, we wish we would have opted for even a little larger engine. There were times we were underpowered in making our way through tides and currents. Fully loaded cruising boats also tend to be heavier than average and need extra power. On any engine changing oil is important: we changed oil every 100 hours, transmission oil every 1,000 hours.

Ground Tackle

For anchoring in Lake Superior we used 50 feet of chain on both a Bruce and CQR plow, our primary anchors. When we left the Great Lakes we changed the CQR to a Delta and increased the chain to 70 feet (5/16" hi-test chain) on each anchor. After a brush with Hurricane Fran in Baltimore and the tides and currents on the East Coast, we increased our chain to 140 feet on both primary anchors. This meant that we are virtually on an all chain rode most of the time. We quickly found out that you don't have to have 300 feet of chain on a single anchor to be anchoring on all chain, nor is it necessary for most anchoring situations. We also took great comfort in anchoring with all chain in areas that had coral. This is one change that has worked so well for us that we won't go back to using less chain.

Sail Management

On Lake Superior our goal was to minimize the time to get the right sails up in changing conditions. Outside of the States our goal was the same except that sailing against strong trade winds forced us to a progression of changes. We sailed to South America with a 155 percent six ounce reefable genoa with strong panels. This sail was a work horse for us and we sailed it in many varied conditions, often reefed in very strong winds. We also had an inside forestay that we kept against the mast to be moved forward with a "hanked on sail" in strong conditions. However, we found that when we were in the strong winds of the Eastern Caribbean and taking green water over the deck that this wasn't a comfortable option to set up and we usually ended up just reefing the genoa. So one of the first things we did when we got to Grenada (along with five other boats) was to put the staystail on a furler. Now having this sail ready to go has bailed us out of rough conditions more than once. We never sail the boat as a cutter, the sails aren't cut right, it's just a means of sail management. Our third head sail was a 110 percent blade that was hanked on a second forestay in a deck bag, but again we were giving it little use because of the ease of reefing the genny. So a year later we added a third furler next to the genoa furler in Trinidad. The system has worked well for us with the blade drum position a little higher than the genoa drum so there is no interference. Now we could change sails at night or in big seas with lots of water on the foredeck, all from the cockpit. A word about cruising spinnakers. They're great for Lake Superior. But in the first two years we only used ours twice — once in the Chesapeake, once in the Virgin Islands. When we did go down wind, the winds were too strong for our 3/4-ounce sail and we ended up taking it home one Christmas. We have two down wind poles on the mast and we did a lot of single sail sailing with either the genny or blade poled out.

Electrical

We now have five batteries. Four house batteries and one for starting the engine. Our solar panels continue to work well and in the tropics they

Dahlfin II under sail in Bequia, St. Vincent, West Indies.
Tim Wright

were wonderful. We found that electrical contacts everywhere on the boat needed to be kept free from corrosion. Sprays and cleaners helped a lot, but sometimes we had to use a small wire brush. Most of our electronics held up very well in salt water. However, our radar "packed it in" in Venezuela and we had to order another from the states from Isla Margarita (duty free). The first few years we had some trouble with the autopilot heads going out, but after I rewired the whole system we never had any more problems. Bonnie had a number of problems with her computer, especially the printer (even though we kept them sealed up in plastic when not in use), and we spent a lot of money getting them repaired.

Radios/Communications

n addition to our VHF, we had a Single Sideband radio that could access all bands including Ham frequencies. A number of boats could only receive, we were very glad we could also transmit. We felt a SSB was essential for cruising in the Caribbean, primarily for getting weather reports. But we also enjoyed keeping up with friends we met through the years via the different nets. Those who had their ham licenses could also send and receive e-mails via a ham frequency. When you are living aboard stateside a cell phone is nice, but the most important communication device for us was Pocketmail. This little device allows us to send and receive e-mail anywhere in the world from almost any touch-tone telephone in the world — and for only $10/month. (Web page for information: *www.pocketmail. com.*)

Refrigeration

Our compressor driven cold plate refrigeration has worked well for many years. The only change we made was when we put in the new engine and we replaced the older Tecumseh compressor with a new rotary Sanders 510, which is so smooth and efficient that we can run the engine at lower rpms. We have a very large freezer — enough to hold 6 months of meat. In the tropics (lat 10°) to keep the freezer and refrigerator going, we had to run the engine 45 minutes twice a day. On Lake Superior, we run the engine for refrigeration about 30 minutes per day. Quite a difference.

Water and Watermakers

On Lake Superior this is not a problem. On our trip south we were able to find good drinking water to Georgetown, Exumas, after that we started the "Pur" watermaker. Having a watermaker really gave us the independence from ports that we desired. Ours is a small model producing about 1.5 gallons per hour. Watermakers run best if they are run every day or at least every other day. A good idea is to make water in a separate container, so if it is a little salty at first you don't contaminate a whole tank. Note that by the second day in the Hudson River, which that far north the water is just brackish, our filter in the galley salt-water pump began to smell so bad that we took the whole unit out for the duration of the trip. This meant we were only on tank water — we had 90 gallons that lasted about three weeks.

Heads

Everyone knows that heads can produce bad odors. We found that salt water in the intake line for head flushing can be as bad or worse. We ended up putting a small system in the line that held replaceable deodorant disks to take away the odors. We also flushed vinegar through the lines every few days to prevent a hard calcified build-up.

Dinghies

Ultraviolet light is incredibly damaging to inflatable dinghies in the lower latitudes. We ended up buying our present dinghy, a 9-foot AB sportboat (Venezuelan made), in Trinidad. It has 16-inch tubes, a soft bottom and fiberglass floor boards. We also had a permanent Sunbrella™ cover made for it to protect it from the sunlight. We still carry it on davits and have added a small crane to lift the outboard motor to the stern rail. (A note of security: in many places we lifted both the dinghy and motor out of the water each night.) In salt water, dinghy bottoms need to be cleaned every two to three weeks if they are left in the water. We used bleach and a scraper.

Heat Management

This was one of the more challenging aspects of the cruise. As you move down the island chain towards South America you have to deal with lots of sunshine and heat. Grenada wasn't so bad, but Trinidad, Venezuela and its offshore islands were incredibly hot. It usually wasn't too bad swinging at anchor in the islands, but the wind often died in harbors and we quickly found we couldn't go ashore to walk the beaches after 10:00 in the morning. We also learned to get our boat work done early in the morning and not go inland to market etc. during the middle of the day. Our sailing bimini was up continuously for more than three years. We installed four two-speed Hella fans and kept two more spares on board. Two of the fans were forward where we slept and one each in the galley and nav-station. The latter two could also be turned around to cool the main cabin. When at anchor or a dock for more than a couple of days, we rigged large awnings forward and aft of the mast to cover the boat, but high enough to let a good flow of air through. On the other side: our forced-air cabin heater, which was a curiosity down south, was quite welcome in the Chesapeake and Intercoastal Waterway in early spring and late fall.

Corrosion and Spare Parts

Between sun and salt, corrosion on a boat on the ocean is relentless. Even the best marine materials need care. Among the worst are exhaust parts (castings, iron pipe), dodger windows (vinyl), raw water pumps and aluminum castings where anodizing is especially thin or hardcoat on the aluminum is chipped. Zippers, even with plastic sliders, need constant care. Stainless rigging, which is 304 stainless, picks up rust color easily, while 316 stainless rigging wire is much better. Spare parts that are critical include a spare starter, electrical connectors and tinned wire, injectors with sealing copper washers, impellers and gaskets to rebuild raw water pumps, belts, a second alternator, parts for the head, cutlass bearing for the propeller shaft—plus electronic backups such as GPS and a VHF radio (not just a handheld model).

Although we miss the Caribbean, I must say that it's nice to be back on water that doesn't eat your boat.

Ron Dahl
November 2000

Appendix IV (2008)

After 29 years and more than 50,000 miles we are still on the same boat. Sure, there were many times we were tempted to buy a bigger one. But the Columbia 10.7 was so well constructed—it seems they don't make boats like they used to. Also we would have had to go to a much bigger boat to justify getting more than what we already had. So we just kept the Columbia, *Dahlfin II*.

I finally have to admit there isn't much more that we can add to the boat. Our efforts are now primarily centered around maintenance and up-grading present systems. With a boat as old as ours we are now in second and third generation of many systems. A case in point is that since the third edition of *Superior Way* we put in a third engine. The decision was made for us when, after having a season of hard starts, a wet/dry compression test showed damage on the rings. This meant that the engine had to be pulled and rebuilt—a very elaborate and costly repair. We decided that if we had to pull the engine out of the boat we weren't going to put an old one back in. In retrospect this was a good decision because the old engine had seen a lot of hard use motoring up and down the Intercoastal Waterway four times and running twice every day for refrigeration for the $4\frac{1}{2}$ years when we were gone to the Caribbean. The next decision was more difficult. It was tempting to put in a larger engine—one of the Yanmar series with 36 horsepower. Our experiences on the East Coast with currents and tides had shown that we were very underpowered with our 28-horsepower Yanmar. The larger engine, however, wouldn't fit without extensive modifications, so we ended putting in another Yanmar 3GM30F. Yes, there are times we would like a larger engine but we continue to enjoy the low fuel consumption of the one we have.

Other upgrades since the third edition have included replacing the genoa with another furling sail with luff-pads and replacing the mainsail traveler with a new one of stainless steel. We also added yet another cabin heater, a forced-air Wallas made in Sweden. An integrated GPS electronic chart plotter was added to our navigational mix and we wonder what we ever did without it. We found it especially useful the second time we went out the Great Lakes and down the Intercoastal Waterway to the Bahamas. A new VHF radio with a remote in the cockpit has also been added. A couple of years ago we improved our system for taking on water from the lake by hooking up a hose with PVC tubing that leads to the deck fills from the wash-down pump in the chain locker. With a couple of integrated charcoal filters we can now take on water while underway. Throughout the years we have become believers in stainless steel for many of our upgrade projects. Stainless steel has proven itself in salt water and fresh for durability and strength.

Systems that continue to work well for us are: the solar panels, below the deck autopilot, side by side furler forestays for sail management, furler staysail (that has proven it's worth countless times), dinghy davits, outboard motor crane, refrigeration/freezer, power windless and multiple navigation instruments.

Aside from general maintenance, one year we pulled the mast, took off all the gear (we have a lot) and repainted it with several coats of polyurethane. It was also a good time to check mast gear and replace any that showed signs of wear. It turned out to be a bigger job than anticipated. On the interior we repainted or varnished all the wood — every locker and under all the cushions. This was another job that took on mammoth dimensions.

In the area of creature comforts we redid the interior and recovered all the cushions for the third time. A flat screen TV replaced the old and we added a CD player and satellite radio. The satellite radio has been a great success since we get music wherever we go, even into the far reaches of the wilderness, and now we can listen to "Prairie Home Companion" every Saturday night.

A parting story on one of our most recent upgrades. Many years back we were on the docks at Little Current in North Channel talking to a European sailor. He remarked that we didn't have our barbecue mounted on the stern pulpit and said, "How very un-American of you." And for years we kept it packed away in the sail locker hauling it out whenever it was needed. We now are "Americanized" and have it mounted on the stern pulpit — with stainless steel of course.

Ron Dahl
September 2007

For further discussion on what has been done on *Dahlfin II* over the years, see: "The Evolution of a Cruising Boat" by Bonnie Dahl. *Good Old Boat* magazine: Part I July/August 2006; Part II September/October 2006.

Appendix V (2024)

After almost 50 years of sailing, we sold our boat and as indicated in the Forward, it is time to pass on the baton to our son, Peter. His dream started many years ago when he commissioned Ted Brewer (January 1933 – October 2021), one of the best-known yacht designers (both production and custom boats) in the country, to design a 38 ft cruising sailboat. It was custom built, hull & deck of aluminum, by Sinek Yachts south of Seattle. The timing couldn't be better because he has just spent three years working with the Port Townsend Shipwrights Co-op, Port Townsend, WA for a total of 20,000 hours. With the Shipwrights, the remainder of the work was completed: mast, rigging, sails, dodger, bimini, life raft, interior, electronics, fitting-out etc. Wayfinder was launched this summer, on 28 June 2024. He spent 3½ months of maiden voyage/shakedown along the wild coast of British Columbia, around Vancouver Island, and up to Prince Rupert, returning to Port Townsend with more lists of things that need to be done. After a number of winter months of final fitting out, he will head down the coast to Baja California to get a good angle on the southern trade winds. And then, turn west… to "carry on his dream".

Ron & Bonnie Dahl
October 2024

Peter Dahl

Wayfinder, at anchor in the Bunsby Islands, British Columbia, Canada.

Wayfinder

Over the years my parents and I have talked extensively about the attributes making a good cruising boat. We often discuss what does and doesn't work. Sailboats are about aesthetics and people have a wide variety of big feelings about what makes a boat beautiful and functional. We have been open to learn as much as we can from others and our own life lessons. For Lake Superior the emphasis is on safety and being able to survive independently between ports.

Some things to think about for the remote areas of the lake:

- An oversized anchor (Rochna, Mantus, or other modern anchor) with ≥60 ft. (20m) chain and nylon rope ≥120' (40m).
- VHF radio, AIS either integral or separate (good source for weather).
- Radar (it is foggy after it rains in the summer).
- Diesel engine with clean filters, a decent sized alternator (≥85A), and tankage for a couple weeks.
- GPS chartplotter.

- Depth and knotmeter.
- Bug screens that seal well, screens on all vents (dorade, engine blowers, etc).
- Sails that will not tear and can take a good blow.
- A good heater, diesel preferred.
- A fridge or electric portable cooler helps avoid eating out of cans all the time.
- A dinghy you trust for exploring. A motor will extend your reach into rivers, islands, and bays.

Peter Dahl
September 2024

Directory of
Marine Interests

Please use with discretion because some of this information may be subject to change over time.

Chapter 1 An Introduction to the Lake

Aerial photos and information on marinas and lighthouses: *www.marinas.com*
   Select marina, then U.S., then state, then marina name, or
   Select lighthouse, then U.S., then state, then lighthouse name

Boating on Lake Superior: *www.lakesuperiorboating.com*

Lake Superior Magazine: 218-722-5002/888-244-5253, *www.lakesuperior.com*

Chapter 2 Cruising Tips for Lake Superior

Army Corps of Engineers – dredging:
   www.lre.usace.army.mil/who/operationsofficehomepage/

MCTS – Canadian Coast Guard Marine Communications & Traffic Service:
   807-345-5190

Richardsons' Chartbooks – Lake Superior: 800-873-4057, *www.richardsoncharts.com*

Water levels – Army Corps of Engineers: *www.lre.usace.army.mil/glhh*

Water levels – Thunder Bay: 807-344-3141

Weather sites –

Environment Canada – Eastern Lake Superior: *https://weather.gc.ca/marine/forecast_e.html?mapID=09&siteID=08503*

Environment Canada – Western Lake Superior: *https://weather.gc.ca/marine/forecast_e.html?mapID=09&siteID=08507*

Environment Canada – Whitefish Bay:
   www.weatheroffice.gc.ca/marine/marine_e.html?C-WFB

Nearshore forecast – (within 5 nm from shore – all areas covered by Duluth):
   www.crh.noaa.gov/product.php?site=DHL&product=NSH&issuedby=DLH

Nearshore forecast – Marquette, MI:
   www.crh.noaa.gov/product.php?site=mqtproduct=NSH&issuedby=MQT&glossary=1

NOAA National Weather Service Weather Forecast Office – Duluth, MN:
   Main site – access to near shore and open water forecast, current buoy observations,
   water levels, *www.crh.noaa.gov/dlh/marine.php*

Ocean Prediction Center – Unified Surface Analysis (Northern Hemisphere): From here
   can access surface analysis charts for specific areas, *www.opc.ncep.noaa.gov/UA.shtml*

Open Lake Forecast (from Duluth) – west and east half of Lake Superior:
   www.crh.noaa.gov/product.php?site=DHL&product=GLF&issuedby=LS

Weather Forecasts for Isle Royale
   Michigan: www.crh.noaa.gov/mqt
   Minnesota: www.crh.noaa/gov/dlh

Chapter 3 South Shore: Waiska Bay, Michigan, to Washburn, Wisconsin

Ashland Marina, Ashland, WI: 715-682-7049

Baraga Marina, Baraga, MI: 906-353-8110

Bayshore Marina, Munising, MI: 906-387-3445 (May – Oct.), 906-387-2095 (Off season)

Big Bay, MI: 906-345-9353

Black River Harbor: 906-667-0261 (Ottawa National Forest Office),
   www.fs.fed.us/rg/ottawa

Burt Township Marina, Grand Marais, MI: 906-494-2613

Cinder Pond Marina, Marquette, MI: 906-228-0469 (May-Oct.), 906-228-0460
    (off season), *www.fishweb.com/maps/marquette/harbors/cinderpond.html*

Coast Guard Marquette, MI: 906-226-3312

Coast Guard Station Portage, Hancock, MI: 906-482-1520

Copper Harbor Marina, Copper Harbor, MI: 906-289-4966

Eagle Harbor Marina, Eagle Harbor, MI: 906-289-4416

Houghton County Marina, Hancock, MI: 906-482-6010

L'Anse Marina, L'Anse, MI: 906-524-6116

Lac La Belle Lodge, Bete Grise, MI: 906-289-4293/888-294-7634

Michigan Great Lakes Harbor Guide (Lake Superior Michigan Harbors):
    www.fishweb.com/recreation/boating/harbors/index.html

Michigan's Keweenaw Tourism Council, Calumet, MI: 888-MI-NORTH (888-646-6784),
    www.keweenaw.info

Ontonagon Marina, Ontonagon, MI: 906-884-4225

Pequaming, MI: 906-524-6413

Presque Isle Marina, Marquette, MI: 906-228-0464

Saxon Harbor (Harbor Lights Restaurant): 715-893-2242, *www.saxonharborboatingclub.org*

Washburn Marina, Washburn, WI: 715-373-5050, *www.cityofwashburn.org/marina.htm*

Witz Marina, Skanee, MI: 906-524-7795 (May – Oct.)

Chapter 4 The Apostle Islands: A National Lakeshore

Apostle Islands Charters, La Pointe, WI: 715-747-2983/800-821-3480,
    www.apostlecharters.com

Apostle Islands Marina, Bayfield, WI: 715-779-5661

Bayfield Boating Guide: *www.bayfieldguide.com/boating.html*

Buffalo Bay Marina, Red Cliff, WI: 715-779-3743

Coast Guard Station Bayfield: 775-779-3950

Friends of the Apostle Islands: *www.friendsoftheapostleislands.or*g

Madeline Island Yacht Club, La Pointe, WI: 715-747-2655

NPS Headquarters, Bayfield, WI: 715-779-3397, *www.nps.gov/apis*

Pike's Bay Marina, Bayfield, WI: 715-779-3900/877-841-3900, *www.pikesbaymarina.com*

Port Superior Marina Assoc., Bayfield, WI: 715-779-5360, *www.portsuperior.com*

Roy's Point Marina, Red Cliff, WI: 715-779-5025

Sailboats Inc., Bayfield, WI: 715-779-3269/800-826-7010, *www.sailing-charters.com*

Schooner Bay Marina, Bayfield, WI: 715-779-3266

Superior Charters, Bayfield, WI: 715-779-5124/800-772-5124, *www.superiorcharters.com*

Chapter 5 West End: Cornucopia, Wisconsin, to Grand Portage, Minnesota

Barker's Island Marina, Superior, WI: 715-392-7131/800-826-7010,
    www.barkers-island-marina.com

Coast Guard Station Duluth, Duluth, MN: 218-720-5412

Coast Guard Station North Superior, Grand Marais, MN: 218-387-2574

Grand Marais Marina, Grand Marais, MN: 218-387-1712

Grand Portage Marina, Grand Portage, MN: 218-475-2476

Knife River Marina, Knife River, MN: 218-834-6076, *www.knife-river-marina.com*

Lakehead Boat Basin, Duluth, MN: 218-722-1757/800-777-8436

North Shore Harbors Plan: *www.dnr.state.mn.us/water_access/harbors/index.html*

Sailboats Inc., Barker's Island, Superior, WI: 715-392-7131/800-826-7010, *www.sailing-charters.com*

Silver Bay Marina, Silver Bay, MN: 218-226-3121, *www.silverbay.com/marina.html*

Siskiwit Bay Marina, Cornucopia, WI: 715-742-3337, *www.siskiwitbay.com*

U.S. Customs, Duluth, MN: 218-720-5203

U.S. Customs, Grand Marais, MN: 218-387-1148/218-370-0111 (hours 9-5), 800-505-8381 (after hours)

U.S. Customs, Grand Portage, MN: 218-475-2244

Voyageurs Marina, Grand Portage, MN: 218-475-2412

Chapter 6 Isle Royale: A National Park

Isle Royal Natural History Assoc., Houghton, MI: 800-678-6925, *www.irnha.org*

Isle Royale National Park, Houghton, MI office: 906-482-0984, *www.nps.gov/isro*

Isle Royale Queen IV, Copper Harbor, MI: 906-289-4437, *www.isleroyale.com*

Preregistration/fee payment: Isle Royale, *www.pasty.com/isro/nps.php*

Rock Harbor Lodge and Marina, Rock Harbor, MI: 906-337-4993 (summer), 270-773-2191 (winter), *www.rockharborlodge.com*

Ranger III, Houghton, MI: 906-482-0984, *www.nps.gov/isro*

Seaplane, Houghton, MI: 218-721-0405/877-359-4754, *www.isleroyaleairservice.com*

Voyageur, Grand Portage, MN: 218-475-0024 (May-Oct.), 651-653-5872/888-746-2305 (off season), *www.Grand-Isle-Royale.com*

Weather Forecasts for Isle Royale
  Michigan: *www.crh.noaa.gov/mqt*
  Minnesota: *www.crh.noaa.gov/dlh*

Wenonah, Grand Portage, MN: 218-475-0024 (May-Oct.), 651-653-5872/888-746-2305 (off season), *www.Grand-Isle-Royale.com*

Chapter 7 Gateway to the North: Pigeon Point, Minnesota, to Lamb Island, Ontario

McKellar Marine, Thunder Bay, ON: 807-622-3864

National Marine Conservation Area: *www.pc.gc.ca/progs/amnc-nmca/proposals/LS_proposal_e.asp*

North of Superior Marketing Association, Thunder Bay, ON: *www.tbaytel.net/marinas*

Prince Arthur Landing Marina, Thunder Bay, ON: 807-345-2741 (summer), *www.lakesuperiorboating.com/thunderbay.htm*, *www.thunderbay.ca/waterfront*

Chapter 8 Across the Top of the Lake: Nipigon Strait to Port Coldwell, Ontario

Bowman Island Charters, Nipigon, ON: 807-886-2504, *www.bowmanislandcharters.com*

Nipigon Marina, Nipigon, ON: 807-887-3040

Red Rock Marina, Red Rock, ON: 807-886-2126

Rossport Town Dock, Rossport, ON: 807-824-1143

Chapter 9 East Shore: Marathon to Dog Harbour, Ontario

Marathon Pulp Inc., Marathon, ON: 807-229-1200

Marathon Taxi, Marathon, ON: 807-229-1009

Pukaskwa National Park, Heron Bay, ON: 807-229-0801, *www.parkscanada.gc.ca/pukaskwa*

Chapter 10 East Shore: Michipicoten Harbour to Gros Cap, Ontario

Buck's Marina, Wawa, ON: 705-856-4488/877-273-3319, *www.bucksmarina.com*

Gitchee Gumee Marina, Havilland Bay, ON: 705-649-2101

Lake Superior Provincial Park: 705-856-2284, *www.lakesuperiorpark.com*

Chapter 11 Crossroads of the Upper Great Lakes: Sault Ste. Marie & St. Marys River
American Side

Charles T. Harvey Marina, Sault Ste. Marie, MI: 906-632-6741

Coast Guard Sector Sault Ste. Marie, MI: 906-632-0967

George Kemp Marina, Sault Ste. Marie, MI: 906-635-7670, *www.kempmarina.com*

Drummond Island Yacht Haven, Drummond Island, MI: 906-493-5232/800-543-4743, *www.diyachthaven.com*

U.S. Customs, Sault Ste. Marie, MI: 906-632-7221

Canadian Side

Bondar Marina, Sault Ste. Marie, ON: 705-759-5430/800-361-1522, *www.cityssm.on.ca*

Belle View Marina, Sault Ste. Marie, ON: 705-759-2838

Canadian Customs, Sault Ste. Marie, ON: 888-CAN-PASS (888-226-7277)

Bibliography

Agawa Rock Indian Pictographs (pamphlet). Ontario: Ministry of Natural Resources, n.d.

Apostle Islands (pamphlet). National Park Service, U.S. Department of Interior. GPO, 1979.

Apostle Islands: Official National Park Handbook. Washington, DC: Division of Publications, National Park Service, U.S. Department of the Interior, 1988.

Arthurs, David. "The Mysterious Structures on Thompson Island." *Wanikan* (Monthly newsletter of the Thunder Bay Chapter, Ontario Archeological Society). March 1981, pp. 6-11.

Bogue, Margaret Beattie and Virginia A. Palmer. *Around the Shores of Lake Superior: A Guide to Historic Sites.* University of Wisconsin Sea Grant College Program, 1979.

Boyer, Dwight. *Great Stories of the Great Lakes.* New York: Dodd, Mead & Co., 1966.

Boyer, Dwight. *Ships and Men of the Great Lakes.* New York: Dodd, Mead & Co., 1977.

Boyer, Dwight. *True Tales of the Great Lakes.* New York: Dodd, Mead & Co., 1971.

Breen, Raymond L. and Ron Thompson. *National Parks on the Great Lakes.* Eastern National, 1998.

Chisholm, Barbara and Andrea Gutsche. *Superior – Under the Shadow of the Gods.* Toronto: Lynx Images Inc., 1999.

Coast Navigation School. "Weather: Courses 1-16." *Motorboating & Sailing,* Sept. 1977-Dec. 1978.

Dahl, Bonnie. *The Loran-C Users Guide.* Streamwood, IL: Richardsons' Marine Publishing Inc., 1986.

Dahl, Bonnie. *The Users Guide to GPS.* Streamwood, IL: Richardsons' Marine Publishing Inc., 1993.

Dawson, K.C.A. *The Pukaskwa Religious Stone Features of Lake Superior.* Ontario: Heritage Record No. 8, British Columbia, Provincial Museum, CRARA '77. (Papers from the Fourth Biennial Conference of the Canadian Rock Art Research Associates.)

D'Angelo O'Brien, Annette. "Marathon: The Little Town That Could." Duluth, MN: *Lake Superior Magazine,* December/January 1992, pp. 19-25.

Department of Commerce, National Oceanic and Atmospheric Administration, National Ocean Survey. *United States Coast Pilot #6: Great Lakes.* Washington, DC: Department of Defense, 1979.

Dewdney, Selwyn and Kenneth E. Kind. *Indian Rock Paintings of the Great Lakes.* Toronto: University of Toronto Press, 1962.

Duncanson, Michael E. and Gilbert Tanner. *A Guide to the Apostle Islands and the Bayfield Peninsula.* Eau Claire, WI: The Cartographic Institute, 1976.

Editors of Outdoor World. *The Great Lakes: North America's Inland Sea.* Waukesha, WI: Outdoor World, n.d.

Fountain, Daniel R. *Michigan Gold – Mining in the Upper Peninsula.* Duluth, MN: Lake Superior Port Cities Inc., 1992.

Gard, E. Robert and L.G. Sorden. *Romance of Wisconsin Place Names.* New York: October House Inc., 1968.

Graham, Gerald S. *A Concise History of Canada.* New York: Viking Press, 1968.

Grant, Campbell. *Rock Art of the American Indians.* New York: Crowell, 1967.

Great Lakes Cruising Club Log Book, "Volume on Lake Superior," Data collected from 1930s to 1991.

Hatcher, Harlan. *The Great Lakes.* New York: Oxford University Press, 1944.

Havighurst, Walter. *The Great Lakes Reader.* New York: Macmillan, 1966.

Havighurst, Walter. *The Long Ships Passing.* New York: Macmillan, 1942.

Holzhueter, John O. *Madeline Island & The Chequamegon Region.* The State Historical Society of Wisconsin, 1986.

Irwin, Constance. *Strange Footprints on the Land: Vikings in America.* New York: Harper & Row, 1980.

Isle Royale National Park © Michigan (pamphlet). National Park Service, U.S. Department of the Interior. GPO, 1990.

Lake Superior Provincial Park (pamphlet). Ontario: Ministry of Natural Resources, n.d.

Mahan, John and Ann. *Lake Superior: Story and Spirit.* Gaylord, MI: Sweetwater Visions, 1998.

Malksu, Alida. *Blue-Water Boundary.* New York: Hastings House, 1960.

Marshall, James R. *Lake Superior Journal – Views from the Bridge.* Duluth, MN: Lake Superior Port Cities Inc., 1999.

Marshall, James R. (ed.) *Shipwrecks of Lake Superior.* Duluth, MN: Lake Superior Port Cities Inc., 1987.

McKee. *Great Lakes Country.* New York: Crowell, 1966.

Ninwidjindimin. *Coastal Hiking Trail from Pic River to Oiseau Bay.* Parks Canada: Pukaskwa National Park, 1971.

Nute, Grace Lee. *Lake Superior.* New York: Bobbs-Merrill, 1944.

Peterson, Rolf O. *The Wolves of Isle Royale – A Broken Balance.* Minocqua, WI: Willow Creek Press, 1995.

Radio Technical Commission for Marine Services. *Marine Radiotelephone Users Handbook.* Washington, DC: 1982.

Richardsons' Chartbook & Cruising Guide: Lake Superior Edition. Streamwood, IL: Richardsons' Marine Publishing Inc., 1990.

Sivertson, Howard. *Tales of the Old North Shore.* Duluth, MN: Lake Superior Port Cities Inc., 1996.

Sivertson, Howard. *The Illustrated Voyageur.* Duluth, MN: Lake Superior Port Cities Inc., 1999.

Sillars, Mal & Hill, Don. *The Weather-Wise Boater.* Grosse Pointe, MI: Mal Sillars Weather Consultants Inc.

Stonehouse, Frederick. *Shipwreck of the* Mesquite. Duluth, MN: Lake Superior Port Cities Inc., 1991.

Strzok, Dave. *A Visitor's Guide to the Apostle Islands National Lakeshore.* Ashland, WI: Superior Printing & Specialties, 1981.

Thwaites, R. (ed) 1959. *The Jesuit Relations and Allied Documents, 1610-1791.* 73 volumes. New York: Burroughs.

U.S. Department of Transportation/U.S. Coast Guard. *U.S. Coast Guard 9th District Local Notice to Mariners.* Cleveland, OH: Ninth Coast Guard District, 1989.

Waters, Thomas F. *The Superior North Shore.* Minneapolis, MN: University of Minnesota Press, 1987.

Wolff, Julius F. Jr. *Lake Superior Shipwrecks.* Duluth, MN: Lake Superior Port Cities Inc. 1990

Index

Boldfaced page numbers indicate a particular subject's primary entry.
Italics page numbers indicate photo or chart reference.

Cree 8, 281
Cruising Season 46, 127, 263
Crystal Cove 199, **227-228**
Cumberland Point 199, 200
Current River 248
Customs 35
Customs Clearance 32, 33, 35, 184, 188, 197, 318, 388, 391, 398
Customs Decal 36
Customs User Fee 36

D

Dacres Rock 281
Dahl Shoal 302-303
Dahlfin I 64
Dahlfin II 169, 285, 363
Daily User Fee 197
Daisy Farm 194, 198-9, **213-214**, 219, 232
Daisy Farm Dock 214
Dampier Cove **334-346**
Dampier Island 319, 320
Danforth Anchor 26, 27
Davie's Island **266**
Davieaux Island 356-357, 359
Davieaux Light 356
Davis Island 346-7
Dawson Bay 242
Dead Reckoning 31, 60
Deadman Island 238, 242
Deep Harbour 343, **345**
Delta Anchor 26-27
Detention Island **311-312**
DeTour Harbor **402**
DeTour Passage 394-396, 402
DeTour Reef Light 396
DeTour Village 395, 402
DeTour, Michigan 402, 407
Devil's Chair 365, 367-368
Devil's Warehouse 335, **368-369**
Devils Island 13, 126, 132-3
Devils Island Dock 112
Devils Island Light Station 132
Dinghies 27-28, 63, 127, 141, 220, 261, 296, 298, 330, 342, 353, 357, 377
Distress Communications Form 37, 39
Dixon Island 368-9
Dock Usage by Commercial Vessels 199
Dog Harbour 314, 316, **352-353**
Dog Island 242
Dollar Bay, Michigan 90, 94

Dominion Fish Company 356
Donut Shop 185
Doris Island 256
Douglass Houghton 93, 100, 105
Dr. Bigsby 315
Dredging 15, 55, 71, 74, 77, 83, 89, 97, 98, 107, 108, 188, 395
Drummond Island 368
Drummond Island Yacht Haven 395, **400-401**
DSC – Digital Selective Calling 39-41
Duck Island 102
Duck Lake 79
Duluth and Iron Range Railroad Depot 178
Duluth Coast Guard 117
Duluth Entertainment Convention Center (DECC) 170, 173
Duluth Ship Canal 169, 170
Duluth Yacht Club 173
Duluth, Minnesota 2, 12-15, 17, 19, 23, 32, 35, 40, 48, 52, 95, 99, 115, 164, 166-170, 172-176, 178-179, 196, 212, 220
Duluth/Superior 158, **161**
Duluth/Superior Harbor 168, 172
Duncan Bay 194, 198, 218, **222-224**, 232
Duncan Narrows 198, 223
Dupuis Island 303-4

E

E.M. McSorley 4
Eagle Harbor Light 104, 153
Eagle Harbor, Michigan **104**
Eagle Island 12, **134**, 143
Eagle Island shoals 143
East Bay 152, **153-154,** 162,163
East Neebish Island 395, **397-498**
Edisen Fishery 199, **212-214**, 218
Edmund Fitzgerald 4, 41, 74, 371, 390
Edna G. Tugboat 178
Edward Harbour **257**
Edward Island 255-257, 259, 261
Electronic Bearing Line 59
Electronic Charts 31
Ella Islet 370
Ellwood A. Mattson Lower Harbor Park 81
Emory Jones 166
Emperor 224
ENC-Electronic Navigational Chart 56-57, 60
Encampment Island 179

English Fishery 339
English Harbour 339
Environment Canada **49**, 246
Equaysayway (Madeline) 140
Equipping Your Boat 24
Erie Mining Co. 182
Etienne Brule' 9, 138, 167, 368
Excursion Boats 78, 157

F

Fairlawn Mansion and Museum 172
False Harbour 357
Fanny Hooe Creek 103
Federation Islands 115
Feldtmann Ridge 205
Ferroclad Fisheries 356
Ferry Landing 118
Ferry Service 118
Ferry Traffic 118
Finn Point 206-208
Fire Destruction 193
Fire Restrictions 198
Fish Harbour **333**
Fish Nets 378
Fisherman's Cove **336-337**
Fisherman's Home **204**
Fishermans Bay **99**, 100, 303, **305**
Fitger's Brewery Complex 173
Five Finger Bay 194, **224-226**
Five Foot Reef **222**
Fix with GPS 58
Flag River 166-7
Flatland Island 238
Floating Heart Bay **351-352**
Florence Bay 231
Fluor Island 270, **273-275**, 281-2
Fo'c'sle Inn B&B 165
Fog 3, 32, 41-3, 46-47, 50, 59, 86, 95-6, 104, 133, 149, 186, 195, 235, 261, 272, 309, 314, 358, 367, 396,
Fog signal 133, 149, 247
Fond du Lac 164
Fond du Lac (Duluth) 115
Foreign Ships 167
Forestry Dock 185-6
Fort Camanistigoyan 244
Fort James Marathon Pulp Mill 317
Fort Wilkins 100, 103
Fort William 11-12, 20, 186-187, 245,
Fortress Anchor 26, 27
Foster Island **310-311**

About the Author

Bonnie and Ron Dahl have cruised for more than 30 years. During the summer months they have lived aboard their Columbia 10.7 sailboat, *Dahlfin II,* exploring the waters of Lake Superior and Lake Huron's North Channel and Georgian Bay. In early June 1996 they left the Great Lakes via the Erie Canal and headed down the eastern seaboard to the Bahamas. Taking the Thorny Path through the Turks and Caicos, Dominican Republic and Puerto Rico, they continued to the Virgin Islands and down the eastern Caribbean islands to Trinidad and Venezuela. After 4¹/₂ years, they returned by the same route to Lake Superior. In 2003, they went out of the Great Lakes again to winter in the Bahamas, returning in 2004. They are now back in the Great Lakes where they continue to sail the wilderness waters of lakes Superior and Huron. In early spring and late fall they sail in their home waters in the Apostle Islands of Lake Superior.

Shortly after they began to sail, Bonnie began writing and had her first articles published in *Cruising World.* She has since been published in *Lakeland Boating, Yachting, Great Lakes Sailor, Great Lakes Travel & Living, Lake Superior Magazine, The Compass* (a Caribbean publication) and *Good Old Boat.* These articles have covered all aspects of boating: provisioning, cruising with children, maintenance, chartering and most areas of Lake Superior, North Channel and Georgian Bay. Through the years, her area of specialty has evolved into navigation with radio location systems: Loran-C, radar, SAT NAV and GPS. Bonnie has written two other books: *The Loran-C Users Guide* and *The User's Guide to GPS.* The first edition of *The Superior Way* was published in 1983, the second edition in 1992, the third edition in 2001 and the fourth edition in 2008.